The Psychology of Adjustment

Current Concepts and Applications

The Psychology of Adjustment

Current Concepts and Applications

Edited by

Walter Katkovsky
Northern Illinois University

Leon Gorlow
The Pennsylvania State University

Third Edition

McGraw-Hill Book Company

New York St. Louis San Francisco Auckland
Düsseldorf Johannesburg Kuala Lumpur
London Mexico Montreal New Delhi Panama
Paris São Paulo Singapore Sydney
Tokyo Toronto

Library of Congress Cataloging in Publication Data
Main entry under title:

The psychology of adjustment.

Previous editions, edited by L. Gorlow and W. Katkovsky, entered under Gorlow.
Includes bibliographies and index.
1. Adjustment (Psychology)—Addresses, essays, lectures. I. Katkovsky, Walter. II. Gorlow, Leon, date, Readings in the psychology of adjustment. [DNLM: 1. Adaptation, Psychological. 2. Behavior. BF335 R287]
BF335.G65 1976 155.2′4 75-17619
ISBN 0-07-033345-9

THE PSYCHOLOGY OF ADJUSTMENT
Current Concepts and Applications

1234567890 KPKP 79876

This book was set in Times Roman by Creative Book Services, division of McGregor & Werner, Inc. The editor was Richard R. Wright and the production supervisor was Milton J. Heiberg. Kingsport Press, Inc., was printer and binder.

Contents

Preface

In the second edition of this book of readings, we noted that the years that had elapsed since the publication of the first edition did not constitute a long period for the development of major changes in scientific knowledge. Now an additional number of years have passed, and our review of the literature again has raised the question, What have been the significant changes and trends in the field since publication of the original edition in 1959? Our conclusions when organizing the second edition were that controversies in the field had become more apparent, that positions taken by different theorists were more diverse, and that the problems associated with the field were more demanding. In some respects these conclusions still apply since many of the same positions and controversies exist. However, a number of new ideas have moved into the limelight. Also, trends toward a *rapproachment* and synthesis on other issues are apparent. The following comments summarize our reactions to the present state of the field of adjustment. Our impressions of the continued controversies, the new developments, and the trends toward resolution of differences for the major topics covered in this book have guided our decisions on the selections to retain and those to add.

THE CONCEPT OF ADJUSTMENT

The specific criteria by which behavior and conditions are designated as adjusted or maladjusted remain controversial. Adjustment continues to be a difficult concept to define with precision, and the differences in definitions and criteria used by different authors result in inconsistent findings and different interpretations of the same data. The argument as to whether adjustment-maladjustment should be conceptualized in terms of absolute standards or as relative to specific situations and groups remains an important and basic controversy in the field. One promising development is a growing interest in determining characteristics associated with positive mental health, i.e., in discovering the personality characteristics that foster adjustment, personal growth, and happiness. This emphasis on the positive has come largely from two sources: from the behaviorists, who concern themselves with engineering behavior that has payoff for the individual, and from the existential theorists, who are interested in establishing ideal human values that serve as guides for healthy behavior. This interest in psychological variables associated with positive and healthy behavior is presented in the papers by Shoben, Bugental, Maslow, Jourard, and Kazdin.

In contrast with the interest in developing basic criteria of positive mental health, there is a growing trend on the part of mental health professionals to reject judgments about the adjustment status of specific groups based on theoretical absolutes and instead to accept the variations in styles of life which exist in specific groups as meaningful and justified adjustments to given conditions. Stated differently, the mental health literature currently acknowledges that judgments about mental health involve values and that the application of an absolute criterion about mental health to a given life-style may constitute little more than a value judgment concerning that life-style. This position is exemplified by the large number of professionals involved in developing a behavioral technology that endeavors to train people to behave in specific ways without regard for the ethics of that behavior according to some absolute standard. For example, in the area of sexual counseling, many programs have been initiated in which individuals are trained to perform sexually in ways consistent with their desires without concern with morality and the social acceptability of the behavior. The papers by Friedes, Honigmann, and Katkovsky discuss the issues that encourage the rejection of absolute standards of mental health and argue for the evaluation of the effectiveness of behavior based on its purpose rather than on conformity to values and morals.

PERSONALITY THEORY

The tendency for individual scientists to identify with specific theories of personality continues. As in the past, the major schools of thought are the psychoanalytic, the phenomenological, and the learning approaches, and these have not undergone major change. Theoreticians within each of these schools have their own special issues and controversies, which in turn lead to the development of subgroups representing a distinctive point of view within each of the schools. The papers on personality theory presented in this book represent succinct statements of major theoretical orientations that are meaningful to the study of psychological adjustment. For the most part, we have retained the same selections as were presented in the second edition of this book. This decision was based on the fact that the general framework of these theories has not changed and that the changes that have occurred within the theories represent greater detail and complexity than is required for the student studying psychological adjustment.

However, those interested specifically in developments in personality theory should note that none of the major schools is static; discussions of current developments within each school can be found in the journals and texts on personality theories.

DETERMINANTS OF ADJUSTMENT

The relative importance of genetic versus environmental factors in determining personality, adjustment status, and psychopathology remains a controversial question. While concern with the possible influence of heredity on specific variables and conditions has increased, as shown by recent studies on differences in intelligence and incidence of schizophrenia in different families and racial groups, greatest interest remains in modifying environmental factors to produce changes in personality. This interest is exemplified by the application of behavioral techniques to patients diagnosed as mentally retarded, as chronically psychotic, and as having minimal brain damage, where the concern is with developing programs that successfully train or modify the behavior of patients without regard for hypotheses about the causes of their conditions. In other words, there appears to be a growing empirical and pragmatic movement to manipulate environmental variables that will produce behavior change rather than a concern with determining the significance of heredity in imposing limitations on given individuals.

Among those investigators concerned with the ways that environmental factors influence adjustment, there is continued interest in the effects of early experiences and those associated with childhood rearing on subsequent personality characteristics and disturbances. The articles by Harlow and Harlow, Dollard and Miller, and Erikson focus on this concern. Also, recent attention has turned to the effects on the adjustment of people of many social and political decisions and environmental features, such as housing, discrimination, population expansion, and ecology. The selections by Poussaint and Atkinson, Konopka, Gove, and Sherman refer to a variety of social factors that bear on the problems of the groups they discuss. The selection by Brown describes the effects of several trends, such as urbanization, egalitarianism, and the drive toward success, which have contributed to the alienation of young people.

PSYCHOPATHOLOGY

The medical model for classifying psychopathology, which has been the mainstay of psychiatric diagnoses in the past, has been under very serious attack during the past fifteen years. Increasingly the trend has been to apply multidimensions to an understanding of psychopathology, and this trend is apparent in all of the papers in the psychopathology section. Also in the past fifteen years, greater concern has been given to the possibility that many of the theories and practices in the mental health field have limited applicability to minority-group members. Some of these groups have been militant in opposing the application of traditional theories of psychopathology to them; e.g., women have argued that the Freudian concept of "penis envy" represents no more than the imposing of masculine values on them. Homosexuals have argued that their choice of a same-sex partner represents a sexual preference and not a mental illness. Youth have argued that rebelliousness and illegal behavior may represent a constructive effort to change the social order rather than expressions of psychopathology. One reaction of mental health professionals to these positions has been to focus on the problems in living of distinct groups, such as women, blacks, and the aged, rather than to apply standard psychiatric diagnoses and absolute criteria of mental health to them. For this reason, the selections in the psychopathology section focus on specific groups and the relatively unique factors that influence their adjustment status.

PSYCHOTHERAPY

Approaches to psychotherapy continue to be varied, often with distinct theories and techniques and with advocates who argue that their approach is more valid and useful than the others. Therefore we have presented papers that describe a variety of methods and ideas for helping persons deal with adjustment problems. Some trends are noticeable. Group therapy appears to be gaining in popularity, probably because it enables therapists to deal with larger numbers of patients. Group procedures are utilized by therapists with very different theoretical orientations. Levitsky and Perls describe groups based on gestalt thinking, while Liberman deals with groups utilizing behavioral techniques. Another trend is represented by many efforts to work with problems as they exist in early stages in order to prevent their development into major disturbances. This trend has led to increased therapeutic efforts with children and to the development of the community mental health movement, in which assistance is made readily available through such programs as crisis lines, storefront drop-in centers, and efforts to alter community characteristics. The trend toward prevention has encouraged the participation of paraprofessionals in psychotherapy, which has added to the mental health work force. Also, many professionals now serve in the role of consultant to persons, such as parents and teachers, who make up the lives of the patients rather than work with the patient. Finally, this concern with prevention has promoted the development of programs designed to increase successful adjustment, as seen by the rising popularity of sensitivity training, meditation, and many self-control programs. The papers by Bach, Liberman, Kazdin, and Kubie deal with the importance of and different approaches to early remediation and prevention of adjustment problems.

It is apparent in the readings and comments throughout this volume that numerous questions, problems, and controversies exist in the area of adjustment. These have been emphasized intentionally, since it is the belief of the editors that the controversial issues and the unsolved problems define the study of adjustment as it exists today and will determine its future developments. In addition, the editors hope that by bringing varied and opposing points of view to the attention of the reader, this volume will promote greater involvement with, and a realistic perception of, the total field of study.

We should like to acknowledge the kindness of the authors, editors, and publishers whose permission to reproduce the reading selections made this volume possible. Specific permission citations are noted at the bottom of the first page of each selection. We hope that the organization, editing, and introductory materials, which have been prepared jointly by the editors, facilitate the understanding of the ideas presented by the authors of the papers.

Walter Katkovsky
Leon Gorlow

The Psychology of Adjustment

Current Concepts and Applications

Section One

The Concept of Adjustment

The definition of *psychological adjustment* has many complexities and difficulties. Varied meanings have been given to the dimension *adjustment-maladjustment,* and these have promoted discussion and debate in the psychological literature. One investigator may use as his or her criterion of adjustment the individual's ability to harmonize his or her own needs with those of the environment, while another may stress the extent to which the individual's behavior conforms to the dictates of his or her society, and still another may define adjustment in terms of the individual's subjective state of well-being and happiness. Each of these criteria or emphases will often lead to different judgments as to the behavior and psychological characteristics that will be labeled as maladjustment.

A further complexity in defining adjustment and maladjustment concerns the relationship of these concepts to other terms, such as normal-abnormal, psychopathology, and mental health and mental illness. In some instances the concepts are used interchangeably; in others, different and independent criteria are cited for each; and some psychologists think of normality and adjustment and abnormality and maladjustment as overlapping but not synonymous. One example of overlap is where the dimension *normal-abnormal* is used as the more general and inclusive variable to describe the degree to which a person deviates from culturally approved ways of behaving and where *adjustment-maladjustment* is used to refer to the more specific idea of the extent to which a person is able to *adapt* to the demands of a situation. In this sense, failure to adapt or adjust may or may not constitute abnormality depending on how seriously that failure departs from what is culturally approved. Failure to adapt to the demands of a chemistry course may then be regarded as maladjusted, but not abnormal, behavior whereas failure to adapt to society's requirement that each person must refrain from inflicting bodily injury on others may be regarded as both maladjusted and abnormal behavior. In contrast, other investigators define abnormality in terms of the presence of specific deviant behaviors, such as anxiety, phobias, delusions, or depression. According to this view, the repeated occurrence of deviant acts means that the individual is abnormal or mentally ill; yet he may be able to deal satisfactorily with his everyday activities and the demands of his environment and thus may not be considered maladjusted.

For the purpose of understanding the problems associated with definitions of the concept of adjustment-maladjustment, the student might initially consider this dimension synonymous with such terms as normality-abnormality and mental health–mental illness, since the varied criteria which have been applied to one of these variables have also been applied to the others. In the first selection in this section, Scott discusses the diverse meanings associated with adjustment or mental health. After summarizing many of the definitions and methods of measuring mental health and the limitations associated with each definition, he raises a number of questions concerning the potential overlap and disagreements among different definitions.

Historically the initial focus of investigators of the psychology of adjustment, mental health, or abnormal psychology has been on the pathological. For many years, investigators tended to concentrate on the identification of signs of abnormal behavior and maladjustment and to define normality and adjustment in terms of the absence of such signs. In addition, many scientists applied the medical profession's disease-entity model to pathological or maladjusted behavior and reasoned that the presence of specific signs or symptoms was indicative of a disease process that could be identified in any society or culture in which it occurred. These scientists hoped to discover symptom criteria for mental illness which would be culture-free and universally valid. Thus such terms as normality, adjustment, and mental health could be defined explicitly by the absence of pathological signs.

The paper by Honigmann argues for an absolute, universal definition of abnormality. While he notes that deviance occurs when in someone's judgment behavior exceeds the culturally determined limits of permitted variation, he makes a distinction between two kinds of deviance, the psychiatric and the nonpsychiatric. This distinction is based on the source of the judgment. In the case of psychiatric deviance, the judgments are made by authoritative, objective specialists, and therefore Honigmann believes that they constitute absolute criteria that have been applied successfully cross-culturally. In contrast, nonpsychiatric deviations lack clear-cut criteria and procedures, are subject to cultural bias, and may constitute moral rather than professional judgments. Honigmann cautions against treating troublesome cultural behaviors as psychiatric deviations and thereby confusing the absolutes of psychiatry with the relative variations in standards and norms which exist between cultures. While Honigmann's distinction is interesting and highlights the importance of both cultural norms and authoritative opinion in making judgments about maladjustment and psychopathology, one might question whether professional criteria are as objective, reliable, and consistent as he claims.

One of the major criticisms of the medical model of psychopathology is that the focus is negative, i.e., on indicators of the abnormal and the maladjusted, and positive mental health is defined solely by the absence of negative signs. Many theorists prefer to cite positive characteristics of mental health and to establish that some ways of behaving are healthier psychologically than others. The paper by Shoben presents a theoretical discussion of "the normal personality" and lists a number of characteristics that he regards as possibly universal criteria for good adjustment. Underlying Shoben's thinking is the assumption that human beings by nature (regardless of the culture, society, or group to which they belong) have certain "unique potentialities." The development of these potentialities is regarded as the broad criterion for mental health, and the more an individual actualizes his or her potentialities, the better adjusted he or she is considered. Shoben's position may be termed an *idealistic* conception of adjustment since it stresses what humanity *could* be. If we were able to agree that all people have the same direction or goal, we would be able to evaluate individuals or groups with respect to that goal. The task then, according to this reasoning, is to determine the goal or the specific unique potentialities or ideals of humanity. As Shoben indicates, psychology's efforts along these lines must be considered quite tentative.

Bugental presents another version of mental health, which he refers to as a "growth orientation" and "humanistic ethic." He considers these definitions the antithesis of adjustment defined in a mechanical, conforming sense and as likely to clash with the traditions and values of our culture. The humanistic ethic includes such factors as assuming responsibility for one's own actions and experiences, valuing authenticity and mutual respect in relationships with others, experiencing the present to the fullest possible extent, and being open to new growth-facilitating experiences. Bugental contends that the humanistic ethic is promoted by successful psychotherapy and that persons who live in accordance with its features themselves become agents of change by trying to alter society so that it is consistent with their values.

The positions of Honigmann, Shoben, and Bugental, while they differ in their criteria of illness and health, seek culture-free, absolute criteria. In contrast with the conceptualization of normal-abnormal behavior in absolute terms, there is also the view that, since most of people's behavior is learned within a given cultural context, pathological behavior must be influenced strongly by the particular standards and demands of the culture in which the learning occurs. Behavior that is considered pathological or maladjusted in one culture may be quite acceptable or even desirable in another. To the extent that a theorist attaches importance to the interdependence between specific environmental-cultural norms and demands and the criteria of psychopathology, his or her position is a *relativistic* one and he or she discounts the possibility of establishing a culture-free definition of mental health or mental illness. Some theorists have taken an extreme position on this score and have argued that pathology by necessity must be relativistic since it represents an evaluative judgment made about an individual's behavior for which no absolute standard exists. To call the hostile, aggressive behavior of the jungle inhabitant pathological in an environment where survival itself demands physical domination and assertion over other forms of life would be misleading. Similarly, to establish inner-directed achievement striving as an ideal goal for all humanity because this behavior is deemed appropriate and desirable in our culture may constitute no more than an imposition of our values on others. The paper by Freides adopts a relativistic position and raises criticisms of the idealistic conception of psychological normality. Freides argues that efforts to designate ideal characteristics inevitably become associated with value judgments concerning the desirability or undesirability of certain characteristics or what constitutes a good or bad way of life. He proposes that a choice of values cannot be determined by science and, instead, feels that psychologists can more profitably address themselves to questions about the potential achievements and limitations of specific behavioral characteristics in specific circumstances of life rather than to attempts to generalize about what might best be considered normal or adjusted behavior.

Freides' proposal that the concept of normality, and by implication such concepts as adjustment and mental health, should be dropped completely represents a strong position with which many psychologists would disagree. Other psychologists would argue that despite the relativity of cultural values and demands, similarities between cultures may promote similarities in the forms of pathology and the ideal characteristics of normality. Some theorists attempt to compromise the differences between the search for absolute universal criteria of mental health and the belief that all criteria are culture-bound. Many psychiatrists, in particular, seek basic personality characteristics that they associate with abnormality but concede that the specific ways in which these characteristics will be expressed depend on the cultural context. For example, a suspicious, paranoid attitude toward others is often regarded as an indicator of pathology, but the content of the individual's suspicions and the ways in which he or she makes the suspicions known will vary depending on the environment in which they occur.

Definitions of Mental Health and Illness*

William Abbott Scott

A serious obstacle to research in the area of mental illness lies in the lack of a clear definition of the phenomenon to be studied. The term "mental ill health" has been used by different researchers to refer to such diverse manifestations as schizophrenia, suicide, unhappiness, juvenile delinquency, and passive acceptance of an intolerable environment. Whether some or all of these various reactions should be included in a single category of "mental illness" is not clear from a survey of the current literature. Theories describing the nature and antecedents of one sort of disturbance rarely relate it to another, and there is a paucity of research evidence indicating the extent to which such manifestations are empirically intercorrelated.

In the face of such ambiguity it would appear useful to attempt an organized review of the various definitions of mental illness which are explicit or implicit in recent research, with a view toward highlighting their commonalities and discrepancies on both a theoretical and an empirical level. Such a presentation might help students concerned with causative factors to assess the comparability of previous research findings on correlates of "mental illness," and also point toward some next steps in research to discover the degree to which these diverse phenomena represent either unitary, or multifold, psychological processes.

The research criteria for mental illness to be reviewed here are subsumed under the following categories: (1) exposure to psychiatric treatment; (2) social maladjustment; (3) psychiatric diagnosis; (4) subjective unhappiness; (5) objective psychological symptoms; and (6) failure of positive adaptation. For each category we shall review studies which appear to have employed the definition, either explicitly or implicitly. This will be accompanied by a critical discussion of the adequacy of each definition, together with an assessment, based on empirical data where possible, of the relation between this and other definitions. Finally, we shall attempt to summarize the differences among the definitions, by indicating their divergent approaches to certain basic problems in the conceptualization of mental illness and health.

MENTAL ILLNESS AS EXPOSURE TO PSYCHIATRIC TREATMENT

The most frequently used operational definition of mental illness, at least in terms of the number of studies employing it, is simply the fact of a person's being under psychiatric treatment. And this definition is usually restricted to hospital treatment,

*From William Abbott Scott, "Research Definitions in Mental Health and Mental Illness," *Psychol. Bull.,* 1958, **55,** 29–45. Reprinted by permission of the author and the Managing Editor, the American Psychological Association.

This review was prepared for the Survey Research Center, University of Michigan, as background material for that organization's national survey of mental health, sponsored by the Joint Commission on Mental Illness and Health. The writer is indebted to Dr. Gerald Gurin of the Survey Research Center, and to Dr. Fillmore Sanford, formerly of the Joint Commission, for their contributions to the ideas presented here. Also appreciation is due the following researchers for their suggestions and for data from current studies which they provided: Harry Beilin, John Clausen, Benjamin Darsky, John Glidewell, Marie Jahoda, Morton Kramer, Thomas Langner, Charles Metzner, M. Brewster Smith, and Shirley Star.

rather than outpatient service. Nearly all the ecological studies (e.g., 3, 16, 22, 30, 35, 50) and most of the studies correlating mental illness with demographic characteristics (e.g., 5, 19, 29, 41, 47) use this as a criterion. They obtain their information from hospital records or, in unusual instances (e.g., 28), from psychiatrists in the area who furnish information about persons treated on an outpatient basis.

Such a definition of mental illness is operational rather than conceptual, but its implicit meaning for the interpretation of research results is that anyone who is regarded by someone (hospital authorities, relatives, neighbors, or himself) as disturbed enough to require hospitalization or outpatient treatment is mentally ill, and people who do not fit into such diagnoses are mentally healthy. Use of hospital records, moreover, requires that the criterion of the nature of the mental illness be the diagnosis which appears on the record.

Shortcomings of such an operational definition are recognized by no one better than its users. The reliability of psychiatric diagnosis is of course open to question, and any attempt to determine correlates of particular kinds of mental disturbance must take into account the large error inherent in the measuring process. (One study of the association between diagnosis at Boston Psychopathic Hospital and previous diagnoses of the patients at other hospitals showed only 51 per cent above-chance agreement between the two [cf. 15, pp. 42–43].)

If ''under the care of a psychiatrist'' is to be regarded as the criterion of mental illness, one must realize the automatic limitation on the size of the mentally ill population that such a definition imposes. Kramer (34, p. 124) has estimated that the maximum possible number of mentally ill, under such a definition, would be less than 7,000,000, given the present number of available psychiatrists.

It has been suggested by both sociologists (7, 10) and physicians (17) that different rates of hospital admissions for different geographical areas may indicate more than anything else about the areas the relative degree to which the communities tolerate or reject persons with deviant behavior (11). Or as the Chief of the National Institute of Mental Health puts it: researchers using hospital records are dependent on the public's rather uneven willingness to give up its mentally ill members and to support them in institutions (17); this in addition to the admittedly unstandardized and often substandard methods of record-keeping used by the various hospitals is likely to render incomparable prevalence and incidence data from various geographical areas.

The effects of such differential thresholds for admission in various communities are difficult to estimate, since they cannot be uniform from study to study. In 1938 a house-to-house survey in Williamson County, Tennessee, yielded nearly one person diagnosed as psychotic, but never having been in a mental hospital, for every hospitalized psychotic from the county (48). By contrast, Eaton found in his study of the Hutterites (14) that more intensive canvassing by psychiatrists did not yield a larger number of persons deemed psychotic than did a more superficial count based on community reports.

Eaton's study *did* yield higher proportions of neurotic diagnoses the more intensive the case finding procedure became, and this observation relates to the finding in New Haven that neurotics under out-patient treatment came disproportionately from the upper socio-economic strata (28). At first consideration, such differential rates seem readily attributable to the cost of psychiatric treatment, but Hollingshead and

Redlich prefer to seek an explanation in the greater social distance between lower-class neurotics and the psychiatrists than in the case of middle- and upper-class neurotics. Whatever the sources of rate differences, it is clear that such correlations as have been reported make one wary of the hospital admissions or outpatient figures as indicative of the "true" incidence of psychiatric disorders. Thus the criterion of exposure to psychiatric treatment is at best a rough indicator of any underlying conceptual definition of mental illness.

MALADJUSTMENT AS MENTAL ILLNESS

Adjustment is necessarily determined with reference to norms of the total society or of some more restricted community within the society. Accordingly, one may conceptually define adjustment as adherence to social norms. Such a definition of mental health has an advantage over the preceding in encompassing a range of more-or-less healthy, more-or-less ill behavior, rather than posing a forced dichotomy. The operation for assessing mental health by this criterion might ideally be a community (or other relevant group) consensus concerning a given subject's degree of adjustment. This has been approximated by at least one set of studies (1, 2).

Rather than assess consensus by pooling many divergent individual opinions, it is possible to assume that a law or other visible sign of social norms constitutes the criterion against which adjustment is determined. Such reference is employed in studies of suicide (12, 26) or juvenile delinquency (25) or divorce (39, 53) as indicants of maladjustment. While the operational criterion may become dichotomous in such cases (whether or not the person comes in contact with the law), this is not necessarily so. Gordon (21) has suggested considering the "biologic gradient" of suicide, extending from contemplation of the act to its actual accomplishment.

Finally, it would be possible to assess degree of adjustment with reference to some externally defined set of requirements for a given social system. Thus a work situation might be seen as demanding a high level of productivity from all its members, and the degree of adherence to this standard becomes the criterion of adjustment, without reference to the individual opinions of the group members or to the manifest norms of the group. This criterion of conformity to the requirements of a given social structure has not been explicitly employed by any of the researchers covered in the present review, but it has been hinted at (37) and remains a possibility, provided that the structural requirements of a social system can be determined independently of the members' behaviors.

Theory of social structure suggests that these three criteria of adjustment would tend toward congruence: The demands of a particular social system lead to the development of social norms, which are expressed in laws or customs and also in the individual participants' notions of what is acceptable behavior. Lack of congruence may be taken as evidence of cultural lag, of poor correspondence between manifest and latent function within the social structure, or of defensive psychological processes within the participating individuals. Since all of these factors supporting discrepancy do occur within most social systems, the criteria may be expected to yield somewhat different results.

When maladjustment is assessed by community consensus, one finds considerable divergence of opinion among various segments of the public regarding what constitutes good and poor adjustment. The Minnesota Child Welfare studies (1) showed differences in criteria for assessing adjustment among different occupational groups in the community. Teachers tended to emphasize standards different from those emphasized by ministers, who in turn displayed some differences from a more heterogeneous group of community adults. Beilin concludes that it is meaningless to discuss ''adjustment'' in the abstract or to contemplate the prediction of ''adjustment'' in general. One must specify *adjustment to what, adjustment to whose standards* (2). Lindemann reflects this relativistic conception of mental health when he states: ''We find it preferable not to talk about a 'case' in psychiatry—rather we try to assess functional impairment in specific situations as viewed by different professional groups in the community. So a 'case' is really a relationship of possibly pathogenic situation and appropriate or inappropriate behavior to that situation. It is often a matter of arbitrary choice whether such a person becomes an object of psychiatric care'' (38, p. 130).

Thus, though adjustment appears a more conceptually adequate criterion of mental health than does exposure to treatment, the necessity for considering different personal frames of reference and the demands of different social structures poses seemingly insurmountable obstacles to the establishment of mutually consistent operational definitions. All such difficulties which lie ''hidden,'' as it were, under the psychiatric treatment criterion, come to the fore to plague the researcher trying to establish a criterion for adjustment which applies to the treated and nontreated alike.

PSYCHIATRIC DIAGNOSIS AS CRITERION FOR MENTAL ILLNESS

There have been a few studies in which entire communities or samples of them have been systematically screened, either by direct examination (44, 48) or by evidence from community records or hearsay (13, 14, 54). Here the criterion for mental illness or health need not be dichotomous, but can be divided into several gradations. Such intensive case-finding can be expected to increase the yield of persons classified as neurotic (34, p. 124) over that provided by the criterion of exposure to treatment, but whether the psychotic group is thereby increased will depend on the community (34, p. 124; 48) and, of course, on the standards for diagnosis employed by the particular investigator.

The lack of standardization of diagnostic procedures and criteria contributes to the incomparability of mental illness rates derived from such studies (34, p. 139; 55). So long as the criterion of assessment is largely dependent on the psychiatrist's subjective integration of a different set of facts for each subject, nonuniform results can be anticipated. Expensive and unreliable though the method may be, it at least places the judgment regarding mental illness or health in the hands of professionals, which is not the case when adjustment is the criterion. And though hospitalization is in part determined by the judgment of professionals, *who* is sent to the hospitals for psychiatric diagnosis is, for the most part, out of the hands of the psychiatrists. As Felix and Bowers (17) have observed, it is the community rather than the clinician that operates the case-finding process today, and this will continue to be so until diagnostic examinations are given regularly to all people.

MENTAL ILLNESS DEFINED SUBJECTIVELY

It has been maintained by some that a major indication of need for psychotherapy is the person's own feeling of unhappiness or inadequacy. Conversely, the degree of mental health may be assessed by manifestations of subjective happiness, self-confidence, and morale. Lewis (36) quotes Ernest Jones to the effect that the main criterion for effect of therapy is the patient's subjective sense of strength, confidence, and well-being. Terman (52, 53) has used a "marriage happiness" test, composed largely of subjective items, and Pollak (43) has suggested that old-age adjustment be assessed in terms of the person's degree of happiness or well-being in various areas of his life.

That such criteria of mental health correlate somewhat with independent diagnoses by physicians has been indicated in two sorts of studies. In the Baltimore Eastern Health District (9), cases diagnosed psychoneurotic were found to express complaints about their own physical health; it is suggested that persons who report chronic nervousness can be classified as suffering from a psychiatric condition. Rogers has maintained that a marked discrepancy between one's "perceived self" and "ideal self" constitutes evidence of psychiatric disturbance (45), and some empirical studies lend support to this position. When Q sorts of subjects' self concepts are compared with Q sorts of their ideal selves, it is possible to distinguish psychiatric groups from nonpsychiatric groups on the basis of the degree of discrepancy between these two measures (4). Furthermore, progress in therapy (as judged by the therapist) tends to be associated with increasing similarity between the patient's self concept and ideal self (46).

Though subjective well-being is an appealing criterion for mental health in ordinary daily living, it might be presumed that under some circumstances psychological defense mechanisms could operate to prevent the person's reporting, or becoming aware of, his own underlying unhappiness and disturbance. Jahoda (33) has rejected happiness as a criterion for mental health on somewhat different grounds: Happiness, she says, is a function not only of the person's behavior patterns, but of the environment in which he moves. If one wants to relate mental health to characteristics of the environment, then one must not take as a criterion of mental health something that already presupposes a benign environment. "There are certain circumstances in which to be happy would make it necessary first to be completely sick" (33, p. 105).

Such objections to this criteria imply that it is possible to find persons who are mentally ill by some other criterion, yet who nevertheless report themselves as happy or self-satisfied. Empirical demonstration of this implication is not available at present. In fact, while one study predicted defensively high Q sorts for the self concept of paranoid psychotics, they were found to have a greater discrepancy between self- and ideal-sorts than normals, and no less discrepancy between these measures than psychoneurotics (4).

MENTAL ILLNESS DEFINED BY OBJECTIVE PSYCHOLOGICAL SYMPTOMS

It is generally accepted almost by definition that mental illness entails both a disordering of psychological processes and a deviation of behavior from social norms

(6). The latter aspect of disturbance may be assessed as maladjustment to one's social environment (discussed above); the former aspect can presumably be assessed by psychological inventories aimed at the assumedly critical processes. The distinction between the psychological inventory approach and the subjective assessment procedure discussed above is not really a clear one. Subjective well-being may be regarded as one of the psychological processes which becomes disordered. Yet more "objective" measures of psychological process, which do not require the subject's verbal report of his degree of happiness, are frequently preferred, both to guard against purposeful distortion and to tap areas of disorder which may not be accompanied by subjective counterparts.

Such "objective" psychological inventories may represent various degrees of manifest purpose. For some, the objective of assessment is transparent, and the only reason they are not classed as devices for subjective report is that they stop just short of requiring the subject to report his over-all level of well-being. Such a manifest-level inventory is Halmos' questionnaire concerning the respondent's difficulties in social relations (24).

At a somewhat less obvious level are such inventories as the MMPI, the War Department Neuropsychiatric Screening Battery, and the Cornell Medical Index, which require subjects to check the presence of various subjective and objective symptoms (e.g., "I smoke too much."). Once validated against an accepted criterion, such as psychiatric diagnosis, these are frequently used as criteria themselves. Rennie constructed a composite instrument of this type to assess his respondents' levels of mental health in the Yorkville study (44); at the same time, a validity analysis of the index was undertaken, by correlating each item with independent psychiatric diagnosis on a sub-sample of the respondents. On the basis of their experience with such a composite instrument, one of Rennie's colleagues (Langner, personal communication, August 1956) suggests caution in abstracting parts of previously validated batteries, since the item validities are sometimes not maintained when they are used out of context of the total instrument.

An adaptation of the psychiatric screening battery approach for use with children is suggested in the work of the St. Louis County Public Health Department (20). It involves obtaining information about symptoms from the children's mothers rather than from the children themselves. Naturally, the symptoms covered must be of the "objective" type ("Does Johnny wet the bed?") rather than the "subjective" type ("Does Johnny worry a lot?"). As validated by an outside criterion (teachers' and psychiatric social workers' ratings of the child's level of adjustment), the number of symptoms reported by the mothers appears to be a promising index of the child's mental health.

A general characteristic of the types of psychological inventories reviewed so far is that each item in the battery is assumed, a priori, to involve a "directional" quality, such that one type of answer (e.g., "yes" to "Are you troubled with nightmares?") may be taken as indicative of psychological disorder, and the opposite answer is indicative of normal functioning. Thus the index of disturbance is computed by adding all the positive indicators, weighted equally. That alternative methods of test construction may yield equally, or more, valid indices of mental illness is indicated by the extensive investigations of McQuitty (40).

McQuitty proposes several different methods of diagnostic test scoring, each based on explicit assumptions about the diagnostic procedure which the test is supposed to represent. One of the simplest assumptions, for example, is that an individual is mentally ill to the extent that his psychological processes deviate from the culturally modal processes. Thus, any type of multiple-alternative test may be administered to a group of subjects representing a "normal" population. Each alternative of each item is then scored for its "popularity." The score for a subject is then computed by adding the popularity scores of the items he checks (McQuitty calls this the T method of scoring); a high popularity score is taken as evidence of mental health (by this "typicality" criterion).

An alternative assumption proposed by McQuitty as underlying the diagnostic procedure might be that mental health is manifest to the degree that the subject's responses conform to *any* pattern of answers represented by a significant number of community people, regardless of whether that pattern is the most popular one. Such an assumption leads to a scoring procedure (H method) whereby a subject's index of "cultural harmony" is based on the degree to which his responses to different questions "go together" in the same manner as do the responses of all people in the sample who check the same alternatives he does.

Elaborations on these basic procedures provide for differential weighting of responses depending on their degree of deviance (WH method), and correction for "linkage" between successive pairs of items (WHc method).

The Bernreuter Personality Test and the Strong Vocational Interest Inventory were administered by McQuitty to a group of mental patients and to a group of university students; they were scored by different methods, the scores for the two tests were correlated, and the mean scores of the two groups compared. Results of the comparisons indicate that: (1) when appropriately scored, the Strong can discriminate mental patients from normals, though not so well as the Bernreuter; (2) better results are obtained if, instead of treating each answer as a separate, independent measure, it is evaluated in terms of the pattern of other answers with which it occurs (WHc scoring method); (3) within the Bernreuter, those items which correlated best with the total score (McQuitty's WHc method of scoring) and provided the best discrimination between patients and normals tended to be of the "subjective" type (i.e., they depended on the subject's introspection, as in "Do you often have disturbing thoughts?") rather than the "objective" (items which an observer could report, such as "Do you talk very much?"); (4) different scoring procedures appeared differentially appropriate for the "subjective" and "objective" items; (5) when the "subjective" items were scored by the method most appropriate to them (i.e., the method which best discriminated patients from normals), and the "objective" items by their most appropriate method, the correlation between the two scores on the same group of subjects was about zero, indicating that two independent dimensions of mental health were being tapped by these two sets of items.

A separate study reported by McQuitty (40) indicated that the simple T method of scoring (based on the popularity of the subject's responses) both subjective and objective items significantly discriminated groups of school children classified on the basis of independent criteria of mental health. There is considerable evidence from these studies that, especially with respect to those traits measured by the "objective" items, the person may be regarded as mentally ill to the extent that he deviates from the dominant community pattern.

The foregoing studies provide a certain amount of evidence that measures of mental illness according to psychometric criteria relate to two of the criteria discussed earlier—maladjustment and psychiatric diagnosis. That such concurrent validation may yield somewhat different results from studies of predictive validity is indicated in Beilin's report of the Nobles County study (2). Two indices of student adjustment predictors were constructed, one (the "pupil index") based on students' responses to five different instruments, and the other (the "teacher index") based on teacher ratings. Both were concurrently validated against juvenile court judges' nominations of delinquent youngsters and against teachers' descriptions of the youngsters. Four years later the mental health of the youth was assessed by a number of different criteria—community reputation, interviewers' ratings, self-assessment, and an adaptation of the Rundquist-Sletto morale scale. The predictors correlated significantly with only some of the subsequent criteria, and all of the correlations were at best moderate. The "pupil index" correlated better with the interviewer's rating than with the community reputation criterion; while the "teacher index" correlated better with the subject's subsequent community reputation than with the interviewer's rating. Or, stated more generally, the psychologist's predictor predicted better to a psychologist's criterion, and a community predictor predicted better to a community criterion. Though the time span (four years) between the predictor and criterion measures may have been such as to allow for considerable change in the subjects, one is nevertheless reminded by these results that various criteria for mental health are not necessarily highly correlated.

In summarizing the various studies of mental health and illness defined by psychological testing batteries, we may note that many of them lack an underlying conception of the nature of mental illness from which to derive items and scoring procedures (a notable exception being McQuitty's measures), that some of them challenge the notion of the unidimensional nature of mental health, and that their degree of correlation with other criteria, such as adjustment of psychiatric diagnosis, depends on the nature of the criterion.

MENTAL HEALTH AS POSITIVE STRIVING

A radically different approach to the assessment of mental health is indicated in the definitions proposed by some writers with a mental hygiene orientation. Gruenberg suggests that, though failure to live up to the expectations of those around him may constitute mental illness, one should also consider the person's failure to live up to his own potentialities (23, p. 131). Frank speaks of the "positive" aspect of mental health—healthy personalities are those who "continue to grow, develop, and mature through life, accepting responsibilities, finding fulfillments, without paying too high a cost personally or socially, as they participate in maintaining the social order and carrying on our culture" (18). In a less exhortative tone, Henry (27) discusses successful adaptation of the person in the "normal stressful situation." He sees many normal situations as situations of inherent stress. Some individuals in them develop mental disease, while others may develop out of them a more complex, but more successful, personality. It is this successful coping with the "normal stressful situation" that Henry regards as indicative of mental health.

Jahoda has translated this kind of emphasis on the positive, striving aspects of behavior into a set of criteria amenable to empirical research. She proposes three basic features of mental health (31): (1) The person displays active adjustment, or attempts at mastery of his environment, in contrast to lack of adjustment or indiscriminate adjustment through passive acceptance of social conditions. (2) The person manifests unity of personality—the maintenance of a stable integration which remains intact in spite of the flexibility of behavior which derives from active adjustment. (3) The person perceives the world and himself correctly, independent of his personal needs.

Active mastery of the environment, according to Jahoda, presupposes a deliberate choice of what one does and does not conform to, and consists of the deliberate modification of environmental conditions. "In a society in which regimentation prevails, active adjustment will hardly be possible; in a society where overt regimentation is replaced by the invisible compulsiveness of conformity pressures, active adjustment will be equally rare. Only where there exists social recognition of alternative forms of behavior is there a chance for the individual to master his surroundings and attain mental health" (31, p. 563).

Such an approach is quite at odds with the subjective criterion of personal happiness, and with the conformity criterion referred to above as "adjustment." Attempted adjustment does not necessarily result in success, for success is dependent on the environment. The best mode of adjustment only maximizes the chances of success. It is mentally healthy behavior even if the environment does not permit a solution of the problem (33). Jahoda proposes that the criterion of happiness be replaced with some more "objective" definition of mental health, based on an explicit set of values.

In an unpublished community study, Jahoda apparently attempted to assess only two of the aspects of mental health incorporated in her definition. Veridicality of perception (actually, of judgment) was determined by asking respondents to estimate certain characteristics of their communities concerning which objective data were available (e.g., proportion of people with only grade-school education), and at the same time inferring needs to distort reality from the respondent's evaluative statements about the problem (e.g., how important *R* believed education to be). This method of assessing need-free perception was regarded as something less than satisfactory (Jahoda, personal communication, August 1956), since the need was so difficult to determine, and it was difficult to establish unambiguously that distortion of judgment was due to the operation of a need rather than simply to lack of valid information.

The degree of attempted active adjustment was assessed by first asking a respondent to mention a particular problem in the community, then determining what he had done, or tried to do, about it, and how he felt about the problem at the time of interview (33). Three aspects of respondents' reactions were coded from their replies (32): (1) the stage of problem solution—mere consideration of the problem, consideration of solutions, or actual implementation; (2) the feeling tone associated with the problem—continued worry or improvement in feeling (either through partial solution or through passive acceptance); (3) the directness or indirectness of the approach—i.e., whether *R* went to the heart of the problem in his attempted solution or merely dealt temporarily with recurrent nuisances.

In her analysis Jahoda relates her measures of problem-solving and need-free perception to various characteristics of the respondents and of the communities in which they live. The relationships are interesting (e.g., in one of the communities the level of problem-solving was related to the degree of community participation of the respondent), but they appear to leave unanswered a basic question about the appropriateness of the criteria. If one accepts Jahoda's definition of mental health as involving the two components assessed in the study, then the results can be interpreted as showing what patterns of social interaction are associated with mental health. But if one is skeptical about the meaningfulness of the definition, then he is impelled to search for correlations between her two measures and other, more commonly accepted, criteria of mental health. These are not reported, although it would appear to be a fair question to ask about the relation of her concepts to those employed by other researchers.

If one is wedded to the happiness criterion of mental health, for example, one may speculate about the possibility of a negative relation between it and those provided by Jahoda. Unhappiness could conceivably lead to excessive coping behavior (attempted adjustment), or excessive coping behavior might elicit negative reactions from others which, in turn, would increase one's unhappiness. In like fashion, it could be that need-free perception would lead to increased unhappiness, since psychological defenses are not available to bolster one's self image. Though Jahoda might reject the suggestion that happiness is even relevant to her criteria, it would appear useful to explore, both conceptually and empirically, the interrelations among other measures of mental health and the novel one proposed by her.

Clausen (6) has maintained that researchers must ultimately face the task of relating mental health defined in positive terms to the individual's ability to resist mental illness under stress. At present it is not known whether they represent a common factor or are independent characteristics. Jahoda (personal communication, August 1956) suspects that positive mental health, as she defines it, may indeed represent a dimension orthogonal to that represented by the conventional psychological symptoms of mental illness. Thus, from a different approach than that employed by McQuitty comes the suggestion that mental health and illness may be a multidimensional phenomenon.

In employing these particular criteria, especially that of active adaptation, Jahoda seems willing to defend the evaluative standards implicit in it. And it may well be that values relating to attempted mastery of problems are every bit as defensible as the values of conformity implied in the adjustment criteria discussed above. Nevertheless, the former appear to exemplify the application of the Protestant ethic to the mental health movement in a manner which might introduce culture and class biases into one's conclusions. Miller and Swanson (42) have hypothesized that lower-class children will show more defeatism than middle-class children, as a result of different interpersonal and environmental experiences. Would they thereby be less mentally healthy by any standards besides those of the middle class? Truly, the problems posed in setting up absolute values from which to judge mental health and illness are perplexing.

BASIC PROBLEMS IN THE DEFINITION OF MENTAL HEALTH AND ILLNESS

Underlying the diversities in definition of mental illness one can discern certain basic differences of viewpoint concerning how the phenomena should be conceptualized. We may abstract certain foci of disagreement by posing the following four points of contention: (1) Does mental illness refer to a unitary concept or to an artificial grouping of basically different specific disorders? (2) Is mental illness an acute or chronic state of the organism? (3) Is maladjustment (or deviance from social norms) an essential concomitant of mental illness? (4) Should mental illness be explicitly defined according to values other than social conformity?

Each of the proposed definitions takes a stand, either explicitly or implicitly, on one or more of these issues. It is likely that resolution of disagreements will depend in part on the outcome of future empirical research. But at least some of the divergence inheres in the theoretical formulation of the problem, and is more a matter of conceptual predilection than of empirical fact. In either case, if one is to arrive at consistent theoretical and operational definitions of mental illness, it would be well to make explicit one's bias concerning each of these issues, and attempt to rationalize it in terms of his conception of the causes of disturbance.

THE UNITARY OR SPECIFIC NATURE OF MENTAL ILLNESS

The position that mental illness is manifest in some rather general form, regardless of the specific diagnostic category in which the patient is placed, would appear to be implicit in the subjective definition of the phenomenon. If the person's feeling of happiness or adequacy is regarded as the crucial indicator of his mental state, this would appear to imply that over-all health or illness can be assessed for a particular person, regardless of the area of functioning referred to. Likewise, the definition of mental health in terms of purposeful striving or active adjustment tends to ignore differences in the underlying bases for such striving or lack thereof. Such a position has been stated explicitly by Stieglitz: "The mensuration of health . . . closely parallels the measurement of biological age as contrasted to chronological age. . . . We are no longer seeking to discover specific disease entities, or even clinical syndromes, but attempting to measure biological effectiveness in adaptation" (51, p. 79). And such a unitary view of the phenomenon is implied in Schneider's comment: "The major 'cause' of mental disease is seen as some form of disorientation between the personality and society" (49, p. 31).

By contrast, the specific view of mental illness is taken by Gordon: "What we choose to call mental disease is an artificial grouping of many morbid processes. The first essential, in my opinion, is to separate the various entities, and in the approach to an epidemiology of mental diseases, to center attention on some one condition, or a few selected conditions, which have functions in common with other mass diseases well understood in their group relationships'' (15, p. 107). McQuitty offers empirical evidence in favor of a specific view, in his isolation of two quite independent measures of mental illness (by psychological testing), both of which correlate with external diagnostic criteria. And he further speculates that the number of areas in which the degree of personality integration varies rather independently is probably greater than the two which he has isolated. ''One might expect that mental illness might develop within any one or more patterns. In order to understand the mental illness of a particular subject, we must isolate the pattern, or patterns, of characteristics to which his mental illness pertains'' (40, p. 22).

While the weight of opinion and evidence appears to favor the multidimensional view, this may simply be a function of the operational definitions employed (e.g., mental health defined by responses to a battery of tests is bound to turn out multidimensional to the extent that intercorrelations among the test items are low). But there are yet insufficient empirical data collected from the unitary point of view to test whether its assumption is correct. Indeed, it seems quite plausible that both happiness and active adaptation may be partially a function of the situation; hence the concept of mental health implied by them must become multidimensional to the extent that they allow for intersituational variability.

THE ACUTE OR CHRONIC NATURE OF MENTAL ILLNESS

The psychologist's testing approach to assessing mental illness inclines him toward a view of the condition as chronic. That is, the predisposing conditions within the organism are generally presumed to be relatively enduring, though perhaps triggered off into an actual psychotic break by excessively stressful situations. The epidemiological approach, on the other hand, is usually concerned with the counting of actual hospitalized cases, and this may incline one toward a view of mental illness as predominantly acute. Felix has espoused this position explicitly: ''Unless the kinds of mental illness are specified, I can't conceive that mental illness is a chronic disease. More mental illnesses by far are acute and even short term than there are mental illnesses which are chronic and long term'' (15, p. 163). Of course, the epidemiological approach traditionally considers characteristics of the host, as well as characteristics of the agent and the environment. But the predisposing factors within the organism seem to be regarded, like ''low resistance,'' not as a subliminal state of the disease, but rather as a general susceptibility to any acute attack precipitated by external factors.

It is easier to regard a psychosis as acute than it is similarly to regard a neurosis, since in the former disorder the break with normal behavior appears more precipitate. However, such a judgment, based on easily observable external behaviors, may be unduly superficial. Even in the case of such a discrete disturbance as suicide, at least one writer (21) recommends considering the biologic gradient of the disorder. He distinguishes varying degrees of suicide, with successful accomplishment as merely a possible end product. Where such continuity between morbid and nonmorbid states can be discerned, the possibility of chronic disturbance might well be considered.

THE PROBLEM OF MENTAL HEALTH AS CONFORMITY TO SOCIAL NORMS

The criterion of mental health based on adjustment clearly implies that conformity to the social situation in which the individual is permanently imbedded is a healthy response. And such an assumption would appear to be lurking, in various shapes, behind nearly all of the other definitions considered (with the possible exception of some of the "positive striving" criteria, which stress conformity to a set of standards independent of the person's immediate social group). In fact, McQuitty's methods of scoring psychological inventories are all explicitly based on the assumption that conformity (either to the total community or to a significant subgroup) is healthy.

If the stability of the larger social system be regarded as the final good, or if human development be seen as demanding harmony in relation to that social system, then such an assumption would appear basic and defensible. But one is still impelled to consider the possibility that the social system, or even an entire society, may be sick, and conformity to its norms would constitute mental illness, in some more absolute sense. If any particular behavior pattern is considered both from the standpoint of its adaptability within the social structure to which the individual maintains primary allegiance and from the standpoint of its relation to certain external ideal standards imposed by the observer, perhaps a comparison of the two discrepancy measures would yield information about the degree to which the social system approaches the ideal. On the other hand, such a comparison might be interpreted as merely indicating the degree to which the researcher who sets the external standards is himself adapted to the social system which he is studying. The dilemma appears insoluble.

THE PROBLEM OF VALUES IN CRITERIA FOR MENTAL HEALTH

The mental hygiene movement has traditionally been identified with one or another set of values—ideal standards from which behavior could be assessed as appropriate or inappropriate. The particular set of values adopted probably depends to a considerable degree on who is doing the judging. Such a diversity of evaluative judgments leads to chaos in the popular literature and to considerable confusion in the usage of the term "mental health" in scientific research. Kingsley Davis (8) presented a rather strong case for the proposition that mental hygiene, being a social movement and source of advice concerning personal conduct, has inevitably been influenced by the Protestant ethic inherent in our culture. The main features of this Protestant ethic, as seen by him, are its democratic, worldly, ascetic, individualistic, rationalistic, and utilitarian orientations.

To the extent that research on mental health is based on criteria devolved from such an ideology, it is middle-class-Protestant biased. To the extent that it is based on some other set of "absolute" norms for behavior, it is probably biased toward some other cultural configuration. At least one researcher, Jahoda (33), has clearly taken the position that mental health criteria must be based on an explicit set of values. There is some advantage in allowing the assumptions to come into full view, but in this case the resulting criteria appear to be rather specialized and not comparable with those used by other researchers. Perhaps the difficulty lies not so much in the existence of explicit assumptions as in their level of generality. If a more basic set of assumptions could be found, from which the diverse criteria for mental health and illness can be derived, then comparability among researches might better be achieved. One would be in a better position to state when mental illness, as defined by psychological tests or by absence of active adjustment, is likely to be displayed in mental illness defined by psychiatric diagnosis or deviance from community standards.

SUMMARY

The various categories of definitions of mental illness discussed here have been distinguished primarily on the basis of their differing operational definitions: the dependent variables employed in empirical research on the phenomena are clearly different. Moreover the conceptualizations of mental illness explicit or implicit in the empirical criteria are often quite divergent—viz., the radically different view-points underlying the "maladjustment," "subjective unhappiness," and "lack of positive striving" definitions.

Certain conceptual and methodological difficulties in each of these types of definition have been noted: "Exposure to treatment" is deficient in that only a limited proportion of those diagnosable as mentally ill ever reach psychiatric treatment. "Social maladjustment" is open to question because of the varying requirements of different social systems and the diversity of criteria for adjustment employed by community members. "Psychiatric diagnosis" provides an expensive, and often unreliable, method of assessing the state of mental health. "Subjective unhappiness" can be criticized as a criterion since it may be a function of intolerable environmental conditions as well as the psychological state of the person, and is subject to distortion by defense mechanisms. The validity of "objective testing procedures" appears to depend considerably on the method by which they are scored, and there is strong evidence that a major component of their score may simply be the degree of conformity of the person to the community average. Finally, criteria included under the heading of "positive striving" are subject to question in that they are inevitably based on disputable value systems of their proponents.

While many of these difficulties would not be considered damaging from the point of view of certain of the definitions of mental illness, they run into conflict with others. Also they suggest certain basic incompatibilities among the various approaches to conceptualization of mental illness. Whether these incompatibilities should be reconciled by further theoretical and empirical exploration, or whether they should be regarded as valid indicators that mental health and illness constitute multidimensional phenomena is still a moot question. We can only note that various studies employing two or more of these different categories of criteria have tended to yield moderate, but not impressive, interrelations.

The criterion of "exposure to psychiatric treatment" has been related to "maladjustment," "psychiatric diagnosis," "subjective unhappiness," and "objective psychometrics." Also "maladjustment" has been related to "psychiatric diagnosis" and to certain "objective" measures; and "psychiatric diagnosis" has been related to both "subjective" and "objective" measures of mental illness. The areas of interrelationship for which no empirical studies have been found are between "subjective" measures and both "maladjustment" and "objective" assessment; also between the "positive striving" criteria and all of the other types of measures.

Two directions for future theory and research are indicated by these results. First, more investigations are needed of the extent of relationship among the various criteria, and of the conditions under which the magnitudes of the intercorrelations vary. Second, assuming absence of high intercorrelations under many conditions, it would be worthwhile to explore the implications of poor congruence between one measure and another—implications both for the person and for the social system in which he lives.

REFERENCES

1 Beilin, H. The effects of social (occupational) role and age upon the criteria of mental health. *J. soc. Psychol.,* in press.

2 Beilin, H. The prediction of adjustment over a four year interval. *J. clin. Psychol.,* 1957, **13,** 270–274.

3 Belknap, I. V., & Jaco, E. G. The epidemiology of mental disorders in a political-type city, 1946–1952. In *Interrelations between the social environment and psychiatric disorders.* N.Y.: Milbank Memorial Fund, 1953.

4 Chase, P. Concepts of self and concepts of others in adjusted and maladjusted hospital patients. Unpublished doctor's dissertation, Univer. of Colorado, 1956.

5 Clark, R. E. Psychoses, income and occupational prestige. *Amer. J. Sociol.,* 1949, **54,** 433–440.

6 Clausen, J. A. *Sociology and the field of mental health.* N.Y.: Russell Sage Foundation, 1956.

7 Clausen, J. A., & Kohn, M. L. The ecological approach in social psychiatry. *Amer. J. Sociol.,* 1954, **60,** 140–151.

8 Davis, K. Mental hygiene and the class structure. *Psychiatry,* 1938, **1,** 55–65.

9 Downes, Jean, & Simon, Katherine. Characteristics of psychoneurotic patients and their families as revealed in a general morbidity study. *Milbank Memorial Fund Quarterly,* 1954, **32,** 42–64.

10 Dunham, H. W. Current status of ecological research in mental disorder. *Social Forces,* 1947, **25,** 321–326.

11 Dunham, H. W. Some persistent problems in the epidemiology of mental disorders. *Amer. J. Psychiat.,* 1953, **109,** 567–575.

12 Durkheim, E. *Le suicide.* Paris: F. Alcan, 1897. (English translation, Glencoe, Ill.: Free Press, 1951.)

13 Eaton, J. W. *Culture and mental disorders.* Glencoe, Ill.: Free Press, 1955.

14 Eaton, J. W., & Weil, R. J. The mental health of the Hutterites. In A. M. Rose (Ed.), *Mental health and mental disorder.* N.Y.: Norton, 1955.

15 *Epidemiology of mental disorder.* N.Y.: Milbank Memorial Fund, 1950.

16 Faris, R. E. L., & Dunham, H. W. *Mental disorders in urban areas.* Chicago: Chicago Univer. Press, 1939.

17 Felix, R. H., & Bowers, R. V. Mental hygiene and socio-environmental factors. *Milbank Memorial Fund Quarterly,* 1948, **26,** 125–147.

18 Frank, L. K. The promotion of mental health. *Ann. Amer. Acad. of Pol. Soc. Sci.,* 1953, **286,** 167–174.

19 Frumkin, R. M. Occupation and major mental disorders. In A. M. Rose (Ed.), *Mental health and mental disorder.* N.Y.: Norton, 1955.

20 Glidewell, J. C., et al. Behavior symptoms in children and degree of sickness. *Amer. J. Psychiat.,* 1957, **114,** 47–53.

21 Gordon, J. E., et al. An epidemiologic analysis of suicide. In *Epidemiology of mental disorder.* N.Y.: Milbank Memorial Fund, 1950.

22 Gruenberg, E. M. Community conditions and psychoses of the elderly. *Amer. J. Psychiat.* 1954, **110,** 888–896.

23 Gruenberg, E. M. Comment in *Interrelations between the social environment and psychiatric disorders.* N.Y.: Milbank Memorial Fund, 1953.

24 Halmos, P. *Solitude and privacy.* London: Routledge and Kegan Paul,1952.

25 Hathaway, S. R., & Monachesi, E. D. The Minnesota Multiphasic Personality Inventory in the study of juvenile delinquents. In A. M. Rose (Ed.), *Mental health and mental disorder.* N.Y.: Norton, 1955.

26 Henry, A. F., & Short, J. *Suicide and homicide.* Glencoe, Ill.: Free Press, 1954.

27 Henry, W. E. Psychology. In *Interrelations between the social environment and psychiatric disorders.* N.Y.: Milbank Memorial Fund, 1953.

28 Hollingshead, A. B., & Redlich, F. C. Social stratification and psychiatric disorders. *Amer. sociol. Rev.,* 1953, **18,** 163–169.

29 Hyde, P. W., & Kingsley, L. V. Studies in medical sociology. I: The relation of mental disorders to the community socio-economic level. *New England J. Med.,* 1944, **231,** 543–548.

30 Jaco, E. G. The social isolation hypothesis and schizophrenia. *Amer. sociol. Rev.,* 1954, **19,** 567–577.

31 Jahoda, Marie. Toward a social psychology of mental health. In A. M. Rose (Ed.), *Mental health and mental disorder.* N.Y.: Norton, 1955.

32 Jahoda, Marie. The meaning of psychological health. *Soc. Casewk,* 1953, **34,** 349–354.

33 Jahoda, Marie. Social psychology. In *Interrelations between the social environment and psychiatric disorders.* N.Y.: Milbank Memorial Fund, 1953.

34 Kramer, M. Comment in *Interrelations between the social environment and psychiatric disorders.* N.Y.: Milbank Memorial Fund, 1953.

35 Lemert, E. M. An exploratory study of mental disorders in a rural problem area. *Rural Sociol.,* 1948, **13,** 48–64.

36 Lewis, A. Social aspects of psychiatry. *Edinburgh med. J.,* 1951, **58,** 241–247.

37 Lindemann, E., et al. Minor disorders. In *Epidemiology of mental disorders.* N.Y.: Milbank Memorial Fund, 1950.

38 Lindemann, E. Comment in *Interrelations between the social environment and psychiatric disorders.* N.Y.: Milbank Memorial Fund, 1953.

39 Locke, H. *Predicting adjustment in marriage: a comparison of a divorced and a happily married group.* N.Y.: Holt, 1951.

40 McQuitty, L. L. Theories and methods in some objective assessments of psychological well-being. *Psychol. Monogr.,* 1954, **68,** No. 14.

41 Malzberg, B. *Social and biological aspects of mental disease.* Utica: State Hosp. Press, 1940.

42 Miller, D. R., & Swanson, G. E. A proposed study of the learning of techniques for resolving conflicts of impulses. In *Interrelations between the social environment and psychiatric disorders.* N.Y.: Milbank Memorial Fund, 1953.
43 Pollak, O. Social adjustment in old age. *Soc. Sci. Res. Council Bull.* No. 59, 1948.
44 Rennie, T. A. C. The Yorkville community mental health research study. In *Interrelations between the social environment and psychiatric disorders.* N.Y.: Milbank Memorial Fund, 1953.
45 Rogers, C. *Client- centered therapy.* Boston: Houghton Mifflin, 1951.
46 Rogers, C., & Dymond, Rosalind. *Psychotherapy and personality change.* Chicago: Univer. of Chicago Press, 1954.
47 Rose, A. M., & Stub, H. R. Summary of studies on the incidence of mental disorders. In A. M. Rose (Ed.), *Mental health and mental disorder.* N.Y.: Norton, 1955.
48 Roth, W. F., & Luton, F. H. The mental health program in Tennessee. *Amer. J. Psychiat.,* 1943, **99,** 662–675.
49 Schneider, E. V. Sociological concepts and psychiatric research. In *Interrelations between the social environment and psychiatric disorders.* N.Y.: Milbank Memorial Fund, 1953.
50 Schroeder, C. W. Mental disorders in cities. *Amer. J. Sociol.,* 1942, **48,** 40–47.
51 Stieglitz, E. J. The integration of clinical and social medicine. In I. Galdston (Ed.), *Social medicine—its derivations and objectives.* N.Y. Acad. of Med., 1947. N.Y.: Commonwealth Fund, 1949.
52 Terman, L. M., et al. *Psychological factors in marital happiness.* N.Y.: McGraw-Hill, 1938.
53 Terman, L. M., & Wallin, P. The validity of marriage prediction and marital adjustment tests. *Amer. sociol. Rev.,* 1949, **14,** 497–505.
54 Tietze, C., et al. Personal disorder and spatial mobility. *Amer. J. Sociol.,* 1942, **48,** 29–39.
55 Tietze, C., et al. A survey of statistical studies on the prevalence and incidence of mental disorders in sample populations. *Publ. Hlth. Rep.,* 1943, **58,** 1909–1927.

Toward a Distinction between Psychiatric and Nonpsychiatric Judgments of Abnormality*

John J. Honigmann

DEVIANCE

Abnormality implies deviation from some kind of ideal, or normal, condition. Yet, it is a fact that the norm from which abnormal human behavior departs is often not explicitly defined and, in the case of human well-being, notoriously difficult to define positively, that is, as other than the absence of symptoms. The difficulty encountered in defining behavioral normalcy positively undoubtedly stems partly from the extraordinary flexibility and adaptability of the human being together with the vast range of

*This paper, written especially for *Readings in the Psychology of Adjustment,* 2d ed., represents a substantial revision of an essay bearing a similar title, "Toward a Distinction between Psychiatric and Social Abnormality," *Social Forces,* 1953, **31,** 274–277.

situations in which human beings are required to participate according to some standard of adequacy. From time to time, age to age, place to place, and problem to problem, different and even mutually exclusive demands are made on human beings.

What is normal for one person in one social setting becomes abnormal for another in a different situation. Consequently, the more closely one stays with a particular situation or system of situations—which is what the culture of a community represents—the easier it is to specify what is normal or abnormal for that system. However, the positive definition of behavioral normalcy is only incidentally my problem for, as the title of this paper suggests, I am primarily concerned with various conceptions of abnormality or deviance.

Every society recognizes a range of behavior in which it accepts or permits people to engage.[1] Sometimes those limits apply to a very small segment of society indeed, perhaps only to a small group, a neighborhood, or a culturally distinct community such as the Hopi Indians. Occasionally the range of permitted behavior covers all mankind in a way that ignores cultural boundaries, as when theologians judge what it is for man to be in a state of grace and psychiatrists fix what it means to be psychiatrically disturbed. The society in which such arbiters presume to operate is a truly universal one. When individuals exceed the range of permitted variation, their behavior or resultant condition is no longer fully condoned by others. If they internalize the relevant standards, they may themselves experience qualms of conscience, worry about their health, fear their poor chance at salvation, or whatnot. These remarks allow me to define deviance conveniently for present purposes by saying that it occurs when, in somebody's judgment, behavior—either observable acts or inferred behavioral states—exceeds the culturally determined limits of permitted variation. Abnormal behavior is abnormal because it passes beyond somebody's bounds of acceptability. Who devises the limits of acceptability or helps bring about agreement on them is a question of fundamental importance, both for determining what is going to be judged deviant as well as for distinguishing between psychiatric and nonpsychiatric judgments of abnormality, the topic to which this paper is addressed. To this matter I will return, as well as to the special problems posed when several arbiters of the same or different cultures disagree in their evaluation of what is unacceptable.

One can, of course, also use the term abnormal to refer to permitted deviance, that is, to behavior that exceeds the usual level but is welcome or that, although abnormal, strikingly exemplifies cultural ideals and therefore merits social approval rather than disapproval. Social science has given little thought to this type of abnormality which, however, is not directly related to my problem.

I said that both observable and inferred behavior may be found deviant. Usually social control tries to halt or correct manifest acts that arouse concern or that offend, but it is not unknown for groups and social systems also to venture to regulate thoughts and feelings. I am reminded of the Hopi Indians advising one another to keep a good heart, Catholics enjoined to avoid bad thoughts. Chinese Communists exploring one another's political philosophies, or for that matter, a psychiatrist who having been made aware of a patient's disturbed feelings seeks to restore the feeling tone to proper limits.

[1]J. J. Honigmann, *Understanding Culture*. New York, Harper and Row, 1963; Ch. 12.

PSYCHIATRIC ABNORMALITY

Mental illness or psychiatric abnormality conforms to the general definition of deviance to the extent that it designates behavior exceeding limits of acceptability. The process for establishing psychiatric abnormality is clear-cut, especially if we ignore professionally debated points of nomenclature and disregard rival theories that purport to explain how certain forms of mental illness arise. Basically, the process depends on a judgment made by an authoritative specialist, a psychiatrist (armed, perhaps, with the *Diagnostic and Statistical Manual for Mental Disorder* published by the American Psychiatric Association), who is able to recognize symptoms in a patient's behavior. From those clues, together with additional information provided by the patient's history, the psychiatrist infers a disturbed psychic state wherein the symptoms originate. The identification of mental illness may primarily be nosological or existential, but in any event it constitutes a ruling concerning the acceptability of the behavior in question. The psychiatrist has authority to say validly that the behavior exceeds desirable or healthy limits or, to put it the other way, he determines what is abnormal. That the Church once played a similar role testifies to the importance of authority in the determination of abnormality and indicates the ease with which such authority may be lost.

It is not necessary that the stricken individual or members of his community themselves recognize that the person's behavior has passed beyond the bounds of acceptability in order for the psychiatrist's diagnosis to be valid. The validity of his judgment depends on the accuracy of the observations he makes and on the logic of the reasoning by which he reaches his conclusion. Exotic communities may expect, tolerate, or even reward behavior corresponding, say, to psychosomatic disorder, paranoid suspicion, hallucination, and a high level of anxiety, or they may ignore the underlying psychodynamic source of such symptoms—the chronically upset essential psychical condition, as Alexander Leighton so succinctly designates the motivating source of mental disorder.[2] In those cases such behavior would not be identified as abnormal by anybody in that community. However, regardless of local acceptability, the behavior would still be abnormal if a foreign psychiatrist using a professional theory and standards evaluated it as falling outside desirable limits of mental health.

No one can any longer deny that there is an objective or operational definition of psychiatric abnormality that has been successfully applied cross-culturally. Nor can anyone affirm that mental illness must be solely defined in relation to cultural context.[3] Though psychiatry as we know it represents a cultural specialty that has developed in European and American culture, its theory provides anyone qualified to use it with a yardstick for recognizing and explaining mental illness anywhere in the world, to a large extent independently of local cultural standards, and regardless of whether the people concerned share that yardstick. The theory will continue to be applied universally as long as experience in using it turns up no great inconsistency or other

[2]A. H. Leighton, *My Name Is Legion.* New York, Basic Books, 1959; Ch. 5.

[3]For an instance of extreme cultural relativism see M. J. Herskovits, *Man and His Works.* New York, Knopf, 1948; pp. 66–67.

difficulty, or as long as it works successfully.[4] Psychiatry is far from being the only system of concepts which, though culture-bound in their inception, can be applied successfully cross-culturally. Once the Church could do this with sin, grace, and other ideas pertaining to related states of spiritual being. But its authority has declined in a changing intellectual climate wherein, for many people, those concepts have lost both their compelling emotional significance and their former truth value. When social science rose in authority, it saw little validity or, what is more to the point, use in evaluating people by such ideas as sin or grace. The new, powerful arbiters, interested in function, dysfunction, development, and lag, wouldn't acknowledge the claim of theological concepts to universality, a claim that has ceased to be taken seriously in our society by even some theologians. Practically all the valuable concepts of cultural anthropology are culture-bound in their origin, even though a number have benefited from their authors' cross-cultural experience, and like psychiatric notions of mental illness, work with considerable precision when used cross-culturally.

Since psychiatric judgments are necessarily culture-bound, the arbiter who makes them must be constantly and carefully alert lest they absorb too great a degree of cultural bias from his own, limited social milieu. Unless he is on guard, a psychiatrist may be too ready to evaluate behavior as psychiatrically abnormal that, regardless of its psychodynamic source, is untenable in his own culture. His identification of symptoms may be unduly influenced by what his own community currently regards as social problems. The point I am making is that although psychiatric judgments are always value judgments, the degree to which they betray culture-bound, moral, or other values can be controlled. Recent epidemiological reports indicate a need for such control. I suspect that lower-class metropolitan people come through a psychiatric screening with worse average mental health than middle- and upper-class people not because their psychical condition is more grievously upset but because lower-class symptoms, like the lower-class culture in which those symptoms are learned, depart so outrageously from the psychiatrist's own class-bound values.[5]

PSYCHIATRIC AND NONPSYCHIATRIC DEVIANCE COMPARED

For several reasons nonpsychiatric deviance cannot be so neatly defined operationally as the psychiatric variety. In the first place, the specialists who are regarded as having power confidently to recognize it seldom possess so clear-cut a status as psychiatrists. Second, procedures for identifying it are both less explicit and less standardized. Finally, we lack sufficient faith in a base line comparable to positive mental health, a base line which, even though it is hard to define, like a myth justifies what psychiatrists are doing. A variety of persons evaluate behavior nonpsychiatrically to judge deviance. Fellow workers in a factory do so when they reprimand the rate-buster

[4]For a neat demonstration of such applicability see A. H. Leighton et al., *Psychiatric Disorder among the Yoruba*. Ithaca, Cornell University Press, 1963.

[5]The point is documented in T. S. Langner and S. T. Michael, *Life Stress and Mental Health,* The Free Press of Glencoe, 1963; esp. Ch. 16. That source speaks of socio-economic strata rather than classes. I discuss the question in J. Honigmann, *Personality in Culture,* New York, Harper and Row, 1967; Ch. 13.

and so do teachers who spot abnormal study habits or unacceptable forms of spelling. In the same fashion neighbors complain about a minority group's religious services, thereby rendering them deviant according to segmental criteria of propriety, and the police halt acts that run afoul of legal codes. Everyone in society possesses some power to sanction behavior departing from social standards that he endorses or tries to enforce and extend.[6] A person's area of social power may be extremely circumscribed, perhaps being limited only to his family or peer group. But even very authoritative persons who hold considerable power in a community to say what is wrong and to make their evaluation stick are varied, especially in a large-scale community. Nonpsychiatric abnormality is a considerably less universal concept than psychiatric abnormality. That is, unlike psychiatrists, social scientists lack an explicit theory or even a simple list of criteria specifying deviant behavior across cultural boundaries. With the possible exception of a few types of behavior—defiant homicide is one that comes most quickly to mind—it is practically impossible to say what behavior is deviant in some nonpsychiatric sense from one culture to another. Our lack of concepts powerful enough authoritatively to identify deviance cross-culturally is only partially due to cultural variability, to the fact that the limits of what is acceptable differ greatly from one social system and one time to another. Basically, as I have suggested, our difficulty lies in the lack of persons in our culture possessing authority to enforce one or more theoretical yardsticks that are well-nigh independent of other cultures, that inspire confidence, and that therefore reliably can be applied cross-culturally to determine behavior departing from some hypothetical base line. I do not speak now of the acceptability of the yardstick abroad; what I emphasize is that there is not even agreement on universal criteria of deviance among European-American social scientists. To be sure, from time to time attempts have been made to devise lists and theories pointing out how nonpsychiatric forms of abnormality arise in society, but instead of predicting such behavior specifically and explaining it theoretically, the best such attempts turn out to define social eufunctioning. For example, we have functional prerequisites for continuing social life[7] and universal values that nearly every community is said to try to implement.[8] Such lists are usually brief and for the most part usually very general or obvious. They provide little help in deducing particular forms of behavior that, because they conflict with functional prerequisites or violate basic values, are consequently abnormal. Prescriptions of social eufunctioning and universal values also illustrate the problem I referred to earlier, namely, the difficulty of trying to define in positive and universal terms those norms in terms of which human behavior may be judged as normal or abnormal.[9] The popular sociological theory which views deviance as the product of a hiatus between desired ends and available, legitimate

[6]In large part I follow the theory of social pressure and power advanced by Godfrey and Monica Wilson in *The Analysis of Social Change*. Cambridge, England, University Press, 1945; pp. 28, 49–58.

[7]J. W. Bennett and M. M. Tumin, *Social Life*. New York, Knopf, 1948; pp. 41–44 and Ch. 4.

[8]C. Kluckhohn, "Universal Categories of Culture." In A. L. Kroeber, ed., *Anthropology Today*. Chicago, University of Chicago Press, 1953; p. 520; C. Kluckhohn, "Universal Values and Anthropological Relativism." In *Modern Education and Human Values*. Pittsburgh, University of Pittsburgh Press, 1952.

[9]Alexander Leighton's criteria of social disintegration avoid starting with positive standards of social functioning. However, useful as they may become for identifying "deviant" social systems, they offer slight help when it comes to evaluating nonpsychiatrically the normalcy of individual behavior. See Alexander Leighton, *My Name is Legion,* New York, Basic Books, 1959; Ch. 6.

means for attaining those ends can't reliably identify deviance as I define it.[10] Not only is it also too general in what it predicts, but it is actually a theory of innovation. Only when one of the innovative modes of individual adaptation that it accounts for happens to be regarded as illegitimate in a community does it correspond to abnormality in the present sense of the term.

As though to fill in the void left by the lack of criteria capable of being used to evaluate nonpsychiatric abhormality universally, there has arisen a tendency to expand the concept of mental illness to cover troublesome behaviors that may in fact not always be symptomatic of psychological difficulty. I refer to such behaviors as homosexuality and promiscuity and to conduct that psychiatric textbooks list under the rubics of "personality disorder" and "sociopathic disturbance." The latter category includes the "antisocial reactions" of persons who are always in trouble and maintain no real interpersonal loyalties and "dyssocial reactions" of individuals who, while they may be capable of strong loyalties, manifest a pervasive disregard for the usual social codes. Addiction to alcohol and drugs also comes under the heading of sociopathy. It is quite possible for a type of behavior deemed to be deviant by nonpsychiatric criteria sometimes to be psychiatrically abnormal. For example, an adolescent's reckless mischief may reveal the strain under which he labors. On the other hand, it may express his new-found strength and maturity. It has been suggested that delinquents from stable lower-class families residing in an area where delinquency rates are high who adopt the values of their peers are less likely to be psychiatrically disturbed than delinquents from middle-class homes marked by hostility and lack of love.[11] I don't question the possibility that morally or socially inappropriate acts may sometimes be symptomatic of an underlying psychological disturbance. But I fear the tendency too readily to regard such conduct as psychiatric abnormality. To diagnose homosexuality in general as "sick," the way some psychiatrists have done in print, impresses me as entirely gratuitous and a shocking confusion of moral and professional standards.[12] When the psychiatrist's social system embraces alternative, class-linked forms of behavior, some of which are morally, logically, and aesthetically opposed to others, the temptation may be great to use powerful psychiatric concepts and the prestige attached to his office to evaluate as psychiatrically abnormal alternatives which he and his class find unacceptable. He may experience subtle pressure and see good reasons to employ his authority in this manner, especially when his evaluations are in line with the direction in which one socially powerful class or group desires to alter, educate, or reform another. Professional persons neither oppose change nor embrace unlimited moral relativity if, under such conditions, they recognize that they must proceed warily. Caution is especially warranted if we work in a climate of democratic values and recognize the importance of keeping the limits of tolerance as wide as possible in order to make life congenial for as many people as possible.

[10]Robert K. Merton, *Social Theory and Social Structure*. Revised and enlarged edition. Glencoe, the Free Press, 1957; Ch. 4.

[11]A. J. Reiss, "Social Correlates of Psychological Types of Delinquency." *American Sociological Review*, 1952, **17**, pp. 710–718. But see J. J. Conger and W. C. Miller, *Personality, Social Class, and Delinquency*, New York, John Wiley and Sons, 1966, who, in data obtained in Denver, find little empirical support for the distinction.

[12]O. Herbert Mowrer and Thomas S. Szasz offer a far more general criticism of psychiatry than I do.

Toward a Concept of the Normal Personality*

Edward Joseph Shoben, Jr.

Clinical practice and the behavioral sciences alike have typically focused on the pathological in their studies of personality and behavior dynamics. While much of crucial importance remains to be learned, there is an abundant empirical knowledge and an impressive body of theory concerning the deviant and the diseased, the anxious and the neurotic, the disturbed and the maladjusted. In contrast, there is little information and even less conceptual clarity about the nature of psychological normality. Indeed, there are even those (5, 13) who argue that there is no such thing as a normal man; there are only those who manage their interpersonal relationships in such a way that others are strongly motivated to avoid them, even by committing them to a mental hospital or a prison, as opposed to those who do not incite such degrees of social ostracism.

This argument has two characteristics. First, it appears to dispose of the problem by simply distributing people among a dimension of pathology. All men are a little queer, but some are much more so than others. Second, it has affinities with the two major ideas that have been brought to bear on the question of what constitutes normal or abnormal behavior: the statistical conception of the usual or the average and the notion of cultural relativism. If pathology is conceived as the extent to which one is tolerated by one's fellows, then any individual can theoretically be described in terms of some index number that reflects the degree of acceptability accorded him. The resulting distribution would effectively amount to an ordering of people from the least to the most pathological. Similarly, if the positions on this continuum are thought of as functions of one's acceptance or avoidance by others, then they can only be defined by reference to some group. The implications here are twofold. First, the conception of pathology is necessarily relativistic, varying from group to group or culture to culture. Second, the degree of pathology is defined as the obverse of the degree of conformity to group norms. The more one's behavior conforms to the standards of the group, the less he is likely to be subject to social avoidance; whereas the more one's behavior deviates from the rules, the greater is the probability of ostracism to the point of institutional commitment.

STATISTICAL AND RELATIVISTIC CONCEPTS OF NORMALITY

Yet the issues are fully clarified by these statistical or culturally relativistic ideas. Is it most fruitful to regard normality or integrative behavior as merely reflecting a minimal degree of pathology, or may there be a certain merit in considering the asset side of personality, the positive aspects of human development? This question becomes particularly relevant when one is concerned with the socialization process or with the goals and outcomes of psychotherapy or various rehabilitative efforts.

*From Edward Joseph Shoben, Jr. "Toward a concept of the Normal Personality," *Amer. Psychologist,* 1957, **12,** 183–189. Reprinted by permission of the author and the Managing Editor, the American Psychological Association.

It seems most improbable that the family, the church, and the school, the main agents of socialization, exist for the minimizing of inevitable pathological traits in the developing members of the community. Rather, parents, priests, and educators are likely to insist that their function is that of facilitating some sort of positive growth, the progressive acquisition of those characteristics, including skills, knowledge, and attitudes, which permit more productive, contributory, and satisfying ways of life. Similarly, while psychotherapists may sometimes accept the limited goals of simply trying to inhibit pathological processes, there are certainly those (11, 16) who take the position that therapy is to be judged more in terms of how much it contributes to a patient's ability to achieve adult gratifications rather than its sheer efficiency in reducing symptoms or shoring up pathological defenses.

A general concern for such a point of view seems to be emerging in the field of public mental health (26). Beginning with an emphasis on treatment, the concept of community mental health swung to a preventive phase with the main interest focused on identifying the antecedents of mental disease and on reducing morbidity rates by attacking their determinants. The vogue of eugenics was one illustrative feature of this stage. More recently, there has been a considerable dissatisfaction with the whole notion of interpreting psychological states in terms of disease analogues (15, 23). Maladjustive behavior patterns, the neuroses, and—perhaps to a lesser extent—the psychoses may possibly be better understood as disordered, ineffective, and defensive styles of life than as forms of sickness. In consequence, there seems to be a growing tendency to conceive of the public mental health enterprise as emphasizing positive development with the prevention and treatment of pathology regarded as vital but secondary.

But in what does positive development consist? The statistical concept of the average is not very helpful. Tiegs and Katz (27), for example, reported a study of college students who had been rated for fourteen different evidences of "nervousness." By and large, these traits were normally distributed, suggesting that those subjects rated low must be considered just as "abnormal" (unusual) as those rated high. This conception seems to provide a superficial quantitative model only at the expense of hopeless self contradiction and violence to the ordinary categories of communication. Even in a case that at first blush seems to cause no difficulty, the problem remains. Criminal behavior, for example, is distributed in a J-shaped fashion with most cases concentrated at the point of zero offenses, ranging to a relatively few instances of many-time offenders. Few would argue that the usual behavior here is not also the most "positive." But one suspects that the sheer frequency of law-abiding behavior has little to do with its acknowledged integrative character. If conformity to social rules is generally considered more desirable than criminality, it is not because of its rate of occurrence but because of its consequences for both society and the individual.

Thus, a statistical emphasis on the usual as the criterion of positive adjustment or normality shades into a socially relativistic concept with an implied criteron of conformity. The terms "usual" or "most frequent" or "average" are meaningless without reference to some group, and this state of affairs poses two problems. First, conformity in itself, as history abundantly demonstrates, is a dubious guide to conduct.

Innovation is as necessary to a culture's survival as are tradition and conservation, and conformity has frequently meant acquiescence in conditions undermining the maturity and positive development of human beings rather than their enhancement. On more personal levels, conformity sometimes seems related in some degree to personality processes that can quite properly be called pathological (2, 24). Second, relativistic conceptions of normality pose serious questions as to the reference group against which any individual is to be assessed. Benedict (3), for example, has made it quite clear that behavior which is considered abnormal in one culture is quite acceptable in others, that certain forms of abnormalities which occur in some societies are absent in others, and that conduct which is thought completely normal in one group may be regarded as intensely pathological in another. Such observations, while descriptively sound, can lead readily to two troublesome inferences. One is that the storm trooper must be considered as the prototype of integrative adjustment in Nazi culture, the members of the Politburo as best representing human normality Soviet style, and the cruelest adolescent in a delinquent gang as its most positively developed member. The other is that any evaluative judgment of cultures and societies must by regarded as inappropriate. Since normality is conceived only in terms of conformity to group standards, the group itself must be beyond appraisal. Thus, the suspicion and mistrust of Dobu (10), the sense of resigned futility that permeates Alor (6), and the regimentation that characterizes totalitarian nations can logically only be taken as norms in terms of which individual behavior may be interpreted, not as indications of abnormal tendencies in the cultures themselves.

Wegrocki (28), in criticizing such relativistic notions, argues that it is not the form of behavior, the actual acts themselves, that defines its normal or pathological character. Rather, it is its function. What he calls the "quintessence of abnormality" lies in reactions which represent an escape from conflicts and problems rather than a facing of them. This formulation, implying that integrative adjustments are those which most directly confront conflicts and problems, seems essentially free of the difficulties inherent in statistical conceptions and the idea of cultural relativism. But it presents troubles of its own. For instance, what does it mean to "face" a problem or conflict? On what ground, other than the most arbitrarily moralistic one, can such confrontations be defended as more positive than escape? Finally, does this facing of one's problems have any relationship to the matter of conformity in the sense of helping to clarify decisions regarding the acceptance or rejection of group standards?

To deal with such questions requires coming to grips with certain problems of value. It is at this point that the behavioral sciences and ethics meet and merge, and it seems unlikely that any conception of normality can be developed apart from some general considerations that are fundamentally moral. Once the purely relativistic ideas of normality are swept away, it becomes difficult to avoid some concern for the issues of happiness and right conduct, *i.e.*, conduct leading to the greatest degree of human satisfaction, that are the traditional province of the literary interpreter of human experience, the theologian, and the moral philosopher. A primary challenge here is that of providing a rational and naturalistic basis for a concept of integrative adjustment that is at once consistent with the stance and contributions of empirical science and in harmony with whatever wisdom mankind has accumulated through its history.

SYMBOLIC AND SOCIAL ASPECTS OF HUMAN NATURE

One way to meet this challenge is by frankly postulating a basic principle of value. The fundamental contention advanced here is that behavior is "positive" or "integrative" to the extent that it reflects the unique attributes of the human animal. There are undoubtedly other ways of approaching a fruitful concept of normality. Nevertheless, this assertion is consistent with the implications of organic evolution, escapes the fallacy of the survival-of-the-fittest doctrine in its various forms, and permits a derivation of more specific criteria of positive adjustment from the distinctive characteristics of man. No discontinuity within the phylogenetic scale need be assured. It seems clear, however, that man, while certainly an animal, can hardly be described as "nothing but" an animal; and his normality or integration seems much more likely to consist in the fulfillment of his unique potentialities than in the development of those he shares with infrahuman organisms.

Foremost among those uniquely human potentialities, as Cassirer (4) and Langer (14) make clear, is the enormous capacity for symbolization. What is most characteristic of men is their pervasive employment of *propositional* language. While other organisms, especially dogs (22) and the higher apes (29), react to symbols, their faculty for doing so indicates only an ability to respond to mediate or representative as well as direct stimuli. Man, on the other hand, uses symbols designatively, as a vehicle for recollecting past events, for dealing with things which are not physically present, and for projecting experience into the future. Goldstein (12) makes the same point in his discussion of the "attitude toward the merely possible," the ability to deal with things that are only imagined or which are not part of an immediate, concrete situation. In patients whose speech has been impaired because of brain damage, this attitude toward the possible is disrupted. Thus, aphasics are typically unable to say such things as, "The snow is black," or "The moon shines in the daytime"; similarly, they are incapable of *pretending* to comb their hair or to take a drink of water although they can actually *perform* these acts. Such patients appear to have lost the uniquely human capacity for thinking *about* things as well as directly "thinking things."

It is his symbolic ability, then, that makes man the only creature who can "look before and after and pine for what is not." Propositional speech makes it possible for him to learn from not only his own personal experience but from that of other men in other times and places, to forecast the consequences of his own behavior, and to have ideals. These three symbol-given attributes—the aptitude for capitalizing on experience, including the experience of others over time, the capacity for foresight and the self-imposed control of behavior through the anticipation of its outcomes, and the ability to envision worlds closer than the present one to the heart's desire—constitute a basic set of distinctively human potentialities.

A second set of such potentialities seems related to the long period of helpless dependence that characterizes infancy and childhood. Made mandatory by the relative biological incompleteness of the human body, this phase of development is likely to be lengthened as cultures become more complex. Thus, in such simpler societies as the Samoan (18), children can achieve a higher degree of independence at an earlier age than in the civilizations of the West, for example, where the necessity for learning complicated and specialized economic skills extends the period of dependence through adolescence and even into chronological young adulthood. The central point, however, is that unlike the young of any other species, human children in *all* cultural settings must spend a long time during which the gratification of their most basic needs is mediated by somebody else and is dependent on their relationship to somebody else.

This state of affairs exposes youngsters during their earliest and most formative stages of development to two fundamental conditions of human life. The first is that one's survival, contentment, and need fulfillment involve an inevitable element of reliance on other people. The second is that the relative autonomy, authority, and power that characterize the parent figures and others on whom one relies in childhood are always perceived to a greater or lesser extent in association with responsibility and a kind of altruism. This is, the enjoyment of adult privileges and status tends to occur in conjunction with the acceptance in some degree of the task of in some way mediating the need-gratifications of others. Mowrer and Kluckhohn (20) seem to be speaking of a similar pattern when they describe the socialization process as progressing from childhood *dependency* through *independence* to adult *dependability*.

Moreover, this reciprocal relationship between reliance and responsibility seems to obtain on adult levels as well as between children and parents, with the degree of reciprocity a partial function of the complexity of the culture. In simpler societies, a relatively small number of persons may assume primary responsibility for virtually all of the needs of the group in excess of its bare subsistence demands. Under civilized conditions, however, the specialization made necessary by technology and the pattern of urban living means that each adult is dependent on some other adult in some way and that, conversely, he is responsible in some fashion for the welfare of some other adult. The difference between the simpler and the more complex cultures, however, is only one of degree. The crucial point is that throughout human society, men are in one way or another dependent on each other both in the familiar situation of parents and children and in the course of adult living. This pattern of interdependency gives to human life a social character to be found nowhere else in the animal kingdom. Even among the remarkable social insects, the patterns of symbiosis found there seem to be a result of a genetically determined division of labor rather than the fulfillment of a potentiality for the mutual sharing of responsibilities for each other.

It is in this notion of the fulfillment of distinctively human potentialities that a fruitful conception of positive adjustment may have its roots. From the symbolic and peculiarly social character of human life, it may be possible to derive a set of potential attributes the cultivation of which results in something different from the mere absence of pathology and which forms a standard against which to assess the degree of integration in individual persons. To accept this task is to attempt the construction of a normative or ideal model of a normal, positively developed, or integratively adjusted human being.

A MODEL OF INTEGRATIVE ADJUSTMENT

In the first place, it would seem that as the symbolic capacity that endows man with foresight develops in an individual, there is a concomitant increase in his ability to control his own behavior by anticipating its probable long-range consequences. The normal person is, first of all, one who has learned that in many situations his greatest satisfaction is gained by foregoing the immediate opportunities for comfort and pleasure in the interest of more remote rewards. He lives according to what Paul Elmer More, the Anglican theologian, calls "the law of costingness":

> . . . the simple and tyrannical fact that, whether in the world physical, or in the world intellectual, or in the world spiritual, we can get nothing without paying an exacted price. The fool is he who ignores, and the villain is he who thinks he can outwit, the vigilance of the nemesis guarding this law of costingness . . . all (one's) progress is dependent on surrendering one interest or value for a higher interest or value. (19, p. 158).

Mowrer and Ullman (21) have made the same point in arguing, from the results of an ingenious experiment, that normality results in large part from the acquired ability to subject impulses to control through the symbolic cues one presents to oneself in the course of estimating the consequences of one's own behavior. Through symbolization, the future outcomes of one's actions are drawn into the psychological present; the strength of more remote rewards or punishments is consequently increased; and a long-range inhibitory or facilitating effect on incipient conduct is thereby exercised.

This increase in self-control means a lessened need for control by external authority, and conformity consequently becomes a relatively unimportant issue. The integratively adjusted person either conforms to the standards of his group because their acceptance leads to the most rewarding long-range consequences for him, or he rebels against authority, whether of persons or of law or custom, on *considered* grounds. This considered form of revolt implies two things. The first is an honest conviction that rules or the ruler are somehow unjust and that the implementation of his own values is likely to lead to a more broadly satisfying state of affairs. Such an attack on authority is very different from revolts that occur out of sheer needs for self-assertion or desires for power or as expressions of displaced hostility. The main dimension of difference is that of honesty as opposed to deception. The normal person is relatively well aware of his motives in either conforming or rebelling. The pathological rebel, on the other hand, tends to deceive himself and others about his goals. His reasons for nonconformity amount to rationalizations, and his justifications are typically projections. This kind of self-defeating and socially disruptive deceptiveness is seen daily in clinical practice.

The second characteristic of nonconformity in the normal person is that it is undertaken with an essential acceptance of the possible consequences. Having considered the risks beforehand, he is inclined neither to whine nor to ask that his rebellious conduct be overlooked if he runs afoul of trouble. In keeping with the "law of costingness," he is willing to pay the price for behaving in accordance with his own idiosyncratic values. "We have the right to lead our own lives," John Erskine (8) makes Helen of Troy say to her daughter Hermione, "but that right implies another—to suffer the consequences. . . . Do your best, and if it's a mistake, hide nothing and be glad to suffer for it. That's morality." A psychological paraphrase of this bit of belletristic wisdom is not inappropriate: The assumption of responsibility[1] for one's actions is one of the attributes of personal integration.

But if personal responsibility and self-control through foresight can be derived as aspects of integrative adjustment from man's symbolic capacity, a third characteristic of interpersonal responsibility can be deduced from his social nature. If interdependency is an essential part of human social life, then the normal person becomes one who can act dependably in relation to others and at the same time acknowledge his need for others. The roots of the former probably lie, as McClelland (17) has pointed out, in the role perceptions which developing children form of parent figures and other agents of the socialization process. By conceiving of such people as at least in some degree the nurturant guides of others and through identification with them, the integratively adjusted individual "wants to be" himself trustworthy and altruistic in the sense of being dependable and acting out of a genuine concern for the welfare of others as he can best conceive it. Altruism in this context, therefore, means nothing sentimental. It certainly includes the making and enforcement of disciplinary rules and the imposition of behavioral limits, but only if these steps are motivated by an interest in helping others and express concern and affection rather than mere personal annoyance or the power conferred by a superior status.

Similarly, the acknowledgement of one's needs for others implies a learned capacity for forming and maintaining intimate interpersonal relationships. Erikson (7) refers to this aspect of the normal personality as the attitude of "basic trust," and it is not far from what can be meaningfully styled in plain language as the ability to love. One suspects that the origins of this ability lie in the long experience during childhood of having need gratifications frequently associated with the presence of another person, typically a parent figure. By this association and the process of generalization, one comes to attach a positive affect to others. But as the youngster develops, he gradually learns that the need-mediating behavior of others is maintained only by his reciprocating, by his entering into a relationship of mutuality with others. If this kind of mutuality is not required of him, he is likely to perpetuate his dependency beyond the period his biological level of development and the complexity of his culture define as appropriate; whereas if he is required to demonstrate this mutuality too soon, he is likely to form the schema that interpersonal relationships are essentially matters of traded favors and that instead of basic trust, the proper attitude is one of getting as much as possible while giving no more than necessary. The pursuit in research and thought of such hypotheses as these might shed a good deal of light on the determinants of friendship, marital happiness, and effective parenthood, the relational expressions of effective personal integration.

[1]This conception of responsibility is by no means antideterministic. As Fingerette (8) points out, one can *understand* his own or another's behavior, in the sense of accounting for it or rationally explaining it, by the retrospective process of examining the past. Responsibility, on the other hand, is neither retrospective in orientation nor explanatory in function. It is future oriented and refers to the *act* of proclaiming oneself as answerable for one's own conduct and its consequences. Thus, "responsibility," in this context, is not a logical term, implying causation, but a behavioral and attitudinal one, descriptive of a class of human actions.

But there is still another interpersonal attitude relevant to a positive conception of adjustment that is somewhat different from that bound up with relationships of an intimate and personal kind. There is a sense in which each individual, even if he regards himself as unfortunate and unhappy, owes his essential humanity to the group which enabled him to survive his helpless infancy. As studies of feral children (25) have shown, even the humanly distinctive and enormously adaptive trait of propositional speech does not become usable without the stimulation and nurture of other people. A kind of obligation is therefore created for the person to be an asset rather than a burden to society. It is partly to the discharging of this obligation that Adler (1) referred in developing his concept of social interest as a mark of normality. While the notion certainly implies the learning of local loyalties and personal affections, it also transcends the provincial limits of group and era. Because man's symbolic capacity enables him to benefit from the record of human history and to anticipate the future, and because his pattern of social interdependency, especially in civilized societies, reaches across the boundaries of political units and parochial affiliations, it seems reasonable to expect the positively developed person to behave in such a fashion as to contribute, according to his own particular lights, to the general welfare of humanity, to take as his frame of reference mankind at large as best he understands it rather than his own group or clan.

Ideologies are at issue here, but there need be neither embarrassment nor a lack of room for debate regarding the specifics of policy and values in the hypothesis that democratic attitudes are closely bound up with personality integration. After all, democracy in psychological terms implies only a concern about others, a valuing of persons above things, and a willingness to participate in mutually gratifying relationships with many categories of persons, including those of which one has only vicarious knowledge. Departures from democratic attitudes in this psychological sense mean a restriction on the potentiality for friendship and imply both a fear of others and a valuation of such things as power over people, thus endangering the interpersonal rewards that come from acting on the attitude of basic trust. Democratic social interest, then, means simply the most direct route to the fulfillment of a distinctively human capacity derived from man's symbolic character and the inevitability of his social life.

Finally, man's ability to assume an attitude toward the "merely possible" suggests that the normal person has ideals and standards that he tries to live up to even though they often exceed his grasp. For an integrative adjustment does not consist in the attainment of perfection but in striving to act in accordance with the best principles of conduct that one can conceive. Operationally, this notion implies that there is an optimum discrepancy between one's self-concept and one's ego-ideal. Those for whom this discrepancy is too large (in favor, of course, of the ideal) are likely to condemn themselves to the frustration of never approximating their goals and to an almost perpetually low self-esteem. Those whose discrepancies are too low, on the other hand, are probably less than integratively adjusted either because they are failing to fulfill their human capacity to envison themselves as they could be or because they are self-deceptively overestimating themselves.

This model of integrative adjustment as characterized by self-control, personal responsibility, social responsibility, democratic social interest, and ideals must be regarded only in the most tentative fashion. Nevertheless, it does seem to take into account some realistic considerations. It avoids the impossible conception of the normal person as one who is always happy, free from conflict, and without problems. Rather, it suggests that he may often fall short of his ideals; and because of ignorance, the limitations under which an individual lives in a complex world, or the strength of immediate pressures, he may sometimes behave in ways that prove to be shortsighted or self-defeating. Consequently, he knows something of the experience of guilt at times, and because he tries to be fully aware of the risks he takes, he can hardly be entirely free from fear and worry. On the other hand, a person who is congruent to the model is likely to be one who enjoys a relatively consistent and high degree of self-respect and who elicits a predominantly positive and warm reaction from others. Moreover, it is such a person who seems to learn wisdom rather than hostile bitterness or pathologically frightened withdrawal from whatever disappointments or suffering may be his lot. Guilt, for example, becomes a challenge to his honesty, especially with himself but also with others; and it signalizes for him the desirability of modifying his behavior, or greater effort to live up to his ideals, rather than the need to defend himself by such mechanisms as rationalization or projection. Finally, the model permits a wide variation in the actual behaviors in which normal people may engage and even makes allowance for a wide range of disagreements among them. Integrative adjustment does not consist in the individual's fitting a preconceived behavioral mold. It may well consist in the degree to which his efforts fulfill the symbolic and social potentialities that are distinctively human.

REFERENCES

1 Adler, A. *Social interest: A challenge to mankind.* London: Faber & Faber, 1938.

2 Adorno, T. W., Frenkel-Brunswik, Else, Levinson, D. J., & Sanford, R. N. *The authoritarian personality.* New York: Harper, 1950.

3 Benedict, Ruth. Anthropology and the abnormal. *J. gen. Psychol.,* 1934, **10,** 59–82.

4 Cassirer, E. *An essay on man.* New Haven: Yale Univer. Press, 1944.

5 Darrah, L. W. The difficulty of being normal. *J. nerv. ment. Dis.,* 1939, **90,** 730–739.

6 DuBois, Cora. *The people of Alor.* Minneapolis: Univer. Minnesota Press, 1944.

7 Erikson, E. H. *Childhood and society.* New York: Norton, 1950.

8 Erskine, J. *The private life of Helen of Troy.* New York: Bobbs-Merrill Co., 1925.

9 Fingarette, H. Psychoanalytic perspectives on moral guilt and responsibility: A re-evaluation. *Phil. phenomenol. Res.,* 1955, **16,** 18–36.

10 Fortune, R. F. *Sorcerers of Dobu.* London: Routledge, 1932.

11 Fromm, E. *The sane society.* New York: Rinehart, 1955.

12 Goldstein, K. *Human nature in the light of psychopathology.* Cambridge, Mass.: Harvard Univer. Press, 1940.

13 Hacker, F. H. The concept of normality and its practical significance. *Amer. J. Orthopsychiat.,* 1945, **15,** 47–64.

14 Langer, Susanne K. *Philosophy in a new key.* Cambridge, Mass.: Harvard Univer. Press, 1942.

15 Marzolf, S. S. The disease concept in psychology. *Psychol. Rev.,* 1947, **54,** 211–221.

16 May, R. *Man's search for himself.* New York: Norton, 1953.

17 McClelland, D. *Personality.* New York: William Sloane Associates, 1951.

18 Mead, Margaret. *Coming of age in Samoa.* New York: William Morrow, 1928.
19 More, P. E. *The Catholic faith.* Princeton: Princeton Univer. Press, 1931.
20 Mowrer, O. H. & Kluckhohn, C. A dynamic theory of personality. In Hunt, J. McV. (Ed.), *Personality and the behavior disorders.* New York: Ronald Press, 1944. Pp. 69–135.
21 Mowrer, O. H., & Ullman, A. D. Time as a determinant in integrative learning. *Psychol. Rev.* 1945, **52,**61–90.
22 Pavlov, I. P. *Conditioned reflexes.* London: Oxford Univer. Press, 1927.
23 Riese, W. *The conception of disease.* New York: Philosophical Library, 1953.
24 Riesman, D. *The lonely crowd.* New Haven: Yale Univer. Press, 1950.
25 Singh, J. A. L., & Zingg, R. M. *Wolf-children and feral man.* New York: Harper, 1942.
26 Subcommittee on Evaluation of Mental Health Activities. *Evaluation in mental health.* Bethesda, Md.: Public Health Service, 1955.
27 Tiegs, E. W., & Katz, B. *Mental hygiene in education.* New York: Ronald Press, 1941.
28 Wegrocki, H. J. A critique of cultural and statistical concepts of abnormality. *J. abnorm. soc. Psychol.,* 1939, **34,** 166–178.
29 Yerkes, R. M. *Chimpanzees: A laboratory colony.* New Haven: Yale Univer. Press, 1943.

The Humanistic Ethic*

James F. T. Bugental

In our usual perspective, we think of the individual who seeks psychotherapy for himself as one who desires to change his own life experience. In this paper I want to take a somewhat different perspective and to suggest that many who have had a growthful therapeutic course emerge from that experience as societal change agents themselves. The person who has discovered he can change what he doesn't like in himself may well seek to change that which he doesn't like in his environment as well.

It will be recognized at once that I am speaking of a kind of therapeutic experience that has as its goal something quite other than producing "adjustment" in the patient. Indeed, that to me abhorrent term is almost diametrically opposite to what I hope those who honor me by being my patients will attain. I say "*almost* diametrically opposite" because I do not feel that my patients become anti-adjusted.

I hope—as I suppose many therapists do—that a patient completing therapy with me will support those societal forms which seem authentic to him in his own life and will work to change those that seem anti-authentic. In other words, I believe that we are social beings and that the healthy person will, in greater or lesser degree, express the social aspect of his life through concernedly being pro or con various phases of his world. Of course, these individuals will vary widely in the extent to which they choose to be so involved and in the stands they will take on particular issues. But the points I want to emphasize here are two: first, the patient is apt to emerge

*From James F. T. Bugental, "The Humanistic Ethic—The Individual in Psychotherapy as a Societal Change Agent," *Journal of Humanistic Psychology,* 1971, 11-25. Reprinted by permission of the author and the Editor, *Journal of Humanistic Psychology.*

from his therapeutic experience with heightened concern about his society and with increased potential to express that concern in effective ways; and second, people who have really come to grasp what I want to call here the humanistic ethic are apt to share an impatience—or indignation—with that which is anti-therapeutic in our culture.

I must note also that when I refer to the bloc of growth-oriented persons, of people supporting a humanistic ethic, I am by no means only speaking of those who have had a formal psychotherapeutic experience. We must recognize that this evolution—for that is what it is—is being supported also by those who have come to share some or all of the ethic by reason of unusually fortunate childhoods, by participation in basic encounter or sensitivity training programs, by reading and contemplation, through exceptional churches, classes, or seminars in connection with their work, or through the growth centers (e.g. Esalen).

The bulk of my presentation below will be devoted to setting forth a first survey of this growth orientation.[1] I do not presume to see this statement as an ultimate or definitive one. It is more in the nature of a progress report. As the humanistic ethic emerges more onto the cultural scene, it may evolve in ways I cannot now estimate (Bugental, 1967). That is, indeed, one of its characteristics: It is not to be captured and contained within any one formulation for it is constantly evolving and has many forms and facets (Bugental, 1970). After making this sketch of my perspective on the therapeutic ethic, I will speculate very briefly about the impending collision between the anti-therapeutic and mechanomorphic forces in our culture and the growing numbers of persons who subscribe in some degree to the humanistic ethic.

A HUMANISTIC ETHIC

Centered Responsibility for One's Own Life

A foundation postulation of the humanistic ethic is that each person is the most responsible agency in his own life. While certainly recognizing the influence of contingency, of social pressure, and of concern for others, the humanistic ethic insists that these do not displace the person from being the one who mediates all such influences and in large part determines how they will influence his being. This is an aspect of what Rollo May (1959) has called "centeredness."

This responsibility is not one that can be delegated or displaced. One is certain to find that at times it involves feelings of guilt, of great emotional pain, and of course, of remorse, but it also can lead to an awareness of one's own potency, dignity, and meaningfulness.

To the person who has not grasped the humanistic ethic, this orientation often seems at first to be a counsel of isolation or of unreal self-centeredness. It is neither; indeed, it is in many ways the reverse of both. Claiming and accepting subjecthood

[1]I will use the terms "humanistic ethic," "therapeutic ethic," and "growth orientation" largely interchangeably. This is not only to relieve the repetitiousness which would otherwise result but to make evident that I am not describing a fixed creed so much as an evolving set of attitudes shared in widely varying degrees and with much variation in specifics by a growing number of persons.

in one's own life is a necessary pre-step to any valid encounter with another person, and it means accepting responsibility for one's own actions and experience, rather than acting as though licensed for self-indulgence.

There is in the humanistic ethic an insistence on the right and the necessity of each person to be the subject—and the only subject—of his own life. This tenet is set in opposition to so much in our culture that tends toward transforming persons into semi-human objects: the credibility gap, propaganda and news manipulation, mass-produced entertainment for passive viewers, depersonalized educational curricula and procedures, and so on—including a mechanomorphic psychology that seeks to reduce the human experience to the banalities of rats, pigeons, and robots (Jourard, 1967).

The growth orientation may be illustrated by the way basic encounter groups call on their members to assert their own autonomy. Such groups grow impatient when someone attempts to explain himself largely in terms of outside influences. The following kinds of statements typically are challenged in such groups:

"I can't do that because my husband doesn't like it."
"It wouldn't be right for me to tell her how I feel if it might hurt her."
"What would people think if my feelings just came out?"

These statements do not express an authentic, responsible concern for others, but are instead expressions of a robot-like subservience to rules originating outside the self.

It is a familiar observation in psychotherapy that many of us in our middle class culture find it difficult to recognize our own feelings or to accept them as valid data. Our language is replete with disclaimers of our centered responsibility: We speak in the second and third persons when meaning the first. We say, "It occurred to me. . . ." when meaning "I think. . . ." And probably we find it hardest of all to explain our actions or intentions in such simple terms as "I felt like it," or "I want it" (Bugental, 1962).

Some have seen dynamic psychology—especially when a certain use is made of the concept of psychic determinism—as excusing all because whatever the individual found objectionable to himself could be blamed on his "unconscious." This, to my mind, is a perversion of a valuable concept. Responsibility does not reside only in what is conscious but is intrinsic in the nature of being. "Blame" is, of course, quite distinct from "responsibility" as I am using these terms here (Bugental, 1965).

The humanistic tenet is a recognition that each individual is the chief determinant of his own behavior and experience. This, of course, includes both conscious and unconscious processes in the person and recognizes that one cannot be responsible for all outcomes of his actions. It insists, however, that while we cannot choose all that befalls us, we can choose how we will respond to it—in Frankl's language, "the attitude we take toward it" (1957).

It is a familiar observation that people react very differently to the same event—be it a concentration camp, a professional success, a love relationship, the death of a friend. While, certainly, differences of early history are influential, I don't believe that even these are completely determining. Each person ultimately is the only *aware* influence in determining his own life (Bugental, 1969b).

Mutuality in Relationship

A second tenet of the humanistic ethic is that the ideal for relationship between people is one of mutuality between persons each of whom is the subject of his own life and each of whom values and recognizes the subjecthood of the other. This is Buber's "I-thou" relation. It is also the Hippies' "You do your thing, and I'll do mine," although in that form it is too easily mistaken for a counsel of nonrelationship, of isolation. Neither in the best of the Hippie movement nor in the humanistic ethic is there an implication of detachment from concern for the other. The intent is, on the contrary, a kind of genuineness of encounter in which the autonomy of each is not only respected but is a solid foundation for meaningful relationship. It is, in a paradoxical way, a foundation which makes possible deeper encounter, greater caring, and less selfishness in the limited and pejorative meaning of that word.

So much in our culture teaches a form of relationship which treats the other person as an object to be manipulated, reacted to, or owned. *How to Win Friends and Influence People* stands as an epitome of the subject-to-object kind of pseudo-relating in which "friends" are *won* by stratagems and maneuvered with tactics to serve one's purposes. Until fairly recently, such a philosophy was the almost universal guide in employer-employee relations, and in more intimate relations it has been advanced with notable popular success by many.

The humanistic ethic, growing out of the therapeutic relation, the encounter group, and the teachings of men like Buber, Rogers, and others, insists that one depersonalizes others only at cost to his own humanness. Relationship is too rich in its potentialities to be reduced to the level of operating as a machine. Moreover this is so whether the intent in doing so is exploitative or seemingly beneficient. To treat the other person as an object in order to gain advantage over him is easily recognized as reprehensible. But to so treat him in order to help him is often heralded as a good thing. The humanistic ethic decries both equally, recognizing that the "management" of news by a well-intentioned president, the paternalistic policies of a "benevolent dictator" type of employer, and the soft-hearted reluctance to set limits for his child on the part of a "liberal" parent are all instances of the failure of relationship and the loss of the humanness to both parties to such maneuvers.

Among other generally accepted patterns of relationship, which therapeutically-oriented people are calling into question, would be that of exclusivity in man-woman relations. This means the end to the double-standard, to the myth of the virgin marriage, to the extreme value placed on marital fidelity, to the folk-tale of the wolf with his string of "conquests," and to the pseudo-ideal of sex for its own sake.

Now since this is a paradoxical list of folkways to be lumped together and since this area of man-woman relations is so central to human concerns, let me enlarge on this point.

The relation between a man and a woman which a society considers the expected model provides, it seems to me, a significant index of what that culture views as desirable in human relations generally. In some, but by no means all, antique societies, women were clearly regarded as things, as generally interchangeable, and as seldom capable of attaining subjecthood in their own right. Thus a man might have a number of women among his possessions.

In our culture—especially the middle class segment—we have a hodge-podge of folkways describing ideals for man-woman relations. These are often conflicting, much ignored at the level of behavior, and frequently the causes of emotional and relationship distress. Many are survivals in changed forms of the woman-as-chattel tradition.

The "official" morality is, of course, that of the virginal man and woman who first discover their own and each other's bodies on their wedding night. This model is in some ways laughable, it is so little descriptive of what is lived out. It would be laughable, that is, except for the truly tragic toll it takes in human misery as people blame themselves for falling short of achieving it.

A contrasting morality is that of the virgin woman and the experienced man. This is, in many ways, the more general expectancy in our culture. And it is truly shocking that this is so, for it demonstrates a societal repression of an obvious inequality, with its callous disregard for the girls inevitably branded "bad." A societal model that so clearly ignores the humanity of an appreciable number of its members is only quantitatively different from the Roman acceptance of butchery in the Coliseum.

A third morality is that of the playboy. This is essentially the view that sex is a good thing and that one does well to get as much as possible—at least until marriage. Then the playboy and his playmate are supposed to undergo a metamorphosis and accept the traditional morality thereafter. Sex—before marriage, be it noted—is seen as a relatively simple natural function with only incidental implications for relationship or self-maturing.

The therapeutic ethic does not, as I see it, specify patterns of sexual behavior as such. Rather it focuses on relationship, and it values authenticity in relationship as among the highest goods potential in the human experience. Yet this position has important implications for sexuality. Probably the epitome of intimate encounter is sexual intercourse between a man and a woman who deeply love each other, who are mutually self-and-other respecting, and who are free to invest themselves fully in their coming together—free, that is, of fear, guilt, and of the need to act out other motives than those intrinsic to their own being together. In such an experience there is genuine transcendence possible. It can mean transcending the separateness which is usually part of being human, a transcending of the difference between giving and receiving, a transcending of the boundaries of time and daily concerns. Clearly, the fullest loving and sexual meeting is a psychedelic experience, the potential for which is in our very nature.

The wise lover knows, however, that there is a Gresham's law governing such experiences. One may accept the discipline of being selective in his relationships and thus preserving their transcendent potentials, or he may yield to the invitations of opportunity and content himself with the pale simulations of the fullness that is potential. Although the choice is certainly not completely either-or, it is not possible to be both an indiscriminate playboy and a fully authentic lover.

What is implied here is that realization of the fullest potentials of one's sexual nature calls for realization of one's fullest potentials as a human being. One must come to terms in some measure with his own internal conflicts and one must relate to the other person in a genuine, mutually respecting fashion if there is to be a sexual meeting of meaningfulness. "Sexual," of course, here means much more than "physical." It subsumes emotional, personal, and relational.

What has just been said should make it evident also that the humanistic ethic does not include the idea of exclusivity in relationships, for that would amount to a kind of ownership of the other. Rather it counsels a selectivity or discrimination such as one would exercise in the care of any precious talent. This means that promiscuity will be seen as sad wastefulness but that the same can be said of blind fidelity.

Moreover, this orientation may free the area of sexual relations from the inappropriate annexations which custom has given it. Thus nudity or semi-nudity is not in itself a matter crucial to sexuality. Our culture generally, is coming to realize this, and newspapers can report—as I read recently about a "Love-in"—that many of the girls were near-nude without a fearful outcry resulting. As some encounter groups are discovering and as current styles are demonstrating, exposure of some or all of the body can be pleasant, even stimulating, without engendering mass orgies. Similarly, moderate sensuality—as in touching, embracing, and some caressing—is increasingly being lifted out of the realm of the fearful and forbidden.

All of these developments will surely have their effects on the institution of marriage. Just what evolution in the nature of marriage will result is difficult to foresee at this point; however, I believe that marriage may be becoming more an individual—may I say, creative?—expression of the relationship of particular couples rather than a socially monolithic imposition. The basis for this view may be summarized as follows.

I think the range of possible growth and fulfillment that is potential in human relationship is truly infinite. This means that two people dedicated to exploring all that their relation can yield may well devote their life-times to that exploration without exhausting its possibilities. At the same time it seems self-evident that our existential situation is such that one must choose some experiences and relinquish others. One cannot, accordingly, choose to explore to the full the potentialities of relationship with a number of partners. When a person selects one partner and commits himself with that person to a full exploration of their relation's possibilities, then a marriage has occurred, and it is fitting that it should be celebrated with ceremony.

But note, it is essential to this meaning of marriage that both parties be aware of the commitment they are jointly making and of the meanings each is giving to that commitment. If there are hidden codicils about ownership of one by the other, of urgency for material gain, of attempts to change the other, then the real meaning of marriage as I am depicting it is undermined. Moreover, if the passage of time results in one or the other of the spouses becoming unwilling or unable to continue such a total commitment, then the marriage itself no longer exists and the formal contract needs re-examination.

Further, there is in this conception no implication of exclusivity beyond that intrinsic to the joint exploration to which both are committed. Relations with others—sexual or not—would be evaluated by the extent to which they contributed to or detracted from the common goal. And, I believe, such other relations may at times help and at other times hinder movement toward such a shared goal.

Now, of course, I have presented an extreme, an idealistic picture. Couples may well choose any degree of commitment to such an exploration. It requires dedication and discipline to seek the far reaches of relationship potential. What is called for by the humanistic ethic, it seems to me, is mutuality and openness in the choice and recognition that any affirmative choice also means some relinquishment.

Here-and-Now Perspective

A third tenet of the humanistic ethic may be designated in a shorthand way as the here-and-now perspective. This outlook reminds us that one always lives only at the present moment. It is not devaluing of the past, but it recognizes that in a very real sense the past is mute and only the interpretations we make of it today give it meaning. The here-and-now perspective, similarly, does not counsel that we be blind to the future, but it does insist that we are in this moment doing much that will determine that future and that it is only in the ever-flowing present that we can realize our own potentials.

That somewhat poetic phrase I just used, "the ever-flowing present," evokes an image, I hope, of the process nature of being—an image important to appreciation of the here-and-now perspective. We are accustomed in much of our thinking to regarding ourselves as relatively static entities, having fixed natures, and seeking a consistency and stability in our own lives. The dearly loved homeostasis of the behaviorists is but one instance. Consistency is so highly prized that you have only to show a man how he has said one thing at one time and a contrasting thing at another to evoke from him a flood of rhetoric designed to demonstrate that both statements are really the same or that one is the logical outgrowth of the other. It is rare to hear, "I've learned differently" or "I was mistaken" or "I've changed my view."

Moreover, we press each other to be constant. We say, "But John, you're always so optimistic, how can you be doubtful now?" We resist seeing ourselves or others change and accuse the one who changes of bad faith. Yet one clear outcome of successful psychotherapy—as of other growth experiences—is that the authentic person is constantly flowing, evolving, becoming. Moreover he values his own and others' flowingness and sees greater possibility rather than threat in it.

The here-and-now perspective is expressed when a person seeks to know as well as possible what it is he is experiencing at each moment and what is the genuine nature of the situation in which he finds himself. In familiar terms, such a person seeks to be free of transference or parataxic distortions of his self-and-world view. This means he is less concerned with what he *should* think, feel, or do than are most of us in our culture.

A concomitant result of this present-valuing perspective is reduced emphasis on striving, on deferred living, and competitive attainment. This is not to say that the authentic person imitates the grasshopper in Aesop's fable and idles away all his hours, but neither does he pattern himself on the ant and forego all experiencing of his life as it is in a narrow focus on trying to make it something else. This is certainly not a counsel of irresponsibility but a realistic reminder that living truly today is among the most important opportunities we have and is, at the same time, the best preparation for tomorrow.

Probably one of the places where a collision between the here-and-now perspective and the contemporary culture is most desirable is in the realm of education. I think it no exaggeration to say that our educational philosophy when viewed in the perspective of human history is almost tragically wasteful and even destructive. Twelve to twenty or more years of each person's most formative years are given over to an experience implicit with learnings about deferred living, extrinsic and competitive values, highly authoritarian social accommodation, and devaluing of the individual, the creative, and the immediate. Surely if there are future social historians, they will wonder that we could have been so ruthless with the greatest of our natural resources: our youth.

But I have broadened my indictment beyond our perspective in this paper. Let me return to that by emphasizing that the schools for the most part are organized to treat pupils as interchangeable objects and to enforce uniformity on those who resist it. This means that learning is supposedly fostered in terms of some distant period at which it will be valued, while spontaneous curiosity, investigativeness, and immediate application are regarded as distractions, devalued as "play," or punished as disruptions of discipline. That is a harsh picture, but unfortunately a reasonably accurate one in thousands of classrooms.

In all fairness, I want to acknowledge that not a few educators are aware of this situation and are seeking against great odds to bring about changes. I am here chiefly indicting the culture at large and its complacency in assuming we have an outstanding educational system.

Also let's look at that word "play" for a minute. By and large it means activity engaged in for its own sake rather than as a means to some other end. This latter is termed "work." I commend to you to watch a pre-school child at the beach or in some other setting unfamiliar to him. He will, if undisturbed, quite confound the experts who tell us how short is his attention span as he spends hours in exploring his world and himself. Is he playing or working? Clearly, he is doing both and going to school at the same time as he learns about gravity, about what his body parts can and cannot do, about the properties of water and sand, about heat and cold, and so on through an extensive and vital curriculum. Watch a grammer school child in a sand lot ball game intently learning more about the physical world and broadening his studies to include social relations. Watch a teenager, if you can, in a setting relatively free of adult supervision, and you will see him taking advanced studies in a variety of essential subjects: language and communication, sexuality and intimacy, limits and lack of limits in society, individuality vs. conformity.

In brief, the most life-significant learnings occur outside the educational structure, on a random basis, with little meaningful guidance from the adult world. Is it surprising that an appreciable number of the brighter, more creative, and more independent of our young people are tempted to drop out of the stultifying schools?

Acceptance of Non-hedonic Emotions

A fourth phase of the humanistic ethic is the recognition that such emotions as pain, conflict, grief, anger, and guilt are parts of the human experience to be understood and even valued rather than to be expressed and hidden. In the culture at large there is a general outlook which tends to see these "negative emotions or experiences" as evidence of something wrong or even shameful. While, to be sure, they may signal the need for attention, they are not, in the view of the humanistic ethic, seen as unexpected or disgraceful.

We have had, in our culture, a general attitude toward all of our emotions that seemed to regard them as dangerous potentials which each person carried within him and which might go off without warning or reason. We have feared strong feelings of all kinds and counseled one another not to feel "too happy," "too miserable," "too hopeful," and so on. Concurrently, immense amounts of talent invention, money, and time have been devoted to evoking emotions in controlled and even artificial ways through the arts, literature, sports, news media, and countless other forms. It is obvious that the suppression of the immediate, personal experience of one's emotions is intimately linked to the great demand for vicarious emotion.

Now all that I have just said about emotions in general is even more true when one considers those experiences which may be grouped as non-hedonic: anger, fear, conflict, grief, guilt, pain, and so on. We have treated these as unfortunate defects in our constitution and often have railed at God or nature for including them in the human design.

Those who have come to terms with their own being through psychotherapy or some other means usually learn, however, that these seemingly unwanted parts of life are in fact essential to full human experience. Encounter group members, for example, come to reject premature reassurance to one of their fellows who is troubled and to object to those who seek to smooth over or evade differences and antagonisms. We have learned that emotion of any character is not simply "disorganized response" (as at least some mechanomorphic psychologists see it). It is, rather, an expression of an experienced meaning in the person's life.

Repeatedly the psychotherapist sees how full confrontation of intense, even excruciating, feelings is essential to his patient's (and his own) preservation of what is valid and significant in life (Bugental, 1969a). Moreover, since the non-hedonic emotions are often aroused at life junctures at which choices of lasting significance must be made, the suppression of such feelings—as many attempt—only results in incomplete and ill-founded decisions being made with the inevitable consequences of failing commitment and renewed distress.

An area in which this recognition of the importance of accepting all emotions is finding a new and very practical application is that of human relations training in industry. Where once business people sought conflict-free working environments and regarded personal emotions as intrusions on the supposedly reasonable workaday world, some better informed companies are recognizing today that personal feelings are essential parts of human beings and must be included in the way the firm is administered. Thus work-family encounter groups are being developed in which a new candor between boss and subordinates is encouraged, and conflicts—with their attendant anger and hurt—are brought out into the open (Rogers, 1967).

Similarly, in friendships and marriages, the humanistic ethic recognizes that such feelings—including guilt and grief, as well—are to be expected and that, expected, they may be disclosed and used as the basis for strengthening the bonds between the people involved.

It is difficult, in a way, to convey what a significant change this means for the human experience. It implies an outlook on one's own life and on relations with others in which the threat of catastrophe is materially lessened. It means, as well, that man learns that he, his fellows, and the ties they have to each other are not as fragile or tenuous as he may have feared. In sum it increases our sense of our own durability and our dignity.

Growth-oriented Experiencing

A final aspect of the humanistic ethic with which I will deal here has to do with the seeking for growth-facilitating experiences which is characteristic of people who have incorporated the humanistic ethic. Of course, what I have already said depicts this valuing as much as it does the specifics with which I have dealt. However, since at root the humanistic ethic is more a value statement about how one experiences his life than anything else, it is important to render this statement as explicit as possible.

The centering of attention on the individual person, on his autonomy and dignity, on his seeking to be authentic and the subject of his own life is, of course, a value position of keystone importance. Correlatively, the kinds of life experiences which are sought will be those in which the relations among persons express the valuing of the individual in mutuality. Here it is important to recognize that the value orientation is not in terms of the traditional "good and bad" or "should and should not," but is cast in a perspective which respects each person's efforts to do what he can with his life and appreciates his gains in authenticity while regretting or even challenging his dropping back from what is potential.

This latter point is important to make more evident: If in a relationship one person does something that hurts the other, traditionally the hurt one had the social "right" to blame the doer of the hurt. Alternatively, he could be long-suffering and hide that he was hurt. The growth-orientation would insist that both of these courses are inauthentic and destructive to the relation and thus to the individuals involved. Instead, the ideal would be for the hurt person and the other to face candidly what has occurred; for the anger and regret intrinsic to the situation itself to be expressed, and for the two to attempt then to forestall recurrences. This last step would surely call for the one who was hurt to seek out those ways in which he himself cooperated—perhaps unconsciously—in bringing about the hurt, for it is very much in keeping with the concept of mutual subjecthood that no person in a relationship is seen as solely responsible for what happens.

Notably absent from this account are recriminations, allusions to other matters outside the point at issue, requirements of compensatory pain, or personal charges and countercharges. It is recognized, instead, that people who risk being genuinely open and close to each other will inevitably hurt each other at times and that any attempt to keep score and balance out hurts ignores the omnipresent mutual responsibility and makes one or the other or both into objects rather than subjects.

It may be protested that this is an ideal not humanly attainable, but I do not believe it is so extreme but what many people are working toward it with evident gains for themselves and their relationships. The long-term freeing of relationships and of the individuals involved is a benefit hard to overestimate.

The therapeutic ethic, thus, centers its values around a perception of each person as worthy in his own right and of genuine relationship as one of life's prime fulfillments. This centering is most evident in the communication that exists among people who share commitment to the humanistic ethic.

Among such people there is a sense of rapport which contrasts markedly with the banality of usual conversation. There is a quality of directness, meaningfulness, and self-disclosure that arises from involvement and willingness to risk. Much talk, as we all know, in ordinary situations is superficial, safe, and detached.

As a consequence of the personal feelings arising from this contrast in ways of relating, persons committed to the humanistic ethic frequently express a need and desire to develop social structures to provide more opportunities for such communication. In some cases, these take the form of leaderless encounter groups which meet regularly and provide an opportunity for more meaningful interaction than do the more usual social occasions. Another emerging medium for such encounters is typified by the pioneering of Esalen and other growth centers where people come together for more intense, emotional, and meaningful exchanges. These exchanges contrast radically with the "entertainment" through vicarious emotion described above. At these centers personal experiencing is valued and facilitated.

Similarly, unmarried people who have come to accept the growth ethic frequently find they do not want to marry someone who does not share this perspective, and married persons whose spouses do not have such an orientation are deeply troubled by the resulting discrepancy.

All of this, of course, smacks of cultism, and in our culture that tends to be a bad word. Yet I believe that there is much that is hopeful in the growing numbers of these people whom one social scientist has half-humorously called an "emotional aristocracy." Cultish they may be, in that they still are a minority bound together by values and attitudes that the surrounding majority does not understand or share. But cultish they are not in any invidious sense or with any intent to keep others out. Admission is simply a matter of a person's seeking to come to terms with himself and to deal with others on a basis of mutual dignity and responsibility. In other words, this is an aristocarcy, if you like, that would gladly become a democracy and whose ranks are open to any who will accept the challenge and opportunity to live more genuinely and openly.

THE COLLISION BETWEEN THE HUMANISTIC ETHIC AND CONTEMPORARY SOCIETY

As the number and influence of persons committed to the humanistic ethic grow, there are certain to be points of collision with the environing culture (Bugental, 1968). Although a society must grow and change to survive, every society—ours most certainly—needs and has forces which resist change. These too are essential. However, when a society is affluent, the conservative forces often tend to be disproportionately strong and then there is the danger that evolution will be stifled. Of course, then revolution becomes more likely. This, I think, is what is happening in our own society. There is clearly a Black revolution in process. Less often recognized is the youth revolution, of which the Hippies are one wing. I think a humanistic evolution may be in the offing.

Now the humanistic ethic, as I have tried to show, runs counter to much that has long been traditional in our culture. As it increases in its impact, a counter force is arising. Today psychotherapy, for example, is seen as a good thing by some, as a dangerous influence by others, and is largely outside the perceptual worlds of a majority of people. But as the variance between therapeutic values and traditional values increases, as the contrast between the popular image of the therapist as a wise man who tells people how to adjust to society and the actuality of therapists pioneering new orientations to human relations becomes more evident, then we may well see a backlash. It is likely that many psychotherapists today could be charged with malpractice, communism, atheism, immorality, and creating dissent, and the charges would be supported in many tradition-conserving settings. Tomorrow, when the traditions are more clearly endangered, we may experience just such prosecutions. Then issues of professional discretion, confidentiality, freedom of professional judgment, the right of an individual to choose his therapist, the public meaning of having been in therapy—all these and others may become points of conflict, hurt, and challenge to the well-being of therapists and others. Another Joe McCarthy could have a field day with psychotherapists and their patients, given the right combination of timing and ruthlessness.

For make no mistake about it, we who share this emerging ethic are a threat to the establishment. It is only that the size and pervasiveness of that threat is as yet unrecognized.

If an evolved humanistic ethic is to make its contribution to the evolutionary stream of man's development, it will require our courage, our dedication, and our persistence. The preliminary statement I have offered here of what I have chosen to call a humanistic ethic must be revised, expanded, and better articulated. This process will also call for us to find improved ways of helping more people to fuller realization of their human potentials. But in the end it calls upon us as individuals to try to live as fully human lives as we can and to know that by doing so we are not only gaining a measure of our own living but adding our bits to the humanization of man.

REFERENCES

Bugental, J. F. T. A phenomenological hypothesis of neurotic determinants and their therapy. *Psychological Reports,* 1962, **10,** 527–530.

Bugental, J. F. T. *The search for authenticity.* New York: Holt, Rinehart & Winston, 1965.

Bugental, J. F. T. The challenge that is man. In J. F. T. Bugental (Ed.), *Challenges of humanistic psychology.* New York: McGraw-Hill, 1967, Ch. 1.

Bugental, J. F. T. Psychotherapy as a source of the therapist's own authenticity and inauthenticity. *Voices,* 1968, **4,** 13–23.

Bugental, J. F. T. Intentionality and ambivalence. In R. McLeod (Ed.) *The unfinished business of William James.* Washington: American Psychological Association, 1969, 93–98. (a)

Bugental, J. F. T. Someone needs to worry: The existential anxiety of responsibility and decision. *Journal of Contemporary Psychotherapy,* 1969, **2** (1), 41–53. (b)

Bugental, J. F. T. Changes in inner human experience and the future. In C. S. Wallia (Ed.), *Toward Century 21: Technology, society and human values*. New York: Basic Books, 1970, 283–295.

Frankl, V. W. *The doctor and the soul*. New York: Knopf, 1957.

Jourard, S. N. Experimenter-subject dialogue: A paradigm for a humanistic science of psychology. In J. F. T. Bugental (Ed.) *Challenges of humanistic psychology*. New York: McGraw-Hill, 1967, 109–116.

May, R. Toward the ontological basis of psychotherapy. *Existential Inquiries,* 1959, **1** (1), 5–7.

Rogers, C. R. The process of the basic encounter group. In J. F. T. Bugental (Ed.) *Challenges of humanistic psychology*. New York: McGraw-Hill, 1967, 261–276.

Toward the Elimination of the Concept of Normality*

David Freides

In recent years, the literature concerning the nature of normality in human personality has shown increasing support for an "idealist" conception of psychological normality. Normality is viewed as an approximation to an ideal or combination of ideals, such as health, rationality, honesty, integration, maturity, or morality. This literature has justifiably criticized the traditional approaches to this problem, i.e., a "symptom-free" conception, specified as absence of pathological stigmata, or a "centrist" conception, specified either as the statistical average of normally disturbed characteristics or as the balance between tendencies, which, in their extremes, are considered pathological, like introversion and extroversion. This paper will present a critique of normative perspectives in personality theory, focusing on the "idealist" position (criticism of traditional approaches may be found in works by Hartman, 1939; Maslow, 1954; Mowrer, 1954; Shoben, 1957, and others), and propose an alternative to these approaches.

A common starting point among authors proposing an idealist conception of normality is the recognition of the enormous extrabiological potential for variation inherent in human beings as evidenced by complex cultural activity, symbolization, and altruism. They stress that these inherently human qualities deserve more serious attention than they are getting from students of personality and should be embodied in the concept of normality. Shoben (1967, p. 185), for example, states, "the fundamental contention advanced here is that behavior is 'positive' or 'integrative' to the extent that it reflects the unique attributes of the human animal." As the "unique attributes" of humans are extremely varied and frequently repugnant, the writers go on to specify what they mean. Maslow (1954, Ch. 12) lists 17 characteristics of self-actualizing people including acceptance of self, others, and nature; spontaneity; problem centering; the quality of detachment; autonomy; democratic character struc-

*From David Freides, "Toward the Elimination of the Concept of Normality." *J. consult. Psychol.*, 1960, **24**, 128–133. By permission of the author and the Managing Editor, the American Psychological Association.

ture; creativeness; and resistance to enculturation. Bond (1952) mentions freedom to focus energy on main purposes, ability to work and love with ease, and to achieve happiness and efficiency somewhat in proportion to circumstances. Shoben (1957) writes of self-control, personal responsibility, social responsibility, democratic social interests, and ideals. McLaughlin (1950) enumerates emotional independence and self-reliance; balance between giving and getting; relative freedom from egotism, inferiority feelings, and excessive competitiveness; conscience; genital sexuality; constructive aggressiveness; solid sense of reality; flexibility; and adaptability.

Several major difficulties and limitations are inherent in this approach. First, it establishes as absolute desiderata patterns of behavior and values that grow out of a particular cultural context during a particular period of its history. It assumes that what is good for us is good for everybody everywhere. Several authors explicitly recognize that these criteria of normality involve assumptions in the nature of value judgments. Other writers do not, but cultural anthropology and history provide evidence that freedom from inferiority feelings or genital sexuality or constructive aggressiveness, for example, are not and have not been universally considered desirable goals for human behavior.

Second, this approach generally does not take into account the circumstances under which the personality is to function. It implies that variations in circumstances do not determine or even influence the functioning of the personality and precludes the study of how behavior and circumstance covary. Third, it largely assumes that postulated criteria of normality are positively correlated, or can be positively correlated. As to whether they are correlated, reference can be made to several attempts to study "normal, healthy individuals." Maslow (1954) and Bond (1952), for example, went to great efforts to obtain suitable examples. Bond guarded against his own selection biases by studying almost complete populations of student council members and concluded nonetheless that 57% could benefit from ideal mental health services. Maslow grudgingly devotes two pages to the imperfections of self-actualizing people. Roe's (1950) studies of eminent scientists (to be sure, using criteria of success and not of normality) amply indicate that nonnormal characteristics regularly accompany achievement, creativity, and success. Redlich (1952) reviews several studies of "normal" populations in which "rich pathological" material was found.

Perhaps even more significant is the question of whether it is reasonable to anticipate that characteristics of normality such as those under discussion can be positively correlated. Consider, for example, such positively valued attributes as love and independence. Ideal patterns of loving devotion and enduring commitment to one's beloved, coupled with independence, assertiveness, and freedom from infantile demands of succorance, are generally accepted as positive characteristics of the normal; but the conflictual nature of multiple human needs and aspirations is obscured by an approach which does not recognize that love and commitment *necessarily* and inevitably restrict independence.

Finally, a value based conception of normality tends arbitrarily to slant research so as to preclude investigations of the relationships between devalued patterns of behavior and ideal patterns of behavior.

These criticisms are not to be construed as arguments for banning values from consideration in personality theory. The question is where and how to deal with them in a way that is scientifically appropriate. Values and value systems may be studied objectively as variables, and the task of psychology is to assess their relationships with other variables and with behavior. Such an approach does not imply that every moral and ethical system is as good or as workable as any other nor that the search for the "good" in either individual or culture should be minimized, but it does indicate a way in which such problems may be considered at levels of discourse which are germane to science. In this manner science is not faced with questions it cannot answer.

It is significant that the proponents of the point of view under discussion seem to be all for the good life but are rather vague as to what they mean by it, while theologists and ethicians are quite explicit and vigorous defenders of the positions they take. The apparent proclivity for tolerance, understanding, and minimization of differences, characteristic of this school of thought (with few exceptions), conceals and overrides hard differences in the approach to life embodied in different value systems.[1] Yet, to consider values as variables seems definitely uncongenial to those who hold that the values they profess are the only values worthy of consideration and study. For example, Shoben (1957), while arguing that a normative approach based on a statistical average precludes the criticism of a culture, confuses a conflict of values with a scientific controversy when he disdains the possibility that the storm trooper would be considered the prototype of integrative adjustment in the Nazi culture. Disapproval of Nazi culture has nothing to do with understanding how a man raised in Nazi Germany might be expected to become a storm trooper. Science can do no more than predict the consequences of a value system. Political, religious, or cultural conflicts are fundamentally not resolved in the laboratory or on the couch.

Writers adopting an idealist approach concerning psychological normality take a position that is steeped in contradiction. On the one hand, their conception of normality has an absolutist quality that is laced with culture-bound value assumptions. On the other hand, they show marked reservations concerning a conception of normality based on social conformity and they abhor any taint of absolutism. Maslow (1954), for example, specifies autonomy, independence of culture and environment, and resistance to enculturation as characteristics of the self-actualizing (normal) person. In doing so, Maslow evidently means to divorce himself from purely statistical conceptions of social conformity. Certainly he does not mean compulsive autonomy, or compulsive resistance to enculturation, yet his whole perspective, shared with many others, including Fromm (1941), Mowrer (1954), and Shoben (1957), is one of meeting a specified ideal, and this inevitably involves some form of cultural bias, some form of limitation, some constriction of freedom.

In a discussion of this contradiction, Knight (1946) deals with the problem by (a) specifying that freedom is largely a subjective matter; (b) showing that many subjective feelings of freedom are spurious, and (c) concluding that genuine freedom and mental health involve the sense of inner compulsion and conformity based on a rational appreciation by the individual of the assumptions, conditions, motives, and

[1]See Herberg (1957) for a critical discussion of the ethical inadequacies of theoretical orientations in psychology which minimize differences in value alternatives and preclude the conceptualization of the realities of moral conflict in the individual.

values in his life. It is this bedrock of rationality to which all of these writers ultimately arrive.

Kubie (1954) takes perhaps the extreme position and asserts that the sole criterion for normality is the predominance of conscious and preconscious over unconscious factors in the determination of an act. Since Kubie rules out consciousness, per se, as a criterion (a delusion is conscious but not normal), he can only be interpreted to mean that rational, reasonable, reality-oriented behavior is normal. On the surface, this seems to be a satisfactory solution to the problem. It posits a criterion which is neutral as far as value is concerned and can conceivably lead to objective assessment procedures. However, such a point of view seemingly would label all nonrational behavior and motivation as abnormal and in doing so would devalue and implicitly condemn any manifestation of emotional spontaneity. Arguing, as Kubie does, that it is the origin of the act and not its subsequent automatic execution that must be assessed, would nonetheless require, at some point, meticulous evaluation of matters of taste, preferences in art, religious values and beliefs, and love objects in order to fulfill this criterion. Kubie's disclaimer (1954, p. 187), "Here is no unreal fantasy of a 'normal' individual out of whom all the salty seasoning of secondary unconscious motivations has been dissolved," when followed in the next paragraph by "What was unconscious . . . must become accessible enough to self-inspection to become conscious when needed," suggests that his conception of "salty seasoning" is not so spicy after all.

When the search for the normal leads to the evaluation of the rational, a host of problems concerning the nature of reason, logic, and rationality may be overlooked. These include the distinctions between a rational process and rational content (Hartman, 1956; Reider, 1950), the illogical and prelogical factors which contribute to the development of intelligence and reason (Piaget, 1953), the role of unconscious and regressive factors in creativity (Kris, 1952), and the process of change in form and content of knowledge and logic through a history which has not ended and whose future course is unpredictable by any reliable means.

Finally, and this criticism is germane to practically every attempt to define normality, it assumes that rational, conscious, and preconscious processes, once established, carry on of their own accord without environmental support and stimulation. Recent studies on the effects of sensory deprivation (Hebb, 1955), the classic studies of perception under distorted conditions (Lawrence, 1949), and many studies of behavior under stress (Lazarus, Deese, & Osler, 1952) indicate that this is simply not the case. To specify consciousness or rationality as the essence of normality merely begs the question.

A truly objective, scientific solution to the problem of defining normality when one is concerned with something more than averaging existing traits and behaviors, when one seeks to embody in this definition a particular conception of what man may be, is impossible to attain. As soon as values, symbols, altruism, and the like are specified in the definition of normality, objectivity yields to time-bound and culture-bound assumptions which are not subject to scientific verification and which are of limited generality. That each person deliberately or unconsciously has a scheme of values, beliefs, and ethics which imparts to him his uniquely human character, that, indeed, to be a human requires such a scheme, is a proposition that does not establish a *particular* system of values or logic as an absolute criterion of normality.

Psychology should stop asking the question "What is normal?" Personality theory requires another orientation. It seems to me that, for purposes of scientific theory construction and also for practical clinical purposes, a rather different and potentially more fruitful approach can be taken. This would entail the viewpoint that human beings have a variety of potentialities, and that the achievement of certain potentialities may entail certain limitations and that achievement and limitation vary with conditions.

Consider it is the distant, withdrawn personality who is unable to form close relationships who, it has been said, stands the best chance of enduring the stress of a prolonged flight into space. The suspicious mistrusting individual, difficult to get along with, may, because of these very characteristics, be an excellent tax inspector, research scientist, or counterintelligence agent. The vain narcissistic personality can become a great entertainer. Reverse the point. Is great acting possible without narcissism? Is creative research possible without mistrust? Is prolonged isolation tolerable for a gregarious individual? The legitimate task of science is not to stand back smugly and label the various distributions of energy and effort as abnormal or normal. The task of theoretical psychology is to provide the concepts and principles which would enable us to comprehend achievements and failings *and their interrelationships*.

Such an approach focuses on man's behavior as the data available for scientific study. Existing terms and concepts such as repression, motive, conformity, defense mechanism, and habit need not be discarded as conceptual tools, but with this perspective the scientist does not imply damnation or praise when he uses them to characterize a psychological process. This approach sets no limits on the sophistication of the theories developed to encompass the facts of behavior, but it lessens the likelihood of confounding facts and theories and value assumptions. It avoids positing criterion value systems but freely admits the incorporation of value systems as variables contributing to or limiting different potentialities. It sets the stage for research into the development and exercise of man's potentialities for what, on other grounds, may be considered good or evil, but does not prejudge or condemn. It permits the description and understanding of man as he was, and can be.

Several features of the present position have been elaborated in the literature. Marmor and Pumpian-Mindlin (1950) and Jahoda (1953), for example, have stressed the interaction of personality and situational variables in the determination of behavior. Hartman (1951) points out that conflicts are inherent to human existence and (1939) that rationality and freedom do not necessarily imply health, while regression and defense are not necessarily maladaptive. Schafer (1954, p. 172) writes, "The growth and organization of personality appears to require that certain of each individual's potentialities be cultivated and others neglected or even plowed under." Marzolf (1947) concludes, "In fact there is no need for the term 'mental disease.' " Several writers (Darrah, 1939; Jones, 1942; Wile, 1940) are doubtful about the existence of "normal" personalities. But in one way or another, they all (with the exception of Wile, 1940) cling to the traditional perspective and express or reflect some concept of normality.

If the framework proposed is theoretically acceptable, objections may nevertheless be raised on practical grounds. If no valid conception of normality is possible, is treatment ever indicated and, if so, toward what goals is treatment directed? At present, certain personality patterns can be labeled abnormal and treatment is presumably directed toward changing abnormal personalities or patterns of behavior into normal ones. The definition of what is normal is considered critical to clinical practice and its elimination apparently leaves an enormous conceptual void.

Actually, there are several unwarranted assumptions implicit in the view that a conception of normality is central to clinical practice. First is the assumption that treatment is initiated with the finding of abnormality, however defined. Operationally, treatment is initiated when motivation from some source exists for treatment and when therapists are motivated and prepared to undertake treatment. There is a reciprocal relationship between professional personnel and patient pool in that the professional proffers the expectation of relief from distress and contributes to the development of this anticipation in potential clients. Absence of some relevant form of this expectation seems to be one of the factors underlying failure in the treatment of lower-class patients by predominantly middle- and upper-class professionals (Hollingshead & Redlich, 1958). The point is that the initiation of treatment results less from a finding of abnormality than from the meshing of reciprocally intertwined (more or less) motivations.

Second, the notion that the aim of treatment consists of changing the patient from abnormal to normal is unjustified. In many cases, in those perhaps most amenable to current forms of treatment, therapy consists largely of helping the patient to resolve conflicting trends within his personality rather than making him or helping him to become normal. The patient who has successfully completed this type of treatment (in which the therapist can remain relatively neutral with regard to values) does not by any flight of the imagination meet the usual criteria of normality. (The individual who speaks of his having been analyzed or treated psychotherapeutically and implies that he is ''normal'' is usually labeled a prig.) Furthermore, as already noted, if the patient has been enabled to deal more successfully with certain kinds of problems and conflicts, this may be at the expense of other potentialities.

A third questionable point is the assumption that the goals of treatment are determined by scientific criteria. In many types of cases the resolution of conflict is only a minor part of therapy. Much more than the bolstering or the elimination of defensive patterns within the personality seems indicated in certain types of schizophrenia, in severely schizoid personalities or in antisocial personalities. Very many of these cases require that a way of life be taught. In other words, certain cases require far more than reorganization of the personality; they require education itself and the inculcation of values. Once again, it seems to me that science can contribute to an understanding of the educative process but that the content of this education is largely a matter that must be decided on other grounds. Here, the articulation and specification of the values under which or toward which the therapist operates is of great importance, *but these choices are not scientific matters.* We do the best we can much like any parent living at a particular time and in a particular place.

This point, that values, symbols, and the like *are* involved in psychotherapy

(Hacker, 1945), brings the discussion full circle. Davis (1938, p. 65) in a little cited analysis of the mental hygiene movement has argued that the social function of the mental hygienist "is not that of a scientist but that of a practising moralist in a scientific, mobile world." It seems to me that what Davis is saying is that professionals dealing with "ways of life" inevitably have to rely on *some* consistent framework to fill gaps and resolve conflicts where they exist and that this framework willy-nilly will be that prevalent in the cultural group to which the professionals belong. If this issue may be obscured in the treatment of adults, it is blatantly apparent and quite inevitable in the treatment of children and in the advice given to parents about techniques of child rearing (Erikson, 1950). As a consequence, it seems likely that psychological treatment is a conservative force in any society no matter how radical the theories about psychotherapy sometimes appear to be. But the implicit or explicit commitment to values involved in the practice of psychotherapy is an issue separate and distinct from a scientifically useful specification of the concept of normality. The future development of a scientific understanding of personality depends on a less restrictive perspective which, ironically, should benefit clinical practice as well.

A shift in perspective in personality theory from one which looks upon man as normal or abnormal or somewhere in between to one which views him as having varying potentialities and limitations under varying conditions, seems to offer an orientation more viable, secure, and fruitful than that prevailing at present. The viable aspect of this position comes out of its capacity to conceive of man in different times and different circumstances. The security features result from the elimination of the necessity for the clinician to rationalize about his own normality (Reider, 1950), permitting his work to be evaluated objectively in terms of its results. Finally, the fruitfulness of this approach rests on its reluctance to condemn, to label abnormal, and its emphasis on the potentialities of every person under the proper conditions. It sets the stage for more extensive investigations into the nature of these potentialities and the conditions of their achievement, all the while keeping before us the pitfalls and limitations that such achievement may involve.

REFERENCES

Bond, E. D. The student council study: An approach to the normal. *Amer. J. Psychiat.*, 1952, **109,** 11–16.

Darrah, L. W. The difficulty of being normal. *J. nerv. ment. Dis.*, 1939, **90,** 730–739.

Davis, K. Mental hygiene and the class structure. *Psychiatry,* 1938, **1,** 55–65.

Erikson, E. H. *Childhood and society*. New York: Norton, 1950.

Fromm, E. *Escape from freedom*. New York: Rinehart, 1941.

Hacker, F. J. The concept of normality and its practical significance. *Amer. J. Orthopsychiat.*, 1945, **15,** 47–64.

Hartman, H. Psychoanalysis and the concept of health. *Int. J. Psycho-Anal.*, 1939, **20,** 308–321.

Hartman, H. Ego psychology and the problem of adaptation. In D. Rapaport (Ed.), *Organization and pathology of thought*. New York: Columbia Univer. Press, 1951.

Hartman, H. Notes on the reality principle. *Psychoanal. Stud. Child,* 1956, **11,** 31–53.

Hebb, D. O. The mammal and his environment. *Amer. J. Psychiat.*, 1955, **111,** 826–831.

Herberg, W. Freud, religion and social reality. *Commentary,* 1957, **23,** 277–284.
Hollingshead, A. B., & Redlich, F. C. *Social class and mental illness.* New York: Wiley, 1958.
Jahoda, Marie. The meaning of psychological health. *Soc. Casewk.,* 1953, **34,** 349–354.
Jones, E. The concept of the normal mind. *Int. J. Psycho-Anal.,* 1942, **23,** 1–8.
Knight, R. P. Determinism, "freedom" and psychotherapy. *Psychiatry,* 1946, **9,** 251–262.
Kris, E. *Psychoanalytic explorations in art.* New York: International Univer. Press, 1952.
Kubie, S. The fundamental nature of the distinction between normality and neurosis. *Psychoanal. Quart.,* 1954, **23,** 167–204.
Lawrence, M. *Studies in human behavior.* Princeton: Princeton Univer. Press, 1949.
Lazarus, R. S., Deese, J., & Osler, S. F. The effects of psychological stress upon performance. *Psychol. Bull.,* 1952, **49,** 293–317.
McLaughlin, J. T. Normality and psychosomatic illness. *Ment. Hyg., N.Y.,* 1950, **34,** 19–33.
Marmor, J., & Pumpian-Mindlin, E. Toward an integrative conception of mental disorder. *J. nerv. ment. Dis.,* 1950, **111,** 19–29.
Marzolf, S. S. The disease concept in psychology. *Psychol. Rev.,* 1947, **54,** 211–221.
Maslow, A. H. *Motivation and personality.* New York: Harper, 1954.
Mowrer, O. H. What is normal behavior? In L. A. Pennington & I. A. Berg (Eds.), *An introduction to clinical psychology.* (2nd ed.) New York: Ronald Press, 1954. Pp. 58–88.
Piaget, J. *The origin of intelligence in the child.* London: Routledge & Kegan Paul, 1953.
Redlich, F. C. The concept of normality. *Amer. J. Psychother.,* 1952, **6,** 551–569.
Reider, N. The concept of normality. *Psychoanal. Quart.,* 1950, **19,** 43–51.
Roe, Anne. The use of clinical diagnostic techniques in research with normals. In M. Reymert (Ed.), *Feelings and emotions.* New York: McGraw-Hill, 1950. Pp. 336–342.
Schafer, R. *Psychoanalytic interpretation in Rorschach testing.* New York: Grune & Stratton, 1954.
Shoben, E. J. Toward a concept of the normal personality. *Amer. Psychologist,* 1957, **12,** 183–189.
Wile, I. S. What constitutes abnormality? *Amer. J. Orthopsychiat.,* 1940, **10,** 216–228.

Section Two

Theories of Personality and Psychological Adjustment

When we observe people, the complexity of behavior and differences among individuals are apparent. Individual A loves her children while individual B does not; individual C seems to us to defeat himself while D achieves his goals; E appears to live in a world of fantasy, unfamiliar to most of us; F is happy while G is depressed. How do we account for these differences? Most of us hold some set of implicit or explicit notions that explain human behavior somewhat to our satisfaction. Most of us feel, more or less in a vague way, that we can account for the behavior of the persons who interact with us. Our private systems, however, are incomplete and do not share widespread acknowledgment.

In this section of readings, we present a variety of ways in which contemporary psychology approaches the problem of accounting for adjustment theoretically and systematically. The papers in this section belong to the domain of *personality theory* and provide accounts of some of the major theories or sets of hypotheses about psychological adjustment.

First, we need to come to some more or less convenient definition of the term "personality." Since different theories define the word differently, it is no easy task to find a definition acceptable to all psychologists. In 1937, Gordon W. Allport published *Personality: A Psychological Interpretation,* (New York: Holt, Rinehart and Winston), which is extremely valuable for its report of his scholarly search for definitions of personality in a variety of settings. Allport discovered forty-eight definitions or meanings that the term had acquired in sociology, law, philosophy, theology, psychology, and literature. It became clear to Allport that there were two fundamentally opposed meanings. One meaning defined personality in terms of outward appearance while the other defined personality in terms of inner experience. Allport proposed a forty-ninth definition for psychology, what a man really is, which he elaborated in the following formal statement: "Personality is the dynamic organization within the individual of those psychophysical systems that determine his unique adjustment to his environment." For Allport, this definition was sufficiently broad to represent a "synthesis of contemporary psychological usage." While its generality involves limitations, it serves as a useful and convenient orientation to this section. All the personality theories to be considered involve postulating an *organization of systems* (habits, traits, attitudes, needs, self-concepts, etc.) that determine adjustment.

Before we turn to the specific personality theories, we need to give some consideration to theories in a formal sense. When can we say that we have a theory? Neal E. Miller [in Krech, D., and Klein, G. S. (eds.), *Theoretical Models and Personality Theory*. Durham, N.C.: Duke University Press, 1952], in commenting upon theoretical models, gives an unequivocal reply. He writes that "a system can properly be called a model or theory if, and only if, one can use it to make rigorous deductions about some of the consequences of different sets of conditions." We have a theory when we can make predictions about the consequences of a *great* number of different conditions from a *limited* set of definitions and axioms.

According to the criteria given above, a good many psychological theories are properly not theories at all but points of view or isolated hypotheses. Miller calls them "articles of faith or intuition." We, however, have not utilized any formal definition of theory to preclude a point of view from consideration but rather have used as a criterion for inclusion the presentation of ideas that contribute to an understanding of personal adjustment.

It is also important to indicate that the theories vary in many respects. Some will appear to be more scientifically rigorous than others; the scope of inquiry will differ, and the evidence available to support each will vary in its character.

The section opens with selections relating to the theories of Freud, Adler, and Jung. They are grouped together because they all belong to the psychoanalytic tradition. Both Adler and Jung, however, came to reject Freudian theory and founded what came to be known as "individual" and "analytic psychology," respectively.

The selection from Freud provides the reader with what many view as his fundamental concepts, i.e., an account of his theory of unconscious determinism and his theory of infantile sexuality. The paper is unusually noteworthy in that it provides a historical view of the development of Freud's major concepts concerning human behavior. It summarizes a large share of his total contribution, which has had a significant impact on our view of the nature of human beings. His influence has been felt strongly not only in psychology and psychiatry, but in other disciplines as well. Literature, anthropology, sociology, education, art, law, theology, philosophy, political science, economics, etc., have all felt his impact.

Freud's attempt to account for human behavior is the most ambitious theory of those considered. His concern is with the totality of human experience. While the scope of psychoanalytic theory enables us to speculate about a wide range of human behavior, the method of validating hypotheses, which consists of the careful examination in a treatment situation of the life history of the individual, is not as rigorous as might be desired. Contemporary psychology, however, is continuing to find ways of subjecting Freudian hypotheses to controlled investigation and experimentation.

In contrast with Freud, Adler did not write a coherent and systematic account of his position. However, his position has been summarized by many of his followers. The paper by Ansbacher presents a concise statement of Adler's theory by one of his foremost interpreters. Adler analyzes the adjustment process in terms of an individual's relationships and methods of coping with his or her environment. Especially important in Adler's thinking is the individual's view of his or her own adequacy and his or her particular methods of attempting to exert influence over others. Maladjustment results from the person's efforts to overcompensate for strong feelings of inadequacy by attempting to dominate and to control others. In addition, Adler's position equates adjustment with the ability to evaluate oneself realistically and to develop social relationships that are beneficial to others and are not merely designed for purposes of self-aggrandizement.

Jung's basic unit of investigation is the *psyche*. With this concept he refers to the psychological structure of the human being. He thinks of the psyche as a kind of nonphysical space wherein psychic phenomena occur. In order to describe these phenomena, Jung has developed a vocabulary that is not widely shared and which includes a number of distinctive concepts. The paper by Storr, in giving a historical account of the development of Jung's theory, summarizes and integrates a number of Jung's difficult concepts and ideas with commendable clarity.

Papers reflecting the positions of Karen Horney and Harry Stack Sullivan are given next. Again they are represented by interpreters, Norman Levy in the case of Horney and Patrick Mullahy in the case of Sullivan. Levy offers a synthesis of Horney's work derived from a review of her books. The reader will want to attend to Horney's insistence on the role of the environment in the production of maladjustment. In marked contrast to the biological position of Freud, Horney draws attention to the variety of adverse influences to which children are subjected. These engender *basic anxiety,* and this is the condition that promotes malajusted ways of interacting with others. According to Sullivan's theory, which has become known as the *interpersonal theory of psychiatry,* personality is "the relatively enduring pattern of recurrent interpersonal situations which characterize a human life." The proper field of investigation is the interpersonal situation; the individual does not and cannot exist apart from his or her transactions with other people. Sullivan's fundamental hypothesis, therefore, led him away from preoccupation with biological drives and Freudian instinctual urges to the study of social interactions—mother and child, doctor and patient, etc. Mullahy's selection gives an account of Sullivan's view with respect to the goals of behavior, the modes of human experience, and the evolving of the self through interaction with others.

The next selection deals with a self-theory conception of the nature of human beings. The essential point is that behavior is a function, in some significant part, of one's *self-concept*, one's self-regarding attitudes. The self-concept refers to the totality of attitudes the individual holds with reference to himself or herself. It is learned in evaluational transactions with others (notably, important others such as mother and father), and it influences behavior whether or not it is in accord with reality. The selection from C. H. Patterson consists of a summary of the personality theory of Carl Rogers, whose self-theory was developed concurrently with his client-centered or nondirective psychotherapy.

The next paper, by Pervin, represents a phenomenological conceptualization of human behavior. Pervin presents the *existential* position on the nature of human beings. Here, human beings are described as concerned with "the meaning of life." In recent years, a great deal of interest has been generated for this position which, congruent with the views of some of the great existential writers and philosophers, such as Camus and Sartre, declares that "people are free" and become what *they choose*. Both Pervin's existential philosophy and Roger's self-theory are based on a phenomenological view point that holds that an understanding of human behavior can occur only through awareness of the idiosyncratic perceptions, feelings, and thoughts of the individual involved. This approach calls into question the possibility of objectifying the important aspects of human conduct.

The last two selections define the nature of human beings from the point of view of learning theory. While there are important variations in the personality theories that different theorists have formulated based on learning concepts, the distinctive aspect of a learning approach is that complex human behavior is viewed as explainable and predictable from basic principles of learning. The paper by Maher provides the reader with the basic learning concepts involving conditioning and avoidance learning. These concepts have been investigated extensively in experimental research, and they indicate the possibility of viewing complex human behavior and problems meaningfully with the theoretical concepts that have been developed to explain relatively simple learning tasks. Katkovsky's paper, which follows, describes the social-learning theory of Julian B. Rotter, which represents another systematic effort to apply learning principles to complex human behavior. This approach is referred to as an "expectancy-reinforcement" theory since the major formulation holds that behavior is a function of the individual's expectations concerning the reinforcements that occur as a consequence of his or her behavior. After reviewing the theory, Katkovsky discusses the development and maintenance of maladjustment using social-learning-theory concepts.

Psychoanalytic Theory*

Sigmund Freud

Psycho-analysis is the name (1) of a procedure for the investigation of mental processes which are almost inaccessible in any other way, (2) of a method (based upon that investigation) for the treatment of neurotic disorders and (3) of a collection of psychological information obtained along those lines, which is gradually being accumulated into a new scientific discipline.

History The best way of understanding psycho-analysis is still by tracing its origin and development. In 1880 and 1881 Dr. Josef Breuer of Vienna, a well-known physician and experimental physiologist, was occupied in the treatment of a girl who had fallen ill of a severe hysteria while she was nursing her sick father. The clinical picture was made up of motor paralyses, inhibitions, and disturbances of consciousness. Following a hint given him by the patient herself, who was a person of great intelligence, he put her into a state of hypnosis and contrived that, by describing to him the moods and thoughts that were uppermost in her mind, she returned on each particular occasion to a normal mental condition. By consistently repeating the same laborious process, he succeeded in freeing her from all her inhibitions and paralyses, so that in the end he found his trouble rewarded by a great therapeutic success as well as by an unexpected insight into the nature of the puzzling neurosis. Nevertheless, Breuer refrained from following up his discovery or from publishing anything about the case until some ten years later, when the personal influence of the present writer (Freud, who had returned to Vienna in 1886 after studying in the school of Charcot) prevailed on him to take up the subject afresh and embark upon a joint study of it. These two, Breuer and Freud, published a preliminary paper 'On the Psychical Mechanism of Hysterical Phenomena' in 1893, and in 1895 a volume entitled *Studies on Hysteria* (which reached its fourth edition in 1922), in which they described their therapeutic procedure as *'cathartic'*.

Catharsis The investigations which lay at the root of Breuer and Freud's studies led to two chief results, and these have not been shaken by subsequent experience: first, that hysterical symptoms have sense and meaning, being substitutes for normal mental acts; and secondly, that the uncovering of this unknown meaning is accompanied by the removal of the symptoms—so that in this case scientific research and therapeutic effort coincide. The observations were carried out upon a series of patients who were treated in the same manner as Breuer's first patient, that is to say, put into a state of deep hypnosis; and the results seemed brilliant, until later their weak side became evident. The theoretical ideas put forward at that time by Breuer and Freud

*From Vol. V. of the *Collected Papers of Sigmund Freud,* edited by Ernest Jones, M.D., Basic Books, Inc., Publishers, New York, 1959.

Acknowledgment also to Sigmund Freud Copyrights Ltd., Mr. James Strachey, The Hogarth Press Ltd. for permission to quote from Vol. 18 of the Standard Edition of *The Complete Psychological Works of Sigmund Freud.*

were influenced by Charcot's theories on traumatic hysteria and could find support in the findings of his pupil Pierre Janet, which, though they were published earlier than the *Studies,* were in fact subsequent to Breuer's first case. From the very beginning the factor of *affect* was brought into the foreground: hysterical symptoms, the authors maintained, came into existence when a mental process with a heavy charge of affect was in any way prevented from being levelled out along the normal path leading to consciousness and movement (i.e. was prevented from being '*abreacted*'); as a result of this the affect, which was in a sense '*strangulated*', was diverted along wrong paths and flowed off into the somatic innervation (a process named '*conversion*'). The occasions upon which 'pathogenic ideas' of this kind arose were described by Breuer and Freud as '*psychical traumas*', and, since these often dated back to the very remote past, it was possible for the authors to say that hysterics suffered mainly from reminiscences (which had not been dealt with). Under the treatment, therefore, '*catharsis*' came about when the path to consciousness was opened and there was a normal discharge of affect. It will be seen that an essential part of this theory was the assumption of the existence of *unconscious* mental processes. Janet too had made use of unconscious acts in mental life; but, as he insisted in his later polemics against psycho-analysis, to him the phrase was no more than a make-shift expression, a '*manière de parler*', and he intended to suggest no new point of view by it.

In a theoretical section of the *Studies* Breuer brought forward some speculative ideas about the processes of excitation in the mind. These ideas determined the direction of future lines of thought and even to-day have not received sufficient appreciation. But they brought his contributions to this branch of science to an end, and soon afterwards he withdrew from the common work.

The Transition to Psycho-analysis Contrasts between the views of the two authors had been visible even in the *Studies*. Breuer supposed that the pathogenic ideas produced their traumatic effect because they arose during '*hypnoid states*', in which mental functioning was subject to special limitations. The present writer rejected this explanation and inclined to the belief that an idea became pathogenic if its content was in opposition to the predominant trend of the subject's mental life so that it provoked him into '*defence*'. (Janet had attributed to hysterical patients a constitutional incapacity for holding together the contents of their minds; and it was at this point that his path diverged from that of Breuer and Freud.) Moreover, the two innovations which led the present writer to move away from the cathartic method had already been mentioned in the *Studies*. After Breuer's withdrawal they became the starting-point of fresh developments.

Abandonment of Hypnosis The first of these innovations was based on practical experience and led to a change in technique. The second consisted in an advance in the clinical understanding of neuroses. It soon appeared that the therapeutic hopes which had been placed upon cathartic treatment in hypnosis were to some extent unfulfilled. It was true that the disappearance of the symptoms went hand-in-hand with the catharsis, but total success turned out to be entirely dependent upon the patient's relation to the physician and thus resembled the effect of 'suggestion'. If that relation was disturbed, all the symptoms reappeared, just as though they had never been cleared up. In addition to this, the small number of people who could be put into a deep state of hypnosis involved a very considerable limitation, from the medical standpoint, of the applicability of the cathartic procedure. For these reasons the present writer decided to give up the use of hypnosis. But at the same time the impressions he had derived from hypnosis afforded him the means of replacing it.

Free Association The effect of the hypnotic condition upon the patient had been so greatly to increase his ability to make associations that he was able straight away to find the path—inaccessible to his conscious reflection—which led from the symptom to the thoughts and memories connected with it. The abandonment of hypnosis seemed to make the situation hopeless, until the writer recalled a remark of Bernheim's to the effect that things that had been experienced in a state of somnambulism were only *apparently* forgotten and that they could be brought into recollection at any time if the physician insisted forcibly enough that the patient knew them. The writer therefore endeavoured to insist on his *unhypnotized* patients giving him their associations, so that from the material thus provided he might find the path leading to what had been forgotten or fended off. He noticed later that the insistence was unnecessary and that copious ideas almost always arose in the patient's mind, but that they were held back from being communicated and even from becoming conscious by certain objections put by the patient in his own way. It was to be expected—though this was still unproved and not until later confirmed by wide experience—that everything that occurred to a patient setting out from a particular starting-point must also stand in an internal connection with that starting-point; hence arose the technique of educating the patient to give up the whole of his critical attitude and of making use of the material which was thus brought to light for the purpose of uncovering the connections that were being sought. A strong belief in the strict determination of mental events certainly played a part in the choice of this technique as a substitute for hypnosis.

The 'Fundamental Technical Rule' of this procedure of 'free association' has from that time on been maintained in psychoanalytic work. The treatment is begun by the patient being required to put himself in the position of an attentive and dispassionate self-observer, merely to read off all the time the surface of his consciousness, and on the one hand to make a duty of the most complete honesty while on the other not to hold back any idea from communication, even if (1) he feels that it is too disagreeable or if (2) he judges that it is nonsensical or (3) too unimportant or (4) irrelevant to what is being looked for. It is uniformly found that precisely those ideas which provoke these last-mentioned reactions are of particular value in discovering the forgotten material.

Psycho-analysis As an Interpretative Art The new technique altered the picture of the treatment so greatly, brought the physician into such a new relation to the patient and produced so many surprising results that it seemed justifiable to distinguish the procedure from the cathartic method by giving it a new name. The present writer gave this method of treatment, which could now be extended to many other forms of neurotic disorder, the name of *psycho-analysis*. Now, in the first resort, this psycho-analysis was an art of *interpretation* and it set itself the task of carrying deeper the first of Breuer's great discoveries—namely, that neurotic symptoms are significant substitutes for other mental acts which have been omitted. It was now a question of regarding the material produced by the patients' associations as though it hinted at a hidden meaning and of discovering that meaning from it. Experience soon showed that the attitude which the analytic physician could most advantageously adopt was to surrender himself to his own unconscious mental activity, in a state of *evenly suspended attention,* to avoid so far as possible reflection and the construction of conscious expectations, not to try to fix anything that he heard particularly in his memory, and by these means to catch the drift of the patient's unconscious with his own unconscious. It was then found that, except under conditions that were too unfavourable, the patient's associations emerged like allusions, as it were, to one particular theme and that it was only necessary for the physician to go a step further in order to guess the material which was concealed from the patient himself and to be able to communicate it to him. It is true that this work of interpretation was not to be brought under strict rules and left a great deal of play to the physician's tact and skill; but, with impartiality and practice, it was usually possible to obtain trustworthy results—that is to say, results which were confirmed by being repeated in similar cases. At a time when so little was as yet known of the unconscious, the structure of the neuroses and the pathological processes underlying them, it was a matter for satisfaction that a technique of this kind should be available, even if it had no better theoretical basis. Moreover it is still employed in analyses at the present day in the same manner, though with a sense of greater assurance and with a better understanding of its limitations.

The Interpretation of Parapraxes and Haphazard Acts It was a triumph for the interpretative art of psycho-analysis when it succeeded in demonstrating that certain common mental acts of normal people, for which no one had hitherto attempted to put forward a psychological explanation, were to be regarded in the same light as the symptoms of neurotics: that is to say, they had a *meaning,* which was unknown to the subject but which could easily be discovered by analytic means. The phenomena in question were such events as the temporary forgetting of familiar words and names, forgetting to carry out prescribed tasks, everyday slips of the tongue and of the pen, misreadings, losses and mislayings of objects, certain errors, instances of apparently accidental self-injury, and finally habitual movements carried out seemingly without intention or in play, tunes hummed 'thoughtlessly', and so on. All of these were shorn of their physiological explanation, if any such had ever been attempted, were shown to be strictly determined and were revealed as an expression of the subject's suppressed intentions or as a result of a clash between two intentions one of which was permanently or temporarily unconscious. The importance of this contribution to psychology was of many kinds. The range of mental determinism was extended by it in an unforeseen manner; the supposed gulf between normal and pathological mental events was narrowed; in many cases a useful insight was afforded into the play of mental forces that must be suspected to lie behind the phenomena. Finally, a class of material was brought to light which is calculated better than any other to stimulate a belief in the existence of unconscious mental acts even in people to whom the hypothesis of something at once mental and unconscious seems strange and even absurd. The study of one's own parapraxes and haphazard acts, for which most people have ample opportunities, is even to-day the best preparation for an approach to psycho-analysis. In analytic treatment, the interpretation of parapraxes retains a place as a means of uncovering the unconscious, alongside the immeasurable more important interpretation of associations.

The Interpretation of Dreams A new approach to the depths of mental life was opened when the technique of free association was applied to dreams, whether one's own or those of patients in analysis. In fact, the greater and better part of what we know of the processes in the unconscious levels of the mind is derived from the interpretation of dreams. Psycho-analysis has restored to dreams the importance which was generally ascribed to them in ancient times, but it treats them differently. It does not rely upon the cleverness of the dream-interpreter but for the most part hands the task over to the dreamer himself by asking him for his associations to the separate elements of the dream. By pursuing these associations further we obtain knowledge of thoughts which coincide entirely with the dream but which can be recognized—up to a certain point—as genuine and completely intelligible portions of waking mental activity. Thus the recollected dream emerges as the *manifest dream-content,* in contrast to the *latent dream-thoughts* discovered by interpretation. The process which has transformed the latter into the former, that is to say into 'the dream', and which is undone by the work of interpretation, may be called the *'dream-work'*.

We also describe the latent dream-thoughts, on account of their connection with waking life, as *'residues of the* [*previous*] *day'*. By the operation of the dream-work (to which it would be quite incorrect to ascribe any 'creative' character) the latent dream-thoughts are *condensed* in a remarkable way, are *distorted* by the *displacement* of psychical intensities and are arranged with a view to being *represented in visual pictures;* and, besides all this, before the manifest dream is arrived at, they are submitted to a process of *secondary revision* which seeks to give the new product something in the nature of sense and coherence. Strictly speaking, this last process does not form a part of the dream-work.[1]

The Dynamic Theory of Dream-formation An understanding of the dynamics of dream-formation did not involve any very great difficulties. The motive power for the formation of dreams is not provided by the latent dream-thoughts or day's residues, but by an unconscious impulse, repressed during the day, with which the day's residues have been able to establish contact and which contrives to make a *wish-fulfilment* for itself out of the material of the latent thoughts. Thus every dream is on the one hand the fulfilment of a wish on the part of the unconscious and on the other hand (in so far as it succeeds in guarding the state of sleep against being disturbed) the fulfilment of the normal wish to sleep which set the sleep going. If we disregard the

[1][In *The Interpretation of Dreams, Standard Ed., 5,* 490, secondary revision is regarded as part of the dream-work.]

unconscious contribution to the formation of the dream and limit the dream to its latent thoughts, it can represent anything with which waking life has been concerned—a reflection, a warning, an intention, a preparation for the immediate future or, once again, the satisfaction of an unfulfilled wish. The unrecognizability, strangeness and absurdity of the manifest dream are partly the result of the translation of the thoughts into a different, so to say *archaic,* method of expression, but partly the effect of a restrictive, critically disapproving agency in the mind, which does not entirely cease to function during sleep. It is plausible to suppose that the *'dream-censorship',* which we regard as being responsible in the first instance for the distortion of the dream-thoughts into the manifest dream, is an expression of the same mental forces which during the day-time had held back or *repressed* the unconscious wishful impulse.

It has been worth while to enter in some detail into the explanation of dreams, since analytic work has shown that the dynamics of the formation of dreams are the same as those of the formation of symptoms. In both cases we find a struggle between two trends, of which one is unconscious and ordinarily repressed and strives towards satisfaction—that is, wish-fulfilment—while the other, belonging probably to the conscious ego, is disapproving and repressive. The outcome of this conflict is a *compromise-formation* (the dream or the symptom) in which both trends have found an incomplete expression. The theoretical importance of this conformity between dreams and symptoms is illuminating. Since dreams are not pathological phenomena, the fact shows that the mental mechanisms which produce the symptoms of illness are equally present in normal mental life, that the same uniform law embraces both the normal and the abnormal and that the findings of research into neurotics or psychotics cannot be without significance for our understanding of the healthy mind.

Symbolism In the course of investigating the form of expression brought about by the dream-work, the surprising fact emerged that certain objects, arrangements and relations are represented, in a sense indirectly, by 'symbols', which are used by the dreamer without his understanding them and to which as a rule he offers no associations. Their translation has to be provided by the analyst, who can himself only discover it empirically by experimentally fitting it into the context. It was later found that linguistic usage, mythology and folklore afford the most ample analogies to dream-symbols. Symbols, which raise the most interesting and hitherto unsolved problems, seem to be a fragment of extremely ancient inherited mental equipment. The use of a common symbolism extends far beyond the use of a common language.

The Aetiological Significance of Sexual Life The second novelty which emerged after the hypnotic technique had been replaced by free associations was of a clinical nature. It was discovered in the course of the prolonged search for the traumatic experiences from which hysterical symptoms appeared to be derived. The more carefully the search was pursued the more extensive seemed to be the network of aetiologically significant impressions, but the further back, too, did they reach into the patient's puberty or childhood. At the same time they assumed a uniform character and eventually it became inevitable to bow before the evidence and recognize that at the root of the formation of every symptom there were to be found traumatic experiences from early sexual life. Thus a sexual trauma stepped into the place of an ordinary trauma and the latter was seen to owe its aetiological significance to an associative or symbolic connection with the former, which had preceded it. An investigation of cases of common nervousness (falling into the two classes of *neurasthenia* and *anxiety neurosis*) which was simultaneously undertaken led to the conclusion that these disorders could be traced to *contemporary* abuses in the patients' sexual life and could be removed if these were brought to an end. It was thus easy to infer that neuroses in general are an expression of disturbances in sexual life, the so-called *actual-neuroses* being the consequences (by chemical agency) of *contemporary* injuries and the *psycho-neuroses* the consequences (by psychical modification) of *bygone* injuries to a biological function which had hitherto been gravely neglected by science. None of these theses of psycho-analysis has met with such tenacious scepticism or such embittered resistance as this assertion of the preponderating aetiological significance of sexual life in the neuroses. It should, however, be expressly remarked that, in its development up to the present day, psycho-analysis has found no reason to retreat from this opinion.

Infantile Sexuality As a result of its aetiological researches, psycho-analysis found itself in the position of dealing with a subject the very existence of which had scarcely been suspected previously. Science had become accustomed to consider sexual life as beginning with puberty and regarded manifestations of sexuality in children as rare signs of abnormal precocity and degeneracy. But now psycho-analysis revealed a wealth of phenomena, remarkable, yet of regular occurrence, which made it necessary to date back the beginning of the sexual function in children almost to the commencement of extra-uterine existence; and it was asked with astonishment how all this could have come to be overlooked. The first glimpses of sexuality in children had indeed been obtained through the analytic examination of adults and were consequently saddled with all the doubts and sources of error that could be attributed to such a belated retrospect; but subsequently (from 1908 onwards) a beginning was made with the analysis of children themselves and with the unembarrassed observation of their behaviour, and in this way direct confirmation was reached for the whole factual basis on the new view.

Sexuality in children showed a different picture in many respects from that in adults, and, surprisingly enough, it exhibited numerous traces of what, in adults, were condemned as '*perversions*'. It became necessary to enlarge the concept of what was sexual, till it covered more than the impulsion towards the union of the two sexes in the sexual act or towards provoking particular pleasurable sensations in the genitals. But this enlargement was rewarded by the new possibility of grasping infantile, normal and perverse sexual life as a single whole.

The analytic researches carried out by the writer fell, to begin with, into the error of greatly overestimating the importanceof *seduction* as a source of sexual manifestations in children and as a root for the formation of neurotic symptoms. This misapprehension was corrected when it became possible to appreciate the extraordinarily large part played in the mental life of neurotics by the activities of *phantasy,* which clearly carried more weight in neurosis than did external reality. Behind these phantasies there came to light the material which allows us to draw the picture which follows of the development of the sexual function.

The Development of the Libido The sexual instinct, the dynamic manifestation of which in mental life we shall call *'libido'*, is made up of component instincts into which it may once more break up and which are only gradually united into well-defined organizations. The sources of these component instincts are the organs of the body and in particular certain specially marked *erotogenic zones;* but contributions are made to libido from every important functional process in the body. At first the individual component instincts strive for satisfaction independently of one another, but in the course of development they become more and more convergent and concentrated. The first (pregenital) stage of organization to be discerned is the *oral* one, in which—in conformity with the suckling's predominant interest—the oral zone plays the leading part. This is followed by the *sadistic-anal* organization, in which the *anal* zone and the component instinct of *sadism* are particularly prominent; at this stage the difference between the sexes is represented by the contrast between active and passive. The third and final stage of organization is that in which the majority of the component instincts converge under the *primacy of the genital zones*. As a rule this development is passed through swiftly and unobtrusively; but some individual portions of the instincts remain behind at the prodromal stages of the process and thus give rise to *fixations* of libido, which are important as constituting predispositions for subsequent irruptions of repressed impulses and which stand in a definite relation to the later development of neuroses and perversions.

The Process of Finding an Object, and the Oedipus Complex In the first instance the oral component instinct finds satisfaction by attaching itself to the sating of the desire for nourishment; and its object is the mother's breast. It then detaches itself, becomes independent and at the same time *auto-erotic,* that is, it finds an object in the child's own body. Others of the component instincts also start by being auto-erotic and are not until later diverted on to an external object. It is a particularly important fact that the component instincts belonging to the genital zone habitually pass through a period of intense auto-erotic satisfaction. The component instincts are not all equally serviceable in the final genital organization of libido; some of them (for instance, the anal components) are consequently left aside and suppressed, or undergo complicated transformations.

In the very earliest years of childhood (approximately between the ages of two and five) a convergence of the sexual impulses occurs of which, in the case of boys, the object is the mother. This choice of an object, in conjunction with a corresponding attitude of rivalry and hostility towards the father, provides the content of what is known as the *Oedipus complex,* which in every human being is of the greatest importance in determining the final shape of his erotic life. It has been found to be characteristic of a normal individual that he learns to master his Oedipus complex, whereas the neurotic subject remains involved in it.

The Diphasic Onset of Sexual Development Towards the end of the fifth year this early period of sexual life normally comes to an end. It is succeeded by a period of more or less complete *latency,* during which ethical restraints are built up, to act as defences against the desires of the Oedipus complex. In the subsequent period of *puberty,* the Oedipus complex is revivified in the unconscious and embarks upon further modifications. It is only at puberty that the sexual instincts develop to their full intensity; but the direction of that development, as well as all the predispositions for it, have already been determined by the early efflorescence of sexuality during childhood which preceded it. This diphasic development of the sexual function—in two stages, interrupted by the latency period—appears to be a biological peculiarity of the human species and to contain the determining factor for the origin of neuroses.

The Theory of Repression These theoretical considerations, taken together with the immediate impressions derived from analytic work, lead to a view of the neuroses which may be described in the roughest outline as follows. The neuroses are the expression of conflicts between the ego and such of the sexual impulses as seem to the ego incompatible with its integrity or with its ethical standards. Since these impulses are not *ego-syntonic,* the ego has *repressed* them: that is to say, it has withdrawn its interest from them and has shut them off from becoming conscious as well as from obtaining satisfaction by motor discharge. If in the course of analytic work one attempts to make these repressed impulses conscious, one becomes aware of the repressive forces in the form of *resistance.* But the achievement of repression fails particularly readily in the case of the sexual instincts. Their dammed-up libido finds other ways out from the unconscious: for it *regresses* to earlier phases of development and earlier attitudes towards objects, and, at weak points in the libidinal development where there are infantile fixations, it breaks through into consciousness and obtains discharge. What results is a *symptom* and consequently in its essence a substitutive sexual satisfaction. Nevertheless the symptom cannot entirely escape from the repressive forces of the ego and must therefore submit to modifications and displacements—exactly as happens with dreams—by means of which its characteristic of being a sexual satisfaction becomes unrecognizable. Consequently symptoms are in the nature of compromises between the repressed sexual instincts and the repressing ego instincts; they represent a wish-fulfilment for both partners to the conflict simultaneously, but one which is incomplete for each of them. This is quite strictly true of the symptoms of hysteria, while in the symptoms of obsessional neurosis there is often a stronger emphasis upon the side of the repressing function owing to the erection of reaction-formations, which are assurances against sexual satisfaction.

Transference If further proof were needed of the truth that the motive forces behind the formation of neurotic symptoms are of a sexual nature, it would be found in the fact that in the course of analytic treatment a special emotional relation is regularly formed between the patient and the physician. This goes far beyond rational limits. It varies between the most affectionate devotion and the most obstinate enmity and derives all of its characteristics from earlier erotic attitudes of the patient's which have become unconscious. This *transference* alike in its positive and in its negative form is used as a weapon by the resistance; but in the hands of the physician it becomes the most powerful therapeutic instrument and it plays a part scarcely to be over-estimated in the dynamics of the process of cure.

The Corner-stones of Psycho-analytic Theory The assumption that there are unconscious mental processes, the recognition of the theory of resistance and repression, the appreciation of the importance of sexuality and of the Oedipus complex—these constitute the principal subject-matter of psycho-analysis and the foundations of its theory. No one who cannot accept them all should count himself a psycho-analyst.

Adler's Theory of Individual Psychology*

Heinz L. Ansbacher

Adler was the first to develop a comprehensive theory of personality, psychological disorders and psychotherapy, which represented an alternative to the views of Freud, even long before Freud had reached the climax of his acclaim, and simultaneously with Freud's own later development.

Alternatives to Freud have in recent years been restated by many who found his system inadequate to the problems to which it pertains. These developments are known as existential psychology and psychiatry, client-centered counseling, humanistic psychology, the "third force" in psychology, phenomenological psychology, social psychiatry, rational-emotive psychotherapy, neo-Freudian trends, ego psychology, and by many other names. In the aspects in which they depart from Freud, they all can be reconciled far more easily with the basic assumptions of Adler than with those of Freud. To know Adler is to be well prepared for all these developments.

It seems that in the development of modern psychological thinking the Western world first had to go through the Freudian stage, even as Adler himself did for a short period. Fourteen years younger than Freud, he was from 1902 to 1911 a prominent member of Freud's circle. But then he was the first to free himself from Freud as countless others have done since, although Freud's influence was stimulating and fructifying. Now that one reads with increasing frequency that we have entered the post-Freudian era, the appreciation of and interest in Adler are proportionately growing.

Freud represented a half-way station, so-to-speak. Revolutionary as his theories were and difficult as they seem at first, they were actually more conservative and more easy to understand with reference to the scientific and also to some of the popular thinking then prevailing, than was Adler's thinking. Freud was revolutionary for his day in that he listened to every word of his patients, knowing that this would be valuable basic information for solving the puzzle of mental disorder. But he was scientifically conservative in that he firmly believed that the patient's inner psychological world was ultimately determined by objective causes that rested in his past. Freud was difficult in that he created a large new vocabulary designating numerous drives, stages, areas, and mechanisms which he believed to have "discovered," and which

*This paper appeared originally as "Introduction to the Torchbook Edition" of *Problems of Neurosis* by Alfred Adler (1, pp. ix–xxvi) and is reprinted here, with some omissions and slight modifications, by permission of the author and the publisher, Harper and Row, Publishers, Incorporated.

he considered responsible for the full range of human behavior. And yet all this was relatively easy to grasp in that it still was similar to old ways of thinking, according to which mental disorders, like physical illnesses, were caused by forces beyond the individual's control.

It was scientifically more revolutionary to proclaim, as did Adler, that the inner psychological world of the individual, which had such far-reaching consequences, was not objectively caused, but was ultimately the individual's own creation, and that the individual's course of life received its direction not from relatively objective drives, but from his highly subjective goals and values. And it was more difficult to accept that the individual could be quite unaware of the goals and values which he himself had created or accepted, than that he was the pawn of an "unconscious" which supposedly controlled his conscious self.

The essential difference between Freud's and Adler's ways of thinking is that in the former the conception of man's psychological functioning is patterned after the older physical sciences, whereas in the latter it is patterned after the biological sciences, the sciences of life. In the former a mechanistic, elementaristic, and deterministic orientation was adequate. But in the latter it is today widely appreciated that for an understanding of what is specific to life, an organismic and holistic view is more fruitful. Such a view reckons not only with objective determiners from the past but declares that a living organism is a functional unity whose parts cooperate for the good of the whole and that therefore its properties are best understood from this standpoint. As Sinnott (16) has repeatedly explained, it is scientifically fruitful to approach problems of biology from a teleological viewpoint.[1]

If the organismic-holistic viewpoint is the more adequate for biology in general, this must be true especially for the science concerned with the highest manifestation of life, human psychology. Adler embraced this viewpoint, which was not so well defined then as it is today. Its principal practical significance is that the individual is understood not as completely determined by outside forces but to a considerable extent as self-determined. Such a conception is particuarly useful in psychotherapy in that it gives the patient a feeling of freedom and optimism, so important in enabling him to change.

THEORY OF PERSONALITY

The essential principles of Adler's psychology, which he named Individual Psychology, may be considered to be the following.

Unity of the Individual

The unit to be studied is the individual person and his way of living. All the general similarities one can observe among people, such as drives, emotions, cultural experiences, must be understood as subordinated to the individual's organization, his *style of life,* life-plan. As in Gestalt psychology the organization of the whole figure will determine how the parts will be perceived, so in Individual Psychology, the organiza-

[1]A more detailed description of Adler's organismic position is given in another paper (5).

tion of the whole person will influence all his partial functions. But, beyond Gestalt psychology, Adler conceived the individual as goal-oriented, and all partial functions, including neurotic symptoms, as serving the overall purpose.

One of the important consequences of this understanding is that the Freudian conscious-unconscious antithesis and the notion of intrapersonal conflicts are done away with. The unconscious serves the individual's purposes no less than the conscious; it is not a relatively autonomous function which attempts to rule the individual, while he attempts to repress it. "Individual Psychology distinguishes in the conscious and the unconscious, not separate and conflicting entities, but complementary and cooperating parts of one and the same reality" (p. 29).[2] "We cannot oppose 'consciousness' to 'unconsciousness' as if they were two antagonistic halves of an individual's existence. The conscious life becomes unconscious as soon as we fail to understand it—and as soon as we understand an unconscious tendency it has already become conscious" (p. 163).

Not only the psychological but also the organic functions are subordinated to the style of life, although both were originally factors in its formation. "The organic functions are dominated by the style of life. This is notably the case with the lungs, the heart, the stomach, the organs of excretion and the sexual organs. The disturbance of these functions expresses the direction which an individual is taking to attain his goal. I have called these disturbances the organ dialect, or organ jargon, since the organs are revealing in their own most expressive language the intention of the individual totality" (p. 156).

"The dialect of the sexual organs is especially expressive" (p. 156). "My questioners often appear to have been misled . . . into believing that the sexual impulse is the central motive. . . . Our experience is that the sexual components cannot even be correctly estimated except in relation to the individual style of life" (p. 46).

"We are far from disputing that every mental and bodily function is necessarily conditioned by inherited material, but what we see in all psychic activity is the *use which is made* of this material to attain a certain goal" (p. 30).

The individual is not divided against himself. He is not the battleground of conflicting forces. What appears as inner conflicts is derived from man's self-determination, including the freedom and necessity to choose between alternatives presented by the situation. It includes the freedom to make mistakes. "Rightly understood, the whole of this mental process—working from below to above, expressing an inferiority but compensating with a superiority—is not ambivalence but a dynamic unity. Only if it is not understood as a whole do we see it as two contradictory and warring entities" (p. 87).

Unitary Motivation

As an organism, a unified whole, the individual is not determined by various drives or motives, but there is one dynamic force, of which all others are only partial and subsidiary aspects. This derives from the growth and forward movement of life itself.

[2]Because this paper was written as an introduction to *Problems of Neurosis* (1) nearly all references to Adler are from this book. Where only page references are given, they are to this book.

It is a general forward striving. The recognition of one master motive is common to all organismic psychologies since Adler. Some of the names that have been chosen by recent workers are: self-actualization, self-expansion, self-consistency, competence.

Adler ultimately spoke of striving for perfection, completion, overcoming, or a goal of success. Earlier he spoke of striving to overcome the difficulties of life (p. 32), the upward strivings of the psyche (p. 33), striving for superiority (p. 13), or, most often, a goal of superiority. Superiority may be personal superiority over others, or superiority over general difficulties, in the sense of perfection, completion, or competence. The former is characteristic of mental disorders, the latter of mental health.

Here a problem arises. Adler's theoretical writing started with the concept of organ inferiority and its compensation, and soon afterwards he stressed feelings of inferiority as a dynamic force. In the present volume we find, "The sense of impotence, or the 'feeling of inferiority,' is the root-conception of Individual Psychology" (p. 33). "We soon perceive a greater or lesser degree of the feeling of inferiority in everyone, together with a compensatory striving towards a goal of superiority" (p. 2).

The problem is: Which comes first, the feeling of inferiority or the striving? A theory of motivation which puts inferiority feelings first would include only what Maslow (14) calls deficit motivation. In this respect compensation is actually a parallel construction to drive-reduction: Without the feeling of a deficit, an inferiority, there would be no striving.

Although Adler never became explicit on this issue, he quietly changed the order in his last writings, putting the striving first. "In comparison with unattainable ideal perfection, the individual is continuously filled by an inferiority feeling and motivated by it" (3, p. 117). "In the struggle for perfection, man is always in a state of psychical agitation and feels unsettled before the goal of perfection" (3, p. 116). This is a great improvement of the theory. Not only does it give room for the concept of growth motivation (14), the primacy of the striving also permits one to consider this striving as a human manifestation of the general growth and expansion movement which is characteristic of all of life. Furthermore, it is not possible to verify a universal primary inferiority feeling in the infant. This can be neither observed directly nor ascertained through introspection; it is merely a conjecture, whereas the striving for success or competence can be very readily observed in the infant (18).

In a paper by Adler (2) published during his last year, summarizing the basic assumptions of Individual Psychology, inferiority feeling is not even mentioned. This does not mean that in the psychology of mental disorders strong inferiority feelings with correspondingly low self-esteem do not remain a central factor. It only means that inferiority feelings are no longer considered primary, but the outgrowth of an impeded striving for success.

Self-determination and Uniqueness

Since the human individual is capable of considering himself and his situation, and of extending himself into the future, the master motive derives its direction from the over-all goal the individual sets for himself, his conceptualization of superiority or success. Not all of the goal content is conceptualized; to a greater or lesser extent the individual is only dimly aware of where he is heading. To some extent the subject's goal is also the inference or working hypothesis of the psychologist.

While the objective realities have been used in the formulation of the goal, it is in the end subjectively determined by the inventive or creative power of the individual. This is how individual uniqueness becomes most pronounced. Beyond the uniqueness of the constellation of hereditary and environmental factors in each particular case, the goal of superiority which uses these is capable of infinite individual variation.

"No soul develops in freedom. Each one is in mental, emotional and nutritive dependence upon his immediate environment on the earth and in the cosmos, yet so far independent that he must take up these relations consciously: he must answer them as the questions of life" (p. 36). "As a conscious relation between its organism and environment, the child's psyche seems to have an indefinite *causal* power: so that, normal or abnormal, it never reacts with anything like mathematical exactitude. Life, as opposed to dead material, always reacts thus, in a more or less inaccurate—and spontaneous—manner" (p. 34). "The child's individual conception of the future is the dominant causal factor" (p. 90). "In the world of the psyche there is no principle of individual orientation beyond our own beliefs" (p. 62).[3] Our responses to the world will depend on our conception of it, our beliefs and attitudes. Thus Individual Psychology becomes a cognitive and phenomenological psychology.

As already mentioned, what appears as inner conflicts derives from man's freedom to make choices. This freedom offers particular difficulty for the neurotic, because a choice point marks a step forward while the neurotic is afraid of going ahead. Thus where others speak of inner conflicts, Adler speaks of the "hesitating attitude" (p. 3), wasting time (p. 103) in order to gain time.

From the postulate of the importance of beliefs and attitudes in the guidance of behavior and their ultimate determination by the individual's own creative power, follows an optimistic outlook so important for treatment, also mentioned earlier.

Social Context

Just as the partial functions cannot be considered out of the context of the individual, so the individual must be considered within his larger ecological context, including particularly human society. An important part of what makes us human, namely language, is a social product, showing how unscientific it would be to study the individual without taking his social context fully into account. Thus Individual Psychology becomes the study of interpersonal transactions.

This is reflected in the following description of the situation developing from a child's feeling dethroned. "It is a common thing for the first child to hasten his own dethronement by fighting against it with envy, jealousy and truculence, which lower him in the parental favour" (p. 102).

[3]It is for such statements that Ford and Urban (12) designated Adler's Individual Psychology a "subjectivistic system."

Even the function of the sense organs was understood by Adler in the social context. "Imperfections in the sense organs limit the means which a child has of sharing in the life of others" (p. 65).

With regard to the most significant problems that man faces—society, occupation, love—they are all of a social nature. "We must realize that every adaptation we have to make in life, from kindergarten to business management, from school chums to marriage, is, directly or indirectly, a social action. From the earliest times, we face new thoughts and events in a manner which is dominantly social or antisocial, it cannot be neutral. Suppose, for instance, that a boy is terrified by illness and death in his environment. He may allay his fears by the determination to be a doctor, and to fight against death. This is obviously a more social idea than that of being a grave-digger, the one who buries the *others*—a reaction which I have also found in a boy in that situation" (p. 33).

Social Interest

In the organismic-holistic view, man is not seen in unavoidable conflict with society and its rules. This does not deny the existence of such conflicts, but does deny their unavoidability. The concept of society itself is only an abstraction. In concrete reality there are only individuals and rules that they have made to facilitate the process of living together. Everyone has the capacity of understanding these "rules of the game," of developing them further, and of contributing something which will become a part of "society" which another individual may have to meet. Human nature "includes the possibility of socially affirmative action" (p. 35).

"The high degree of cooperation and social culture which man needs for his very existence demands spontaneous social effort, and the dominant purpose of education is to evoke it. Social feeling is not inborn; but it is an innate potentiality which has to be consciously developed" (p. 31). The German term is *Gemeinschaftsgefühl*, which has also been translated as social interest.[4] It is not an innate altruistic motive, opposed to a selfish motive. This would be a motivational dualism, foreign to a holistic theory. Social interest is rather a cognitive function which must be *consciously* developed through education. It may, however, acquire secondary motivational attributes like any developed capacity such as typing or skiing. Man likes to do what he is capable of doing well.

The concept of social feeling or social interest is today recognized as one of Adler's extremely important contributions. It is particularly important for a definition of positive mental health which offers such great difficulty to other theories which do not have this concept.

[4]*Gemeinschaft* in the composite term *Gemeinschaftsgefuhl* is actually not limited to the social aspect. It rather stands for communality or community, a broader concept. *Gemeinschaftsgefuhl* has thus rightly been translated also as community feeling, community interest, communal intuition, or sense of solidarity. It is quite possible to have a feeling of communality with life and the universe in general, to identify with the order of the universe. It is this that Adler meant when he said that the mentally healthy individual "feels at home in life . . . at home upon the crust of the earth," as quoted below.

THEORY OF MENTAL HEALTH, NEUROSIS, AND PSYCHOTHERAPY

Mental Health

While the definition of positive mental health is still an extensively discussed problem, Adler clearly recognized the necessity of formulating a widely serviceable answer. He generally did not describe mental disturbances as ''illness'' but showed how they were mistaken ways of living, mistaken life styles. He designated those with mistaken life styles as ''failures.'' Thus mental health could never be the mere absence of illness, but was a less faulty way of living. The aim of his therapeutic efforts was ''to replace the great mistakes by small ones. . . . Big mistakes can produce neuroses, but little mistakes a nearly normal person'' (p. 62).

Adler phrased his therapeutic aim in this modest fashion because he had no absolute answer to the right way of living. We still do not have the answer and probably never shall have, as we have no absolute answer to the meaning of life.

In the face of this dilemma, presented by the necessity of a definition of the right way of living on the one hand, and the impossibility of giving an absolute answer, Adler resorted to a pragmatic answer. Adler observed that those who could be called mentally healthy led lives which in the long run were socially more useful in a broad sense than the lives led by those who could be called mentally ''sick.'' Consequently he made social usefulness the criterion of mental health.

''By useful I mean in the interests of mankind generally. The most sensible estimate of the value of any activity is its helpfulness to all mankind, present and future, a criterion that applies not only to that which subserves the immediate preservation of life, but also to higher activities such as religion, science, and art'' (p. 78). The healthfulness of such striving is determined by the order of the world according to which a self-centered goal is bound to be limited and precarious, whereas a self-transcending useful goal has the greatest validity attainable.

Such usefulness is the outcome of a well developed social feeling or social interest. ''It is almost impossible to exaggerate the value of an increase in social feeling. The mind improves, for intelligence is a communal function. The feeling of worth and value is heightened, giving courage and an optimistic view, and there is a sense of acquiescence in the common advantages and drawbacks of our lot. The individual feels at home in life and feels his existence to be worthwhile just so far as he is useful to others and is overcoming common instead of private feelings of inferiority. Not only the ethical nature, but the right attitude in aesthetics, the best understanding of the beautiful and the ugly will always be founded upon the truest social feeling'' (p. 79).

A similar passage reads: ''Courage, an optimistic attitude, common sense, and the feeling of being at home upon the crust of the earth, will enable him to face advantages and disadvantages with equal firmness. His goal of superiority will be identified with ideas of serving the human race and of overcoming its difficulties by his creative power'' (pp. 47–48). Here Adler characterizes the way of life of the individual ''who has been well prepared for social life'' (p. 47) through development of his social interest. Such a person will also ''solve all love-problems with loyalty to the partner and responsibility to society'' (p. 47).

Neurotic Style of Life

By contrast, the neurotic life style is essentially that of the pampered child. Such a person does not contribute, but rather leans on others and is likely not to take responsibility for his actions but to shift responsibility and blame upon other factors or other people.

"In the investigation of a neurotic style of life we must always suspect an opponent, and note who suffers most because of the patient's condition. Usually this is a member of the family, and sometimes a person of the other sex, though there are cases in which the illness is an attack upon society as a whole. There is always this element of concealed accusation in neurosis, the patient feeling as though he were deprived of his *right*—i.e., of the center of attention—and wanting to fix the responsibility and blame upon someone. By such hidden vengeance and accusation, by excluding social activity whilst fighting against persons and rules, the problem-child and the neurotic find some relief from their dissatisfaction" (p. 81).

The dissatisfaction stems from the fact that such a person is not prepared when he comes to face the general life problems of society, work, and love, all of which require cooperation and social interest for their satisfactory solution. "All neurotic persons who have developed from a pampered prototype expect to be appreciated *before* they will do anything of social value instead of *after* having done it, thus expecting the natural course of things to be reversed in their own favor" (p. 77). Such people want "to take without giving" (p. 95), want "everything for nothing" (p. 94) and "all or nothing" (p. 55). The result often is nothing.

When an impasse is reached, the neurosis breaks out into the open. The patient shows disabling symptoms. These serve to safeguard his self-esteem and to provide excuses for his failure before himself and others. At the same time the symptoms are hidden accusations of others whom he considers not to have done enough for him. "Neurosis invariably gives relief to the subject, not, of course, in the light of objectivity and common sense, but according to his own private logic: it secures some triumph or at least it allays the fear of defeat. Thus neurosis is the weapon of the coward, and the weapon most used by the weak" (p. 80). "The problem of every neurosis is, for the patient, the difficult maintenance of a style of acting, thinking, and perceiving which distorts and denies the demands of reality" (p. 1).

This description of the neurotic may seem harsh. But Adler also makes the important categorical statement: "Every neurotic is partly in the right" (p. 24). By this is meant that he has "good" reasons for his behavior—only, they are not sufficient reasons. The neurotic generally suffered from organ inferiorities or was pampered or neglected as a child (pp. 34–37), all three situations being conducive to the development of the pampered, non-contributive style of life, as Adler formulated it in a later publication. "In these three types of children we encounter the three typical accentuations of the feeling of inferiority. They all weaken the social contact, and tend to isolate the individual in an ever-narrowing sphere of interest" (p. 37).

The point is that the individual was misled by such situations toward his mistaken style of life. To understand a case means to arrive at the conclusion: Considering the circumstances of the patient and his original mistaken interpretation, he is acting quite logically, and we would respond the same way given the same premises. Thus we can empathize and sympathize with the neurotic, and also remain hopeful regarding the possibility of change.

Psychotherapy

If mental health is striving for a goal of superiority or success which is one of general benefit, and if mental disorder is a mistaken striving for a goal which has no general validity, one of personal superiority, then the task of psychotherapy becomes a re-orientation of the patient toward a more useful objective for his striving. The patient came to the therapist because he reached an impasse with regard to a specific life situation with which he is presently confronted. "We must make a change in the deeper motive, in the underlying style of life, and then the patient will see all his life-tasks in a new perspective" (p. 19). The outcome is a cognitive reorganization.[5]

The mistaken goal stems, as we have seen, from an underdeveloped social interest and increased inferiority feelings. It thus becomes the task of the therapist to encourage the patient and to strengthen his social interest. This is done by the therapist himself first extending a sincere social interest to the patient. Thus psychotherapy is at once repudiated as a detached technology, and becomes a sincere interpersonal relationship.

"The patient must be appealed to in a friendly way, coaxed into a receptive frame of mind. Indeed, the task of the physician or psychologist is to give the patient the experience of contact with a fellow-man, and then to enable him to transfer this awakened social feeling to others. This method, of winning the patient's good will, and then transferring it to his environment, is strictly analogous to the maternal function. The social duty of motherhood is to interpret society to the individual, and if the mother fails in this, the duty is likely to devolve much later upon the physician who is heavily handicapped for the task. The mother has the enormous advantage of the physical and psychic relation; she is the greatest experience of love and fellowship that the child will ever have. . . . This is the two-fold function of motherhood, to give the child the completest possible experience of human fellowship, and then to widen it into a life-attitude towards others" (pp. 20–21).

"What the Freudians call transference (so far as we can discuss it apart from sexual implication) is merely social feeling" (p. 73). "We are far from denying that other schools of psychiatry have their successes in dealing with neuroses, but in our experience they do so less by their methods than when they happen to give the patient a good human relation with the physician, or above all, to give him encouragement" (p. 40).

The task of the therapist is to enable the patient "to realize what he is doing, and to transfer his egocentric interest to social life and useful activity" (p. 40). The cure depends on the patient's understanding his self-centered goal "which has been hitherto a heavily-guarded secret" (pp. 73–74) from his own understanding.

But Adler made the cure not dependent on such insight alone. He also had a place for therapy without insight, such as milieu therapy, or as we often say today, social therapy. "It is true, that, in lighter cases, a patient with very varied symptoms may

[5]Sundberg and Tyler (17) have very appropriately classified Adler with cognitive and value change theorists of psychotherapy among whom they include Adolph Meyer, Albert Ellis, F. C. Thorne, G. A. Kelly, Lakin Phillips, O. H. Mowrer, and the existentialists, particularly Rollo May and V. E. Frankl.

lose them before he himself or the doctor have come to grasp their coherence. When this happens it is either because of a favorable change in the patient's situation or because the doctor, by encouragement or by change, renews the patient's interest in others'' (p. 54).

CONCLUDING COMMENTS[6]

Adler was convinced that it was necessary and possible to communicate basic principles of mental health and adjustment convincingly and effectively to the broadest sectors of society. As we have seen, he considered mental disorder not an illness in the usual sense but a mistaken way of living; the whole community could contribute to reducing this mistake, not only the expert and the individual himself.

Working in this direction, Adler created a network of over 30 child guidance clinics in connection with the Vienna public schools, staffed by volunteers who conducted their counseling sessions in front of qualified audiences. He conducted adult-education classes on a large scale. He considered it most important that teachers be alerted to the social principles of mental health. He fully appreciated that he was in many ways restating principles of religious guidance. In all, Adler thus anticipated many trends of what today is called community psychiatry (15).

In accordance with his practical efforts Adler kept his terminology as simple as possible, limited his theorizing to broad outlines of the essentials and showed indefatigably how these apply to individual cases. Today this plain, minimal theory has been found a suitable framework for the new developments in the hospital treatment of mental patients (6, 7). Rudolf Dreikurs, a foremost Adlerian psychiatrist, has written a series of books presenting principles which have proved directly applicable by teachers in their classrooms (9) and by parents and married couples in their homes (8, 10). And in general it has been stated that ''Adler's ideas . . . have become the accepted clinical common sense of our time'' (19).

But Adler's simplicity in theory has also had positive scientific advantages in that his terms were kept at the lowest possible level of abstraction, close to the operational level (5), a widely accepted scientific requirement. At the same time Adler seems to have identified truly significant concepts of rather general validity. When Farberow and Shneidman (11, pp. 306–313) asked six clinicians of different orientations (Freudian, Jungian, Adlerian, Sullivanian, Kelly, Rogerian) to make Q-sorts for one suicidal patient, the Adlerian Q-sort showed the highest communality with the other five (.74), the Freudian the next to the lowest (.43), and the Jungian the lowest (.39) (13). These results would seem to offer some tentative experimental confirmation for our initial statement that to know Adler is to be well prepared for many current theoretical developments.

From his main concern with the wide practical applicability of his work Adler expressed the following conviction about his Individual Psychology with which we may conclude: ''There may be more venerable theories of an older academic science. There may be newer, more sophisticated theories. But there is certainly none which could bring greater gain to all people'' (4, p. 364n).

[6]This section has been newly written for the present volume.

REFERENCES

1 Adler, A. *Problems of neurosis: a book of case histories* (1929). New York: Harper Torchbooks, 1964.

2 Adler, A. The progress of mankind (1937). In K. A. Adler and Danica Deutsch (Eds.), *Essays in Individual Psychology*. New York: Grove Press, 1959, Pp. 3–8.

3 Adler, A. *The Individual Psychology of Alfred Adler: a systematic presentation in selections from his writings*. Edited by H. L. and Rowena R. Ansbacher, New York: Basic Books, 1956; Harper Torchbooks, 1964.

4 Adler, A. *Superiority and social interest: a collection of later writings*. Edited by H. L. and Rowena R. Ansbacher. Evanston, Ill.: Northwestern University Press, 1964.

5 Ansbacher, H. L. The structure of Individual Psychology. In B. B. Wolman and E. Nagel (Eds.), *Scientific psychology*. New York: Basic Books, 1965. Pp. 340–364.

6 Brooks, G. W., Deane, W. N., and Ansbacher, H. L. Rehabilitation of chronic schizophrenic patients for social living. *J. Indiv. Psychol.*, 1960, **16,** 189–196.

7 Deane, W. N., and Ansbacher, H. L. Attendant-patient commonality as a psychotherapeutic factor. *J. Indiv. Psychol.*, 1962, **18,** 157–167.

8 Dreikurs, R. *The challenge of marriage*. New York: Duell, Sloan and Pearce, 1946.

9 Dreikurs, R. *Psychology in the classroom: a manual for teachers*. New York: Harper and Bros., 1957.

10 Dreikurs, R., and Soltz, Vicki. *Children: the challenge*. New York: Duell, Sloan and Pearce, 1964.

11 Farberow, N. L., and Shneidman, E. S. (Eds.) *The cry for help*. New York: McGraw-Hill, 1961.

12 Ford, D. H., and Urban, H. B. *Systems of psychotherapy*. New York: Wiley, 1963.

13 Kelly, G. A. Nonparametric factor analysis of personality theories. *J. Indiv. Psychol.*, 1963, **19,** 115–147.

14 Maslow, A. H. Deficiency motivation and growth motivation (1955). In *Toward a psychology of being*. Princeton, N.J.: Van Nostrand, 1962. Pp. 19–41.

15 Papanek, Helene. Adler's concepts in community psychiatry. *J. Indiv. Psychol.*, 1965, **21,** 117–126.

16 Sinnott, E. W. *Cell and psyche: the biology of purpose* (1950). New York: Harper Torchbooks, 1961.

17 Sundberg, N. D., and Tyler, Leona E. *Clinical psychology*. New York: Appleton-Century-Crofts, 1962.

18 White, R. W. Adler and the future of ego psychology (1957). In K. A. Adler and Danica Deutsch (Eds.), *Essays in Individual Psychology*. New York: Grove Press, 1959. Pp. 437–454.

19 White, R. W. Is Alfred Adler alive today? *Contemp. Psychol.*, 1957, **2,** 1–4.

C. G. Jung*

Anthony Storr

Jung, who died in June 1961 at the age of eighty-five, was the last survivor of the great trio of European psychiatrists whose names are household words. Freud, Jung and Adler were all, in their different ways, pioneers; each contributed ideas that have had a powerful influence, not only upon psychiatry, but upon the general conception that twentieth-century man has of his own nature.

Of the three contributions, that of Jung is the least generally appreciated. Adler, during his lifetime, exerted considerable personal influence. His ideas were easy to grasp, and expressed in a style so popular that they are liable to be undervalued by the sophisticated. Freud's work has been widely accepted; and, although his originality and iconoclasm at first made him enemies, he wrote with such admirable clarity that his books have long been familiar to educated people. But Jung remains unread, and this is not altogether surprising. For the man who picks up a book on psychology usually does so in the hope of finding some illumination of his personal problems, and if he turns to Adler or Freud he will inevitably find something that applies to himself. But if he happens to light on Jung he is likely to be nonplussed. For he may well find that he is confronted by an erudite discussion of the Trinity, or by an excursion into Chinese Yoga, or by a disquisition on medieval alchemy. What possible relevance can such esoteric subjects have to the day-to-day problems of living for which the average person seeks advice? It is understandable that some conclude either that Jung is too deep for them, or else that he is a crank who has deserted science for some crazy mixture of religion and speculative philosophy.

That this is not so it is the purpose of this article to demonstrate. Jung's point of view is, in some ways, unusual, and during the latter part of his life he was chiefly concerned with patients who differed from the common run of psychiatric cases. But the fact that Jung's viewpoint has not won more general appreciation is not because it is intrinsically bizarre, but because he himself had some difficulty in communicating it. As a talker Jung was superb; anyone who has heard him in private conversation who has read the verbatim record of his seminars must realize that he was a tough, realistic thinker who could not be dismissed as a crank. But his writings are often obscure, and nowhere did he himself make an adequate summary of his ideas, as did Freud, for instance, in his *Outline of Psychoanalysis*. Jung's influence has been both wide and deep; but his ideas have penetrated by a process of diffusion rather than as a result of detailed study of his actual writings. As he himself said: "I have such a hell of a trouble to make people see what I mean."

Jung's work can best be appreciated by way of an outline of the development of his thought. He was the son of a Swiss pastor, brought up in the country, and as a child somewhat isolated, since his sister was nine years younger. Quite early he developed an interest in the past and originally wanted to be an archeologist. But the

*From Anthony Storr, "C. G. Jung," *The American Scholar*, 1962, **31**, 395–403. Reprinted by permission of the author and the publisher, *The American Scholar*.

family did not have the money for him to pursue a purely academic career, so he turned to medicine as a second choice. At the time when Jung qualified as a doctor, psychiatry was a specialty of negligible importance; but Jung embraced it eagerly, since he saw that in the study of the mind he could combine both his interest in natural science and his extensive knowledge of philosophy and the history of ideas. He obtained a post in the Burghölzli mental hospital in Zurich, where he worked from 1900 to 1909.

During this time he produced a great deal of original work, including the studies in word-association in which he introduced the word "complex," and his famous book on *The Psychology of Dementia Praecox.* By the end of 1900 Jung had read Breuer and Freud's *Studies on Hysteria,* and Freud's *The Interpretation of Dreams.* He at once perceived the value of Freud's conceptions and became his enthusiastic advocate. *The Psychology of Dementia Praecox* was the first attempt to apply psychoanalytic ideas to the study of insanity, and one of the first in which it was demonstrated that there was a hidden meaning in the apparently incomprehensible words and gestures of the insane. Jung sent this book to Freud, and the two men first met in 1907 when Jung went to Vienna at Freud's invitation.

There followed a period of some six years of collaboration, during which Jung was Freud's favorite lieutenant. But a certain intransigence, characteristic of genius, precluded Jung from remaining *in statu pupillari;* with the publication in 1913 of his next book, *The Psychology of the Unconscious,* communication with Freud came to an end. There were many reasons for the break. The temperamental gulf between the two men was a wide one, and there was a considerable difference in age. But, in addition to this, their training and experience were quite dissimilar. Freud's interest, in his early days, was centered upon neurosis; his original theories of mental structure were based upon the study of hysteria. He never worked in a mental hospital for more than a brief period and had little experience of psychotic patients. It was natural enough that his views should derive from the study of repressed, infantile patterns and the tangle of early interpersonal relationships, since this is the material that comes to light in the analysis of neurotic patients.

Jung, on the other hand, was fascinated by schizophrenia, and remained so until the end of his life. While accepting Freud's theory of repression as applied to neurosis, he came to the conclusion that it was inadequate to explain the extraordinary depth and richness of the material produced by patients suffering from schizophrenia. Psychotic phantasies, and many dreams of both normal and abnormal people, could not, he concluded, be explained in terms of the vicissitudes of infancy. There must be a deeper region of the unconscious mind which lay below the level of personal repression; this region Jung named the collective unconscious. Because of his interest in the past, Jung already had a considerable knowledge of the myths of primitive people; he was thus able to demonstrate remarkable parallels between the dreams and phantasies of his patients and recurrent patterns of myth from all over the world. The variations on these mythological themes might be infinite but the underlying patterns remained the same; to these patterns and the figures that appeared in them Jung gave the name of archetypes. In *The Psychology of the Unconscious* Jung took the phantasies of a patient who later became psychotic and showed, with a wealth of detailed parallels, that the production of phantasy was governed not only by the personal experiences of childhood, but also by determinants that the individual shared with all mankind, even with peoples who might be remote both geographically and in time from himself. In Jung's view the child was not born into the world with a mind like a sheet of blank paper on which anything could be imprinted. The child was already predisposed to feel and think along the same lines as his ancestors had done since the beginning of time. The unconscious could not be regarded simply as a part of the mind to which unpleasant emotions were banished. It was the very foundation of our being, and the source not only of mental disturbances but also of our deepest hopes and aspirations.

Freud could not accept this view, and the two men parted. But it is interesting to record the fact that, in one of his last works, Freud reached a similar conclusion about the nature of the unconscious. "Dreams bring to light material which could not originate either from the dreamer's adult life or from his forgotten childhood. We are obliged to regard it as part of the archaic heritage which a child brings with him into the world, before any experiences of his own, as a result of the experiences of his ancestors." Jung's concept of the collective unconscious, common to all mankind, was, therefore, not so controversial as it at first appeared: many Freudians accept something of the kind. The rift between Jung and Freud, like all such rifts, was surely based on personal conflict, not simply on theoretical differences; and it is time that curiosity about this ancient controversy was replaced by an objective appraisal of the great contribution that each man has made to our understanding of the mind.

The conflict with Freud had, however, one positive result. It set Jung thinking about how it happened that he, Freud and Adler studied the same material and yet produced such different points of view about it. From his reflections sprang the idea for which he is best known to the general public, the idea of differing psychological types. Jung saw that men approached the study of the mind, and indeed life in general, from different basic preconceptions, of which they were not always aware. The extravert valued the outer world, the relation to external objects, whereas the introvert gave his chief esteem to the world he discovered within himself. Both attitudes were necessary for a full comprehension of reality, but men were usually one-sided and tended toward one or the other extreme. Adlerian psychology, with its emphasis on power, was the product of an introvert, for Adler was concerned with exalting the subject at the expense of the object, as if the object were a threat that might overwhelm the subject. Freudian psychology, on the other hand, was an extraverted construction since Freud regarded sexuality as paramount, and it is in the sexual relationship above all others that the object is most highly valued.

Jung's further subdivision of both types into thinking, feeling, sensation and intuition has not been generally accepted; but his original terms "extravert" and "introvert" have become part of everyday speech. For, as he rightly perceived, this particular dichotomy reflects something fundamental in human nature; many other psychologists, including William James, Kretschmer, Eysenck and Melanie Klein, have found a similar classification valuable. Jung regarded himself as predominantly an introvert, in whom thinking was the best developed function. His difficulty in communicating his ideas is characteristic of the introverted type who is often, as Jung said of himself, "at variance with the reality of things" and thus may not realize what it is that prevents other people from understanding him. A gross example of this is the misunderstanding that led to the accusation that Jung was antisemitic and a Nazi sympathizer, a slander that has already been refuted by his Jewish pupils and need not detain us here.

The next step in Jung's thought follows naturally as a result of combining his view of the unconscious with his typology. Neurosis, Jung concluded, was due to a one-sided development of consciousness which certainly had its roots in earliest childhood, but which was chiefly manifested in a lack of adaptation to the present situation. The extravert's danger was that he might lose himself in the press of external affairs; the introvert ran the risk of failing to maintain contact with the outer world. The ideal man would be equally well adapted to the reality of both inner and outer worlds; but such perfect adaptation was a goal toward which to aim rather than a reality that was ever completely achieved. It seemed to Jung that there was a reciprocal relationship between conscious and unconscious, and that the unconscious compensated for a one-sided attitude of consciousness. Hence neurotic symptoms were not simply unpleasant relics of the repressions of childhood, but were also abortive attempts on the part of the mind to remedy its own lack of balance. The psyche, in other words, was a self-regulating entity; and dreams, phantasies and other derivations of the unconscious could not be regarded solely as childish wish-fulfillments, but often as revelations of latent potentialities and as pointers toward the future development of the individual.

The idea that the mind is a self-regulating system is valuable in clinical practice. It is, moreover, a conception that accords well with modern ideas in physiology and cybernetics. The body itself is self-regulating; there are within it numerous devices that serve the purpose of keeping the internal environment constant, so that each cell may function at its optimum efficiency. Such devices, for example, regulate the hormonal system, the acid-base equilibrium of the blood, and body temperature. Automation existed within himself before man ever applied it to machines; and the checks and counterchecks that prevent the internal environment of the body from straying too far from an ideal balance are more complex and more subtle than those in any automatic factory.

It is surprising that Jung's theory of the self-regulating psyche has not attracted more attention. Of all his hypotheses it is the easiest to substantiate with clinical evidence; it is in line with physiology and thus scientifically respectable; it is borne out by the experience of everyday life. We are all familiar with the tough writer who at heart is a sentimentalist; with the frail, emotional woman who is actually ruthless; with the office tycoon who, at home, is a dependent child; with the hard-bitten rationalist who suddenly succumbs to the allure of an outlandish creed. Men are all a mixture of opposites; and the more extreme a person's conscious attitude, the more certainly will one find its opposite within. Jung concluded that the aim of man's development was the integration of the personality, which he conceived as a balance between opposites, between inner and outer reality, between reason and emotion, between extraversion and introversion. The individual who achieved integration was one who had succeeded in reconciling the opposites within himself and making a whole out of the disparate elements of his personality. It was not possible for a man to attain complete integration, any more than it was possible for an artist to create a perfect work of art; but this appeared to be the goal of human life toward which the unconsciously directed process of development was tending.

In Jung's view this search for integration and wholeness was characteristic of the second half of life; it is in dealing with the problems of older patients that Jung's analytical psychology comes into its own. Freud and his followers tended to assume that a man's development was complete with the achievement of freedom from parental ties and the establishment of sexual maturity: psychoanalysts have generally been reluctant to treat patients of middle age and over. Jung, however, found that his practice largely consisted of such patients. They were often people who had achieved both sexual maturity and professional success and who did not fit into the usual categories of neurosis. Nevertheless, they had come to a point at which they felt "stuck," and at which life seemed arid and without significance. The study of such people convinced Jung that at about the age of thirty-five or forty a change took place, at least in the people who consulted him. It was a time at which the individual might find that the pursuits of his youth had palled and that many of the activities that used to give him pleasure were no longer enthralling. At such a time the study of the products of unconscious phantasy is often particularly rewarding: Jung found that, in some people, a process of development seemed to be taking place that could be followed both in dreams and in the paintings, poems and other works of the imagination that he encouraged his patients to produce. This sequential development Jung called the individuation process; its study became the chief preoccupation of his own latter years.

Having formulated the idea that there was, in the second half of life, a psychological process of development tending toward the integration of the individual, Jung started to look about for historical parallels. For he believed that man's essential nature did not alter much in the course of time, and he therefore felt that there must be evidence in the past of men seeking the same integration for which his patients were looking in the present.

He found his parallel in alchemy. Those who are unfamiliar with Jung's thought have found it hard to understand why he should preoccupy himself with such matters as the alchemist's quest for the philosopher's stone. Alchemy, like astrology, which was also one of Jung's interests, has long been discredited by science. Of what possible interest can it be today?

The explanation of Jung's interest is simple. Alchemy is interesting psychologically just because there is nothing in it scientifically. It is equivalent to the projection tests that psychologists use in the assessment of personality. Like a Rorschach inkblot, alchemy contains nothing objective, and, since it is far removed from external reality, it provides an admirable field for the study of unconscious processes. The alchemists were searching for something that had no existence in the outside world, but that nonetheless seemed to them of extreme importance. Like Jung's patients, they were looking for integration and wholeness: the symbolism in which they described their quest was remarkably similar to the symbolism that Jung found in the dreams and phantasies of his patients.

In essential terms the alchemical quest was a search for salvation, but one that could not be contained within the framework of conventional religion. Jung found that many of his older patients were also attempting to find a meaning in life in a way that could only be described as religious, although most of them could not accept any orthodox creed. If a man were to attain his full stature as an individual it would seem that he must acquire some philosophy of life, some view as to the meaning of his own existence. As Jung himself said: "Man cannot stand a meaningless life."

It was not only in alchemy that Jung found evidence of the individuation process. He made wide-ranging researches into the fields of comparative religion, Chinese philosophy, Yoga and other arcane subjects; in doing so, he incurred the suspicion of scientists who, without understanding what he was doing, felt that he had abandoned science for mysticism. But the truth is that the less a subject is based on external reality, the more fruitful a field is it likely to be for the study of unconscious processes; Jung's later researches follow logically from his original premises.

Jung has been generally recognized as one of the great original minds of the twentieth century. Freud's psychoanalysis and Jung's analytical psychology have sometimes been regarded as incompatible; but in many respects the two approaches are complementary, and it is only the fanatics of either school who cannot see any value in the other's point of view. Freud's contribution to psychology took a generation to establish. It will probably take at least as long for the full impact of Jung's thought to be assimilated. But Jung's influence has been felt in many fields outside psychiatry, and his place in history is already assured. The concept of the collective unconscious, for instance, has been used by the writer J. B. Priestley in his book *Literature and Western Man,* by the historian Arnold Toynbee in *A Study of History,* and by the physicist W. Pauli in his work on the astronomer Kepler. Sir Herbert Read has acknowledged his debt to Jung in his writings on art, and many creative artists have felt that Jung understood their aims in a way that no previous writer on psychology had been able to do.

Although he was the first to demand that the analyst himself be analyzed, Jung was reluctant to have his teaching codified, and for many years he resisted the setting up of an institute to train pupils in his methods. He believed that his ideas were no more than a preliminary venture into a new field of research and referred to them as a subjective confession. Science takes a long time to catch up with intuitive genius; so far, there have been only a few experimental investigations based on Jung's later concepts. But it should be possible to formulate a series of propositions in such a way that his findings can be objectively demonstrated. A start has already been made in the study of dreams.

Jung maintained that our ignorance of ourselves is profound. He considered that man's most urgent task today is to deflect his gaze from the further conquest of the material world toward the study of his own nature. In a world in which opposites are so far divided that they threaten each other with mutual annihilation, we should do well to listen to Jung's counsel.

Karen Horney's Concept of Human Motivation*

Norman J. Levy

In *Neurosis and Human Growth* (5), Horney describes the neurotic process as a special and unfortunate form of human development which involves a waste of constructive energies. The development is both different in quality from and antithetical to healthy human growth. When conditions are favorable man will put his energies into realizing his own potentialities. Such development will vary naturally with his particular physical endowment, temperament and gifts. With these determinants together with his background and experiences, he will evolve as a person, softer or harder, more cautious or more trusting, more self reliant or less, more contemplative or more outgoing, attempting to actualize his special gifts.

To the extent the growing child is subjected to inner and outer stresses, he will become alienated from that which is real in himself. He will shift the major part of his energies to the task of molding himself by a rigid system of inner dictates into a being of absolute, god-like perfection and will strive to fulfill his idealized image of himself. In this way he aims at satisfying his pride in those qualities he feels he has, could have, or should have.

Unless a child is a mental defective he will learn in some way to cope with others and acquire some skills. Some forces, however, cannot be acquired or even developed by learning. As an illustration Horney (5) points out that an acorn neither has to be nor can be taught to grow, but given a chance it will develop its intrinsic potentialities and become an oak tree. Similarly, man, given a chance to develop his particular human potentialities, will also develop the unique alive forces of his real self (5) that "central force common to all human beings and yet unique in each which is the deep source of growth." By clarifying his feelings, thoughts, wishes and interests and by tapping his resources, he will be more able to express himself and relate to others spontaneously. Thus in time he will find his values and aims in life and grow toward self realization.

In order to develop his given potentialities, a man needs favorable conditions for his growth. He must have an atmosphere of warmth to give him both a feeling of inner security and inner freedom. This will enable him to have and express his own feelings and thoughts. The good will, guidance and encouragement of others are necessary for him to become a mature, fulfilled individual. In addition to love he also needs the strengthening effect of healthy friction with the wishes and wills of others.

When, through a variety of adverse influences, a child is not permitted to grow according to his individual needs and possibilities, he may develop neurotic difficulties. If the people in his environment are too involved in their own neuroses to be able to love the child, or even to conceive of him as the particular individual he is, if their attitudes toward him are determined by their own neurotic needs and responses, they may be dominating, over protective, intimidating, irritable, over-exacting, over-indulgent, erratic, partial to other siblings, hypocritical and indifferent. One single factor

*From Norman J. Levy, "Karen Horney's Concept of Human Motivation," *Psychologia,* 1960, **3,** 113–118. By permission of the author and the Editor, *Psychologia.*

is rarely, if ever, the total determinant in development of a neurosis. The whole constellation of interpersonal reactions may exert untoward influences on the child's growth.

A child who does not develop the experience of being part of or of being accepted will experience an insecure, apprehensive feeling called basic anxiety (1), the feeling of being isolated and helpless in a world conceived as potentially hostile. Cramped by the pressure of his basic anxiety the child is prevented from relating to others with the spontaneity of his real feelings. Instead he must deal with them in ways which do not arouse or increase basic anxiety but rather attempt to allay it. Without going into detail, the particular attitudes of the child are determined both by his given temperament and the impact of the environment. Briefly he may try to cling to the most powerful person around him; he may try to rebel and fight against others or he may try to shut them out of his inner life and emotionally withdraw from them. In principle this means he can move toward, against or away from others. The ability to want and to give affection, to comply through cooperation, the ability to fight and the ability to spend time by oneself occasionally are all necessary for good human relations. They do not mutually exclude one another. These moves become extreme and rigid, however, in a child who feels shaky because of his basic anxiety. Affection, for instance, becomes clinging; compliance becomes appeasement. He may be driven to rebel or to retreat into himself, without reference to his real feelings and regardless of the inappropriateness of his attitude in a particular situation. The degree of compulsiveness, blindness and rigidity in his attitudes is in proportion to the intensity of the basic anxiety lurking within him. The child, driven not just in one but in all of these directions, develops fundamentally contradictory attitudes towards others, and the three moves clash in what Horney calls in "Our Inner Conflict", the basic conflict. In time he tries to solve his basic conflict by making one of these moves consistently predominant. His prevailing attitude then becomes one of compliance, or aggressiveness, or aloofness.

This first attempt at solving neurotic conflicts has a determining influence upon the further course of his neurotic development. Changes of personality occur not only toward others but also in relation to himself. According to his main direction, the child also develops certain appropriate needs, sensitivities, inhibitions and the beginnings of moral values. The child who is predominantly compliant, for instance, will not only tend to ingratiate himself with others and to cling to them, but will also try to be unselfish and good. Similarly the predominantly aggressive child valuing strength will emphasize capacity to endure and to fight. This early solution aims chiefly at a unification of relations with others and since the individual is still divided he needs a firmer and more comprehensive integration. The constant need to be on the defensive drains his inner strength and makes large areas of his personality unavailable for constructive uses. Lacking self confidence he is less well equipped for life. Living in a competitive (1) society, and feeling isolated and hostile, he must strive desperately to lift himself above others.

This need to evolve artificial, strategic ways to cope with others has forced him to become alienated from himself and to override his genuine feelings, wishes and thoughts. When safety becomes paramount, innermost feelings and thoughts must recede in importance. Since his feelings and wishes cease to be determining factors, he becomes driven rather than the driver. He no longer knows where he stands, what he stands for or "who" he is. Needing a feeling of identity to become meaningful to himself and to get a feeling of power and significance, gradually and unconsciously he sets to work through his imagination to create in his mind an idealized self-image. By means of this process he endows himself with unlimited powers and exalted faculties and believes he is all things to all people and all things to himself, hero, genius, supreme lover, saint or god.

This personal idealized image is constructed from the materials of his own special experiences, his earlier fantasies and his particular needs as well as his given faculties. Shortcomings or flaws are dismissed or retouched. Compliance and self-effacement become goodness, love, saintliness; aggressiveness and arrogance become strength, leadership, heroism, omnipotence; aloofness and fear of involvement become wisdom, self-sufficiency and independence.

There are a variety of ways a person may deal with his contradictory trends. He may glorify one aspect of his personality while openly denying but secretly admiring the other two trends. He may so isolate them in his mind that they may seem neither contradictory nor conflicting. He may attempt to elevate all of his qualities to positive accomplishments and gifts. In this way he considers his self-minimizing as humility, his domineering tendencies as leadership and his detachments as objectivity. They become compatible aspects of a rich personality and in his mind he becomes the universal man of the Renaissance.

Eventually the individual begins to make efforts to actualize this secretly cherished image. While the healthy course would be a move toward what was real in himself he now starts to abandon it definitely for the idealized self which represents to him what he could be or should be. It becomes the perspective from which he looks at himself, the measuring rod with which he measures himself. The goal of proving his idealized image in action infiltrates his aspirations, his goals, his conduct of life and his relations to others.

In this search for glory there is a need for perfection which he tries to achieve by a complicated system of shoulds and taboos; neurotic ambition, the drive for external success with emphasis on competition; and the need for a vindictive triumph. This need for a vindictive triumph, this need for vindication, is experienced and expressed as the need to rise to prominence and put others to shame or defeat them and to seek revenge for real or imagined humiliations suffered earlier in life.

The drives for glory aim at the absolute in wisdom, infinite virtue or unlimited powers. A well functioning man needs both the vision of possibilities, the perspective of infinitude *and* the realization of limitations, the necessity of the concrete. If his thinking and feeling are primarily focused upon the infinite, he loses his sense for the concrete, for the here and now. Losing his capacity for living in the moment, his thinking may become too abstract. His feelings for others may evaporate into sentimentality for mankind in the abstract. If, on the other hand, he does not see beyond the narrow horizon of the concrete, the finite, he becomes narrow and petty. Both qualities, the capacity to perceive possibilities and to deal with the concrete are necessary for growth.

The more his irrational imagination has taken over, the more he will be disturbed by anything real, definite, concrete or final. He will tend to resent the definiteness of time, the concreteness of money, the finality of death. There are countless ways in which he disregards evidence which he strategically must avoid. Horney (5) quotes one patient as saying: "If it were not for reality, I would be perfectly all right."

The difference, then, between healthy strivings and neurotic drives for glory is one between spontaneity and compulsion, between recognizing and denying limitations, between focussing on the end-product and a feeling for evolution, between seeming to be and being, illusion and truth.

No matter how averse the neurotic may be to checking with reality, no matter how talented he may be, he still is in all essentials like everybody else. Actually he is not god-like and others do not treat him as though he were god-like. Like everyone else he must perform the biologically necessary functions of eating, sleeping, excreting, breathing etc.; a day has 24 hours, others may act as though he were just an ordinary mortal. What does such a person do who is almost constantly faced with puzzling painful discrepancies? As long as he must cling to his personal aggrandizement, he must therefore find the world at fault. Instead of probing his illusions, he presents a claim to the outside world that it should be different. Others should treat him in accordance with his grandiose notions about himself. When they do not cater to his illusions, he considers it unfair. Feeling he deserves a better deal, his wishes and needs become claims. When these claims are not fulfilled he experiences them as unfair frustrations about which he thinks he has a right to feel outraged.

When the neurotic looks at himself he ignores what he actually is but rather sets to work to mold himself into a being of his own creation. How he feels he should be may encompass the utmost of honesty, generosity, considerateness, justice, dignity, courage, unselfishness. He should be the perfect lover, husband and teacher. He should be able to endure everything, should like everybody, should love his parents, his wife, his country, or he should not be attached to anything or anybody, nothing should matter to him, he should never feel hurt and he should always be serene and unruffled. He should always enjoy life or he should be above pleasure and enjoyment. He should know, understand and foresee everything. He should be able to solve every problem of his own or of others in no time. He should be able to overcome every difficulty of his as soon as he sees it. He should never be tired or fall ill. He should always be able to find a job. He should be able to do things at once and without effort which can actually only be done by putting in time and work. Horney (4) calls these inner dictates, the tyranny of the shoulds. These demands on himself, these inner dictates like political tyranny in a police state, operate with complete disregard for the person's own psychic condition—for what he actually can feel or do. A person operating under the yoke of the shoulds feels the strain in terms of disturbed human relations and impaired spontaneity of feelings, wishes, thoughts and beliefs.

When a person recognizes that he cannot measure up to his inner dictates, he ceases to be proud of the human being he actually is and starts to hate and despise himself. Since neurotic pride is false pride, it collapses whenever it is hurt. The typical reactions to hurt pride are shame and humiliation, rage and fear. Any hurt to our pride may provoke vindictive hostility ranging all the way from dislike to hate, from irritability to anger to a blind murderous rage. Fear, anxiety and panic may occur as reactions to anticipated or actual humiliations or they may be repressed contributing to psychotic episodes, depressions, alcoholism, psychosomatic disorders or the need to sit tight on these emotions of anger and fear with a general flattening of emotion.

Neurotic pride while vitally important to the individual renders him extremely vulnerable at the same time. There is an urgent need to save face and to restore pride when it is hurt or to avoid injuries when it is endangered. Some of the measures employed are the impulse to take revenge for what is felt as humiliation, the striving for safety through restricting one's life and the philosophy that it is safer not to try than to try and fail. The neurotic must develop a system of private values to determine what to like and accept in himself, what to glorify and of what to be proud. This system of values by necessity also determines what to reject, to be ashamed of, to despise, to hate. Pride and self-hate are bound together inseparably. The hatred results from awareness of the discrepancy between what a person would be and what he is. Self-hate results in feeling guilty, inferior, cramped and tormented. Surveying self-hate and its ravaging forces we cannot help but see in it a great tragedy. The great tragedy is that in reaching out for the infinite and absolute, a man starts destroying himself. In terms of the devil's pact, the abandoning of the self corresponds to the selling of one's soul. In psychiatric terms we call it the alienation from the self, the remoteness of the neurotic from his own feelings, wishes, beliefs, and energies. The alienated person can not feel he is an active determining force in his own life.

What are the consequences of unresolved conflicts? The protective structure gives rise to fears that its equilibrium will be disturbed, fear of insanity, fear of exposure, and of changing anything in oneself. Living with unresolved conflicts involves a devastating waste of energies, indecisiveness, ineffectualness, and inertia, unconscious pretenses—of love, goodness, interest, knowledge, honesty, fairness and suffering, an unconscious arrogance, and inability to take a definite stand, undependability and a lack of responsibility. Although neurotic entanglements invariably generate a measure of hopelessness, people do manage to carry on in one way or another. They may submerge themselves in work; they may resign themselves to living. They may give up all serious or promising pursuits and turn to the periphery of life, devoting themselves to shallow, frivolous pastimes. They may actually drift in an aimless fashion and gradually deteriorate. Finally persons without hope may turn aggressively destructive and live vicariously through others in a sadistic way. Horney (5) describes in great detail the three major attempts at solving these intrapsychic difficulties, the expansive solution or the appeal of mastery, the self effacing solution or the appeal of love; and the resigned solution or the appeal of freedom.

And what are the goals of the doctor and the patient in psychoanalytic therapy? Since symptoms are not the essential constituents but the outgrowths of the neurotic character structure, the focus must be on resolving the intrapsychic and interpersonal conflicts. The work to be done with regard to himself concerns all that is involved in self-realization. It means striving toward a greater spontaneity in experiencing all of one's feelings, wishes and beliefs. In addition to expressing himself freely he will be capable of voluntarily disciplining himself. By enabling him to tap his resources and to use them for constructive ends, he develops the feeling of being an active force in his life. This makes possible taking responsibility for himself, making decisions and taking the consequences for such decisions. As the patient achieves a sense of inner independence, he is able to establish his own hierarchy of values and apply it to actual living. To the extent he approximates wholeheartedness he will be living with less pretense and with more emotional sincerity. With regard to others it means working toward relating himself to them in a spirit of mutuality with his genuine feelings and toward respecting their individuality with their assets, liabilities and distinctive features. With regard to work it means that he will become more able to enjoy the process of the work itself. This aspect of the job rather than end product will become the major source of his satisfaction. He will aim at becoming more productive by realizing and developing his particular talents and capacities.

In a forward moving analysis, as the individual outgrows his neurotic egocentricity he will become more aware of the broader issues involved in his particular life and in the world at large and will come to experience himself as part of a bigger whole. Whether it be in the family, in the community or even in a larger activity he will be willing and able to assume his share of responsibility in it, contributing constructively in whichever way he is capable. In this way through active participation he not only widens his personal horizon but also achieves the feeling of belonging that comes when a person finds and accepts his place in the world. None of these goals is wholly attained but they are approached in a successful analysis.

To conclude this presentation of Horney's concepts of human motivation I should like to present her philosophy as expressed in the introduction of her book *Our Inner Conflicts:* My own belief is that man has the capacity as well as the desire to develop his potentialities and become a decent human being, and that these deteriorate if his relationship to others and hence to himself is, and continues to be, disturbed. I believe that man can change and go on changing as long as he lives. And this belief has grown with deeper understanding.

REFERENCES

1 Horney, Karen: *The neurotic personality of our time.* New York: W. W. Norton and Company, Inc., 1937.
2 Horney, Karen: *New ways in psychoanalysis.* New York: W. W. Norton and Company, Inc., 1939.
3 Horney, Karen: *Self analysis.* New York: W. W. Norton and Company, Inc., 1942.
4 Horney, Karen: *Our inner conflicts.* New York: W. W. Norton and Company, Inc., 1945.
5 Horney, Karen: *Neurosis and human growth.* New York: W. W. Norton and Company, Inc., 1950.

Some Aspects of Sullivan's Theory of Interpersonal Relations*

Patrick Mullahy

THE GOALS OF HUMAN BEHAVIOR

We begin our exposition of Sullivan with some preliminary distinctions and assumptions. He differentiates ''human performances,'' which include revery processes, such as day dreaming, and thought, into a two-part classification. In more popular language, the purposes, the goals or end states of human behavior are divided into two actually interrelated classes. These two classes refer to the pursuit of satisfactions and the pursuit of security. Satisfactions include sleep and rest, food and drink, sexual fulfillment (the satisfaction of lust). Loneliness is also listed as a ''middling example.'' These satisfactions are closely connected with the bodily organization of man. Hence, loneliness is included by Sullivan because, among other things, we have a desire to touch one another and to be physically close.

The class of pursuits pertaining to security refer more directly to man's cultural equipment than to bodily organization. The concept of security, in Sullivan's sense, is not easy to explain. Roughly, it refers to the state of well-being, of ''good feeling,'' of euphoria. All ''those movements, actions, speech, thoughts, reveries and so on which pertain more to the culture which has been imbedded in a particular individual than to the organization of his tissues and glands, is apt to belong in this classification of the pursuit of security.''[1]

The process of becoming a human being, for Sullivan, is synonymous with the process of acculturation or socialization. The need for security arises from the fact that every person undergoes this process of acculturation which begins at birth. From the very beginning of life in this world, everyone, at first through ''empathy,'' which we discuss below, is made to feel some of the effects of the culture by the attitudes of the significant person or persons who take care of him: mother, nurse, or their surrogates. The attitudes of those who take care of the child are themselves socially conditioned. Because of empathy, long before the infant can understand what is happening, he experiences something of the attitudes of the significant people around him. Later he is deliberately taught what is right and wrong, ''good'' and ''bad.'' In this way, the impulses, the biological strivings of the infant are socially ''conditioned,'' that is, moulded, both as to form of expression and fulfillment, according to the culturally approved patterns. As we shall see, because of the experiences of approval and disapproval from the parents or their surrogates, the achievement of satisfactions according to the culturally ''correct'' or approved patterns causes a profound feeling of well-being, of good feeling, of security. When, for certain reasons, the felt needs of a person, the biological strivings, cannot be fulfilled according to

*From Patrick Mullahy, *Oedipus: Myth and Complex,* Thomas Nelson and Sons, New York, 1948. Pages 280–301 reprinted by permission of the author and the publisher.

[1]Harry Stack Sullivan, *Conceptions of Modern Psychiatry,* The William Alanson White Psychiatric Foundation, Washington, D.C., 1947, p. 6.

culturally approved patterns, which he learned in early life, he feels intense and painful uneasiness and discomfort, insecurity, or *anxiety*.

It is not very difficult to see that the distinction between the pursuit of satisfactions and the pursuit of security and their attainment is logical or conceptual. The two are inextricably bound up together. But these two broad classifications are helpful for preliminary discussion. In general terms they explain what one is after in any situation with other persons, whether real or "fantastic" or a blend of both ("eidetic"). Hence, they represent "integrating tendencies." They explain why a situation in which two or more people—"all but one of which may be illusory" (or eidetic)—are involved or "integrated" becomes an interpersonal situation. It is because of these needs that one cannot live and be human except in communal existence with others.

THE CONCEPT OF TENSION

Because of the great role which anxiety and tension play in Sullivan's theories, we need first to mention some of his ideas about the latter. The achievement of satisfactions causes a decrease of tonus, tension, of the unstriped, involuntary muscles. But the effort at warding off anxiety (insecurity) is accompanied by heightened tonus, often of the striped, skeletal muscles, often of the unstriped, visceral muscles.

> The facts seem to indicate that tonic changes in the unstriped, involuntary muscles of the viscera—the internal organs of the body—are, from birth onward, intimately related to the experiencing of desires, needs for satisfaction. Heightened tone of the stomach wall is called out by depletion of our chemical supplies and the occurrence of vigorous contractions in these tense muscles gives rise to the "pangs of hunger." The taking of food—the ingestion of which probably leads to a release of nutritive substance stored in the liver—promptly relieves the excess tone and the contractions quiet down to the churning of the stomach contents. Hunger, in a way of speaking, is from the first influx of food, more a matter of the oral dynamism than of the stomach. In infants, at least, once this dynamism has discharged itself, alertness disappears, vigilance is withdrawn from circumambient reality, and sleep supervenes. Throughout life the pursuit of satisfactions is physiologically provoked by increased tone in some unstriped muscles; and the securing of the satisfactions is a relaxation of this tone, with a tendency towards the diminution of attention, alertness, and vigilance, and an approach to sleep.[2]

In the securing of satisfaction, the striped, skeletal muscles are "of relatively instrumental value" in very early infancy. They are said to do what is necessary—we are not told what that is—and then relax. But as soon as the mother begins to include prohibitions and disapprovals in educating the youngster, things get complicated. He develops a need for security against primarily "noxious emotional states empathized from the personal environment." Here the skeletal muscles take on a new function.

This function is to get rid of empathized discomfort and painful tension of various origins.

[2] *Op. cit.*, p. 43.

> The oral dynamism [the respiratory apparatus, the food-taking apparatus, from which the speaking apparatus is evolved] has been the channel for performances needed to appease hunger—and pain and other discomforts. It may be presumed that its function in emitting the cry has been quite automatic. This may not have worked too well, and delayed response to the cry may be one of the first experiences that tend to focus alertness. But in any case, the oral dynamism is not effective in securing relief from the discomfort set up by empathy; on some occasions, it is simply ineffectual, and on other occasions, its activity is accompanied by increase of the empathized discomfort. This leads gradually to a differentiation of empathized from other discomforts, and to the *inhibition* of the cry as a universal tool. The inhibiting of a complex pattern of behavior is not as simple as was its automatic initiation. Some of the movements are cut off, but the increase of tone in the appropriate muscles may not be inhibited. The experience of empathized hostility or unfriendly prohibition or, as it later comes to be observed, a forbidding gesture becomes colored by and associated with heightened tone in some striped muscles—at first those concerned with the cry.
>
> The course of acculturation, in so far as it pertains to toilet habits, is also a learning to suffer increasing tension in the bladder and rectum, and to resist the automatic relaxation of the sphincter muscles concerned in retaining the urine and feces. Failures in this are often accompanied by empathized discomfort [due to parental disapproval], and success is often the occasion of empathized comfort which is added to the satisfaction from relief of the tension.[3]

Action which avoids or relieves any of these tensions is experienced as continued or enhanced *self-respect* or self-esteem. Thus a person who has become tense at an expression of hostility from someone he is talking to may subsequently, let us say, be made to laugh heartily at some remark or occurrence. When this happens, he suddenly feels a relief from tension; he "feels better" about himself and others. While the effort to ward off anxiety involves an increase of tension, the relief from anxiety is associated with actions which, among other things, decrease muscle tension.

Anxiety is not synonymous with muscle tension, but the latter is a necessary condition for its experience. As we shall see, *anxiety is always related to interpersonal relations*.

THE POWER MOTIVE

Even more important and logically more fundamental than the impulses resulting from a feeling of hunger or thirst is the "power motive," the impulse to obtain and maintain a feeling of ability. To be able to obtain satisfactions and security is to have power in interpersonal relations; not to be able to do so is to be powerless, helpless. According to Sullivan, the development of actions, thoughts, foresights, etc., which are "calculated" to protect one from insecurity, is based on and springs from the disappointments and frustrations of early infancy. When one achieves power or ability in interpersonal relations, one respects oneself and therefore others. While the attitude toward the self is first determined by the attitude of those who take care of the child,

[3] *Op. cit.*, p. 44. Sullivan has changed his mind about empathizing comfort before the epoch of childhood, feeling that there is no certain evidence of its existence before then. (Personal communication to the writer.)

his subsequent attitude toward others is determined by the attitude he has toward himself. "If there is a valid and real attitude toward the self, that attitude will manifest as valid and real toward others."[4]

EMPATHY

There is said to be "a peculiar emotional relationship" between the infant and those who take care of him. Long before he can understand what is happening to him, this "emotional contagion or communion" between him and the significant adult, the mother or nurse, exists. Sullivan surmises its greatest importance is between the ages of six and twenty-seven months. For example if a mother looks with disfavor on her offspring or she suffers a fright around feeding time, there may be great feeding difficulties. This unclear mode of emotional communication is thought to be biological, for certain animals are said to exhibit a similar phenomenon. Since the attitudes of the mother or nurse are socially conditioned, this mode of emotional communication, which does not seem to occur, in Sullivan's view, through ordinary sensory channels, is very important for understanding acculturation. In later years, however, empathy is not much in evidence.

THREE MODES OF EXPERIENCE

All experience occurs in one or more of three "modes"—the prototaxic, parataxic, and syntaxic. As the Greek roots of this horrendous term indicate, the prototaxic mode refers to the first kind of experience the infant has and the order or arrangement in which it occurs. As grownups, we experience things in terms of time and space, of here and "out there," of before and after. We break up our experience, so to speak, into constituent elements for the purposes of getting along in the world. Furthermore, our experience, or at least much of it, is referable to a self who does the experiencing, the self being a center of reference. "I went for a walk in the park at four o'clock." These are examples of every day distinctions we make. Others, of course, are much more subtle and refined.

Now in the beginning, the infant, Sullivan hypothecates, makes no such distinctions for a variety of reasons. Aside from structural and functional limitations, the organism at birth has had, of course, no direct experience with the cultural heritage. We shall avoid saying he has no mind as yet—for we shall not deal here with the problem of the nature of mind nor with the problem of what he inherits from his life in the womb, concerning which apparently not a great deal is known, at least regarding mind.

According to Sullivan's hypothesis all that the infant "knows" are momentary states, the distinction of before and after being a later acquirement. The infant vaguely feels or "prehends" earlier and later states without realizing any serial connection between them. He has no ego in any distinctive sense because the self has not yet developed. For such reasons, he has no awareness of himself as an entity separate from

[4] *Op. cit.*, p. 7.

the rest of the world. In other words, his felt experience is all of a piece, undifferentiated, without definite limits. It is as if his experiences were "cosmic." This mode of experience is often marked in certain schizophrenic states.

The terms "parataxic" and "syntaxic"[5] also are etymologically related to the order and arrangement of experience. At the risk of confusion, we shall remind the reader that parataxic (like syntaxic) is a grammatical term as well, which refers to the ranging of clauses or propositions one after another without connectives such as "and," "or," "since," etc., to show the relations between them.

Gradually the infant learns to make some discrimination between himself and the rest of the world. As Sullivan puts it, he no longer reaches out to touch the moon. In other words he gradually learns to make elementary differentiations in his experience.

> We learn in infancy that objects which our distance receptors, our eyes and ears, for example, encounter, are of a quite different order of relationship from things which our tactile or our gustatory receptors encounter. That which one has in one's mouth so that one can taste it, while it may be regurgitated to the distress of everyone is still in a very different relationship than is the full moon which one encounters through one's eye but can in no sense manage.[6]

As the infant develops and maturation proceeds, the original undifferentiated wholeness of experience is broken. However, the "parts," the diverse aspects, the various kinds of experience are not related or connected in a logical fashion. They "just happen" together, or they do not, depending on circumstances. In other words, various experiences are felt as concomitant, not recognized as connected in an orderly way. The child cannot yet relate them to one another or make logical distinctions among them. What is experienced is assumed to be the "natural" way of such occurrences, without reflection and comparison. Since no connections or relations are established, there is no logical movement of "thought" from one idea to the next. The parataxic mode is not a step by step process. Experience is undergone as momentary, unconnected states of being.

The parataxic mode of organizing experience occurs mainly through visual and auditory channels. Dreams are often examples of this mode of experiencing. But it occurs a good deal of the time in waking life. In other words, we do not—and cannot—always organize our experience into a logically connected, related totality, in which the various elements are compared, contrasted, and ordered in a precise fashion. Ordinarily we do not indulge in careful ratiocination as we dress in the morning, proceed to work, and so on. It is not necessary, and in any case there is not enough time.

As the infant learns the rudiments of language, he is said to pass into the "epoch" of childhood. And here we introduce another term, the "autistic." The autistic is a verbal manifestation of the parataxic. But the capacity for verbal communication is just beginning to be manifested, and the tools, vocabulary, grammar, etc., are scarcely

[5]Or "syntactic."
[6]*Op. cit.*, p. 16.

formed and learned. Because of the child's limited equipment and experience with the symbol activity and experience of others, his own symbol activity is arbitrary, highly personal, unchecked and untested. Hence his imagination is not curbed to conform to everyday "reality." Autistic symbols, however, are useful in recall and foresight.

Let us take an example of a child who has been given a picture book also containing words, say, to name or describe the pictures. It will have a picture of a cat, and below or above or somewhere on the page there is written what the child eventually learns is c-a-t. Then, too, to complete the example, the animal who runs around the house also is referred to by the same name as that of the colored or black and white pattern in the book. Sullivan comments on the significance of such a frequent phenomenon in our culture as follows:

> I am sure no child who can learn has not noticed an enormous discrepancy between this immobile representation in the book which, perhaps, resembles one of the momentary states that kitty has been in on some occasion. I am certain that every child knows that there is something very strange in this printed representation being so closely connected with the same word that seems to cover adequately the troublesome, amusing, and very active pet. Yet, because of unnumbered, sometimes subtle, sometimes crude experiences with the carrier of culture, the parent, the child finally comes to accept as valid and useful a reference to the picture as "kitty" and to the creature as "kitty."
>
> The child thus learns some of the more complicated implications of a symbol in contradistinction to the actuality to which the symbol refers, which is its referent; in other words, the distinction between the symbol and that which is symbolized. This occurs, however, before verbal formulation is possible.
>
> From the picture book and the spoken word in this culture one progresses to the printed word and finally discovers that the combination of signs, c-a-t, includes "kitty" in some miraculous fashion, and that it always works. There is nothing like consistent experience to impress one with the validity of an idea. So one comes to a point where printed words, with or without consensually valid meaning, come to be very important in one's growth of acquaintance with the world.
>
> There was first the visually and otherwise impressive pet, which was called "kitty" (an associated vocalization); then came the picture of the kitten; now comes the generic *c a t* which includes, kitty, picture of kitten, a kitten doll, and alley cats seen from the windows. And all this is learnt so easily that—since no one troubles to point it out—there is no lucid understanding of the sundry types of reality and reference that are being experienced. Familiarity breeds indifference in this case. The possibilities for confusion in handling the various kinds of symbols, naturally, remain quite considerable.[7]

The child gradually begins to catch on to patterns of relationships, to the grammatical structure of the language, and to the usual relationships and distinctions obtaining in his society. There is a more discriminating realization of the other fellow, the responder. The child now more clearly realizes that, for example, when he cries "dada," the other person responds in a more or less characteristic fashion. And so the child learns to anticipate the responses of others. These responses become associated with the use of certain words and gestures. In other words, the characteristic reactions of the other people give meaning to the language, a meaning that is thus

[7] *Op. cit.*, p. 16.

implicitly agreed upon. Of course, the child does not set out systematically to learn the everyday meaning of the language. He learns by the trial and error method. Hence, he also learns that not only one's own experience is important, but that of others. He also learns to use verbal symbols as an economical way to get a lot to happen in a short time, with little use of energy.

Of course, there is a great deal more than this to be said about the learning process, but this sketch may indicate some of the ways by which, according to Sullivan, a child learns to use language with an interpersonal reference.

In any case, the child gradually learns the "consensually validated" meaning of language—in the widest sense of language. These meanings have been acquired from group activities, interpersonal activities, social experience. Consensually validated symbol activity involves an appeal to principles which are accepted as true by the hearer. And when this happens, the youngster has acquired or learned the syntaxic mode of experience.

But the learning process is not always consistent—because the significant others are not always consistent in their behavior. Furthermore, as we know, people do not always take the trouble to teach the child the distinctions between various symbols and that to which they refer. The trial and error method by which a good deal of learning necessarily occurs is not ideally suited for acquiring precise distinctions. For such reasons, language thus comes to have a double meaning—a personal meaning and a consensually validated meaning or a blend of both. In this way, among others, people come to maintain a wide margin of misinformation and illusion about others, themselves, and the world.

Tension, when it occurs in connection with needs, such as those of food and sex, is experienced in the syntaxic and parataxic modes. The tension of anxiety, however, is experienced by grown-ups mainly in the parataxic mode.[8]

THE MEANING OF DYNAMISM

Before taking up an exposition of the self dynamism (or self system or, simply, self) we must try to indicate what the term "dynamism" means. It has been defined as "a relatively enduring configuration of energy which manifests itself in characterizable processes in interpersonal relations."[9] In other words dynamism refers to the way energy is organized and channeled in the human organism. Dynamism implies only a relatively enduring capacity to bring about change. It is analogous to any structure or organization or processes which always contains numerous sub-structures.

For Sullivan energy always means physical energy. He rejects the notion of "psychic energy."

THE EVOLUTION OF THE SELF

As everyone knows, certain restraints are put on the young offspring's freedom which are or are considered to be necessary for his socialization, for training him and making

[8]Anxiety is always *felt*. Contrary to previous formulations, Sullivan now is convinced it never occurs in the prototaxic mode but that it occurs mainly in the parataxic. (Personal communication to the writer.)

[9]Harry Stack Sullivan, "Introduction to the Study of Interpersonal Relations," *Psychiatry,* vol. 1, p. 123, footnote, 1938.

him the sort of person considered right and desirable in the society in which he will live and have his being. These restraints, above everything else, bring about the evolution of the self dynamism. In this evolution, other aspects of the personality, such as *the selectively inattended* and *disassociated* processes, those which occur outside of self-awareness, are also developed.

We shall begin our exposition of Sullivan's theories concerning the evolution of personality with the "epoch" of infancy. Infancy refers to the period from birth to the maturation of the capacity for language behavior. During this period certain of the attitudes of the parent or nurse are said to be conveyed empathically. Suppose the mother is tired or upset or angry when she is in close contact with the infant, let us say, when she nurses or bathes him. Something of her attitude is then conveyed to him. His sense of well-being, his euphoria, is markedly decreased. The mother who observes or at least senses this gets anxious, which state is then communicated to the infant, further lowering his feeling of well-being, further increasing his insecurity. And so the process goes on. It is "dynamic."

Euphoria and anxiety are, conceptually, direct opposites, "polar constructs." In actuality there is no such thing as "pure" euphoria, in which there is no tension and therefore no action, something like an empty state of bliss. Perhaps the nearest approximation to euphoria in the "ideal" sense is deepest sleep. Nor is there any actual state of absolute anxiety. In the state of terror—in which there is a complete but temporary disorganization of personality—the most extreme degree of tension ordinarily observable occurs. Euphoria and anxiety are inversely related.

It is not difficult to see that a chronically hostile mother will induce an intense and more or less chronic anxiety in the offspring. Furthermore, such a mother will deprive him of the experience of tenderness—a deprivation which will have fateful consequences for his future well-being and happiness.

One of the characteristics of anxiety is that it interferes with observation and analysis, with the acquisition of information and understanding and with recall and foresight. It interferes with alertness to the factors in a situation that are relevant to its occurrence. Therefore it interferes with effective action.

Sooner or later the infant is recognized as educable. And when this happens, there is said to be a restriction of tender cooperation. The exhibition of tenderness by the parents tends to be modified so that it will be used more on "suitable" occasions. The mother, for example, begins to train the child in the "proper" toilet habits, those considered proper in the society in which she lives. She will express or withhold tenderness and approval as the child learns to conform or not to her desires and methods in this matter. Thus, training involves the expression of tenderness and approval for some acts and disapproval and the withholding of tenderness for others. In other words, some performances bring tenderness and approval with the consequent increase of euphoria, while others bring disapproval and hence anxiety. These experiences of rewards and punishments come to be regarded as something special. Gradually the child catches on to the fact that they are related to his feelings of euphoria and anxiety. The more or less abrupt supervention of anxiety gradually teaches or forces him to focus awareness on the performances which bring approval and disapproval. He learns, for example, to recall incidents occurring before anxiety. After a while a forbidding gesture will be sufficient to change his behavior. In other words, as his observation improves, his grasp on the patterns of approval and disapproval becomes more refined. He learns that when anxiety is present and something is done which brings tenderness and approval, the painful discomfort is assuaged or banished.

Hence, the child gradually learns to focus attention on behavior which brings approval and disapproval in order to win rewards, tenderness and approval, and escape punishment, disapproval and disapprobation.

In infancy a vague idea of "my" body arises. From the sentience of the body as a basis, there gradually evolve three "personifications" of "me"—"good me," "bad me," and "not-me." The "good me" is an organization of experiences of approval, tenderness, and general good feeling. The "bad me" is an organization of experiences related to increasing anxiety states. The "rudimentary personification" of "not-me" evolves very gradually. The processes labeled "not-me" belong to the most poorly grasped aspects of living and refer to "uncanny" experiences like horror, dread, loathing, awe. What these uncanny experiences are about is not known, but they seem to originate in the experiences of anxiety in infancy, "primitive anxiety." They occur in the parataxic mode. The personification, "not-me," is not constituted by communicative processes and hence not much can be said about it. Nightmares and certain schizophrenic experiences are examples of uncanny experiences of the "not-me."

The "personifications" of "good me" and "bad me" belong to the self system. In other words, to put this crudely, there are times when "I" am "good me" and times when "I" am "bad me." Whether or not the self is predominantly one or the other depends on the course of experience, especially in early life. But the "good me" is essentially desirable, for it is organized on the basis of experiences of security. Hence "I" shall tend to regard "my" self as essentially the "good me"—at least unless my life experience has been extraordinarily unfortunate.

We can now state in general terms the origin, nature, and function of the self dynamism. It has its basis in the need for alertness to approval, tenderness and disapproval. We should like, too, to call attention to its *restrictive* function.

> The self-dynamism is built up out of this experience of approbation and disapproval, of reward and punishment. The peculiarity of the self-dynamism is that as it grows it functions, in accordance with its state of development, right from the start. As it develops, it becomes more and more related to a microscope in its function. Since the approbation of the important person is very valuable, since disapprobation denies satisfaction and gives anxiety, the self becomes extremely important. It permits a minute focus on those performances of the child which are the cause of approbation and disapprobation, but, very much like a microscope, it interferes with noticing the rest of the world. When you are staring through your microscope, you don't see much except what comes through that channel. So with the self-dynamism. It has a tendency to focus attention on performances with the significant other person which get approbation or disfavor. And that peculiarity, closely connected with anxiety, persists thenceforth through life. It comes about that the self, that to which we refer when we say 'I,' is the only thing which has alertness, which notices what goes on, and, needless to say, notices what goes on in its own field. The rest of the personality gets along outside awareness. Its impulses, its performances are not noted.[10]

[10]*Conceptions of Modern Psychiatry,* pp. 9–10.

Among the peculiarities of anxiety is the fact that it is always "at 180° to any other tension with which it coincides."[11] In other words, it directly opposes the tensions of somatic needs and thereby prevents or hinders the satisfaction of somatic needs. An extremely anxious person cannot obtain proper sexual satisfaction or may be prevented from enjoying food by nausea, vomiting, etc. While all other tensions are followed by activities, either overt or covert, which resolve the tensions and satisfy needs, the tension of anxiety, in Sullivan's lanaguage, does not result in energy transformations directed to its relief by the removal of the situational factors obviously concerned in its provocation. The tension of fear, on the other hand, is often manifested in activities which remove the situational factors provoking fear, escapes them, neutralizes their importance or defers being afraid until the near future when the real or apparent danger is over.

As one grows, one learns, if only in a dim way, how to avoid most situations which provoke intense anxiety, but the capacity for it remains. And it will manifest itself throughout life. In this respect, the difference between the "normal" person and the "neurotic" is only one of degree.

Because experiences of approbation and disapproval occur long before one can think, long before one can discriminate what occurs, the earliest attitudes, and the most "deep seated" and pervasive, are acquired unthinkingly with little or no discrimination. Furthermore, the infant, and to a large extent also, the child, is biologically and psychologically helpless. Not only does he depend on the parents for the necessities of life itself, but he has no or only an incipient ability to think and no or insufficient social experience. Hence, in earliest years the attitudes, codes, and behavior of the parents and their surrogates are necessarily accepted without criticism or discrimination. In Sullivan's language he is still pretty much restricted to the parataxic mode of experience. Later, at least to some degree, he will develop the ability to question, compare and relate his experiences.

The "facilitations and deprivations," that which is approved and disapproved by the parents and others close to the child, becomes the source of the material built into the self dynamism. By and large their behavior will be sufficiently consistent to give the self-system a form and direction which it will maintain throughout life. Any experience which promises to threaten the form and direction of the self will provoke anxiety. When this happens, the person will not clearly notice what is happening; its significance will not be realized. And he will usually, without being aware of it, indulge in behavior calculated to nullify the experience or its importance.

Thus, anxiety, is the instrumentality by which the self limits and restricts awareness. It functions so as to maintain its own form and direction.

> Even when the self is a derogatory and hateful system it will inhibit and misinterpret any disassociated feeling or experience of friendliness towards others; and it will misinterpret any gestures of friendliness from others. The direction and characteristics given to the self in infancy and childhood are maintained year after year, at an extraordinary cost, so that most people in this culture, and presumably in any other, because of inadequate and

[11]Harry Stack Sullivan, "The Meaning of Anxiety in Psychiatry and in Life," *Psychiatry,* vol. 11, no. 1, p. 4, 1948.

> unfortunate experience in early life, become "inferior caricatures of what they might have been." Not only the family, but various other cultural institutions less directly, all combine, more or less unwittingly, to produce this effect.[12]

Actions, including thinking, phantasy, and emotions and feelings, if they are to occur within self-awareness, must conform to the characteristics of the self. Otherwise they are "disassociated" or "selectively inattended."

The self may be said to be made up of or at least circumscribed by *reflected appraisals*. The child lacks the equipment and experience necessary for a careful and unclouded evaluation of himself. The only guide he has is that of the significant adults who take care of him, and who treat and regard him in accordance with the way in which they have developed from their own life experience. Hence, the child experiences himself and appraises himself in terms of what the parents and others close to him manifest. By empathy, facial expression, gestures, words, deeds they convey to him the attitudes they hold toward him and their regard or lack of it for him.

These he "naturally" accepts because he is not yet a questioning, evaluating being. If the significant people express a respecting, loving attitude toward him, he acquires a respecting, loving attitude toward himself. If they are derogatory and hateful, then he will acquire a derogatory and hateful attitude toward himself. Throughout life, save perhaps for the intervention of extraordinary circumstances and allowing for some modification through later experience, he will carry the attitude toward himself he learned in early life around with him just as surely as he will carry his skin.

Sullivan suggests, however, that the controlling limiting function of the self is not absolute. Certain impelling needs, such as the need of sexual satisfaction, if thwarted, may prove too powerful even for the self system. Fortunately children retain a capacity for change. A loving teacher may undo somewhat the effects of a destructive parent, but a hateful destructive teacher may limit or slow up the effects of the loving care of tender parents.

To the extent to which limitations and peculiarities of the self interefere with biologically necessary satisfactions and security, then to that extent a person is mentally ill.

The self-dynamism is not synonymous with momentary self-awareness. It is a more or less stable organization or configuration of interpersonal processes, past, present, and of the prospective future. The self has a before and after. Since it merges with other processes occurring outside discriminating awareness, it has "background," it shades imperceptibly into marginal processes of awareness. These marginal processes of awareness may often be noted just before one "drops off" to sleep. Because the self also manifests itself in focal awareness, it has a "foreground."

SELECTIVE INATTENTION AND DISASSOCIATION

It does not seem necessary to emphasize the fact that much of human experience and behavior occurs outside self-awareness. Freud formulated phenomena occurring out-

[12]Patrick Mullahy, "A Theory of Interpersonal Relations and the Evolution of Personality," *Psychiatry*, vol. 8, no. 2, p. 191, 1945.

side self-awareness in terms of the "preconscious" and "unconscious." But for Freud these concepts have "topographical" and other features which are foreign to Sullivan's thought. Hence the latter usually avoids the use of such terms because they are "loaded" with meaning to which he does not subscribe.

The concepts by which he tries to formulate his thoughts on such matters are labeled "selective inattention" and "disassociation." The difference between the two is one of degree, measured by the difficulty of access to discriminating awareness.

The child gradually learns to pay close attention to behavior which is approved and disapproved. He must in order to maintain security and avoid anxiety. His attention becomes focused on these performances. This process is analogous to what goes on when, say, a music lover is present at a thrilling concert. Such a person becomes absorbed in the music, "wrapped up" in it. His attention will be entirely focused on the performance and enjoyment of it. To everything else he will pay little heed. In fact, he will not be conscious of anything else, such as the people around him, the passage of time, and so on. For the child his security is at issue, which of course is vitally important, and he will pay close attention to what goes on when approval or disapproval is involved. Certain other experiences either of himself or others will not be so clearly noticed because they entail no particular approval and tenderness or disapproval. Hence, his attention and inattention become selective. To some of his experience and behavior he will be inattentive, and this will then not be carefully discriminated. It will go on outside of discriminated awareness.

Some of these processes can more easily become the object of careful awareness than others. Thus, a friend may call attention to some of them, point them out, and in this case they then become subject to the person's awareness. Such processes are said to be selectively inattended. They can be accepted by the self.

But there are other processes which, when pointed out, do not get careful attention and scrutiny. In spite of the friend's efforts, they will not be clearly noticed. On the contrary, the person will not be able to become consciously aware of them. He will deny their existence, perhaps becoming tense and angry at the efforts of his friend. Nor will he, usually, be able to recall any experience of them. Such experiences are said to be disassociated. The self refuses to grant them awareness.

Motivational systems or dynamisms existing in disassociation are not necessarily "abnormal." And they may find expression in an interpersonal situation without those who participate becoming consciously aware of what is going on. In general, disassociated tendencies are expressed in dreams, phantasies and in unnoticed everyday behavior. In fact, if this were not so, the self system of "normal" people would disintegrate. In other words, the disassociated tendencies would prove too powerful for the inhibitions of the self, thus causing unbearable anxiety, and the person would "go to pieces."

THE MEANING OF INTERPERSONAL

There is a final point to be mentioned. The term "interpersonal" refers not only to real people existing in space and time but also to "fantastic personifications" or to people who exist physically but who serve rather as "potent representations" of other people once significant in a person's past, say, one's mother or father. In general, any frame of reference, whether constituted by real people, imaginary people existing only in story books, illusory personifications of real people (eidetic persons), or any idea or object given traits or characteristics possessed by human beings, along with one other real person, can serve to make up an interpersonal situation. We can personify and become "integrated" with almost anything, including cultural entities like the government, the church, the school, who "have their being and their manifestation so far as any particular person is concerned in other people who are significant for one reason or another to him. . . ."[13]

The Self in Recent Rogerian Theory*

C. H. Patterson

The objective of this paper is to sketch the place of the self in the current client-centered approach to personality. While the self is today becoming of central importance in all theories of personality, it constitutes the core of the Rogerian approach which has, in fact, been designated by some writers (e.g., 9, 15) as "self-theory." Perhaps this is because client-centered theory is based upon the observations of individual clients in therapy.

ROGERS' FORMULATIONS

1947

Rogers' earliest formulation was presented in 1947 (17): "The self is a basic factor in the formation of personality and in the determination of behavior." As the perception of self changes, behavior changes. The person's feeling of adequacy is basic to psychological adjustment. The absence of threat is important for the development of an adequate self-concept and is a condition for changes in the self-concept. The self-concept is, by definition, a phenomenological concept: it is the self as seen by the experiencing person.

1951

In 1951 Rogers (18) amplified and extended his discussion of the self in nineteen propositions. The point of view remained perceptual and phenomenological; there is no reality for the individual other than that given by his perceptions. The self is the central concept of personality and behavior. While the basic drive of the organism is the maintenance and enhancement of the organism, the psychological self may take precedence over the physiological organism.

Once the self has developed, experiences are perceived and evaluated in terms of their relevance and significance to the self. Behavior is normally consistent with

[13] *Conceptions of Modern Psychiatry,* p. 23.

*From C. H. Patterson, "The Self in Recent Rogerian Theory," *J. Indiv. Psychol.* 1961, **17**, 5–11. By permission of the author and the Editor, *Journal of Individual Psychology.*

the self-concept, even at the expense of the organism. However, organic experiences or needs which are unsymbolized (because they are unacceptable) may at times lead to behavior inconsistent with the self-concpet ("I was not myself"), or to psychological tension and maladjustment. Experiences which are inconsistent with the self-concept may be perceived as threatening, and may be rejected, denied, or distorted; the self-concept is defended.

Psychological adjustment or integration, on the other hand, exists when the self-concept is congruent with all the experiences of the organism. Under conditions of absence of threat to the self, all experiences—including the organismic—may be examined and assimilated into the self-concept, leading to changes in the self-concept. This occurs in therapy.

1959

The most recent and most detailed of Rogers' theoretical discussions, a more systematic and extended formulation of earlier expressions, appeared in mimeographed form in 1955 and in print in 1959 (19). Self-actualization becomes an important aspect of a general actualizing tendency.

The self-concept is defined as "the organized, consistent conceptual Gestalt composed of characteristics of the 'I' or 'me' and the perceptions of the relationships of the 'I' or 'me' to others and to various aspects of life, together with the value attached to these perceptions" (19, p. 200). The ideal self is introduced into the theory and is defined as "the self-concept which the individual would most like to possess, upon which he places the highest value for himself" (19, p. 200).

Several concepts having to do with regard are included. Rogers postulates a basic, though secondary or learned, need for positive regard from others—that is for warmth, liking, respect, sympathy, and acceptance—and a need for positive self-regard, which is related to or dependent upon positive regard from others.

Unconditional self-regard is a state of general positive self-regard, irrespective of conditions. Positive self-regard may be conditional, however, when the individual "values an experience positively or negatively solely because of . . . conditions of worth which he has taken over from others, not because the experience enhances or fails to enhance his organism" (19, p. 209). In this case the individual is vulnerable to threat and anxiety.

The central ideas in Rogers' theory of the self may be stated as follows:

1 The theory of the self, as part of the general personality theory, is phenomenological. The essence of phenomenology is that "man lives essentially in his own personal and subjective world" (19, p. 191).

2 The self becomes differentiated as part of the actualizing tendency, from the environment, through transactions with the environment—particularly the social environment. The process by which this occurs is not detailed by Rogers, but is presumably along the lines described by the sociologists Cooley (8) and Mead (13).[1]

[1]Sociology, I think, anticipated psychology in reacting against behaviorism and recognizing the importance of the self. In the middle thirties, as an undergraduate in sociology at the University of Chicago, I was exposed to the writings of Cooley (8) and Mead (13) on the self. This was where I took on the phenomenological approach. Not until several years later were the self and phenomenology introduced, or rather reintroduced, into psychology. I say reintroduced because James (12) had recognized the importance of the self, and was a phenomenologist as well.

3 The self-concept is the organization of the perceptions of the self. It is the self-concept, rather than any "real" self, which is of significance in personality and behavior. As Combs and Snygg note, the existence of a "real" self is a philosophical question, since it cannot be observed directly (6, p. 123).

4 The self-concept becomes the most significant determinant of response to the environment. It governs the perceptions or meanings attributed to the environment.

5 Whether learned or inherent, a need for positive regard from others develops or emerges with the self-concept. While Rogers leans toward attributing this need to learning, I would include it as an element of the self-actualizing tendency.

6 A need for positive self-regard, or self-esteem, according to Rogers, likewise is learned through internalization or introjection of experiences of positive regard by others. But, alternatively, it may be an aspect of the self-actualizing tendency.

7 When positive self-regard depends on evaluations by others, discrepancies may develop between the needs of the organism and the needs of the self-concept for positive self-regard. There is thus incongruence between the self and experience, or psychological maladjustment. Maladjustment is the result of attempting to preserve the existing self-concept from the threat of experiences which are inconsistent with it, leading to selective perception and distortion or denial of experience.

This highly condensed summary does not include the vicissitudes of the self through the processes of disorganization, or the processes of reorganization which take place in therapy.

While a number of persons have contributed to the theory, including Raimy (16), Snygg and Combs (21), and many others who have been associated with Rogers, there has been no other comparable exposition of the theory nor are there any adequately stated alternatives or variations of it. Rogers' terminology differs in some respects from that used by other client-centered writers, but the basic concepts are similar if not identical. For example, some theorists, including myself (14), have used the term self-esteem to refer to what Rogers designates as positive self-regard.

COMPARISON WITH OTHER FORMULATIONS

"Me" Versus "I"

Several theorists (2, 4, 13, 22) have emphasized two aspects of the self, essentially distinguishing between the *self as object,* the "me," and the *self as subject,* the "I." The first is often referred to as the *self-concept,* the second as the *ego,* although, as Hall and Lindzey (9, p. 468) point out, there is no general agreement upon terms. James called the "me" the empirical self and the "I" the pure ego—the sense of personal identity or the judging thought. This personal identity, he suggested, may not exist as a fact, "but it would exist as a *feeling* all the same; the consciousness of it would be there, and the psychologist would still have to analyze that" (12, p. 333). The ego would appear to be self-consciousness. Mead's conceptions of the "I" and the "me" appear to be similar, although his discussion is difficult to follow. The "I" appears to be the awareness of the self as of the moment of action (13, pp. 173–178, 192).

These concepts, while preferable to the idea of the "I" as an executive, which lends itself to reification, are vague and difficult to pin down. At least I am not able to differentiate actually, practically, or operationally between the executive aspects of the self, and the self as an object to the self. The self of Snygg and Combs is both an object and doer. Others, including Allport (1) and Sherif and Cantril (20), also appear to adopt this view. Hilgard (10) suggests that the concept of the self as a doer is an error into which psychologists have been led by the commonsense or lay view that behavior seems to be self-determined.

In Rogers' theory the self-concept, although an important determiner of behavior, is not an executive or doer. There is no need for positing such an executive. The organism is by nature continually active, seeking its goal of actualization, and the self as part of the organism is also seeking actualization through its constant activity. The self-concept thus influences the direction of activity, rather than initiating it and directing it entirely. Thus Rogers avoids the problem of reification and the ambiguousness of the concept of the "I" or the ego as an executive. James' sense of personal identity might be considered a part of the self-concept, and the ego or "I" as the awareness of the self-concept. However, I am not sure that this solution is entirely satisfactory.

Ideal Self

In his recent formulation of the concept of the ideal self Rogers indicates that the perception of the ideal self becomes more realistic, and the self becomes more congruent with the ideal self, as an outcome of therapy. This suggests that personality disturbance is characterized by an unrealistic self-ideal, and/or incongruence between the self-concept and the self-ideal. This formulation has been the basis of some research by the client-centered school (e.g., 3). But it is not incorporated in Rogers' statement of the theory. The theory apparently does not recognize conflict between the self-concept and the self-ideal as a source of disturbance, but emphasizes the conflict between the self-concept and organismic experiences as its source. This is in contrast to some other theories in which the self-ideal is a central concept and an important factor in psychological adjustment of maladjustment, e.g., Horney (11).

The Self

The notion of the self, or the self-structure, is broader than the self-concept. It includes the self-concept and the ideal self. What else it includes, is not clear. Combs and Snygg speak of the phenomenal self, defined as the "organization of all the ways an individual has of seeing himself" (6, p. 126). The self-concept includes "only those perceptions about self which seem most vital or important to the individual himself" (6, p. 127). How these are to be differentiated is not indicated. Rogers considers the self-concept to be in the person's awareness, whereas the self may include aspects not in awareness.

PROBLEMS OF OPERATIONAL DEFINITION

Rogers made an effort to keep his constructs and concepts so that they can be operationally defined. The phenomenological approach, it seems to me, fosters this effort. One is not concerned about the "real" self, the "real" environment, etc., but the perceptions of particular individuals. The self-concept and the self-ideal are perceptions which can be studied and objectified by instruments such as the Q-sort, or by tests of the "Who am I" variety. The latter, though ideally suited for use with client-centered theory, have not, however, to my knowledge, been used in connection with this theory.

Rogers points out the problem of operationally defining the organismic experiences which, it is assumed, conflict with the self-concept. The aspects of the self other than the self-concept and the self-ideal, are also not operationally defined. Maybe we do not need these concepts. I see no need for unconscious elements of the self, for example. Aspects of the self which are not in awareness but which can be brought into awareness, can be tapped by instructions such as "Sort these statements in terms of your concept of yourself as a father." The self, insofar as it is behaviorally effective, may consist only of the various self-perceptions—thus resolving the problem posed above about the area of the self apart from the self-concept and the self-ideal. The organismic experiences, on the other hand, as an essential aspect of the theory, must be brought within the realm of measurement. The approach of Chodorkoff (5), using Q-sorts of self-referent items by clinicians as an "objective description" of the total experience of the individual, though operational, may be questioned as to its validity.

There is also the problem, pointed out by Combs and Soper (7), that although the self-concept may be operationally defined as the individual's statements about himself, these statements do not necessarily correspond to his perception of himself. His statements may be inaccurate for a number of reasons, including inability or unwillingness to give an accurate report. Yet there is no other approach to determining the self-concept, since by definition it is the perception of the self by the individual, and no one else can report upon it or describe it.

In general, what is needed is a more formal theoretical statement which would lead to testable hypotheses for research, not only with clients in therapy, but in many other situations, with many other kinds of subjects.

SUMMARY

The aspects of Rogers' theory which relate to his central formulation of the self-concept have been summarized. A comparison with the thinking of others regarding the self attempted to clarify some differences and showed other differences in need of resolution. Some problems of operational definition were briefly discussed.

REFERENCES

1 Allport, G. W. The ego in contemporary psychology. *Psychol. Rev.*, 1943, **50,** 451–468. Also in *Personality and social encounter: selected essays*. Boston: Beacon Press, 1960. Pp. 71–93.

2 Bertocci, P. A. The psychological self, the ego and personality. *Psychol. Rev.*, 1945, **52,** 91–99.

3 Butler, J. M., & Haigh, G. V. Changes in the relation between self-concepts and ideal concepts consequent upon client-centered counseling. In C. R. Rogers & R. F. Dymond

(Eds.), *Psychotherapy and personality change.* Chicago: Univer. Chicago Press, 1954. Pp. 55–76.

4 Chein, I. The awareness of the self and the structure of the ego. *Psychol. Rev.,* 1944, **51,** 504–514.

5 Chodorkoff, B. Self-perception, perceptual defense, and adjustment. *J. abnorm. soc. Psychol.,* 1954, **49,** 508–512.

6 Combs, A. W., & Snygg, D. *Individual behavior.* Rev. ed. New York: Harper, 1959.

7 Combs, A. W., & Soper, D. W. The self, its derivative terms, and research. *J. Indiv. Psychol.,* 1957, **13,** 134–145. Also in A. E. Kuenzli (Ed.), *The phenomenological problem.* New York: Harper, 1959. Pp. 31–48.

8 Cooley, C. H. *Human nature and the social order.* New York: Scribner's, 1902.

9 Hall, C. S., & Lindzey, G. *Theories of personality.* New York: Wiley, 1957.

10 Hilgard, E. R. Human motives and the concept of the self. *Amer. Psychologist,* 1949, **4,** 374–382. Also in H. Brand (Ed.), *The study of personality.* New York: Wiley, 1954. Pp. 347–361.

11 Horney, K. *Neurosis and human growth.* New York: Norton, 1950.

12 James, W. *The principles of psychology.* Vol. 1. New York: Holt, 1890.

13 Mead, G. H. *Mind, self and society.* Chicago: Univer. Chicago Press, 1934.

14 Patterson, C. H. *Counseling and psychotherapy: theory and practice.* New York: Harper, 1959.

15 Pepinsky, H. B., & Pepinsky, P. N. *Counseling: theory and practice.* New York: Ronald, 1954.

16 Raimy, V. C. Self-reference in counseling interviews. *J. consult. Psychol.,* 1948, **12,** 153–163. Also in A. E. Kuenzli (Ed.), *The phenomenological problem.* New York: Harper, 1959. Pp. 76–95.

17 Rogers, C. R. Some observations on the organization of personality. *Amer. Psychologist,* 1947, **2,** 358–368. Also in A. E. Kuenzli (Ed.), *The phenomenological problem.* New York: Harper, 1959. Pp. 49–75.

18 Rogers, C. R. *Client-centered therapy.* Boston: Houghton Mifflin, 1951.

19 Rogers, C. R. A theory of therapy, personality, and interpersonal relationships, as developed in the client-centered framework. In S. Koch (Ed.), *Psychology: a study of a science.* Vol. 3. New York: McGraw-Hill, 1959. Pp. 184–256.

20 Sherif, M., & Cantril, H. *The psychology of ego-involvements.* New York: Wiley, 1947.

21 Snygg, D., & Combs, A. W. *Individual behavior.* New York: Harper, 1949.

22 Symonds, P. M. *The ego and the self.* New York: Appleton-Century-Crofts, 1951.

Existentialism, Psychology, and Psychotherapy*

Lawrence A. Pervin

Recently there has been a growing interest in existentialism. While it has already gained some determined adherents and some vehement enemies, the majority of psychologists and social scientists of related disciplines remain confused about the place of existentialism in their particular field of endeavor. The reasons for this are

*From Lawrence A. Pervin, "Existentialism, Psychology, and Psychotherapy," *Amer. Psychologist,* 1960, **15,** 305–309. Reprinted by permission of the author and the Managing Editor, the American Psychological Association.

many: the philosophical nature of existentialism, the varying approaches and emphases commonly called existential, the lack of clarity and completeness in the existential approaches. While thus there are many reasons for the evident confusion, very likely the main reason is the lack of familiarity with existential writings, concepts, and approaches. The following attempts to introduce the reader to some of the basic elements of existentialism and to point to its relevance to psychology and psychotherapy.

FUNDAMENTAL CONCEPTS OF EXISTENTIALISM

As described by Tillich (1944), "Existence" emerged in the 1840's and was represented in the works of Schelling, Kierkegaard, and Marx. The movement then subsided until the 1880's. A rebirth was experienced in the *"lebensphilosophie"* or Philosophy of Life of Neitzsche. Contemporary philosophy of experienced existence, represented in the works of Heidegger and Jaspers, has resulted from a combination of Neitzche's Philosophy of Life with Husserl's phenomenology.

While the existential philosophers express a good deal of variability in their views, there is also some common ground or group of common traits which justifies calling them all existential philosophers. Perhaps most important is the concern with Existence—man in a situation. It is out of this particular common concern that common emphases emerge.

One major aspect of the "existential view" is that of the significance of the individual. As described by Tillich: "Where there is an Existentialist point of view there is the problem of the human situation experienced by the individual" (1952, p. 130). Historically, it was the threat of the loss of the individual person which drove the revoutionary existentialists of the nineteenth century to their attack. The attack has led to a particular view of the individual, for he is now seen as singular, unique, and irreplaceable. The individual is not just a member of the crowd and the herd, he is unrepeatable. For Kierkegaard the only existential problem is to exist as an individual. This view of the individual has, in part, led to the existentialist's concern with death, for it is here as nowhere else that the individual is himself alone and completely irreplaceable.

The attack and the rebellion further revolve around the existential view of the singular and unique individual. For the existentialists man is free. For Kierkegaard freedom is the self. Nietzsche's individual freely affirms. For Jaspers existence is freedom, and for Sartre consciousness is freedom. Compare Tillich's statement: "Man is essentially 'finite freedom'; freedom not in the sense of indeterminancy but in the sense of being able to determine himself through decisions in the center of his Being" (1952, p. 52) with Freud's: "what we call our ego is essentially passive. . . . We are 'lived' by unknown and uncontrollable forces" (1957, p. 214). Freud's deterministic view of man represents a complete opposite to the existential view of man as absolute freedom. This freedom is highly valued, for it is part of that which distinguishes man from other animals and makes him a human being. Part of this is also the ability of man to see himself as a self, to have consciousness, to be reflective, to question his own existence. These are powers and possibilities of man and man alone.

Freedom involves freedom from and freedom to. Both involve freedom of the instincts, and both involve responsibility. Man is responsible for Being—for his own existence, for his freedom and his choices, for the realization of himself. Man is responsible for being himself and so for being authentic. To flee from one's freedom and responsibility is to be inauthentic, to live in despair and "Bad Faith." Life in Nietzsche's Philosophy of Life is "the process in which the power of being actualizes itself" (Tillich, 1952, p. 27). For Tillich, man is "asked to make of himself what he is supposed to become, to fulfill his destiny. In every act of moral self-affirmation man contributes to the fulfillment of his destiny, to the actualization of what he potentially is" (Tillich, 1952, p. 52).

Existentialists are concerned with the meaning of life. Contemporary existential philosophers are particularly concerned with the problem of restoring meaning to life. According to Tillich, twentieth century man has experienced the universal breakdown of meaning, he has "lost a meaningful world and a self which lives in meanings" (1952, p. 139). This concern about the meaning of life and self enters into the existential view of psychopathology and psychotherapy.

As one examines the above points, he realizes that he has seen similar points made by noted men of a variety of disciplines. The ideas of Fromm correspond in a number of ways to those of the existentialists. Fromm (1941) talks of man as wanting to have a sense of personal identity, to become a unique individual. Because he has fewer predetermined courses of behavior than any other animal, man has gained freedom. But, not freedom to develop as an individual. Concern with the problems of existence, freedom, meaning, and the realization of the individual exemplifies Fromm's indebtedness to existential thought. Goldstein's emphasis upon the unique individual and the realization of potentialities are similarly existential in character.

While existentialism is a European creation and the above theorists are of European heritage, the spirit of the existential rebellion and the need for a new view of man have not left our American scholars untouched. The theory of Carl Rogers is phenomenological in character and stresses the individual and self-realization. Also, the psychology of George Kelly corresponds, in part, to the "existential view." There is a concern with the personal meaning of events to the individual. As we shall soon see, Binswanger and the existential psychoanalysts stress the world-design of the individual. Kelly (1955), in a similar way, stresses the understanding of the construct system of the individual—the way he construes the world. Furthermore, Kelly emphasizes the future as a factor in human behavior and that the individual's construction of the past is open to change—he is not bound to the past.

Some theorists openly avow their indebtedness to the existentialists. In others the influence has been more subtle. And, finally, some have independently arrived at similar points of view. In any case, it must be recognized that existentialism has had and does have something to offer. The possibility that psychology can independently arrive at the desired goals should not be the basis for an evaluation of existentialism. If existentialism can aid in the achievement of the desired goals, psychologists cannot afford to remain ignorant of its concepts. On the other hand, uncritical acceptance forebodes a similarly unhealthy situation.

TWO EXISTENTIAL APPROACHES

The existentialists are concerned with the beings that we are. It seems natural, therefore, that at least some of these philosophers should turn to the problems of normal man, abnormal man, and the process of "making" the latter into the former. In the following, two existential approaches will be briefly discussed: the approach represented in the new volume of *Existence* (May, Angel, & Ellenberger, 1958) and the approach represented in "On Logotherapy and Existential Analysis" (Frankl, 1958). The two are especially noteworthy since the former culminates primarily from work with psychotic patients while the latter culminates almost entirely from work with neurotic patients.

Existential Analysis

The existential analysts emphasize the study of the experiencing individual. Events are looked at in terms of their meaning for the individual. He is seen as a Being-in-the-World. The belief is that the individual reveals himself through his world-project or world-design. According to Kuhn, the world-design is that "which is laid by every human upon everything that exists, through which he interprets everything that exists, and from which he gets a context of reference, wherein each person's existence *(Dasein)* is determined" (May *et al.*, 1958, p. 396).

In an attempt to get at the patient's inner universe of experience, the existential analyst studies how the phenomenological coordinates of time, space, causality, and materiality are experienced. Within the time dimension the future is seen as particularly significant. Medard Boss calls man's capacity to transcend the immediate situation the basic and unique characteristic of human existence. The approach to the future is seen as particularly significant because it affects the view of the past and determines those parts which will be influential in the present. The Being of a person is characterized in terms of three modes: *Umwelt*—the biological world; *Mitwelt*—the world of one's fellow men; and *Eigenwelt*—the mode of relationship to oneself. The three are simultaneous modes of Being-in-the-World. Anxiety, hostility, and aggression are normal states and part of Being-in-the-World.

Human psychopathology is seen in a number of ways by the existentialists. According to Tillich, in the neurotic the self which is affirmed is a reduced one and some or many of its potentialities are not admitted to actualization. From Kierkegaard's view the neuroses and psychoses would be accompanied by a loss of self, an inner alienation. Jaspers views the psychotic as one who has lost his own existence and so has lost the existence of reality. In general, existential analysis points to the deviations of the structure of existence as representative of psychopathology.

The process of existential psychotherapy remains somewhat ill-defined. The central aspect of the process appears to be the patient's recognition and experiencing of his own existence. The patient is oriented toward fulfillment of his existence. As regards technique, there is little that is specific. The belief is that a flexible approach is necessary to understand the person-in-his-world. Technique is varied from patient to patient and from one phase of treatment to another: "What will best reveal the existence of this particular patient at this moment in history?"

Logotherapy

The "school" of Victor Frankl has been known under various names: Logotherapy, Existential Analysis, and Medical Ministry. The name Existential Analysis refers to the influences of Kierkegaard, Heidegger, Jaspers, and other existential philosophers. It is neither related to Binswanger's Daseinanalyse nor to Sartre's Existential Psychoanalysis.

Like all existentialists, Frankl is concerned with preserving the unity of being. An interpretation of nature in terms of concentrically layered structures is felt to preserve this unity. For Frankl, man lives in three dimensions: the somatic, the psychic, the spiritual. Furthermore, human existence is characterized by its spirituality, freedom, and responsibility.

Logotherapy focuses upon the search for meaning in human existence. While psychoanalysis emphasizes the will-to-pleasure and individual psychology the will-to-power, existential analysis emphasizes the will-to-meaning. "This will-to-meaning is the most human phenomenon of all since an animal never worries about the meaning of its existence" (Frankl, 1955, p. 9). Ultimate meaning is represented in the individual's unique task in life, which awaits realization in his personality. Meaning is found through actualizing value, through self-realization.

As stated above, man is both responsible and free. Responsibility springs from the singularity and uniqueness of existence. One is responsible to life for the fulfillment of the spiritual and the realization of values. Freedom means freedom in the face of instincts, inherited disposition, and environment. It involves the fundamental possibility of choosing. Man can decide whether he shall be at all—he can choose suicide—and in this way is distinguished from all other kinds of being.

The will-to-meaning can remain frustrated and unfulfilled. This condition is called existential frustration. Existential frustration is not something pathological itself. But, when it does become pathogenic, it is called a noogenic neurosis. This neurosis is rooted in spiritual conflicts and ethical problems.

For Frankl, the neurotic lacks "instinctive sureness" in sensing his task. He blocks the realization of his own potentialities and plays one life task off against the other. The outstanding feature of the neurotic is his escape from freedom and responsibility. It is seen as a mode of existence in which the person blames his destiny, his childhood, and his environment for what he is.

While not all neuroses are noogenic, there is a psychotherapy appropriate to them: "When a neurosis is really noogenic, spiritually rooted, it requires a psychotherapy having a spiritual basis, and that is what I call Logotherapy, in contrast to psychotherapy in the narrower sense of the word" (Frankl, 1958, p. 34).

As a therapy, Logotherapy calls upon the spiritual in man and upon his will-to-meaning. Frankl proposes two mottos for all psychotherapy: "He who knows a Why of living surmounts almost every How" (Neitzsche) and "If we take people as they are, we make them worse. If we treat them as if they were what they ought to be, we help them to become what they are capable of becoming'' (Goethe). Logotherapy, then, seeks to help the patients become what they are capable of becoming, to bring out the ultimate possibilities of the patients, to enable them to find meaning in existence.

The two theories and techniques of psychotherapy described here may be characterized as outgrowths of the existential movement. There are a number of criticisms appropriate to their systems. The two systems are deficient in both theory and technique. While Western belief is seen as holding that understanding follows technique, existential psychoanalysis holds that technique follows understanding. For understanding to be of use to psychology as a science it must be lawful understanding and thus available for formulation into theory. But, theory furnishes another problem for existential analysis. Kuhn states: ''Existential analysis is not a finished, beautifully rounded theory which allows us to explain some, or all, events that occur in a psyche. Furthermore, we are at present still at the beginning of work in this direction'' (1958, p. 397). Frankl similarly states: ''We have not systematically delineated a theory of the neuroses'' (1955, p. 201).

While each of these approaches is lacking in certain aspects, they do have contributions to make. The emphasis upon actualization of potentialities, the fulfillment of Being, has found its way into a number of psychotherapies. The attention Logotherapy calls to the significance of meaning in a person's life is well worth the attention of all psychotherapists: ''The old question still faces us as it has faced humanity for ages past: what is the meaning of life . . . what might be called the moral and spiritual side of life, something that is basic in man'' (Nehru, 1958, p. 110). It is probable that the finding of a personal and meaningful task in life can alleviate many neurotic difficulties. Edith Weisskopf-Joelson goes so far as to say: ''Helping patients develop effective and socially acceptable defenses against anxiety—such as a supportive system of ethical values—seems a more realistic, even though perhaps a less ambitious goal of therapy than getting to the roots of the disorder'' (1955, p. 702). Weisskopf-Joelson further points out the wisdom in de-emphasizing happiness as a goal and the wisdom of a philosophy that accepts suffering. Frankl's therapy should be an especially useful aid in dealing with situations of unavoidable suffering.

Finally, the two systems have an approach or view to offer. They represent a badly needed ''new view'' of man—a view of man worthy of attention, study, and emulation. It is a view of man which allows for and emphasizes man's freedom and courage.

CONCLUSION

Existentialism and existential analysis can be criticized and found lacking on philosophical grounds. They can also be criticized and found lacking on psychological grounds. While I applaud the existentialists for their emphasis upon the unique individual, I find fault with their conclusions from this. Their emphasis has led them to abandon hope of understanding and predicting human behavior in a lawful way. The existentialists see science and objective reality as appealing to the universal person and to no one in their individuality. Since the individual is unique, they insist that he cannot be covered by laws for all men. Frankl states: "A real human person is not subject to rigid prediction. Existence can neither be reduced to a system nor deduced from it" (1955, p. 169). This emphasis is worthy in cautioning us against unrealistic generalizations and abstractions. The individual is free and unique. But, does this mean that he behaves unlawfully and unpredictably? There is something common to all these individuals that we are, and this may be a subject for scientific endeavor. The understanding of patterned and lawful aspects of human behavior is the subject of inquiry for psychology. If in some way all or part of behavior is lawful, then to that extent human behavior can be predicted. While the laws we ultimately arrive at may not lead to a complete understanding and prediction of each and every individual, or any individual, they may represent a considerable advance beyond the present darkness and mystery. The individual and the human must not be forgotten in abstractions, but psychology's attempt at a lawful understanding of human behavior must be pushed to its limit.

But, the realization of the inadequacies of a view should not blind us to the potential contributions. In Europe, under the direction of such men as Buhtendijk, van Lennep, and Wellek, existential psychology and the phenomenological method have made some progress. There are continued reports of the growth in popularity of existential psychotherapy. At Harvard, tests derived from existential categories have already been formulated. Existentialism and existential analysis are far from representing a complete system or theory. It would be foolhardy to accept or reject them in their entirety. Perhaps they can be useful to psychology in terms of the approaches and views they offer. The existential view of man, his uniqueness, his freedom, his responsibility, his own frame of reference, and will-to-meaning are worthy of serious attention and investigation. Their emphasis upon that which distinguishes man from other animals, upon normal guilt, hostility, and anxiety, and upon such categories as that of temporality and spatiality are similarly noteworthy. They represent possible suggestions for further study by psychology. If approached in this light, I think that existentialism may have much to offer and psychology considerable to gain!

REFERENCES

Frankl, V. E. *The doctor and the soul.* New York: Knopf, 1955.

Frankl, V. E. On logotherapy and existential analysis. *Amer. J. Psychoanal.,* 1958, **18,** 28–37.

Freud, S. The ego and the id. In J. Rickman (Ed.), *A general selection from the works of Sigmund Freud.* New York: Doubleday Anchor, 1957.

Fromm, E. *Escape from freedom.* New York: Farrer & Rinehart, 1941.

Kelly, G. A. *The psychology of personal constructs.* New York: Norton, 1955. 2 vols.

May, R., Angel, E., & Ellenberger, H. F. (Eds.) *Existence.* New York: Basic Books, 1958.

Nehru, J. The tragic paradox of our age. *New York Times,* 1958, Sept. 7, Section 8.

Tillich, P. Existential philosophy. *J. Hist. Ideas,* 1944, **5**(1), 44–70.

Tillich, P. *Courage to be.* New Haven: Yale Univer. Press, 1952.

Weisskopf,-Joelson, Edith. Some comments on a Viennese school of psychiatry. *J. abnorm. soc. Psychol.,* 1955, **51,** 701–703.

Learning: Conditioning and Avoidance*

Brendan A. Maher

Definitions of *learning* are numerous. . . . we shall define learning as *the process which changes the probability that a given response will be elicited by a given stimulus*. Having defined learning as a process in this way, we can recognize that the investigation of learning is largely directed to discovering the environmental influences which affect it and the biological variables which may modify it. On the whole, the majority of learning theorists have paid less attention to biological variables than they have to environmental ones, and our body of scientific knowledge is consequently more advanced with regard to the effects of the latter. Indifference to biological processes and their effects upon behavior is most plausible when the investigator is fairly sure that he is dealing with biologically normal behavior. We may proceed as though the organism is "empty" when we know that it is full but intact. Psychopathologists, on the other hand, may make no such assumption unless they are bent on futility. Behavioral consequences of biological aberration are of great significance in psychopathology. . . . However, since simplicity will be better served by considering environmental variables separately from biological ones. . . . Let us now turn to examine the influence of environmental variables upon the learning process.

CONDITIONING

For practical purposes the simplest example of learning is the acquisition by a subject of a *conditioned response* (CR). In what is called *classical conditioning,* a stimulus which already has the power to elicit a response is presented in contiguity with another stimulus which does not yet have this power. Repeated presentations of these two stimuli in contiguity eventually lead to a situation where the formerly neutral stimulus will now elicit the response when it is presented alone. The response remains essentially the same—the occurrence of learning is demonstrated by the fact that the probability that it would occur to the neutral stimulus was originally zero. Following the conditioning procedure, it has been raised to some positive level of probability.

Certain technical terms are used to describe this process. The stimulus which originally elicits the response is referred to as the *unconditioned stimulus* (US) and the response, when made to it, is an *unconditioned response* (UR). The previously neutral stimulus is described as the *conditioned stimulus* (CS) and the response, when made to the CS alone, is called the *conditioned response* (CR). An example of this procedure would be provided by the acquisition of a conditioned eyeblink response. A puff of air, delivered to the eye, will elicit an eyeblink. At this point the air puff is the US and the eyeblink the UR. If the delivery of the air puff is preceded by a short audible sound stimulus, and if this sequence of stimuli is repeated sufficiently often, the sound will elicit the eyeblink response. Now the sound is a CS, and the eyeblink response to the CS is a CR.

*From Brendan A. Maher, *Principles of Psychopathology,* McGraw-Hill Book Company, Inc. New York, 1966. Pages 43–52 reprinted by permission of the author and the publisher.

Learning may be demonstrated by a different sequence of events in a procedure generally known as *operant conditioning*. This refers to the procedure wherein a reinforcing stimulus is presented to the subject whenever he makes a given response. The response in question is not being elicited by the reinforcing stimulus, the latter usually being concealed until after the desired response has occurred. Conditioning is defined as having been established when the rate of occurrence of the reinforced response increases in the situation. For some purposes we may wish to use increases in the speed of responding or in the magnitude of the response.

The best-known illustration of experimental operant conditioning is the acquisition of a bar-pressing response by a rat (or a key-pecking response by a pigeon) in an apparatus which is constructed so as to deliver food when the bar is pressed. This kind of apparatus is usually called an "operant-conditioning chamber"—or more colloquially, a "Skinner box," referring to the major contribution of B. F. Skinner to our understanding of operant conditioning. A typical operant-conditioning chamber is illustrated in Figure 1.

More specific developments of the operant-conditioning technique involve the use of special schedules of reinforcement, whereby the response is not reinforced each time it is made. Schedules may include reinforcement of a predetermined percentage of the responses made, of responses made only in the presence of some special stimulus such

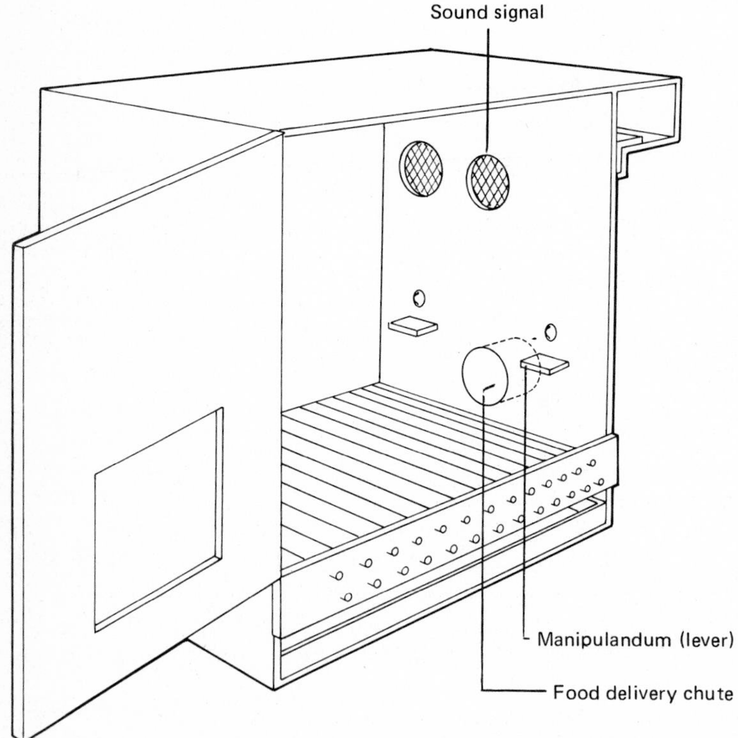

Figure 1 Operant-conditioning chamber of the kind used in laboratory procedures.

as a light, or of responses made during specified time intervals. Much work has gone into the study of effects of different schedules of reinforcement, but we cannot discuss them in detail here.

Extinction

After establishing a conditioned response, we may proceed to *extinguish* it: that is to say, we may reduce its rate, speed, or magnitude by eliminating the reinforcement related to the response. In the case of classical conditioning, for example, we may establish a CR of salivation to a bell (CS) by presenting the CS in contiguity with food (US). When the CR has been well established, we may extinguish it by giving repeated presentations of the bell alone, never pairing it again with food. The salivation response will begin to diminish in magnitude and frequency and will eventually extinguish.

Extinction of operant conditioning is achieved by removing the reinforcement entirely so that the conditioned response is never followed by reinforcement. Here again we will find a slowing down of the rate of responding until it is extinguished. We should note, however, that the attainment of complete extinction of a previously conditioned response is a questionable phenomenon. When a response has been extinguished, and is then neither elicited nor emitted for a period of time away from the conditioning environment, the return of the subject to the conditioning environment will be accompanied by the reappearance of the response at higher strength than that which it had at the end of the extinction procedure. This reappearance of a conditioned response that had been apparently extinguished is called *spontaneous recovery,* and the phenomenon is of considerable importance in the application of learning theory to human behavior.

If for some reason we wish to extinguish a certain response which has been conditioned, we may use both the procedure of extinction and that of *counterconditioning*. Counterconditioning consists simply of the reinforcing of a new response which is incompatible with the one which it is desired to extinguish. As we shall see later on, certain aspects of psychotherapy may be regarded as instances of the counterconditioning of new and more adaptive responses to take the place of the undesirable pathological behaviors which have brought the patient into treatment.

Reinforcement

Of all the concepts which are crucial to the understanding of learning, that of *reinforcement* is perhaps the most central. It is, at the same time, the most troublesome to define. As a beginning, let us turn to Verplanck (1957). He defines reinforcement as "the operation of presenting to the animal in operant conditioning, after it has made a response (and therefore contingent on its occurrence), a reinforcing stimulus or of withdrawing a negative reinforcing stimulus," and "in classical conditioning, the operation of presenting, contiguously in time, a conditioned stimulus and an unconditioned simulus" (p. 25).

The problem of this definition is that we do not know what will be a reinforcement until learning has occurred. Commonsense observation has led to the assumption that food is a reinforcing stimulus to a hungry subject, or that reduction of pain is a reinforcement to almost any living organism. Most of the time this assumption is supported, i.e., animals learn responses which are reinforced by food or by pain reduction, etc. However, at the present time, there is no adequate definition of reinforcement that is independent of observation of learning. In effect, any consequence of a response that will occur again under like conditions is a reinforcement. If this change is one of increasing the probability, then it is a *positive* reinforcement; if it is a change to a lower probability, then it is a *negative* reinforcement.

Animal experimentation makes major use of *biological* or *primary* reinforcements. Typical biological reinforcers include food for a hungry animal, water for a thirsty animal, sexual activity after a period of deprivation, and removal of excessive heat, cold, painful stimulation, etc., from the environment. These reinforcements are classed together as primary because they appear to be effective for any animal in a given species without training.

By and large, in Western society much behavior does not appear to be supported by direct primary reinforcers. Social reinforcers, such as the acquisition of success, prestige, acceptance by others, and the like, appear to be responsible for much social learning which takes place. Likewise, social punishment, failure, and rejection seem to act as negative reinforcers. Social learning theorists have suggested many lists of social reinforcers. We shall not be concerned here with these lists, except to note that among them have been included such events as the acquisition of material wealth, the construction of objects or of systems, praise, prestige, friendship, pity, and so on.

Theoretical interest attaches to the question of whether social reinforcers are acquired on the basis of experience with primary reinforcers, or whether some of them at least are as fundamental to human behavior as the primary biological reinforcers. From a practical point of view this distinction is of less importance. Adult behavior may be so greatly determined by the occurrence of social reinforcers that the origin of these reinforcers may be irrelevant to the problem of the extinction or change of specific behaviors.

Secondary Reinforcement

Stimuli which are present and contiguous with the delivery of a reinforcer may, after a number of such presentations, acquire the power to act as reinforcers for the response in the absence of the original reinforcer. When this state of affairs has been reached, the stimuli in question are described as *secondary reinforcers*. It is clear that the development of a secondary reinforcer may sometimes be accidental. Contiguities between situational simuli and existing reinforcers may occur in an unlimited number of ways, leading to the establishment of the situational stimuli as secondary reinforcers. There may be no "logical" or obvious connection between the secondary reinforcer and the response when they occur together at some much later time.

Stimulus Generalization

Once a response has been conditioned to a particular CS, it will also be evoked by any other stimulus which has some similarity to that CS. Similarity of one stimulus to another is a rather complicated matter. Any physical characteristic of a stimulus might vary—size, color, shape, brightness, etc., in visual stimuli: pitch, loudness, etc., in an auditory stimulus. Where the variation is measurable in physical units, such as inches, lumens, decibels, frequency in cycles per second, and so forth, we speak of *primary stimulus generalization.* An illustration of a curve or gradient of primary stimulus generalization is given in Figure 2.

Questions of theoretical interest have been raised about the shape of the gradient of stimulus generalization, but we may here concern ourselves only with the observation that with decreasing similarity to the original CS, other stimuli evoke the response with decreasing strength, probability, and speed. By the same token, the extinction of the response is more rapid when extinction is established with a generalization stimulus than it is when extinction procedures use the original CS.

Generalization of Extinction

We may establish a response to a particular CS and then proceed to extinguish it to a similar generalized stimulus. After some measure of extinction has been achieved with the generalized CS, we may once more present the original CS and will find that the response to it has been weakened by the intervening extinction process. This phenomenon is referred to as the *generalization of extinction.* Apart from its interest for learning theorists, the procedure is of some importance in understanding clinical techniques involved in the extinction of pathological behavior.

Semantic Generalization

Much human behavior is verbal. Human social, interpersonal behavior is predominantly verbal. Consequently the significant stimuli and responses are spoken or written words, the physical attributes of which are much less important than the symbolic meanings that they have acquired. Similarity between words may exist on the basis of meaning rather than on the basis of the number and order of letters which they have in common. Experiments by Lacey and Smith (1954) and Lacey, Smith, and Green (1955) demonstrate that the establishment of conditioned responses of the autonomic system to a stimulus word "cow" also generalized to other rural words such as "corn" and

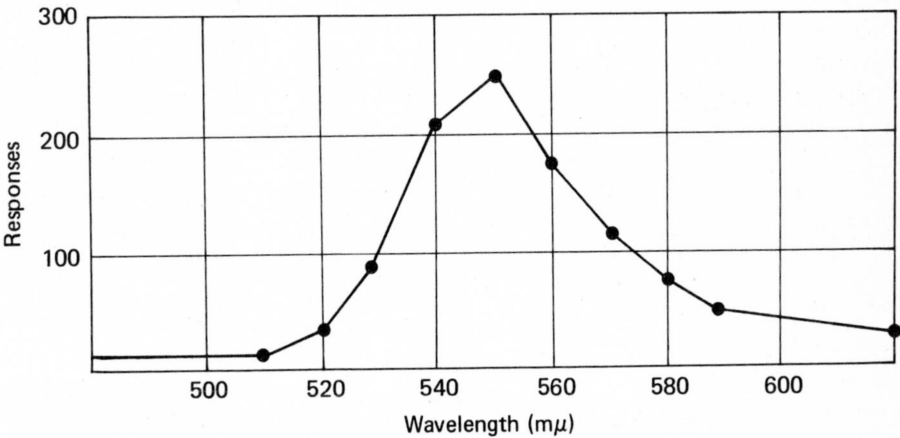

Figure 2 A stimulus generalization gradient. *(From Guttman and Kalish, 1958.)*

"tractor" when these were presented to the subject. Here, presumably, the basis of generalization was the rural connotation of the words.

There is some reason to believe that the dimensions of semantic generalization change in the period of childhood and the transition to adulthood. Reiss (1946), for example, established a conditioned GSR to words and found that stimulus generalization was most apparent to homophones (words of the same sound but with different spelling and meaning) between the ages of 7 and 9; for antonyms (words of opposite meaning) for the age range 10 to 12; and for synonyms between 14 and 20 years.

Partial Reinforcement Effect

When a response is learned under conditions in which the CS is not always accompanied by the US, an interesting and paradoxical effect is obtained. The response learned under these conditions is harder to extinguish than one which is learned under conditions of 100 per cent reinforcement. To this phenomenon is given the name *partial reinforcement effect* (PRE). Sophisticated theoretical explanations have been developed to account for this effect, and sophisticated experiments have been made to discover the limits within which it occurs. None of these will be discussed here, but we may note that the existence of PRE suggests that learned behaviors may be kept at fairly high strengths if an occasional reinforcement is provided. It is not necessary for CS-US contiguities to be consistent or frequent in order for an established CR to be maintained. In fact, the PRE indicates that behaviors which were acquired under conditions of partial reinforcement will be relatively difficult to eliminate.

LEARNING: AVOIDANCE LEARNING

Responses which are conditioned to stimuli associated with a painful US exhibit certain features which make it necessary to treat avoidance learning as a somewhat special problem. Let us consider some concepts first.

Avoidance Response

In establishing an *avoidance response,* we pair a CS with a painful US (in the experimental laboratory, the latter is typically a painful electric shock) under conditions in which the subject can avoid receiving the shock at all provided that he makes a predetermined response when the CS appears. Technical steps usually involve the response being one which will break the shock circuit before the shock is delivered, as for example by pressing a bar, or the response may involve the movement of the subject from the region where the shock will occur. In either case, the response is said to be learned when the subject is able to successfully avoid shock a significantly large number of times.

Escape Responses

A different procedure is one in which the subject is not able to avoid the shock completely but may terminate it, after it starts, by some predetermined response. The main difference between the *escape* and avoidance situations is that in the former the US is always applied, whereas in the latter it never appears once the response has been learned.

Conditioned Emotional Response

A third type of conditioning to painful stimulation is one in which the CS is paired with the US and in which there is no way in which the US may be avoided or terminated. Under these conditions, the subject's response represents the UR typical of the species in the presence of unavoidable pain and has been termed an ''emotional'' response. After sufficient conditioning trials, the CS alone will evoke the pattern of response elicited by the US. When produced by the CS alone, it may be termed the *conditioned emotional response* or CER. Clearly the CER will be quite variable from one kind of organism to another, and will also be influenced by the manner and site of delivery of the US. In the case of the laboratory rat, for example, delivery of shock across a grid floor on which the subject is placed commonly elicits a pattern of responses which includes immobility or ''freezing'' to the floor, defecation and urination, and flattening of the ears as the major components.

From these three procedures, we may now turn to the theoretical explanations and problems which the phenomena of avoidance learning have created.

Learned Fear

One explanation of avoidance learning is that the painful stimulation produces both pain and fear (Miller, 1948)—*fear* being a term for a group of responses which accompany pain but are independent of them, in the sense that they can be elicited when no pain is present. A complete description of the fear responses might be difficult to provide, but we may note that many of them would be functions of the visceral nervous system and would include increases in heart rate, respiration, perspiration and generalized muscular tension. Miller suggested that the effect of pairing a CS with a painful US was to produce a conditioned fear response such that the onset of the CS would then produce the pattern of fear responses—a process very similar to the conditioned emotional response.

A second aspect of this explanation is that the termination of fear is a reinforcer and that any response which terminates fear will be acquired. Many experiments have demonstrated that once a subject has developed a conditioned fear response to a stimulus, he will learn further responses the only reinforcement of which is that they remove the CS and thus presumably terminate the fear. Removal of the CS in such a case is clearly acting as a secondary reinforcer in much the same way that the presence of the CS may act in learning based on positive reinforcements. Particular importance attaches to this phenomenon, because it illustrates the fact that an individual may develop many responses which serve to avoid a CS, responses which may not have occurred at all in the presence of the US.

Extinction of Avoidance Responses

During the previous discussion of extinction, we noted that the essential step in extinguishing a response is to present the CS without the US, so that the response is made but is not followed by reinforcement. Unreinforced responses then diminish in strength and extinguish. Avoidance learning presents a rather unusual problem in this respect, as the avoidance response—by definition—ensures that the US is not experienced. Speaking colloquially, we might say that the subject doesn't stay around to find out whether or not there is going to be a painful stimulus. Thus the very nature of avoidance behavior is such that extinction is difficult to achieve unless special techniques are involved. Inasmuch as it is necessary that the subject be given repeated trials in which the CS is not accompanied by the US, it is necessary that the avoidance response not be permitted to occur. In a word, the subject must be induced or compelled to undergo the extinction process.

Limits of Extinction of Avoidance Responses Every clinical psychologist knows from experience that the removal of pathological behaviors based upon fear is an extremely difficult task. Many forms of pathological behavior receive punishment from society, in the form of social rejection, contempt, and the like. Psychological symptoms are obviously the occasion of much distress to the patient himself. In the light of this we ask ourselves, "Why does someone persist in behavior which is receiving no positive reinforcement and is, indeed, being punished?" There seems to be every reason why symptoms should extinguish without the need for special procedures. This phenomenon has been called *the neurotic paradox* (Mowrer and Ullman, 1945).

The resolution of the paradox is comparatively straightforward. Provided that we are dealing with symptomatic behavior which is being reinforced by avoiding exposure to fear-producing situations, all the conditions necessary to the maintenance of the symptom are present, and present in sufficient degree to outweigh the effects of such social punishment as the symptom is receiving. In order to extinguish symptoms which are being reinforced by removing the patient from fear-producing stimuli, we must prevent the symptoms from serving this purpose. Provided that we can keep the patient in contact with the feared situation long enough and often enough for him to learn that the feared danger (the US) will not occur, extinction *should* take place.

Unfortunately the problem is much less simple than that. We have touched upon the possible nature of the fear response itself and have suggested that the reduction of it constitutes the reinforcement which maintains avoidance behavior. Visceral responses, of the kind which are commonly thought to constitute the major features of the fear response, have considerably longer latencies than many avoidance responses which are supposed to be based on them. In a word, much experimental avoidance behavior has been shown to occur so rapidly after the CS appears that the fear response could not have had time to develop (Solomon & Wynne, 1953, 1954). If the avoidance response terminates the fear stimulus, then some of the major components of the fear response will not occur in the presence of that stimulus, and it will thus be difficult to extinguish the fear response.

Conservation and Partial Irreversibility of Anxiety From the foregoing we might summarize the situation by saying that since the speed with which motor avoidance responses may be made is greater than the speed with which visceral components of fear can occur to the same stimulus, there is an inherent psychological reason for the difficultues experienced in extinguishing avoidance behavior. In the case of human behavior, we all are probably familiar with the situation where a sudden emergency while driving on the highway produces a rapid, skilled reaction of swerving from the path of danger—but may be followed some seconds after the danger is over by a very unpleasant experience of fear or distress. The important point here is that we recognize that avoidant behavior may occur without any conscious feeling of fear on the part of the individual. This feeling may come later. If the avoidance response is well learned, it may never come at all. As a descriptive term for the fact that fear tends to be saved from extinction by the speed of the avoidance response, Solomon and Wynne have suggested the phrase *the principle of anxiety conservation.*

So far, so good. However, in the nature of things some avoidance responses may be delayed by random variations in the circumstances in which they are elicited. Thus, from time to time, the response may be made slowly enough for the fear response to develop. When this happens often enough and the US does not occur, the process of extinction should begin, and in the long run responses should become slower, extinction be hastened even further, and so on. Yet where the original US was an intense traumatic stimulus, ultimate extinction of the avoidance response seems to be very rare. Solomon and Wynne have suggested that fear reactions of this kind may be impossible to extinguish completely. Thus for this hypothesis they have offered the principle of *partial irreversibility* of fear responses.

Generalization of Avoidance Responses

Just as other kinds of conditioned responses are elicited by stimuli which are somewhat similar to the original CS, so avoidance responses will occur to generalized stimuli. No special concepts are necessary here. However, some questions have been raised regarding the probability that the gradient of stimulus generalization for avoidance responses may be steeper than that for positively reinforced responses when the two are acquired and compared in similar situations. The rationale behind this suggestion is rather complex. It is dealt with in our discussion of conflict in a later chapter.

Punishment and the Suppression of Behavior

The child who raids the cookie jar may find that this response leads to punishment. If this were the only and regular result of his behavior, we should expect that he would develop avoidance behaviors of some kind toward cookie jars, parents, or other stimuli which were regularly associated with the punishment. Common sense indicates that this is not the case and that punishment of this kind does not eliminate the behavior for which it is given. We must recognize that the effect of punishment upon behavior which is being independently reinforced is different from the effect of punishment upon behavior which is not being reinforced. The child who is burned by a hot radiator is likely to stay away from it indefinitely, because the response of touching the radiator has not been positively reinforced in any way. On the other hand, the response of raiding the cookie jar is likely to be reinforced at least some of the time, unless the child has an unusually alert mother! The effect of punishment under such circumstances is to suppress the response when the stimuli associated with punishment are present, but it is likely that the response will occur when these stimuli are absent. When his mother is in the room, the child will stay away from the cookies; when she is absent he will go ahead with his depredations. Thus the effect of the conditioned stimuli for punishment is to *suppress* the behavior, not to eliminate or extinguish it.

A simple laboratory demonstration is illustrated in Figure 3. In this experiment a hungry rat has learned the operant response of pressing a bar to obtain food. After the response has been acquired, the animal maintains the bar-pressing response at a fairly stable rate. Then the experimenter proceeds to deliver punishment (electric shock) preceded by a light, which acts as a conditioned stimulus. The effect of the shock is to produce the CER of freezing in the rat, and this effectively prevents the occurrence of the bar-pressing response. After the experimenter gives a number of these punishments, he eliminates the shock but presents the CS from time to time. In this final stage of the demonstration, the animal will not press the bar while the CS is present, but it soon returns to its normal rate of pressing when the CS is absent. We may describe this situation as one in which the CS *suppresses* the bar pressing but does not extinguish it.

We should note that the suppression of ongoing behavior may be achieved by delivering punishment which is in no way contingent upon the subject's responses (as in the experiment just described) or by punishing the response if it is made when some warning stimulus is present (as in the example of the child and the cookie jar).

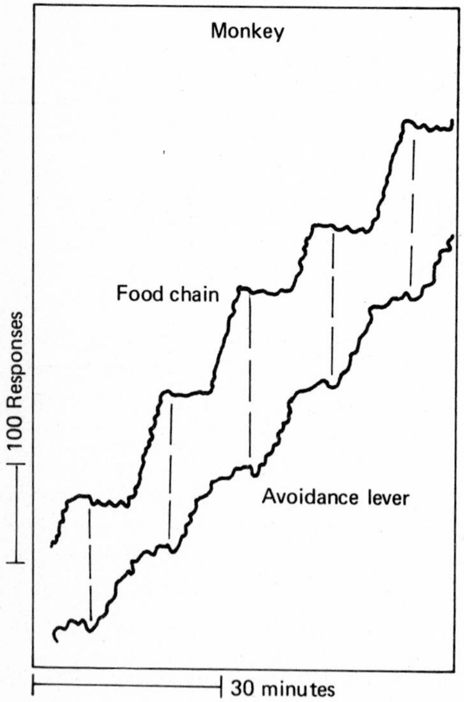

Figure 3 Suppression in a chain of operant responses. When a warning signal for punishment is on, the responding for food is suppressed while the animal makes an avoidant response. The vertical broken lines indicate the onset of the warning stimulus. *(From Sidman, 1958.)*

REFERENCES

Guttman, N., & Kalish, H. Experiments in discrimination. *Sci. Amer.*, 1958, **198,** 77–82.

Lacey, J. I., & Smith, R. L. Conditioning and generalization of unconscious anxiety. *Science,* 1954, **120,** 1045–1052.

Lacey, J. I., Smith, R. L., & Green, A. Use of conditioned autonomic responses in the study of anxiety. *Psychosom. Med.*, 1955, **42,** 208–217.

Miller, N. E. Studies of fear as an acquirable drive. I: Fear as motivation and fear reduction as reinforcement in the learning of new responses. *J. exp. Psychol.*, 1948, **38,** 89–101.

Mowrer, O. H. & Ullman, A. D. Time as a determinant in integrative learning. *Psychol. Rev.*, 1945, **52,** 61–90.

Reiss, B. F. Genetic changes in semantic conditioning. *J. exp. Psychol.*, 1946, **36,** 143–152.

Sidman, M. *Tactics of scientific research.* New York: Basic Books, 1958.

Solomon, R. L., & Wynne, L. C. Traumatic avoidance learning: acquisition in normal dogs. *Psychol. Monogr.*, 1953, **67,** No. 4 (Whole No. 354).

Solomon, R. L., & Wynne, L. C. Traumatic avoidance learning: the principles of anxiety conservation and partial irreversibility. *Psychol. Rev.*, 1954, **61,** 353–385.

Verplanck, W. S. A glossary of some terms used in the objective science of behavior. *Psychol. Rev.*, 1957, **64** (supplement).

Social-learning Theory Analyses of Maladjusted Behavior*

Walter Katkovsky

Social-learning theory represents a personality theory comprised of a set of systematic assumptions and concepts which are based on learning principles and empirical findings. The aim of the theory is to understand and predict complex human behavior, and thereby to provide the clinical psychologist with a framework for developing hypotheses about personality, its development, psychological problems, and personality change. Associated with the theory, attention has been given to the development of reliable and valid measures of the concepts which can be used both in applied clinical activities and controlled research.

This paper will concentrate on interpretations and analyses of adjustment problems and behaviors typically associated with psychopathology based on the concepts and hypotheses derived from social-learning theory. Other presentations of the application of the theory to maladjustment and psychopathology can be found in Jessor, Liverant & Opochinsky (1963), Rotter (1970), and Phares (1972). Before considering specific analyses of maladjustment, some of the basic assumptions and concepts of the

*This paper is a revision and expansion of "Social-learning theory and maladjustment" which was published in the second edition of this book.

theory will be reviewed. A detailed presentation of social-learning theory can be found in Rotter (1954, 1972).

BASIC ASSUMPTIONS

Social-learning theory defines its area of interest with an initial postulate which reads, "The unit of investigation for the study of personality is the interaction of the individual and his meaningful environment" (Rotter, 1954, p. 85). A number of assumptions and ideas are associated with this postulate and these are presented below.

1 The study of personality is regarded as the study of learned behavior, i.e., behavior which develops and changes with experience. Included as learned behaviors are not only the individual's actions, but also his thoughts, feelings, desires, motives, etc. The social-learning theorist elects to restrict his investigation to learned reactions because he believes these to be most important in understanding complex human interpersonal behavior. This is not to imply that unlearned behaviors are considered unimportant. Reflex actions, biological conditions within the organism, maturational changes, and physiological adaptation are regarded as significant in establishing the conditions in which learning first occurs. However, the social-learning theorist assumes that it is unnecessary and often unprofitable to attempt to trace learned reactions back to inherited, instinctual, or physiological processes. Instead, he regards the meanings, feelings, and actions which the individual acquires in connection with unlearned behaviors as more significant in explaining his later behavior than the unlearned behaviors *per se*. For example, in the study of sexual behavior, the values, attitudes, and physical responses learned in prior experiences dealing with sex are likely to predict the nature of an individual's sexual reactions better than an assessment of his physiological or biochemical state.

2 When studying personality, the theorist must decide to what extent he will conceptualize human behavior as having unity or interdependence and to what extent behaviors may be studied as independent and discrete. Social-learning theory takes the point of view that personality has unity and that the prediction of any specific behavior is enhanced by studying its relation to the individual's past experiences and other behaviors. The unity of personality results from the influence an individual's experiences have on one another. New experiences are colored by what has happened to the person in the past, and old learning is changed by new experiences. Personality unity is also fostered by the fact that different behaviors often lead to the same outcome or consequence for the individual and these then become *functionally related*. For example, the person who receives recognition and praise from others for telling jokes as well as for performing well academically will learn to associate these two behaviors with the same outcome. As a consequence, diverse actions may take on the same meaning to the individual, and while he may behave differently in different situations, the same purpose may motivate his actions.

3 Another point of emphasis on which the personality theorist must take a position is the degree to which human behavior will be viewed as stable and unchanging and the degree to which it will be seen as alterable and varying under changing conditions. Social-learning theory's position is that all learned responses can be modified by new experiences and the emphasis is on flexibility and amenability to change. While it is assumed that as a person grows older, his behavior will become increasingly stable, the possibility of change will depend on his specific past experiences and not on age *per se*. No developmental stage is arbitrarily cited as a cutoff point after which change or new learning can no longer occur. The potential for change is always present.

4 The study of personality tends to emphasize people's characteristic or typical ways of behaving as contrasted with behaviors which are highly specific to a given situation. In social-learning theory, concepts have been developed which pertain both to general characteristics of behavior and to specific acts, although somewhat greater interest is placed on behavioral generality. The generality of behavior can be explained by the fact that different situations may take on essentially the same meaning to the individual because of similar learning experiences in those situations. If a person categorizes both the college classroom and the corner coffee shop as places where he might attract the attention of members of the opposite sex, his behavior in these two different situations is likely to be more similar than if he learns to associate one situation with academic efforts and the other with heterosexual pursuits. While the social-learning theorist is interested in behavioral generality, he also is concerned with circumstances which evoke specific actions and variations in behavior. In addition, the degree of behavioral generality depends on the individual's unique experiences, and individual differences in the generality or specificity of behavior are regarded as an important topic of study.

5 In accord with field theory, social-learning theory places considerable importance on environmental factors in determining human behavior. Emphasis is on the "meaningful" environment as perceived and interpreted by the individual as well as on the objective environment. Each person attends selectively to his surroundings at any given time and attaches significance and meaning to the stimuli that confront him. The particular aspects of the environment with which he deals and the meanings he gives them are based on previous learning experiences. The unique learning experiences of a person result in individualistic perceptions and interpretations, and in order to explain the impact of situational conditions on his behavior, one must know the meaning which those conditions have for him. To the extent that social-learning theory stresses the individual's subjective interpretation of his environment, the theory assumes a phenomenological slant and rejects the position that behavior can be explained without inferring a mediational process between a stimulus and the individual's response. At the same time, the social-learning theorist notes that since the members of a given society—or for that matter, all human beings—share many common learning experiences, people's subjective interpretations of the environment have much similarity. Consequently it is unnecessary to rely completely on a subjective or phenomenological frame of reference to explain and predict human behavior.

6 The theory is called a *social*-learning theory because it postulates that the major ways of behaving are learned in social situations and that other people constitute the most important aspects of the environment. The development of personality is seen as dependent primarily on the child's interactions and relationships with other people. While much of the behavior of an infant is motivated by biological needs (hunger, thirst, physical pain, etc.), the learning which occurs in conjunction with these needs promotes new social needs which involve the persons who care for him. Subsequently, the social needs are more significant in determining the individual's behavior than are the biological needs. Similarly, personality problems and ways of coping with them deal chiefly with an individual's relationships with other people; i.e., they involve his social adjustment.

In stating that the most important aspects of the environment are social, theorists with a social-learning point of view do not rule out the idea that a person interacts with and reacts to himself. Subjective awareness of personal characteristics or conditions, e.g., hunger, pain, sexual excitement, and emotional reactions, may serve as stimuli for the individual's actions. In actuality, however, his response is to the meaning he gives these characteristics or conditions, and these are learned in his experiences with other people. A person may also react to himself in terms of a learned social norm as, for example, when he reacts to himself as thin or fat, handsome or ugly, intelligent or unintelligent. Whatever his reaction, it is based on learned meanings and on how he believes others who are important to him evaluate and react to that characteristic.

7 The method of social-learning theory in investigating personality is historical; i.e., events are studied in sequence, and a particular behavior is related to past learning. However, it is unnecessary to attempt to trace a person's experiences since birth or early childhood in order to explain a particular behavior or predict its future occurrence. Also, the idea of a single or basic cause is rejected since any behavior can be related to numerous conditions and events in the past as well as in the present. Instead, the theorist or clinician is concerned with describing relevant antecedent conditions, and he recognizes that there are always numerous conditions that can be related to the behavior and that they can always be traced further back in time. The particular antecedents he chooses to emphasize and the scope of his historical analysis will depend on his purpose and on practical considerations, such as time and efficiency.

8 One of the most important assumptions made by social-learning theory is that human behavior has direction or purpose. Behavior is described as *goal-directed,* i.e., as oriented toward or away from some aspect of the environment. A person may seek to gain a particular outcome or reward or to avoid a particular outcome or punishment. In social-learning theory, both *needs* and *goals* are inferred from the same directional interaction of an individual with his environment. When the description of the direction of the behavior pertains to the person, the term need is used; when attention is placed on the environmental conditions which determine the aim of the behavior, the term goal is used. For example, a child who asks his teacher to explain to him how to solve an arithmetic problem is described as expressing the need for dependence and as seeking instrumental help. Both the need and the goal are inferred from the direction or purpose of the child's behavior.

9 The assumption that behavior has direction is based on the fact that an event which follows a behavior affects the probability of that behavior occurring again. If the consequence of a person's behavior is favorable to that person, the consequence is described as a *positive reinforcement* and this reinforcement strengthens the probability that the same behavior will occur again. If the consequence is unfavorable or undesirable to the person, it is a *negative reinforcement* and decreases the probability of that behavior occurring again. The influence of consequences on the subsequent occurrence of preceding behaviors is often called the *principle of reinforcement* or the *law of effect*. Some other learning theories which employ the law of effect define a positive reinforcement on the basis of the drive reduction of a "tissue need," i.e., in terms of the diminution of a physiological drive such as hunger, thirst, or sex. Social-learning theory, however, regards this definition as too restrictive to explain complex human behavior and defines reinforcement in a broader sense to include "any action, condition or state that affects movement toward a goal" (Rotter, 1954, p. 98). The effect of a reinforcement on the behavior which precedes it will depend on its value to the individual; the higher the reinforcement value, the greater the reinforcing effect on the behavior. The specific conditions or events which act as reinforcers and the values attached to the reinforcements must be determined empirically through the study of a given group, culture, or individual.

10 The use of language is a major factor in the interactions between people and is regarded as very significant in the learning and maintaining of behavior and personality characteristics. Words, ideas, and statements direct attention to specific cues and thereby play an important part in defining the environment. Language enables the individual to group varying situations together as similar and to generalize and apply behavior which has been learned in one situation to another. Conversely, language helps the individual to discriminate between situations and thereby promotes changes in behavior from one set of conditions to another. An additional important function of language is that it reinforces behavior. In some instances, words act as symbols of reinforcements for tangible objects and in other instances, as with statements of praise or criticism, as direct reinforcements.

CONCEPTS

In an attempt to explain and predict the behavior of an individual in any given situation, personality theories implicitly or explicitly ask such questions as, In what ways has he acted in similar situations in the past? What are alternative ways in which he might behave? What are the differential probabilities that he will act in one way or another? These questions are expressed in social-learning theory by the concept *behavior potential,* which refers to the idea that in any given situation, a variety of behaviors might occur and the potential occurrence of each will depend on the individual's past experiences with each. The behavior which most frequently led to positive reinforcement in comparable situations is the behavior with the greatest potential for occurring again. When the theorist is interested in more general personality characteristics rather than in a single behavior, the concept *need potential* is employed. This term refers to the potential occurrence of behaviors which are functionally related, i.e., which are directed toward the same or similar reinforcements. The distinction between the terms behavior potential and need potential is one of generality; the former refers to a single behavior, whereas the latter is more inclusive and may refer to a number of different acts which are associated with one another because in the past they have all led to the same reinforcement. Thus, one might speak of a student's behavior potential for studying. Or one might be concerned more generally with the student's need potential for academic achievement, which would include all behaviors associated with his academic work.

A second major concept in social-learning theory is *expectancy*. This is defined as "the probability held by the individual that a particular reinforcement will occur as a function of a specific behavior on his part in a specific situation" (Rotter, 1954, p. 107). The definition points to three separate factors as important to the concept. First, reference is made to "a particular reinforcement"; that is, a specific event which has meaning or value to the person serves as the directional force for the behavior in that the purpose is to bring about that event. Second, the definition notes that the expectancy pertains to "a specific behavior." Theoretically a different expectancy will be held for each behavior which in the past has been associated with the reinforcement. The behavior most likely to occur is the one for which the expectancy is highest that it will lead to the reinforcement. Third, attention is drawn to the importance of "a specific situation." The expectancy for a given reinforcement in one situation may be similar to or different from the expectancy for the occurrence of that reinforcement in another situation. To the extent that different situations are perceived as similar, the expectancy concerning a particular behavior will generalize from one situation to another and thus will be the same or similar.

When the concern is with more general characteristics about the anticipation of future events, two additional concepts involving expectancies are used. *Freedom of movement* refers to the mean expectancy held when a variety of functionally related behaviors are considered. We might speak of the freedom of movement (or mean expectancies) for affiliation, achievement, dominance, or love, each of which represents a separate group of reinforcements which are functionally related. At a still higher level of abstraction and generality, we might describe a person's total state of adjustment in terms of this concept. That is, if an individual expects to be able to gain a great deal of success and satisfaction as a result of his behavior, he is described as having high freedom of movement for life's satisfactions, whereas someone with expectancies for failure, frustration, and punishment is described as having low freedom of movement.

Generalized expectancy refers to the influence of experience from similar situations on the expectancy held in a particular situation. The more an individual perceives a situation as similar to situations he has experienced in the past, the more his expectancies in the new situation will generalize from past happenings. Generalized expectancies may be developed concerning varied aspects of situations. Different generalizations may be made concerning expectancies in situations with men as compared with women, or in classrooms as compared with social situations. One type of generalized expectancy to which social-learning theory has given considerable attention is *the belief in internal versus external control of reinforcements* (Rotter, 1966). The occurrence of a reinforcement may be viewed as a function of one's own behavior (internal control) or as a function of external influences over which one has little or no control (external control). An individual's belief in internal control is based on his assessment of his abilities, knowledge, personality characteristics, physical attributes, or any other characteristics he identifies with himself. Beliefs in external control, on the other hand, may be associated with ideas concerning chance, luck, fate, supernatural forces, or ways in which other people may control or influence the events in one's life. Beliefs in internal versus external control appear to be highly relevant to adjustment and maladjustment. An extreme external orientation may prevent the individual from seeing the part he plays in the difficulties he is having and thus may discourage change. On the other hand, an extreme internal orientation, in which an individual erroneously attributes many events to his own actions, may be associated with delusions of grandeur, guilt reactions, and self-punitive behavior.

Reinforcement value is defined as the degree of preference for one reinforcement to occur if the possibilities of several reinforcements occurring are equal. For example, the reinforcement value of attending a baseball game may be higher or lower than the reinforcement value of attending a concert, depending on an individual's preferences and the degree to which he expects one will be more satisfying than the other. The value of a given reinforcement is a function of the reinforcements it has been associated with in past experiences. The more an event has led to satisfying consequences in the past, the higher its positive value will be; and conversely, the more it has been associated with unpleasant happenings, the higher its negative value. A more generalized concept of reinforcement value is termed *need value;* this is defined as "the mean preference value of a set of functionally related reinforcements" (Rotter, 1954, p. 189). Corresponding in level of abstraction with the concepts need potential and freedom of movement, need value pertains to the importance placed on one set of reinforcements, which through experience have become identified with one another, in comparison with another set. For example, the need value of attaining vocational success may be higher or lower than the need value of being liked by others.

Another concept of social-learning theory which refers to a special instance of reinforcement value is termed *minimal goal.* It is possible to place the reinforcements which might occur in any given situation on a continuum in terms of their preference value. Some of these reinforcements will lead to satisfaction and others to dissatisfaction. Minimal goal is the theoretical dividing point between those reinforcements which are experienced as satisfactions and those which are experienced as dissatisfactions and is defined as "the lowest goal in a continuum of potential reinforcements for some life situation or situations which will be perceived as a satisfaction" (Rotter, 1954, p. 213). If we consider course grades on the usual continuum from A to F, one student may be satisfied with his performance as long as he receives a D or better, while another may be dissatisfied with any grade less than a B. The minimal goal of the latter clearly is considerably higher than that of the former. An individual's minimal goals for affection, affiliation, dominance, or any other need describe the extent to which that need must be reinforced before he feels satisfied. The higher the minimal goal, the more reinforcement of that need is required before satisfaction is experienced.

The major concepts of social-learning theory may be brought together into two basic formulas. The first is

$$BP_{x,s_1,R_a} = f(E_{x,R_a,s_1} \ \& \ RV_a)$$

This formula reads "The potential for behavior x to occur in situation 1 in relation to reinforcement a is a function of the expectancy of the occurrence of reinforcement a following behavior x in situation 1 and the value of reinforcement a" (Rotter, 1954, p. 108). The second formula is

$$NP = f(FM \ \& \ NV)$$

This reads, "The potentiality of occurrence of a set of behaviors that lead to the satisfaction of some need (need potential) is a function of the expectancies that these behaviors will lead to these reinforcements (freedom of movement) and the strength or value of these reinforcements (need value)" (Rotter, 1954, p. 110).

CRITERIA OF MALADJUSTMENT

Social-learning theory makes no effort to designate certain behaviors as healthy and desirable, and others as pathological and undesirable in an absolute sense. The question of what constitutes maladjusted behavior is viewed as an ethical question of "What should be?", rather than a scientific one dealing with "What is?" Labeling a particular act as maladjusted is in effect a value judgment which must be based on an ethical position and not on a scientific theory. The theory may describe some behaviors as more or less effective, efficient, or successful than others. Such judgments, however, can be made only in terms of the purpose or goal of the behavior, which in itself can be evaluated as healthy or pathological only as it conforms to or deviates from a particular ethical value.

The psychologist can turn to a number of different sources to provide criteria of maladjustment based on an ethical position. Rotter has designated one source as "the social-centered approach" which refers to values upheld by the society or culture. Included under this designation are judgments that particular actions are pathological because they deviate from the statistical norm, or from what others consider socially desirable, or from society's definitions of constructive, adaptive, or ideal actions. A second source of criteria of maladjustment focuses on the specific individual and is designated by Rotter as "the self-centered approach." Behavior which results in unhappiness, suffering, or internal conflict for the individual concerned is regarded as maladjusted, and acts which contribute to his subjective sense of harmony and well-being are regarded as adjusted behavior. Here the individual's personal goals and potential also might influence judgments concerning desirable and undesirable behavior for him. A third source of criteria for designating behavior as adjusted or maladjusted might be designated "values associated with professional opinion." In recent years there has been increasing acknowledgement that many of the theories and professional practices involving diagnosis, treatment, hospitalization, etc., in the mental health fields perpetuate values and ethical assumptions. What Szasz has referred to as "the mental health ethic" (Szasz, 1970) often functions as a set of moral values for making judgments about maladjustment based on the opinions of professionals. These values might be regarded as a special instance of social-centered values, i.e., those that are accepted by the professional authorities in a society. The significant point made by Szasz and others is that professional values often are presented as scientific facts and indisputable indicators of mental health and illness rather than as moral values.

Under many circumstances, a social-centered and a self-centered value system will be consistent and complimentary, e.g., where the individual's personal state of happiness and the reinforcements from other people which follow his behavior stem from the same value system. However, where these two points of view differ and a particular behavior is regarded as maladjusted by one of these criteria and not by the other, the professional worker and his client must decide which criteria to follow or emphasize. In any case, the social-learning theorist stresses the point that the judgment is made on the basis of ethical considerations and not from the theory itself.

In a general sense, what constitutes maladjustment depends chiefly on the values which predominate in the particular culture and represents the failure of members of that culture to learn to behave in accord with those values. In any given instance, a behavior or condition is designated as maladjusted or pathological because it is discrepant with the values of society (or some aspect of society) or the values of the individual involved, i.e., with what others want or expect of the individual, or with what he wants and expects for himself. Since values and expectations vary with different situations, the specific situation in which the behavior or condition occurs is a crucial factor in designating it as adjusted or maladjusted. Stated differently, definitions of maladjustment and psychopathology are relative, and not absolute, to a given context based on the appropriateness of the behavior to that context as judged by representatives of society or the individual himself.

The fact that social-learning theory does not specify criteria of maladjustment in no way indicates disinterest in this question. Professional workers in mental health are called upon to make judgments concerning adjustment and maladjustment and to promote changes in their clients consistent with some criteria. Therefore, they must be familiar with the various possible approaches of establishing criteria and potential inconsistencies between these. In addition, social-centered criteria of maladjustment highlight specific areas of learning and specific behaviors within a given society which are likely to cause problems for persons in that society. For example, the areas of sex, aggression, and achievement are involved in many of the problems and conflicts experienced by persons in the United States, and these problems can be traced directly to inconsistencies and confusion within the society in the values associated with these areas. It is important that the mental health worker be aware of confusion and inconsistencies in value judgments in society since these will assist him in understanding the problems presented by his clients.

Just as social-learning theory makes no effort to specify criteria of maladjustment, the theory proposes no special concepts to cover psychopathology. Rather, behavior designated as deviant, disturbed, maladjusted, neurotic, etc., is regarded as complex social behavior which can be understood on the basis of the same principles as any other social behavior. Once a judgment regarding the inappropriateness, maladaptiveness, or pathology of a specific behavior or condition is made, social-learning theory offers principles and hypotheses concerning the development, maintenance, and change of that behavior or condition.

CLASSIFICATION OF MALADJUSTED BEHAVIOR

An initial endeavor on the part of any scientific field is to classify the phenomena being studied. Considerable time and effort have been devoted to this in the psychiatric and psychological literature and a variety of classificatory schemes have been presented. While social-learning theory takes the position that there is no one correct or absolute way of classifying maladjustment, and presents no special classificatory scheme, the theory specifies four factors that must be considered: 1) the individual's purpose, goal, or need at the time he engages in a certain behavior, 2) the extent to which his behavior succeeds in achieving his goal or satisfying his need, 3) his expectancy that his behavior will satisfy his need, and 4) the specific situations in which the behavior occurs, i.e., the situational demands and the behaviors most likely and least likely to be rewarded in that situation.

The most popular classicatory scheme consists of the American Psychiatric Association's *Diagnostic and Statistical Manual of Mental Disorders* (DSM-II). While the psychiatric classifications are not based on a consistent framework for making distinctions (some designations are based on causes, others on distinguishing features of the predominant behavior involved, others on prognosis, and some on the basis of personality typologies), they rely considerably on the medical or disease model. This model assumes that maladjusted behavior is symptomatic of an underlying pathological condition and that each condition can be classified according to its cause, symptoms, and prognosis analogous to a physical disease. Social-learning theory regards this system of classification as deficient for a number of reasons. Many of the classifications represent over-generalized categories that include such varied behaviors within a single grouping that they ignore significant differences between individuals classified in the same way. Also, insufficient attention is given to situational variations in behavior, and the assumption is made that an individual classified as having a certain condition will exhibit that condition regardless of the situation. The language used by this classificatory scheme tends to focus on negative conditions and undesirable behavior, ignoring positive and desirable behaviors, and encourages the fallacy of thinking that the condition causes the behavior, when in fact the condition often represents no more than another term for the behavior.

In recent years, with the growing popularity of behavior therapy and behavior modification, efforts have been made to classify maladjustments in terms of the specific problematic behaviors involved. While this approach avoids many of the over-generalizations associated with the medical model, and has the advantage of clearly specifying target behaviors for remediation, classification based on behavior alone ignores the fact that the same behavior may have different meanings, serve different purposes, and be differentially appropriate depending on the specific individual and situation. Classification of maladjustment should consider not only the problematic behavior, but also the individual's purpose in behaving that way and the effectiveness of the behavior in meeting that purpose.

Several classificatory schemes have been proposed which take into consideration variables cited as important by social-learning theory. One of these is Kanfer and Saslow's analysis of behavioral excesses and deficits, with consideration given to situational demands, motivational patterns, biological features, and self-control of the individual (Kanfer and Saslow, 1969). Bandura has proposed a schema which includes a number of the categories cited by Kanfer and Saslow and has added "defective or inappropriate incentive systems" (reinforcement values in social-learning theory terms), "defective and inappropriate stimulus control of behavior" (situational factors), and "aversive self-reinforcing systems" (Bandura, 1968). Two other approaches to classification often used informally by clinical psychologists, though incomplete, also are compatible with social-learning theory. One is to classify maladjustment or psychopathology into the life area which is most involved, e.g., marital problems, vocational difficulties, identity problems. These categories focus on the situational pressures and demands as well as the individual's ability to meet these. Another informal approach is to assess problems in terms of the need area involved, e.g., sexual difficultues, aggression problems, dependency problems. This type of categorization cites the specific needs of the person which are creating problems for him and the likelihood that his behavioral repertoire and the real life situations he is in will result in his being able to satisfy those needs.

THE ONSET OF MALADJUSTED BEHAVIOR

Social-learning theory holds to the assumption that the initiation of much pathological behavior occurs as a result of trial-and-error efforts by the individual to gain the reinforcements he seeks. Any of the following situations in life may encourage engaging in novel or new behaviors: (a) where a previously learned behavior is no longer reinforced, (b) where the individual finds himself in a new situation in which he is uncertain of what is expected of him, (c) where experimentation and behavior flexibility are encouraged by others, and (d) where real-life or fictional models are observed acting in ways that are new to the individual. Some of his trial-and-error actions are likely to deviate from cultural values and to conflict with situational demands or other needs of the individual. In other words, it seems a safe assumption that all persons in the course of their psychological development have at various times behaved in maladjusted or pathological ways. More important than the fact that maladjusted behavior occurs is the question of what reinforcements follow that behavior. If the behavior is followed by a negative consequence to the individual, the maladjusted behavior is not likely to occur again. However, if it is followed by a positive consequence, the behavior potential of that act occurring again has increased despite the fact that it is inappropriate or undesirable according to other criteria.

THE MAINTENANCE OF MALADJUSTED BEHAVIOR

According to social-learning theory, when a positive consequence or reinforcement follows a specific behavior, the individual's expectancy that he will achieve that reinforcement with that behavior is strengthened. That is, the expectancy is reinforced, and therefore the likelihood of that behavior occurring again has increased. Also, the more desirable the consequence to the individual, i.e., the higher the reinforcement value, the greater the subsequent likelihood of the behavior occurring. Thus, maladjusted behavior is maintained as long as the individual continues to expect that it will lead to a reinforcement he values.

When conceptualized within a reinforcement schema such as this, a basic and significant question concerning the continuation of maladjusted behavior is: Why does behavior persist (or its potential remain high) if the behavior is negatively sanctioned by the culture and generally leads to discomfort or punishment for the individual? In other words, the problem in understanding maladjusted behavior is to explain why a person subjectively expects to gain some type of satisfaction for a behavior which his culture regards as undesirable and which experience should teach him will lead to negative consequences. Social-learning theory offers a number of hypotheses in answer to the above question. These hypotheses, in essence, constitute a way of conceptualizing maladjustment and psychopathology utilizing the specific concepts of the theory.

I High Need Value and Low Freedom of Movement

The most common formulation of maladjustment from social-learning theory is where a person desires certain reinforcements (high need value), but has low expectancies of attaining them (low freedom of movement). The consequence is that he will experience frustration, failure, and disappointment. The latter in themselves are aversive and negatively reinforcing. In effect, then, he expects not to be able to obtain what he wants and also expects punishment for trying to do so. Two likely consequences of these circumstances are that he will engage in avoidance behaviors to minimize the punishment associated with his failures, and will seek substitute ways of trying to obtain the reinforcements he desires. Each of these consequences is likely to result in further complications for him.

Avoidance behaviors may involve direct physical withdrawal and distance from the aversive situations or various forms of conceptual withdrawal such as repression, defensiveness, distortions, and fantasies. The acts of avoidance and withdrawal may constitute maladjustments for specific situations and lead to direct negative consequences, as for example, when an individual avoids going to his job because of anticipated failure and therefore is fired. In addition, avoidance behaviors typically involve other less direct negative consequences. Both physical and conceptual avoidance result in removing the individual from the situation so that no new learning can occur. Opportunities for attempting new behaviors which might change the individual's expectancy for success are not possible. Also, the avoidance feeds on itself; i.e., each time the individual avoids a situation where he expects failure or frustration, the behavior potential for avoiding increases since it has successfully protected him from the aversive consequences he anticipates. Conceptual avoidance frequently involves the additional problem of distorting reality, which in itself can cause increased difficulties with the environment.

As noted, the individual with high need value and low freedom of movement is likely to seek new ways of gaining the reinforcements he desires. However, his efforts and the subsequent substitute behaviors he engages in are likely to be confused with his efforts to avoid expected failures. The result is that he will seek novel, idiosyncratic, or symbolic ways of avoiding the expected punishment and somehow gaining the unexpected reward. Because of their idiosyncratic and symbolic nature, these behaviors usually constitute distortions and unconstructive attempted solutions. Such behaviors as obsessions, compulsions, paranoid projections, hysterical reactions, and phobias usually can be analyzed as representing efforts to avoid an anticipated punishment and, symbolically and idiosyncratically, to gain the desired reinforcement. Again, these idiosyncratic behaviors complicate the individual's interactions with his environment by leading to new failures and punishments.

Where the above formulation exists, the individual's adjustment will improve by effecting a better balance between his need value and freedom of movement. This might be accomplished by increasing his expectancies of being able to attain need satisfactions by helping him develop more effective behaviors and eliminating the avoidance and symbolic behaviors in which he has engaged. In addition, his need value might be lowered by encouraging him to feel satisfied with realistic rewards available to him and by increasing the value of other needs.

II Problems Associated with Freedom of Movement and Generalized Expectancies

A low expectancy is the result of unsuccessful past performance. In most instances, the failure to gain rewards per se need not cause maladjustment. Instead, the individual may engage in constructive efforts to develop the behaviors which ultimately will be rewarding. As noted above, problems are likely when avoidance behaviors block possible constructive change and when the individual engages in symbolic, idiosyncratic behavior. The latter may be motivated not only by anticipated frustrations and failures because the individual's need value is high, as described above, but also because of pressures from the environment. Where the individual is expected to behave in certain ways by the environment, and finds himself unable to do so, he will fear punishment. Similarly, where the standards of the environment for reward are extremely high, the individual will regard his behavior as inadequate to meet the situational demands. In either case, social learning theory describes the individual as having low freedom of movement. Avoidance and symbolic substitute behaviors again are likely, with their subsequent complications. The broader the scope of the individual's low expectancies, i.e., the more need areas involved, the greater his frustrations and fears will be. Where the individual finds himself unable to achieve satisfactions in need areas which are an essential part of social living, e.g., personal recognition, achievement, sex, affiliation, etc., he is likely to experience demoralization, low self-esteem, and generalized feelings of inferiority and inadequacy. Depression frequently results when low freedom of movement is pervasive and involves many needs of the individual.

The concept of generalized expectancy also helps to explain many maladjustments. That is, an individual may have low expectancies for success which have generalized to a variety of diverse situations. The more situations involved, the more pervasive his expected failure and the more situations he will avoid. Conditions of diffuse or free-floating anxiety are often found to involve a fear of failure that has generalized to practically all aspects of the individual's life. Maladjustments may be associated with specific generalized expectancies which are unrealistic, inappropriate, or inaccurate. For example, a strong generalized expectancy that outcomes are caused by the person's own behavior (belief in internal control of reinforcements), even where his responsibility is not apparent, will encourage guilt and possible self-punitive reactions. Conversely, a strong generalized expectancy that outcomes are caused by external factors rather than one's own behavior may promote irresponsibility and paranoid projections of blame. Rotter (1967) has described individual differences in generalized expectancy of interpersonal trust. Excessive generalized trust may lead to gullibility and disappointment in many interpersonal situations, whereas excessive distrust may result in suspiciousness and fear of others.

Where an individual's freedom of movement is low for important need areas, or where his generalized expectancy for success is low in a variety of situations, his adjustment will improve by assisting him in the development of behaviors likely to achieve rewards in real-life situations. Where extreme generalized expectancies promote maladjusted reactions, the individual may be helped by encouraging his anticipation of negative consequences because of overgeneralized expectancies and his development of situationally appropriate expectancies.

III Problems Associated with Reinforcement and Need Values

A variety of problems may be attributable to the values placed on reinforcements and need satisfactions. Maladjusted behavior is often associated with high need values, i.e., where too great an importance is attached to a particular need. The person then is prone to perceive diverse situations in terms of that one need and to behave in accord with it, possibly at the expense of other needs or of objective reality. For example, the person who continually is concerned with gaining achievement rewards will interpret non-achievement situations, such as those involving friendships, love and affection, in terms of achievement and is apt to act in assertive, competitive ways where this type of behavior is inappropriate. The consequences might well be that his preoccupation with achievement leads to conflict with others and to frustration of his achievement needs as well as other needs.

Conflicts between needs of high value frequently exist in persons experiencing adjustment problems. A given act might result in the satisfaction of one need, but the frustration of another. An example is where forceful leadership behavior satisfies dominance needs, but results in social rejection and frustration of affiliation needs. Conflicts between needs foster frustration and confusion, which in turn may lead to indecision, ambivalence, and deviant efforts to gain satisfactions. Cultural values and stereotypes tend to promote conflicts between some needs. Behavior and the successful attainment of reinforcements associated with one need area may be culturally incompatible with another. An example of the latter which is receiving increased attention today is conflict between successful achievement on the part of women, on the one hand, and successful fulfillment of the feminine role as defined by society, on the other. Horner (1972) has postulated "a motive to avoid success" on the part of many women because successful achievement might lead to social rejection and loss of self-esteem as a woman. Other examples of frequent incompatibilities fostered by cultural sterotypes are between dependence and masculinity needs and behaviors, between creativity and conformity, acquiescence and assertiveness, and between sexual and religious needs.

A third formulation of maladjustment based on reinforcement values involves the concept of minimal goal, i.e., the lowest goal in a reinforcement hierarchy that is perceived as reinforcing. The higher a person's minimal goal level, the greater his skills and behavioral effectiveness must be in order for him to experience satisfaction. If his behavioral repertoire and competence are sufficient to achieve his goals, no problems will result. However, many maladjustments involve unrealistic minimal goals which cannot be achieved despite reasonable accomplishment. Minimal goals which involve such notions as being best, special, perfect, and fulfilling absolute standards of good, all foster feelings of failure, frustration, and inadequacy. Depression, despair, avoidance of effort, distortions of reality, and fantasied success are among the consequences of unrealistically high minimal goals.

Low minimal goals also may be associated with maladjustment because of discrepancies with society's expectations or demands. The individual who is too easily satisfied has little reason to strive to develop the behaviors and skills consistent with societal norms and expectations. The result might be behavior which is deviant and inappropriate in the eyes of others, such as indifference to the standards and potential rewards offered by society, vagrancy, the absence of drive and motivation, and unwillingness to assume responsibilities.

According to social-learning theory, the value of a reinforcement can be changed by pairing it with other reinforcements of different value. Thus, where problems are associated with reinforcements, needs, and minimal goals of high value, improved adjustment will result if the importance of the reinforcements is diminished in the eyes of the individual by associating them with less desirable consequences to him. Conversely, reinforcement values and minimal goals may be raised by associating them with other reinforcements which are desirable to the individual. Conflict between incompatible needs can be lessened by encouraging predominance of one need over another and by promoting clear-cut relationships between specific behaviors and their effects for different needs.

IV Problems Involving Situational Discriminations

Much of what is called maladjusted or pathological behavior consists of past learning of ways of acting appropriate for some situations which the individual has generalized to other situations where the action is inappropriate. Where he fails to discriminate between important differences between situations and the likely consequences of his action in them, there may be over-generalization of expectancies and reactions. Discrimination failures and over-generalization may take a variety of forms. Failure to note differences between different situations may result in rigid and inappropriate actions. For example, the student who brings to social situations the detached intellectualizing which was rewarded in his academic work is apt to find that others regard him as pedantic, cold, and artificial. Similarly, important distinctions must be drawn between different groups and individuals with whom one interacts. Adjustment problems might well occur when both parents and peers are treated in the same way. Age clearly constitutes an important factor in defining society's expectations and demands. Failure to discriminate between different societal expectations with increasing age often results in the maintenance of behavior learned in childhood which is inappropriate for adults. A common example is carrying over many of the sexual taboos learned as a child which interfere with the successful sexual adjustment of the adult.

As noted earlier, social-learning theory holds that behaviors, expectancies, reinforcements, and situations become functionally related. That is, diverse behaviors and their expectancies are associated with one another because they result in the same reinforcement; diverse reinforcements are equated because they occur together; and diverse situations are seen as the same because of similar experiences in them. Another way of presenting this idea is in terms of generalization. Different stimuli and different responses take on the same meaning to the individual. Problems may occur where the functional relationships involve over-generalizations. An example of an over-generalized expectancy is where experienced failure in one sport becomes associated with other sports resulting in fear of failure and avoidance of all athletic activities. An example of an over-generalized reinforcement or need is where the individual emphasizes one need in all social interactions, such as achievement success as described earlier. Effective adjustment to a major extent involves making discriminations, and more specifically, developing clear distinctions that will answer the question, which behaviors will lead to which reinforcements in which situations?

A special instance of the importance of discriminations involves distinguishing between the immediate versus the long-term or delayed reinforcements which follow behavior. Frequently the immediate consequences of an act differ from its long-term consequences, and such discrepancies help explain the maintenance of maladaptive behavior. The behavior potential of an action will increase when the immediate consequence is rewarding to the individual even though with time that same act may result in punishing consequences. The individual's failure to associate the delayed negative consequences to the maladjusted behavior encourages the continuation of that behavior. Many behaviors associated with psychopathology appear to involve immediate reward, but long-term aversive consequences, such as the use of alcohol and drugs, deviant sexual behavior, theft, and other illegal acts. Avoidance behavior in situations involving expected failure constitutes an especially important example where the short-term positive consequence outweighs the long-term negative consequence in promoting its occurrence. The anxiety relief that follows either physical or conceptual withdrawal and avoidance reinforces the likelihood of these behaviors occurring again despite the fact that over time the avoidance is likely to increase the fears and problems of the individual. That is, the immediate reward of avoiding feared situations is more effective in maintaining the avoidance behavior than the delayed punishment is in discouraging it. Where positive, short-term consequences maintain maladjustment, awareness of the relationship between the maladjusted behavior and the negative long-term consequences will help lessen the frequency of that behavior.

V The Direct or Indirect Reinforcement of Maladjusted Behavior

An assumption which follows from social-learning theory concerning the maintenance of maladjusted behavior is that, despite negative social consequences and suffering on the part of the individual involved, the maladaptive act is reinforced by some aspect of the present life of the individual, at least intermittently. The reinforcement of maladjusted behavior can occur in a direct, blatant way, or indirectly and quite subtly. Four conditions are described below where maladjusted behavior can be reinforced. These are in no way mutually exclusive, and most maladjusted conditions are likely to involve all of them to some extent.

First, a common, but often over-looked, reason for the existence of maladjusted behavior is that persons important to the individual directly encourage it. The behavior can be positively reinforced by the attention, concern, sympathy, and special privileges it brings, i.e., by the secondary gains described by psychoanalysts. Also, the maladjusted behavior sometimes satisfies the needs of important people in the individual's life; e.g., a dominant mother might encourage dependence in her child; or a wife with strong guilt feelings might encourage her husband's infidelity so that she can feel like a martyr. Direct reinforcement also occurs where the individual belongs to a subculture that prizes a behavior which the larger culture considers maladjusted. For example, some adolescent peer groups promote behavior which is antagonistic to the adult culture.

A second way in which maladjusted behavior can be reinforced is indirect and involves the complex and subtle interactions and relationships between people. For example, the wife who becomes forgiving and pleasant following her husband's atonement for infidelity indirectly reinforces it. Similarly, the parent who tells his child he should not smoke, but does so himself, also communicates that smoking is an enjoyable and valued experience. Determination of the indirect and subtle reinforcement of maladjusted behavior requires detailed study of the individual's interactions and relationships with persons important to him.

A third and even more subtle way in which maladjusted behavior is reinforced is through the idiosyncratic and symbolic meanings people give to the consequences of their acts. While most people might regard the consequence of a particular act as clearly punishing, the unique reinforcement history of a given individual might result in that same consequence being positive or desirable for him. For example, being arrested and jailed is aversive to most persons; but to the individual who has learned that he can gain companionship, attention, or status by being jailed, the consequence is personally rewarding and the individual is likely to maintain his antisocial behavior. Conversely, a consequence that is rewarding to most people may be punishing to some. For example, being in the company of an attractive member of the opposite sex may seem rewarding, but to the individual who expects rejection, the situation may be so anxiety-provoking that it constitutes a punishment and is to be avoided. In discussing the personal meanings and values of reinforcements, Phares (1972) has noted that determining the reinforcements an individual regards as important requires a careful analysis and considerable "clinical sensitivity."

A fourth way in which reinforcement of maladjusted behavior occurs, and which also requires detailed knowledge about the individual, is through self-reinforcement. As described by Bandura (1968), self-administered reinforcers frequently out-weigh the influence of external reinforcers in maintaining social and maladjusted behavior. An important aspect of self-reinforcement involves the minimal goals of the individual discussed previously. Where a person has a high, perfectionistic minimal goal, which is unknown to an observer who sees him as relatively competent and successful, the person may be described as having inexplicable feelings of worthlessness and inadequacy. The problem here is that the person's high self-standards lead to self-criticism and subsequent low freedom of movement. Reverse situations also exist in which a person experiences self-satisfaction for behavior not condoned by society at large. Aggressive, assaultive behavior may represent to the individual desired masculinity which increases his self-esteem, and therefore is continued, even though the behavior creates other problems for him. Many maladjusted behaviors are maintained because the involved person symbolically attributes a desirable outcome to them, which, in effect, constitutes a self-reinforcement of the behavior.

Where direct or indirect reinforcement of maladjustment exists, the first task in assisting the person is to determine the source of reinforcement. Subsequently, termination of the positive reinforcement of maladjusted behavior is necessary, and this might be accomplished by a variety of methods from discussions which emphasize aversive consequences to making specific changes in the person's living arrangements that remove the reinforcements.

THE ABSENCE OF ADJUSTED BEHAVIORS

While maladjustment generally is associated with the presence of deviant or undesirable behavior, failure or inability to act in ways which a culture regards as necessary also is regarded as maladjustment. The specific behaviors which a culture expects or demands of its members vary with different situations and are related to many variables pertaining to the individual, such as his age, sex, occupation, and social standing. Membership in special groups within a culture usually carries with it requirements that certain actions be performed, and failure to perform them constitutes maladjustment in those groups. Thus, the criteria of maladjustment based on failure to perform adjusted acts is highly relative. However, the inability or refusal to behave in certain ways is regarded as deviant and maladjusted in most societies for all persons beyond the first few years of life. For example, feeding and clothing oneself, controlling bladder and bowel functions, learning some form of communication with others, and engaging in rational thinking and purposive behavior are required of all but very young children, and deviations are regarded as maladjustment. As an individual matures and reaches adulthood, an increasing number of behaviors are expected of him, the particular nature of which depends upon his sex and socioeconomic class; these include such behaviors as learning skills which will enable him to earn a living, participating in activities appropriate to his sex, and developing the social behaviors necessary for harmonious interaction with others.

Under reinforcement theory, we might expect all persons to learn to behave in ways their culture sanctions and rewards. The initial occurrence of desirable behaviors is likely to be encouraged by the direct teaching of others and by observation and imitation. Furthermore, the continuation of socially sanctioned actions once they occur is promoted by the fact that they lead to positive reinforcements. Why then do some individuals fail to learn to behave in ways which are considered desirable and adjusted and which society generally encourages and rewards? Social-learning theory postulates two possibilities: first, the individual's particular environment may deviate from the general culture and not provide the necessary learning conditions, and second, the prior learning of the individual may interfere with or block his learning of behaviors regarded as desirable. Each of these possibilities is discussed below and, as is true in trying to understand the basis for the presence of maladjusted behavior, the social-learning theorist adopts an ideographic and historical approach in determining reasons for the absence of desirable behavior.

Inappropriate conditions for learning a behavior may consist of circumstances which prevent or discourage its initial occurrence or may result when the behavior is followed by no reinforcement or a negative reinforcement. Although most persons in a culture act in a given way, the unique life conditions of a person may prevent him from witnessing or being able to try out a particular act. Physical ailments during childhood may restrict exploratory behavior and may make it difficult or impossible to behave in a given way. Parental restrictions and taboos may have this same result. The absence of a same-sex parent from the home also may discourage the initial occurrence of many sex-appropriate behaviors because of the lack of a model to imitate. Homes described as impoverished or disadvantaged economically and/or culturally are likely to lack stimuli which encourage the child to try new behaviors.

Even when culturally appropriate behaviors occur, the person's life situation may not reinforce them or may negatively reinforce them. The mother who prefers that her child remain close and dependent on her may discourage appropriate independent behavior to such an extent that the child fails to learn essential skills for caring for himself. Frequently conditions discourage the learning of behavior despite deliberate efforts on the part of others to promote that behavior. To illustrate, a parent may work intensely with his child to teach him to swim, but if the parent's reactions are critical and frightening to the child, they in effect constitute negative reinforcement for that activity and the child may learn that swimming is something he cannot do and should avoid.

Assuming adequate exposure to cultural influences, in most instances when a behavior which society deems desirable or essential for adjustment is not learned, the failure occurs because of interference from prior learning of the individual. This is especially true with adults; even though one's childhood background may not have provided the conditions for learning the desired behavior, adult experiences are likely to have communicated the nature of the behavior that has not been learned and the potential rewards which follow it. When this is the case, the person knows that he should act in a given way to be in harmony with his culture, but finds himself unable to do so because of other responses he has learned.

Many of the same theoretical ideas which in social learning explain the presence of maladjusted behavior may account for the interference of past experiences on the learning of adjusted responses. Probably the most common interference occurs from avoidance and withdrawal responses. As noted before, responses which remove a person from a stimulus or situation in which he expects negative reinforcement prevent him from learning any other response in that situation. Consequently they block the development of behaviors which are culturally desirable in those situations.

The interference often consists of the learning of fears which do not apply at a later time, such as childhood fears which are inappropriate for an adult. Negative reinforcement of curiosity and assertiveness during childhood also often interferes with the occurrence of these characteristics in the adult when they are desired. In such cases, the individual can be described as having learned too well, or overlearned, so that he is unable to change even though conditions have changed.

The failure to develop appropriate and adjusted responses may result from the failure to discriminate correctly between different times, places, and people. If a behavior resulted in a negative reinforcement in the past, but is positively reinforced in the present, the individual who fails to discriminate between past and present will not become aware of the change. Another example consists of failure to note and respond to differences in behaviors which are appropriate in different groups. Responses which are punished when they occur with authority figures may be desired in peer interactions, and the lack of discrimination between the behavioral demands of these two groups of people may impede the learning of appropriate peer responses. Sometimes a person learns not to behave in a particular way, even though that behavior is desirable, because he has concentrated on the immediate reinforcements which are negative and has ignored delayed or long-term positive consequences of that behavior. For example, the college student who has failed to learn to devote himself to his studies may be responding only to the negative reinforcement that studying prevents him from engaging in enjoyable social activities and not to the delayed positive reinforcements, such as receiving a good grade on the final exam, graduating successfully, and obtaining a desired position following graduation.

An important aspect of learning adjusted, appropriate, and successful behavior is the development of certain broadly conceived behaviors that facilitate adaptation to difficult circumstances. Changes, frustrations, and problem situations will always be encountered, and individuals able to deal with these constructively will be better able to adjust than those who are not. Behaviors which often facilitate new adjustments are problem-solving, flexibility, self-awareness, and the seeking of alternative solutions.

As we have seen, social-learning theory concepts can be used to analyze and develop hypotheses concerning maladjustment. The validity of these hypotheses can be determined only by their value to the practicing clinician in helping maladjusted persons and by their accuracy in the prediction of human behavior. Further elaboration and development of the theory's application to the understanding and prediction of personality difficulties and maladjustments are likely to result from research and clinical practice which utilizes social-learning theory concepts.

REFERENCES

American Psychiatric Association. *Diagnostic and statistical manual of mental disorders,* ed. 2. Washington, D.C. 1968.

Bandura, A. A social learning interpretation of psychological dysfunctions. In P. London and D. Rosenhan (Eds.), *Foundations of abnormal psychology*. New York: Holt, Rinehart and Winston, Inc., 1968.

Horner, M. Toward an understanding of achievement-related conflicts in women. *Journal of Social Issues,* 1972, **28,** 157–175.

Jessor, R., Liverant, S., and Opochinsky, S. Imbalance in need structure and maladjustment. *Journal of Abnormal and Social Psychology,* 1963, **66,** 271–275.

Kanfer, F. H. ad Saslow, G. Behavioral diagnosis. In C. M. Franks (Ed.), *Behavior therapy: Appraisal and status*. New York: McGraw-Hill Book Co., 1969.

Phares, E. J. A social learning theory approach to psychopathology. In J. B. Rotter, J. E. Chance, and E. J. Phares (Eds.), *Applications of a social learning theory of personality*. New York: Holt, Rinehart and Winston, Inc., 1972.

Rotter, J. B. *Social learning and clinical psychology*. Englewood Cliffs: Prentice-Hall, 1954.

Rotter, J. B. Generalized expectancies for internal versus external control of reinforcements. *Psychological Monographs,* 1966, **80,** (1, Whole No. 609).

Rotter, J. B. A new scale for the measurement of interpersonal trust. *Journal of Personality,* 1967, **35,** 651–665.

Rotter, J. B. Some implications of a social learning theory for the practice of psychotherapy. In D. J. Levis (Ed.), *Learning approaches to therapeutic behavior change*. Chicago: Aldine, 1970.

Rotter, J. B. An introduction to social learning theory. In J. B. Rotter, J. E. Chance, and E. J. Phares (Eds.), *Applications of a social learning theory of personality*. New York: Holt, Rinehart and Winston, Inc., 1972.

Szasz, T. S. *Ideology and insanity*. Garden City: Doubleday & Co., Inc., 1970.

Section Three

The Determinants of Adjustment

The readings in this section report on some of the variables that generally are considered significant in determining adjustment patterns. Whenever the topic of causal factors in behavior is approached, the question of the relative importance of heredity and environment usually is raised. The influences of heredity and environment on behavior are, however, so complex and interdependent that we cannot meaningfully separate one from the other. While we may note differences among infants at birth, we are unable to determine the extent of the hereditary influence apart from that of the prenatal environment. Infants with the same hereditary potential may differ markedly because of variations, deficiencies, and mishaps in the maternal condition while the child is in utero. Because of the difficulty in isolating hereditary factors, most investigators of the determinants of adjustment focus on environmental factors, which lend themselves more readily to research.

The readings on the determinants of adjustment which follow present a representative picture of environmental influences. The first selection provides a discussion of the significance of cultural factors in individual differences in adjustment, mental health, and personality. Leighton and Hughes muster the evidence in support of a number of basic propositions about the relationships between culture and personality. They persuade us that mental health and other related attributes of individuals need to be seen in the context of culture, and that culture does, in fact, have a powerful impact on adjustment.

The second reading alerts us to an important attribute of our own culture which appears to have relevance for determining adjustment—the variable of *social class*. Dividing our culture into groups based on class structure (determined by an index of ecological area of residence, occupation, and education), Hollingshead and Redlich present findings that indicate significant relationships between social class and the incidence of psychiatric disorders. The enthusiasm of the authors for relating social concepts to particular adjustment patterns seems warranted. As they point out, however, it is important to go beyond showing that statistical relationships exist between social class and mental illness; we must seek the specific ways in which social conditions function to influence the adjustment of individuals. The final report by Hollingshead and Redlich on this project, entitled *Social Class and Mental Illness* (Wiley, New York, 1958), suggests that their research constitutes a very fruitful approach to understanding ways in which social factors determine problems and patterns of adjustment.

The next two selections deal with the developing organism and give accounts of events and experiences that are critical for adequate adjustment. They both share a belief in the fundamental hypothesis that early experience has important consequences for adult behavior.

Many psychologists have attributed paramount importance to early childhood experiences because they are viewed as providing the foundation for the nature of subsequent adjustment. The first paper describes four training situations in early childhood which are thought to produce long-lasting effects on the personality characteristics of the individual. Dollard and Miller discuss some of the typical problems and reactions of the child concerning feeding, cleanliness, sex, and hostility. They also specify some of the habits that are acquired in the context of experiences with each of these. One example of how a habit is acquired would be that of the child who is repeatedly punished by a parent. The child may learn to perceive all authority figures with the fear and anger felt toward his or her parent.

The next selection provides us with a summary report from the Harlows on their well-known research on the effects of rearing conditions on behavior. They have been pursuing the consequences on behavior of a number of early life situations in rhesus monkeys, and, while the extent to which their findings can be generalized to human beings is open to question, their observations are exciting. Their general finding that the longer and more complete the social deprivation, the more devastating are the behavioral effects supports the hypothesis that early experience is an important determinant of later adjustment.

For a large number of investigators, psychosexuality is of central importance in human development and adjustment. Many investigators regard the individual's sexual drive and its expression as having a good deal of relevance for personality formation. Rutter's paper provides us with a review of the literature of normal sexual development in relation to physical maturation, sexual activity, object choice, gender role, sexual competence, etc. In a sense, his paper provides us with a normative description of both physical and psychological sexual development.

Konopka's paper conceptualizes a set of requirements for healthy development in adolescents. Following some introductory material on the common experiences of early adolescents, her paper addresses both the conditions for healthy development of youth and the obstacles to normal development. Among these obstacles, she gives attention to society's view of adolescence as preparatory and prolonged economic dependence, limited possibility for experimentation, societal confusion about success, and adult dominance of youth organizations that occur during adolescence. Her paper concludes with a set of recommendations concerning the kinds of programs that she believes would facilitate the healthy development of young people.

Erikson's paper provides us with an extremely well-known and far-reaching conceptualization of *psychosocial* developmental stages. The interest here is broader than the orthodox Freudian analysis of progress through *psychosexual* stages. Erikson sees the individual as passing through eight social stages, each of which is devoted to the establishment of alternative basic attitudes: basic trust versus basic mistrust, autonomy versus shame and doubt, initiative versus guilt, etc. Continuity is provided for in Erikson's scheme by the assertion that the character of the resolution of basic attitudes that occurs at earlier stages has consequences for the kind of resolution that occurs at later stages. In this sense, the events occurring at various stages of life are determinants of later behavior.

The selection by Brown endeavors to account for the widespread sense of alienation that is present today. In his view there are five societal pressures that define conditions for alienation in youth. They are (1) the trend toward urbanization, (2) the egalitarian trust, (3) the drive to "succeed," (4) the concept of "fit," and (5) the absence of "caring." These factors are implicated by Brown in widespread poverty, delinquency, and illness. He sees alienation as thwarting productivity, demeaning self-esteem, and rendering the individual a burden to his society.

Cultures as Causative of Mental Disorder*

Alexander H. Leighton and Jane H. Hughes

INTRODUCTION

A review of the previous papers makes it evident that mental disorder is considered to be the product of multiple factors. The present paper is in harmony with this orientation, and its title, which was assigned to us, should not be interpreted as implying ideas of mono-causal relationship.

The discussion of our topic will be necessarily limited and selective, since talking about culture in its global sense touches on virtually all aspects of human behavior. Some areas such as family relationships and social change have been discussed earlier. Others such as cultural history and philosophy are too vast to be treated adequately in one chapter. We shall attempt, therefore, to present some points from

*From Alexander H. Leighton and Jane H. Hughes, "Cultures as Causative of Mental Disorder," in *Causes of Mental Disorders: A Review of Epidemiological Knowledge, 1959,* Milbank Memorial Fund, New York, 1961. Reprinted by permission of the authors and the publisher.

salient literature, and to give impressions derived from several years of research dealing with socio-cultural factors and mental disorder.

DEFINITION OF CONCEPTS

Culture

As used here "culture" is a label for an abstraction that encompasses the total way of life of a group of human beings.

Many other definitions have been proposed, and several variants are current in the social sciences (25). Leslie White, for example, employs the word to mean a pattern of history which can be analyzed and understood without reference to the human beings in whom it is expressed (46). Culture in this sense is a determinant force which follows its own laws irrespective of individual psychology and acts upon, rather than interacts with, human personalities. Such a conceptualization provides a way of explaining other phenomena by means of culture as the causal element. We think, however, that despite some possible usefulness in White's "culturology" with regard to understanding the evolutionary path of society as a whole, it is too divorced from human variation to have relevance for the malformations and malfunctionings of personality known as mental disorders.

Other ways of defining culture point to the material artifacts produced by certain societies and to the relationship between patterns of livelihood and environmental resources. Our concept includes all these factors—history, adaptation to physical environment, technology—but its focal point is what Hallowell has termed the "psychological reality" of culture (15). By this emphasis, culture refers primarily to the shared patterns of belief, feeling, and adaptation which people carry in their minds as guides for conduct and the definition of reality. Besides concerning all aspects of human life—social relationships, economics, and religion, for example—culture as a totality contains patterns of interconnections and interdependencies.

Although all societies have a cultural heritage which is transmitted from one generation to the next, the particular style varies from one group to another. Where contrast is marked, it is impossible to speak of different cultures. Thus cultures have been grouped as "Western and non-Western," "hunting and gathering," "agricultural," and "industrial" (17), or as "peasant societies" and "great traditions" (39).

In studying cultural factors which affect mental disorder, modern urbanities are, of course, as much the focus of attention as non-literate tribal groups. It is a common practice, however, to direct analysis toward situations which offer contrast to what prevails in our own culture with the hope of moving thereby into greater understanding of problems to which we are somewhat blinded by their being too close to us. It is for this reason that the examples to be cited here deal mainly with non-Western cultures, and the literature reviewed is primarily from the field of anthropology and the subfield "culture and personality" in which anthropologists and psychiatrists have collaborated.

Mental Disorder

Coming as it does at the end of the symposium, our definition of mental disorder should need little elaboration. It is in keeping with the symposium's inclusion of all those behaviors, emotions, attitudes, and beliefs usually regarded as in the field of psychiatry. Such breadth of definition means that neuroses are encompassed as well as psychoses, sociopathic disorders as well as psychophysiological disturbances. It also means the inclusion of brain syndromes and mental retardation—conditions not primarily based on psychological experience but subject nonetheless to the influences of culture through practices of breeding, diet, care of the ill, use of drugs and intoxicants, and the training of the defective child.

HOW CULTURAL FACTORS MAY BE THOUGHT TO AFFECT PSYCHIATRIC DISORDER

As a means of organizing pertinent ideas, what follows will be presented as a series of statements, each one supplying a different way of completing the sentence ''Culture may be thought to. . . .''

1 Culture May Be Thought to Determine the Pattern of Certain Specific Mental Disorders

Names representing culture-specific disorders are well known in anthropological literature although they are not part of the standard nomenclatures of Western psychiatry. A list would include ''amok'' and ''lâtah'' both found in Malay (2, 43, 48), ''imu'' among the Ainu of Japan (47), ''koro'' in China (44), ''witiko'' among the Ojibwa Indians of the Northeast Woodlands (27), ''piblokto'' in the eastern Arctic (3), and ''arctic hysteria'' in Siberia (20). Each one embodies a constellation of symptoms found primarily in a given culture area, and often there is association between cultural beliefs or practices and the content of the symptoms.

''Witiko,'' for example, takes the form of a homicidal spree during which the individual may kill and eat members of his own family (7). In what could be called a delusional excitement the patient believes himself possessed by a spirit from his cultural mythology, the Witiko, a hoary cannibalistic monster with a heart of ice. ''Koro'' is an anxiety state in which delusions concern withdrawal of the male sexual organs into the abdomen. It is associated with fear of death in a culture where it is believed that the sexual organs do disappear from corpses. Among the Eskimos, ''piblokto'' refers to a temporary derangement during which various bizarre acts are carried out such as dashing out naked into subzero weather or mimicking the sounds of Arctic birds and animals.

''Lâtah,'' ''imu'' and ''arctic hysteria'' are characterized by involuntary imitating, automatic obedience, shuddering, and fright. It is believed that women are more frequently sufferers from this disability than men. In some cultures certain people, especially old women, are known for this affliction, and it is considered sport to use gestures or words which will set off a reaction in which the victim goes into unseemly postures, dances to exhaustion, disrobes, and even harms herself or others.

There are accounts of whole groups of individuals becoming afflicted with a kind of mass hysteria, recalling the ''dancing crazes'' in Europe during the Middle Ages. One report tells of an instance in which a Cossack officer was drilling a group of Siberian natives. Each order he issued was shouted back first by one individual and then gradually by a chorus of all in the ranks. Every man appeared trapped in an exhausting and self-defeating repetition of the orders (and then curses) uttered by the increasingly infuriated officer (8).

A number of explanations have been invoked to account for such disorders. These comprise the ideas that they are:

1 Reactions based on physical disease such as malaria, tuberculosis, or leutic infection, but patterned in expression by cultural elements (43).

2 Reactions to the stress of severe environment, starvation, or long periods of isolation (37).

3 Reactions to the stress and strain of role characteristics in the culture (1).

4 "Hysteria" (6), that is, variations of a syndrome familiar in Western clinics and which is referred to in the American Psychiatric Association nomenclature as "dissociative reaction" (4)

These explanations are not mutually exclusive. Some of the culturally localized syndromes can be considered as neurotic states involving suggestibility, and in which the content of symptoms is produced by the experience of growing up in a particular culture and being inculcated with its shared sentiments. Contributing factors may then be the stress of environment or roles. Dynamic mechanisms or noxious agents can also be regarded as components in the origin and course of the disorder.

The idea that these disorders are hysterical should, however, be treated with some caution. This is said partly from our feeling that such a conclusion is deceptively complete and hence may cut off effort toward penetrating to a less superficial level of understanding. There is also the possibility that it expresses a bias of the Western clinician who may have some tendency to consider any seemingly bizarre behavior as hysterical if there is no organic basis and if it cannot be called schizophrenia. This is further encouraged if the person exhibiting such behavior is uneducated from the Western point of view, is "simple" and "child-like"—qualities which are part of the stereotype we hold of "primitives." It would seem wise not to blanket aberrant behaviors found among the people of this or that culture with the term and concepts of "hysteria" (or of schizophrenia for that matter), but rather examine to see if some cases, at least, may not be on a somewhat different basis from what we are accustomed to see in the West. And even when "hysteria" turns out to be a valid label such an approach might, through comparisons and contrasts, increase our knowledge regarding the nature of the condition, not only as it occurs among non-Western peoples, but also among ourselves.

2 Culture May Be Thought to Produce Basic Personality Types, Some of Which Are Especially Vulnerable to Mental Disorder

The concepts of "basic personality type" (21, 22, 23), "modal personality" (16, 19), and "national character" (35, 14) were developed by anthropologists and psychiatrists to account for the fact that certain personality traits and certain inclinations to symptoms of psychiatric significance seemed to be associated with growing up in particular cultures. Being middle class American, Japanese, Russian—or, as described in Ruth Benedict's classic volume, being Zuñi, Kwakiutl, or Dobu (5)—appears to predispose individuals toward particular kinds of symptoms. In the employment of these concepts, culture and personality were held to be essentially two aspects of a single phenomenon (42). This opened the way for studying personality through cultural data rather than through the behavior of individuals. The early work in this field by Kardiner and Linton had its foundation in exploring ethnographies and the folklore of non-literate tribes. Through analysis of child-rearing practices, kinship arrangements, socio-structural stresses, and especially religion and myths considered as projections of common, underlying personality attributes, "basic personality types" were postulated for different cultures.

Basic personality was thought of as a central core of values and attitudes which culture stamps into each of its members—a common denominator underlying each person's individual elaboration of life experience. Once a type had been described, it could be assessed from the psychiatric point of view as to its vulnerabilities. Thus, if at the cultural level—that is, group practices and beliefs—patterns were found that had psychiatric implications it was assumed that individuals in that culture would have these as psychological weaknesses. Whole cultures were described with psychiatric terms heretofore reserved for diagnosing individuals. If a society exhibited patterns of suspiciousness, hostility, witchcraft fears, and ideas of grandeur as in the potlaching Indian groups of the Northwest coast, there was a tendency to call such cultures "paranoid."

Since a major component of almost every clinical definition of psychiatric disorder is some deviation from the expected behavior and shared sentiments of the group to which the individual belongs, the use of clinical terms for conforming, group-oriented behavior involves a contradiction. At best, it is the employment of unclear descriptive labels to characterize patterns of behavior manifested by a society. At worst, the clinical implications of the words are transferred to the group behavior, and dynamic interpretations are made in this framework. Since the behavior of people in accord with and at variance with group patterns implies major differences of psychological process, these usages can be exceedingly misleading. To say that a group is "paranoid," for instance, may be passable though not admirable if by this is meant behavior that is suspicious and hostile. If, however, the word is intended as some kind of explanation based on individual psychology, then many pre-judgments and unsound inferences from individual to group behavior may enter the picture. One runs the risk of anthropomorphizing the group and regarding it as a deviant individual among a number of other anthropomorphized groups. It is one thing to say that functioning at the personality level and functioning at the socio-cultural level display similarities, and that how well they fit together is significant for adequate functioning at each level. It is another thing, however, to go beyond this and use identical terms in referring to these different levels of abstraction. This is especially true when the psychiatric terms invoked to identify and classify cultural patterns are not well standardized even at their source—psychiatry.

Theories concerning basic personality may also be criticized for a tendency to consider cultural factors as overriding variations based on genetic influences affecting temperament (13) and for ignoring the possible effects of endemic disease and other physiological factors. For the most part "basic personality types" have been derived solely from cultural behavior or from the results of projective tests like the Rorschach.

Thus far vulnerability to, or resistance against, mental illness has been postulated without concomitant investigation of the actual distribution and patterning of psychiatric disorder in the population.

Our own inclination is toward a less specific functional view of sociocultural groups and the personalities which compose them. By this is meant the aim of understanding how psychiatric disorder can arise, take shape, and endure, as a result of interaction between individual functioning (personality) and group functioning. Since a discussion of this viewpoint has been previously published by one of us (30), we shall not here elaborate it further.

3 Culture May Be Thought to Produce Psychiatric Disorders through Certain Child-rearing Practices

This point is closely allied to its predecessor. The difference is that while basic personality types have been formulated from looking at cultures as wholes, the focus here is directly and more exclusively levelled at socialization practices and the early years of life experience. Freudian theory has provided a means of organizing data from different cultures with regard to toilet training, nurturing, control of aggression, weaning, and encouraging independence (11). It has also provided a way of interpreting cultural variations with regard to probable significance for mental disorder among adults. Cultures portray remarkable variation in customs such as swaddling, use of a cradle-board, bottle or breast feeding, varying modes of punishment and reward, the permissive or restraining parental attitudes. This has given impetus to many hypotheses regarding the differential occurrence of psychiatric disorders.

The risk of this approach is to give undue emphasis to one set of factors, and to one period on the life-arc of individuals, to the exclusion of all other factors and periods of personality growth and development. Few would quarrel with the importance of the early years of life, but to assume that the experiences of infancy determine everything that comes afterward so far as origin, course, and outcome of psychiatric disorder is concerned, is to assume more than the knowledge currently at our disposal warrants. Different sets of dynamics are relevant to individual functioning at different stages of life. Physiological and psychological changes in maturation and involution are probably of considerable significance in some kinds of mental disorders. Since our interest is in discovering cultural factors relevant to the whole range of psychiatric illnesses, it is important to recognize that adolescence, maturity, and senescence are viewed and defined as variously in different cultures as is child-rearing.

4 Culture May Be Thought to Affect Psychiatric Disorders through Types of Sanction

It has long been accepted that there is a relationship between some kinds of disorder and the manner in which a patient handles the problem of conformity or nonconformity —the sense of being right or wrong in the eyes of his social audience. There is considerable variation among cultures regarding how punishment is meted out to those who defy accepted beliefs and standards about what ought and ought not to be done. Cultures also vary in what is defined as transgression and the kinds of responsibility demanded of members. Some groups operate on the principle that society at large is the controller of moral conduct; others appear to maintain social control by implanting in individuals the job of self-monitoring conduct. These two types—"other-directed" and "inner-directed" in Reisman's terminology (40)—have usually been called "shame" and "guilt" cultures in anthropological literature. A critical discussion of this orientation is given by Piers and Singer (38). It has been thought that distinctive forms of psychopathology may be found in "shame" cultures where the atonement for sin calls for some kind of public demonstration such as a confession, while other kinds of symptomatology may be fostered in "guilt" cultures where expiation is left to the lonely world of conscience. One can theorize that where the group as a whole is the court to which account must be made, there would be a tendency for psychiatric disorder to take the form of antisocial behavior, aggression of the sociopathic type. Where individual super-ego is stressed, there might be an inclination to self-directed punishment and depression. In short, and in overly simple terms, one type of culture can be thought to encourage symptoms which are disturbing to the group, while the other encourages symptoms which are disturbing to the individual who has them.

With regard to the kinds of behavior for which people are punished, it has been noted that some cultures institute negative sanctions only against what is defined as controllable, while others include involuntary behavior as well (23). Among some peoples, menstruation, multiple births or impotence are thought to be defiling to the whole group or at least an affront to cultural expectations. In a personal communication Dr. T. A. Baasher of Khartoum North has told one of us[1] of the Ingassuma tribe in the Sudan where it is believed that the mother of twins has the evil eye. He reported an instance in which such a mother committed suicide by running her head against a rock while the members of her village looked on.

The psychological burden related to the occurrence of certain uncontrollable and not uncommon events and to some kinds of physiological processes, e.g. menstruation, may be of a magnitude that makes it appropriate to say that a given culture has a serious potential for psychiatric disorder. At least it seems clear that sanctions of this nature have a quite different meaning with regard to mental health from those which relate the occurrence of insanity to more or less self-willed acts such as breaking incest taboos among the Navaho (41), or masturbation as found in some of the folk beliefs of our own culture.

5 Culture May Be Thought to Perpetuate Psychiatric Malfunctioning by Rewarding It in Certain Prestigeful Roles

Under the last point attention was focussed only on negative sanctions. We turn now to the positive side—reward—and also more explicitly to the concept of role (32). The relationship between socio-cultural role and mental disorder is complex, and we shall deal with it in two parts: here in terms of roles which may attract individuals who have certain disorder tendencies and in Statement 6, below, in terms of roles which may produce some types of psychiatric disorder through being seats of conflict and stress.

In non-Western cultures the roles of medicine-man and holy-man—shaman or sahu—are examples of social positions for which, it has been thought, personnel are recruited from unstable members of the culture—hysterics and psychotics (24, 9).

Taking the shaman as an instance, behaviors connected with the role have been described as indicative of disorder because emotional lability and frenzy characterize the seance, because the shaman has charismatic dominance over the group of individuals for whom the curing ceremony is held, because the shaman believes that he loses his own identity and becomes possessed by an over-world spirit, and because a fit or epileptic-like seizure culminates the performance.

There are, however, some considerations to be taken into account in following this line of thought. Just because the shaman's behavior resembles psychiatric symptoms is not a warrant for assuming that they are in fact psychiatric symptoms. Whatever else it may be, his behavior is part of the role of shaman and hence it may or may not have a relationship to his personality as a whole which would qualify him as mentally ill in Western terms. The settling of this question would require a thorough psychiatric examination of the person. To make a clinical diagnosis on the basis of role behavior alone is scarcely on a firmer basis than making a diagnosis from cultural patterns as noted [earlier].

What in shamanistic behavior may appear hysterical or psychotic to the Western psychiatrist is, to the people concerned, a time-honored ritual through which practitioners heal sick people or divine the future. Hence the "symptoms" of the shaman may in fact be the result of learning and practice. His role embodies a traditional plan for serving particular ends, and it is available in the culture as a model. The patterning of behavior after this model can, of course, vary greatly in its success, from excellent to poor.

It can also be assumed that a variety of personality types will be attracted to the model and role for a variety of reasons, some making a conscious selection while others act in response to both unconscious factors and extraneous circumstances. In the cultures where shamans are found, there is usually much less diversification of roles than is the case in Europe and America. There the business of life may be managed through nearly all the men being hunters, farmers or warriors, with the women in the main being homemakers. The role of shaman, consequently, may be almost the only variant possible and it is thus likely to collect incumbents for a wide variety of reasons, some of a psychiatric nature, some for matters of temperament, some related to superior and creative qualities, and some based on physical abnormality—blindness or loss of a limb—which makes achievement of the more prevailing roles impossible. It seems to us, that while some shamans or medicine-men may be suffering from psychiatric disorder, this is probably not by any means the case with all.

The concept of role is traceable in part to 'role' as it is known in the theater. This may serve as a reminder that any given role as performed by an actor is not necessarily a direct and simple reflection of his own personality. Very few Ophelias have really been mad, and mad actresses do not necessarily perform Ophelia well. At the same time we do not wish to suggest that, because they may learn their part, most shamans are conscious fakers. On the contrary, it would seem likely that the ability to perform is enhanced by belief in the importance of the part.

In our own culture there are doubtless certain roles which resemble that of shaman in that they not only offer opportunity to mentally healthy personalities but also provide shelter for those with a certain amount of deviance. The artist comes to mind in this connection. Of course, many artists are mentally healthy, but it is possible for the arts to provide an opportunity for an ill person to express himself creatively and thus have a position in the social system. Artists are often accorded leeway—indeed, may acquire prestige—in the expression of psychiatric symptoms which, if evinced by people in other social roles, might be reason for sanctions, or even hospitalization. Places such as the Left Bank, Greenwich Village, and North Beach give a social medium where fairly large numbers of sick people can float. These areas contain not only the genuine artist but shelter many who act like poets and painters without ever becoming highly original or productive. Certain religious groups and colonies have similar sheltering characteristics for malfunctioning personalities.

6 Culture May Be Thought to Produce Psychiatric Disorders through Certain Stressful Roles

With this statement attention shifts to the effects of roles rather than their patterning and appearance. It is possible to conduct analysis so as to identify roles considered to be psychologically damaging, even to the extent of producing psychiatric disorder. For the most part this approach has been typical of sociology, in contrast to anthropology's focus on child-rearing.

Roles can be considered stressful in a number of ways. One is the problem of ambiguous definition regarding expected behavior. This is especially true of new roles developed in situations of socio-cultural change where tradition gives no guidelines for assisting the recently emancipated to adapt and fulfill his new state. The principle is pertinent whether we observe a freed slave, a modern career woman, or a person in the limbo between magical and rational thought.

Roles may also present the person with inherently conflicting standards of behavior; the man who dedicates his life to humanitarian goals may come to feel he can reach a position effective for launching such a program only by being ruthless and competitive. Or a person may have to fill at one time several roles which make contradictory demands on his personality. We see this for example in students who have cast themselves in the role of liberals yet attempt to be loyal offspring to conservative parents.

The relationship between role stresses and a particular kind of psychiatric disorder has been reported by Linton as occurring among the Tanala of Madagascar (34). These people have a condition called "tromba" which occurs mainly among second sons and childless wives. This is to be understood in the context of a culture in which inheritance and privilege are based on primogeniture and in which marriages are polygamous with the value of women related chiefly to child-bearing. Not only are role stresses and lack of social value involved, but also the mental illness itself gives opportunity for compensating prestige ("secondary gain."). Normally the family gives little attention to people filling such subservient roles as younger sons and wives without children, but for this illness the family group will finance an elaborate curing rite with attention focussed on the tromba-sufferer.

Innumerable other examples could be given of role stresses peculiar to this or that culture, and it seems probable that many of them are associated with some kind of psychiatric disturbance. It is a hard matter to pin down, however, for while individually persuasive cases can be found, research encounters problems of definition and the assembling of statistics adequate for conclusive statements.

7 Culture May Be Thought to Produce Psychiatric Disturbance through Processes of Change

It was intimated in the last section that some of the most striking examples of stressful roles pertain to cultural change—that is to say a given role is conflict-laden because of changes in the web of socio-cultural situations with which it is related. Being a wife and mother may take on this character if, in the changing cultural situation, a woman is also expected to hold a job, vote, be educated, and so forth.

Literature on the relationship between mental disorder and social change through immigration, mobility connected with war, acculturation, and detribalization was reviewed in the last paper. It is not, therefore, appropriate to develop it further here except to indicate that culture is not static social organization and that in the world today, any study of culture is of necessity a study of change—changes of various sorts, at various rates, and with varying degrees of integration and conflict. Although there are numerous methodological problems connected with the use of hospital admission rates or projective tests, we feel that with advances in methods of case finding it is in the area of cultural change that some of the most revealing findings will occur that bear on the relationship between culture and mental disorder (31).

8 Culture May Be Thought to Affect Psychiatric Disorder through the Indoctrination of Its Members with Particular Kinds of Sentiments

There is now considerable literature in the social sciences on the differences between cultural groups in regard to socially shared feelings and ideas about man, nature, and reality (18). For the most part this has been concerned with values or beliefs held by relatively normal individuals. Implications regarding psychiatric disorders have, however, been pointed up in a number of ways. It seems probable that some cultures equip people with patterns of fear, jealousy, or unrealistic aspiration, which may foster mental illness; other cultures may be based on themes of self-acceptance and a relationship to natural forces which are more conducive to mental health.

Reality-testing in the tradition of Western empiricism is, for instance, a criterion advanced by modern psychiatry as an essential component of sanity and mental health. With such a base for discrimination, it has been suggested by Kroeber that the practice of magic and witchcraft and the adherence to non-objective beliefs characteristic of "primitive" peoples indicates a diffuse and subtle paranoia (24). Few would argue against the value of reality-orientation as a mark of psychiatric health, but, as many have pointed out, the standard cannot be determined exclusively by scientific rationalism. A better criterion is whether or not a person is capable of assessing and acting in response to reality as it is defined by the group in which he grows up. This opens the way for understanding the relationship of religious faith, folk belief, and emotional coloring of attitudes to the development and maintenance of healthy adjustments and maladjustments. From such a perspective have come attempts to employ concepts which emphasize equally the cognitive, effective, and basic-urge (largely instinctual) forces which come into play in human functioning, and in that light to analyze the significance of differences in the cultural patterning of belief. The Eaton and Weil study of mental illness among the religious communities of Hutterites takes this aspect as one of its points for analysis (10). And it is central in the Stirling County Study (30).

9 Culture Per Se May Be Thought to Produce Psychiatric Disorder

All human beings are born and develop in cultural contexts which impose regulation of basic human urges. It has been thought that this is both universal and psychologically noxious with repercussions evident throughout the human race. We may all be, in short, like Chinese women with bound feet. Variations, however, are to be found in the degree of impulse-repression. Thus according to this view, simple and "primitive" societies with cultures which permit expression of sex and aggression are, on the whole, a healthier environment than complex, modern civilizations which compress infants into highly artificial patterns of existence. This is the kind of thing Freud had in mind when he spoke of 'civilization and its discontents' (12).

Most social scientists today would not accept such inherent assumptions about the character of "primitive" and "civilized" cultures. The distinction has limited usefulness and then only when the terms are carefully defined. The more we have learned about "primitive" cultures, the more impressed we are with their potential for being both repressive and suppressive. There is much in favor of the general idea that some kinds and degree of psychiatric disorder may be the price paid for being socialized, somewhat as backache and curvature of the spine may be part of the price paid for walking on our hind legs.

10 Culture May Be Thought to Affect the Distribution of Psychiatric Disorders through Patterns of Breeding

This statement and its successor—the final point we shall present as a way in which culture may be thought to relate to mental illness—stand on a different basis from all the previous items. Until now each statement has shared with others the characteristic of assuming that psychological transactions are the main, if not the only intermediary between cultural factors and the emergence and shaping of psychiatric disorder. This has, in fact, been the principal orientation of those concerned with culture and its bearing on mental disorder.

Culturally-prescribed inbreeding is found in many groups of people, particularly with reference to some non-Western cultures, elite families, and small communities which for one reason or another live in isolation. If such groups begin with a prevalence of hereditary factors which make for mental retardation, schizophrenia, manic-depressive psychosis or other forms of emotional instability, it is to be expected that these conditions will become accentuated and prevalent in the group. Laubscher's early work in the field of cross-cultural psychiatry illustrates an attempt to relate the amount of schizophrenia among the Bantu of Africa to the pattern of cross-cousin marriage (29).

The same kinds of factors may be at work at more subtle levels, and in larger groups. Thus the accumulating evidence in the West that there is greater prevalence of psychiatric disorder in the lower socio-economic ranges, has one explanation in terms of a socio-cultural process which produces a downward drift and interbreeding of people with genetically determined disabilities.

Heredity as a factor in psychiatric disorder suffers both from overemphasis and neglect. Heredity as such is considered *the* matter of importance in many centers of psychiatry, particularly in Europe. But the question of cultural patterns and their shaping of hereditary processes is scarcely considered, at least in any systematic way. In other psychiatric centers—especially in the United States—and among most social scientists, the whole of heredity is by-passed in favor of psychological factors. Here culture is apt to be given more emphasis but not in connection with the distribution of genes.

11 Culture May Be Thought to Affect the Distribution of Psychiatric Disorder through Patterns Which Result in Poor Physical Hygiene

Our concern here is the role of physiological factors as the intermediary between culture and psychiatric disorder. Culture and cultural variation can be supposed to influence the distribution of noxious agents and traumata, and also the distribution of compensating factors and capabilities for resistance. In many non-Western cultures, for instance, contacts with the West which have demanded acculturation and abrupt industrialization have been accompanied by the spread of syphilis, tuberculosis, and many other diseases. Directly and indirectly these can foster disorder, although some have more potential in this regard than others. Of equal importance to the introduction of disease through contact, is the lack of native preventive and therapeutic measures.

Diet, based not only on availability of resources but also cultural preferences, may result in vitamin deficiency and malnutrition which in turn can affect the nervous system. There may also be cultural practices about child delivery, or the use of herbs and concoctions which make for brain damage. In some areas drugs have widespread use in native therapy, in reaction, and in religious ceremonies. There may thus be long-term degenerative effects as well as more immediate toxicities.

CONCLUDING NOTES

Given the impressions sketched above, what conclusions can be drawn with regard to epidemiological studies of psychiatric disorder in different cultures as a means of expanding knowledge of etiology?

One can say to begin with that if the emphasis is on a primary target of inquiry such as genes, damage to the brain, or family relationships, the cultural context will be of some importance even if secondary. It will be one of the sets of factors to be considered in understanding how the damage comes about—whether *via* hereditary, physiological or psychological means—how it is spread and perpetuated and how it may be controlled.

If we take culture-in-relation-to-psychiatric-disorder as the primary matter for attention, then a major gap is apparent: an incomplete descriptive account of the varieties of psychiatric disorder to which human beings are susceptible across the world. The magnitude of this gap becomes apparent as soon as one begins to look into it. We do not even have a reasonably complete account of psychiatric disorders as these occur in a selection of contrasting cultures. Many of the localized types of illness such as those mentioned earlier are actually based on very few observations, some of them carried out years ago by non-psychiatrists. Despite the fact that psychiatric clinics exist in many non-Western societies, problems of nomenclature, variable criteria, and a Procrustean emphasis on Western systems of classification make assessment and comparison very difficult. Beyond this is a void consisting in the unknown numbers of persons who, though disturbed, do not ever come to clinical attention.

The importance of supplying this lack in our knowledge bears first of all on the descriptive aspect of scientific procedure. While we recognize that not everyone would accept systematic description as a basic component of the scientific process, it would be a digression to argue the case in general terms here. Suffice it to say, then, that if one does believe as a principle that this has its place and contribution to make in the study of man (no less so than in the study of other creatures, or of the earth's crust, or of the stars) then the gap is in obvious need of filling. Although it will take years of painstaking work by many observers, it is a necessary foundation on which to base other kinds of study.

Stepping down, however, from the level of general scientific desirability with its implied faith in serendipity, it is possible to point out a number of more specific goals and opportunities. For one thing, description paves the way for assessment of frequency—be this in terms of prevalence or incidence. Such counts will be essential ultimately, both in critical problems of basic research into etiology and in providing information for programs concerned with treatment and prevention.

Description and the use of these descriptions as criteria for counts of frequency (epidemiology), bring with them the need for developing a system of classification that will stand up across cultures. While this may look on the surface like a rather dry and laborious exercise in taxonomy, shafts run out from it into the foundations of psychiatry, and there may be consequences that will profoundly alter many accepted ideas and change significantly the way the field is perceived.

Psychiatry itself, like most of the rest of medicine, is a product of Western culture. As such, it embodies ideas of illness and wellness, of normal and abnormal, of well-functioning and malfunctioning, of adaption and maladaption which have their roots in our own shared sentiments regarding the character of reality, of what is desirable, and of what ought to be desired. While the range in these matters is considerable in the West itself, cultural studies make it clear that it is not so great as when the whole world is considered. In other words malfunction, one of the major components of a definition of psychiatric disorder, shifts its character from culture to culture.

This problem is not necessarily limited to differences of shared preference and shared belief as supplied by one culture in comparison to another. It may involve not only feeling and knowing but also the process of thinking. The studies of Mertens and his co-workers using psychological tests in the Belgian Congo suggest that natives who have had a European kind of education think like Europeans, while those who do not, retain a framework quite different from the Aristotelian logic which is second nature to most Westerners (36, 28, 45).

The indications of such plasticity and difference should not lead one to hold that the range of psychological variation is limitless and that there are no transcultural consistencies. Even today there is good reason for believing that universals exist. While definition of malfunction and threshold of tolerance may vary from culture to culture, it is almost certain that mental retardation is known in all, as are also symptoms very like schizophrenia and depression. One of the opportunities in cross-cultural studies is to discover and more precisely specify universals and differentiate them from more localized disorders. Such a step would be a major advance in narrowing the field of possible etiological factors requiring investigation and would point to some as being more important than others.

A system of classification, together with its definitions and underlying concepts, which would stand up across cultures and take into account the variable and less variable factors, would probably result in some rearrangement and reorientation for psychiatry. At the least it would call for assessment of etiological theories against a broader background and it should bring to the fore the notion that the etiology of diagnosis in this or that cultural setting is a matter that has to be understood before there can be understanding of the etiology of disorder.

Psychiatric disorders are not, however, the only relevant area in need of taxonomic consideration. A problem of equal importance is the development of a system of classification for ordering the socio-cultural environment in a manner relevant to our interests in the effect of socio-cultural factors on the origin and pattern of psychiatric disorders. While some consideration has already been given to cross-cultural and trans-cultural classification of psychiatric illness, very little has been given to categorizing cultures and social groups from this point of view. Yet without this there is severe limitation in generalization, in cross-comparison, and in the identification of salient socio-cultural factors.

While it is our opinion that the problems just mentioned are of first-order importance, it is not our intention to assert that they are the only questions worth tackling. Our inclination is rather to feel that the broad context needs to be kept in mind in any specific study and the limitations recognized which will prevail pending development of systematic knowledge in the wider areas. With this reservation, there is much to be said for pushing ahead with particular studies such as those concerned with relating culture, personality, and psychiatric disorder.

It may well be that descriptive studies of psychiatric disorders in non-Western cultures could be combined and articulated with investigations of culture and personality. For instance a common syndrome in the Western Region of Nigeria is excitement (26). It apparently shows up in the clinics there with far greater frequency than it does in Europe or North America. It is also a component of disorders which have other features as well. One has the impression, moreover, that excitement at a somewhat lower level, though still high by Western standards, is a prominent aspect of many personalities. It also seems that the culture itself sets a positive value on states of frenzy under certain conditions. What are the relationships of these behaviors to each other?

Are there also hereditary and physiological factors to be considered? Is there, for instance, any connection with what appears to be an unusual frequency of malignant hypertension? What is the part played by cultural change?

The promise in pursuing such questions is not at present in terms of revealing highly specific relationships such as was done by Pasteur in his work with micro-organisms, but rather in assembling evidence as a means of feeling out the more and less probable hypotheses for later, more crucial investigation. It is largely a matter of finding suitable targets and discovering the right questions to ask of nature—questions which are answerable by the further procedures of science.

What has been observed above with regard to studies of culture, personality and psychiatric disorder, apply also to investigations of roles, child-socialization, and other questions of a similar type.

With all cultural studies, the possible contribution of hereditary and physiological factors should be given consideration. Their recognition is important, just as is the case with culture when the primary emphasis is on one of these other topics.

In concluding our paper, we should like to return again to a point mentioned earlier. This is our impression that comparative study of change is one of the most fruitful opportunities for uncovering the nature of socio-cultural factors in relation to psychiatric disorder. We regard descriptions and analyses of cultures at a given time as prerequisite to this, as fixing-points in terms of which to understand shifts. If, following a suggestion made earlier, we were to attempt to build a system for classifying cultures in such a manner as to have maximal relevance for mental health and mental illness, we would choose types of socio-cultural change as our starting point.

REFERENCES

1 Aberle, D. F.: 'Arctic Hysteria' and 'Laîah' in Mongolia. *Transactions of the New York Academy of Sciences,* May, 1952, 14, **7,** 291–297.

2 Abraham, J. J.: 'Laîah' and 'Amok.' *The British Medical Journal,* February 24, 1912: 438–439.

3 Ackerknecht, E. H.: Medicine and Disease Among Eskimos. *Ciba Symposia,* July-August, 1948, **10:** 16–921.

4 American Psychiatric Association, Committee on Nomenclature and Statistics: Diagnostic and Statistical Manual [for] Mental Disorders. Washington, D.C.: The Association, 1952. 130 pp.

5 Benedict, R.: Patterns of Culture. Boston and New York, Houghton Mifflin, 1934. 290 pp.

6 Brill, A. A.: Piblokto or Hysteria Among Peary's Eskimos. *The Journal of Nervous and Mental Disease,* August, 1913, **40:** 514–520.

7 Cooper, J. M.: The Cree Witiko Psychosis. *Primitive Man,* January, 1933, **6:** 20–24.

8 Czaplicka, M. A.: Aboriginal Siberia: A Study in Social Anthropology. Oxford, Clarendon Press, 1914. 374 pp.

9 Devereux, G.: Normal and Abnormal: The Key Problem of Psychiatric Anthropology. Chapter 2 *in* Some Uses of Anthropology: Theoretical and Applied. Washington, D.C., The Anthropological Society of Washington, 1956. 120 pp.

10 Eaton, J. W.; Weil, R. J.: Culture and Mental Disorders: A Comparative Study of Hutterites and Other Populations. Glencoe, Illinois, The Free Press, 1955. 254 pp.

11 Erikson, E. H.: Childhood and Society. New York, W. W. Norton, 1950. 397 pp.

12 Freud, S.: Civilization and Its Discontents. (J. Riviere, Trans.) London, Hogarth, 1930. 144 pp.

13 Gorer, G.: The Concept of National Character. Personality in Nature, Society, and Culture. (C. Kluckhohn; H. A. Murray; D. M. Schneider, Eds.) New York, Knopf, 1953. 701 pp.; 246–259.

14 Gorer, G.; Rickman, J.: The People of Great Russia. New York, Chanticleer Press, 1950. 235 pp.

15 Hallowell, A. I.: Culture and Experience. Philadelphia, University of Pennsylvania Press, 1955. 434 pp.

16 Honigmann, J. J.: Culture and Personality. New York, Harper, 1954. 499 pp.

17 Howells, W. W.: Back of History: The Story of Our Own Origins. New York, Doubleday, 1954. 384 pp.

18 Hughes, J. M.; Hughes, C. C.; Leighton, A. H.: Notes on the Concept of Sentiment. Appendix A *in* Leighton, A. H.: My Name Is Legion. Foundations for a Theory of Man in Relation to Culture. New York, Basic Books, 1959. 452 pp.

19 Inkeles, A.; Levinson, D. J.: National Character: The Study of Modal Personality and Sociocultural Systems. Handbook of Social Psychology (G. Lindzey, Ed.) Cambridge, Addison-Wesley, 1954. 2 vols.; Vol. 2: 977–1020.

20 Jochelson, Waldemar, [V. I.]: . . . The Koryak. (Publications of the Jessup North Pacific Expedition, Vol. 6.) Memoirs of the American Museum of Natural History, Vol. X, Part II. New York, G. E. Stechert, 1908. 842 pp.

21 Kardiner, A.: The Individual and His Society: The Psychodynamics of Primitive Social Organization. New York, Columbia University Press, 1939. 503 pp.

22 Kardiner, A.: The Psychological Frontiers of Society. New York, Columbia University Press, 1945. 475 pp.

23 Kroeber, A. L.: Anthropology: Race, Language, Culture, Psychology, Prehistory. New York, Harcourt, Brace, 1948. 856 pp.

24 Kroeber, A. L.: Psychosis or Social Sanction. The Nature of Culture. Chicago, University of Chicago Press, 1952. 437 pp.; 310–319.

25 Kroeber, A. L.; Kluckhohn, C.: Culture: A Critical Review of Concepts and Definitions. (Papers of the Peabody Museum of American Archaeology and Ethnology, Harvard University. Vol. 47, No. 1.) Cambridge, Massachusetts, The Museum, 1952. 223 pp.

26 Lambo, T. A.: Neuropsychiatric Observations in the Western Region of Nigeria. *British Medical Journal,* December 15, 1956, **2:** 1388–1394.

27 Landes, R.: The Abnormal Among the Ojibwa. *The Journal of Abnormal and Social Psychology,* January, 1938, **33:** 14–33.

28 Laroche, J. L.: "Recherche sur les aptitudes des ećoliers noirs au Congo Belge." [Thèse de doctorat] Louvain, Institut de Psychologie Appliqueé, 1958.

29 Laubscher, B. J. F.: Sex, Custom and Psychopathology: A Study of South African Pagan Natives. New York, Humanities Press, 1952. 347 pp.

30 Leighton, A. H.: My Name Is Legion. Foundations for a Theory of Man in Relation to Culture. New York, Basic Books, 1959. 452 pp.

31 Leighton, A. H.: Mental Illness and Acculturation. Medicine and Anthropology (I. Gladston, Ed.) New York, International Universities Press, 1959. 170 pp.

32 Linton, R.: The Study of Man. An Introduction. New York, Appleton-Century, 1936. 503 pp.

33 Linton, R.: The Cultural Background of Personality. New York, Appleton-Century, 1945. 157 pp.
34 Linton, R.: Culture and Mental Disorders. Springfield, Illinois, Thomas, 1956. 139 pp.
35 Mead, M.: National Character. Anthropology Today. An Encyclopedic Inventory. (A. L. Kroeber, Ed.) Chicago, University of Chicago Press, 1953. 966 pp.; 642–667.
36 Mertens de Wilman C., Vers une étude plus systemátique des variables psychologiques de l'acculturation. *Revue de psychologie appliqueé,* January, 1958, **8:** 1–23.
37 Novakovsky, S.: Arctic or Siberian Hysteria as a Reflex of the Geographic Environment. *Ecology,* April, 1924, **5:** 113–127.
38 Piers, G.; Singer, M. B.: Shame and Guilt: A Psychoanalytic and a Cultural Study. Springfield, Illinois, Thomas, 1953. 86 pp.
39 Redfield, R.: Peasant Society and Culture: An Anthropological Approach to Civilization. Chicago, University of Chicago Press, 1956. 162 pp.
40 Reisman, D.: The Lonely Crowd: A Study of the Changing American Character. New Haven, Yale University Press, 1950. 386 pp.
41 Spencer, K.: Mythology and Values: An Analysis of Navaho Chantway Myths. Philadelphia, American Folklore Society, 1957. 240 pp.
42 Spiro, M. E.: Culture and Personality: The Natural History of a False Dichotomy. *In* Readings in Child Development. (W. E. Martin; C. B. Stendler, Eds.) New York, Harcourt, Brace, 1954. 513 pp.: 117–141.
43 van Loon, F. H. G.: Amok and Laŧah. *The Journal of Abnormal and Social Psychology,* January–March, 1927, **21:** 434–444.
44 Van Wulfften Palthe, P. M.: Psychiatry and Neurology in the Tropics. Chapter 8 *in* A Clinical Textbook of Tropical Medicine. (C. D. de Langen, and A. Lichtenstein, Eds.) Amsterdam, G. Kolff, 1936. 557 pp.
45 Verhaegen, P.: Utilite áctuelle des tests pour l'étude psychologique des autochtones congolais. *Revue de psychologie appliqueé,* 1956, **6:** 139–151.
46 White, L. A.: The Science of Culture: A Study of Man and Civilization. New York, Farrar, Straus, 1949. 444 pp.
47 Wielawski, J.; Winarz, W.: Imu—A Psychoneurosis Occurring Among Ainus. *Psychoanalytic Review,* 1936, **23:** 181–186.
48 Yap, P. M.: The Laŧah Reaction: Its Pathodynamics and Nosological Position. *The Journal of Mental Science,* October, 1952, **98:** 515–564.

Social Class and Psychiatric Disorders*

August B. Hollingshead and Frederick C. Redlich

INTRODUCTION

The research reported here grew out of the work of a number of men, who, during the last half-century, have demonstrated that the social environment in which individuals live is connected in some way, as yet not fully explained, to the development of mental illness (1). Medical men have approached this problem largely from the

*From August B. Hollingshead and Frederick C. Redlich, "Social Class and Psychiatric Disorders" in *Interrelations between the Social Environment and Psychiatric Disorders,* Milbank Memorial Fund, New York, 1953. Pages 195–207 reprinted by permission of the authors and the publisher.

viewpoint of epidemiology (2). Sociologists, on the other hand, have analyzed the question either in terms of ecology (3), or of social disorganization (4). Neither psychiatrists nor sociologists have carried on extensive research into the question we are concerned with, namely, interrelations between the class structure and the development of mental illness. However, a few sociologists and psychiatrists have written speculative papers in this area (5).

The present research, therefore, was designed to discover whether a relationship does or does not exist between the class system of our society and mental illnesses. Five general hypotheses were formulated to test some dimension of an assumed relationship between the two. These hypotheses were stated positively; they could just as easily have been expressed either negatively or conditionally. They were phased as follows:

1 The *prevalence* of psychiatric disorders is related significantly to the class structure.
2 The *types* of psychiatric disorders are connected significantly to the class structure.
3 The type of *psychiatric treatment* is associated with an individual's position in the class structure.
4 The *psycho-dynamics* of psychiatric disorders are correlative to an individual's position in the class structure.
5 *Mobility* in the class structure is neurotogenic.

Each hypothesis is linked to the others, and all are subsumed under the general theoretical assumption of a functional relationship between stratification in society and the prevalence of particular types of mental disorders among given social classes or strata in a specified population. Although our research was planned around these hypotheses, we have been forced by the nature of the problem of mental illness to study *diagnosed* prevalence of psychiatric disorders, rather than *true* or *total* prevalence. This point should be kept in mind, when we present some of our preliminary findings.

METHODOLOGICAL PROCEDURE

The question of how these hypotheses are being tested leads us to a brief discussion of methodological procedures. In the first place, the research is being done by a team of four psychiatrists,[1] two sociologists,[2] and a clinical psychologist.[3] The data are being assembled in the New Haven urban community, which consists of the city of New Haven and surrounding towns of East Haven, North Haven, West Haven, and Hamden. This community had a population of some 250,000 persons in 1950.[4] The New Haven community was selected because the community's structure has been

[1]Drs. F. C. Redlich, B. H. Roberts, L. Z. Freedman, and Leslie Schaffer.
[2]August B. Hollingshead and J. K. Myers.
[3]Harvey A. Robinson.
[4]The population of each component was as follows: New Haven, 164,443; East Haven, 12,212; North Haven, 9,444; West Haven, 32,010; Hamden, 29,715; and Woodbridge, 2,822.

studied intensely by sociologists over a long period. In addition, it is served by a private psychiatric hospital, three psychiatric clinics, and twenty-seven practicing psychiatrists, as well as state and Veterans Administration facilities.

Four technical operations had to be completed before the hypotheses could be tested. Briefly these operations were: (1) the delineation of the class structure of the community; (2) selection of a cross-sectional control of the community's population; (3) the determination of who was receiving psychiatric care; and (4) the stratification of both the control sample and the psychiatric patients.

August B. Hollingshead and Jerome K. Myers took over the task of delineating the class system. Fortunately, Maurice R. Davie and his students had studied the social structure of the New Haven community in great detail over a long time span (6). Thus, we had a large body of data we could draw upon to aid us in blocking out the community's social structure.

Stated categorically, the community's social structure is differentiated *vertically* along racial, ethnic, and religious lines; each of these vertical cleavages, in turn, is differentiated *horizontally* by a series of strata of classes. Around the socio-biological axis of race two social worlds have evolved: A Negro world and a white world. The white world is divided by ethnic origin and religion into Catholic, Protestant, and Jewish contingents. Within these divisions there are numerous ethnic schisms. The Irish hold aloof from the Italians, and the Italians move in different circles from the Poles. The Jews maintain a religious and social life separate from the gentiles. The *horizontal* strata that transect each of these vertical divisions are based upon the social values that are attached to occupation, education, one's place of residence in the community, and associations.

The vertically differentiating factors of race, religion, and ethnic origin, when combined with the horizontally differentiating ones of occupation, education, place of residence, and so on, produce a social structure that is highly compartmentalized. The integrating factors in this complex are twofold. First, each stratum of each vertical division is similar in its cultural characteristics to the corresponding stratum in the other divisions. Second, the cultural pattern for each stratum or class was set by the "Old Yankee" core group. This core group provided a cultural model that has shaped the status system of each sub-group in the community. In short, the social structure of the New Haven community is a parallel class structure within the limits of race, ethnic origin, and religion.

This fact enabled us to stratify the community, for our purposes, with an *Index of Social Position.*[5] This *Index* utilizes three scaled factors to determine an individual's class position within the community's stratificational system: (1) ecological area of residence; (2) occupation; and (3) education. Ecological area of residence is scaled into a six point scale; occupation and education are each scaled on a seven point scale. To obtain a social class score on an individual, we must know his address, his occupation, and the number of years of school he had completed. Each of these factors is given a scale score, and the scale score is multiplied by a factor weight determined by a

[5]A detailed statement of the procedures used to develop and validate this *Index* will be described in a forthcoming monograph on this research tentatively titled *Psychiatry and Social Class,* August B. Hollingshead and Frederick C. Redlich.

standard regression equation. The factor weights are as follows: Ecological area of residence—5; occupation—8; and education—6. Then the three factor scores are summed. The resultant score is taken as an index of this individual's position in the community's social class system.

This *Index* enabled us to delineate five *main* social class strata within the horizontal dimension of the social structure. These principal strata or classes may be characterized as follows:

Class I This stratum is composed of wealthy families whose wealth is often inherited and whose heads are leaders in the community's business and professional pursuits. Its members live in those areas of the community generally regarded as the best; the adults are college graduates, usually from famous private institutions, and almost all gentile families are listed in the New Haven *Social Directory,* but few Jewish families are listed. In brief, these people occupy positions of high social prestige.

Class II Adults in this stratum are almost all college graduates; the males occupy high managerial positions, many are engaged in the lesser ranking professions. These families are well-to-do, but there is no substantial inherited or acquired wealth. Its members live in the "better" residential areas; about one-half of these families belong to lesser ranking private clubs, but only 5 per cent of Class II families are listed in the New Haven *Social Directory.*

Class III This stratum includes the vast majority of small proprietors, white-collar office and sales workers, and a considerable number of skilled manual workers. Adults are predominantly high school graduates, but a considerable percentage have attended business schools and small colleges for a year or two. They live in "good" residential areas; less than 5 per cent belong to private clubs, but they are not included in the *Social Directory.* Their social life tends to be concentrated in the family, the church, and the lodge.

Class IV This stratum consists predominately of semi-skilled factory workers. Its adult members have finished the elementary grades, but the older people have not completed high school. However, adults under thirty-five have generally graduated from high school. Its members comprise almost one-half of the community; and their residences are scattered over wide areas. Social life is centered in the family, the neighborhood, the labor union, and public places.

Class V Occupationally, Class V adults are overwhelmingly semi-skilled factory hands and unskilled laborers. Educationally most adults have not completed the elementary grades. The families are concentrated in the "tenement" and "cold-water flat" areas of New Haven. Only a small minority belong to organized community institutions. Their social life takes place in the family, on the street, or in the neighborhood social agencies.

The second major technical operation in this research was the enumeration of psychiatric patients. A Psychiatric Census was taken to learn the number and kinds of psychiatric patients in the community. *The Psychiatric Census was limited to residents of the community who were patients of a psychiatrist or a psychiatric clinic, or were in a psychiatric institution on December 1, 1950.* To make reasonably certain that all patients were included in the enumeration, the research team gathered data from all public and private psychiatric institutions and clinics in Connecticut and nearby states, and all private practitioners in Connecticut and the metropolitan New York area.

It received the cooperation of all clinics and institutions, and of all practitioners except a small number in New York City. We are convinced that we have data on at least 98 per cent of all individuals who were receiving psychiatric care on December 1, 1950.

Forty-four pertinent items of information were gathered on each patient by a team composed of a sociologist and a psychiatrist, and placed on a schedule. Sociological data were collected by the sociologists, and psychiatric data by the psychiatrists. The schedule included such psychiatric items as symptomatology and diagnosis; onset of illness and duration; referral to the practitioner and the institution; the nature and intensity of treatment. On the sociological side, we were interested in age, sex, occupation, education, religion, race and/or ethnicity, family history, marital experiences, and so on.

The third technical research operation was the selection of a control sample from the normal population of the community. The sociologists drew a 5 per cent random sample of households in the community from the 1951 New Haven *City Directory*. This directory covers the entire communal area. The names and addresses in it were compiled in October and November, 1950, a period very close to the date of the Psychiatric Census. Therefore, there were comparability of residence and date of registry between the two population groups. Each household drawn in the sample was interviewed, and data on the age, sex, occupation, education, religion, and income of family members, as well as other items necessary for our purposes were placed on a schedule. This sample is our Control Population.

Our fourth basic operation was the stratification of the psychiatric patients and of the control population with the *Index of Social Position*. As soon as these tasks were completed, the schedules from the Psychiatric Census and the 5 per cent Control Sample were edited and coded, and their data were placed on Hollerith cards. The analyses of these data are in process.

SELECTED FINDINGS

Before we discuss our findings relative to Hypothesis I, we went to reemphasize that our study is concerned with *diagnosed* or *treated* prevalence rather than *true* or *total* prevalence. Our Psychiatric Census included only psychiatric cases under treatment, diagnostic study, or care. It did not include individuals with psychiatric disorders who were not being treated on December 1, 1950, by a psychiatrist. There are undoubtedly many individuals in the community with psychiatric problems not being treated by psychiatrists who escaped our net. If we had *true* prevalence figures, many findings from our present study would be more meaningful, perhaps some of our interpretations would be changed, but at present we must limit ourselves to the data we have. With this caveat in mind, we shall turn to a discussion of our findings relative to our hypotheses.

Hypothesis I

To recapitulate, Hypothesis I, as revised by the nature of the problem, stated: *The diagnosed prevalence of psychiatric disorders is related significantly to an individual's position* in the class structure. A test of this hypothesis involves a comparison of the normal population with the psychiatric population. If no significant difference between the distribution of the normal population and the psychiatric patient population by social class is found, Hypothesis I should be abandoned as untenable. However, if a significant difference is found between the two populations by class, Hypothesis I should be entertained until more conclusive data are assembled. Pertinent data for a limited test of Hypothesis I are presented in Table 1. The data included in Table 1 show the number of individuals in the normal population and the psychiatric population by class level. What we are concerned with in this test is how these two populations are distributed by class.

When we analysed these population distributions by the use of the chi square method, we found a *very significant* relation between social class and treated prevalence of psychiatric disorders in the New Haven community. A comparison of the percentage distribution of each population by class readily indicates the direction of the distortion of psychiatric cases. For example, Class I comprises 3.1 per cent of the community's population, but only 1.0 per cent of the psychiatric cases. Class V, on the other hand, includes 17.8 per cent of the comunity's population, but it contributed 36.8 per cent of the psychiatric patients. The chi square test show that these differences are far beyond the limits of chance even at the .001 level of probability. On the basis of our data Hypothesis I clearly should be accepted as tenable.

Hypothesis II

Hypothesis II postulated a significant connection between the *type* of psychiatric disorder and social class. This hypothesis involves a test of the ideas that there may be a functional relationship between an individual's position in the class system and the type of psychiatric disorder that he may present. This hypothesis depends, in part,

Table 1 Distribution of Normal and Psychiatric Population by Social Class

	Normal population[1]		Psychiatric population	
Social class	No.	Per cent	No.	Per cent
I	358	3.1	19	1.0
II	926	8.1	131	6.7
III	2,500	22.0	260	13.2
IV	5,256	46.0	758	38.6
V	2,037	17.8	723	36.8
Unknown[2]	345	3.0	72	3.7
Total	11,422	100.0	1,936	100.0

$P < .001$ $\chi^2 = 408.16$

[1]These figures are preliminary, they do not include Yale students, transients, institutionalized persons, and refusals.

[2]The unknown cases were not used in the calculation of χ^2. They are (1) individuals drawn from the sample and (2) psychiatric cases whose class level could not be determined because of paucity of data.

on the question of diagnosis. Our psychiatrists based their diagnoses on the classificatory system developed by the Veterans Administration (7). For the purposes of this paper, we grouped all cases into two categories: the neuroses and the psychoses. The results of this grouping by social class are given in Table 2.

A study of Table 2 will show that there is a distinct inverse relationship between neuroses and psychoses by social class. The neuroses are concentrated at the higher levels, and the psychoses at the lower end of the class structure. Our team advanced a number of different theories to explain the sharp differences between the neuroses and psychoses by social class. One assumption was that the low percentage of neurotics in the lower classes was a direct reaction to the cost of psychiatric treatment. But as we accumulated data in a series of case studies, for tests of Hypotheses IV and V, we became skeptical of this simple interpretation. Our detailed case records indicate that the social distance between psychiatrist and patient may be more potent than economic considerations in determining the character of psychiatric intervention. This question requires further research.

The high concentration of psychotic patients in the lower strata is probably the product of a very unequal distribution of psychotics in the general population. To test this idea, Hollingshead selected schizophrenics for special study. Because of the severity of this disease the probability is that few schizophrenics are not receiving some kind of psychiatric care. This diagnostic group comprises 44.2 per cent of all patients, and 58.7 per cent of the psychotics, in our study. Ninety-seven point six per cent of these schizophrenic patients had been hospitalized at one time or another, and 94 per cent were hospitalized at the time of our census. When we analyze these patients in terms of their class level we find that there is a highly significant inverse relationship between social class and schizophrenia.

Hollingshead decided to determine, on the basis of our data, what the probability of the prevalence of schizophrenia by social class might be in the general population. To do this he used a proportional index to learn whether or not there were differentials in the distribution of the general population, as represented in our control sample, and the distribution of schizophrenics by social class. If a social class exhibits the same

Table 2 Distribution of Neuroses and Psychoses by Social Class Based on the Psychiatric Census

	Neuroses		Psychoses	
Social class	No.	Per cent	No.	Per cent
I	10	52.6	9	47.4
II	88	67.2	43	32.8
III	115	44.2	145	55.8
IV	175	23.1	583	76.9
V	61	8.4	662	91.6
Total	449		1,442	

$P < .001$ $\chi^2 = 296.45$

proportion of schizophrenia as it comprises of the general population, the index for that class will be 100. If schizophrenia is disproportionately prevalent in a social class the index will be above 100; on the other hand, if schizophrenia is disproportionately low in a social class the index will be below 100. The bias for or against the probability of schizophrenia in a given social class is given in the last column of Table 3.

The fact that the Index of Prevalance in Class Level I is only one-fifth as great as it would be if schizophrenia was proportionately distributed in this class, and that it is two and one-half times as high in Class Level V as we might expect on the basis of proportional distribution, gives further weight to the tenability of Hypothesis II. The fact that the Index of Prevalence is 11.2 times as great in Class V as in Class I is a remarkable finding.

Hypothesis III

Hypothesis III stipulated that the type of psychiatric treatment a patient receives is associated with his position in the class structure. A test of this hypothesis involves a comparison of the different types of therapy being used by psychiatrists on patients in the different social classes. We encountered many forms of therapy, but they were grouped under three main types; psychotherapy, organic therapy, and custodial care. The patient population, from the viewpoint of the principal type of therapy received, was divided roughly into three main types; psychotherapy, organic therapy, and custherapy; 31.7 per cent received organic treatments of one kind of another; 31.7 per cent received organic treatments of one kind or another; and 36.3 per cent received custodial care without treatment. When we analyzed these types of therapy by class a distinctly significant increase occurred in the percentage of cases who received no treatment, other than custodial care, as one moved from the higher to the lower classes. The same finding applies to organic treatment. Psychotherapy, on the other hand, was concentrated in the higher classes. Within the psychotherapy category there were sharp differences between the types of psychotherapy administered to the several classes. For example, psychoanalysis was limited to Class I and II, whereas patients in Class V who received any psychotherapy were treated by group methods in the state hospitals.

Table 3 Comparison of the Distribution of the Normal Population with Schizophrenics by Class, with an Index of Probable Prevalence

	Normal population (5 per cent sample)		Schizophrenics		
Social class	No.	Per cent	No.	Per cent	Index of prevalence
I	358	3.2	6	.7	22
II	926	8.4	23	2.7	33
III	2,500	22.6	83	9.8	43
IV	5,256	47.4	352	41.6	88
V	2,037	18.4	383	45.2	246
Total	11,077	100.0	847	100.0	

The number and percentage of patients who received each type of therapy is given in Table 4.

The data of Table 4 shows very definitely that Hypothesis III should be retained.

At the moment we do not have data available for a test of Hypotheses IV and V. These hypotheses will be put to a test as soon as we complete work on a series of cases now under close study. Preliminary materials give us the impression that they too will come out positively.

CONCLUSIONS AND INTERPRETATIONS

This study was designed to throw new light upon the question of how mental illness is related to social environment. It approached this problem from the perspective of social class to determine if an individual's position in the social system was associated significantly with the development of psychiatric disorders. It proceeded on the theoretical assumption that if mental illnesses were distributed randomly in the population, then the hypotheses we phrased to test the idea that psychiatric disorders are connected in some functional way to the class system would not be found to be statistically significant.

The data we have assembled demonstrate conclusively that mental illness, as measured by diagnosed prevalence, is not distributed randomly in the population of the New Haven community. On the contrary, psychiatric difficulties of so serious a nature that they reach the attention of a psychiatrist are distributed in highly significant ways along social class lines. In addition, types of psychiatric disorders, and the ways patients are treated are strongly associated with social class position.

The objective statistical tests of our hypotheses indicate that there are definite connections between particular types of social environments in which people live, as measured by the social class concept, and the emergence of particular kinds of psychiatric disorders, as measured by psychiatric diagnosis. They do not tell us: (1) what these connections are; nor (2) do they tell us how they are functionally connected to a particular mental illness in a given individual. They do indicate, however, that we are proceeding on promising and safe ground. The next step, we

Table 4 Distribution of the Principal Types of Therapy by Social Class

	Psychotherapy		Organic therapy		No treatment	
Social class	No.	Per cent	No.	Per cent	No.	Per cent
I	14	73.7	2	10.5	3	15.8
II	107	81.7	15	11.4	9	6.9
III	136	52.7	74	28.7	48	18.6
IV	237	31.1	288	37.1	242	31.8
V	115	16.1	234	32.7	367	51.2

$P < .001$ $\chi^2 = 336.58$

believe, is to turn from the strictly statistical approach to an intensive study of the social environments associated with particular social classes, on the one hand, and of individuals in these environments who do or do not develop mental illnesses, on the other hand. Currently the research team is engaged in this next step, but we are not ready to make a formal report of our findings.

REFERENCES

1 For example, *see:* Rosanoff, A. J.: Report of a Survey of Mental Disorders in Nassau County, New York. New York: National Committee for Mental Hygiene, 1916; Stern, Ludwig: *Kulturkreis und Form der Geistigen Erkrankung* (Sammlung Zwanglosen Abshandlungen aus dem Gebiete der Nerven-und-Geitesdrankheiten), X, No. 2, Halle a. S:C. Marhold, 1913, 1–62; Sutherland, J. F.: Geographical Distribution of Lunacy in Scotland. *British Association for Advancement of Science,* Glasgow, Sept. 1901; White, William A.: Geographical Distribution of Insanity in the United States. *Journal of Nervous and Mental Disease,* XXX (1903), 257–279.

2 For example, *see:* Braatoy, Trygve: Is It Probable that the Sociological Situation Is a Factor in Schizophrenia? *Psychiatrica et Neurologica,* XII (1937), 109–138; Gerard, Donald L. and Siegel, Joseph; The Family Background of Schizophrenia. *The Psychiatric Quarterly,* 24 (January, 1950), 47–73; Hyde, Robert W. and Kingsley, Lowell V.: Studies in Medical Sociology, I: The Relation of Mental Disorders to the Community Socio-economic Level. *The New England Journal of Medicine,* 231, No. 16 (October 19, 1944), 543–548; Hyde, Robert W. and Kingsley, Lowell V.: Studies in Medical Sociology; II: The Relation of Mental Disorders to Population Density. *The New England Journal of Medicine,* 231, No. 17 (Oct. 26, 1944), 571–577; Hyde, Robert W. and Chisholm, Roderick M.: Studies in Medical Sociology, III: The Relation of Mental Disorders to Race and Nationality. *The New England Journal of Medicine,* 231, No. 18 (Nov. 2, 1944), No. 3, Malamud, William and Malamud, Irene: A Socio-Psychiatric Investigation of Schizophrenia Occurring in the Armed Forces. *Psychosomatic Medicine,* 5 (Oct. 1943), 364–375; Malzberg, B.: Social and Biological Aspects of Mental Disease, Utica, N.Y. State Hospital Press, 1940; Roth, William F. and Luton, Frank H.: The Mental Health Program in Tennessee: Statistical Report of a Psychiatric Survey in a Rural County. *American Journal of Psychiatry,* 99 (March, 1943), 662–675; Reusch, J. and others, Chronic Disease and Psychological Invalidism.: New York: American Society for Research in Psychosomatic Problems, 1946; Reusch, J. and others, Duodenal Ulcer—A Socio-psychological Study of Naval Enlisted Personnel and Civilians, Berkeley and Los Angeles: University of California Press, 1948; Reusch, Jurgen; Jacobson, Annemarie; and Loeb, Martin B.: Acculturation and Illness. *Psychological Monographs: General and Applied,* 62, No. 5, Whole No. 292, 1948 (American Psychological Association, 1515 Massachusetts Ave., N.W., Washington 5, D.C.); Tietze, C.; Lemkau, Paul; and Cooper, M.: A Survey of Statistical Studies on the Prevalence and Incidence of Mental Disorders in Sample Populations. *Public Health Reports,* 1909–27, 58 (Dec. 31, 1943); Tietze, C.; Lemkau, P.; and Cooper, Marcia: Schizophrenia, Manic Depressive Psychosis and Social-Economic Status. *American Journal of Sociology,* XLVII (Sept. 1941), 167–175.

3 Faris, Robert E. L. and Dunham, H. Warren: Mental Disorders in Urban Areas. Chicago: University of Chicago Press, 1939; Dunham, H. Warren: Current Status of Ecological Research in Mental Disorder, *Social Forces,* 25 (March 1947), 321–326; Felix, R. H. and Bowers, R. V.: Mental Hygiene and Socio-environmental Factors. The Milbank Memorial

Fund Quarterly, XXVI (April 1948), 125–147; Green, H. W.: Persons Admitted to the Cleveland State Hospital, 1928–1937, Cleveland Health Council, 1939.

4 Faris, R. E. L.: Cultural Isolation and the Schizophrenic Personality. *American Journal of Sociology,* XXXIX (Sept. 1934), 159–169; Faris, R. E. L.: Reflections of Social Disorganization in the Behavior of a Schizophrenic Patient. *American Journal of Sociology,* I (Sept. 1944), 134–141.

5 For example, *see:* Davis, Kingsley: Mental Hygiene and the Class Structure. *Psychiatry* (February 1938), 55–56; Parsons, Talcott: Psychoanalysis and the Social Structure. *The Psychoanalytical Quarterly,* XIX, No. 3 (1950), 371–384; Dollard, John and Miller, Neal: Personality and Psychotherapy. New York: McGraw-Hill, 1950; Reusch, Jurgen: Social Technique, Social Status, and Social Change in Illness. Personality in Nature, New York: Alfred A. Knopf, 1949, 117–130; Warner, W. L.: The Society, the Individual and His Mental Disorders. *American Journal of Psychiatry,* 94, No. 2 (September, 1937), 275–284.

6 Davie, Maurice R.: The Pattern of Urban Growth. Studies in the Science of Society, edited by G. P. Murdock, New Haven, 1937, 133–162; Kennedy, Ruby J. R.: Single or Triple Melting-pot Intermarriage Trends in New Haven, 1870–1940. *American Journal of Sociology,* 39 (January 1944), 331–339; McConnell, John W.: *The Influence of Occupation Upon Social Stratification.* Unpublished Ph.D. thesis, Sterling Memorial Library, Yale University, 1927; Myers, Jerome K.: Assimilation to the Ecological and Social Systems of a Community. *American Sociological Review,* 15 (June 1950), 367–372; Minnis, Myra: The Relationship of Women's Organizations to the Social Structure of a City. Unpublished PhD. thesis, Sterling Memorial Library, Yale University, 1951.

7 *Psychiatric Disorders and Reactions,* Veterans Administration, Technical Bulletin 10A–78, Washington, October 1947.

Critical Training Situations in Childhood*

John Dollard and Neal E. Miller

The culture, of course, takes a position—a traditional position—on the various needs of the child. It has a design for the feeding situation, for cleanliness training, for sex training, for the treatment of anger responses in the child; and as the society imposes its will through the acts of the parents, the child reacts in its blind emotional way. Each one of the above-mentioned training situations can produce long-lasting effects on the character and habits of the individual and each is worth a brief discussion. We are by no means sure that these four are all of the dilemmas which can produce acute emotional conflicts, but we do know that each one of them has, in known cases, done so.

1 THE FEEDING SITUATION: CONFLICTS AND ATTITUDES

Much important learning takes place in reference to the hunger drive and the strong responses it excites. During the nursing period the child cannot "comfort" itself. It

*From John Dollard and Neal E. Miller, *Personality and Psychotherapy,* McGraw-Hill Book Company, Inc. New York, 1950. Pages 132–154 reprinted by permission of the authors and the publisher.

cannot, so to say, tell itself "It won't be long now," or "Only twenty minutes 'til feeding time." The hunger of the child is an urgent, incessant, and timeless pressure which, obviously, produces the most intense activation. If the child is fed when hungry, it can learn that the one simple thing it can do to get results (i.e., cry) can make a difference in what happens. Learning to cry as a signal for food is one small unit in its control of the world. Such a trait could be the basis of a later tendency to be "up and doing" when in trouble, of a belief that there is always a way out of a painful situation.

Apathy and Apprehensiveness

If the child is not fed when it is crying, but is instead left to "cry itself out," it can, similarly, learn that there is nothing it can do at that time to change the painful circumstances. Such training may also lay the basis for the habit of apathy and not "trying something else" when in trouble. In the second case, when drive is allowed to mount, the child can also learn that being a little bit hungry is followed by being very painfully hungry. When the child is then fed, only its most violent responses are reinforced. In this case the child can learn to fear being very hungry when it is only slightly hungry and to make the frightened response appropriate to severe hunger when only mild hunger exists. It is thus learning to "overreact," to be apprehensive of evil even when the circumstances of life seem calm. This learning occurs through the behavior mechanism of anticipation.

Sociability and "Love"

On the other hand, probably the feeding experience can be the occasion for the child to learn to like to be with others; that is, it can establish the basis of sociability. When the hungry infant is fed, some of the wonderful relaxation responses which it experiences can be conditioned to the stimuli of those persons who are caring for the child. Thereafter the mere appearance of the mother can produce a momentary feeling of well-being. The child will learn to stop crying at the sound of her footstep, the rustle of her dress, or the sound of the tap water which is warming its bottle. These experiences have an intense emotional quality which is often attached thereafter to the word "mother" as the source of all beneficence.

Likewise, if the child is properly held, cared for, and played with, the blessed relaxing quality of these experiences also will attach to those who care for it. Since the mother or caretaker stands at the very head of the parade of persons who become "society" for the child, it is quite important that she evoke such benign and positive responses in the child.

Lack of Social Feeling

The reverse of all this can also take place if the child is stuffed when it is not hungry. If its food rewards are in various ways cut down and spoiled, it may not care much whether "the others" are there or not. It may tend to be "low in social feeling." If the child is actually punished for crying when it is hungry, as by being slapped, a true hunger-anxiety conflict will be created. Though this may be rare, it does undoubtedly happen, especially when the child is overactive as a result of gastric upset and so is able to provoke anger in the ill-disciplined parent.

One Origin of Fear of Being Alone

The child can learn another dangerous habit in this period. It can learn to fear being alone. Teaching a child to fear being alone is easy to do and is often done inadvertently. Let the child get very hungry when it is alone, let it cry and not be heard or attended to, but let the quantity of stimulation in its body from hunger and from crying continue to rise. When the child is finally fed, these very strong terminal responses are reinforced and can be attached to all the stimuli which were present during the period of its intense hunger. These responses can produce stimuli of drivelike strength. Similarly responses which produce strong drives can be attached to the darkness, to the immobility of objects, to quietness, to absence of parental stimuli. Once the child has inadvertently learned to "fear" darkness and quietness and immobility, it will also learn to escape from the darkness into the light, from the quietness into noise, and from immobility into the presence of others.

This escape may be perceived by the parents as an additional nuisance when they are expecting their hours of relaxation; the child insists on being with them even though "there is nothing wrong with it." They may then take punitive measures, forcing the child back into the dark or the quiet and creating a true conflict between fear of darkness and the newly learned fear of the irate parent. This must indeed be a very common conflict, since fear of quietness and darkness are not innate in children and yet are frequently seen.

If this fear persists into adult life, it can be an element in the character of a person who is compulsively driven to social contacts, who cannot tolerate being alone. Compulsive sociability may also involve a sacrifice in creativeness, since in order to be creative the individual must be able to tolerate a certain amount of loneliness.

Weaning

In the case of weaning also, severe traumatic circumstances may arise. If the child is suddenly changed from one type of food or mode of feeding to another, it may go on a hunger strike which the parents obstinately oppose, saying "It will eat when it gets hungry enough." Indeed it will, but in the meantime it may have learned some of the fears or the apathy already listed. If parents punish the child for its refusal to eat the new food a genuine conflict is created which in turn will have its consequences. There seems hardly anything valuable that an infant can learn by punishment under such circumstances, and parents should take the greatest pains to avoid this.

Colic and Recurring Hunger

The child with colic is also a sore trial to itself and its parents. One of the simplest circumstances producing "colic" is that the infant has eaten too much and must regurgitate some of the food or the gases which its digestion produces. Once it has been laboriously walked or patted into parting with food or gas it may be hungry again. Unimaginative parents, not understanding that hunger has innocently recurred, will fail to feed the child. If the mother does feed it, the child may overeat again and the cycle of gastric tension, vomiting, and hunger may recur. However, until an infant learns to make its gastric distress anticipatory and thus to check itself while eating, there is no way of avoiding these circumstances. The sequence overeating, gastric distress, vomiting, and recurring hunger seems more likely to occur with children fed on schedule since they will get much hungrier while waiting for the scheduled moment of feeding and are more likely to overeat.

If parents lose their tempers and punish the young child at any phase of this awkward kind of learning to eat just the right amount, severe conflict concerning feeding may ensue. If the infant is punished before it is burped, the result may be that it has anxiety attached to burping and regurgitating, and it is thus condemned to bear gastric tension. If it is punished after regurgitating when it is again hungry, anxiety responses will be attached to hunger stimuli. Under these conditions punishment cannot teach the infant anything that will help it along its road to development. Nevertheless this unavoidable circumstance of colic is one to test the character of the most devoted parents.

The foregoing discussion is by no means a check list of all the things that a child can learn during the first year or so of life. For example, in learning to crawl and walk the child is also learning to fear bumps. It learns not to poke its head under the table and then suddenly try to stand erect. It is learning a few words and common commands. Those interested in the somatic development of the child can consult Gesell (1940). Various specialists in pediatrics such as Spock (1946) have described the behavior problems that are most frequent among young children in the home.

Secret Learning of Early Years

What we have attempted to do here is to show that the seemingly innocuous feeding situation can be fraught with important emotional consequences. Outsiders who cannot know what is going on in a home may see no reason to suppose that the infant is learning anything at all. Yet observant insiders may see the child becoming apathetic, apprehensive, learning to fear the dark, on the one hand, or becoming loving, sociable, and confident, on the other. It is this secret learning of the early years which must be made the object of scientific research. We are firmly of the opinion that anything that can be sensed can be scaled and thus that apathy, sociability, and fear can be scientifically treated if we but trouble to study the child in the home—where these habits are being learned.

Early Conflicts Unlabeled, Therefore Unconscious

The young child does not notice or label the experiences which it is having at this time. It cannot give a description of character traits acquired during the first year of life nor yet of its hardships, fears, or deep satisfactions. What was not verbalized at this time cannot well be reported later. An important piece of history is lost and cannot be elicited by questionnaire or interview. Nevertheless, the behavioral record survives. The responses learned occur and may indeed recur in analogous situations throughout life. They are elicited by unlabeled cues and are mutely interwoven into the fabric of conscious life. The fact that different children learn different things during this period undoubtedly accounts for some of the variability between children which is often attributed to innate factors.

2 CLEANLINESS TRAINING CAN CREATE CONFLICTS

If the child has come safely and trustfully through the early feeding and weaning experience it may learn for the first time in its cleanliness training that the culture patterns lying in wait for it have an ugly, compulsive aspect. No child may avoid this training. The demands of the training system are absolute and do not take account of individual differences in learning ability. The child must master cleanliness training or forfeit its place in the ranks of socially acceptable persons. Freud describes the culture's task as building within the personality of the child the psychic dams of loathing and disgust (Freud, 1930, p. 40) for urine and feces and particularly for the latter. The attempt to construct these inward barriers immediately puts the child in a conflict situation.

Observation of children within the home indicates that children begin with the same naïve interest in their feces and urine that they have in the other parts and products of their bodies. Development of the ability to grasp and finger objects makes it possible for the young child to handle and play with fecal material. The morning will arrive in every nursery when the astonished parents will observe their beloved child smearing feces over his person, his hair, and his immediate environment with gurgling abandon. This may be the first occasion for sharp, punishing exhortations, for angry dousing, for the awakening of anxiety in connection with fecal materials. On pain of losing the parents' love and so exposing itself to the high drives and tensions which occur when they do not support it, and on further pain of immediate punishment, the child must learn to attach anxiety to all the cues produced by excretory materials—to their sight, smell, and touch. It must learn to deposit the feces and urine only in a prescribed and secret place and to clean the body. It must later learn to suppress unnecessary verbal reference to these matters, so that, except for joking references this subject matter is closed out and excluded from social reference for life.

Difficulty of Cleanliness Learning

Cleanliness training is difficult because culture must work a reversal of a strong innate connection between a cue and a response. The swelling bladder or bowel produces a strong drive stimulus which at a certain strength releases the urethral sphincter or touches off the evulsion response in the anus. To meet cultural demands this sequence must be rearranged. The connection between bowel stimulus and the evulsion response must be weakened. The child must learn to suppress the evulsion response to the bowel drive-stimulus alone. It must then insert other responses in the sequence. At first it must learn to call to the parents. It must later learn to insert walking, unbuttoning, and sitting on the toilet chair while it is still suppressing the urgent evulsion response. Only to a new pattern of cues—the bowel stimulus, the cues of the proper room, the sense of freedom of clothes, the pressure of the toilet seat on the child's thighs—may the evulsion response occur without anxiety.

In short, this response occurs not only to the pressure of the primary drive involved but also to the complex stimulus pattern just named. If one can once get the child to order the responses correctly, the strong tension reduction produced by defecation will reinforce the responses to the pattern of cues enumerated. The real problem, therefore, is getting the child to suppress the naïve evulsion response and to insert a considerable series of responses into the sequence before evulsion.

We do not revel in the details of this analysis but offer the detailed analysis because we believe it is impossible to understand the difficulty of the learning involved unless one sees all the new units which must be learned. For instance, buttoning and unbuttoning is a difficult habit for small children to learn and may hold up the perfect learning of the sequence for some time. The child, however, is not really trained until it can carry out the whole sequence by itself.

Learning without Verbal Aids

The difficulties which produce conflict in this learning arise chiefly from the fact that the child must accomplish it in a period of life when it has to learn mainly without verbal aids, that is, by trial and error. Learning cleanliness control by trial and error is a slow and vexing business. The child must learn to wake up in order to go to the toilet, though sleep seems good. It must learn to stop its play even when social excitement is strong. It must learn to discriminate between the different rooms of the house—all this by crude trial and error. In this case, "trial" means urinating or defecating in an inappropriate place, and "error" means being punished for the act so that anxiety responses are attached to the cues of this place. In the trial-and-error situation this must be repeated for each inappropriate place—bed, living room, dining room, kitchen, "outside."

The function of this training is to attach anxiety responses to the defecation drive so that they win out over the immediate evulsion response. These anxiety responses also motivate and cue off the next responses in the series, such as calling to the parents, running to the bathroom, unbuttoning the clothes, and the like. When accomplished by trial-and-error means, this training necessarily takes considerable time, perhaps several years in all, in which child and parent are under severe pressure.

Strong Emotions Aroused in Cleanliness Training

Learning cleanliness is no mere behavioral routine. It arouses strong emotions—perhaps as strong as are ever evoked in the child again. Anger, defiance, stubbornness, and fear all appear in the course of such training. Fear may generalize to the toilet itself and excite avoidance responses in the very place where the child is expected to "go." Unable to discriminate between the safe and the unsafe place, the child may try "not to defecate at all." This behavior is perfectly automatic, but it may seem willful to the parents, and they may particularly resent the final loss of control after the protracted attempt to inhibit defecation. Once hit on, this response would be strongly reinforced and tend to become habitual since the drive reduction after prolonged withholding would be much more intense than after a normal period of withholding. When "losing control," instead of deliberately relaxing, is strongly rewarded, the habit of "losing control" should become anticipatory and thus prolong the problem of cleanliness training. In other words, great strictness at early ages may block rather than advance the child in his cleanliness learning.

Learning to Escape from Sight of Parents

The child may become, from the parents' standpoint, furtive by the following means: When it is punished for a cleanliness error by the parent, anxiety is attached to the sights and sounds produced by that parent. In order to escape that anxiety the child may attempt to escape from the parental presence and attempt to keep to a minimum the amount of time it spends near the parent. This state of affairs has the disadvantage that the child is escaping from one of its natural teachers. It may learn to speak less well than it might because it simply does not remain near those people who could teach it to speak. Infliction of punishment may also arouse anger toward the inflicting agent. The child may attempt struggling with the parents, biting them, or slapping at them and, in turn, be punished for this behavior. Thus, an anger-anxiety conflict is learned.

Excessive Conformity and Guilt

Again, the child may get the impression that it is pursued by an all-seeing, punishing guardian and may try making as few responses as possible—and certainly not innovating any novel responses. Its conclusion on the basis of punishments received may be that unless a response is known to be correct it should not be risked. Thus may be laid the characterological basis of the excessively timid, conforming individual. Similarly, the child may not be able to discriminate between parental loathing for its excreta and loathing for the whole child himself. If the child learns to adopt these reactions, feelings of unworthiness, insignificance, and hopeless sinfulness will be created—feelings which sometimes so mysteriously reappear in the psychotic manifestations of guilt.

Advantages of Verbal Aids

From this discussion it will be clear that the trial-and-error method of early training, with its many punishments, has much more risk attached than training carried on at a time when the child can be verbally aided to hit on the right sequence of responses in a few early trials. Once the child has acquired the words "living room," "kitchen," "bedroom," and "outside," a single punishment trial, if properly conducted, can attach anxiety to all these cues at the same time and so spare the brutal repetition of punishment. If the child has already learned to call for help when it needs help, it can much more easily learn to call for aid when it needs to defecate. If it has learned to stop various activities to the word "stop," it is much easier to get it to check the evulsion response when this is occurring to its innate stimulus. If certain promises of the parents already have reward value attached to them, the child can be aided to make the right responses by being promised simple rewards. If the child already attaches anxiety to certain instructions of the parents, these instructions can have some of the same effect as repeated, direct punishments.

In this case also the reinforcement of the act of defecation itself will fix the correct series of responses into place. This will happen whether the course of the training has been stormy or smooth. However, in the case of the smooth, verbally aided learning there is much less danger of arousing furious anger or of creating maladaptive habits such as retention of feces and loss of control. Extremely strong anxiety reactions do not occur and feelings of excessive worthlessness are less likely. The end result is the same so far as mere cleanliness training is concerned. The difference lies in the fact that the later, verbally aided method of getting out the response has much less risk of violent side reactions and character distortions.

Freud's Superego

The foregoing analysis employs the thoughts and sentences of Freud reworked from the standpoint of behavior theory. The course of cleanliness training is unlabeled and unconscious. Any one of us may have been through a stormy period of this kind and yet have no recollection of it. The results may show themselves in our symptoms, our most deeply embedded "character" traits, in our dreams, in our intuitive presuppositions about life, but they will not show themselves in our verbal behavior. The record of this training will be found in no man's autobiography, and yet the fate of the man may be deeply influenced and colored by it.

The first broad strands of what Freud calls the Superego are laid down at this time. Anxiety reactions, never labeled, are attached to stimuli, also unlabeled. When these stimuli recur later the anxiety reactions automatically recur. The resulting effect Freud has called the "Superego" or unconscious conscience. When unconscious guilt reactions are severe, the personality is suffused with terror. It is hard to say whether a morbid conscience is a worse enemy of life than a disease like cancer, but some comparison of this kind is required to emphasize the shock produced in the witness when he sees a psychotic person being tortured by such a conscience. Enough is known now to convince us that we should make the humble-seeming matter of cleanliness training the subject of serious research.

3 CONFLICTS PRODUCED BY EARLY SEX TRAINING

Sex-anxiety conflicts seem frequently to be involved in neuroses arising in civilian life. The recurrent appearance of sex as a conflict element does not seem to be due to the fact that sex is the strongest of human drives. At their highest levels, pain, hunger, and fatigue certainly outrank it. Many strong secondary drives such as anxiety, ambition, and pride can also be stronger than sex. Sex seems to be so frequently implicated because it is the most severely attacked and inhibited of primary drives. Even though relatively weaker, sex can exert a strong pressure which produces great activation in the organism and great misery if blocked for long periods. In no other case is the individual required to wait so many years while patiently bearing the goading drive.

Source of First Sex Conflict—The Masturbation Taboo

Erection of the penis can be observed in male infants as a reflexive response to interrupted feeding or to urethral drive pressure (Halverson, 1938). At the age of a year the child is able to grasp an object quite perfectly. The sensitivity of the genital and the ability to prehend make masturbation possible. It seems likely also that there is some kind of reward associated with masturbating. On the basis of his observations, Kinsey *et al.* (1948) believes that small boys acquire the capacity for orgasm long before they become able to ejaculate; similarly an experiment by Sheffield, Wulff, and Backer (1950) demonstrates that sexual responses short of ejaculation can serve to reinforce learning in the albino rat. It is certainly a fact that, if unchecked, children do learn to masturbate and that they sometimes obstinately persist even when quite severe sanctions are applied.

The sight of a child masturbating evokes intense anxiety in the adults of our culture and they promptly apply sanctions, ranging from persistently removing or jerking the child's hand away from its genital to slapping and spanking it. The result is to set up in the child the same sex-anxiety conflict which the adults have. As in other cases, masturbatory conflicts established in the first years of life are invariably unconscious. A vague negative feeling, a tendency to withdraw, an unease is established at the act, sight, or thought of masturbatory behavior. These conflicts differ for different individuals in many ways and for many reasons. Some individuals may be caught in the act more often than others; some may be punished more severely than others; some may have stronger innate sex drive than others. Some may have had more time to learn the habit before being caught and punished and may thus have a stronger appetite for this behavior than other persons. Some may, so to say, scare easier than others because they already have strong anxieties established in the cleanliness-training situation. Such anxieties generalize easily from urethral to the genital stimuli. Often both are called "nasty" and the cue produced by the common verbal response helps to mediate generalization of fear. In this case it is easy to train the individual out of the masturbatory habit, since the fear does not have to be learned but only generalized to the sex stimuli.

Parents Don't Notice Effects of Taboo

The imposition of a masturbation taboo can have important effects on the child's life. There may be immediate and direct changes in behavior. . . . When behavior changes occur it seems quite surprising that parents do not notice them as results of conflict over masturbation. The fact that they do not so notice is, however, easily explained: Intimate as their contact is with the child they may yet be very poor observers of cause and effect. Most of the young child's emerging life is mysterious to parents anyway. They may further have particular avoidances against noticing matters and connections which arise in the sexual sphere. Likely, they believe themselves to have been sexless in childhood and can do no less than believe the same in respect to their children. Whether correctly evaluated by parents or not, the masturbatory taboo is the first of the important sex taboos, and it sets up a sex-anxiety conflict in each of us.

Sex Typing of Personality

The sexual development of the child cannot be understood without understanding the forceful training in sex typing which it receives. The unspecialized or less specialized human being, the infant, is identified as boy or girl and its relationship with others is defined in terms of sex type. Sex typing is a strictly conventional arrangement that varies from society to society (Mead, 1949). Our own society is strongly organized around sex specialization of personality. This begins with male and female names, clothes, play patterns, toys, and continues throughout life by defining specialized sex roles for man and woman. The ultimate love object of the child is defined as a member of the opposite sex. The nascent sexual reactions of the child are directed toward stimuli of the opposite sex. The child is led to expect eventual sex rewards from persons of the opposite sex.

The Taboo on Homosexuality

Training in sex typing has the indirect effect of imposing a vigorous taboo on homosexuality. Homosexual objects are not presented, are treated by neglect or, if need be, vigorously condemned. The errors children make while learning sex typing are the source of much amusement to adults. The little girl declares she is going "to marry mommie" when she grows up or the little boy states he will marry his admired older brother. Children are carefully corrected and trained into making the appropriate distinctions. Furthermore, it seems probable that parents, already sex-typed, help to develop this turning toward the opposite sex by themselves "favoring" the child of the opposite sex.

Students of sexual abnormalities have suspected that the failure to define sharply the sex type is a factor in producing perverse sex adjustment (Henry, 1948). Thus, if a boy child were ardently desired, the parents might fail to impose sharp feminine sex typing on the girl who actually arrived. Or, in the opposite case, a mother who prefers her son to remain her "baby" may make him effeminate when she should be emphasizing his masculine character. Such inversions of social sex typing cannot directly produce a sexual perversion since sex responses must be attached to same-sex cues before a perverse sex appetite can exist; but they might tend to confuse the child about what its socially expected sex goals were and thus contribute to deviation.

After sex typing has been imposed and well learned, the child is in about this net position: masturbation has been tabooed, and it cannot give itself sex rewards by this means; sex behavior between siblings has been suppressed; on the other hand, a new channel, though a long one, has apparently been opened through the fact of sex typing. The child is vaguely led to expect something rewarding in the general direction of the opposite sex. These two circumstances set up the situation of the Oedipus complex.

How Fear Is Attached to Heterosexual Approach Responses

The anxiety which adolescents, and often adults, show at the prospect of heterosexual contact must be explained. It does not arise by chance. It arises rather in the family situation which is the child's most important early learning situation. The first definition of sexual responses is learned in relation to parents and siblings and only later transferred to others. Freud calls this the Oedipus situation.

We will illustrate from the case of the boy child, where the matter seems to be clear, and rehearse and paraphrase the familiar facts discovered by Freud. The boy child turns to his mother in fact or thought in the hope of getting sex rewards when he can no longer get them by himself. He expects sex rewards partly by generalization (Miller, 1948*b*; von Felsinger, 1948) of expectation of reward—that is, by analogy to the many rewards the mother has already given him—and partly from the fact that by sex typing he has learned to expect sex rewards from a woman and his mother is the woman at hand. Doubtless some of the anxiety already learned in connection with masturbation generalizes to the sex impulse when it begins to show itself toward family women.

A new source of anxiety appears, however; that is, fear of the father. The five-year-old boy knows his father is the head of the house, the symbolic source of punishments and discipline. He also knows that his father is the husband of his mother and has some unique relationship to her. This rivalry of the father does not exist merely in the boy's mind. It is often made very concrete in the father's behavior. The father may complain that the little boy sleeps in the mother's bed when he is already "too old" for such behavior. The father may object to the fact that the child or children sop up so much of the mother's time and leave so little to him. The father may impose certain restrictions about entering the parents' room which leave the child with a mystery on his hands. Whenever the male child makes emotional demands on the mother, the father may become more critical of him in other and more general respects, saying that the boy talks too much, that he does not work enough, and so forth. If the boy reacts with fear toward his father as a rival, it is because the father, consciously or unconsciously, is acting in a way that seems fearsome and rivalrous. The child is usually unable to discriminate between opposition on ground of sexual learnings and that evoked by its other claims on the mother. The whole thing may be played out as a kind of dumb show. The heterosexual strivings of the boy toward the mother may be behaviorally real and active but not labeled in the boy's mind. On the other hand, the opposition of the father, though active and effective, may be oblique and unconscious.

Often the mother herself rejects the claims of the boy. She has anxiety at any overtly sexual responses from the child, stops fondling him, and may suddenly and inexplicably change from being loving and approving to being horrified, disgusted, and disapproving.

In this case there is less need for the father to be harsh and hostile. But if the mother does not reject and does not clearly show her separate loyalty and adherence to the father, a great burden is placed upon him to maintain his control of his wife. The mother, for example, may use the seeming need of the child as a way of escaping from her husband and from the sexual conflicts which she has in regard to him. She may favor and cozen the son while avoiding her husband, and unconsciously this may seem to the father like a genuine kind of preferment. The father may then react by very actively arousing the boy's fears.

Specific Genital Anxiety

If the boy's motives are sexual, the increased threat from the father produces anxiety which is directly attached to the sexual motives and interpreted as a sexual threat. This is one way in which castration anxiety may become an important factor in the boy's life even though the father never threatens castration in so many words. The boy has learned that the punishment often fits the crime.

There are other and less ghostly sources of the castration threat. Very often it has been specifically associated with the masturbation taboo—*i.e.*, that if the boy plays with his penis, the penis will be cut off. The threat may appear in the fables of childhood which are told so eagerly. One of the authors as a six-year-old boy was permitted to participate in an after-dark session of older boys. They were telling the tale of how Bill Smith, a prominent citizen of the town, had come home and surprised his wife in bed with her lover. Smith thereupon pulled out a spring-labeled jackknife (demonstration of length and viciousness of same by boy telling the story) and proceeded to unman the lover. Such a story does not remain, however, as a mere "fable." It is taken to heart and has the effect of teaching straight-out castration fear to sex motives.

The castration idea may occur in still another way; that is, as an inference from the lack of penis in the girl. The parents do not explain the different nature of the girl's genital. The uninstructed boy may assume that the girl once had an external genital but has been deprived of it, perhaps as a punishment. There is no doubt that this inference is often made. The authors have repeatedly heard it in those in-family situations where children are first questioning their elders about sexual matters. It is further surprising in the history of adults how often the idea of bodily damage occurs in relation to sex "sins." Castration fear has been shown clinically to be connected with fears of bodily damage, especially in the cases of heart and brain, to aversion to crippled people, and to avoidance of women in their genital aspect. Castration fear is frequently escaped by approaching the bachelor girl (who has no husband or father at her side) or by recourse to women of lower class or racial status (whose normal protectors are not allowed to function).

In any case, and engendered by whatever of these several means or combination of them, the sex conflict takes a new twist when it is worked out within the family. Anxiety which was once attached only to the masturbation impulse is now attached to the heterosexual approach situation. If this anxiety is made very strong it can produce a certain relief in the intensity of the conflict. This is the so-called "resolution" of the Oedipus complex. When anxiety is greatly dominant over approach tendencies, the conflicted individual stays far from his goal and but few of the acquired elements in the sexual appetite are aroused. Thus, that part of the intensity of the conflict which is produced by appetitive sex reactions is missing, and the conflict is therefore lessened. However, this conflict should and does recur when the individual is placed near his goal object and cannot easily escape, as frequently happens in adolescence. Then again the full strength of the sex reactions is pitted against the terror of sexual injury. Marriage evidently seems to some adults a similar situation—that of being held close to a feared goal—and they make the blind escape responses which would be expected.

Heterosexual Conflict Not Labeled

If the prior intimidation of the person has been very great, and if the mother's stand is correct, much less fear need be imposed by the father. If sex appetite is weak rather than strong, there is much less pressure from the child's side and less anxiety need be imposed to counteract it.

All these events are but poorly labeled at the time they occur. The culture is niggardly about giving names to sexual organs, sexual feelings, or the fears attached to them. The child is therefore not able to make a logical case for itself and, so to say, "put it up to the parents." Furthermore, repression sets in in two ways: Children are frequently forbidden to talk to others about their sexual reactions. Such sentences or thoughts as do occur tend to make the conflict keener both by arousing sex appetites and by cueing off the anxiety attached to them. The child is pained when it tries to think about sexual things and relieved when it stops. The result is repression. This repression has one unfortunate consequence for science. When the individual is later interviewed he is not able, promptly and freely, to give account of these matters. The renaming and mental reestablishment of these bygone events can thereafter only be made through the weary work of psychotherapy.

Science is not the only loser. The individual himself has lost his opportunity to use higher mental activities in solving the conflicts involving sex and authority. There are many ways in which the person can be victimized. A sexual perversion may lurk behind the blank surface of repression. The individual may never again be able cheerfully and amiably to accept a measure of authority exerted over him. Acute anxiety may be attached to his heterosexual impulses and when the time comes that society expects, almost requires, that he marry, he may be unable to do so. Even though he is able to get over the line into marriage, he may find the years of his marital life haunted and poisoned by constant, unconscious anxiety. In this case, the individual has automatically generalized to all women the anxiety proper only to the incest situation. He has failed to discriminate, as a free mental life would enable him to do, between the tabooed sexual feelings and objects of childhood and the relative freedom permitted to adults. To every authoritarian figure in his life he generalizes the intense anxiety that he once experienced when attempting to rival his father in the sexual field. Only when higher mental processes are restored can the individual make those discriminations which allow him to proceed freely and constructively with his life as an adult.

4 ANGER-ANXIETY CONFLICTS

At this point we are more interested in the connection between angry emotions and fear than we are in the problem of how angry feelings are aroused in the child. We assume, however, as before (Dollard *et al.,* 1939) that anger responses are produced by the innumerable and unavoidable frustration situations of child life. In the frustration situation, new and strong responses are tried out. Some of these have the effect of inflicting pain on other people. Society takes a special stand toward such anger responses, generally inhibiting them and allowing them reign only in a few circumstances (self-defense, war, etc.). Many of these attack, or "put through the act," responses produce strong stimuli, and these we recognize as the emotion of anger. Lift the veil of repression covering the childhood mental life of a neurotic person and you come at once upon the smoking responses of anger.

Patriarchal Code on Child's Anger

Parents intuitively resent and fear the anger and rage of a child, and they have the strong support of the culture in suppressing its anger. Direct punishment is probably used much more frequently when the child is angry and aggressive than in any other circumstance. More or less without regard to what the child is angry about, fear is attached to the stimuli of anger. The virtuous chastisement of the rebellious child is an age-old feature of our patriarchal culture. According to the old Connecticut Blue Laws, a father could kill a disobedient son (Blue Laws of Connecticut, 1861, Section 14, p. 69). Even though this code was never exercised in this extreme in recent times, it shows the complete freedom to punish which was once culturally allowed parents. As the domestic representative of the patriarch in his absence, the mother is free to punish children "in their own interest."

How Fear Is Attached to Anger Cues

We have already noted the situation of early cleanliness training as one tending to produce angry confusion in the small child. At earliest ages the cultural practice seems to be that of extinguishing anger rather than punishing it; that is, the child is segregated, left to "cry and thresh it out." However, parents' motivation to teach the child cleanliness training is so strong that they frequently also use punishment, especially in the case of what they interpret as stubborn or defiant behavior. Anxiety responses therefore become attached not only to the cues produced by the forbidden situation but also to the cues produced by the emotional responses which the child is making at the time. It is this latter connection which creates the inner mental or emotional conflict. After this learning has occurred, the first cues produced by angry emotions may set off anxiety responses which "outcompete" the angry emotional responses themselves. The person can thus be made helpless to use his anger even in those situations where culture does permit it. He is viewed as abnormally meek or long-suffering. Robbing a person of his anger completely may be a dangerous thing since some capacity for anger seems to be needed in the affirmative personality.

Other Frustrations Producing Anger

The same state of affairs can prevail and be additionally reinforced as a result of the frustrations occurring in the sex-training situation. If the child is punished for masturbating it may react with the response of anger. The parent may not notice the provocative circumstance but see only that the child has become mysteriously "naughty." Its naughtiness may be punished and the connection between anger and fear be strengthened.

Parental rejection or desertion may likewise produce anger in the child. If the child feels secure only when the parents are present, it may react with fear when the parents leave or when they threaten to leave again. When the parents return, the child may make excessive claims, want unusual favors, "be clingy." To these demanding and possessive gestures on the part of the child the parent may react with unintelligent punishment, thus again teaching the child to fear.

The new tasks involved in growing up impose many frustrations on the child. Giving up long-standing privileges may arouse rage. Being forced to try out new responses, such as putting on his own clothes or tying its own shoe laces, can anger the child. If it screams, lunges, slaps at the parent in these circumstances, punishment is the almost inevitable answer, and the connection between anger and fear is additionally strengthened.

Sibling Rivalry

Rivalry between siblings is a constant incitement to anger, and such rivalry occurs in every household, without exception, where there are siblings of younger ages. The occasions for rivalry seem innumerable. Siblings may compete for evidences of parental love. If the parent disappoints a child, that child may "take it out" on the luckier brother or sister. Younger children may anger older ones by being allowed to assume too quickly privileges which the older have long waited and worked for. Older children may tease and torment younger ones in retaliation. Sometimes the younger child is resented merely for existing and for having displaced the older one and alloyed its satisfaction in being the unique child.

The younger children may enjoy privileges which the older have been forced to abandon and thus create some degree of unconscious resentment. Younger children may tyrannize over older ones by too freely playing with or even destroying their toys and precious objects. Parents should intervene and prevent such behavior but often they do not, and the older child revenges himself in roundabout ways. Younger children may resent the privileges enjoyed by the older and attempt to punish older siblings for their greater freedom. These angry displays result in punishment of the one or the other child by the parents—and sometimes of both. The younger children tend to "catch it" more from the older, and the older children more from the parents. Though parents may mitigate these angry relationships between siblings by just rules which are honestly enforced, there seems no way to take all the hostile strain out of such relations.

Mental Limitations

Small children confront an unintelligible world. Many of their frustrations result from this fact. They do not have the mental units to be patient and foresightful. They do not know how to comfort themselves while waiting. They cannot live in the light of a plan which promises to control the future. Since so much is frustrating to them that is later bearable, they are especially prone to anger. They want to know "Why isn't the circus here today?" "Why do I have to wait 'til my birthday to get a present?" "Why does Daddy have to go to work just when it's so much fun to play with him?" Living in the present and being unable to reassure themselves about the future, young children resort to anger at these inevitable frustrations. Adults experience the hostile or destructive behavior of young children as a nuisance, do not understand its inevitability, and frequently punish aggressive responses.

Devious Aggression

If anger must be abandoned as a response in a frustrating situation, other responses will be tried out such as pleading for what one cannot take by force or submitting to frustrations which can only be worsened through opposition. Devious forms of aggression are particularly likely to occur in this case. The individual can be punished for direct anger responses but it is much harder to catch him at roundabout aggression. He may learn to lie in wait and take revenge by hastening and sharpening punishment which his opponent has invoked in some other way. Gossip, deceit, creating dangerous confusion about agreements and life relationships may all be indirect modes of angry reaction.

Anger Conflict Unlabled

As in the case of sex-anxiety conflicts, the anger-anxiety conflict is likely to be poorly labeled. Verbal skills are at a low level when much of this training is going on. Repression of the language describing anger-anxiety conflicts may occur because conflict is thus, momentarily at least, reduced. As a result, the individual cannot, in later life, be selectively angry, showing anger in just those social situations in which it is permitted and rejecting anger where it is not.

The Overinhibited Person

Inhibition of anger may occur in two different degrees. The overt, or some of the overt, responses of direct aggression may be inhibited. Some such inhibitions must occur if a child is to live in our culture. The process may, however, go farther and the emotion of anger itself be throttled. If the response-produced drives of anger evoke intense fear, the individual may be incapable of a normal life. The victim loses the core of an affirmative personality. He may be unable to compete as is demanded by our society in school or business spheres. He may be additionally shamed because he cannot bring himself to fight. He may depend unduly on others, waiting for them to give him what is everyone's right to take. Such a child cannot be a self-maintaining person because he cannot produce any anger responses at all, let alone those which are "legitimate and proper."

Since many outlets for anger are permitted adults which are not permitted to children, the person who is overtrained to inhibit anger may seem childish in that he is still following the age-graded code of childhood and is unable to embrace the freer standards of adulthood. One of the chief tasks of psychotherapy, in the case of unduly inhibited persons, is to enable them to name and describe their angry feelings so that they may extinguish undue fear and begin to learn a proportionate self-assertiveness.

FRUSTRATED MOBILITY ASPIRATIONS PRODUCE AGGRESSION

There is little doubt that adults can be in conflict concerning their mobility strivings and that these conflicts can lead to pathological results in behavior (Ruesch, Loeb, *et al.*, 1946). The conflict could be described somewhat as follows: In order to be strong and safe, or stronger and safer, the person wants to identify with and possess the symbols of a social group above that of his original family. In order to make this transition, however, certain prescribed routes must be followed. The person must have a talent which brings him in touch with and makes him useful to the group into which he wants entry. This talent could be intellectual, could be a facility for making money, could be beauty, could be an exceptionally loving and understanding personality. If an individual has the wish to change position but does not have such a talent or does not enjoy it to a sufficient degree, he may find it impossible to make the transition. He may find himself unable to establish the contacts which will enable him to learn the rituals of behavior of the superordinate group. He may gradually come to know that, though "the promised land" is in sight, he will never enter it. Meanwhile the group he is trying to leave punishes him for being "different" and the group he tries to enter rejects him as presumptuous. The realization, conscious or unconscious, that his campaign has failed may serve as a severe frustration and produce varying types of aggressive and compensatory behavior. The resentment of the person who fails of mobility is likely to be severely punished and thus to create an acute anger-fear conflict.

Mobility Conflicts Which Are Unconscious

Except in one circumstance, which we shall come to in a moment, it does not seem likely that conflicts such as the one just described are engendered in early childhood. The conflict may nevertheless be unconscious. This unconsciousness of the elements of an adult conflict can arise because the mobile person gets little help from his society in labeling his behavior. He is not told what he is trying to do, and he has no clear understanding of what the techniques are. If he hits on the means of mobility, it is, from his point of view, a matter of luck or accident. He is ordinarily not permitted to think that different social classes exist because the social beliefs which protect the class system forbid this recognition. Usually the mobile individual sees himself only as rising in some value such as "wealth" or occupation but he does not realize that his real mobility will be founded on a complex set of behavioral adaptations and changes in taste and outlook. Usually, therefore, the mobile person does not know what is happening to him while it is happening, does not know how he failed if he fails, and does not know until "afterward" how he succeeds if he succeeds. This is a set of conditions which is bound to baffle and to arouse a confusion of angry, rebellious, apathetic, and submissive responses.

Children of a Mixed-class Marriage

The one circumstance that we can see under which difference in social class can have an effect on a small child is the case where the child is born of a mixed-class marriage. If the mother is superordinate, she might in some ways "look down" on the father, apologize for him, and limit his usefulness as a model to her male child. Such a mother may be unduly "ambitious" for her children, attempting to speed them over the landscape of childhood instead of allowing them to find their natural pace through it. She may get satisfaction in imposing early cleanliness training because it seems to her like a guarantee of the future precocity of the child. She may inculcate the sex taboos strongly because she feels that the "goodness" of the child in this respect will keep it out of "bad company" and aid its development in the schools. She may handle its angry tendencies severely in the hope of making it amenable and yet urge it to highly competitive performance outside the home. One would predict that this kind of family training would give a special coloring to the circumstances which ordinarily produce conflict in small children (Davis and Havighurst, 1947; Warner, 1949, pp. 70–72).

A child in a class-stable family with parents matched from the class standpoint would not ordinarily discover in the early years of life that there is any group "above" its parents. During the formative period these parents would play their august roles, majestic in their competence and authority so far as the child could see. It would only be later in life, perhaps first during school days, that the child would learn that there are any people who look down upon it or its parents. Undoubtedly such knowledge would have some kind of effect on the career of the child, but we cannot say what the possible outcomes might be. We can be sure, however, that the evaluation put on the self and the family by the surrounding society will be a fact of importance in the developmental history of every child.

REFERENCES

Blue Laws of Connecticut. Capital Laws. Code of 1650, Section 14, Duane Rulison, Philadelphia, 1861.

Davis, Allison, and Havighurst, Robert, *Father of the Man,* Houghton Mifflin, Boston, 1947.

Dollard, John, Doob, L. W., Miller, N. E., and Sears, R. R., *Frustration and Aggression,* Yale University Press, New Haven, 1939.

Freud, Sigmund, *Three Contributions to the Theory of Sex,* 4th ed., Nervous and Mental Disease Publishing Company, Washington, D.C., 1930.

Gesell, Arnold, *The First Five Years of Life,* Harper, New York, 1940.

Halverson, H. M., "Infant sucking and tensional behavior," *J. gen. Psychol.,* **53**:365–430, 1938.

Henry, G. W., *Sex Variants,* 1-vol. ed., Hoeber-Harper, New York, 1948.

Kinsey, A. C., Pomeroy, W. B., and Martin, C. E., *Sexual Behavior in the Human Male,* Saunders, Philadelphia, 1948.

Mead, Margaret, *Male and Female,* Morrow, New York, 1949.

Miller, N. E., "Theory and experiment relating psychoanalytic displacement to stimulus response generalization," *J. abnorm. soc. Psychol.,* **43**:155–178, 1948*b*.

Ruesch, Jurgen, Loeb, M. B., *et al., Chronic Disease and Psychological Invalidism: A Psychosomatic Study,* American Society for Research in Psychosomatic Problems, New York, 1946.

Sheffield, F. D., Wulff, J. J., and Backer, Robert, 1950. "Reward Value of Sexual Stimulation without Ejaculation" (in preparation).

Spock, Benjamin, *Baby and Child Care,* Pocket Books, New York, 1946.

von Felsinger, John, "The Effects of Ovarian Hormones on Learning," Ph.D. dissertation, Yale University, New Haven, 1948.

Warner, W. L., and Associates, *Democracy in Jonesville,* Harper, New York, 1949.

The Effect of Rearing Conditions on Behavior*

Harry F. Harlow and Margaret K. Harlow

A wealth of clinical evidence shows that human children who have never had adequate maternal care or who have been separated from adequate maternal care within some critical state, suffer disturbance and delay or even irreparable damage in terms of subsequent personal-social development. The importance of maternal ministrations in the child's development is further supported by many clinical investigations and by some limited experimental data.

Personality malfunctions that have been attributed to maternal inadequacy include such syndromes as marasmus, hospitalism, infantile autism, feeble-mindedness, inadequate maternal responsiveness, and deviant or depressed heterosexuality. If these disorders are the results of maternal inadequacy, only research with human subjects can establish the conditions and kinds of maternal behavior that produce them. Unfortunately, experiments critical to the resolution of these problems cannot be done with human subjects. We cannot rear babies in illuminated black boxes during the first half-year, year, or two years of their lives. We cannot have mothers rear their children in isolation from other children and from adults for the first two, four, or eight years. We dare not have human children reared with either no mothers or inadequate mothers while providing them with maximal opportunity to interact with age-mates, either identically reared or differentially reared. Yet these are the kinds of experiments which are required if we are to assess the effects of maternal variables unconfounded with other experiential variables on the child's personal-social development.

Most clinical investigations have given primary attention to the effects of maternal privation, defined as absence or inadequacy of maternal responsiveness, or to maternal deprivation, defined as infant separation after the infant has established profound, or at least adequate, maternal attachments. Relatively little attention has been given to the effects of the absence or inadequacy of opportunity for the child to interact with other children and to form adequate affectional patterns with and for them. We know that it is important for the child to form effective infant-mother affectional patterns, but it also is likely that he must form effective child-child affectional patterns if he is to attain normal personal-social, sexual, and paternal patterns. Obviously these affectional systems are not independent. It is possible, but by no means a certainty, that at the human level, normal child-child affection requires previous affectional bonds between mother or mother-figure and child. It is certain that the mother plays an important role in the formation of peer affections by providing for and encouraging associations between infants or children, or by preventing or discouraging such associations. Human mothers may also markedly influence the nature and course of child-child relationships.

Psychoanalytic theory, which looks for temporal reduction and temporal primacy, will ascribe primary importance to the earliest causes and conditions whether or not

*From Harry F. Harlow and Margaret K. Harlow, "The Effect of Rearing Conditions on Behavior," *Bull. Menninger Clinic,* 1962, **25,** 213–226. Reprinted by permission of the authors and the Editor, *Bulletin of the Menninger Clinic.*

these are of greatest importance. Initial traumas have a false clarity as causative agents since they are not confounded by preceding events, whereas the role of all subsequent events is confounded by the role of these events operating during previous experience. Yet primacy in time need not, and often should not, be equated with primacy in importance.

EFFECTS OF TOTAL SOCIAL DEPRIVATION ON MONKEYS

Six years ago we took two newborn rhesus monkeys, one male and one female, and subjected them to total social deprivation for the first two years of life. Each was placed in a solid, illuminated cage such that it never saw any other animal—monkey or human—even though it was tested for food responsiveness and learning by remote-control techniques. During isolation these monkeys adapted to solid food slowly and learned with great difficulty, but they were found to have normal weight and good coats when removed—there were no signs of marasmus. At the conclusion of the two years' isolation, they were tested for social responsiveness to each other and to normal monkeys smaller and younger than themselves. They did not respond to each other and either froze or huddled in a corner when abused by the younger animals. Placed together in a cage in a room with many caged monkeys, they showed withdrawal from the new external world, and in the more than two years they lived together, they remained abnormally frightened, showed minimal interaction, and engaged in no sex activities. In follow-up social tests at four years of age with smaller and weaker monkeys, they made no effort to defend themselves except for one brief episode with one of the pair, after which it curled into a ball and passively accepted abuse. The potential for social behaviors in these animals had apparently been obliterated.

We have preliminary, incomplete data on the effects of such total social deprivation confined to a six-month period and are obtaining other data on the effects of such deprivation over a twelve-month period. The results to date indicate severe but not complete withdrawal from external environmental stimulation. Repeated testing in our playroom situation, shown in Figure 1, reveals that one of these monkeys is almost totally unresponsive socially and the other only occasionally engages in brief, infantile-type social interactions. Normally, the playroom is a highly stimulating situation for monkeys. It is 8 feet high with 36 square feet of floor space, and it contains multiple stationary and mobile toys and tools, flying rings, a rotating wheel, an artificial tree, a wire-mesh climbing ramp, and a high, wide ledge, offering opportunities to explore and play in a three-dimensional world.

We also have data on eight monkeys subjected to total social isolation from other monkeys during the first 80 days of life. Although they neither saw nor contacted nor heard other monkeys, they did see and contact human experimenters, who removed them from their isolation boxes and tested them repeatedly on learning problems after the second week of life. A year later these animals appear to be normally responsive to external environmental stimulation and they are socially responsive to each other when tested in the playroom. This social responsiveness as measured by the appearance of increasingly complex play patterns has become qualitatively normal, but probably it is depressed somewhat quantitatively. Whether there will be subsequent effects on heterosexual and maternal behavior remains for future observation.

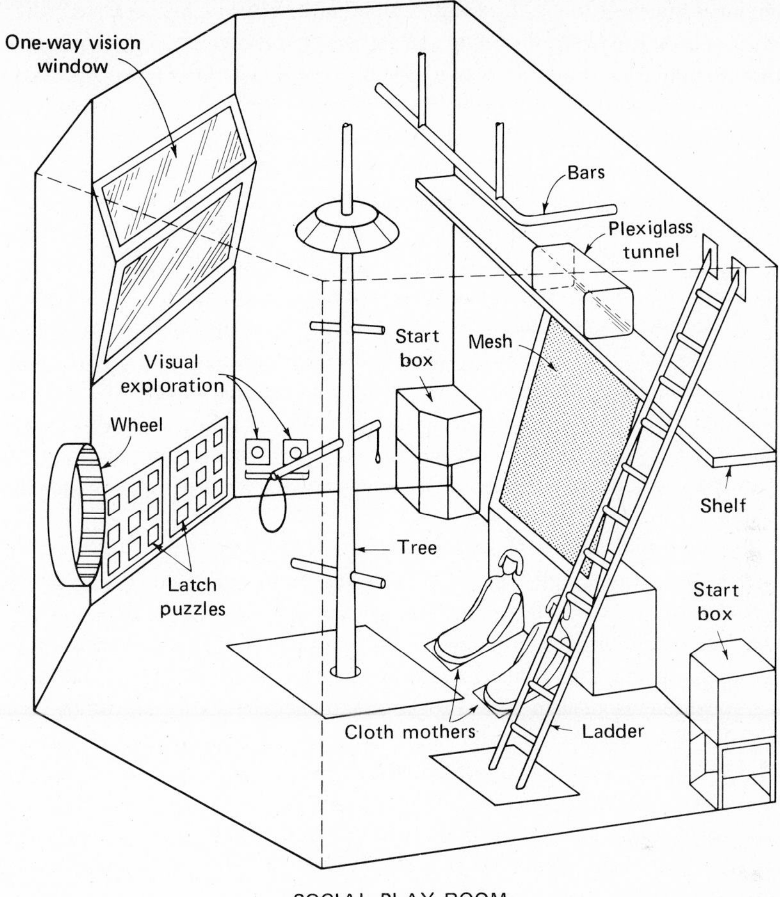

Figure 1

If we assume a rough developmental ratio of four to one for monkey to man, the results on these eight monkeys are not completely in accord with human clinical data, which at best are only roughly comparable to our experimental situation. Social isolation up to eight or ten months of age is reported to endanger or impair the personal-social development of human infants. It may be that the stimulation and handling of the monkeys in the learning experiments played a positive role in preparing them for subsequent exposure to a monkey environment, thus minimizing the isolation effects. It is also possible that the human infant is more susceptible than the monkey infant to damage from social isolation.

EFFECTS OF EARLY PARTIAL SOCIAL DEPRIVATION

We have data on various groups of monkeys raised from the day of their birth without their mothers and without any monkey companionship at least through the first half-year. One group of 56, now ranging in age from five to eight years, was raised in individual bare wire cages where they could see and hear other monkeys, but not touch them. A group of four was similarly housed for up to five years, but had access to a single wire surrogate[1] during the first half-year of life. A third group of over 100 monkeys was raised identically except for access to a cloth surrogate[2] or to both a cloth surrogate and a wire surrogate during at least six months of the first year.[3] Approximately half of these animals have been housed after six months or one year of age with another monkey of like age and like or unlike sex for part or all the time since.

Although there may be differences in the personal-social behaviors of the monkeys comprising these groups, we cannot be sure at the present time, and for this reason we group them together. Many members of all three groups have developed what appear to be abnormal behaviors, including sitting and staring fixedly into space, repetitive stereotyped circling movements about the cage, clasping the head in the hands and arms while engaging in rocking, autistic-type movements, and intrapunitive responses of grasping a foot, hand, arm, or leg and chewing or tearing at it with the teeth to the point of injury.

The sex behavior of the six oldest wire-cage-raised monkeys was first measured by Mason[4] in 1960 and compared with that of rhesus monkeys of equal age which had lived in the wild during most of the first year of life. All the wild-raised monkeys, male and female, showed normal sex behavior, characterized in the male by dorsoventral mounting, clasping the legs of the female by the feet, and holding the buttocks by the hands. The females in turn sexually presented themselves by elevating their buttocks and tails, lowering their heads, and frequently looking backward without threatening. No laboratory-raised male or female showed normal sex behavior. Attempted mounting by the male was random in regard to body part, and the most frequent pattern was grasping a side of the female's body and thrusting laterally. The female's patterns were totally disordered and often involved sitting down and staring aimlessly into space. Although none of these animals was sexually mature, heterosexual positioning in both male and female normally develops during the second year.

Attempts to breed the cage-raised monkeys approximately two years later also ended in complete failure. When the oldest wire-cage-raised females were between five and seven years of age and the oldest surrogate-raised females were between three and five years, repeated attempts were made to breed 11 of the wire-cage-raised females and four of the cloth-surrogate-raised females with highly selected males from our breeding colony. The females were placed in the large breeding cages during estrus, and if no fighting ensued within 15 minutes, they were left overnight. Eventually one wire-cage-raised female and three cloth-surrogate females became

[1]A wire surrogate mother is a bare, welded wire cylindrical form surmounted by a wooden head with a crude face and supported semiupright in a wooden frame.

[2]A cloth surrogate differs from the wire surrogate in that the wire cylinder is cushioned with a sheathing of terry cloth.

[3]Harlow, H. F.: The Nature of Love. *Amer. Psychologist,* 1958, **13,** 673–685. Harlow, H. F.: Love in Infant Monkeys. *Sci. Amer.,* 1959, **200,** 68–74.

[4]Mason, W. A.: The Effects of Social Restriction on the behavior of Rhesus Monkeys: I. Free Social Behavior. *J. Comp. Physiol. Psychol.,* 1960, **53,** 582–589.

pregnant. Although observation did not reveal clear-cut differences in the behavior of these two groups, the differences in pregnancy approach significance in spite of—or possibly because of—the greater immaturity of the cloth-surrogate-raised females. Actually, no female, impregnated or not, demonstrated a normal pattern of sexual behavior. Many females tried to avoid the males; some actually threatened the males and would probably have been injured had our males not been carefully screened. When the males approached and positioned the females, the females usually collapsed and fell flat on the floor. Impregnation of the four females was achieved only through the patience, persistence, knowledgeability, and motor skill of the breeding males.

We have subsequently tested many wire-cage- and surrogate-mother-raised males and females with experienced breeding females and experienced breeding males, respectively, in a large 8-foot by 8-foot by 8-foot room especially designed for breeding studies. All the males have continued to show the disorganized and inappropriately oriented sexual responsiveness which we have already described, and no male has ever appropriately mounted our experienced and cooperative breeding-stock females, let alone achieved intromission.

With a single exception we have never seen normal, appropriate sexual posturing in our wire-cage- or surrogate-raised females. The females do not approach the males, nor do they groom or present. One cloth-surrogate-raised female was not impregnated throughout six mating sessions, and during this time she began to respond positively and appropriately to the males and eventually developed a normal, full-blown pattern of sexual presentation and sexual posturing during copulation.

EFFECTS OF MATERNAL CONDITIONS

Direct comparison of the effects of being raised by real monkey mothers and cloth surrogate mothers on subsequent personal-social development has been measured by the use of our playpen test situation. In two playpen situations babies were housed with their real mothers, and in a third setup the babies were housed with cloth mothers. The playpen, whose floor plan is given in Figure 2, consists of large living cages each housing a mother and an infant and adjoining a compartment of the playpen. A small opening in each living cage restrains the mother, but gives the infant continuous access to the adjoining playpen compartment. During two daily test sessions, each an hour in length, the screens between playpen compartments were raised, permitting the infant monkeys to interact as pairs during the first six months and as both pairs and groups of four during the second six months. Two experimenters independently observed and recorded the behavior exhibited during test sessions.

The infants raised by real monkey mothers were more socially responsive to each other than were the infants raised by the cloth surrogates. They showed a wider range of facial expressions, and, probably of paramount importance, they developed simple interactive play patterns earlier than the surrogate-raised monkeys and achieved a level of complex play patterns not achieved by the surrogate-raised monkeys during an 18-month test period.

All the male, mother-raised infants have at one time or another responded sexually toward the mother with pelvic thrusting and in at least two cases by

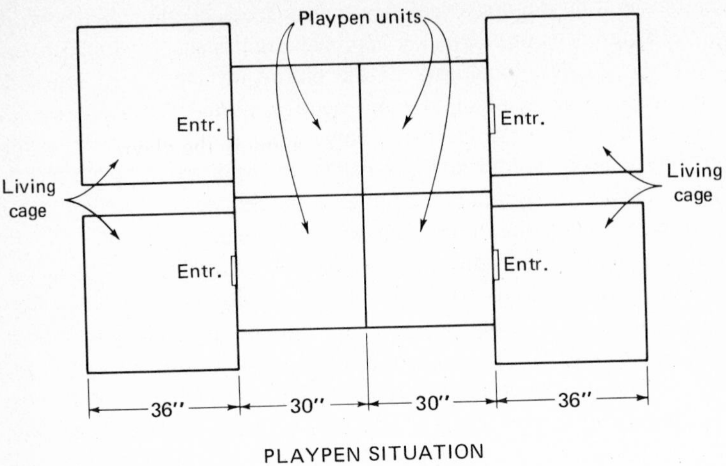

Figure 2

dorsoventral mounting. In three cases pelvic thrusting to a female was observed before 50 days of age and in a fourth case, before 100 days of age. Only two (one male and one female) cloth-surrogate-raised monkeys were observed to show pelvic thrusting to the surrogate, and this occurred initially at approximately 100 days of age. Frequency of this sexual play was much higher toward real mothers than toward surrogates. In both situations maximal frequency occurred at about five months and then declined, apparently being superseded by thrusting directed toward other infants.

Surrogate babies and mothered babies showed no significant differences in first-observed, infant-directed thrusting, but the actual mean score of the surrogate group was lower. The frequency of sexual play was higher for the real-mothered babies than for the surrogate babies. Finally, seven of eight mother-raised monkeys showed appropriate adult-form sex behaviors during the first 18 months, including ankle clasp by the males, whereas adult-oriented sex behavior was not observed in the cloth-surrogate-raised babies.

There is every reason to believe that normal mothering facilitates the development of heterosexual behavior in rhesus monkeys. This may be in part the result of direct contacts with the mother growing out of the intimate bonds between mother and child. One must not, however, underestimate the importance of the role which the real mother apparently plays, indirect though it is, in stimulating the infants to associate with other infants. This is accomplished from the third month on by discouraging the infant from constant clinging as it matures. From time to time the mother restrains the infant's approaches or cuffs it if it nips her or pulls her hair. The chastised infant seeks the companionship of other babies until the storm subsides—the other mothers by this time generally reject all but their own babies—and in the infant-infant interchanges, strong affectional bonds develop along with behaviors, sexual and nonsexual, appropriate to the sexes.

In the present study, as in all ordinary human situations, there is confounding in the roles played by the mother-infant affectional systems and the infant-infant and peer-peer affectional systems in determining later behavior. We expect to resolve this in part by raising two groups of monkey babies with real mothers, but denying them any opportunity to interact with other infants for six months in the one group and 12 months in the other before subjecting them to social testing.

Some information is supplied by another experiment involving eight rhesus babies raised on cloth surrogate mothers, but tested 20 minutes a day in the playroom, which is a more stimulating environment than that afforded by the relatively cramped and bare confines of the play compartments of the playpen situation. These surrogate-mothered babies showed excellent and appropriately timed play behaviors and very early came to assume both sexual and nonsexual behaviors appropriate to males and females. The males threatened, the females did not; the males initiated rough-and-tumble play, but not the females. Male chased males and males chased females, but females practically never chased males and seldom chased females. By a year of age considerable appropriate male and female sex behavior had occurred, and full and complete copulation, other than insemination, was repeatedly observed in the two males and two females on which observations were continued during the second year of life.

It is obvious that we must not underestimate the importance and role of the infant-infant affectional system as a determiner of adolescent and adult adjustments. It is more than possible that this system is essential if the animal is to respond positively to sheer physical contact with a peer, and it is through the operation of this system, probably both in monkey and man, tht sexual roles become identified and, usually, acceptable.

The role of the mother in the formation of the adult personality is obviously important, but the exact mechanics are open for experimentation. The most tender and intimate associations occur at a stage in which the monkey infant and human infant can to a considerable extent be molded. Monkey and human mother both have the obligation of gradually dissolving the intense physical bonds which characterize the early mother-child relationship. For the monkey mother it is easy and natural—when the infant becomes mature enough and strong enough to become bothersome, she rejects or punishes it and the baby retreats for a time. Subsequently, she welcomes the baby back. Independence is gradually established. For the human mother, with her more complicated motivational systems and her complex culture, it may be difficult to achieve this gradual separation. The overprotective mother is a well-known clinical extreme in the human problem of weaning the infant and child emotionally. Probably the surrogate monkey mother is a parallel of the overprotective human mother, failing usually to equal the normal mother in rearing socially and sexually adjusted monkeys because, at least in part, she is ever available to provide comfort and security. She never discourages contact and thereby never encourages independence in her infant and affectional relationships with other infants and children. The normal state of complete dependency necessary in early infancy is prolonged until it hinders normal personal-social development.

As we have already pointed out, four of our laboratory-raised females never had real mothers of their own, one being raised in a bare wire cage and three with cloth surrogates. The first week after the birth of the baby to the wire-cage-raised female, the mother sat fixedly at one side of the cage staring into space, almost unaware of her infant or of human beings, even when they barked at and threatened the baby.

There was no sign of maternal responses, and when the infant approached and attempted contact, the mother rebuffed it, often with vigor.

The next two unmothered mothers constantly rebuffed the approaches of their infants, but, in addition, frequently engaged in cruel and unprovoked attacks. They struck and beat their babies, mouthed them roughly, and pushed their faces into the wire-mesh floor. These attacks seemed to be exaggerated in the presence of human beings, and for this reason all formal testing was abandoned for three days for the third unmothered mother because we feared for the life of the infant. The fourth unmothered mother ignored and rejected her infant but did not exhibit excessive cruelty.

In strong contrast to the frailty of the maternal affectional system was the vigor and persistence of the infants' bondage to the mother—time after time, hour after hour, the infants returned, contacted, and clasped the mother in spite of being hit, kicked, and scraped unceremoniously off the mother's body. The physical punishment which these infants took or sought for the privilege of brief contact even to the back or side of the mother's body testified to the fact that, even in infants, attachment to the mother may be prepotent over pain and suffering. One could not help but be reminded of children, removed from indifferent or cruel, indigent, and alcoholic parents, whose primary insistent wish is to return home.

The degree to which monkey data are generalizable to the human being will remain an unsolved dilemma. Nevertheless, we are so struck by the many apparent analogies that we are tempted to say the monkey experiments give us faith in the human clinical observations.

SUMMARY

Infant rhesus monkeys have been reared starting on the first day of life in a variety of situations, including total isolation; partial isolation, either in individual bare wire cages in a colony room for two years or longer, or in individual wire cages with access to one or two mother surrogates for at least the first six months; and in situations with real or surrogate mothers plus contact with other infants for the first year or two of life.

Total isolation for two years resulted in failure to display social or sexual behavior in the next two years, spent in a joint living cage. Results on six months of such isolation are still being gathered and suggest severe, but not complete, social deficits. Only mild effects have been observed thus far in monkeys isolated through the first 80 days of life.

Partial isolation has produced behavioral aberrations in many monkeys and sexual inadequacy in all males and in all but one female. Four females were impregnated, in spite of inadequate posturing, and proved to be completely inadequate mothers.

Infants raised by the live mothers were more advanced in social and sexual behavior than infants raised by surrogate mothers in a controlled playpen situation. The mother's role is not entirely clear, however, because in a more stimulating playroom situation, surrogate-mothered babies have shown normal social and sexual behavior.

Over all, it appears that the longer and the more complete the social deprivation, the more devastating are the behavioral effects. Further research is needed to evaluate the relative contributions of live mothers and infant companions to later adjustment.

Normal Psychosexual Development*

Michael Rutter

Psychosexual issues occupy a central place in child development both because of the importance of sexual interests in any consideration of social and emotional behavior and because theories of development have so often regarded sexual drive and its focus as causal influences in relation to personality formation.

In examining what happens in normal psychosexual development it will be necessary to consider many different and disparate areas, for sexuality is a complex subject which incorporates many relatively independent subdivisions. In order to set the scene for psychological issues, the physical changes associated with sexual development will be described.

HORMONAL CHANGES

Before puberty there are no sizeable sex differences in sex hormone production. In both boys and girls small amounts of androgens and oestrogens are produced—probably by the adrenals (Tanner, 1962). The production of androgens increases in both sexes at about 8–10 yr with a further much sharper rise in adolescence. This later rise is present in girls and boys but it is much more marked in the latter so that greater androgen excretion in the male is first evident only at puberty. The excretion of oestrogens gradually rises in both sexes from about age 7 yr. During adolescence there is a very large and sharp further increase in girls but only a very small increase in boys. The adolescent increase in androgens and oestrogens is due to increasing hormone production by the gonads stimulated by gonadotrophins from the anterior pituitary gland (Fitschen and Clayton, 1965).

GROWTH OF GONADS AND DEVELOPMENT OF SECONDARY SEXUAL CHARACTERISTICS

There is very little growth in the weight of the gonads in either sex up to the time of adolescence, when, of course, there is a very marked development (Tanner, 1962).

In boys, the first sign of impending puberty is usually an acceleration of the growth of the testes and scrotum, accompanied by slight and later great growth of pubic hair. At the same time there is development of the penis, a considerable height spurt, enlargement of the larynx and deepening of the voice. About 2 yr after the beginning of pubic hair growth, axillary and facial hair first appear and there are changes in physique associated with an acceleration in the development of muscular strength. There are two main points to notice in relation to the physical changes at adolescence. First, the development spans a period of at least 4–4½ yr and second there is an immense variation in the age at which puberty occurs. For example, the average age of first ejaculation in the Kinsey study was just under 14 yr but in 10

*From Michael Rutter, "Normal Psychosexual Development," *Journal of Child Psychology, Psychiatry and Related Disciplines*, 1971, **11**, 259–283. Reprinted by permission of the author and the Editor, *Journal of Child Psychology, Psychiatry and Related Disciplines*.

percent of cases it occurred either before the eleventh or after the sixteenth birthday (Kinsey *et al.*, 1948). Thus, in normal boys there is a 5 yr range for the age at which puberty is reached. A similar range is found if puberty is assessed by height spurt, pubic hair growth or gonadal development (Tanner, 1962).

In girls, puberty begins some 2 yr earlier and extends over a slightly shorter period (3 or 4 yr rather than 4 or 5). However, individual variation is equally great. The average age of menarche is about 13 yr but the range extends from 10 to 16½ yr. Breast development is usually the first sign of pubescence; this begins between 8 and 13 yr, being followed, usually within a year or so, by the appearance of pubic hair, a height spurt and changes in general physique. It should be noted, however, that there is considerable individual variation in the ordering and timing of these physical changes.

In short, physically speaking there is very little sexual development until puberty, the changes at adolescence spread over some 4 yr, there is enormous individual variation in the timing of this development, and girls reach puberty 18 months or 2 yr before boys.

The age when puberty is reached is of some psychological significance. Boys who are late in reaching puberty tend to be less popular, less confident and less assertive, but eager and talkative and attention-seeking (McCandless, 1960; Mussen and Jones, 1957, 1958; Jones and Bayley, 1950). They are also likely to be late in establishing heterosexual behaviour (Schofield, 1965). The Fels longitudinal study suggested that adolescent boys with non-masculine interests during early childhood tended later to be anxious about sexuality and to have less heterosexual activity (Kagan and Moss, 1962). The possible reasons for this are not hard to find. Manliness and sexual vigour are highly regarded attributes among adolescent boys, and youths who have still not reached puberty by 16 yr or so may well begin to doubt their masculinity and become anxious and introspective about their development. A further reason is that *early* puberty is associated with muscular physique (McCandless, 1960; Tanner, 1962), and again athletic abilities are highly valued in most adolescent groups. The extent to which late puberty is a handicap in boys varies somewhat in different cultures, emphasizing that the disadvantages are largely due to society's reaction to continuing physical immaturity (Mussen and Bouterline-Young, 1964). To some extent the social disadvantages of late puberty in boys persist into adulthood but they tend to diminish with age (Jones, 1965). A further point is that early maturers of both sexes tend to have a higher I.Q. and educational attainment at all ages (Douglas and Ross, 1964).

Girls' reactions to early or late puberty are more complex and so far as can be judged from the limited studies available there are not the clear-cut advantages to early maturing that are found in boys (McCandless, 1960). Indeed, very early maturing may sometimes be associated with undue selfconsciousness and anxiety together with an attempt to conceal breast development through altered posture.

PSYCHOSEXUAL DEVELOPMENT

In contrast to physical development, much *psycho*sexual development takes place before puberty. For the sake of clarity this development will be subdivided into three parts; (1) sexual activity and interests, (2) concepts of sexual differences and the creation of babies, and (3) sex role differentiation.

SEXUAL ACTIVITY AND INTERESTS

Although, in the light of later evidence, Freud's account of psychosexual development was incorrect in some important aspects (see below), numerous studies have amply confirmed his view of the extent and importance of infantile sexuality.

In the male infant, erections of the penis have been noted to occur from birth (Halverson, 1940), the frequency in the first few months of post-natal life ranging from 3 to 11 times per day. At first these erections seem to be largely associated with bladder and bowel distension and, so far as can be judged by the infant's reaction, appear unpleasant in quality. But elimination is then associated with detumescence. Incidentally, this association suggests how anal activities may acquire an erotic component. These early erections are just reflex but infants soon begin to touch and rub their genitals. At first this is just one aspect of general bodily exploration and, probably, touching the genitals occurs no more often than touching other parts of the body. At this stage, it would be misleading to call this infantile sexuality. However, gradually infants learn that genital stimulation may be particularly pleasant and from observations it would seem that genital manipulation then gains a more definitely erotic quality. The exact incidence of genital manipulation in very young children is not known but it is evident from several studies that the rate is quite high. For example, the Newsons (1963) found that 36 per cent of the mothers of 1 yr olds reported genital play in their children. Pulling the penis by boys was said to be much commoner than genital stimulation by girls. When such masturbatory activities lead to orgasm-like responses varies greatly from child to child; they have been noted from as early as 5 months but usually it is not until somewhat later (Kinsey *et al.*, 1948, 1953). From Kinsey's (Kinsey *et al.*, 1948) longitudinal observations of boys from infancy up to late childhood, it appears that the later reactions were sufficiently similar to the earlier behaviour to suggest the orgastic nature of the infantile experiences. Even so there are clear physiological differences. Obviously, ejaculation does not occur before puberty but also there is not the male post-orgasm refractory period so that boys may have several "orgasms" in quick succession (Kinsey *et al.*, 1948).

Oral activities are also very common in infancy and it is clear that much pleasure is gained from non-nutritional sucking. To what extent this can be regarded as erotic clearly depends on how wide a definition of eroticism is employed.[1] The same difficulty applies to any attempt to examine changes with age. Thus, thumb-sucking gradually diminishes during the pre-school period but, in marked contrast, nail-biting shows a very considerable rise in frequency over the same years (Macfarlane, 1939; Macfarlane *et al.*, 1954; Wechsler, 1931; Billig, 1941).

[1]In psychoanalytic terminology erotic activities are not confined to those with a genital association or aim. Sexuality and eroticism are seen as an *intrinsic aptitude* to release the genital. Thus, emotional reactions of all kinds—desire, hope, fear, anger—and associated activities may derive from sexuality (Dalbiez, 1941).

During the 2–5 yr period, genital interest, however defined, evidently increases. In a study of middle-class American pre-school children, Sears, Maccoby and Levin (1957) found that about half were reported to indulge in sex play or genital handling. Levy (1928) studying slightly younger children found that masturbatory activities occurred in at least 55 per cent of boys but only 16 per cent of girls. A similar sex difference was reported by Koch (1935) and it may be concluded that manual stimulation of the genitals in much commoner in boys than girls. Thigh rubbing is an alternative source of genital pleasure in girls, but how often this occurs is not known.

Games involving undressing or sexual exploration (often under the guise of "mothers and fathers" or "doctors") are common by age 4 yr (Isaacs, 1933; Newson and Newson, 1968) although again the frequency is not known. Nevertheless, that sex play is a common occurrence with nursery school children is evident from Susan Isaacs' early studies. She also showed the diverse nature of pre-school children's sex games. Exhibitionistic and voyeuristic activities with both other children and adults are characteristic, masturbation occurs, children attempt to fondle their mother's breasts, and it appears from the nature of their play that urination is associated in children's minds with sex activities.

There has been some controversy over the extent to which sexual pleasure in girls at this age is centred on the clitoris or vagina (Greenacre, 1950). The matter remains unresolved but in view of the finding that clitoral and vaginal orgasm are physiologically indistinguishable in adults (Masters and Johnson, 1966) the issue probably has little importance.

The years between 5 or 6 and puberty were once thought to be a sexually latent period with a repression of sex interest and little psychosexual development (Fries, 1959). It is now clear that this is very far from the truth. Anthropologists first pointed out that whatever happened in Western societies, in sexually permissive cultures sex play and love-making were common during middle childhood (Malinowski, 1929; Ford and Beach, 1951). In recent years, a number of studies have produced somewhat similar findings for the U.S.A. Although there may possibly still be some greater concealment of sex interests during middle childhood than either before or after, nevertheless overt sex activities and interests are common and widespread (Bernick, 1965; Reese, 1966). Ramsey (1943) found that the accumulative incidence of masturbation in boys rose from about 10 per cent at 7 yr to over 80 per cent at 13 yr. Heterosexual play in the same survey rose from less than 5 per cent at 5 yr to a third of boys at 8 yr and two-thirds at 13 yr. The rates in the Kinsey study (1948) were lower but the trend was the same—that is, a gradual rise during the pre-pubertal years. Both studies showed also a rise in the accumulative incidence of coital play during the years before adolescence, although this occurred in only a minority of the children.

Similar findings are reported for girls except that the rates of sexual activity are lower at all ages. These results leave no doubt that sexual activity occurs during the so-called latency years, but it should not be concluded from these figures that there is necessarily a continuity between pre-pubertal sex play and adult sex activity (Broderick, 1966). In the early school years sexual activity is a much more sporadic activity than it is later and it has neither the intensity nor complexity of later sex behaviour.

Homosexual play in boys (which mostly consists of mutual handling of genitals) also shows a gradual rise during childhood (Ramsey, 1954; Kinsey *et al.,* 1948) reaching 25 to 30 per cent at 13 yr. The figures for girls are similar (Kinsey *et al.,* 1953). In this country Schofield (1965) reported lower rates of homosexual behaviour (although he thought his figures an underestimate) but he did note that in both boys and girls homosexual activities were very much commoner in boarding schools than in day schools. This suggests that the development of homosexual behaviour is probably much influenced by the social setting and by the presence or absence of heterosexual opportunities. Whether this transient phase of homosexual activity has any bearing at all on persisting adult homosexuality is doubtful (West, 1968).

The rates of various sexual activities are in themselves of limited interest in view of the known marked differences between different societies. What is much more important is the light thrown on the process of psychosexual development through the information given on age differences. In this connection, Broderick's study of 10–12 yr old children provides some useful findings (Broderick and Fowler, 1961; Broderick and Rowe, 1968). He found that the majority of the children claimed to have a sweetheart and between 10 and 12 yr there was a rise in the proportion of children preferring an opposite sex companion in various situations. By 10 yr two-thirds of them had been kissed and by 12 yr this was so for 5 out of 6 children. Broderick developed a scale of social heterosexuality and showed that in the preadolescent period there was a gradual progression from wanting to marry someone to having a particular girl-friend, to being "in love" with this particular girl-friend and finally social activities in the company of this friend.

As Broderick's data refer only to children aged over 9 yr it is not possible to state at what age this process begins. An early study by Campbell (1939) showed that up to the age of 7 or 8 yr children played with both boys and girls, there was then a phase of playing only with children of the same sex as themselves, followed at about puberty by increasing social interaction with the opposite sex. Broderick also found that at age 10–12 yr children had many more friends of the same sex than of the opposite sex. However, as already discussed, even during the period while friendships were mostly same-sex there was considerable heterosexual interest and some sexual activity. It may be concluded that same-sex friendships remain a feature of middle childhood but the inference from this that sex is latent is evidently wrong. It is somewhat disguised but still it is obviously active. The latency is accurate only in so far as it refers to heterosexual *social* activities rather than sexual interests.

Although much remains to be learned about sexual interests and activities in early and middle childhood, it is abundantly clear that these years constitute a time of active psychosexual development.

During and after adolescence, however, there is a very marked upsurge in sexual activity in both sexes. In Schofield's English study of teenagers (1965) he found that by the age of 13, a quarter of the boys and almost a third of the girls had had their first date. During the next 2 yr there is a rapid rise in the incidence of dating so that by age 16 yr over 70 per cent of the boys and over 85 per cent of the girls had experienced dating. The figures for kissing are closely similar and again boys lag behind girls in the age at which they start. Deep kissing and breast fondling occurs somewhat later, but by 17 yr the majority of adolescents have progressed to this stage of sexual activity. After 15 yr the curve for sexual experience rises fast. At 15 less than a fifth of the boys have touched the genitals of a girl but by 17 nearly half have done this. By the age of 18, a third of the boys and about 1 in 6 of the girls will have had sexual intercourse.

In keeping with their slower physical development, boys begin sexual activities later than girls, but by 17 yr there is no longer any difference. Youngsters of both sexes who start dating and kissing at an early age are also more likely to have early sexual intercourse. However, there are differences between boys and girls in the pattern of sexual activity in later adolescence. Fewer girls have intercourse but once they have started they are more active sexually. The boys have more sexual partners (implying a small core of promiscuous girls) but the girls more often have an enduring sexual association. There are also differences in attitudes to sex. Girls tend to look for a romantic relationship while boys seek a sexual adventure. At the time of Schofield's survey in the early 1960s most adolescents were not using birth control although nearly all had some knowledge of it. About half of them either said that they did not like the idea of contraceptives or could not be bothered with them. It is uncertain how far this is a rationalization of more deep-seated reasons for avoiding contraception.

To summarize the main findings on psychosexual development; genital play often begins in the preschool period, during the early school years there is a gradual increase in both heterosexual interests and sexual activity, at puberty there is a marked increase in both, and after puberty there are differences between boys and girls in their patterns of sexual behaviour and in their attitudes towards sex. Homosexual behaviour occurs as a transient phase or isolated occurrence during early adolescence in perhaps up to a quarter of both boys and girls.

THE DEVELOPMENT OF SEX "DRIVE"

Before discussing the development of sex "drive" and factors influencing it, it is necessary to examine the concept of drive itself. Drive is a hypothesis which has been invoked to account for the internal motivation of behaviour and it has usually been described in terms of some biologic need such as hunger, thirst or sex. Frequently (as in the case of psychoanalysis, some learning theories and Lorenz's variety of ethology),[2] the drive is supposed to have an energy component of a quantitative nature giving rise to a hydraulic view of energies flowing in certain directions, becoming dammed up and then released. Energy models of motivation, however, lead to so many wrong predictions and fail to account for so many phenomena (Hinde, 1960; Hunt, 1960; Barnett, 1963) that they may be dismissed as only a very partial truth at best. Mason *et al.* (1959) showed that monkeys would work to solve puzzles regardless of any satisfaction of hunger, thirst or other biological drives. Studies by both Levin and Kaye (1964) and by Bridger (1962) have shown that neonates suck when they are awake or aroused, regardless of degree of hunger. Numerous workers have shown that

[2]The type of drive in each of these theories differs somewhat (Rapaport, 1960).

children and animals explore even when they are not hungry and thirsty, and indeed hunger and thirst may actually inhibit such behaviour (Montgomery, 1953).

Even drives apparently meeting a biological need do not have a one-to-one relationship with that need. Thus, hunger and thirst may be satiated by swallowing, mechanical gastric distension or saccharine even though none serve a useful nutritive purpose and starvation may lead to a loss of hunger (Barnett, 1963; Hebb, 1961; Deutsch and Deutsch, 1966). Appetite and hunger are not the same thing (Janowitz and Grossman, 1949). Experiments such as these clearly show that even with apparently basic drives such as hunger there are important learned components, diminution of drive is not necessarily associated with the satiation of the biological need and many behaviours are motivated by other means.

The same applies to sex. In so far as sex meets a biological need it might be thought that orgasm was required to fulfil that need. However, Sheffield, Whalen and others have shown that penile stimulation is inherently reinforcing and that orgasm or ejaculation is not necessary for reinforcement to occur (Sheffield *et al.,* 1951; Whalen, 1961; Whalen, 1966). It appears that these are at least two basic mechanisms involved in the energy component of sexual drive—first the sexual arousal mechanism and secondly the orgasm mechanism (Beach, 1956). Although they are related they are by no means the same thing. The fact that men have a refractory period after orgasm in which they are not easily aroused has been used to argue for an energy component or sex drive, but this is a weak argument because females have no refractory period (Masters and Johnson, 1966). Many women can have repeated orgasms in quick succession.

There are biological components which help to determine the strength of sexual motivation (see below) but also there are strong psychological components (Hardy, 1964; Whalen, 1966). Increasing sexual activity may serve to whet the appetite rather than deplete the drive. Sexual abstinence may lead to increased sexual arousal in some circumstances (Barnett, 1963) but it may also lead to the reverse effect. There have been several investigations of the effects of learning on sex drive in animals, the results being ambiguous and contradictory (Deutsch and Deutsch, 1966) but remarkably few attempts to study this problem in man. However, a recent study by Barrett (1970) does provide some relevant information. He studied the frequency of coitus in a large number of married couples in order to determine the extent to which coitus on any one day was or was not contingent on whether coitus had occurred on the previous day. He found that in most couples there were no contingency effects. This would suggest that drive was not operating (although he did not investigate the issue for this purpose). In about a third of couples there was an alternating pattern, so that if on day X coitus had occurred on day X + 1 coitus did not occur. This pattern is consonant with drive mechanism although obviously it is open to several other interpretations. However, in about 10 per cent of couples there was the opposite effect. That is, if coitus occurred on one day it was *more* likely to occur on the following day. This is more in keeping with a learning view of motivation, that sexual intercourse leads to an increase in desire, not a diminution.

In no sense of the word did this study provide a crucial test of the drive hypothesis as the effect of prolonged periods of abstinence was not studied. But so far as it goes it suggests that sex drive involves learned components as well as biological aspects.

It is sometimes thought that sexual intercourse is necessarily pleasurable by some innate mechanism but this is not so. Schofield (1965) found that many youths of both sexes did not enjoy their first experience of intercourse. Sexual behaviour includes many learned components, and depending upon whether a person's first sexual experience is enjoyable or unpleasant he may either never try again (or at least not for many years) or he may have intercourse again within a few days and continue to have sex regularly and frequently (Schofield, 1965). Sexual appetite is to a considerable extent learned, not inborn. Even so, it would be quite wrong to conclude that internal factors are of no importance in sexual activity. On the contrary, they are most influential (although not the only influences). It has been demonstrated in many different studies that androgens have a powerful effect on eroticism in both sexes. The sexual responsiveness of individuals whose glands fail to secrete androgens remains at a relatively weak and immature level in spite of their reaching adulthood in other respects (Money, 1961). Hypogonadal men on substitution hormone therapy show a diminution of erotic interest if therapy is discontinued. On the other hand the effects of post-pubertal castration are more variable, and in some cases there is no effect on sexual capacities, emphasizing the importance also of non-hormonal mechanisms. However, castration either surgical or functional (through the administration of oestrogens which lead to testicular atrophy) usually produce some loss of sexual desire and potency. It may be concluded that androgens have an important (but far from exclusive) controlling function on sex drive in the male.

It appears that androgens have the same effect in the female, the hormones being secreted by the adrenal. Women with excessive circulating androgens, as in the adrenogenital syndrome, often show an unusually high level of eroticism which diminishes when the androgen level is lowered by treatment (Money, 1961). Similarly, women for whom androgen therapy is prescribed often report an increase of sexual desire as a side effect (Money, 1961). Conversely, normal women deprived of their normal adrenal androgens by either adrenalectomy or hypophysectomy experience a lessening or loss of libido (Schon and Sutherland, 1960; Waxenberg *et al.*, 1959). That this does not happen after ovariectomy (which deprives them of oestrogens but not androgens) illustrates the *un*importance of female hormones in this connection. The limited evidence on hypogonadal women taken off substitution hormone therapy also suggests that oestrogens have little effect on libido (Money, 1961) other than through their effect on end orgasms. Oestrogens affect the vascularity and mucous content of the vagina which may have a secondary effect on the enjoyment of sex.

Until recently it has been thought that female hormones have no effect on libido. While it remains clear that androgens have the main influence on female libido, there is some evidence that female hormones may have some impact. There are variations in the incidence of sexual intercourse according to the stage of the menstrual cycle which suggest hormonal influences (Udry and Morris, 1968) and loss of libido is seen in some women on progestagenic steroids (Grant and Mears, 1967). Experiments in sub-human primates suggest that the sexual attractiveness of the female to the male is under hormonal control, one of the mechanisms possibly being the male's smelling of an oestrogen-dependent vaginal pheromone (Michael, 1968). Whether there is any parallel to this in the human is unknown.

Thus, the regulation of libido in the human is a complex matter with arousability determined by hormonal state, feedback effects of copulation and experience. Androgens play an important part in the maintenance of sexual interest in both sexes. As already discussed, there is a marked increase in androgen secretion at puberty (much more marked in the male) and it has been shown that hormonal production plays a most important part in the upsurge of sexuality about the time of adolescence. The role of androgens also explains why the upsurge is generally more marked in boys than girls.

THE DEVELOPMENT OF PSYCHOSEXUAL COMPETENCE AND MATURITY

It may be asked not only what provides sexual impetus but also what factors are associated with the achievement of psychosexual maturity and competence. To what extent does "it all come naturally" in some innate fashion and to what extent are skills acquired?

As we have seen, sexual activity and interests including genital play is a normal part of childhood preceding puberty. Nonetheless, there is a difference between childish sexuality and adult sexuality. Hormones seem to be necessary for this transition in that hypogonadal males remain psychosexually immature in their late teens unless there is hormone therapy (Money, 1961). It is difficult to say whether androgens have any direct effect on psychosexual maturity in that hypogonadal adolescents are likely to be treated as children by other people and few are able to have a social life normal for their age. This social handicap, doubtless, plays some part in their psychosexual immaturity. Also, of course, without androgens the male cannot ejaculate and so is unlikely to have erotic ejaculatory dreams or images.

On the other hand, hormonal maturity seems not to be sufficient to lead to psychosexual maturity. Children of both sexes who have precocious puberty usually remain rather immature in their sexual imagery and behaviour unless they have been treated by other people in a way that is ahead of their social maturity. On the whole, premature puberty leads to an increase in sexual arousal but not to adult type psychosexual behaviour. Although there may be some advance in psychosexual development (especially in boys), psychosexual behaviour tends to remain roughly in keeping with chronological age and social experiences (Money, 1961; Connor and McGeorge, 1965).

The fact that sexual competence has to be learned and is not instinctively known is evident from Harlow's studies of the long-term effects of severe social deprivation in infant monkeys (Harlow and Harlow, 1969). Animals reared in total isolation showed little sexual behaviour when adult and such sexual approaches as they made were extremely inept. Males failed to copulate successfully and the females presented themselves so badly that even experienced males frequently could not impregnate them.[3] Social experiences with other animals during infancy were necessary for the development of both normal sexual interests and also sexual competence. Interestingly, however, for this purpose it was sufficient for monkeys to be raised with *either*

[3]In that the monkeys also showed *disturbed* behaviour, it is possible that the findings may, in part, represent a *disruption* of sexual activities rather than a true failure to develop competence.

a mother *or* with peers. To a considerable extent, interaction with peers and interaction with a mother served equally well as the basis for future social and sexual behaviour.

Obviously, such extreme conditions of rearing are not to be found in the human, but probably, in humans as well as other animals, social experience is necessary for the development of sexual competence. Schofield (1965) in his general population study of sexual behaviour in teenagers found that a third of the boys and half of the girls did not like their first experience of sexual intercourse. A fifth of the boys did not achieve orgasm and the majority of the girls failed to reach a climax. Sexual competence does not come innately; social and sexual experiences both before and after puberty are probably crucial in its development.

BIOLOGIC FACTORS INFLUENCING GENDER ROLE (PSYCHOLOGIC SEX)

Let us now turn our attention to what biologic factors determine gender role—that is, whether a person feels himself to be male or female. Biologic sex takes five distinct forms (chromosomal sex, gonadal sex, hormonal sex, internal reproductive structures, and external genital morphology) (Hampson and Hampson, 1961), each of which may be considered with respect to its part in the development of gender role or psychologic sex. Normally, of course, all of these are the same for any individual but there are a number of medical disorders in which they are at variance. In these conditions, there are various sexual abnormalities which lead to mistakes at birth in the decision as to whether the child is male or female. Accordingly biologic males may be reared as girls and vice versa. These disorders have been extensively studied from the psychologic viewpoint by Money and the Hampsons (Money, 1961, 1965; Money and Ehrhardt, 1968; Hampson and Hampson, 1961) and their studies have provided evidence which allows reasonably firm conclusions on the influence of biologic factors in the determination of gender role.

First, it seems clear that chromosomal sex is quite unimportant in this respect. In a series of 20 hermaphroditic individuals who had been assigned to and reared in a sex contrary to their chromosomal sex, in *every* case the person's gender role was in accord with their assigned sex and rearing rather than their chromosomal sex (Hampson and Hampson, 1961). Furthermore, chromosomal studies of transvestites and transsexuals have shown that the sex chromatin pattern agrees with the external genital morphology and *not* with the gender role (Barr and Hobbs, 1954).

Gonadal sex also seems to play but a minor part in the development of gender role. Among 30 patients in whom the sexual status of the gonads disagreed with the sex of assignment and rearing, in all but 3 cases the gender role was fully concordant with the sex rearing. In these 3 cases the gender role was neither firmly male nor female (Hampson and Hampson, 1961).

As the adrenals produce sex hormones and as the gonads may not secrete the appropriate hormones it is possible to examine the effects of hormones independently of gonadal sex. In the Hampsons' series of 31 patients whose sex hormones and secondary sexual body development contradicted their assigned sex and rearing, 5 became ambivalent with respect to their gender role. As restoration of normal hormonal balance had no effect on psychologic sex it was concluded that hormones had no direct effect on gender role. However, animal experiments force one to be cautious about accepting this conclusion. It is well established that prenatal androgen administration in guinea pigs leads to the animals later behaving in a male way (Young *et al.,* 1964). Prenatal oestrogens, on the other hand, have no feminising effect. More recent work by Goy (1968) and his colleagues suggest that a somewhat similar effect is found in rhesus monkeys. In humans also, prenatal androgens probably have some effect on sex-related behaviour. A group of progestin induced hermaphrodites and adrenogenital hermaphrodites have been studied by Money and Ehrhardt (1968) (both are conditions in which there is foetal exposure to excess androgens). In many of these girls there was a masculine-like interest in athletic pursuits, in boys' toys, and male-type clothing, suggesting the presence of a hormone effect in foetal life. On the other hand, the gender role was usually female so that the foetal hormonal effect is probably much less marked than it is in other species. It is also important to note that this is strictly a *prenatal* effect. The administration of androgens to the adult or child has no effect on gender role (Money, 1961).

The Hampsons' study of hermaphrodites suggests that there is no correlation between psychologic sex and *internal* accessory organs. Even the *external* genital appearance seems to have surprisingly little effect on gender role. They studied 25 hermaphrodites in whom there was a marked degree of contradiction between their external genital appearance and their assigned sex and rearing. It is remarkable that 23 of these 25 patients had a gender role in keeping with their assigned sex and rearing in spite of having external genitalia which contradicted their given sex. Nevertheless, this acceptance of their paradoxical appearance had given rise to considerable psychologic distress in many cases (Hampson and Hampson, 1961). It may be concluded that although, in general, the external genitalia are not the most important influence on psychologic sex, nevertheless body appearance does have an important bearing on the development of gender role.

Inevitably, the evidence from the Hampson and Money studies derives from very abnormal populations and some writers have suggested that this may have influenced the findings. Because the individuals had low hormone levels and were biologically ambiguous they may have been more susceptible than normal to psychological "imprinting" (Diamond, 1965). There are a few reports of isolated cases where members assigned to one sex felt that they belonged to the opposite sex and at puberty they developed some sort of cross-sex change, in effect confirming their earliest gender wishes (Dewhurst and Gordon, 1963; Baker and Stoller, 1968). These, and accounts of a successful late change in gender role, suggest that in some individuals biological factors may play some part in determining gender (Dewhurst and Gordon, 1963; Berg *et al.,* 1963).

However, the evidence taken altogether seems clearly to indicate that although biologic factors do have some influence on the acquisition of gender role, much the most important factor is the sex the child is assigned by his parents and thus the sex in which he has been brought up. What aspects of parental care are important in this respect will be considered below.

BIOLOGIC FACTORS DETERMINING DIRECTIONS OF SEXUAL INTEREST

Sexuality has several other components which we must consider. So far we have discussed the strength of sexual appetite, the development of sexual competence and the acquisition of gender role, aspects which are all to some extent independent. Quite separate from all these dimensions is the direction of sexual interest or the object choice. By this we mean those persons or objects toward whom an individual directs his sexual activities (Whalen, 1966). In this connection, biological factors concerned with sexual characteristics appear unimportant in the vast majority of cases. In the series of cases studied by the Hampsons (1961) whenever psychologic sex differed from biologic sex (however it was assessed—chromosomes, gonads, hormones, etc.), the direction of sexual orientation was practically always in accord with psychologic sex. Similar negative results stem from studies of homosexuals and transsexuals where it has been found that the direction of sex interest is very rarely explained by chromosomal anomalies (Pare, 1956; Pritchard, 1962; Raboch and Nedoma, 1958) or by hormonal abnormalities (Perloff, 1949; Migeon *et al.,* 1969). Androgens increase sex drive but they are without influence on its direction.

Chromosomal and hormonal factors, therefore, are usually unimportant in the determination of object choice. However, genetic factors (not concerning chromosomal sex) may well be important in some cases of homosexuality. Kallman's early report (1952) of 100 per cent concordance in monozygotic twin pairs where one twin was homosexual has *not* been confirmed by more recent studies (Parker, 1964; Heston and Shields, 1968). However, although the matter requires further evidence, it does seem that concordance is higher in monozygotic pairs than dizygotic pairs suggesting the importance of hereditary factors.

In many cases the development of homosexual inclination (and of course this is a matter of degree rather than presence or absence) seems to be related to a person's early life experiences (West, 1968; Bancroft, 1970; Kenyon, 1970). The evidence suggests that poor relationships with parents, perhaps particularly the parent of the same sex, may play a part in the development of homosexual interests. At present, this remains too general an explanation to be of much value and it fails to explain why some transvestites are homosexual but most are not (Randall, 1970). All that can be concluded with any certainty is that early family relationships in some way play some part in the development of object choice but how and in what way remains unknown. In any case, these considerations take us some way from the discussion of normal psychosexual development so let us return to examine a further element—that of the concept of sexual differences.

CONCEPTS OF SEXUAL DIFFERENCES AND THE CREATION OF BABIES

It has long been known that most young children show an interest in sexual matters and ask their parents questions about sex (Hattendorf, 1932). Some 40 yr ago, Hattendorf (1932) in a systematic study found that by the age of 5 yr the majority of children had asked about sex and even by age 3 yr nearly half had. From 4 yr until puberty children continue to ask questions at the same frequency emphasizing again the active sexual interests in the middle years of childhood. However, it should be noted that most children do not ask many questions. At every age, all sorts of questions are asked but there is a different emphasis as the children grow older, in parallel with their increasing cognitive sophistication. The pre-school child asks about the origin of babies, physical sex differences, body organs and functions and the coming of another baby. The young school child shows an increased interest in the process of birth, and the pre-adolescent tends to focus on the father's role in reproduction and on marriage. This development in the type of questions asked is associated with a similar development in the extent and detail of children's understanding of the origins of babies, as shown by Conn (1947) using a doll-play interview technique.

A recent Israeli study by the Kreitlers (1966) emphasized that at age 5 yr, children's understanding of the procreative process is still incomplete and often inaccurate. Nearly all knew that babies come from the mother's belly but most children were vague and uncertain about the role of the father and over half thought that the belly had to be cut open to get the baby out. There was an interesting sex difference in children's theories about how the baby got into the mother's belly. Among children from Western families, most boys thought that the baby was formed from the food eaten by the mother. Some girls also thought this, but more believed that the baby had always been in the belly. Oriental boys were most inclined to think that the baby was swallowed, but very few Western children suggested this.

The same study clearly showed that most 4–5 yr olds from Western families were well aware that boys have a penis whereas girls do not. Children from Oriental families were not quite so well informed, just less than half being knowledgeable on the topic. An ingenious American study by Katcher (1955), which involved getting pre-school children to link upper and lower halves of nude and clothed bodies on a picture puzzle, showed that young children first recognize sex differences by hair style and adult clothing. Whether this would still be so today with the emphasis on "unisex" is uncertain! The proportion of children making errors in genital recognition fell steadily from age 3 yr–8 yr, over 50 per cent of children making no errors by age 5 yr. Interestingly, as both Katcher and Conn found, most children seemed unaware of the significance of the breasts as a female characteristic.

Children's reactions to the discovery of genital differences were investigated by Conn (1940; Conn and Kanner, 1947) using his doll-play technique. He interviewed children aged 5–13 yr attending a paediatric clinic. Children who had had the opportunity of seeing the genitals of the opposite sex were asked about their reaction, and a third were able to describe how they felt and responded at the time. Most children accepted the genital differences as natural, although some were surprised and several thought the difference odd or funny. About a third of the children believed at first that the girls had had a penis but had lost it in some way or it had grown small, or it had been cut off. Not all of this third were perturbed by the thought of penis loss and Conn and Kanner (1947) concluded that castration anxiety was an infrequent occurrence. Levy (1940) has criticized this view and to some extent the matter must remain open because of the large number of Conn's children who could not recall how they felt when they first saw genitals of the opposite sex. However, even on Conn's own findings, a third of children (boys more than girls) had had castration thoughts, which can hardly be regarded as infrequent.

SEX ROLE DIFFERENTIATION

The last aspect of psychosexual development to be considered is that of sex role differentiation and sex typing. Three distinct aspects are involved, (1) gender role (that is, the child's identification of himself as male or female as already described), (2) sex role preference (that is, the sex the child would like to be), and (3) sex role standards (the acquisition of behaviour and attitudes which are culturally appropriate for the child's sex). The facts about when a child acquires these various aspects of sex role are reasonably well established, but *how* he does so is still a matter for vigorous controversy.

As to when a child first regards himself as a boy or a girl, two approaches provide answers. First, there are the observational studies on when children correctly answer the question "Are you a girl or a boy?". Gesell (1940) reported that over two-thirds of 3 yr olds answered this correctly while the majority of 2½ yr olds did not do so. Rabban (1950) found the same results for 2½-3½ yr olds and showed that correct sex awareness was almost complete a year later. An alternative approach to the same question is to see at what age it is possible to change a child's gender role in cases where, owing to some anatomical abnormality, a wrong sex assignment had been made. The Money and Hampson studies (Money, 1961, 1968; Hampson and Hampson, 1961) show that it is often difficult to do this successfully after age 3 yr, although other workers have shown that there are important exceptions (see above). Both approaches suggest, then, that by age 3 yr sex role identity is becoming well established, although the difficulties involved in a late change of gender role are probably not as great as the early studies suggested (Dewhurst and Gordon, 1963; Berg *et al.*, 1963).

However, the correct recognition by a child of his own sex does not mean that he has correctly sorted out the concept of sex differences. Rabban's study as well as those already discussed under concepts of sex differences show that a child first appreciates his own sex (usually by age 3 yr), that within the next 2 yr or so he gradually learns to generalize this to the correct recognition of other people's sex, and that this generalization comes at the same time as the child learns which physical criteria define sex.

Several studies (Brown, 1956, 1957; Hartup and Zook, 1960; Hetherington, 1967) have examined children's sex preferences using a projective technique involving a figure of ambiguous sex called "It". Children are asked to choose the toys and games for "It" to play with and to give "It" a name. Sex preference is considered to be the sex role or sex of the name chosen for "It". It has been found that even at an age as early as 3 yr there is a strong tendency for children to exhibit a same-sex preference (Hartup and Zook, 1960), but this preference tends to become even stronger as children grow older (at least in boys). The reality of this difference is demonstrated by the fact that similar findings have been obtained by asking children directly what toys they prefer or which parent they would like to be when they grow up (Kohlberg, 1967; Rabban, 1950). Pre-school children have also been found to choose the same-sex parent more often than the other-sex parent as a model to emulate (Kagan and Lemkin, 1960). So it is clear that children begin to establish same-sex preferences very early. What, in a way, is more interesting from a developmental point of view is that boys do so both earlier and more consistently than girls (Hetherington, 1967; Kohlberg, 1967; Hartup and Zook, 1960; Brown, 1957). Furthermore, the same studies show that girls tend to have a similar or even a slightly stronger degree of feminine preference in the pre-school period to that shown later—in contrast to the marked age trend in boys. In our culture, it seems that more girls prefer to be male than boys prefer to be female (Kohlberg, 1967). This conclusion is supported by reports from adults which indicate that between a third and two-thirds of women wanted to be male at some point in their lives (Terman, 1938; Terman, 1956; Landis *et al.*, 1940), whereas very few men ever wanted to be female. Almost certainly the reason for this is that the male is more highly regarded in most societies (McKee and Sherriffs, 1957; Rutter, 1970). Men have many advantages in terms of job opportunities, most religions are explicit on male superiority, and even the heroes in children's stories are twice as likely to be male as female (Child *et al.*, 1946). As girls grow up they become increasingly aware of the higher prestige of the male role and their sex preferences are influenced accordingly (Kohlberg, 1967).

Sex differences in children's behaviour and attitudes are also evident from early childhood. To what extent these represent biological differences of a constitutional kind and to what extent the learned acquisition of sex role standards set by society is quite uncertain. In terms of behaviour perhaps the most obvious difference is the greater aggressiveness of boys which is evident from age 2 yr upwards (Kagan, 1964; Maccoby, 1967). In that sex differences in behaviour *precede* the child's knowledge of whether he is a boy or girl, clearly the behaviour cannot be secondary to his conscious learning of the rules laid down by society regarding appropriate sex role behaviour. Instead one must turn either to hypotheses that they are constitutional differences or to hypotheses that, by the way parents treat male and female infants, they differentially reinforce aggressive behaviour in boys.

On the constitutional hypothesis there is a good deal of evidence in support. First, the finding that males are more aggressive than females in other primates, and indeed in many animal species (Hamburg and Lunde, 1967; Goy, 1968; Lawick-Goodall, 1968), argues in favour of some biological explanation. However, more direct supporting evidence is provided by the studies of Young, Goy and their colleagues (Young *et al.*, 1964; Goy, 1968) which show that the administration of androgens during foetal life affects the later manifestation of aggressive behaviour. It seems that androgens act on the brain during a critical period in development. Note that this is a biological effect on brain development, not the direct effect of hormones on behaviour. It is uncertain whether or not there is a similar effect in the human but recent work by Money and Ehrhardt (1968) suggests that there may be.

With regard to the possible differential reinforcement of aggression in male and female infants there is no satisfactory evidence either for or against. Whereas there are sex differences in early mother-infant interaction both in human and non-human primates (Rutter, 1970) these are complicated and age-related in a way that does not allow any conclusions on the differential rearing hypothesis. Furthermore, as these studies and others (Hamburg, 1967) also show sex differences in infant behaviour it seems just as likely that differences in the infants' behaviour leads to parental differences as the other way round. It may be concluded that these very early sex differences in behaviour probably are due at least in part to biological factors, but in addition there may also be the influence of differential child-rearing.

The later development of sex differences in attitudes, choice of games and other activities, however, is almost certainly socially determined in view of findings that what is regarded as masculine in one culture may not be in another (Mischel, 1967; D'Andrade, 1967). The age at which these sex differences in behaviour and interests become apparent vary from behaviour to behaviour, but on the whole they are quite marked at age 4–5 yr, although differences continue to increase up to 8 or 9 yr (Kagan, 1964; Kohlberg, 1967). However, for reasons already discussed, the sex typing of activities occurs earlier and is more marked for boys than it is for girls.

PSYCHOSEXUAL STAGES OF DEVELOPMENT

It may seem surprising that up to this point no mention has yet been made of the psychoanalytic psychosexual stages of development (Abraham, 1927; Freud, 1905, 1928a, b, 1923; Buxbaum, 1959; Fries, 1959). Until recently the concepts of oral, anal, phallic, latency, pre-adolescent and adolescent genital stages have dominated most textbook accounts of child development. However, Anna Freud (1966) has come to describe development in rather broader terms, Erikson (1963) has pointed to other crises in growing up, and contemporary accounts by psychoanalysts now lay much less emphasis on these stages (Gillespie, 1968), although many of the original concepts remain. The best critique has been provided by White (1960), who suggested that the Freudian model of psychosexual stages is in some respects inadequate and misleading. He went on to argue that development was better viewed as the acquisition of various types of social competence.

Let us consider then what evidence there is on the various psychosexual stages. The oral stage is thought to last for approximately the first year of life during which time oral activities are considered to constitute the chief libidinal activities. Of course, sucking is an important feature of infancy—that is not in dispute. Also, in many but not all babies the oral area is more sensitive to stimulation than are other parts of the body (Lustman, 1956). However, young infants spend much time in exploratory play activities of a non-oral kind (Piaget, 1951; Gesell, 1940; Millar, 1968; White, 1959). It is now evident that the mother-child attachment does *not* primarily depend on sucking and feeding (Bowlby, 1969); sucking is not due to an innate desire (Watson, 1965), whether the child is breast-fed or bottle-fed is of no importance for later development (Caldwell, 1964), and genital play of a sexual kind is already common (see above). Thus, the concept of an oral stage is accurate in so far as it implies that oral activities are common in infancy, but it is seriously misleading in implying that these are the only or even the most important behaviours at this stage.

The second and third years of life are said to constitute the anal stage during which libidinal energies are primarily centred on eliminatory functions. Again, it is obviously true that this is the age when the child begins to gain control of his bowels and bladder and his attempts to do so constitute sources of both interest and exploration for him. But, on the other hand, there is nothing to suggest that methods of toilet training have any effect on adult personality (Caldwell, 1964). Toilet training probably involves less parental investment of energies than was once the case (Caldwell, 1964), and there are many other developments of greater importance in the second and third years (White, 1960; Thompson, 1962; Elkind, 1967). Also, genital play and exploration is very common at this age, as we have already discussed.

Freud was probably more correct about the phallic stage. Although systematic studies of the prevalence of sex play at age 4–6 yr are lacking, numerous observational studies have shown that there is an obvious genital interest in many of children's games at this time (see above). Castration anxiety and the Oedipus complex are two essential elements of this stage according to psychoanalytic views. Because of the supposed unconscious nature of many of the child's sexual feelings, these hypotheses have proved difficult to test and previous reviewers have tended to interpret the evidence in contradictory ways (Sears, 1951; Friedman, 1951; O'Connor and Franks, 1960; Zigler and Child, 1969). Castration anxiety undoubtedly occurs, probably more in boys than girls, but it seems doubtful whether it is universal and its importance for development is even more doubtful.

The Oedipus complex, which refers to the child's attachment to the opposite-sexed parent and hostility to the same-sexed parent, has been more difficult to examine. Direct questions to children as to which parent they love most have usually failed to demonstrate the supposed sex difference. On the other hand, projective techniques have produced age-specific findings which tend to support the Oedipus hypothesis (Friedman, 1952). Direct observational studies of early infancy have shown variations between children in the parent to whom they are most attached (Schaffer and Emerson, 1964). Studies using projective methods indicate an even greater individual variation in whether children show the Oedipal pattern of relationships at age 5 yr or so (Friedman, 1952). Cross-cultural studies (Honigmann, 1954) also suggest that the development of hostility to the same-sexed parent depend very much on the family pattern of relationships characteristic of particular societies. The evidence regarding the Oedipus complex is too contradictory and unsatisfactory to give rise to any firm conclusion but it seems highly probable that many children do go through a phase in which there is some antipathy to the same-sexed parent. Whether this is based on feelings of sexual rivalry is quite unknown, and what significance, if any, it has for later development is equally uncertain. It should also be said that the Oedipus complex seems to be far from universal and it is quite dependent on family circumstances rather than on any innate predisposition.

Freud's view that the emergence of castration anxiety led to a repression of sexual interests during middle-childhood—the so-called "latency period" has been shown to be basically wrong. Sexual interests and activities remain active and lively during this period.

It is sometimes suggested that Freud did not mean latency to be interpreted in absolute terms. That he *did* intend that, however, is evident from what he wrote in a review article in 1922 (Freud, 1922). "Towards the end of the fifth year this early period of sexual life normally comes to an end. It is succeeded by a period of more or less complete *latençy* (original italics). . . . The latency period appears to be a biological peculiarity of the human species.'' Furthermore, Anna Freud (1947) has made it clear that a real break in sexual development is thought to occur. She states that during the latency period . . . ''infantile sexuality comes to a standstill. Instead of developing further until sexual maturity is reached (as happens in the animal world), the libidinal urges diminish and fade into the background . . . this break in the course of sexual development is an important characteristic of the human race.'' She thought that it was partly due to a biological decrease in libido and partly to repression. It may be that in Vienna at the beginning of this century social pressures led to a concealment or even a repression of sexual interests in middle childhood. But, as we have seen, this is not the case in Western world today and certainly there is no indication of a biological decrease in libido in the early school years.

The psychoanalytic view of adolescence as a period of revival of Oedipal conflicts remains largely untested. The view that this is a period of greatly increased and more specific sex interests is, of course, one that is shared by all developmental theories and is well borne out by the available evidence.

In summary, Freud's concept of sexuality beginning in infancy or early childhood has been well established and is undoubtedly right. His description of the oral and anal stages has proved to be too narrow and, in some respects, quite misleading. He was probably right that the period of increasing genital interests about the age of 4 or 5 yr is sometimes associated with castration anxiety and hostility to the same-sexed parent. However, this pattern seems not to be universal and its presence appears to be related to particular patterns of upbringing. The concept of a latency period seems to be simply wrong and for once Freud can be accused of underestimating the importance of sex! The psychosexual mechanisms suggested for the adolescent period remain largely untested. As already discussed, the concept of innate sexual drive or libido seems to be only a half-truth and it is most unlikely that its energy component can be regarded in the hydraulic terms suggested by Freud.

PSYCHO-SOCIAL THEORIES OF SEXUAL DEVELOPMENT

Repeatedly, throughout this paper, it has been concluded that, although biological factors play some part, the way a child is brought up is the prime determinant of his gender role, of his sex type and of the direction of his sexual interests. This conclusion seems reasonably well based but it is important to note that it is based entirely on circumstantial evidence and that we have next to no idea of *what* aspects of child-rearing are important with respect to psychosexual development.

Several major hypotheses have been put forward to explain how a child develops his sex role. Perhaps the most widely held view is that identification with the same-sexed parent serves as the basis for sex role identity (Kagan, 1964). While identification with a parent is an important part of social development it seems rather unlikely that this is an adequate explanation in that sex role identity is well on the way to being established by age 4 yr at a time when both sexes probably still identify with the mother (Kohlberg, 1967). An alternative social-learning view that sex-typed behaviours are learned in the same way as any other sort of behaviour by response to parental expectations and reinforcement (Mischel, 1967) seems to explain some aspects of psychosexual development, but it probably underestimates the importance of a child's own feelings in recognizing himself as a boy or a girl and it remains too general a theory to be of much predictive value at present. The psychoanalytic theory has already been discussed in part. It only remains to add that a further important aspect of it is the view that sexuality develops from identification. In boys father-identification is thought to be the result of an anxiety-based defensive repression of sexual impulses leading to an identification with the parent perceived to be the aggressor. The weakness in the emphasis on identification has already been noted and there is very little experimental support for the notion of "identification with the aggressor" (Kohlberg, 1967; Bandura *et al.*, 1963; Bandura, 1969). Kohlberg (1967) has put forward cogent arguments for the view that sexual awareness and sex role differentiation are part of cognitive development and follow the same maturational and learning processes shown by other aspects of cognition. Undoubtedly this is true as far as it goes, but whether this is the whole explanation is another matter.

All the theories associate psychosexual development with parental identification and suggest that this is influenced by the nature of parent-child relationships. A number of studies have shown that identification tends to be greater when the parent is warm and nurturant (Kagan, 1964; Kohlberg, 1967) and that it is also influenced by which parent is dominant (Hetherington, 1967). However, the correlations are often weak, key studies have given rather different findings on replication (Yarrow *et al.*, 1968), and often findings rely on retrospective data which have been shown to have both rather low reliability and important biases (Yarrow *et al.*, 1970). How little we know and how much we have still to learn is obvious.

This still leaves the question of the acquisition of direction of sex interests. The fact that most homosexuals are not transsexuals serves to emphasize that object choice does not necessarily determine gender role. Money and the Hampsons (1961) have suggested the possible importance of a sort of imprinting mechanism operative at a critical period in early childhood. This could be so. There are anecdotal and experimental accounts in the literature of how animals (including cats and primates as well as birds) may be imprinted at least for a while on to abnormal objects by virtue of their early experiences (Beach, 1948; Micheal, 1961; Sluckin, 1970). Whether this can occur in the human and, if it can, how often it accounts for deviant sex interests is unknown. Others have laid emphasis on the importance of which parent is dominant and on patterns of identification and dependence (West, 1968). There is some evidence in support of those views but again we still have a long way to go before the mechanisms are understood (Gagnon, 1965).

CONCLUSIONS

Before puberty there are no sizeable sex differences in sex hormone production and physically speaking there is very little sexual development until puberty. The age when puberty is reached is of some psychological significance. In contrast to physical development psychosexual development begins in infancy. Genital play is common in the preschool child and during middle childhood heterosexual interests continue to develop. In both sexes there is a marked upsurge in sexual activity at puberty. Homosexual behaviour occurs as a transient phase in perhaps up to a quarter of young adolescents. The regulation of libido is a complex matter with arousability determined by hormonal state, feedback effects of copulation and experience. Androgens are important in the maintenance of sexual interest in both sexes. Sexual competence does not come innately but is to some extent learned.

Although biologic factors have some influence on the acquisition of gender role, the most important factor is the sex assigned by the parent and thus the sex in which he has been brought up. Early family relationships also play a part in the development of sexual object choice but genetic factors (not concerning chromosomal sex) may be important in some cases of homosexuality.

Throughout childhood, children continue to ask questions about sexual differences and the creation of babies. Their knowledge on these topics parallels their cognitive development and acquisition of concepts. Sex-role identity is becoming well established by age 3 yr, but it is not until later that children reliably recognize the sex of other people. Preference for their own sex begins to be evident about the same age but this appears earlier and more consistently in boys than girls. Sex differences in behaviour are evident by age 2 yr, before children know their own sex. In part these differences may be biologically determined but the later development of sex differences in attitudes, choice of games and other activities is almost certainly socially determined.

Freud's concept of sexuality beginning in early childhood has been shown to be correct but his description of the oral and anal stages have proved to be too narrow, and somewhat misleading. Castration anxiety and the Oedipal situation have been shown to be common about age 4–5 yr but they are not universal occurrences and their significance for later development is unknown. Freud's description of the latency period had been found to be wrong in most respects and his concept of innate sex drive with a quantifiable energy component only a half-truth.

At present there is insufficient evidence to decide between the various psychosocial theories of sexual development.

SUMMARY

The course and process of normal sexual development is reviewed with respect to physical maturation, sexual activity and interests, sex "drive", psychosexual competence and maturity, gender role, object choice, children's concepts of sexual differences, sex role preference, sex role standards, and psychosexual stages. Biologic, psychoanalytic and psychosocial theories of sexual development are briefly considered in the light of these findings.

REFERENCES

Abrahams, K. (1927) *Selected Papers on Psychoanalysis*. Hogarth Press, London.

Baker, H. J. and Stoller, R. J. (1968) Can a biological force contribute to a gender identity? *Am. J. Psychiat.* **127,** 1653–1658.

Baldwin, A. C. (1968) *Theories of Child Development,* pp. 349–373. Wiley, New York.

Bancroft, J. H. J. (1970) Homosexuality in the male. *Br. J. Hosp. Med.* **3,** 168–181.

Bandura, A. (1969) Social-learning theory of identificatory processes. In *Handbook of Socialization Theory and Research* (Edited by Goslin, D. A.), Rand McNally, New York.

Bandura, A. Ross, D. and Ross, S. A. (1963) A comparative test of the status envy, social power and secondary reinforcement theories of identificatory learning. *J. Abn. soc. Psychol.* **67,** 527–534.

Barnett, S. A. (1963) *A Study in Behaviour.* Methuen, London.

Barr, M. C. and Hobbs, G. E. (1954) Chromosomal sex in transvestites. *Lancet* **2,** 1109–1110.

Barrett, J. C. (1970) An analysis of coital patterns. *J. biosoc. Sci.* **2,** 351–357.

Beach, F. A. (1947) A review of physiological and psychological studies of sexual behaviour in mammals. *Physiol. Rev.* **27,** 240–307.

Beach, F. A. (1948) Sexual behaviour in animals and man. *The Harvey Lectures* **43,** 259–279.

Beach, F. A. (1956) Characteristics of masculine sex drive. In *Nebraska Symposium on Motivation.* Vol. 8, pp. 1–31. University of Nebraska Press, Lincoln.

Berg, I. Nixon, H. H. and MacMahon, R. (1963) Change of assigned sex at puberty. *Lancet* **2,** 1216–1217.

Bernick, N. (1965) The development of children's sexual attitudes as determined by the pupil-dilation response. Unpublished doctoral dissertation. Univ. Chicago cited Kohlberg (1967).

Billig, A. (1941) Fingernail biting: Its incipiency, incidence and amelioration. *Genet. Psychol. Mon.* **24,** 123–218.

Bowlby, J. (1969) *Attachment and loss.* Vol. 1. *Attachment.* Hogarth Press, London.

Bridger, W. H. (1962) Ethological concepts and human development. In *Recent Advances in Biological Psychiatry* (Edited by Wortis, J.), Vol. 4, 95–107. Grune & Stratton, New York.

Broderick, C. B. (1966) Sexual behaviour among preadolescents. *J. Soc. Issues* **22,** 6–21.

Broderick, C. B. and Fowler, S. E. (1961) New patterns of relationships between the sexes among preadolescents. *Marriage and Family Living* **23,** 27–30.

Broderick, C. B. and Rowe, G. P. (1968) A scale of preadolescent heterosexual development. *J. Marriage and the Family* **30,** 97–101.

Brown, D. Z. (1956) Sex-role preference in young children. *Psychol. Monogr.* **70** (Whole No. 287).

Brown, D. Z. (1957) Masculinity-femininity development in children. *J. consult. Psychol.* **21,** 197–202.

Buxbaum, E. (1959) Psychosexual development: the oral, anal and phallic phases. In *Readings in Psychoanalytic Psychology* (Edited by Levitt, D.). Appleton, New York.

Caldwell, B. M. (1964) The effects of infant care. In *Review of Child Development Research* (Edited by Hoffman, M. C. and Hoffman, L. W.), Vol. 1. Russell Sage Foundation, New York.

Campbell, E. H. (1939) The social-sex development of children. *Genet. Psychol. Mon.* **21,** 461–552.

Child, I. L., Potter, E. H. and Levine, E. M. (1946) Children's textbooks and personality development: an exploration in the social psychology of education. *Psychol. Mon.* **60** (Whole No. 279).

Conn, J. H. (1940) Children's reactions to the discovery of genital differences. *Am. J. Orthopsychiat.* **10,** 747–754.

Conn, J. H. (1947) Children's awareness of the origins of babies. *J. Child Psychiat.* **1,** 140–176.

Conn, J. H. and Kanner, L. (1947) Children's awareness of sex differences. *J. Child Psychiat.* **1,** 3–57.

Connor, D. V. and McGeorge, M. (1965) Psychological aspects of accelerated pubertal development. *J. Child Psychol. Psychiat.* **6,** 161–178.

Dalbiez, R. (1941) *Psychoanalytic Method and the Doctrine of Freud.* Longmans, Green, London.

D'Andrade, R. G. (1967) Sex differences and cultural institutions. In *The Development of Sex Differences* (Edited by Maccoby, E. E.). Tavistock, London.

Deutsch, J. A. and Deutsch, D. (1966) *Physiological Psychology.* Dorsey Press, Homewood, Illinois.

Dewhurst, C. J. and Gordon, R. R. (1963) Change of sex. *Lancet* **2,** 1213–1216.

Diamond, M. (1965) A critical evaluation of the ontogeny of human sexual behaviour. *Q. Rev. Biol.* **40,** 147–175.

Douglas, J. W. B. and Ross, J. M. (1964) Age of puberty related to educational ability, attainment and school leaving age. *J. Child Psychol. Psychiat.* **5,** 185–196.

Elkind, D. (1967) Cognition in infancy and early childhood. In *Infancy and Early Childhood* (Edited by Brackbill, Y.). Free Press, New York.

Erikson, E. H. (1963) *Childhood and Society,* 2nd Ed. Norton, New York.

Fitschen, W. and Clayton, B. E. (1965) Urinary excretion of gonadotrophins with particular reference to children. *Arch. Dis. Child.* **40,** 16–26.

Ford, C. S. and Beach, F. A. (1951) *Patterns of Sexual Behaviour.* Harper, New York.

Freud, A. (1947) Emotional and instinctual development. In *Indications for Child Analysis and Other Papers* 1945–1956 (1969). Hogarth Press, London.

Freud, A. (1966) *Normality and Pathology in Childhood.* Hogarth Press, London.

Freud, S. (1905) Three essays on the theory of sexuality. In *The Standard Edition of the Complete Works of Sigmund Freud* (Edited by Strachey, J.), Vol. VII, pp. 125–143. Hogarth Press, London.

Freud, S. (1908a) On the sexual theories of children. In *The Standard Edition of the Complete Works of Sigmund Freud* (Edited by Strachey, J.), Vol. 9, pp. 205–227. Hogarth Press, London (1959).

Freud, S. (1908b) Character and anal eroticism. In *Collected Papers,* Vol. 2, pp. 45–50. Hogarth, London (1924).

Freud, S. (1922) Two encyclopaedia articles. In *The Standard Edition of the Complete Works of Sigmund Freud* (Edited by Strachey, J.), Vol. XVIII. Hogarth Press, London.

Freud, S. (1923) The infantile genital organization of the libido. In *Collected Papers,* Vol. 2, pp. 244–249, Hogarth, London (1924).

Friedman, S. M. (1952) An empirical study of the castration and Oedipus complexes. *Genet. Psychol. Mon.* **46,** 61–130.

Fries, M. E. (1959) Reivew of the literature on the latency period. In *Readings in Psychoanalytic Psychology* (Edited by Levitt, M.). Appleton, New York.

Gagnon, J. H. (1965) Sexuality and sexual learning in the child. *Psychiatry* **28,** 212–228.

Gesell, A. (1940) *The First Five Years of Life.* Methuen, London.

Gillespie, W. H. (1968) The psychoanalytic theory of child development. In *Foundations of Child Psychiatry* (Edited by Miller, E.). Pergamon, London.

Goy, R. W. (1968) Organising effects of androgen on the behaviour of rhesus monkeys. In *Endocrinology and Human Behaviour* (Edited by Michael, R. P.). Oxford University Press, London.

Grant, E. C. G. and Mears, E. (1967) Mental effects of oral contraceptives. *Lancet* **2,** 945–946.

Greenacre, P. (1950) Special problems of early female sexual development. *Psychoanalyt. Stud. Child.* **V,** 122–138.

Halverson, H. M. (1940) Genital and sphincter behaviour of the male infant. *J. Genet. Psychol.* **56,** 95–136.

Hamburg, D. A. and Lunde, D. T. (1967) Sex hormones in the development of sex differences in human behaviour. In *The Development of Sex Differences* (Edited by Maccoby, E. E.). Tavistock Publications, London.

Hampson, J. L. and Hampson, J. G. (1961) The ontogenesis of sexual behaviour in man. In *Sex and Internal Secretions* (Edited by Young, W. C. and Corner, G. W.), Vol. II, 3rd Edn. Williams & Wilkins, Baltimore.

Hardy, K. R. (1964) An appetitional theory of sexual motivation. *Psychol. Rev.* **71,** 1–18.

Harlow, H. F. and Harlow, M. K. (1969) Effects of various mother-infant relationships on rhesus monkey behaviours. *Determinants of Infant Behaviour IV* (Edited by Foss, B. M.). Methuen, London.

Hartup, W. W. and Zook, E. A. (1960) Sex-role preference in three and four year old children. *J. Cons. Psychol.* **24,** 420–426.

Hattendorf, K. W. (1932) A study of the questions of young children concerning sex: a phase of an experimental approach to parent education. *J. Soc. Psychol.* **3,** 37–65.

Hebb, D. O. (1961) *The Organization of Behaviour: a new psychological theory.* Science Edit., New York.

Heston, L. L. and Shields, J. (1968) Homosexuality in twins: a family study and a registry study. *Arch. Gen. Psychiat.* **18,** 149–160.

Hetherington, E. M. (1967) The effects of familial variables on sex typing, on parent-child similarity and on imitation in children. In *Minnesota Symposia on Child Psychology* (Edited by Hill, J. P.), Vol. 1. University of Minnesota Press, Minneapolis.

Hinde, R. A. (1960) Energy models of motivation. *Symp. Soc. exp. Biol.* **14,** 199–213.

Honigmann, J. J. (1957) *Culture and Personality.* Harper Bros., New York.

Hunt, J. M. (1960) Experience and the development of motivation: some reinterpretations. *Child Develop.* **31,** 489–504.

Isaacs, S. (1933) *Social Development in Young Children.* Routledge & Kegan Paul, London.

Janowitz, H. D. and Grossman, M. I. (1949) Hunger and appetite: Some definitions and concepts. *J. Mt. Sinai Hosp.* **16,** 231–240.

Jones, M. C. (1965) Psychological correlates of somatic development. *Child Develop.* **36,** 899–911.

Jones, M. C. and Bayley, N. (1950) Physical maturing among boys as related to behaviour. *J. Educ. Psychol.* **41,** 129–148.

Kagan, J. (1964) Acquisition and significance of sex typing and sex-role identity. In *Review of Child Development Research* (Edited by Hoffman, M. L. and Hoffman, L. W.), Vol. 1. Russell Sage Foundation, New York.

Kagan, J. and Lenkin, J. (1960) The child's differential perception of parental attributes. *J. abn. soc. Psychol.* **61,** 440–447.

Kagan, J. and Moss, H. A. (1962) *Birth to Maturity.* Wiley, New York.

Kallman, F. J. (1952) Comparative twin study on the genetic aspects of male homosexuality. *J. nerv. ment. Dis.* **115,** 283–297.

Katcher, A. (1955) The discrimination of sex differences by young children. *J. genet. Psychol.* **87,** 131–143.

Kenyon, F. E. (1970) Homosexuality in the female. *Br. J. Hosp. Med.* **3,** 183–206.

Kinsey, A. C., Pomeroy, W. B. and Martin, C. E. (1948) *Sexual Behaviour in the Human Male.* Saunders, Philadelphia.

Kinsey, A. C., Pomeroy, W. B., Martin, C. E. and Gebhardt, P. H. (1953) *Sexual Behaviour in the Human Female,* Saunders, Philadelphia.

Koch, H. L. (1935) An analysis of certain forms of so-called 'nervous habits' in young children. *J. Genet. Psychol.* **46,** 139–170.

Kohlberg, L. (1967) A cognitive-developmental analysis of children's sex-role concepts and attitudes. In *The Development of Sex Differences* (Edited by Maccoby, E. E.). Tavistock, London.

Kreitler, H. and S. (1966) Children's concepts of sexuality and birth. *Child Develop.* **37,** 363–378.

Landis, C., Landis, A. T. and Bolles, M. M. (1940) *Sex in Development.* Hoeber, New York.

Lawick-Goodall, J. N. (1968) The behaviour of free-living chimpanzees in the Gombe stream reserve. *Anim. Behaviour. Mon.* **1,** 165–311.

Levin, G. R. and Kaye, H. (1964) Non-nutritive sucking by human neonates. *Child Develop.* **35,** 749–758.

Levy, D. M. (1928) Fingersucking and accessory movements in early infancy: an ethologic study. *Am. J. Psychiat.* **7,** 881–918.

Levy, D. (1970) 'Control-situation' studies of children's response to the difference in genitalia. *Am. J. Orthopsychiat.* **10,** 755–762.

Lustman, S. L. (1956) Rudiments of the ego. *Psychoanal. Stud. Child* **11,** 89–98.

McCandless, B. R. (1960) Rate of development, bodybuild and personality. In *Child Development and Child Psychiatry* (Edited by Shagass, C. and Pasamanick, B.), Vol. 88, 42–57. American Psychiatrical Association, Washington, D.C.

Maccoby, E. E. (Ed.) (1957) *The Development of Sex Differences.* Tavistock, London.

MacFarlane, J. W. (1939) The relation of environmental pressures to the development of the child's personality and habit patterning. *J. Pediat.* **15,** 142–152.

MacFarlane, J. W., Allen, L. and Honzik, M. R. (1954) *A Developmental Study of the Behaviour Problems of Normal Children between 21 months and 14 years.* University of California Press, Berkeley.

McKee, J. P. and Sheriffs, A. C. (1957) The differential evaluation of males and females. *J. Pers.* **25,** 356–371.

Malinowski, B. (1929) *The Sexual Life of Savages in North-western Melanesia.* Harcourt, Brace & World, New York.

Mason, W. A., Harlow, H. F. and Rueping, R. R. (1959) The development of manipulatory responsiveness in the infant rhesus monkey. *J. comp. physiol. Psychol.* **52,** 555–558.

Masters, W. H. and Johnson, V. E. (1966) *Human Sexual Response.* Churchill, London.

Michael, R. P. (1961) Hypersexuality in male cats without brain damage. *Science* **127,** 553–554.

Michael, R. P. (1968) Gonadal hormones and the control of primate behaviour. In *Endocrinology and Human Behaviour* (Edited by Michael, R. P.). Oxford University Press, London.

Migeon, C. J., Rivarola, M. A. and Foreat, M. G. (1969) Studies of androgen in male transsexual subjects: effects of oestrogen therapy. In *Transexualism and Sex Reassignment* (Edited by Green, R. and Money, J.). John Hopkins Press, Baltimore.

Millar, S. (1968) *The Psychology of Play.* Penguin, London.

Mischel, W. (1967) A social-learning view of sex differences in behaviour. In *The Development of Sex Differences* (Edited by Maccoby, E.). Tavistock, London.

Money, J. (1961) Sex hormones and other variables in human eroticism. In *Sex and Internal Secretions* (Edited by Young, W. C. and Corner, G. W.), 3rd Edn. Vol. II. Williams & Wilkins, Baltimore.

Money, J. (1965) Influence of hormones on sexual behaviour. *Ann. Rev. Med.* **16,** 67–82.

Money, J. and Ehrhardt, A. A. (1968) Prenatal hormonal exposure: possible effects on behaviour in man. In *Endocrinology and Human Behaviour* (Edited by Michael, R. P.). Oxford University Press, London.

Montgomery, K. C. (1953) The effect of the hunger and thirst drives upon exploratory behaviour. *J. comp. Psychol.* **46,** 315–319.

Mussen, P. and Bouterline-Young, H. (1964) Relationships between rate of physical maturing and personality among boys of Italian descent. *Vita Humana* **7,** 186–200.

Mussen, P. H. and Jones, M. C. (1957) Self-conception motivations and interpersonal attitudes of late and early maturing boys. *Child Develop.* **28,** 243–256.

Mussen, P. H. and Jones, M. C. (1958) The behaviour motivations of late and early maturing boys. *Child Develop.* **29,** 61–67.

Newson, J. and Newson, E. (1963) *Patterns of Infant Care in an Urban Community.* Allen & Unwin, London.

Newson, J. and Newson, E. (1968) *Four Years Old in an Urban Community.* Allen & Unwin, London.

O'Connor, N. and Franks, C. (1960) Childhood upbringing and other environmental factors. In *Handbook of Abnormal Psychology* (Edited by Eysenck, H. J.). Pitman, London.

Pare, C. M. B. (1956) Homosexuality and chromosomal sex. *J. Psychosom. Res.* **1,** 247–251.

Parker, N. (1964) Homosexuality in twins: a report on three discordant pairs. *Br. J. Psychiat.* **110,** 489–495.

Perloff, W. H. (1949) The role of the hormones in human sexuality. *Psychosom. Med.* **11,** 133–139.

Piaget, J. (1951) *Plays, Dreams and Imitation in Childhood.* Norton, New York.

Pritchard, M. (1962) Homosexuality and genetic sex. *J. Ment. Sci.* **128,** 616–623.

Rabbon, M. (1950) Sex-role identification in young children in two diverse social groups. *Genet. Psychol. Mon.* **42,** 81–158.

Raboch, J. and Nedoma, K. (1958) Sex chromatin and sexual behaviour. *Psychosom. Med.* **20,** 55–59.

Ramsey, C. V. (1943) The sexual development of boys. *Am. J. Psychol.* **56,** 217–233.

Randall, J. (1970) Transvestism and transsexualism. *Br. J. Hosp. Med.* **3,** 217–233.

Rapaport, D. (1960) On the psychoanalytic theory of motivation. In *Nebraska Symposium on Motivation,* Vol. 8, pp. 173–247. Univ. Nebraska Press, Lincoln.

Reese, H. W. (1966) Attitudes toward the opposite sex in late childhood. *Merill-Palmer Quart.* **12,** 157–163.

Rutter, M. (1970) Sex differences in children's responses to family stress. In *The Child in His Family* (Edited by Anthony, E. J. and Koupernik, C.). Wiley, Interscience, New York.

Schaffer, H. R. and Emerson, P. E. (1964) The development of social attachments in infancy. *Monogr. Soc. Res. Child Development.* **29,** No. 3 (serial no. 94).

Schofield,M. (1965) *The Sexual Behaviour of Young People.* Longmans, London.

Schon, M. and Sutherland, A. M. (1950) The role of hormones in human behaviour III. Changes in female sexuality after hypophysectomy. *J. Clin. Endocrinol. Metabol.* **20,** 833–841.

Sears, R. R. (1951) *Survey of objective studies of Psychoanalytic Concepts.* Social Science Research Council, New York.

Sears, R. R., Maccoby, E.E. and Levin, H.(1957) *Patterns of Child Rearing.* Harper & Rowe, New York.

Sheffield, F. D., Wulff, J. J. and Becker, R. (1951) Reward value of copulation without sex drive reduction. *J. comp. physiol. Psychol.* **44,** 3–8.

Sluckin, W. (1970) *Early Learning in Man and Animal.* Allen & Unwin, London.

Tanner, J. M. (1962) *Growth at Adolescence,* 2nd Ed. Blackwell, Oxford.

Terman, L. M. (1938) *Psychological Factors in Marital Happiness.* McGraw-Hill, New York.
Terman, L. M. (1956) Personal communication to Brown, D. G. (1956) *op. cit.*
Thompson, G. C. (1962) Developmental trends in social awareness and interactive skills. In *Child Psychology,* Chap. 12. Houghton Mifflin, Boston.
Udry, J. R. and Morris, N. M. (1968) Distributions of coitus in the menstrual cycle. *Nature* **220,** 593–596.
Watson, R. I. (1965) *Psychology of the child, 2nd Edn., pp. 262–267.* Wiley, New York.
Waxenberg, S. E., Drellich, M. G. and Sutherland, A. M. (1959) The role of hormones in human behaviour—I. Changes in female sexuality after adrenalectomy. *J. clin. Endocrinol. Metab.* **19,** 193–202.
Wechsley, D. (1931) The incidence and significance of fingernail biting in children. *Psychoanal. Rev.* **18,** 201–209.
West, D. J. (1968) *Homosexuality,* 3rd Edn. Duckworth, London.
Whalen, R. E. (1961) Effects of mounting without intromission and intromission without ejaculation on sexual behaviour and male learning. *J. comp. physiol. Psychol.* **54,** 409–415.
Whalen, R. E. (1966) Sexual motivation. *Psychol. Rev.* **73,** 151–163.
White, R. W. (1959) Motivation reconsidered—the concept of competence. *Psychol. Rev.* **66,** 297–333.
White, R. W. (1960) Competence and the psychosexual stages of development. *Nebraska Symposium on Motivation,* Vol. 8, pp. 97–141.
Yarrow, M. R., Campbell, J. D. and Burton, R. V. (1970) Recollections of childhood: a study of the retrospective method. *Mon. soc. Res. Child Develop.* **35,** No. 5 (serial No. 138).
Young, W. C., Goy, R. W. and Phoenix, C. H. (1964) Hormones and sexual behaviour. *Science* **143,** 212–218.
Zigler, E. and Child, I. L. (1969) Socialization. In *The Handbook of Social Psychology* (Edited by Lindzey, G. and Aronson, E.), Vol. 3. Addison-Wesley, London.

Requirements for Healthy Development of Adolescent Youth*

Gisela Konopka

INTRODUCTION

In the spring of 1973 the Office of Child Development of the Department of Health Education and Welfare asked Gisela Konopka and the Center for Youth Development and Research, University of Minnesota to develop a statement on their concept of normal adolescence and impediments to healthy development. The statement was viewed as a possible base for national policy. . . .

We are talking about adolescent youth in the cultural context of the United States of America in the 1970's. Our objectives are:

- to present a positive developmental model of adolescence by describing what we regard as the key concepts and qualities of adolescence;

*From Gisela Konopka, "Requirements for Healthy Development of Adolescent Youth," *Adolescence,* 8, **31,** 291–316. Slightly edited and reprinted by permission of the author and the Editor, *Adolescence.*

- to set forth some of the conditions for healthy development of adolescent youth;
- to discuss specific obstacles to such development.

Within this framework we offer a few recommendations concerning programs and research that could facilitate healthy development of adolescent youth. . . . [W]e emphasize that we do not see adolescence purely as preparation for adulthood. Rather we see it as one part of the total developmental process—a period of tremendous significance distinguished by specific characteristics. *Basic to our view is the concept that adolescents are growing, developing persons in a particular age group—not pre-adults, pre-parents, or pre-workers, but human beings participating in the activities of the world around them.* In brief, we see adolescence not only as a passage to somewhere but also as an important stage in itself.

In setting down what we consider to be the significant characteristics or key concepts of adolescence, we call attention again to the fact that they will not apply *in toto* to any person, group, or subgroup. Circumstances and timing, combined with individual differences, make for an infinite variety of behavior patterns, interactions, and outcomes.

Key Concepts of Adolescence

Experience of Physical Sexual Maturity A phenomenon particular to adolescence that never occurs again in the life of the individual is the process of developing sexual maturation, different from the state of accomplished sexual maturation. Biologically this is a totally new experience. Its significance is due partly to its pervasiveness and partly to the societal expectations surrounding it. It creates in adolescents a great wonderment about themselves and the feeling of having something in common with all human beings. It influences their whole relationship to each other, whether male or female. Entering this part of maturity also stimulates them to newly assess the world. Indicative of the importance attached universally to maturation of the sex organs are the puberty rites and initiation rituals that mark the transition from childhood to adulthood in many cultures, including present day USA.

Experience of Withdrawal of and from Adult Benevolent Protection Along with biological maturity attained in adolescence come varying degrees of withdrawal of and from the protection generally given to dependent children by parents or substitutes. We know that some young people were never protected, even as children, but we assume a modicum of protection as a healthy base. Whatever the degree of previous protection, the adolescent is moving out from the family toward interdependence (not independence, but *inter*dependence) in three areas: (1) with his peers, his own generation; (2) with his elders, but now on an interacting or a rebellious level instead of a dependent level (adults often increase their attempt to control and direct adolescents, which tends to promote active rebellion); and (3) with younger children, not on a play level but on a beginning-to-care-for-and-nurture level. This process of moving away from dependency creates tensions and emotional conflicts.

Consciousness of Self in Interaction The development of self and the searching for self starts in childhood, but the intellectual as well as the emotional consciousness of self in interaction with others is particularly characteristic of adolescence. It is a time when personal meaning is given to new social experiences. The young person defines for himself what he is experiencing in his relationships with others. His "meaning" may be different from that of those with whom he is interacting, but so long as it makes sense to him he can grow and move forward. The kind of categories he used as a child to figure out the world begin to break down. What may have been clear and explicable may suddenly become inexplicable.

Re-evaluation of Values Though the formation of values is a lifelong developmental process, it peaks in adolescence.It is related to both thinking and feeling, and is influenced by human interaction. In our culture where young people are likely to be exposed to a variety of contradictory values, questioning begins even in childhood. The adolescent engages in re-evaluation of values that have been either accepted at an earlier age or simply rejected because of individual resistance. He moves beyond simple perception (if I burn my hand it hurts) and sees things in a moral framework as "good" and "bad." He is consciously searching for value clarification. He becomes a moral philosopher concerned with "shoulds" and "oughts." Given the inconsistency of a society whose institutions frequently do not follow the general intent of the ideological system, value confrontations are inevitable. The young, because of the intensity of their total being, tend to be uncompromising. They may opt clearly for a thoroughly egalitarian value system, or they may give up and become cynics. The wish of each generation to start over again is not new. What is new in our time, however, is the intensity and the worldwide drive to translate this wish into reality.

Again, the younger child is constantly developing mastery of the outer world, but the adolescent encounters his world with a new intellectual and emotional consciousness. He meets his world less as an observer and more as a participator who actually has a place to fill.

Experimentation The young are possessed of greater physical, mental, and emotional capacity and therefore of a great thirst to try out those capacities. Experimentation is writ large—as important as eating or sleeping. Human beings learn through experimentation from childhood on. The child explores, for instance, by touching, putting things into his mouth, etc. Adolescents need to experiment with wider circles of life—meet various kinds of people, see other cultures. They need to experiment with their own strength and value systems—lead a group, try out intimate relationships, engage in some form of adventure. The experimentation necessary to adolescents usually includes a feeling of *risk*. It is their way of learning about their own and the surrounding reality.

This need is fraught with danger because adolescents are not as cautious as adults, yet it must have some outlet. It can become a major form of positive healthy development of the young.

Qualities of Adolescence

Linked inseparably with the major phenomena of adolescence outlined above are a number of qualities or characteristics peculiar to this period; at least they are present in heightened form. We look on them as healthy and normal, not as detrimental or negative. A few of the more significant ones are highlighted here.

The drive to experiment is coupled with a mixture of *audacity* and *insecurity*. The audacity is related to not being experienced enough to envision the harmful consequences of a given action; the insecurity is related to the uncertainty that accompanies inexperience and the lessening or withdrawal of protection.

A deep sense of *loneliness* and a high degree of *psychological vulnerability* are two other specific qualities of adolescence. Every attempt at experimentaion, and reaching out is new and very intense. If the outcome is negative it is exceedingly painful because youth do not have a "bank" of positive experiences to draw from when defeats occur. Adults can say, "Oh well, you'll get over it," but such remarks annoy more than they comfort.

Enormous *mood swings* are usually cited as characteristic of adolescence. Many factors contribute to the swings. Physiological changes are related to emotional changes. Moving from dependence to interdependence creates a whole series of tensions and conflicts. The impact of peers is magnified. Ambivalence is common. The yearning to jump into the next stage of development co-exists with the desire to have things stay as they are. The feeling of omnipotence tangoes with the feeling of helplessness and inadequacy. The cocksure conviction that "it won't happen to me" plays hide and seek with the fear that it will. Being expected to act like an adult one minute and being treated like a child the next is experienced as confusing. How can one be too young to do almost everything one wants to do, and adult enough to behave as "they" think one should? Seeing parents as mere humans with frailties can be terrifying after having depended on them as all-wise.

Adolescents have a strong *peer group need*. They stress cooperation with that segment of the group with which they identify. The sub-groups they form are often very tightly knit. To gain group acceptance the individual seems to relegate his personal competitive drives to second place, whether the goal is positive or negative—manning a hotline emergency service, for example, or "ripping off" a certain store.

Finally, adolescents need to be *argumentative* and *emotional* since they are in the process of trying out their own changing values and their own relationships with the outer world.

* * * * * *

Summarizing the attributes of adolescence into *one* concept is difficult and may be an oversimplification. Erik Erikson gave us the concept of the age of identity-seeking; therefore his stress on provision of a moratorium as condition for healthy development.

I (Konopka) prefer to think of adolescence as the AGE OF COMMITMENT. It is the move into the *true interdependence of men*. The struggle between dependency and independence—so often described in the literature—is an expression of this entrance into interdependence.

Commitment includes the search for oneself, as Erikson stressed, but it also points toward the emotional, intellectual, and sometimes physical reach for other people as well as ideas, ideologies, causes, work choices.

This move toward *commitment* is so serious and so significant that providing healthy conditions to let it unfold becomes just as crucial for human development as providing healthy conditions for growth in early childhood. It elevates adolescence from a stage frequently regarded as one that must be endured and passed through as rapidly as possible to a stage of earnest and significant human development.

CONDITIONS FOR HEALTHY DEVELOPMENT OF YOUTH

Looking back now on our view of man and adolescence in the cultural context of the United States in the 1970's, we begin to see clusters or constellations of associated imperatives, skills, and tasks that—taken together—create a climate conducive to healthy development of youth.

A pluralistic society with egalitarianism as an ideal demands participation of people. Therefore it is quite clear that creation of conditions that facilitate healthy adolescent development begins with the encouragement of equal and responsible participation by youth in the family or other societal units.

Because we are living in a complex society, *choice-making* becomes increasingly important. It cannot be based on instinct. Therefore youth must develop the capacity to make decisions in many areas: school interests, work interests, use of discretionary time, the kind of friends they want to cultivate, and so on. Practical learning opportunities are essential.

As the protections normally associated with childhood are withdrawn and adolescents move toward wider interdependence, particularly with their peers, they need to have a sense of *belonging* to their own age groups and to adults as well. They need to find ways to interact with peers—both male and female. They need to acquire the skills to handle their sex drives, to develop and maintain friendship, to experience intimacy. They may choose to join a youth organization or a gang, take up a "cause," concentrate on dancing or listening to records in a group, or adopt some other activity—and they should have the opportunity to do so.

Because of the conflicting values adolescents encounter in a rapidly changing world, they should have the opportunity to thrash out their reactions, consider the pluses and minuses, and try to determine where they themselves stand so that they will be better able to deal with ideas of all shades—including demagoguery. Those working and living with youth can foster healthy value formation by *encouraging open discussion* and refraining from trying to superimpose their values upon them.

Although "Who am I?" is a question that recurs throughout life, the search for identity becomes more conscious and highly emotional during adolescence. Therefore the young need a *chance to reflect on self* in relation to others (some use their peers as mirrors) and to test self in a variety of settings. The process is a healthy one so long as it does not consist entirely of looking inward.

In recent years people in the helping professions, and laymen as well, seem to have become engrossed in a very individualistic approach to healthy psychological development. Value clarification is discussed in terms of one person examining his own values; participants in therapy groups delve endlessly into themselves; books on self-analysis keep rolling off the presses. While we believe it is a condition of growth to be able to discover who one is, we also believe that inordinate preoccupation with self in the search for identity can become very unhealthy. Hence we emphasize the importance of looking outward as well as inward.

Since experimentation is essential to learning, adolescents should have the opportunity to discover their own strengths and weaknesses in a host of different situations, to experience success and also learn how to cope with adversity and defeat. These skills are usually acquired through active participation. Therefore adolescents should have a genuine *chance to participate as citizens, as members of a household, as workers—in general, as responsible members of society.*

Experimentation involves risks. With audacious but inexperienced youth doing the experimenting, the risks are magnified. If experimentation is essential to learning, as we have said, then it can be argued that adolescence should be a period in which youth can experiment without suffering disastrous consequences when they fail or make mistakes; in other words, that the means for a psychosocial moratorium should be provided. It can also be argued that learning and growth will not occur unless youth are held responsible for their actions, and that participatory activity without such responsibility becomes tokenism.

Our view is that some allowance for experimentation is important for healthy development, but that the "moratorium" should not be total. Adolescents should be *allowed to experiment with their own identity, with relationships to other people, and with ideas, without having to commit themselves irrevocably.* They should be able to *try out various roles* without being obligated to pursue a given course—in school or in the world of work, for example. They should also have the opportunity to practice with limited hurt if they fail, because while their inexperience does not make them inferior to adults, it does make them different. On the other hand, youth should understand that genuine *participation* and genuine *responsibility go hand in hand;* that a basic tenet of our social system is: for every right or set of rights there is a corresponding responsibility or set of responsibilities. To illustrate: young or old, a bona fide voting member of a governing board or some other decision-making body is responsible for his vote. Also we believe that youth should be helped to develop a feeling of *accountability* for the impact they have on other human beings—accountability not in a hierarchic sense, but *in the context of a relationships among equals.*

Finally, a climate that facilitates healthy development should provide opportunities to cultivate the *capacity to enjoy life,* to be creative, to be frivolous, to do things on one's own, and to learn to interact with all kinds of people—people of different races, different interests, different life styles, different economic and cultural backgrounds, different ages.

* * * * * *

To recapitulate, conditions for healthy development should provide young people with opportunities

- to participate as citizens, as members of a household, as workers, as responsible members of society;

- to gain experience in decision making;
- to interact with peers and acquire a sense of belonging;
- to reflect on self in relation to others and to discover self by looking outward as well as inward;
- to discuss conflicting values and formulate their own value system;
- to experiment with their own identity, with relationships to other people, with ideas; to try out various roles without having to commit themselves irrevocably;
- to develop a feeling of accountability in the context of a relationship among equals;
- to cultivate a capacity to enjoy life.

Given these conditions, adolescents will be enabled to gain experience in forming relationships and making *meaningful commitments*. They are not expected by the adult world to make final lifelong commitments; the expectation is related to their own need for interdependence and humanity's need for their commitment to others without losing themselves.

OBSTACLES TO PROGRESS OF NORMAL DEVELOPMENT

Having looked at some of the conditions that facilitate healthy development, we now look at the other side of the coin: obstacles to the progress of normal development. Both the presence of unfavorable factors and the absence of favorable factors constitute obstacles.

The factors selected for discussion here are closely related to the key concepts and qualities of adolescence described earlier. Those that impede normal development of all human beings—such as *lack of nutrition, inadequate housing, poverty in general, racial discrimination—are exceedingly important and are acknowledged here as basic*. In addition, we wish to underline the following specific obstacles to healthy development of adolescent youth.

Violation of Adolescents' Self-Respect by Adult World

Violation of self-respect is detrimental to all human beings. In adolescence, because of increasing self-consciousness and interdependence with peers, anything that violates self-respect—such as racial discrimination, or being disregarded as a significant human being, or being labeled a failure—is taken with special hurt. It may result in withdrawal, complete destruction of self, mental illness, drug abuse, or enormous hostility. The adolescent sees many inconsistencies in the adult world which were less definable in childhood. He often perceives simple criticism as a demeaning "put-down." To ignore or to laugh off his hurt and frustration is to violate his self-respect in a very real way.

Society's View of Adolescence as Preparatory

The prevailing cultural view that adolescence is only a time of preparation for adulthood is harmful because it places youth in an ambivalent situation where they are neither children nor adults. It causes expectations to be extremely confused: in one instance, "You're too old to behave like that;" in another, "You're still a child, you know." The very rhetoric that adolescence is transition may be an obstacle in itself.

Prolonged Economic Dependence of Youth

Youth's bursting energy, thirst for adventure, and yearning for a productive role in society make it difficult for some to accept prolonged economic dependence. School dropouts, especially in the middle class economic bracket, often are motivated by wanting to make it on their own. A sense of violation of self-respect, inflicted by school or community, contributes to dropouts at all economic levels, perhaps more so at the lower level. While modern technology has increased the need for the more extensive knowledge and training that long schooling makes possible, educational requirements for many jobs are "standard" rather than job-related. They should be less rigid.

Limited Outlet for Experimentation by Youth

Urbanization and population density diminish possibilities for experimentation. Though mobility increases at adolescence, space and places to go are limited. Opportunities for part time work experience are limited by the inability or unwillingness of business and industry to accept large numbers of young people into their operations and by the desire of labor organizations to lock up jobs and entrance to jobs.

Mistrust is another basis for many restrictions on experimentation. Some restrictions are warranted on the grounds of reasonable protection, but others—such as some youth-serving organizations not allowing 16- and 17-year-olds to go on hikes without an adult present—are exaggerated.

Popular Acceptance of the Generation Gap Concept

In recent years the concept of a generation gap has been widely accepted as inevitable —a notion reinforced by the media. Worse, the so-called gap has been acted out as hostility by both adults and young people, each placing the other in the role of adversary. This state of affairs is an obstacle to the healthy development of adults as well as youth, since they are interdependent.

Influences That Encourage Adolescent Egocentricity

An outcome of increased personal alienation and separation from responsibilities and participation has been the problem of adolescent egocentricity. The lack of effective interpersonal competencies, both within the teenage generation and across teenage and adult generations, escalates the tendency toward a narrow individualism. The relativism inherent in the fad to "do your own thing" too often leads to further withdrawal and separation. Such experience can act as an effective negative barrier by preventing the development of needed interpersonal competency.

Lack of Opportunity for Moral Development

It is important to note that many adolescents stabilize their value system at levels well below universal values of social justice. Society's failure to provide for significant experience and careful examination/reflection of that experience for most teenagers literally stunts their moral development. Simple precepts are no more acceptable. Critical to our statement is the finding that there is almost no increase in the level of moral maturity beyond that reached during adolescence. Clearly, according to Kohlberg[1] and Konopka[2], the time to stimulate maximal psychological and moral maturity is during this stage.

Society's Confusion about Sex

A conspiracy of silence about sex or banal exchange on the level of advertising cliches are still characteristic of the wider society. Such practice prevents young people from clarifying their own attitudes about one of the most forceful drives at this age. It pushes them into clandestine experimentations that often frighten or demean them. Such ignorance has helped to increase the incidence of venereal disease in young people.

Society's Belief That Family is the Only Place for Youth

For certain young people the fact that the traditional family (father, mother, children) is considered the only unit conducive to healthy growth, with no alternatives, is damaging. With no legitimate substitute available they are forced into runaway episodes, hiding, drugs.

Dominance of Youth Organizations by Adults

Organizations are instruments of our society. Causes are fought and won by organizations. Yet when the young organize they are seldom permitted to run their own show. Adult needs often supersede the healthy development of youth. Adult leaders of youth organizations tend to view teenagers as minds to be molded and shaped as if they were young children. Governing boards are dominated by adults who make policy, "know what is best." Adult "advisers" engineer subtle (and sometimes not so subtle) roadblocks to action. Formal organizations which presumably exist to serve youth become top-heavy bureaucracies impervious to the suggestions youth offer. Such tactics prevent youth from gaining experience as genuinely functioning citizens and breed cynicism.

Denial of Equal Participation to Youth

In almost every aspect of society—family, school, civic organizations, political groups, social and religious groups—youth are usually not permitted equal participation. They may not even be allowed free passage into the organizations. This denial is inconsistent with the notion that people learn and develop by doing.

Uneven Laws Pertaining to Youth

Laws pertaining to youth vary from state to state. Some are outmoded; some are ambiguous; all are variably administered. For those youngsters who run into legal

[1]L. Kohlberg and R. Kramer, "Continuities and Discontinuities in Childhood and Adult Moral Development," *Human Development,* 1969, **12:** pp. 93–120.

[2]Gisela Konopka, "Formation of Values in the Developing Person," *American Journal of Orthopsychiatry,* **43**(1), January 1973.

difficulties the obstacles to healthy development are multiplied tenfold. If the offenders are institutionalized they are cut off from normal interaction with their associates and their development is stunted—contrary to the philosophy of the juvenile court which was established so that young persons could be protected and rehabilitated instead of being punished. ''Juvenile status offenses'' (truancy, chronic absenting, and incorrigibility, for example) are offenses only if committed by the young. Teenagers are punished for behavior often necessary at that age. Laws making it impossible for young people to get medical care without parental consent are obstacles to physical health, and to mental and emotional health as well.

RECOMMENDATIONS

Several considerations influenced our approach to recommendations concerning the kind of programs and research endeavors we believe would facilitate the healthy development of adolescent youth.

The fact that this statement is addressed to a governmental agency led us to direct our suggestions primarily toward action that could be instituted by government.

We do not adhere to the simplistic view that by government action alone or by individual action alone will healthy development of youth be assured. At best it can only be facilitated, and that pursuit will require the best efforts of both worlds—public and private.

It is understood that the fulfillment of basic needs is the foundation on which facilitation of any kind of human development rests. This statement is concerned for the most part with the psychosocial aspects of healthy development. Our recommendations are directly related to our previously stated view of adolescence, taken as a whole.

* * * * * *

Two approaches to recommendations were considered: (1) giving attention individually to each system in which adolescents live and move—educational, family, work, discretionary time, correctional, and governmental; (2) looking at the total picture and thinking in terms of remedial or rectifying programs and research efforts. The second approach was agreed upon, chiefly because each system is so closely related to other systems that any program, to be effective, necessarily would have to involve more than one system. The pivotal position of the *educational system* should be specially noted. In the life of adolescent youth the schools are of critical importance. Unless they are supportive of programs aimed at reform in other areas, those programs are likely to fall short.

We begin with some general observations that apply to all systems.

Priority Concerns Related to All Systems Serving Youth

We assign top priority to actuating a major effort to *educate adults who work with youth* about conditions that facilitate healthy development, and how such conditions can be created. Envisioned is an interdisciplinary focus on youth in formal and informal educational programs designed to improve the skills, insight, and understanding of persons involved with youth—teachers, parents, counselors, social workers, recreation directors, correction officers, health professionals, and other youth-serving personnel.

We also urge greater emphasis on the *education of youth* (1) to improve their competency and self-confidence in using the resources and power to which they have access, and (2) to develop in each individual the strength or courage to cope with the system as it affects him.

Changes in structure and program are recommended wherever required *to facilitate significant input by youth.* Experience with federal programs such as Model Cities, Housing, and Community Action could provide direction. In the educational system, for example, consideration might be given to student membership on the school board or on key committees, or the development by students of student rights statements, or the legitimization of organizations run by youth for youth. This is not, however, to suggest the development of a professional group of adolescents who are presumed to speak for the adolescent community. Adolescents, like any other population group, are not all of one mind.

Criteria for Programs and Systems Serving Youth

The effectiveness of programs and systems serving youth can be judged by the opportunities they offer youth and the credibility they enjoy. We believe those which merit support are distinguished by:

- Provision of opportunity for youth to have experience in (1) making choices; (2) making commitments; (3) experimenting with a variety of roles to ''try out'' the choices and commitments they make
- Credibility: validity of the program in the eyes of those served.

* * * * * *

Unless real options are available, choice-making becomes an empty phrase. Pseudo decision-making does not promote developing commitment. Therefore, *intervention* logically should be focused on the removal of limiting factors.

Carrying this line of reasoning further, *law* should be used to support healthy development rather than as it is now, presumably to curb socially disapproved behavior (often including behavior that actually has become more common.)[3] The formulation and use of *policy* should be guided by the same principle.

Greatest Urgency

It can always be said (and all too often is) that progress on this or that front cannot be made until such and such changes are made on some other front. While we are well aware of the complex interrelationships that make remedial action difficult, we believe an intensive national effort must be made to rectify conditions in areas where youth are being most cruelly battered and mangled.

[3]The population of delinquency institutions for girls consists in the majority of girls whose ''crime'' is involvement in sexual experimentaion.

1 We have singled out the correctional system as the greatest offender because it is the one in which youth are most powerless, once they enter it. A total and concerted effort should be made to:
   a Close mass juvenile institutions;
   b Develop substitute living situations for young people who cannot live at home;
   c Provide access of juveniles to legal aid.
2 We suggest support of programs to make education (formal and informal) a base for healthy growth instead of humiliation and frustration. We recommend:
   a Creation of options and alternatives within and outside of existing school systems. The deliberate promotion of pluralistic learning environments staffed by adults from a variety of backgrounds would provide for greater learning experience and participation by a larger segment of teenagers. These options would include the development of adolescents as teachers and counselors—staff participants—in schools. Prior in-service (or other) education of participating teachers would be essential.
   b Provision of experiential education for young people, through community participation.
   c High priority given to programs which educate teachers and other youth workers to genuinely respect and work effectively with adolescents from various backgrounds.
3 Our final suggestion is the creation of significant employment opportunities for youth. Our concern here is for underemployed and unemployed youth in need of meaningful job opportunities as well as educational and vocational counseling.

We have refrained from making detailed proposals for programs because that must be done by the people who will carry them out.

We suggest that the Office of Child Development convene a small conference to develop priorities and exchange ideas for additional projects. . . .

EPILOGUE

> "How can I establish a figure, even the crudest outline, if I don't know what I'm doing? . . . What do I know of the causes? The vital structure of a man that lies beneath the surface, and that my eye can't see? How can I know what creates from within, the shapes I see from without?"[4]

Those are always the questions artists, scientists, educators, and finally all people must ask. They ask them all their lives, but especially in adolescence. The preceding statement raises the questions of deeper understanding of one age group related to our present day culture. It is set within the value system of a democratic society with all its possible advantages and its desperate search for realization.

It is my conviction that each life period has its sorrows and exhilarations for the individual who experiences them as well as for those surrounding him and that each period has its significance for the continuous development of the human race. Youth is neither golden nor rotten. It has the potential of all human experience. Only—the adult generation is still partially responsible for helping youth to be healthy, sturdy,

[4]Irving Stone, *The Passionate Journey* New York: Doubleday and Co., 1959, p. 187.

able to cope with its own problems and also with the problems of the total society. And all human beings have a responsibility neither to demean others nor to hinder others from developing. Observation alone is never sufficient. It leaves the door open to negative forces sweeping over us. We must take the initiative first, to eliminate the destructive forces impinging on our youth and second, to strengthen those forces that will enhance their health and thus the fate of all of us. The world may never be perfect, but much can be done!

SELECTED BIBLIOGRAPHY

Adolescence

Alissi, A. S. "Concepts of Adolescence," *Adolescence,* Vol. VII, No. 28, Winter, 1972, pp. 491–510.

Buhler, Charlotte. *From Birth to Maturity,* London: Kegan Paul, Trench, Trubner & Co., Ltd., 1935.

Coleman, James S. *The Adolescent Society,* New York: The Free Press, 1961.

Konopka, Gisela. *The Adolescent Girl in Conflict,* Englewood Cliffs, N.J.: Prentice-Hall, Inc., 1966.

———. "Adolescence in the 1970s," *Child Welfare,* Vol. L. No. 10, 1971, pp. 553–559.

———. "Formation of Values in the Developing Person," *American Journal of Orthopsychiatry,* Vol. 43, No. 1, January 1973, pp. 86–96.

———. "An Integrated View of Adolescence," March 1971, unpublished.

Muuss, Rolf E., ed. *Theories of Adolescence,* New York: Random House, 1962, second edition.

———. ed. *Adolescent Behavior and Society: A Book of Readings,* New York: Random House, 1971.

Man

Dewey, John and James H. Tufts. *Ethics.* New York: Henry Holt and Co., 1932.

Ellwood, Charles A. *A History of Social Philosophy.* New York: Prentice-Hall, Inc., 1938.

Kluckhohn, Clyde and Henry A. Murray. *Personality in Nature, Society, and Culture.* New York: Alfred A. Knopf, 1961, second ed.

Konopka, Gisela. *Social Group Work: A Helping Process.* Englewood Cliffs, N.J.: Prentice-Hall, Inc., 1963.

Nelson, Leonard. *System of Ethics.* New Haven: Yale University Press, 1956.

Smuts, J. C. *Holism and Evolution.* London: Macmillan and Co., Ltd., 1926.

Stern, William. *General Psychology from the Personalistic Standpoint.* New York: The Macmillan Co., 1938.

Culture

Adamic, Louis. *A Nation of Nations.* New York: Harper and Brothers Publishers, 1945.

Hoebel, E. Adamson. *Anthropology: The Study of Man.* New York: McGraw-Hill Book Co., 1972, fourth ed.

Maritain, Jacques. *Reflections on America,* New York: Charles Scribner's Sons, 1958.

Eight Ages of Man*

Erik H. Erikson

INDUSTRY VS. INFERIORITY†

Thus the inner stage seems all set for "entrance into life," except that life must first be school life, whether school is field or jungle or classroom. The child must forget past hopes and wishes, while his exuberant imagination is tamed and harnessed to the laws of impersonal things—even the three R's. For before the child, psychologically already a rudimentary parent, can become a biological parent, he must begin to be a worker and potential provider. With the oncoming latency period, the normally advanced child forgets, or rather sublimates, the necessity to "make" people by direct attack or to become papa and mama in a hurry: he now learns to win recognition by producing things. He has mastered the ambulatory field and the organ modes. He has experienced a sense of finality regarding the fact that there is no workable future within the womb of his family, and thus becomes ready to apply himself to given skills and tasks, which go far beyond the mere playful expression of his organ modes or the pleasure in the function of his limbs. He develops a sense of industry—that is, he adjusts himself to the inorganic laws of the tool world. He can become an eager and absorbed unit of a productive situation. To bring a productive situation to completion is an aim which gradually supersedes the whims and wishes of play. His ego boundaries include his tools and skills: the work principle teaches him the pleasure of work completion by steady attention and persevering diligence. In all cultures, at this stage, children receive some *systematic instruction,* although it is by no means always in the kind of school which literate people must organize around special teachers who have learned how to teach literacy. In preliterate people and in nonliterate pursuits much is learned from adults who become teachers by dint of gift and inclination rather than by appointment, and perhaps the greatest amount is learned from older children. Thus the *fundamentals of technology* are developed, as the child becomes ready to handle the utensils, the tools, and the weapons used by the big people. Literate people, with more specialized careers, must prepare the child by teaching him things which first of all make him literate, the widest possible basic education for the greatest number of possible careers. The more confusing specialization becomes, however, the more indistinct are the eventual goals of initiative; and the more complicated social reality, the vaguer are the father's and mother's role in it. School seems to be a culture all by itself, with its own goals and limits, its achievements and disappointment.

*From Erik H. Erikson, *Childhood and Society,* Second Editon, W. W. Norton & Co., Inc., New York, 1963. Pgs. 259–269. Reprinted by permission of the author and the publisher.

Editor's note: Erikson discusses human development and its consequences for adjustment in terms of eight stages through which individuals pass. He characterizes each stage as involving a particular crisis or issue in personality development. His position is that if the issue is dealt with in a satisfactory fashion, the person will advance competently and confidently to the succeeding stage. The earliest stage of development, which is an elaboration of Freud's oral stage of infantile sexuality, is resoved in favor of *basic trust* or *basic mistrust.* The second stage, somewhat like Freud's anal stage, is resolved in terms of *autonomy* or *shame and doubt.* The third stage, constituting an elaboration of Freud's phallic stage, is characterized by exploratory sex and is resolved in terms of *initiative* or *guilt.* The selection given here presents Erikson's material for succeeding five stages.

The child's danger, at this stage, lies in a sense of inadequacy and inferiority. If he despairs of his tools and skills or of his status among his tool partners, he may be discouraged from identification with them and with a section of the tool world. To lose the hope of such "industrial" association may pull him back to the more isolated, less tool-conscious familial rivalry of the oedipal time. The child despairs of his equipment in the tool world and in anatomy, and considers himself doomed to mediocrity or inadequacy. It is at this point that wider society becomes significant in its ways of admitting the child to an understanding of meaningful roles in its technology and economy. Many a child's development is disrupted when family life has failed to prepare him for school life, or when school life fails to sustain the promises of earlier stages.

Regarding the period of a developing sense of industry, I have referred to *outer and inner hindrances* in the use of new capacities but not to aggravations of new human drives, nor to submerged rages resulting from their frustration. This stage differs from the earlier ones in that it is not a swing from an inner upheaval to a new mastery. Freud calls it the latency stage because violent drives are normally dormant. But it is only a lull before the storm of puberty, when all the earlier drives re-emerge in a new combination, to be brought under the dominance of genitality.

On the other hand, this is socially a most decisive stage: since industry involves doing things beside and with others, a first sense of division of labor and of differential opportunity, that is, a sense of the *technological ethos* of a culture, develops at this time. We have pointed in the last section to the danger threatening individual and society where the schoolchild begins to feel that the color of his skin, the background of his parents, or the fashion of his clothes rather than his wish and his will to learn will decide his worth as an apprentice, and thus his sense of *identity*—to which we must now turn. But there is another more fundamental danger, namely man's restriction of himself and constriction of his horizons to include only his work to which, so the Book says, he has been sentenced after his expulsion from paradise. If he accepts work as his only obligation, and "what works" as his only criterion of worthwhileness, he may become the conformist and thoughtless slave of his technology and of those who are in a position to exploit it.

IDENTITY VS. ROLE CONFUSION

With the establishment of a good initial relationship to the world of skills and tools, and with the advent of puberty, childhood proper comes to an end. Youth begins. But in puberty and adolescence all sameness and continuities relied on earlier are more or less questioned again, because of a rapidity of body growth which equals that of early childhood and because of the new addition of genital maturity. The growing and developing youths, faced with this physiological revolution within them, and with tangible adult tasks ahead of them, are now primarily concerned with what they appear to be in the eyes of others as compared with what they feel they are, and with the question of how to connect the roles and skills cultivated earlier with the occupational prototypes of the day. In their search for a new sense of continuity and sameness, adolescents have to refight many of the battles of earlier years, even though to do so they must artificially appoint perfectly well-meaning people to play the roles of adversaries; and they are ever ready to install lasting idols and ideals as guardians of a final identity.

The integration now taking place in the form of ego identity is, as pointed out, more than the sum of the childhood identifications. It is the accrued experience of the ego's ability to integrate all identifications with the vicissitudes of the libido, with the aptitudes developed out of endowment, and with the opportunities offered in social roles. The sense of ego identity, then, is the accrued confidence that the inner sameness and continuity prepared in the past are matched by the sameness and continuity of one's meaning for others, as evidenced in the tangible promise of a "career."

The danger of this stage is role confusion.[1] Where this is based on a strong previous doubt as to one's sexual identity, delinquent and outright psychotic episodes are not uncommon. If diagnosed and treated correctly, these incidents do not have the same fatal significance which they have at other ages. In most instances, however, it is the inability to settle on an occupational identity which disturb individual young people. To keep themselves together they temporarily overidentify, to the point of apparent complete loss of identity, with the heroes of cliques and crowds. This initiates the stage of "falling in love," which is by no means entirely, or even primarily, a sexual matter—except where the mores demand it. To a considerable extent adolescent love is an attempt to arrive at a definition of one's identity by projecting one's diffused ego image on another and by seeing it thus reflected and gradually clarified. This is why so much of young love is conversation.

Young people can also be remarkably clannish, and cruel in their exclusion of all those who are "different," in skin color or cultural background, in tastes and gifts, and often in such petty aspects of dress and gesture as have been temporarily selected as *the* signs of an in-grouper or out-grouper. It is important to understand (which does not mean condone or participate in) such intolerance as a defense against a sense of identity confusion. For adolescents not only help one another temporarily through much discomfort by forming cliques and by stereotyping themselves, their ideals, and their enemies; they also perversely test each other's capacity to pledge fidelity. The readiness for such testing also explains the appeal which simple and cruel totalitarian doctrines have on the minds of the youth of such countries and classes as have lost or are losing their group identities (feudal, agrarian, tribal, national) and face world-wide industrialization, emancipation, and wider communication.

The adolescent mind is essentially a mind of the *moratorium,* a psychosocial stage between childhood and adulthood, and between the morality learned by the child, and the ethics to be developed by the adult. It is an ideological mind—and, indeed, it is the ideological outlook of a society that speaks most clearly to the adolescent who is eager to be affirmed by his peers, and is ready to be confirmed by rituals, creeds, and programs which at the same time define what is evil, uncanny, and inimical. In searching for the social values which guide identity, one therefore confronts the problems of *ideology* and *aristocracy,* both in their widest possible sense which connotes that within a defined world image and a predestined course of history, the

[1]*See* "The Problem of Ego-Identity," *Journal of the American Psychoanalytic Association,* **4** (1956), 56–121.

best people will come to rule and rule develops the best in people. In order not to become cynically or apathetically lost, young people must somehow be able to convince themselves that those who succeed in their anticipated adult world thereby shoulder the obligation of being the best.

INTIMACY VS. ISOLATION

The strength acquired at any stage is tested by the necessity to transcend it in such a way that the individual can take chances in the next stage with what was most vulnerably precious in the previous one. Thus, the young adult, emerging from the search for and the insistence on identity, is eager and willing to fuse his identity with that of others. He is ready for intimacy, that is, the capacity to commit himself to concrete affiliations and partnerships and to develop the ethical strength to abide by such commitments, even though they may call for significant sacrifices and compromises. Body and ego must now be masters of the organ modes and of the nuclear conflicts, in order to be able to face the fear of ego loss in situations which call for self-abandon: in the solidarity of close affiliations, in orgasms and sexual unions, in close friendships and in physical combat, in experiences of inspiration by teachers and of intuition from the recesses of the self. The avoidance of such experiences because of a fear of ego loss may lead to a deep sense of isolation and consequent self-absorption.

The counterpart of intimacy is distantiation: the readiness to isolate and, if necessary, to destroy those forces and people whose essence seems dangerous to one's own, and whose "territory" seems to encroach on the extent of one's intimate relations. Prejudices thus developed (and utilized and exploited in politics and in war) are a more mature outgrowth of the blinder repudiations which during the struggle for identity differentiate sharply and cruelly between the familiar and the foreign. The danger of this stage is that intimate, competitive, and combative relations are experienced with and against the selfsame people. But as the areas of adult duty are delineated, and as the competitive encounter, and the sexual embrace, are differentiated, they eventually become subject to that *ethical sense* which is the mark of the adult.

Strictly speaking, it is only now that *true genitality* can fully develop; for much of the sex life preceding these commitments is of the identity-searching kind, or is dominated by phallic or vaginal strivings which make of sex-life a kind of genital combat. On the other hand, genitality is all too often described as a permanent state of reciprocal sexual bliss. This then, may be the place to complete our discussion of genitality.

For a basic orientation in the matter I shall quote what has come to me as Freud's shortest saying. It has often been claimed, and bad habits of conversation seem to sustain the claim, that psychoanalysis as a treatment attempts to convince the patient that before God and man he has only one obligation: to have good orgasms, with a fitting "object," and that regularly. This, of course, is not true. Freud was once asked what he thought a normal person should be able to do well. The questioner probably expected a complicated answer. But Freud, in the curt way of his old days, is reported to have said: "Lieben und arbeiten" (to love and to work). It pays to ponder on this simple formula; it gets deeper as you think about it. For when Freud said "love" he meant *genital* love, and genital *love;* when he said love *and* work, he meant a general work-productiveness which would not preoccupy the individual to the extent that he loses his right or capacity to be a genital and a loving being. Thus we may ponder, but we cannot improve on "the professor's" formula.

Genitality, then, consists in the unobstructed capacity to develop an orgastic potency so free of pregenital interferences that genital libido (not just the sex products discharged in Kinsey's "outlets") is expressed in heterosexual mutuality, with full sensitivity of both penis and vagina, and with a convulsionlike discharge of tension from the whole body. This is a rather concrete way of saying something about a process which we really do not understand. To put it more situationally: the total fact of finding, via the climactic turmoil of the orgasm, a supreme experience of the mutual regulation of two beings in some way takes the edge off the hostilities and potential rages caused by the oppositeness of male and female, of fact and fancy, of love and hate. Satisfactory sex relations thus make sex less obsessive, overcompensation less necessary, sadistic controls superfluous.

Preoccupied as it was with curative aspects, psychoanalysis often failed to formulate the matter of genitality in a way significant for the processes of society in all classes, nations, and levels of culture. The kind of mutuality in orgasm which psychoanalysis has in mind is apparently easily obtained in classes and cultures which happen to make a leisurely institution of it. In more complex societies this mutuality is interfered with by so many factors of health, of tradition, of opportunity, and of temperament, that the proper formulation of sexual health would be rather this: A human being should be potentially able to accomplish mutuality of genital orgasm, but he should also be so constituted as to bear a certain amount of frustration in the matter without undue regression wherever emotional preference or considerations of duty and loyalty call for it.

While psychoanalysis has on occasion gone too far in its emphasis on genitality as a universal cure for society and has thus provided a new addiction and a new commodity for many who wished to so interpret its teachings, it has not always indicated all the goals that genitality actually should and must imply. In order to be of lasting social significance, the utopia of genitality should include:

1 mutuality of orgasm
2 with a loved partner
3 of the other sex
4 with whom one is able and willing to share a mutual trust
5 and with whom one is able and willing to regulate the cycles of
  a work
  b procreation
  c recreation
6 so as to secure to the offspring, too, all the stages of a satisfactory development.

It is apparent that such utopian accomplishment on a large scale cannot be an individual or, indeed, a therapeutic task. Nor is it a purely sexual matter by any means. It is integral to a culture's style of sexual selection, cooperation, and competition.

The danger of this stage is isolation, that is, the avoidance of contacts which commit to intimacy. In psychopathology, this disturbance can lead to severe "character-problems." On the other hand, there are partnerships which amount to an isolation à deux, protecting both partners from the necessity to face the next critical development—that of generativity.

GENERATIVITY VS. STAGNATION

The term *generativity* encompasses the evolutionary development which has made man the teaching and instituting as well as the learning animal. The fashionable insistence on dramatizing the dependence of children on adults often blinds us to the dependence of the older generation on the younger one. Mature man needs to be needed, and maturity needs guidance as well as encouragement from what has been produced and must be taken care of.

Generativity, then, is primarily the concern in establishing and guiding the next generation, although there are individuals who, through misfortune or because of special and genuine gifts in other directions, do not apply this drive to their own offspring. And indeed, the concept *generativity* is meant to include such more popular synonyms as *productivity* and *creativity,* which, however, cannot replace it.

It has taken psychoanalysis some time to realize that the ability to lose oneself in the meeting of bodies and minds leads to a gradual expansion of ego-interests and to a libidinal investment in that which is being generated. Generativity thus is an essential stage on the psychosexual as well as the psychosocial schedule. Where such enrichment fails altogether, regression to an obsessive need for pseudo intimacy takes place, often with a pervading sense of stagnation and personal impoverishment. Individuals, then, often begin to indulge themselves as if they were their own—or one another's—one and only child; and where conditions favor it, early invalidism, physical or psychological, becomes the vehicle of self-concern. The mere fact of having or even wanting children, however, does not "achieve" generativity. In fact, some young parents suffer, it seems, from the retardation of the ability to develop this stage. The reasons are often to be found in early childhood impressions; in excessive self-love based on a too strenuously self-made personality; and finally (and here we return to the beginnings) in the lack of some faith, some "belief in the species," which would make a child appear to be a welcome trust of the community.

As to the institutions which safeguard and reinforce generativity, one can only say that all institutions codify the ethics of generative succession. Even where philosophical and spiritual tradition suggests the renunciation of the right to procreate or to produce, such early turn to "ultimate concerns," wherever instituted in monastic movements, strives to settle at the same time the matter of its relationship to the Care for the creatures of this world and to the Charity which is felt to transcend it.

EGO INTEGRITY VS. DESPAIR

Only in him who in some way has taken care of things and people and has adapted himself to the triumphs and disappointments adherent to being, the originator of others or the generator of products and ideas—only in him may gradually ripen the fruit of these seven stages. I know no better word for it than ego integrity. Lacking a clear definition, I shall point to a few constituents of this state of mind. It is the ego's accrued assurance of its proclivity for order and meaning. It is a postnarcissistic love of the human ego—not of the self—as an experience which conveys some world order and spiritual sense, no matter how dearly paid for. It is the acceptance of one's one and only life cycle as something that had to be and that, by necessity, permitted of no substitutions: it thus means a new, a different love of one's parents. It is a comradeship with the ordering ways of distant times and different pursuits, as expressed in the simple products and sayings of such times and pursuits. Although aware of the relativity of all the various life styles which have given meaning to human striving, the possessor of integrity is ready to defend the dignity of his own life style against all physical and economic threats. For he knows that an individual life is the accidental coincidence of but one life cycle with but one segment of history; and that for him all human integrity stands or falls with the one style of integrity of which he partakes. The style of integrity developed by his culture or civilization thus becomes the "patrimony of his soul," the seal of his moral paternity of himself (". . . pero el honor/Es patrimonio del alma": Calderón). In such final consolidation, death loses its sting.

The lack or loss of this accrued ego integration is signified by fear of death: the one and only life cycle is not accepted as the ultimate of life. Despair expresses the feeling that the time is now short, too short for the attempt to start another life and to try out alternate roads to integrity. Disgust hides despair, if often only in the form of "a thousand little disgusts" which do not add up to one big remorse: *mille petis dégoûts de soi, dont le total ne fait pas un remords, mais un gêne obscure*" (Rostand).

Each individual, to become a mature adult, must to a sufficient degree develop all the ego qualities mentioned, so that a wise Indian, a true gentleman, and a mature peasant share and recognize in one another the final stage of integrity. But each cultural entity, to develop the particular style of integrity suggested by its historical place, utilizes a particular combination of these conflicts, along with specific provocations and prohibitions of infantile sexuality. Infantile conflicts become creative only if sustained by the firm support of cultural institutions and of the special leader classes representing them. In order to approach or experience integrity, the individual must know how to be a follower of image bearers in religion and in politics, in the economic order and in technology, in aristocratic living and in the arts and sciences. Ego integrity, therefore, implies an emotional integration which permits participation by followership as well as acceptance of the responsibility of leadership.

Webster's Dictionary is kind enough to help us complete this outline in a circular fashion. Trust (the first of our ego values) is here defined as "the assured reliance on another's integrity," the last of our values. I suspect that Webster had business in mind rather than babies, credit rather than faith. But the formulation stands. And it seems possible to further paraphrase the relation of adult integrity and infantile trust by saying that healthy children will not fear life if their elders have integrity enough not to fear death. . . .

Alienated Youth*

William Neal Brown

One of the central problems of contemporary society is the large number of people who fail to find a place for themselves in the mainstream of living. In large measure, this segment of the population is reflected in the statistics from our courts and correctional institutions, our public welfare caseloads, and the standing pool of chronically or sporadically unemployed. A substantial number of these people are between the ages of 16 and 21, and could well be categorized as *alienated youth.* In various ways they have been caught up in the change characteristics of the current world and have been unable to make the necessary and timely adaptations to ensure survival in a highly complex, competitive, social order.

These people have been unable to deal with the results of high population mobility and the resultant shift from rural to urban living. They have been shunted aside, like the "rejects" on an assembly line, in the explosive technological expansion, with its premium on high levels of literacy or technical understanding. They have been unable to make personal adjustment to the dislocations and marked changes in patterns of family living and the increased employment of mothers. They have been unable to deal in any functional way with the generational conflict occasioned by the rapidity of change in the world and the loss of communication between them and their elders, because they are, in fact, talking about two different worlds, seen from completely different perspectives and evolving widely different sets of values. They are, in the main, poorly educated for the tasks expected of them. Caught up in this maelstrom, these young people are nonplused, frustrated, and, finally, embittered; they give up, "walk away from it," cease to struggle, and move into another world—their own stream, or rivulet, or cesspool.

Alienation is often equated with delinquency. One writer (1) has even equated it with poverty, commenting that poverty involves a state of mind, carrying with it "apathy, inertia, indifference and loss of initiative." He goes on to say that poverty may cause "envy, bitterness and self-depreciation of the ego." Another writer (2) speaks of a lack of community integration and of a sense of belonging to the larger culture. Other theories of delinquency revolve around anomie and the lower classes' feeling of dissociation, rejection by the larger world, and helplessness. (3-5) It is not difficult to see how these equations could be made, since some of the same variables—tenuous parent-child relationships, financial difficulty, limited education—are perceived as contributing factors in both instances. However, it is the position of this paper that this is too limited a view, that alienation equated with delinquency suggests consideration of only those persons statistically available to us. Alienation as a factor in current society should be perceived in broader perspective. It is conceived here as including all those who are "shut off," who are unprepared and unable to move into the mainstream of life, unsuited to assume the normal roles of mating, making a living, and producing a home and family.

*From William Neal Brown, "Alienated Youth," *Mental Hygiene,* 1968, **52,** 330–336. Reprinted by permission of the author and the Editor, *Mental Hygiene.*

Who, then, are the alienated? They are the underachievers in education, the underemployed in industry, the school dropouts, the unemployed, and the adjudicated delinquents.

The significant role of education in survival and in upward social and economic mobility has been widely documented. This fact notwithstanding, we are faced with a problem of considerable proportion in educational underachievement. A part of the cause for this would seem to lie in the structure and nature of school organization (especially for large numbers of lower-class youth); but a substantial cause seems to relate to values evolving from what has been described as the "adolescent culture."

Coleman (6) conducted a two-year study of the "climate of values" among students in nine public high schools of the Midwest. He included schools typical of America, with a range in social class, size of school, type of community, and parental economic status. He concluded from this study "that the interests of teenagers are not focused around studies, and that scholastic achievement is at most of minor importance in giving status or prestige to an adolescent in the eyes of other adolescents." In fact, he produced evidence that scholastic achievement was negatively valued. Important to boys were athletic prowess, cars, and social success with girls. The girls valued social success, including personality, beauty, clothes, and dates with boys. It was found that not all students yielded to group pressure; in large schools scholastically oriented subgroups did form. But, for most students, it appeared that social activities, sports, dates, and cars took precedence over intellectual activities.

The significance of such a value system for later life adjustment is obvious and need not be belabored here. What does need to be answered is the question, Why do some emerge from such a value system and move relatively smoothly into adult adjustment whereas others are lost and become alienated? The answer seems to hinge on two sets of factors: (1) whether the underachievement is based solely on the adolescent value structure rather than on a combination of the value structure plus school curriculum organization that does not take the needs of the individual child into account, and (2) the nature of the social and economic supports available to the underachiever. Where the underachievement is related primarily to the adolescent value system, the individual, with social and economic support from his family, can recoup. Where both factors are involved, the obstacles to readjustment become insurmountable; and the individual becomes first frustrated, then alienated. This is most often the case with the lower-class child.

The social problems of unemployment and underemployment are closely related to the educational problems of underachievement and dropping out of school. Keyserling (7) states, ". . . among both families and unattached individuals, there is a very high correlation (regardless of causation) between the amount of education and the amount of poverty."

The phenomenon of school dropouts is highly concentrated among the families of the poor. It is estimated that annually 400,000 boys and 350,000 girls drop out of school, that 7.5 million pupils will drop out between 1962 and 1970. Of these, 31 per cent will have only an eighth grade education or less; 30 per cent will have completed the ninth grade; and 39 per cent will have completed the tenth or eleventh grades. A high correlation has been suggested between school dropouts and juvenile delinquency. The price of this to our society is incalculably high. The young dropout pays in limited job opportunities, lower earnings, and lack of security—perhaps for the rest of his life. (7)

Juvenile delinquency as an avenue toward alienation and a symptom of it is so manifest and so well documented in the literature that there is little need to attempt any delineation of its scope and dimension here.

What causes alienation? Obviously, there are no hard-and-fast, black-and-white answers to this question. Bernard (8) has observed that one of the prime reasons for community disorganization, for social chaos, is an incompatible rate of change in the ecological, social, or technological structure of the system. We live in an age in which "change" is the "consistency"; rapid change in all areas of living is the rule rather than the exception. It is a state of affairs to which we are little accustomed and to which we accustom slowly. Thus, we see all about us the social dislocation accruing from changes that apparently occur too rapidly for the human integrative capacity. The explosive forces of change create conditions of stressful living for the average adult; for the child who looks to the adult—the parent, the teacher, the youth leader—for support, encouragement, and guidance, the stresses are compounded.

In my view, there are five societal pressures that make for alienation in the youth of today. They are: (1) the trend toward urbanization, (2) the egalitarian thrust, (3) the drive to "succeed," (4) the concept of "fit," and (5) the absence of "caring."

THE TREND TOWARD URBANIZATION

The trend toward urbanization is viewed as a factor in alienation largely within the context of the generally accepted image of the city as a place of more complex, decentralized, and depersonalized living. (9, 10) It is a fact that we are rapidly becoming an urban society. (By the time of the 1950 census, more than half the population lived in 168 metropolitan centers; by 1960 more than half the population lived in 212 metropolitan centers.) Such basic life factors as housing, education, transportation, and health services are in profound contrast in rural and urban living.

If one accepts the view of Sir Henry Maine that "whereas in the past men had been related to one another on the basis of status, they were now related on the basis of contract," then *work,* as the primary source of contract in this society, becomes a key determinant of satisfaction or dissatisfaction with the human condition. If this is accepted as a premise and one couples it with the fact that we are finding it increasingly difficult to provide work for all who can work, then many people are left in the position of non-access to a basic source of life satisfaction. Assuming that the revolutionary change from rural to urban living has deprived men of the opportunity and necessity for close personal relationships and that the human needs that were met in those ways are supplanted by contractual obligations, then, when these obligations are removed or *denied* (as in the case of alienated youth), a vacuum is created that must be filled with something. If these assumptions are correct, we would seem to be facing a future of increasing numbers of people with feelings of alienation or "anomie."

One of the major pressures in the child's world today is the instability that accrues from the complexities of urban living and creates such uncertainty for the adults to whom the child is responsible.

THE EGALITARIAN THRUST

The child growing up in today's world is faced with a society torn by the uncertainties of social and cultural upheaval. School people are most familiar with this in terms of the disruptive repercussions of the decisions and issues surrounding the 1954 Supreme Court decision on desegregation in the public schools, the Civil Rights Act of 1964, and the aggressive drive for equality by the American Negro during the past decade. However, the struggle of the Negro is but a small bubble in what seems to be a boiling cauldron of worldwide egalitarian unrest.

A spirit of freedom is walking abroad throughout the earth. From the bowels of Africa, across the face of Europe, in the Near East and the Far East, there is the throbbing manifestation of a "straining at the leash" against any conditions that tend to hem men in. Consider how many nations that once were colonies have attained statehood over the past 25 years—India, Morocco, Egypt, Libya, Ghana, and Nigeria, to name only a few.

Today's children ask the same questions that children have always asked: Who am I, and why? Who are "they," and why? The questions are the same, but adults must search for new answers. The old answers related to conditions that either no longer exist or are in a state of rapid, revolutionary change. The inability of adults to find answers consonant with changed life conditions results in widespread disorganization within the community, including the public school system, with its manifold influences on the life of the child. The young are confused and disillusioned by the old answers. The disparity between our behavior in relation to these changes and the idealized abstractions we espouse and the schools must teach, creates an insidious pressure on the growing child.

THE DRIVE TO SUCCEED

There is tremendous pressure in today's society for a person to succeed. To be successful is certainly a worthwhile and laudable goal. How, then, can one define the drive toward success as a factor in alienation?

The pressure accrues from the criteria by which success is determined and the avenues through which it can be achieved. In the main, success is measured in this society by the attainment of financial stability and the acquisition of visible material goods. Given the nature and conditions of the present society, I do not know that there is a better measuring rod. I do know that the drive toward success—held in many instances for children by parents before the children have any real understanding of what success is, and by other parents for children who face systemic obstacles to any real attainment of success—creates a real pressure on children at a very early age.

It has been noted that education has been shown to be one of the primary avenues by which people enhance their economic position and thereby their chances of vertical movement up the social scale. Thus, competition is institutionalized in systems of formal education in contemporary urban societies. For the child, practical emphasis is placed on securing good grades rather than on learning. (Only the naïve assume that the two—good grades and learning—are necessarily synonymous.) An individual child may not be "competing"; but, by the very nature of the structure, he is "in competition." This fact is emphasized in schools by the system of rewards, grades, promotions, honor lists, and extracurricular positions of status and prestige. The fact of competition has significant implications, often negative, for the person who does not want to compete, who shies away from competition, or, worse, who has areas of strength that fit the rules of another game but do not mesh with the expectations of the system as currently defined. Unless the school looks for such areas of strength and attempts to build on them, the child fails but does not understand why. It is only a short step from this point to frustration, and the child is then well on the road to alienation.

THE CONCEPT OF FIT

The concept of "fit" is an emerging derivative of research in social psychology. With the increased complexity of living and the trend toward urbanization noted above, more and more emphasis is placed on the smooth functioning of the system. Individuals tend to be viewed in terms of whether their behavior is functional or dysfunctional to the system—whether that system be the family, the peer group, the school, or the community. This places a premium on adaptation or "adjustment," and correspondingly reduces opportunity and incentive for expression of individuality and creativity. The concepts of status and role pinpoint and describe the nature of the individual's "fit" into the society, and standards of conduct are reflective of expectations embodied in roles that people occupy.

For the urban machine to move in its accustomed ways, people are expected to "manage," "to get along"; and anyone or any group that does not is dysfunctional to the "system" and creates a hardship for the others that make it up. The system itself has institutionalized a selecting and sorting process that results in the class structure of communities. Within this process, competition is inherent, and the individual is expected to compete in a sufficiently successful way so that he will not be a burden to others. Failure to do so is viewed as a form of deviance.

This definition of "deviance" has been used to encompass the indigent, the mentally ill, adult and juvenile offenders, truants, and school dropouts. From this perspective, the social scientist is not particularly concerned with etiology but more with the facts of existence. For example, Simmons and Wolff (11) at Cornell, have experimented with ignoring classifications of physical illness and studying it by treating it generically and situationally by age, ethnic grouping, occupation, and other factors. From this approach they found that the correlates are remarkably similar for who gets sick, who gets arrested, and who develops a mental disorder—in short, for those who might be considered examples of deviance, of people who do not "fit." Merton's (12) theory of deviance emphasizes the "success" theme. In this competitive society, success is what is valued, what is important—thus, the ends justify the means. Deviant persons seek the standard ends of success, but through deviant means.

This concept of "fit" and the need for it is quite functional for the system. It is an added pressure of considerable proportion for the person who must grow up within the system. This is especially true at the present time when the child must balance his "fit" against the unclear, ambivalent, and often contradictory expectations of the adult world.

THE ABSENCE OF "CARING"

The final factor in the press toward alienation that I have chosen has been designated simply "the absence of caring." The simplicity of the term "caring" conveys most clearly the area of my concern and is an expression of my conviction that, in the highly complex order of our existence, in the way our lives are structured for survival, we have screened out, in large measure, the capacity or the inclination to care. *Doing* is very important: achieving has our highest priority. *Caring* can be sandwiched in to close the chinks; or, if doing and achieving make a tight union, then caring can be left out altogether. The irony is that this state of affairs renders doing and achieving all the more difficult and makes for exceeding pressure on children.

I was intrigued recently when, leafing through a journal published by the American Academy of Psychotherapists, I came across several pages of photographs of children and animals. Impressed by the pictures, I went back to look at the narrative that preceded them. The article was entitled "Scenes of Tenderness: Photo-Essay." The following comment by the editors (13) is pertinent to our present consideration:

> Six months before Issue #3 went to press the editors began to plan a photo essay on "scenes of tenderness." We were motivated by the classic work in human portraiture, *The Family of Man*. We naïvely thought that we could, without great strain, capture public scenes of tenderness. It did not take us long to realize that we are not photographers, and that the world outside the therapist's office contains little public display of what could be called "tenderness." We agreed after much effort that, in effect, people, adults at least, simply do not show much tenderness. Kids do, with pets and sometimes with each other, when adults aren't looking . . . but otherwise, there is just not much that is tender.

It should be emphasized that this absence of caring is caused as much or more by structure as by intent, and by the diffuse nature of the parent role in an urban society. As our society has developed to its present highly complicated, intricate state of technological and business organization, the place of the father has increasingly become that of economic provider. As the maze through which the father must thread his way daily in the task of economic provision becomes more complex, the focus of life energies and time is increasingly telescoped into the provider role, and other aspects of fathering are consequently diminished. (And, for many alienated youngsters, father can not provide, so he disappears completely.) Father becomes a hazy image—for the lower-class child, someone who is doing a "double" or working overtime to make ends meet; for the middle- and upper-class child, someone supposedly important who does something supposedly important, who "works" or "goes to business" every day (nowadays in some other place, usually the nearest metropolitan complex), who leaves early in the morning and returns late in the evening, often fatigued and irritable, and, worse, from the point of view of the child, who sometimes has another meeting or community "commitment" to occupy a portion of his evening.

The role of the mother has changed, too. In April 1956, there were 21,194,000 employed women in the United States, two-thirds of whom were holding full-time jobs. (14) By June 1958, the Children's Bureau (15) had established that there were more than 7 million full-time working mothers with children under 18, almost 3 million with children under 12, and 2.5 million with children under 6. Financial pressure was a major factor in a mother's decision to work.

There is no intent here to imply a malicious lack of concern on the part of parents for the well-being of children; there is intent to demonstrate the extent to which our lives are ordered by contractual obligations that are, of necessity, given high priority. Whatever the expressive intent of parents, the fact is that millions of today's children spend their lives in the care of alternative parents, relatives, neighbors, or older siblings; and a sizable number of parents rely on the public school as their primary source of daytime care of their children.

It has been suggested that the pressures toward alienation operate across the spectrum of society. Nevertheless, it is readily apparent that their impact is more immediate and more devastating on young people from broken and/or impoverished families.

ALIENATION'S PRODUCTS

Finally, what are the results of alienation? This is a question that defies an easy answer. There are, for example, no statistical analyses of normative behavior in relation to alienation. They would be difficult to accomplish; for the alienated, like the poor, are largely invisible, "hidden" in the matrix of the society. The terms most commonly used to describe them are "apathy," "frustration," and "aggression." Certainly, every welfare worker has seen the signs of apathy, and the correctional worker daily views the manifold signs of frustration and aggression. We are all familiar with the "long, hot summers" of recent years and the explosive reactions of Harlem, Rochester, and Watts—smoldering apathy and frustration turned suddenly to aggression.

Michael Harrington, (16) in writing of the poor in *The Other America,* suggests that one reason we don't notice a large number of the poor is that over 8 million of them are under 18 years of age. Further, it is no accident that 90 per cent of our welfare caseloads and 92 per cent of the inmates of our correctional institutions are non-white. These are the most alienated people.

It would seem that the manifest results of alienation are most surely poverty, delinquency, and illness. The simplest answer is that alienation thwarts productivity, demeans the sense of self, and renders the individual an undue burden to his society.

REFERENCES

1 Cohen, A.: Delinquent Boys. Glencoe, Ill., The Free Press, 1955.
2 Herzog, E.: Social Service Review, **37**:389 (December), 1963.
3 Yablonsky, L.: The Violent Gang. New York, Macmillan, 1962.

4 Ferguson, T.: The Young Delinquent in His Social Setting. London, Oxford University Press, 1952.
5 Glueck, S.: Family Environment and Delinquency. Boston, Houghton Mifflin, 1962.
6 Coleman, J. S.: Harvard Educational Review, **29**:338 (Fall), 1959.
7 Keyserling, L. H.: Progress or Poverty: the U.S. at the Crossroads. Washington, D.C., Conference on Economic Progress, 1964, pp. 40–41.
8 Bernard, J.: American Community Behavior. New York, Holt, Rinehart and Winston, 1962.
9 Mumford, L.: The City in History. New York, Harcourt, Brace and World, 1961.
10 Wood, R. C.: Metropolis Against Itself. New York, Committee for Economic Development, 1964.
11 Simmons, L. W., and Wolff, H. G.: Social Science in Medicine. New York, Russell Sage Foundation, 1954, pp. 109–169.
12 Merton, R. K.: Social Theory and Social Structure. Glencoe, Ill., The Free Press, 1957, pp. 161–181.
13 Voices—The Art and Science of Psychotherapy, **2**:25 (Spring), 1966.
14 U.S. Department of Labor, Women's Bureau: Handbook on Women Workers, Bulletin No. 261. Washington, D.C., U.S. Government Printing Office, 1956.
15 Lajewski, H. C.: Child Care Arrangements of Full Time Working Mothers. Washington, D.C., U.S. Department of Health, Education, and Welfare, Children's Bureau, 1959.
16 Harrington, M.: The Other America. Baltimore, Penguin Books, 1962.

Section Four

Dynamics of Adjustment

The papers is this section discuss another set of factors that influence adjustment, viz., the interaction between the individual as he or she exists at a given point in time and the situational forces and pressures that call for a reaction on his or her part. We refer to this interaction as the "dynamics of adjustment." While the authors of the papers frequently differ in their theoretical orientations and specific ideas concerning adjustment, they adopt the general view that an individual's behavior is a dynamic process resulting from the interplay of forces impinging on him or her. They base their ideas on the assumption that a human being is a changing, modifiable organism. The personality characteristics and behavior an individual displays are the result of the continuous interaction of internal and external stimulation. Conflicts and frustrations are viewed as inevitable, and, in order to resolve them, a person learns to adopt different modes of thinking, believing, and acting. In this group of readings the adjustment process is analyzed, and some of the methods, techniques, and styles of adjustment that are typical in our culture are considered.

The first selection, by Lazarus, discusses the effects of stress on the individual. After reviewing definitions and different sources of stress, he notes that stress can have either a disorganizing or an organizing effect on behavior, i.e., stress can lead to confusion and a disruption of established behaviors or to the stimulation of motivation and efforts to eliminate the stress through new learning or behavior. The consequences to the individual's adjustment status will depend on the specific nature of the old behaviors that are disrupted and the new ones that are developed and on the extent to which the changes successfully reduce the stress and anxiety experienced by the individual. The papers that follow Lazarus's in this section expand on this thesis, each describing a different conceptualization of ways of dealing with stress and their likely consequences to psychological adjustment.

In recent years considerable attention has been devoted to the various methods of adjustment or patterns of behavior characteristic of individuals and groups when dealing with conflict and frustration. Since Freud's description of the "ego defenses," increasing emphasis has been placed on the classification of specific styles of adjusting and the motivations and purposes underlying them. The study of characteristic methods of dealing with conflict and anxiety is especially relevant to an understanding of the adjustment process. On the one hand, defensive techniques enable the individual to maintain a sense of equilibrium and mitigate the anxiety and discomfort he or she would experience without them. On the other hand, some defensive maneuvers appear to result in negative consequences that, in turn, give rise to additional stress and anxiety for the individual. It follows then that the relationship between adjustment and defense mechanisms is a complex one depending on numerous factors such as the frequency of the occurrence of a particular method of defense, the situations in which it occurs, and the reactions of others to it. For example, an individual's tendency to retreat into fantasy whenever he or she encounters frustration may enable the individual to maintain a sense of composure and balance under adverse conditions. But a frequent or intense withdrawal into fantasy, its occurrence at inappropriate times, or the intolerance of others for this type of reaction may promote further difficulty for the individual rather than aid him or her.

McCall distinguishes between two alternatives in responding to threats to self-esteem. One may cope with threat in a realistic manner or one may engage in defensiveness. The paper consists of an analysis of the latter alternative and describes the variety of ways in which individuals attempt to nullify threat to their self-esteem and integrity. While acknowledging the contributions of Freud and his daughter, Anna, to this area, McCall chooses to describe the mechanisms of defense logically and phenomenologically rather than psychoanalytically. The mechanisms therefore are not viewed solely as protective devices against anxiety arising from sexual impulses, but also are viewed as arising from *any* threat to self-esteem—"incompetence, stupidity, selfishness, indecisiveness. . . ."

The papers by Karen Horney and Erich Fromm provide us with still other ways of conceptualizing patterns of adjustment to anxiety, frustration, and conflict. Horney adopts the position that conflict is the basis of maladjustment and specifies the importance of conflicts associated with the individual's interactions with others. She refers to a *basic conflict* underlying all maladjustment which involves the individual's ambivalences about the role he or she wishes to play with others. Where the individual overemphasizes one style of relating to others (for example, a highly aggressive attitude) at the expense of other possible modes of interacting, the basis for increased conflict and friction is present. Adjustment, according to Horney, consists of a harmonious, flexible style of interacting with others; maladjustment consists of rigid interpersonal styles, and these may consist of *moving toward people* (compliance, dependence, seeking of affection), *moving against people* (distrust, hostility, aggression), or *moving away from people* (avoidance, detachment, isolation).

The excerpt from Fromm's book *Man for Himself* describes variations in what the author refers to as the *nonproductive personality*. For Fromm, healthy individuals have developed a sense of identity that enables them to actualize their abilities and potentials so that they are, in effect, productive members of society. The nonproductive character orientations, however, are *types* of persons who have not learned to relate to others in ways that enable them to fulfill their basic needs and potentials. Instead these individuals continue to seek adjustment by ineffective styles of behavior that serve to increase the frustrations and conflicts they experience. In addition, it is worth noting that Fromm pays a good deal of attention to the role culture plays in promoting differences in adjustment.

In summary, the defense mechanisms of McCall, the rigid interpersonal styles of Horney, and the nonproductive character orientations of Fromm may all be viewed as behavior serving the function of allaying anxiety, distress, loss of esteem, etc. While the papers by McCall, Horney, and Fromm make some references to healthy and normal approaches to dealing with problems and stresses, the remaining papers in this section deal directly with reactions that facilitate adjustment.

The Jourard paper proposes a close relationship between self-disclosure and mental health: the mentally healthy person is a discloser, and self-disclosure is a technique for achieving mental health. In addition, it should be noted that disclosure and the inhibition of disclosure may be in the service of anxiety-fear reduction and may be properly viewed as an adjustment pattern.

The selection by Maslow represents another constructive approach to living, which he associates with self-actualization. Similar to the criteria of the healthy individual described by Bugental in Section One as living in accord with "a humanistic ethic", the self-actualizing person is described by Maslow as one who engages in "intrinsic learning" involving "the process of learning to be the best human being you can." He discusses a number of approaches to living which he believes lead to self-actualization, including becoming totally and selflessly absorbed in events and experiences, making day-to-day choices that promote growth rather than defense, acknowledging oneself, and being honest and responsible for one's actions. The final paper, by Smitson, constitutes a further elaboration of some of the characteristics of the emotionally mature person identified by Maslow. Smitson calls attention to such attributes as independence, ability to accept reality, adaptability, and empathic understanding.

Adjustment and Stress*

Richard S. Lazarus

The most widespread regulative principle of human behavior is a homeostatic one in which the person alters either himself or his external environment when disequilibrium has been produced in order to restore the equilibrium (Cannon, 1939). An alternative or supplementary view involves the postulation of growth tendencies within the individual (e.g., Rogers, 1951). These lead him to seek mastery or control over himself and his environment in order to realize his highest potential and to produce the most harmonious relationship possible between himself and the environment. From either point of view, adjustment refers to the processes of this self or environmental alteration that produce some given state such as equilibrium or self-actualization.

Because the biological and psychological needs of an individual, as well as the external pressures to which he is exposed, are continually changing, adjustment is always taking place. But what if the adjustive capacities are taxed beyond their scope and the demands (internal or external) become excessive? Disturbances in function arise. These disturbances can include such subjective states and behavior patterns as psychological misery, somatic malfunctioning (psychosomatic disorders), abnormal forms of thought, socially reprehensible or deviant forms of behavior, and failure to execute successfully or normally the life tasks within the context of an individual's ability. The processes of adjustment are, therefore, important to us not only because under normal circumstances of living they determine our actions but also because, when they fail under conditions of unusual demand, our welfare is endangered. When this happens we talk about the existence of a state of *stress,* an extreme instance of disturbed equilibrium.

It is important to study stress states in order to understand their consequences for adjustment and to learn the nature of the (stressor) conditions that bring them about in the first place. We shall discover that the concept of stress is a central one in our conceptions of psychopathology. It is probably also an essential feature of normal human development. For example, Sullivan (1953) considered anxiety as a crucial and even positive force in man's efforts to improve himself and the world. Rank (1945) considered the conflict of wills associated with the life and death fears as a basic part of life itself and as the basis of human creativeness. Davis (1952) also emphasized the importance of anxiety in the normal process of socialization. The crucial problem in normal versus pathological development is the amount of stress and the resources available for mastering it. Let us examine some of the main ways of viewing the nature of stress.

STRESS AS ENVIRONMENTAL CONDITIONS

A wide variety of meanings have been given to the term "stress." One of the most common notions is that stress represents some circumstance or situation *external* to an individual that makes sudden or extraordinary demands upon him. Thus, we might

*From Richard S. Lazarus, *Adjustment and Personality,* McGraw-Hill Book Company, Inc., New York, 1961. Pages 303–315 reprinted by permission of the author and the publisher.

think of unusual conditions, such an anticipated surgery (Janis, 1958) or disasters (floods, storms, fires, explosions, or military bombings) as examples of stress. Also see Wallace (1960).

One of the most fascinating investigations of such crisis situations was performed by Cantril (1952), who described and analyzed the panic that gripped thousands of persons after the famous Orson Welles radio broadcast, "The Invasion from Mars" (1938). Welles had produced a dramatization of such an imaginary invasion so realistically that large numbers believed it and fled for their lives. Persons all over the country rushed aimlessly through the streets, packed their families into automobiles to flee the danger, cried, or otherwise behaved as though the end of the world were imminent.

Cantril asked what conditions were important in bringing about this extraordinary reaction in so many persons. He observed that panic occurred mostly in persons who tuned in after the program had gotten under way and did not hear the introductory announcement that would indicate that the program was only a dramatization. When such persons attempted to check their hypothesis of a real Martian invasion against other facts, for example, looking out the window or turning to other radio stations, they did not use correctly the information because of their fear. Some noticed the streets were empty and assumed that this was the result of the crisis. Others saw crowded streets and assumed that everyone was fleeing. When they heard regular radio programs on the other stations, they assumed that efforts were being made to reassure the populace. Whatever conflicting information they obtained was integrated into their fear-generating hypothesis of an invasion from Mars.

The essential difficulty with this approach, which defines stress as the threatening situation, is that what is a source of stress for some persons is not necessarily so for others. Although it is true that extreme conditions of actual disaster will severely disturb a high percentage of persons, individual reactions to these situations are extremely varied. Even in floods or military bombings, there are some persons who respond in a cool and collected fashion and others who become disorganized. Moreover, it seems unwise to restrict the term "stress" to those extremely unusual conditions that have a very great impact on nearly everyone. There are many more ordinary conditions of everyday life that can produce great impact.

In the case of the Orson Welles broadcast, only a small percentage of those hearing the broadcast responded to the situation as stressful. In his study of the effects of the program, Cantril also attempted to determine what it was about these persons that made them especially vulnerable. For one thing, degree of education was an important factor. Those whose knowledge was limited had less information against which to check the concept of a Martian invasion. There were, no doubt, important personality factors as well, which made some persons more likely to respond in the fashion they did.

Another study of mass hysteria (Johnson, 1952) concerned persons who believed surging rumors about a killer who struck with a paralyzing gas. It was found that those who reacted with panic had personalities like persons who develop neurotic attacks of hysteria. Most of the reports of attacks came from women. The number affected represented a small part of the total population of the town involved in the supposed crisis.

There have been many experimental attacks on the problem of the effects of stressor conditions. It has been only in recent years, however, that experimenters have begun to explore systematically the factors behind individual differences in reaction. For example, Lazarus and Eriksen (1952) performed an experiment in which a group of subjects were exposed to a situation of failure. The stressed subjects, as a group, seemed not to be affected differently in their performance from a control group, which received no stressor experience. However, a careful analysis showed that the stressed group was much more variable, some subjects showing improvement in performance and others showing impairment. The fact that some subjects were affected in one way and others in the opposite direction cancelled out any obvious group differences. The experimenters then asked what personality factors accounted for the differences in reaction to the stressor condition (Eriksen, Lazarus, & Strange, 1952), but they were unable to find satisfactory evidence in their study. More recent research on the problem has begun to show that differences in motivational characteristics of people determine in part whether stress will occur (Vogel, Raymond, Lazarus, 1959). Differences in coping mechanisms are also a basic factor in determining the consequences of stress for behavior and cognition. But there is still relatively little systematic knowledge about the personality and situational factors that influence reactions to crisis or stressor conditions.

There are great differences between individuals in their sensitivity to various situations as stressors, and it is necessary to discover the reasons why one individual is disturbed by a given situation and another is not. We must go beyond the stimulus definition of stress, which treats all persons as essentially alike and assumes that their perceptions of danger or threat are based on exactly the same conditions. We must also consider the ordinary stresses of life, such as getting a job, getting married, the death of a loved one, seeing a disturbing movie, etc. These experiences have different impacts on different persons, and we must come to understand why.

STRESS AS A STATE WITHIN THE INDIVIDUAL

A second major way of viewing stress treats it as a *state of the individual* rather than as an external condition that he faces. For example, the famous physiologist Selye (1956) makes stress synonymous with what he calls the "adaptation syndrome," an organized set of biological reactions to noxious stimulation such as physical injury. If bodily tissues are damaged, certain systematic biochemical changes take place as a result, these changes being part of the organism's efforts to repair the damage. However, these adaptations to the noxious or damaging circumstances in themselves, especially when chronic, can produce further injury to the organism. For example, when a person responds to a chronic fear-provoking situation with an outpouring of adrenalin (a hormonal substance that produces vast changes in metabolism), this outpouring of the adrenal-hormonal substance can be quite damaging to the long-range functioning of the organism. Psychosomatic disturbances such as ulcers, colitis, and high blood pressure are thought to involve this chronic adaptation process to psychological danger. Selye's emphasis is on the internal state of the organism and its consequences rather than on the situation that produces it.

This diversity in the meaning of stress can be confusing, because different writers use the term to mean different things. I am inclined to lean toward the latter approach in my definition of stress. However, the problem still remains to identify for any person or class of persons the conditions (internal and external) that can be defined as stressors because they bring about the stress state. One of the consequences of the state is the elicitation of adjustment mechanisms, which are associated with both healthy and pathological behavior.

We are now prepared to divide the area of stress and adjustment into four issues or problems. The first is the conditions or sources of stress. The second is the nature of the stress state itself. The third is the coping mechanisms elicited by the stress. The fourth is the behavioral consequences of stress.

SOURCES OF STRESS

It is especially when the demands upon a person tax him to the limit of his resources or beyond that we speak of "psychological stress." The concept of stress is concerned, therefore, with demands that are in degree more severe than ordinary. These demands must produce thwarting of motives in some way. This thwarting can be in the form of threats to the maintenance of life and the avoidance of pain, or it can restrict a person's opportunity to satisfy motives of great importance to him. Therefore, what is thwarting to one man may not be to another because of different patterns of motivation.

Mahl (1949) made some observations that are very pertinent to this point. He wished to discover the psychological and physiological bases of ulcer formation, and to this end he experimented with the conditions that produce excessive hydrochloric acid secretion (thought to be an important cause of ulcers) in the stomach. Stomach acidity in human subjects was measured just prior to an important college examination and also during nontension controls periods. Six of the eight subjects showed a marked increase in acid secretion prior to the examination, but two of the subjects showed no increase; in fact, a slight decrease. Mahl then examined the interview material he had obtained from the subjects during the experiment in order to understand better the reasons for these individual differences. He found that the two students who failed to show an increase in stomach acidity under the stressor condition were rather casual about the examination and did not regard it as threatening. One of them had already been accepted into a medical school of his choice and believed that the examination could not endanger his status. The other was content to obtain the gentleman's grade of C. He too was indifferent to the coming examination. These motivational factors in the two subjects reduced the prospect of their being threatened by the same examination that was a source of stress to the other six.

Another experimental example of the importance of motivation in determining whether a situation will be stressful can be found in a recent experiment by Vogel, Raymond, and Lazarus (1959). They found that subjects who were motivated primarily toward achievement (success academically and vocationally) rather than toward affiliation (establishing warm, friendly interpersonal relations) were not stressed by a threat to the latter motivation but were considerably disturbed by the implication that they were failing on a test of their capacity to succeed academically and vocationally. Conversely, subjects with a strong motivation toward affiliation and weak motivation toward achievement were

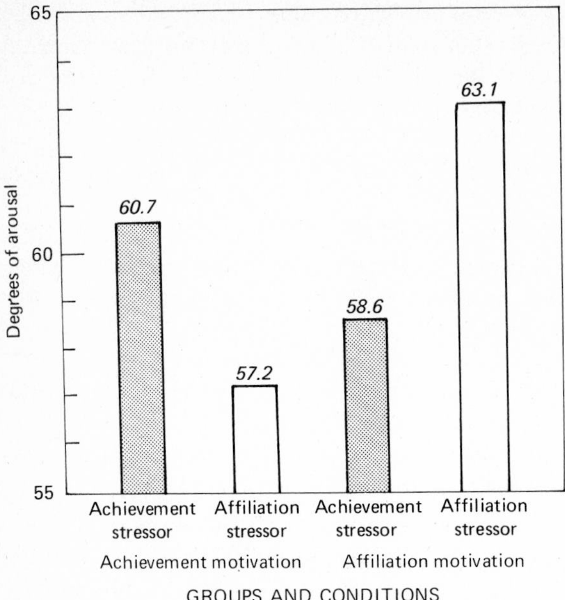

Figure 1 Groups and Conditions—degree of arousal and the relevance of the stressor condition to the basic motivational pattern. Shaded bars show degree of arousal when the stressor was relevant to the subjects' motive preference. *(After Vogel et al., 1959.)*

> disturbed only when their capacity to establish friendly relations with others were impugned and not when they failed in a test of their achievement potential. These results are shown in the form of a bar graph in Figure 1.

Stress must always be regarded in terms of the relation between the pattern of motivations of the person and the life situation to which he is exposed. So far as human beings share similar motive patterns, similar situations produce thwarting. Later on, some of the life situations regarded as typically thwarting, because they impinge upon more or less universal or widely shared motivations, will be discussed.

It is useful to distinguish as sources of stress two kinds of situations; one that produces deprivations of biological needs, or makes extreme physical demands upon the individual, and one that involves threats to the self-esteem of the person. Examples of the former might be exposure to extreme temperatures or to conditions of starvation or semistarvation. Many adventure stories have been built around stress themes of this kind: truck drivers carrying high explosives over treacherous roads; man's struggles with the elements while manning a ship through a hurricane; military battles; in general, man's search for solutions to physical threats to his survival. During World War II, an extensive experimental study of the psychological and physiological effects of semistarvation was made by Franklin and his colleagues (1948). Many consequences of this prolonged physical stress were observed, but these were transitory, disappearing after the body weight of the subjects was restored by a normal diet.

Psychologists generally believe that the second type of stress source, threats to self-esteem, is far more potent in producing maladjustments, including neuroses and psychoses, than the former. Some examples of such sources of stress are the conflict in wartime between a man's wish to escape the dangers of combat and his wish to appear courageous or heroic in the eyes of his fellow soldiers; the conflict between man's hostile impulses toward others and the internalized attitude that such hostility is reprehensible; the conflict between sexual impulses and the attitude that these impulses are wrong or tabooed; or man's wish to be secure and dependent upon some protective persons (often the parents) and his need to be autonomous and independent.

These threats to self-esteem (or "ego motives") are often described as pathogenic conflicts. They result in the *thwarting* of some important motivation of the individual, and this thwarting itself can be viewed as the source or antecedent of stress. The term "thwarting," however, is often applied when a person is deprived in some physical way or when his physical security is in some way threatened. Rosenzweig (1944) applied the term *frustration* to thwartings that have the character of threats to self-esteem in order to distinguish them from simple physical deprivation. I prefer this latter usage because it avoids some of the confusion that arises as a result of these terms (thwarting and frustration) having been frequently used interchangeably.

If we concern ourselves with sources of stress that psychologists generally regard as very common, we can approach the question in two ways. On the one hand, as has been completely done by Mussen and Conger (1956), we could look at periods of development in which characteristically different problems are faced. For example, in childhood there are the problems of weaning, toilet training, social adjustments, and school adjustments. When we study adolescence, we might concentrate on the biological and social changes that take place as the child becomes initiated into an adult role in society. For the period of senescence, new problems emerge from a person's deteriorating physical condition and his reduced usefulness and independence, particularly in our own society.

Although these developmental periods are associated with certain characteristic problems, the exact form and degree of these problems varies from person to person. For instance, some elderly persons are not faced with idleness and are able to function usefully and serenely within society. Similarly, many adolescents are guided through the transition to adulthood in such a way as to minimize or eliminate the stresses common to this period of life. This point is embedded in the anthropological studies of Margaret Mead (1934, 1935).

In contrast with the analysis of sources of stress by developmental periods, we can approach the field in a second way, by ignoring specific periods of life and considering timeless problems, which psychologists have considered potentially stressful to anyone at any age. The nature of these problems would vary according to the theoretical approach to personality we adopt, although it would not be difficult to obtain some agreement among psychologists about certain focal areas. We can then list as important sources of stress the expression and control of sexual impulses; the attainment of social acceptance in the context of competitive behavior; the reaction to the deprivation of love and affection through parental rejection; the conflict between dependency needs and striving for independence; the achievement of social and occupational success in the face of physical and intellectual inferiorities; and the mastery of, or adjustment to, continuing social change (which has become increasingly important in modern times because of the accelerated changes in society and its patterns of living). These sources of stress tend to cut across developmental periods, although they can be accentuated at some periods of life and reduced in others. The relative importance of each varies in the different personality theories discussed.

THE NATURE OF STRESS

The problem now is to consider the effect of these sources of stress upon the individual. Up to now we have theorized that the frustration of ego motives is the general source of stress. There is, moreover, an intimate relationship between frustration and emotion, such that when frustration occurs a person reacts with disturbing emotion (as opposed to positive or pleasant emotion such as delight), probably to the degree of the original motive strength itself. If frustration did not have negative emotional consequences, then we probably would not speak of stress as a special problem. We would consider a person as faced merely with the task of overcoming obstacles to the gratification of motives, and we could apply relatively simple learning principles to understand how he acquires an adaptive solution. When emotions enter into the picture, however, the ordinary course of problem solving is changed in some important respects. There are certain special consequences of the emotional state associated with stress (such as the development of nonadaptive behavior) that make the study of stress of great importance to the understanding of personality and adjustment.

The state of stress is dependent upon the nature of the emotion (i.e., degree and type) aroused and the ways in which persons attempt to cope with it. However, stress is not entirely equivalent to emotion because a person can succeed in reducing or eliminating the disturbing emotional state by mechanisms of defense. In that instance, we may find little or no evidence of emotional arousal, but the person's cognitive behavior in the presence of somatic symptoms may suggest that he is under stress.

In order to clarify this point more fully, let us consider some essential features of emotional states. An emotion is a hypothetical construct in that the emotional process cannot be directly observed but can only be inferred from certain behavioral and subjective consequences.

Generally speaking, there are three classes of observable events that define the state of emotion. One is the *visceral expression,* that is, the many biochemical and tissue reactions stimulated by the activity of the autonomic nervous system. We shall not elaborate these here except to note that emotional states are associated with noticeable visceral changes, such as increased heart rate, respiratory changes, perspiring, and gastric secretions. It was once thought that particular emotional experiences, such as fear or anger, were somatically undifferentiated and that, although persons had different subjective experiences of emotion, the biochemical reactions were the same. The work of Wolff (1950), however, has shown that in anger the mucous membranes of the body become engorged with blood (as in red-faced anger) and bathed with secretions, and in fear reduction of blood flow (paling of the face) and drying out of the tissues is common. Recently Funkenstein and his associates (1957) and Ax (1953) have been able to demonstrate different adrenal gland chemical secretions associated with fear and anger, fear leading to the secretion of adrenalin and anger to noradrenalin.

The second aspect of emotion lies in *motor expression,* the innervation of the smooth and striated muscles of the body sometimes described as "physical tensions." In his studies of stress, Malmo (1953, 1955) and his associates have measured muscle-action potentials, that is, increase in tension in muscle groups of the body as manifested in increased electrical potential. He has observed, for example, that persons who are prone to headaches seem to show their emotional reaction under stress-producing situations in increased tension of muscle groups at the back of the neck.

The third class of activities in which emotions can be expressed has been referred to as *affect,* the subjective experience of emotion, one of the most important of which is anxiety. A person can tell us that he is anxious, uneasy, or apprehensive or that he is delighted, exhilarated, or relaxed.

The field of emotions is one of the most important and baffling in psychology. Relatively little is known about the complex interrelationships between frustration and emotion and between the three classes of emotional manifestation: somatic, motor, and affective. It should be noted that emotions are regarded most often in their negative or uncomfortable sense, with relatively little attention given to positive emotional states, which are also important to behavior. In the field of adjustment and psychopathology, anxiety and fear rather than joy or delight have been given central theoretical positions.

The role of emotion and its manifestations in adaptive behavior has been handled in different ways. Some writers have suggested that mild states of tension are actually sought by man. For example, Lecky (1945) talked about man as a tension-producer rather than as a tension-reducer. Most psychological theories, however, tend to regard tension and affect an unpleasant states, which man attempts to eliminate or reduce by his actions. It is generally agreed that strong affects are unpleasant and can *disorganize* the productive efforts of man. Typically, this disorganization is conceived of as excessive stimulation interfering with cognitive behavior or adaptive functioning; that is, it obstructs the performance of the adaptive tasks at hand.

In contrast, Leeper (1948) argued that emotion actually tends to organize human behavior functionally to avoid danger. Similarly, Freud (1936) and Dollard and Miller (1950) have also stressed the organizing properties of emotion, regarding fear or anxiety as a drive; that is, an unpleasant stimulus, which motivates the organism to discover and apply ways of reducing it. The same point has been developed by social psychologists, such as Davis (1952), who has pointed out that, in the socialization of the child, parents intentionally produce anxiety (a subjective manifestation of stress) by punishing or disapproving socially inappropriate behavior and rewarding or approving acceptable behavior. The child comes to learn the socially approved attitudes and patterns of conduct because failure to do so is associated with disapproval and consequent anxiety. In order to be comfortable and free from anxiety, the child learns to adopt the appropriate patterns. As we shall see shortly, when the value systems to which the child is exposed are in conflict, or when they result in the frustration of biologically powerful impulses, various ego defenses can be learned to reduce the anxiety; the behavioral consequences of these defenses, which are maladaptive in certain respects (for example, the distortion of reality), make it appear that emotions disorganize behavior. In reality, anxiety has important organizing properties, but its indirect effects often have the appearance of behavioral confusion.

The evidence of the effects of emotion is consonant with both views of emotion, as a disorganizer, or source of interference, and as an organizer of behavior, depending upon what perspective is employed. In some studies, such as that of Postman and Bruner (1948), perceptual behavior was made poverty-stricken by stressing the subjects (in this case the subjects were required to form hypotheses about the nature of a stimulus presented on a screen too rapidly for complete recognition). In other studies, such as that of Deese, Lazarus, and Keenan (1953), the introduction of a stressor yielded improvements in learning in a particular group of subjects and decrements in another. Two groups of subjects were employed in the latter study, a highly anxious group and one normally low in anxiety. These subjects learned a list of nonsense syllables under control, or nonstressor, conditions, and under a stressor condition, which consisted of a painful electric shock administered whenever the subject made an error. As can be seen from the bar graph in Figure 2, which summarizes some of the data from the experiment, the normally anxious group's performance was actually facilitated by the stressor condition (they gave more correct responses under the electric-shock condition), and the group normally low in anxiety did far worse. Still other patterns were found under different types of stressor conditions. Both the organizing (facilitating) and disorganizing (impairing) effects of emotion can be readily confirmed in experimental research of this sort.

By extension of the above discussion, we can say that stress can affect the process of adjustment in two ways. In the first place, it can interfere with cognition, thus making the ordinary adaptive tasks of life more difficult to perform (the disorganizing effect). Secondly, and perhaps more important, mechanisms of defense designed to

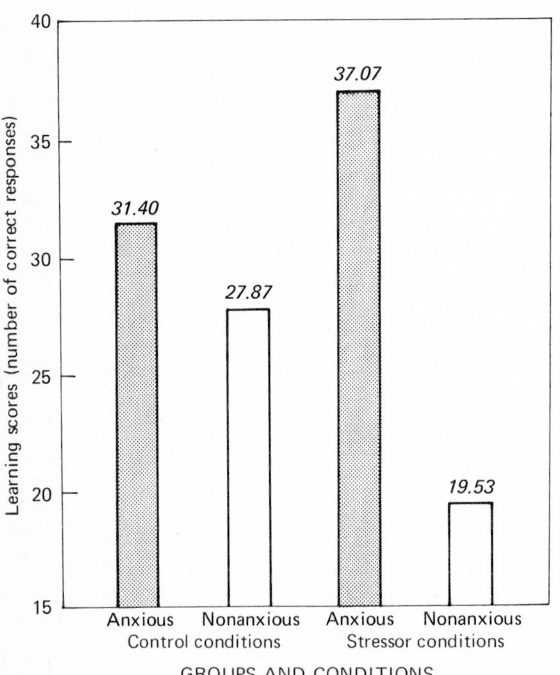

Figure 2 Groups and conditions—effects of stress on learning as a function of level of anxiety. Shaded graphs are those of the subjects who showed a high level of anxiety under normal, nonexperimental conditions as measured by a questionnaire. *(After Deese et al., 1953.)*

reduce the stress are produced (the organizing effect). These defenses in themselves are maladaptive in the sense that they are generally self-deceiving, thus making it difficult or impossible for the person to approach realistically the actual conflict or source of frustration that aroused the state of stress. However, they may be regarded as adaptive in the sense that they serve to reduce anxiety.

It should be understood that the absence of subjective manifestations of emotion (affect such as anxiety) is not in itself a suitable sign of the absence of stress, because defensive operations can reduce or eliminate the emotion at the expense of effective adaptation. For example, if a person deals with stress by repressive defense mechanisms (and is therefore totally unaware of the internal conflicts), he may succeed in reducing anxiety to such a degree that he appears entirely comfortable. The expression *la belle indifférence,* used to describe a characteristic of the disorder known as "conversion hysteria," reflects this absence of anxiety, although the conversion symptom (blindness, deafness, anesthesias, paralysis, etc.) suggests a severe state of stress and the operation of the mechanism of repression. Often we infer a state of stress not from the subjective reports of the person, but on the basis of other evidence such as physiological reactions or the behavioral manifestations of ego-defense mechanisms.

We have considered the sources of, and the nature of, stress, primarily in terms of its relation to emotion. An equally important aspect of the stress state is the attempt to reduce it in some way. We must now consider the ways in which persons cope with stress and the consequences of these coping mechanisms for human behavior and adjustment.

REFERENCES

Ax, A. F. The Physiological Differentiation between Fear and Anger in Humans. *Psychosom. Med.,* 1953, **15,** 433–442.

Cannon, W. *The Wisdom of the Body.* (rev. ed.) New York: Norton, 1939.

Cantril, H. The Invasion from Mars. In G. E. Swanson, T. M. Newcomb, and E. L. Hartley (Eds.), *Readings in Social Psychology.* New York: Holt, 1952. Pp. 198–207.

Davis, A. & R. F. Havighurst. Social Classes and Color Differences in Child Rearing. In G. E. Swanson, T. M. Newcomb, & E. L. Hartley (Eds.), *Readings in Social Psychology.* New York: Holt, 1952. Pp. 539–550.

Deese, J. E., R. S. Lazarus, & J. Keenan. Anxiety, Anxiety Reduction, and Stress in Learning, *J. exp. Psychol.,* 1953, **46,** 55–60.

Dollard, J., & N. E. Miller. *Personality and Psychotherapy.* New York: McGraw-Hill, 1950.

Eriksen, C. W., R. S. Lazarus, & J. R. Strange, Psychological Stress and Its Personality Correlates: Part II. The Rorschach Test and Other Personality Measures. *J. Pers.,* 1952, **20,** 277–286.

Franklin, J. C., B. C. Schiele, J. Brozek, & A. Keys. Observations of Human Behavior in Experimental Semistarvation and Rehabilitation. *J. clin. Psychol.,* 1948, **4,** 28–45.

Freud, S. *The Problem of Anxiety.* New York: Norton, 1936.

Funkenstein, D. H., S. H. King, & Margaret Drolette. *Mastery of Stress.* Cambridge, Mass.: Harvard University Press, 1957.

Janis, I. L. *Psychological Stress.* New York: Wiley, 1958.

Johnson, D. M. The "Phantom Anesthetist" of Mattoon: A Field Study of Mass Hysteria. *J. abn. soc. Psychol.,* 1945, **40,** 175–186.

Lazarus, R. S., & C. W. Eriksen. Effects of Failure Stress upon Skilled Performance. *J. exp. Psychol.*, 1952, **43,** 100–105.
Lecky. P. *Self-consistency*. New York: Island Press, 1945.
Leeper, R. W. Lewin's Topological and Vector Psychology: A Digest and Critique. *Univ. Ore. Publ. Stud. Psychol.*, 1943, No. 1.
Malmor, R. B., & A. A. Smith. Forehead Tension and Motor Irregularities in Psychoneurotic Patients Under Stress. *J. Pers.*, 1955, **23,** 391–406.
————, H. Wallerstein, & C. Shagass. Headache Proness and Mechanisms of Motor Conflict in Psychiatric Patients. *J. Pers.*, 1953, **22,**163–187.
Mead, G. H. *Mind, Self, and Society*. Chicago: University of Chicago Press, 1934.
Mead, Margaret. *Coming of Age in Samoa*. New York: Morrow, 1928.
————. *Sex and Temperament in Three Primitive Societies*. New York: Morrow, 1935.
Mussen, P. H., & J. J. Conger. *Child Development and Personality*. New York: Harper, 1956.
Postman, L., & J. S. Bruner. Perception Under Stress. *Psychol. Rev.* 1948, **55,** 314–323.
Rank, O. *Will Therapy*. Translated by Julia Taft. New York: Knopf, 1945.
Rogers, C. R. *Client-centered Therapy*. Boston: Houghton Mifflin, 1951.
Rozenzweig, S. An Outline of Frustration Theory. In J. McV. Hunt (Ed.), *Personality and the Behavior Disorders*. New York: Ronald, 1944.
Selye, H. *The Stress of Life*. New York: McGraw-Hill, 1956.
Sullivan, H. S. *The Interpersonal Theory of Psychiatry*. New York: Norton, 1953.
Vogel, W., Susan Raymond, & R. S. Lazarus. Intrinsic Motivation and Psychological Stress. *J. abnorm. soc. Psychol.*, 1959, **58,** 225–233.
Wallace, A. F. C. *Tornado in Worcester*. Washington. D.C.: National Academy of Sciences–National Research Council, Disaster Study No. 3, 1956. Publication 392.
Wolff, H. (Ed.) Life Stress and Bodily Disease. *Proc. Ass. Res. nerv. ment. Dis.* Baltimore: Williams & Wilkins, 1950.

The Defense Mechanisms Re-examined*

Raymond J. McCall

THE PHENOMENOLOGY OF DEFENSE MECHANISMS

. . . No one who writes in this area can be unaware of the fact that we are all standing on Freud's shoulders, and there is good reason to commend Anna Freud as well for her attempt to present systematically the Freudian position. But in acknowleding our debts to the Freuds, *père et fille,* we may still be chary of subscribing to Freudian constructs and postulates which are far removed from simple phenomenological description and which constitute a kind of systematic mythology of the libido. In this mythology is included the highly dubious assumption that the "ego" is entirely the vassal of the "instinctual apparatus" (the "id"), that sexual and destructive impulses, the latter arising from the "death instinct," are the only sources of anxiety, and that the subject of the defense-mechanisms is always this same anxiety. Because

*From Raymond J. McCall, "The Defense Mechanisms Re-examined: A Logical and Phenomenal Analysis," *Catholic Psychological Record,* 1963 **1,** 45–64. Pages 47–64 reprinted by permission of the author and the Editor, *Catholic Psychological Record.*

we employ the generic term "defense mechanism" and in most instances the specific terms (such as *rationalization, compensation, displacement, projection)* for particular instances thereof, terms which were coined by Freud or his immediate followers, we perhaps commit ourselves to general concepts like "psychic conflict" and "unconscious motivation" but in no significant degree are we bound to the elaborate theoretical system which Freud and his followers have built up to account for these phenomena, or to specific aspects of this system which are supposedly related directly to "ego defense." We may, for example, accept the notion of hostility as frequently involved in the defense mechanism of *projection* without committing ourselves to the "death instinct" as its ultimate root, or to infantile "spitting out" as its prototype, or to homosexuality as its concomitant (Fenichel, 1945).

Adhering, then, as closely as possible to a phenomenological method, we may begin by describing defense mechanisms as *self-protective maneuvers, pertaining to perception and motivation, mental or psychic, yet largely unconscious, designed to soften or disguise what is unacceptable in or to the self.* Though not deliberately adopted, defense mechanisms have an apparent utility as disguises of our weaknesses and baser motives.

Not only Freud and the orthodox Freudians, but many others, have seen the defense mechanisms as essentially protection against *anxiety,* particularly of the sort deriving from aberrant sexual impulse. However important this particular kind of defense may be—and we should be careful not to underestimate it—there is little evidence in favor of regarding all defense mechanisms as deriving from it. We run less risk of over-generalization (or misplaced concreteness), therefore, if we maintain that *whatever* is threatening to our self-esteem is a fitting subject for cognitive-appetitive self-defense. Perhaps sexually derived anxiety has a special importance and intensity, but it would seem that the defense mechanisms may be evoked by anything that conflicts with our *minimum ideal* of what the self must be. This might include imcompetence, stupidity, selfishness, indecisiveness, or any other self-devaluating experience or circumstance. It may be that the three interrelated conditions of the self —*anxiety, hostility* and *sexuality*—are peculiarly suited to elicit the *habitual and exaggerated* employment of defenses which seems to characterize the neurotic, but our description and analysis of the defense mechanisms should take cognizance of the fact that they are employed by normal as well as by neurotic and other types of abnormal persons.

On this, as well as on other accounts, defense mechanisms should not be confused with *symptoms* of neuosis or other abnormal conditions.[1] The mechanisms are purely *endopsychic* or mental (congitive-appetitive) devices, ways of perceiving and desiring, giving a protectively distorted registration of the self and its world, and connoting a matching wish to have them free of threats to our self-regard. Symptoms, on the other hand, are not limited to the psychic, to ways of thinking and wishing, but attach themselves to our behavior in any of a thousand ways as well as to our thoughts and feelings, and may disturb our physiological as well as our psychological functioning. Thus, *perceiving* your boss as though he were your tyrannical father connotes the

[1]This confusion detracts from much of Anna Freud's analysis in her widely admired book, *The Ego and the Mechanisms of Defense* (1954).

defense-mechanism of *displacement,* while developing a severe *phobia* at the prospect of going out of the house on work days (without knowing why) would be a *neurotic symptom,* just as developing high blood pressure after a short time on the job might be designated a *psychosomatic* or *psychophysiologic symptom.* In many instances the defense mechanism and the symptom may be related as antecedent and consequent, but there is no justification for confusing relatively simple cause with its more heterogeneous and often distant effects.

To say that the defense mechanisms are largely *unconscious* is to stress by implication that they are always in corresponding degree *self-deceptive.* If, indeed, the individual were not taken in by them they would not serve to defend his self-esteem against the intimation of inadequacy or dereliction. That unconscious *defense* is less effectively adjustive than conscious *coping* is evident if we consider that, however variously the ideal of self-realization may be construed, the self-directively adjustive life is a *conscious* life; a never-ending task of modifying situations to suit the demands of the self, modifying the latter to suit the requirements of the former, or (most often) effecting some compromise between the two.[2] From any perspective, this involves insightful awareness in such matters as understanding the limitations of one's own powers and performance; recognizing our social dependence and the need of acquiescing in the reasonable demands of others; acknowledging the irrational and imperfect elements in ourselves (not just in others or in the institutions of our society); admitting to oneself at least failure of adaptation when it occurs and the consequent need for self-correction, renewed effort, and variation in our approach. Not only, we should add, are these modes of coping different from defense; they are made difficult or impossible by the subjectively protective set of the defense mechanisms which in effect blinds us to our own real requirements other than those dictated by self-esteem.

It would appear, therefore, that the self which is defended by defense mechanisms is not the insightful, reality-oriented, and socialized self. Rather, it is the infantile self with its islands of self-ignorance, its imperfectly socialized dependency, its delusive over-valuation of itself ("narcissism"), and its defective reality-contact. However important it may be for self-realization that the individual retain his energizing self-regard, it seems that when subjectively oriented defense assumes primacy over objectively oriented coping, we have an immature and intrinsically maladaptive organization, perhaps indeed the very *Anlage* of the neurotic personality structure.

DESCRIPTIVE ANALYSIS OF DEFENSE MECHANISMS

Lists of defense mechanisms are variable in length and in the intricacy of the logical and psychological considerations offered in their support. We shall consider an even dozen in what appears to be the most nearly logical order for an understanding of their pertinence to abnormal psychology. They are:

1 Repression
2 Isolation
3 Rationalization

[2]Recall the famous prayer: "O Lord, give me the courage to change what has to be changed, the patience to bear what cannot be changed, and the wisdom to tell the difference between the two."

4 Reaction-formation
5 Compensation
6 Defensive devaluation
7 Displacement
8 Projection
9 Withdrawal
10 Identification
11 Undoing
12 Autism

1 Repression

The attempted exclusion from awareness of self-devaluating experiences such as shameful memories and unacceptable motives whether hostile, fearful, sexual, pettily selfish, crude, dishonest, or contemptible.

Repression is said to be the most fundamental of defense mechanisms, since unless the self-devaluating memory or motive is somehow removed from the center of consciousness, it is difficult to see how we can be deceived into using other means to defend against it. All other mechanisms would thus seem to depend upon at least an initial repression. At the same time, the very existence of other mechanisms indicates that repression is not entirely successful in "warding off" the self-depreciating experience. If to rationalize or project or displace a hateful impulse or shortcoming I must be less than perfectly aware of that impulse or shortcoming, by the same token there would be no need for me to rationalize, or project, or displace if through repression I had succeeded in putting the whole matter out of mind. It is for this reason that the term "*attempted* exclusion" has been incorporated in our definition of repression.

The Freudians speak of repression in quasi-topographical terms as a process by which "drives and memories" are "pushed down into the unconscious." Pursuing the metaphor, they hold that such repressed material continues to exist *unchanged* "in the unconscious," but being barred from direct expression, can return only in symbolic or disguised form as "symptoms," "sublimations," or other "derivatives." One possibility, however, which they acknowledge but to which they seem not to have devoted sufficient attention, is that repression may be *from the beginning* less than an all or none affair, and that what they are pleased to call "the return of the repressed" may sometimes signalize only its failure to depart.

There is a tendency, too, for them to regard conscious-unconscious as a simple dichotomy, and to speak of mental states as one *or* the other. It is more in accord, however, both with scientific usage and with everyday experience to think of conscious and unconscious as the opposite ends of a continuum rather than as dichotomous contraries, and to recognize that the departure from and approach to consciousness may be gradual. Of some experiences I may be quite unconscious, as of events taking place prior to my second birthday, and you may be utterly unaware of crassly selfish reasons for wanting to do someone a good turn. Frequently, on the other hand, we are able to bring past events to the margin of consciousness, if not to its center—as psychoanalysis has made very clear—and frequently, too, we dimly sense an element of self-seeking in our more "unselfish" attitudes.

There is thus much in our psychic life that is neither clearly conscious nor entirely unconscious. Perhaps if we imagine clear and focal consciousness as the center of a spiral, and unconsciousness as exemplified by increasing removal from that focal center but having its exact boundaries fluid and unspecified we shall have a topographical analogy that limps a little less than the one implied by the sharply divided surface and subsurface of the Freudian iceberg. It would seem, at any rate, more descriptively accurate to think of repression as initially incomplete, and of the unconscious as a relative condition, than to assume a total repression into total unconsciousness of a totally unchangeable psychic content that can be re-admitted to awareness only by way of symbolization. Only the Freudian penchant for an over-simplified, two-valued logic and for a mechanical model of the human psyche requires thinking in such rigid categories.

In discussing repression and the unconscious it also seems worthwhile to keep in mind the difference between the psychic *process* of repression, and its *product,* the repressed experience. Even if we assume that the act of repression is totally unconscous, it does not follow that the self-devaluating experience is always rendered totally unconscious, or even rendered unconscious in all its self-devaluating aspects. Though I am not conscious of repressing, I may remain conscious of certain parts of an experience which has self-depreciating implications, and perhaps even vaguely conscious of the self-depreciating elements themselves. It is possible, in short, that at times repression is only partially successful because it is only partial. This does not rule out the possibility that some repressed material may return to awareness in symbolic form, but leaves open the additional possibility that in some instances only part of the original experience is repressed.

2 Isolation

Isolation may be defined as *the cutting off or blunting of unacceptable aspects of a total experience.* To accept isolation as a mechanism underscores the partial nature of at least some repression, since isolation seems to be nothing but a special kind of partial repression, one indeed whose partial nature is most evident. Thus in the most common manifestation of isolation the individual appears to be in possession of all the facts of a situation but not to recognize them for what they are, or not to register the whole situation in its most obvious implications of a derogatory sort. This is likely to impress the ordinary observer as peculiar or queer as when the mother of a severely retarded child regards her child's behavior as little different from that of other children despite its gross deficiencies; or when the long-suffering wife of the alcoholic sees her husband's trouble only in his being a little too sociable; or when the notably homely girl fails to appreciate the unmistakable implications of her unattractiveness. This kind of isolation seems to defend against deficiency in ourselves or in those close to us.[3]

We should note, however, that it is not so much the *existence* of the fact which is nullified by the partial repression as is its *motivational relevance* and *emotional implications,* from which its existence is isolated. In another kind of isolation—that

[3]Allport (1937) especially has noted the manner in which the self tends with maturity to broaden so as to include those closest to us. I am thus not only my physical and isolated self but, in a very real sense, those with whom I "identify."

found in certain types of obsessional neurosis and concerned with unacceptable impulses in the self—it is again not the fact which is denied to consciousness. In these cases the individual acknowledges the unacceptable desire but cannot recognize its relevance to his own motivational system. (''I love my wife. Why should I feel this crazy impulse to strangle her?'') Perhaps, too, the homely girl *knows* that she is homely but fails to see this fact as relevant to her seldom being invited out by eligible males. Such ''selective imperception'' is very palpably defensive, not denying the experience but separating or isolating it from elements threatening to self-esteem.

3 Rationalization

Rationalization may be described as *pseudo-explanation of criticizable behavior or attitude which substitutes acceptable (often fancied) motives for its actual motives.* The rationalizer will view his idleness as needed relaxation, his cowardice as caution, his impatiently severe discipline as in the child's best interests.

In the classical view rationalization always involves repression of an unacceptable motive and its return in some disguise which is still close enough to the original to awaken defensive processes. Though it may in many instances be true, this smacks a little of cloak-and-dagger melodrama. Less mysterious and equally worth noting again is the palpable incompleteness or partial failure of the repression. It would seem, indeed, that *the sense of having an unacceptable purpose behind our action must be at least vaguely present in order for there to be any occasion to rationalize,* and this means that what is threatening to self-esteem has not been effectively repressed. Without recourse to the notions of banishment and return incognito, we might assume that in some instances a particular evil inclination has been repressed but that a residual, in the form of a vague or general feeling of guilt or unworthy disposition, abides with us and demands that somehow it be ''explained away.''

The compulsory character of this demand for explanation is not hard to understand when we recall that from infancy on each of us is expected to be able to account for his conduct according to the standards of ''reason'' and ''common sense'' dictated by his culture and sub-cultures. The *fear of disapproval* by others for what is base and unworthy in one's conduct is one of the most powerful motives in human existence, and a plausible basis for that nameless but often unsettling apprehension which we call ''anxiety'' (McCall, 1962). In this sense there can be no reasonable doubt that rationalization operates as a defense against anxiety, reinforcing our efforts to escape disapproval by concocting allegedly laudable purposes for our behavior.

The task of rationalization is made somewhat easier by the fact that most of our actions are *multiply motivated* (''over-determined'' is the Freudian barbarism), so that there may be ''good'' as well as ''bad'' reasons for our behaving as we do. The work of rationalization in this case is to point up, rather than invent, the good reasons for our action when repression has reduced, without quite eliminating, our awareness of the bad.

4 Reaction-formation

A singularly unhappy term for *defending self-esteem against one's partially repressed and unacceptable dispositions by over-desiring their opposite.* If rationalization is a kind of "refutation by argument" of implied unworthiness, reaction-formation is a "refutation by action." I lay the ghost of suspected meanness by behaving so very, very nobly that no one could possibly doubt the purity of my motives. Least of all we should add, myself!

Though overworked in certain circles, reaction-formation ("antithetic counteraction" or "counteractive inversion" would be a more precisely descriptive term) is probably important in the genesis of certain moralistic compulsions and attitudes. It is fanciful to suppose that all perfectionism is motivated, as Freud thought, by the repressed desire for the exact opposite: that extreme neatness, for example, is simply "warding off" a powerful disposition to be disgustingly messy, that the ideal of perfect benevolence is motivated by an unacknowledged but uncompromising hostility and a savage cruelty, or that those who are most on the side of the angels are the biggest devils at heart. It is possible, nevertheless, to cite enough examples of "antithetically counteractive" motivation to give plausibility to such exaggerations; and where an individual's ethical attitudes are extreme and inflexible at the same time that he gives evidence of excessive preoccupation with the violation of ethical standards (especially by others), we may reasonably suspect something like reaction-formation to be at work.

To justify suspicion of reaction-formation, however, there should be indications of the persistence in some form (perhaps only symbolic) of the rejected motive while the reaction against it is truly immoderate, a "bending over backwards," a tendency to "protest too much" in action as well as in words, and an obsessive concern with morality and immorality in this particular area. Sexual irregularities may offer a special occasion for reaction-formation since sexual motivation is likely to be at once powerful and devious, yet subject to much restriction and criticism. Certainly those who spend a great deal of time investigating and exposing the sexual depravities of others are thereby afforded an opportunity to wallow in the shocking details thereof themselves. This may offer simultaneously a partial gratification of their own repressed sexual impulses (perhaps voyeuristic or Peeping Tom-like in nature) and the appearance of absolute virtuousness.

The Reverend Davidson in Somerset Maugham's classic "Rain" is close to an ideal embodiment of reaction-formation. His implacable hatred of sexual immorality, his relentless persecution of the loose woman, Sadie Thompson, his consuming joy at her "conversion," the aridity of his own married life, even his dreams of mountains which resemble a woman's breasts, point to the defensive and self-deceptive nature of his own rejection of sex. It is not then from an ideal morality that reaction-formation springs but from a rigid and uninsightful moralistic excess, through which symbolic glimpses of a very different sort of motivation appear. And, of course, it is not merely sexuality that may thus emerge. As Plato said of Antisthenes' contempt for worldly honors and other goods: "His vanity peeps out through the holes in his cloak."

Reaction-formation is not, however, to be confused with hypocritical pretense. The person employs this mechanism indeliberately rather than with full awareness, and there is usually little doubt of the sincerity of his desire for ethical righteousness. It is, in fact, the extremity of this desire which gives him away, making clear the defensive rather than adjustively coping nature of his love of virtue.

5 Compensation

If what remains threatening to self-esteem in the way of deficiency or dereliction cannot be "explained away" (rationalization) or "acted away" (reaction-formation), it can perhaps be *made up for*. This is the way of *compensation*. Compensation may then be described as a *defense mechanism which enables us to offset unacceptable tendencies or weakness by overvaluing and overstressing acceptable motives or strengths*. The interdependence of the two elements, "*over*valuation" and "weakness" is essential to the notion of compensation as a defense mechanism rather than as a mode of coping; and in defensive compensation there is always in all probability some repression, so that the deficiency or aberration is not consciously faced.

Alfred Adler, who invented the term "compensation," saw clearly that every style of life demands the stressing of certain values and the subordination or diminution of others. We have no warrant to speak of compensation as an unrealistic and uninsightful defense, however, unless the valuation of one goal is exaggerated as a means of defending self-esteem against an unacknowledged imperfection. So, to set great store by intellectual accomplishment is not compensation unless it is extreme and designed (unconsciously) to make up for physical or other defects; and striving for a successful career may well be nothing but adjustive coping unless it serves as a means of offsetting social unattractiveness or a comparable shortcoming.

Compensation is also to be distinguished from deliberate emphasis upon certain capacities and dispositions where these reflect natural endowment or general group expectation. Thus for the musically talented child in 18th century Germany to devote more of his energies to music than to any other interest, or for the athletically endowed American boy to work in and out of season to perfect his skills in fielding or foul-shooting, is by no accounting necessarily compensatory.

Nor should a direct attack on a weakness, designed to overcome whatever incapacity that weakness may connote, be confused with defensive compensation. The boy with polio who becomes a distance runner, the stutterer who will one day be a great orator, the frail child who develops into a partisan of the vigorous life are manifesting an actively coping rather than a defensive orientation. We should be chary of labeling as compensatory any behavior that does not imply unrealistic over-valuation and unadmitted defect.

A form of supposed compensation said to be common among modern women, due to their inferior status in our society and their resentment of male superiority and privilege, was designated by Adler "masculine protest." Whatever the merits of this notion (which has considerable currency among clinicians working with neurotic women), it too should not be overworked. In his later years Adler gave up the contention that one's entire style of life is determined by the mode of compensation for the sense of inferiority originating in childhood, and he relegated the famous "inferiority complex" to a secondary though still significant place in the development of personality. In any case, it would be a dangerous oversimplification to disregard the constructively adjustive aspect of much feminine striving, and to reduce all the efforts of women to overcome their dependent and subordinate status in our culture to a "masculine protest." Even to conjoin under this heading all instances of aggressive feminism, from the fastidiousness of the D.A.R. to the zealousness of the

W.C.T.U., not excluding the manipulative proclivities of women executives, matriarchal dictators, and lady wrestlers, is to dilute the meaning of "masculine protest" to that of an anti-feminine expletive. Even following a more restrained usage, however, it is doubtful that much of what is called "masculine protest" has any bearing on compensation as a defense mechanism.

6 Defensive Devalution

If we cannot compensate for weaknesses and transgressions, we can divert our own and others' attention from them by concentrating on the faults of others. Though not included in the classical lists of defense-mechanisms, defensive devaluation appears to be an important self-protective maneuver, of a cognitive sort basically, *a focusing upon the weaknesses and aberrations of others as a means of calling attention away from one's own deficiencies.*

Behaviorally, defensive devaluation is likely to be expressed by endless and unwarranted "griping" at the bosses, the "brass," the government, or "people" generally. But the true defensive devaluator does not criticize in the hope of effecting reform but as a defense against his own sense of inadequacy and perhaps guilt. The presence of repression is indicated by his general insensitivity to faults in himself in the face of an extreme sensitivity to the inconsiderateness, stupidity, and similar faults of others. He sees the mote of his neighbor's eye but misses the splinter in his own, and with a vengeance. Yet he does not directly overemphasize his own assets as in compensation, nor does he attribute his own motives to others, as is supposed to take place in *projection.* Nor does defensive devaluation connote the profound lack of insight, characteristic of reaction-formation and, as we shall see, projection. It is thus perhaps the "least abnormal" of mechanisms, enabling us to say in effect "I know I have my weaknesses, but what do they amount to when you consider . . .," followed by a litany of the foibles and iniquities of others, thereby mitigating the threat to self-esteem of our own failings without denying their existence.

7 Displacement

Attaching an unacceptable motive and its accompanying affect to an alternative object which can provide partial (usually symbolic) release for the original motive without bringing the latter to awareness. Examples are numerous, as in the peculiar joy derived from beating a business rival at golf or bridge, satisfying a prying tendency by taking a job which involves conducting investigations into the lives of others (perhaps that of a psychologist!), carrying over a repressed hatred and fear of one's father to one's relations with his boss or with older authority figures generally.

Whether displacement plays as enormous a role in human motivation as postulated by Freud is open to considerable doubt, but there is no question that as a defense mechanism it has unusual importance in the genesis of neurotic symptoms and of neurotic "tendencies" found even in the normal person.

The symbolic and defensive nature of displacement is manifested by the presence of intense feeling quite disproportionate to the acknowledged importance of the current circumstance. When, for example, a man attaches a value to winning at bridge that the card game in itself could not by any reckoning warrant, when he is upset for days over a bad play or at losing to a neighbor, playing and replaying every trick in his mind, planning his strategy for the next game in great and anxious detail, we infer that beating his opponent at bridge is symbolic to him of something larger, that not the game itself but his self-regard is somehow at stake. So when a man is hatefully resentful of a superior where there is little or nothing in the behavior of the superior to justify this malevolent attitude, we may again look beyond the present situation to some other relation of which it may be symbolic and which, having been repressed, has been denied expression, such as resentment toward a domineering parent, rivalry with an older brother, and the like.

We may note in such cases a *reason to repress* the original motive and feeling. Thus the love and respect which we are supposed to feel, and often actually do feel, toward our parents or siblings, may make attitudes of dislike or resentment unacceptable and self-devaluating. This does not seem to be the case with all symbolic displacements, however, which therefore may not serve any special defensive purpose but take place simply as a result of the inevitable human disposition to symbolize. Thus my transfer of negative feeling from an earlier experience to a present one may be maladaptive without serving to protect self-esteem, as when I react to a new acquaintance on the basis of his (unrecognized) resemblance to an old rival. Though maladaptive, such displacements are unlikely to be productive of neurosis since the aberrant tendency is not reinforced by the continuing need to safeguard self-esteem and may be more readily modified by corrective experience.

In postulating that the defensive symbolism of displacement renders intelligible much peculiar feeling and behavior, and that phobias and compulsions and conversion symptoms often "make sense" in the light of their symbolically defensive purpose, Freud unquestionably contributed more than any other person to our understanding of neurotic and other abnormal phenomena. Freud also seems to have had reason on his side in arguing that sexual motives, because of their intrinsic urgency and the severe disapproval with which their manifestation in the young is likely to be greeted, are specially subject to symbolization and displacement, following inadequate repression.

It is something less than necessary, however, to concur in Freud's speculations regarding the unlimited displaceability of sexual motives and to conclude with him that not only many neurotic symptoms but many entirely normal activities of a higher order such as religious rituals, artistic endeavor, and intellectual interests equally represent symbolic fulfilments of sexual urges. To interpret prayer as satisfying the impulse to masturbate, painting as a displacement of the motive to smear excrement, and intellectual curiosity as a symbolic equivalent of the wish to play Peeping Tom in the parental bedroom, requires a degree of credulity in the magical power of symbolism which is so far fortunately confined to some psychoanalysts and psychotics.

Some instances of apparent displacement involve little or no symbolism and most probably denote a rather obvious kind of "safety-valve" mechanism, as when the business man who has had to contain his ire all day takes it out on his wife and children in the evening; or when we, having put up with a series of frustrations or indignities, "blow up" at some trifling contretemps. These bear only a superficial resemblance to the systematically symbolic and elaborately self-deceptive displacements we find in many neurotics, and should not be considered to exemplify the defense-mechanism in any strict sense. Symbolism as well as self-defense is thus probably, as Freud thought, essential to the kind of displacement which contributes to neurosis.

8 Projection

Projection is one of the most important mechanisms for the understanding of psychological abnormality, but it is more pertinent to psychosis and the so-called personality pattern disturbances than it is to the relatively minor abnormalities or neuroses. To project is *to defend against unacceptable motives by attributing to others either the motives themselves or the criticism of oneself for having such motives.* The unacceptable is not explained away, counteracted, or made up for (as in rationalization, reaction-formation, and compensation); one gets rid of it projecting it onto others, by regarding it as the creation of others and not of oneself. Projection is instanced by interpreting neutral behavior in another as hostile, while not recognizing the reality and primacy of one's own hostility; by reacting to homosexual or other deviant sexual tendencies in oneself by first over-vigorously denying the possibility of any such tendencies, and thereupon ascribing to others unjust accusations against the self of having such tendencies. The two examples illustrate what may be distinguished as *primary projection* (direct attribution of our unacceptable motives to another); and *secondary projection* (attribution to others of critical attitudes toward the self for allegedly having unacceptable motives). What is projected in the latter case is *one's own* self-devaluating attitude which may well be a greater threat to self-esteem than the original (unacceptable) motive.

Since both kinds of projection ascribe to others what is actually our own motivational or attitudinal stance, the use of projection as a defense mechanism presupposes a profound lack of insight and a deep repression of our irrational and censurable dispositions. To project is thus not just to blame others for our problems, it is to blame others for our own baser motives and consequent self-critical attitudes. It would seem then that projection could be sustained only by a defensively "touchy" and uninsightful view of the self as irreproachable, combined with a basically suspicious and hostile view of others, a singularly unappealing combination but one whose existence is supported by the clinical impression that those with a high quota of hostility and low insight find projection relatively easy. It is worth noting, too, that when hostile motives are projected the inner need which they connote can still be satisfied by the counter-hostility we feel justified in manifesting after we have projected our original hostility to others. Projection may thereby be reinforced through rationalization, while a defensively devaluative attitude toward others may prepare the ground for it.

Since friction is an inevitable consequence of social closeness, and insight is achieved with difficulty, while the empathic understanding of others is rare indeed, it is not surprising that some tendencies toward hostile projection—sometimes called "paranoid trends"—are found everywhere. Extensive and elaborate use of projection is, however, rare in normal persons, probably because it involves so much distortion of the self-picture and so many uncritical suppositions regarding the motives of others. The deepening and stabilization of primary projection is characteristic of what is known as paranoid personality disorder, rather than of neurosis; and the elaboration of self-deceptive notions regarding the accusatory attitude of others toward oneself for sexual irregularities and the like (secondary projection) is generally symptomatic of paranoid psychosis. Perhaps the tendency to project is ubiquitous, but it is fortunately subject to limitation and correction where reality contact is good and insight at all present.

9 Withdrawal

This is a so-called minor mechanism, representing a defensive reaction to weaknesses or ineptitude which is at the opposite pole to compensation. It should not be confused with the symptomatic behavior of *social withdrawal,* though it may be antecedent thereto. In itself, defensive withdrawal is a purely mental mechanism, an *endopsychic retreat from what is desired but considered unattainable.* Like other defense mechanisms it presupposes the operation of repression, in this case at least to reduce the awareness of failure or incompetence. The complementary function of withdrawal is thus to reduce motivation or desire for the object whose attainment is thought to be beyond reach.

Coping or constructive adjustment demands, of course, that we learn our limitations and cease trying to reach the unattainable. Defensive withdrawal is something else: a subtle self-deception in which we convince (or all but convince) ourselves that we don't care about the loss of something we very much wanted. By relinquishing interest, by saying to myself ''I don't care,'' I defend myself against the highly self-devaluating experience of failure, prospective or retrospective. ''I didn't fail,'' I say in effect, ''I just didn't try. And I didn't try because it doesn't really matter to me.'' What makes withdrawal essentially maladjustive is its prevention of further effort to attain the desired goal or even of the attempt to re-assess the situation. Perhaps what is needed in many cases is not a psychological ''leaving the field'' but the taking of a new tack, or a hard look at our past efforts in order to discover the reason for their failure. The stabilization of the withdrawal mechanism, however, so lowers the attraction of the goal—at least to consciousness—that re-appraisal and renewed effort are most unlikely to occur. If the habitual ''withdrawer,'' then, ''wards off'' failure by giving up almost in advance, he effectively ''wards off'' success as well. Withdrawal-in-advance may thus be the mark of the inept or inadequate personality, while withdrawal after the event may be akin to the rationalization of failure. The fable of the fox and the sour grapes, though often interpreted quite differently, appears to exemplify this kind of withdrawal more than any other defense-mechanism.

10 Identification

Identification is *defending against the conviction of inadequacy and weakness by viewing oneself as somehow the same as or one with some figure of power or status.* It is probably less dependent on repression than most other mechanisms, though it may involve a diminished awareness of one's separate identity as a creature of weakness. In its original, childish form identification results in a detailed and intense imitation of a parent or other status person. It may be very thoroughgoing because it is a kind of natural extension of the process of learning by imitation, and because it may also involve a normal expression of affection. But behind this extreme imitation there is likely to be the primitive, magical thinking of identification which concludes in effect: "If I am like him in every act, I will take on his attributes of power and competence." Identification in this sense is undoubtedly important for the development of personality in childhood and early adolescence. It is to a great extent by "trying on" the attitudes and manners of acting suggested by others—most often through deeds rather than words—parents to begin with, but also older siblings, teachers, peer group leaders, and various other status figures, that we find for ourselves the style of life that (more or less) fits.

Despite the importance of identification for personality development, the persistence into adulthood of its childlike mode of thinking results in a neurotic immaturity. The individual may have to begin by identifying with a father or other mentor, but as he matures he must alter and adapt the model to the dimensions of circumstance and the substance of his own individuality. The ideal self must come closer to the capacities of the real self and to the possibilities determined by the actual and present life situation. To behave exactly like your father, for example, when your own capacities and temperament are quite different from your father's, and where the surroundings in which you find yourself are also quite different, is certainly maladjustive, however impressive your father's behavior may have been.

If identification does not disappear, it becomes radically altered in the normal adult, acquiring flexibility, becoming more broadly socialized, object-oriented, coping rather than defensive. The normal adult manifests a great deal of what is sometimes loosely called "group identification." He "identifies" with his profession or trade, his family, his country, his political party, his local community, his religion. If his identifications are thereby multiplied, they are also less total and involuntary and have only a limited resemblance to the defense mechanism found in the abnormal and the developmental contrivance employed by the immature. Adult identifications reflect what Allport has called the objectification and extension of the self: they manifest what through socialization the individual has become (Allport, 1937). Defensive identification, on the other hand, reflects what the individual is *not* but would become, as a means of escape from the self-devaluating reality of his own limitations.

In normal persons, too, identification (whether developmental or adult) seems closely related to affiliation and affection. The normal child loves and admires the parent with whom he identifies. The normal man "cathects" his family, his religion, his profession, his school. There is little affection manifested, however, in what the Freudians aptly call "identification with the aggressor," as when a child imitiates to the letter in his actions toward a younger sibling the behavior of a brutal father whom he fears and hates; or when lighter-skinned Negroes exhibit prejudice toward their darker fellows; or when, as has been reported, concentration camp inmates outdo their guards in brutality toward their fellow prisoners, not stopping at murder and torture, and even sewing scraps of Gestapo uniform to their prison garb that they might resemble more closely their tormentors.

11 Undoing

Undoing is *symbolic restitution for a present impulse or past behavior considered unacceptable.* Distinction must again be made between restitution as a conscious and deliberate social act, designed to make up at least partially for a wrong done to another, and defensive undoing, a self-deluding kind of magical thinking by which we annul our delinquencies. The latter, like other defense-mechanisms, is based upon at least partial repression, while social reparation, which the psychoanalysts and others often confuse with undoing, presupposes a consciousness of wrong done and of a connection between the restitutional act and the original transgression. Nor is the thinking involved in the latter necessarily magical. When we apologize for an insult for example, we do not ordinarily deceive ourselves or others into thinking that thereby the offending action is undone. Rather we express a wish, recognized as contrary-to-fact, that we had not committed the injury and we signify an intention not to repeat it. It is as an expression of present attitude and augury for the future that reparative behavior has social meaning. So the husband who brings flowers to his wife after he has treated her badly need not suppose that his past action is nullified, but simply that his present behavior gives some indication of his positive feeling toward her, which may serve to offset the earlier evidence of disregard. It is only when he is unaware of the relation between the two acts, or when he has displaced both actions to an entirely symbolic and unreal plane, that he gives evidence of employing undoing as a defense-mechanism in the strict sense.

Of course, there is some connection between defensive undoing and social reparation, especially developmentally. For the child who can see no connection between his behavior (which has been adjudged wrong) and the verbal formula, "I'm sorry," the latter may appear to be simply an incantation which prevents the evil consequences to him of the former. With the development of intelligence, however, he should acquire some understanding of the real, as opposed to the magical, effect of efforts to redress socially harmful actions. It is only when, as an adult, he reverts to a childishly magical use of symbolic restitution that we can regard his behavior as self-deceptively defensive and potentially neurotic.

12 Autism

A special kind of daydreaming by which *achievement in fantasy substitutes for achievement in fact and defends self-esteem against the sense of inadequacy and failure*. Autism goes farther than isolation and withdrawal since it substitutes a kind of activity for the deficiency or failure. It does not, however, go as far as compensation since the substituted activity is merely fantasy. This fantasy, moreover—and this is significant in differentiating autism as a defense-mechanism from ordinary fantasy—tends to prevent further effort toward real goals by consuming our time and attention in the effortless and empty satisfactions of reverie. Such fantasy neither prepares for nor relaxes from endeavor but substitutes therefor, and since its rewards are as faint as they are easy, it has a natural tendency to proliferate and expand.

James Thurber's short story "The Secret Life of Walter Mitty" remains the perfect literary expression of autism as a defense, but the mechanism does not require the elaborately inventive imagination manifested by Thurber's character. The tendency to use fantasy as an unconscious substitute for the motive and effort to achieve and as a means of disengagement from the self-devaluating experience of nonachievement suffices. And if, in this age of wonders, the personal fantasy-making mechanism falters, we have but to turn on the television set, make for the nearest movie house, or open the pages of any of the many unfunny "comic books" or apocryphal "true story" magazines, to have available a pre-packed fantasy world in which even the effort of imagination has been minimized.

Where achievement in the direction of self-realization *(coping)* is prevented by reason of age (as in childhood, adolescence, and old age), or by reason of inability to accept the approved goals of one's culture or subculture—consider the man of integrity living in a dictatorship or the creative artist forced to live and work among Philistines—the autistic mechanism may prove a useful buffer against a too harsh reality. Where good adjustment is impossible, as it may be for the best of men in a bad society, or when caught in the web of adverse circumstance, fantasy may mitigate frustration and ward off despair. The self-depreciating but by no means ingenuous query "I can dream, can't I?" summarizes the understandably defensive posture of the normal man blocked by external factors over which he has little control, but not surrendering hope. What differentiates this from the autism found in the abnormal is that the adequate person will prefer coping to fantasy, where coping is possible; the inadequate may not.

SUMMARY

This paper provides a phenomenological analysis of 12 major defense mechanisms. The mechanisms are viewed as self-deceptive psychic strategies for protecting self-esteem against self-devaluating experiences. The debt to Freud is acknowledged, but the analysis is for the most part based on grounds other than the psychosexual.

Defense mechanisms are distinguished sharply from psychopathological symptoms, and while repression is admitted to be fundamental, its partial and unsuccessful nature is also stressed. Departing from classical views, isolation is defined in terms of motivational relevance; rationalization is related to "over-determination"; "antithetic counteraction" is regarded as a more precise term than "reaction-formation"; the coping types of compensation including masculine-protest are distinguished from the defensive variety; a new mechanism, somewhere between compensation and projection and labeled "defensive-devaluation" is introduced; the Freudian overuse of displacement is criticized; distinction is made between primary and secondary projection; the developmental is contrasted both with the mature and the defensive use of identification; undoing is differentiated from realistic social reparation; and the normality of some kinds of autism acknowledged.

REFERENCES

Allport, G. W. *Personality: A psychological interpretation.* New York: Holt, 1937.

Fenichel, O. *The psychoanalytic theory of neurosis.* New York: Norton, 1945.

Freud, Anna. *The ego and the mechanisms of defense.* London: Hogarth, 1954.

McCall, R. J. Invested Self-expression: Toward a Theory of Human Structural Dynamics. In A. A. Schneiders and P. J. Centi (Eds.), *Selected Papers from the ACPA Meetings of 1960–1961. New York, Fordham Univer., 1962.*

The Basic Conflict*

Karen Horney

Conflicts play an infinitely greater role in neurosis than is commonly assumed. To detect them, however, is no easy matter—partly because they are essentially unconscious, but even more because the neurotic goes to any length to deny their existence. What, then, are the signals that would warrant us to suspect underlying conflicts? In . . . examples cited . . . their presence was indicated by two factors, both fairly obvious. One was the resulting symptoms—fatigue in the first case, stealing in the second. The fact is that every neurotic symptom points to an underlying conflict; that is, every symptom is a more or less direct outgrowth of a conflict. We shall see gradually what unresolved conflicts do to people, how they produce states of anxiety, depression, indecision, inertia, detachment, and so on. An understanding of the causative relation here helps direct our attention from the manifest disturbances to their source—though the exact nature of the source will not be disclosed.

The other signal indicating that conflicts were in operation was inconsistency. In the first example we saw a man convinced of a procedure being wrong and of injustice done him, making no move to protest. In the second a person who highly valued friendship turned to stealing money from a friend. Sometimes the person himself will be aware of such inconsistencies; more often he is blind to them even when they are blatantly obvious to an untrained observer.

Inconsistencies are as definite an indication of the presence of conflicts as a rise in body temperature is of physical disturbance. To cite some common ones: A girl wants above all else to marry, yet shrinks from the advances of any man. A mother oversolicitous of her children frequently forgets their birthdays. A person always generous to others is niggardly about small expenditures for himself. Another who longs for solitude never manages to be alone. One forgiving and tolerant toward most people is oversevere and demanding with himself.

Unlike the symptoms, the inconsistencies often permit of tentative assumptions as to the nature of the underlying conflict. An acute depression, for instance, reveals only the fact that a person is caught in a dilemma. But if an apparently devoted mother forgets her children's birthdays, we might be inclined to think that the mother was more devoted to her ideal of being a good mother than to the children themselves. We might also admit the possibility that her ideal collided with an unconscious sadistic tendency to frustrate them.

Sometimes a conflict will appear on the surface—that is, be consciously experienced as such. This would seem to contradict my assertion that neurotic conflicts are unconscious. But actually what appears is a distortion or modification of the real conflict. Thus a person may be torn by a conscious conflict when, in spite of his evasive techniques, well-functioning otherwise, he finds himself confronted with the necessity of making a major decision. He cannot decide now whether to marry this woman or that one or whether to marry at all, whether to take this or that job, whether

*From Karen Horney, *Our Inner Conflicts,* W. W. Norton and Company, Inc., New York, copyright, 1945. Pages 34–37 and 40–47 reprinted by permission of the publisher. Slightly edited.

to retain or dissolve a partnership. He will then go through the greatest torment, shuttling from one opposite to the other, utterly incapable of arriving at any decision. He may in his distress call upon an analyst, expecting him to clarify the particular issues involved. And he will necessarily be disappointed, because the present conflict is merely the point at which the dynamite of inner frictions finally exploded. The particular problem distressing him now cannot be solved without taking the long and tortuous road of recognizing the conflicts hidden beneath it.

In other instances the inner conflict may be externalized and appear in the person's conscious mind as an incompatibility between himself and his environment. Or, finding that seemingly unfounded fears and inhibitions interfere with his wishes, a person may be aware that the crosscurrents within himself issue from deeper sources.

The more knowledge we gain of a person, the better able we are to recognize the conflicting elements that account for the symptoms, inconsistencies, and surface conflicts—and, we must add, the more confusing becomes the picture, through the number and variety of contradictions. So we are led to ask: Can there be a basic conflict underlying all these particular conflicts and originally responsible for all of them? Can one picture the structure of conflict in terms, say, of an incompatible marriage, where an endless variety of apparently unrelated disagreements and rows over friends, children, finances, mealtimes, servants, all point to some fundamental disharmony in the relationship itself? . . .

Proceeding now to evolve my own position, I see the basic conflict of the neurotic in the fundamentally contradictory attitudes he has acquired toward other persons. Before going into detail, let me call attention to the dramatization of such a contradiction in the story of Dr. Jekyll and Mr. Hyde. We see him on the one hand delicate, sensitive, sympathetic, helpful, and on the other brutal, callous, and egotistical. I do not, of course, mean to imply that neurotic division always adheres to the precise line of this story, but merely to point to a vivid expression of basic incompatibility of attitudes in relation to others.

To approach the problem genetically we must go back to what I have called basic anxiety,[1] meaning by this the feeling a child has of being isolated and helpless in a potentially hostile world. A wide range of adverse factors in the environment can produce this insecurity in a child: direct or indirect domination, indifference, erratic behavior, lack of respect for the child's individual needs, lack of real guidance, disparaging attitudes, too much admiration or the absence of it, lack of reliable warmth, having to take sides in parental disagreements, too much or too little responsibility, overprotection, isolation from other children, injustice, discrimination, unkept promises, hostile atmosphere, and so on and so on.

The only factor to which I should like to draw special attention in this context is the child's sense of lurking hypocrisy in the environment: his feeling that the parents' love, their Christian charity, honesty, generosity, and so on may be only pretense. Part of what the child feels on this score is really hypocrisy; but some of it may be just his reaction to all the contradictions he senses in the parents' behavior. Usually, however, there is a combination of cramping factors. They may be out in the open or quite hidden, so that in analysis one can only gradually recognize these influences on the child's development.

[1]Karen Horney, *The Neurotic Personality of Our Time,* W. W. Norton, 1937.

Harassed by these disturbing conditions, the child gropes for ways to keep going, ways to cope with this menacing world. Despite his own weakness and fears he unconsciously shapes his tactics to meet the particular forces operating in his environment. In doing so, he develops not only *ad hoc* strategies but lasting character trends which become part of his personality. I have called these "neurotic trends."

If we want to see how conflicts develop, we must not focus too sharply on the individual trends but rather take a panoramic view of the main directions in which a child can and does move under these circumstances. Though we lose sight for a while of details we shall gain a clearer perspective of the essential moves made to cope with the environment. At first a rather chaotic picture may present itself, but out of it in time three main lines crystallize: a child can move *toward* people, *against* them, or *away from* them.

When moving *toward* people he accepts his own helplessness, and in spite of his estrangement and fears tries to win the affection of others and to lean on them. Only in this way can he feel safe with them. If there are dissenting parties in the family, he will attach himself to the most powerful person or group. By complying with them, he gains a feeling of belonging and support which makes him feel less weak and less isolated.

When he moves *against* people he accepts and takes for granted the hostility around him, and determines, consciously or unconsciously, to fight. He implicitly distrusts the feelings and intentions of others toward himself. He rebels in whatever ways are open to him. He wants to be the stronger and defeat them, partly for his own protection, partly for revenge.

When he moves *away from* people he wants neither to belong nor to fight, but keeps apart. He feels he has not much in common with them, they do not understand him anyhow. He builds up a world of his own—with nature, with his dolls, his books, his dreams.

In each of these three attitudes, one of the elements involved in basic anxiety is overemphasized: helplessness in the first, hostility in the second, and isolation in the third. But the fact is that the child cannot make any one of these moves wholeheartedly, because under the conditions in which the attitudes develop, all are bound to be present. What we have seen from our panoramic view is only the predominant move.

That this is so will become evident if we jump ahead now to the fully developed neurosis. We all know adults in whom one of the attitudes we have sketched stands out. But we can see, too, that his other tendencies have not ceased to operate. In a predominantly leaning and complying type we can observe aggressive propensities and some need for detachment. A predominantly hostile person has a complaint strain and needs detachment too. And a detached personality is not without hostility or a desire for affection.

The predominant attitude, however, is the one that most strongly determines actual conduct. It represents those ways and means of coping with others in which the particular person feels most at home. Thus a detached person will as a matter of course use all the unconscious techniques for keeping others at a safe distance because he feels at a loss in any situation that requires close association with them. Moreover, the ascendant attitude is often but not always the one most acceptable to the person's conscious mind.

This does not mean that the less conspicuous attitudes are less powerful. It would often be difficult to say, for instance, whether in an apparently dependent, compliant person the wish to dominate is of inferior intensity to the need for affection; his ways of expressing his aggressive impulses are merely more indirect. That the potency of the submerged tendencies may be very great is evidenced by the many instances in which the attitude accorded predominance is reversed. We can see such reversal in children, but it occurs in later life as well. Strickland in Somerset Maugham's *The Moon and Sixpence* would be a good illustration. Case histories of women often reveal this kind of change. A girl formerly tomboyish, ambitious, rebellious, when she falls in love may turn into a compliant, dependent woman, apparently without ambition. Or, under pressure of crushing experiences, a detached person may become morbidly dependent.

Changes like these, it should be added, throw some light on the frequent question whether later experience counts for nothing, whether we are definitely channeled, conditioned once and for all, by our childhood situation. Looking at neurotic development from the point of view of conflicts enables us to give a more adequate answer than is usually offered. These are the possibilities: If the early situation is not too prohibitive of spontaneous growth, later experiences, particularly in adolescence, can have a molding influence. If, however, the impact of early experiences has been powerful enough to have molded the child to a rigid pattern, no new experience will be able to break through. In part this is because his rigidity does not leave him open to any new experience: his detachment, for instance, may be too great to permit of anyone's coming close to him, or his dependence so deep-rooted that he is forced always to play a subordinate role and invite exploitation. In part it is because he will interpret any new experience in the language of his established pattern: the aggressive type, for instance, meeting with friendliness, will view it either as a manifestation of stupidity or an attempt to exploit him; the new experience will tend only to reinforce the old pattern. When a neurotic does adopt a different attitude it may look as if later experiences had brought about a change in personality. However, the change is not as radical as it appears. Actually what has happened is that combined internal and external pressures have forced him to abandon his predominant attitude in favor of the other extreme—but this change would not have taken place if there had been no conflicts to begin with.

From the point of view of the normal person there is no reason why the three attitudes should be mutually exclusive. One should be capable of giving in to others, of fighting, and of keeping to oneself. The three can complement each other and make for a harmonious whole. If one predominates, it merely indicates an overdevelopment along one line.

But in neurosis there are several reasons why these attitudes are irreconcilable. The neurotic is not flexible; he is driven to comply, to fight, to be aloof, regardless of whether the move is appropriate in the particular circumstance, and he is thrown into a panic if he behaves otherwise. Hence when all three attitudes are present in any strong degree, he is bound to be caught in a severe conflict.

Another factor, and one that considerably widens the scope of the conflict, is that the attitudes do not remain restricted to the area of human relationships but gradually pervade the entire personality, as a malignant tumor pervades the whole organic tissue. They end by encompassing not only the person's relation to others but also his relation to himself and to life in general. If we are not fully aware of this all-embracing character, the temptation is to think of the resulting conflict in categorical terms, like love *versus* hate, compliance *versus* defiance, submissiveness *versus* domination, and so on. That, however, would be as misleading as to distinguish fascism from democracy by focusing on any single opposing feature, such as their difference in approach to religion or power. These are differences certainly, but exclusive emphasis upon them would serve to obscure the point that democracy and fascism are worlds apart and represent two philosophies of life entirely incompatible with each other.

It is not accidental that a conflict that starts with our relation to others in time affects the whole personality. Human relationships are so crucial that they are bound to mold the qualities we develop, the goals we set for ourselves, the values we believe in. All these in turn react upon our relations with others and so are inextricably interwoven.

My contention is that the conflict born of incompatible attitudes constitutes the core of neurosis and therefore deserves to be called *basic*. And let me add that I use the term *core* not merely in the figurative sense of its being significant but to emphasize the fact that it is the dynamic center from which neuroses emanate. This contention is the nucleus of a new theory of neurosis. . . . Broadly considered, the theory may be viewed as an elaboration of my earlier concept that neuroses are an expression of a disturbance in human relationships.

The Nonproductive Character Orientations*

Erich Fromm

A THE RECEPTIVE ORIENTATION

In the receptive orientation a person feels "the source of all good" to be outside, and he believes that the only way to get what he wants—be it something material, be it affection, love, knowledge, pleasure—is to receive it from that outside source. In this orientation the problem of love is almost exclusively that of "being loved" and not that of loving. Such people tend to be indiscriminate in the choice of their love objects, because being loved by anybody is such an overwhelming experience for them that they "fall for" anybody who gives them love or what looks like love. They are exceedingly sensitive to any withdrawal or rebuff they experience on the part of the loved person. Their orientation is the same in the sphere of thinking: if intelligent, they make the best listeners, since their orientation is one of receiving, not of producing, ideas; left to themselves, they feel paralyzed. It is characteristic of these people that their first thought is to find somebody else to give them needed information rather than to make even the smallest effort of their own. If religious, these persons have a concept

*From Erich Fromm, *Man for Himself,* Rinehart and Company, Inc., New York, 1947. Pages 62–73 reprinted by permission of the author and the publisher.

of God in which they expect everything from God and nothing from their own activity. If not religious, their relationship to persons or institutions is very much the same; they are always in search of a "magic helper." They show a particular kind of loyalty, at the bottom of which is the gratitude for the hand that feeds them and the fear of ever losing it. Since they need many hands to feel secure, they have to be loyal to numerous people. It is difficult for them to say "no," and they are easily caught between conflicting loyalties and promises. Since they cannot say "no," they love to say "yes" to everything and everybody, and the resulting paralysis of their critical abilities makes them increasingly dependent on others.

They are dependent not only on authorities for knowledge and help but on people in general for any kind of support. They feel lost when alone because they feel that they cannot do anything without help. This helplessness is especially important with regard to those acts which by their very nature can only be done alone—making decisions and taking responsibility. In personal relationships, for instance, they ask advice from the very person with regard to whom they have to make a decision.

This receptive type has great fondness for food and drink. These persons tend to overcome anxiety and depression by eating or drinking. The mouth is an especially prominent feature, often the most expressive one; the lips tend to be open, as if in a state of continuous expectation of being fed. In their dreams, being fed is a frequent symbol of being loved; being starved, an expression of frustration or disappointment.

By and large, the outlook of people of this receptive orientation is optimistic and friendly; they have a certain confidence in life and its gifts, but they become anxious and distraught when their "source of supply" is threatened. They often have a genuine warmth and a wish to help others, but doing things for others also assumes the function of securing their favor.

B THE EXPLOITATIVE ORIENTATION

The exploitative orientation, like the receptive, has as its basic premise the feeling that the source of all good is outside, that whatever one wants to get must be sought there, and that one cannot produce anything oneself. The difference between the two, however, is that the exploitative type does not expect to receive things from others as gifts, but to take them away from others by force or cunning. This orientation extends to all spheres of activity.

In the realm of love and affection these people tend to grab and steal. They feel attracted only to people whom they can take away from somebody else. Attractiveness to them is conditioned by a person's attachment to somebody else; they tend not to fall in love with an unattached person. We find the same attitude with regard to thinking and intellectual pursuits. Such people will tend not to produce ideas but to steal them. This may be done directly in the form of plagiarism or more subtly by repeating in different phraseology the ideas voiced by others and insisting they are new and their own. It is a striking fact that frequently people with great intelligence proceed in this way, although if they relied on their own gifts they might well be able to have ideas of their own. The lack of original ideas or independent production in otherwise gifted people often has its explanation in this character orientation, rather than in any innate lack of originality. The same statement holds true with regard to their orientation to material things. Things which they can take away from others always seems better to them than anything they can produce themselves. They use and exploit anybody and anything from whom or from which they can squeeze something. Their motto is: "Stolen fruits are sweetest." Because they want to use and exploit people, they "love" those who, explicitly or implicitly, are promising objects of exploitation, and get "fed up" with persons whom they have squeezed out. An extreme example is the kleptomaniac who enjoys things only if he can steal them, although he has the money to buy them.

This orientation seems to be symbolized by the biting mouth which is often a prominent feature in such people. It is not a play upon words to point out that they often make "biting" remarks about others. Their attitude is colored by a mixture of hostility and manipulation. Everyone is an object of exploitation and is judged according to his usefulness. Instead of the confidence and optimism which characterizes the receptive type, one finds here suspicion and cynicism, envy and jealousy. Since they are satisfied only with things they can take away from others, they tend to overrate what others have and underrate what is theirs.

C THE HOARDING ORIENTATION

While the receptive and exploitative types are similar inasmuch as both expect to get things from the outside world, the hoarding orientation is essentially different. This orientation makes people have little faith in anything new they might get from the outside world; their security is based upon hoarding and saving, while spending is felt to be a threat. They have surrounded themselves, as it were, by a protective wall, and their main aim is to bring as much as possible into this fortified position and to let as little as possible out of it. Their miserliness refers to money and material things as well as to feelings and thoughts. Love is essentially a possession; they do not give love but try to get it by possessing the "beloved." The hoarding person often shows a particular kind of faithfulness toward people and even toward memories. Their sentimentality makes the past appear as golden; they hold on to it and indulge in the memories of bygone feelings and experiences. They know everything but are sterile and incapable of productive thinking.

One can recognize these people too by facial expressions and gestures. Theirs is the tight-lipped mouth; their gestures are characteristic of their withdrawn attitude. While those of the receptive type are inviting and round, as it were, and the gestures of the exploitative type are aggressive and pointed, those of the hoarding type are angular, as if they wanted to emphasize the frontiers between themselves and the outside world. Another characteristic element in this attitude is pedantic orderliness. The hoarder will be orderly with things, thoughts, or feelings, but again, as with memory, his orderliness is sterile and rigid. He cannot endure things out of place and will automatically rearrange them. To him the outside world threatens to break into his fortified position; orderliness signifies mastering the world outside by putting it, and keeping it, in its proper place in order to avoid the danger of intrusion. His compulsive cleanliness is an other expression of his need to undo contact with the outside world. Things beyond his own frontiers are felt to be dangerous and "unclean"; he annuls the menacing contact by compulsive washing, similar to a religious washing ritual prescribed after contact with unclean things or people. Things have to be put not only in their proper place but also into their proper time; obsessive punctuality is characteristic of the hoarding type; it is another form of mastering the outside world. If the outside world is experienced as a threat to one's fortified position, obstinacy is a logical reaction. A constant "no" is the almost automatic defense against intrusion; sitting tight, the answer to the danger of being pushed. These people tend to feel that they possess only a fixed quantity of strength, energy, or mental capacity, and that this stock is diminished or exhausted by use and can never be replenished. They cannot understand the self-replenishing function of all living substance and that activity and the use of one's powers increase strength while stagnation paralyzes; to them, death and destruction have more reality than life and growth. The act of creation is a miracle of which they hear but in which they do not believe. Their highest values are order and security; their motto: "There is nothing new under the sun." In their relationship to others intimacy is a threat; either remoteness or possession of a person means security. The hoarder tends to be suspicious and to have a particular sense of justice which in effect says: "Mine is mine and yours is yours."

D THE MARKETING ORIENTATION

The marketing orientation developed as a dominant one only in the modern era. In order to understand its nature one must consider the economic function of the market in modern society as being not only analogous to this character orientation but as the basis and the main condition for its development in modern man.

Barter is one of the oldest economic mechanisms. The traditional local market, however, is essentially different from the market as it has developed in modern capitalism. Bartering on a local market offered an opportunity to meet for the purpose of exchanging commodities. Producers and customers became acquainted; they were relatively small groups; the demand was more or less known, so that the producer could produce for this specific demand.

The modern market[1] is no longer a meeting place but a mechanism characterized by abstract and impersonal demand. One produces for this market, not for a known circle of customers; its verdict is based on laws of supply and demand; and it determines whether the commodity can be sold and at what price. No matter what the *use value* of a pair of shoes may be, for instance, if the supply is greater than the demand, some shoes will be sentenced to economic death; they might as well not have been produced at all. The market day is the "day of judgment" as far as the *exchange value* of commodities is concerned.

The reader may object that this description of the market is oversimplified. The producer does try to judge the demand in advance, and under monopoly conditions even obtains a certain degree of control over it. Nevertheless, the regulatory function

[1]Cf., for the study of history and function of the modern market, K. Polanyi's *The Great Transformation* (New York: Rinehart & Company, 1944).

of the market has been, and still is, predominant enough to have a profound influence on the character formation of the urban middle class and, through the latter's social and cultural influence, on the whole population. The market concept of value, the emphasis on exchange value rather than on use value, has led to a similar concept of value with regard to people and particularly to oneself. The character orientation which is rooted in the experience of oneself as a commodity and of one's value as exchange value I call the marketing orientation.

In our time the marketing orientation has been growing rapidly, together with the development of a new market that is a phenomenon of the last decades—the "personality market." Clerks and salesmen, business executives and doctors, lawyers and artists all appear on this market. It is true that their legal status and economic positions are different: some are independent, charging for their services; others are employed, receiving salaries. But all are dependent for their material success on a personal acceptance by those who need their services or who employ them.

The principle of evaluation is the same on both the personality and the commodity market: on the one, personalities are offered for sale; on the other, commodities. Value in both cases is their exchange value, for which use value is a necessary but not a sufficient condition. It is true, our economic system could not function if people were not skilled in the particular work they have to perform and were gifted only with a pleasant personality. Even the best bedside manner and the most beautifully equipped office on Park Avenue would not make a New York doctor successful if he did not have a minimum of medical knowledge and skill. Even the most winning personality would not prevent a secretary from losing her job unless she could type reasonably fast. However, if we ask what the respective weight of skill and personality as a condition for success is, we find that only in exceptional cases is success predominantly the result of skill and of certain other human qualities like honesty, decency, and integrity. Although the proportion between skill and human qualities on the one hand and "personality" on the other hand as prerequisites for success varies, the "personality factor" always plays a decisive role. Success depends largely on how well a person sells himself on the market, how well he gets his personality across, how nice a "package" he is; whether he is "cheerful," "sound," "aggressive," "reliable," "ambitious"; furthermore what his family background is, what clubs he belongs to, and whether he knows the right people. The type of personality required depends to some degree on the special field in which a person works. A stockbroker, a salesman, a secretary, a railroad executive, a college professor, or a hotel manager must each offer different kinds of personality that, regardless of their differences, must fulfill one condition: to be in demand.

The fact that in order to have success it is not sufficient to have the skill and equipment for performing a given task but that one must be able to "put across" one's personality in competition with many others shapes the attitude toward oneself. If it were enough for the purpose of making a living to rely on what one knows and what one can do, one's self-esteem would be in proportion to one's capacities, that is, to one's use value; but since success depends largely on how one sells one's personality, one experiences oneself as a commodity or rather simultaneously as the seller *and* the commodity to be sold. A person is not concerned with his life and happiness, but with becoming salable. This feeling might be compared to that of a commodity, of handbags on a counter, for instance, could they feel and think. Each handbag would try to make itself as "attractive" as possible in order to attract customers and to look as expensive as possible in order to obtain a higher price than its rivals. The handbag sold for the highest price would feel elated, since that would mean it was the most "valuable" one; the one which was not sold would feel sad and convinced of its own worthlessness. This fate might befall a bag which, though excellent in appearance and usefulness, had the bad luck to be out of date because of a change in fashion.

Like the handbag, one has to be in fashion on the personality market, and in order to be in fashion one has to know what kind of personality is most in demand. This knowledge is transmitted in a general way throughout the whole process of education, from kindergarten to college, and implemented by the family. The knowledge acquired at this early stage is not sufficient, however; it emphasizes only certain general qualities like adaptability, ambition, sensitivity to the changing expectations of other people. The more specific picture of the models for success one gets elsewhere. The pictorial magazines, newspapers, and newsreels show the pictures and life stories of the successful in many variations. Pictorial advertising has a similar function. The successful executive who is pictured in a tailor's advertisement is the image of how one should look and be, if one is to draw down the "big money" on the contemporary personality market.

The most important means of transmitting the desired personality pattern to the average man is the motion picture. The young girl tries to emulate the facial expression, coffiure, gestures of a high-priced star as the most promising way to success. The young man tries to look and be like the model he sees on the screen. While the average citizen has little contact with the life of the most successful people, his relationship with the motion-picture stars is different. It is true that he has no real contact with them either, but he can see them on the screen again and again, can write them and receive their autographed pictures. In contrast to the time when the actor was socially despised but was nevertheless the transmitter of the works of great poets to his audience, our motion-picture stars have no great works or ideas to transmit, but their function is to serve as the link an average person has with the world of the "great." Even if he can not hope to become as successful as they are, he can try to emulate them: they are his saints and because of their success they embody the norms for living.

Since modern man experiences himself both as the seller and as the commodity to be sold on the market, his self-esteem depends on conditions beyond his control. If he is "successful," he is valuable; if he is not, he is worthless. The degree of insecurity which results from this orientation can hardly be overestimated. If one feels that one's own value is not constituted primarily by the human qualities one possesses, but by one's success on a competitive market with ever-changing conditions, one's self-esteem is bound to be shaky and in constant need of confirmation by others. Hence one is driven to strive relentlessly for success, and any setback is a severe threat to one's self-esteem; helplessness, insecurity, and inferiority feelings are the result. If the vicissitudes of the market are the judges of one's value, the sense of dignity and pride is destroyed.

But the problem is not only that of self-evaluation and self-esteem but of one's experience of oneself as an independent entity, of one's *identity with oneself*. . . . the mature and productive individual derives his feeling of identity from the experience of himself as the agent who is one with his powers; this feeling of self can be briefly expressed as meaning *"I am what I do."* In the marketing orientation man encounters his own powers as commodities alienated from him. He is not one with them but they are masked from him because what matters is not his self-realization in the process of using them but his success in the process of selling them. Both his powers and what they create become estranged, something different from himself, something for others to judge and to use; thus his feeling of identity becomes as shaky as his self-esteem; it is constituted by the sum total of roles one can play: *"I am as you desire me."*

Healthy Personality and Self-Disclosure*

Sidney M. Jourard

For a long time, health and well-being have been taken for granted as "givens," and disease has been viewed as the problem for man to solve. Today, however, increasing numbers of scientists have begun to adopt a reverse point of view, regarding disease and trouble as the givens, with specification of positive health and its conditions as the problem to solve. Physical, mental and social health are values representing restrictions on the total variance of being. The scientific problem here consists in arriving at a definition of health, determining its relevant dimensions and then identifying the independent variables of which these are a function.

Scientists, however, are supposed to be hard-boiled, and they insist that phenomena, to be counted "real," must be public. Hence, many behavioral scientists ignore man's self, or soul, since it is essentially a private phenomenon. Others, however, are not so quick to allocate man's self to the limbo of the unimportant, and they insist that we cannot understand man and his lot until we take his self into account.

I probably fall into the camp of those investigators who want to explore health as a positive problem in its own right, and who, further, take man's self seriously—as a reality to be explained and as a variable which produces consequences for weal or woe. This paper gives me an opportunity to explore the connection between positive health and the disclosure of self. Let me commence with some sociological truisms.

Social systems require their members to play certain roles. Unless the roles are adequately played, the social systems will not produce the results for which they have been organized. This flat statement applies to social systems as simple as that provided by an engaged couple and to those as complex as a total nation among nations. Societies have socialization "factories" and "mills"—families and schools—which serve the function of training people to play the age, sex and occupational roles which they shall be obliged to play throughout their life in the social system. Broadly

*From Sidney M. Jourard, "Healthy Personality and Self-Disclosure," *Ment. Hyg. N.Y.*, 1959, **32**, 499–507. Reprinted by permission of the author and the Editor, *Mental Hygiene*.

speaking, if a person plays his roles suitably, he can be regarded as a more or less normal personality. Normal personalities, however, are not healthy personalities (Jourard 1958, 16–18).

Healthy personalities are people who play their roles satisfactorily, and at the same time derive personal satisfaction from role enactment; more, they keep growing and they maintain high-level physical wellness (Dunn 1958). It is probably enough, speaking from the standpoint of a stable social system, for people to be normal personalities. But it is possible to be a normal personality and be absolutely miserable. We would count such a normal personality unhealthy. In fact, normality in some social systems—successful acculturation to them—reliably produces ulcers, paranoia, piles or compulsiveness. We also have to regard as unhealthy personalities those people who have never been able to enact the roles that legitimately can be expected from them.

Counselors, guidance workers and psychotherapists are obliged to treat with both patterns of unhealthy personality—those people who have been unable to learn their roles and those who play their roles quite well but suffer the agonies of boredom, frustration, anxiety or stultification. If our clients are to be helped they must change, and change in valued directions. A change in a valued direction may arbitrarily be called growth. We have yet to give explicit statement to these valued directions for growth, though a beginning has been made (Fromm 1947, Jahoda 1958, Jourard 1958, Maslow 1954, Rogers 1954). We who are professionally concerned with the happiness, growth and well-being of our clients may be regarded as professional lovers, not unlike the Cyprian sisterhood. It would be fascinating to pursue this parallel further, but let it suffice for us to be reminded that we do in fact share membership in the oldest profession in the world. Our branches of this oldest profession probably began at the same time that our sisters' branch began, and all branches will continue to flourish so long as they meet the needs of society. We are all concerned with promoting personality health in the people who consult with us.

Now what has all this to do with self-disclosure?

To answer this question, let's tune in on an imaginary interview between a client and his counselor. The client says, "I have never told this to a soul, doctor, but I can't stand my wife, my mother is a nag, my father is a bore, and my boss is an absolutely hateful and despicable tyrant. I have been carrying on an affair for the last ten years with the lady next door and at the same time I am a deacon in the church." The counselor says, showing great understanding and empathy, "Mm-humm!"

If we listened for a long enough period of time we would find that the client talks and talks about himself to this highly sympathetic and empathic listener. At some later time the client may eventually say, "Gosh, you have helped me a lot. I see what I must do and I will go ahead and do it."

Now this talking about oneself to another person is what I call self-disclosure. It would appear, without assuming anything, that self-disclosure is a factor in the process of effective counseling or psychotherapy. Would it be too arbitrary an assumption to propose that people become clients because they have not disclosed themselves in some optimum degree to the people in their life?

An historical digression: Toward the end of the 19th century Joseph Breuer, a Viennese physician, discovered (probably accidentally) that when his hysterical patients talked about themselves, disclosing not only the verbal content of their memories but also the feelings that they had suppressed at the time of assorted "traumatic" experiences, their hysterical symptoms disappeared. Somewhere along the line Breuer withdrew from a situation which would have made his name identical with that of Freud in history's hall of fame. When Breuer permitted his patients "to be," it scared him, one gathers, because some of his female patients disclosed themselves to be quite sexy, and what was probably worse, they felt quite sexy toward him.

Freud, however, did not flinch. He made the momentous discovery that the neurotic people of his time were struggling like mad to avoid "being," to avoid being known, and in Allport's (1955) terms, to avoid "becoming." He learned that his patients, when they were given the opportunity to "be"—which free association on a couch is nicely designed to do—they would disclose that they had all manner of horrendous thoughts and feelings which they did not even dare disclose to themselves, much less express in the presence of another person. Freud learned to permit his patients to be, through permitting them to disclose themselves utterly to another human. He evidently didn't trust anyone enough to be willing to disclose *himself vis à vis,* so he disclosed himself to himself on paper (Freud 1955) and learned the extent to which he himself was self-alienated.

Roles for people in Victorian days were even more restrictive than they are today, and Freud discovered that when people struggled to avoid being and knowing themselves they got sick. They could only become well, and stay relatively well, when they came to know themselves through self-disclosure to another person. This makes me think of George Groddeck's magnificent *Book of the It (Id)* in which, in the guise of letters to a naive young woman, Groddeck shows the contrast between the public self —pretentious role-playing—and the warded off but highly dynamic *id*—which I here very loosely translate as "real self."

Let me at this point draw a distinction between role relationships and interpersonal relationships—a distinction which is often overlooked in the current spate of literature that has to do with human relations. Roles are inescapable. They must be played or else the social system will not work. A role by definition is a repertoire of behavior patterns which must be rattled off in appropriate contexts, and all behavior which is irrelevant to the role must be suppressed. But what we often forget is the fact that it is a person who is playing the role. This person has a self—or, I should say, he *is* a self. All too often the roles that a person plays do not do justice to all of his self. In fact, there may be nowhere that he may just *be* himself. Even more, the person may not *know* his self. He may, in Horney's (1950) terms, be self-alienated.

This fascinating term "self-alienation" means that an individual is estranged from his real self. His real self becomes a stranger, a feared and distrusted stranger. Estrangement—alienation from one's real self—is at the root of the "neurotic personality of our time" so eloquently described by Horney (1936). Fromm (1957) referred to the same phenomenon as a socially patterned defect.

Self-alienation is a sickness which is so widely shared that no one recognizes it. We may take it for granted that all the clients we encounter are self-alienated to a greater or lesser extent. If you ask anyone—a client, a patient, or one of the people here—to answer the question, "Who are you?" the answer will generally be, "I am a psychologist, a guidance worker, teacher or what have you." The respondent will probably tell you the name of the role with which he feels most closely identified. As a matter of fact, the respondent spends a greater part of his life trying to discover who he is, and once he has made some such discovery, he spends the rest of life trying to play the part. Of course, some of the roles—age, sex, family or occupational roles—may be so restrictive that they fit a person in a manner not too different from the girdle of a 200-pound lady who is struggling to look like Brigitte Bardot. There is Faustian drama all about us in this world of role-playing. Everywhere we see people who have sold their souls—the real self, if you wish—in order to be a psychologist, a guidance worker, a nurse, a physician, a this or a that.

Now I have suggested that no social system can exist unless the members play their roles and play them with precision and elegance. But here is an odd observation, and yet one which you can all corroborate just by thinking back over your own experience. It's possible to be involved in a social group, such as a family or a work setting, for years and years, playing one's roles nicely with the other members—and never getting to know the *persons* who are playing the other roles. Roles can be played personally and impersonally, as we are beginning to discover in nursing. A husband can be married to his wife for fifteen years and never come to know her. He knows her as "the wife." This is the paradox of the "lonely crowd" (Riesman 1950). It is the loneliness which people try to counter with "togetherness." But much of today's "togetherness" is like the "parallel play" of 2-year-old children, or like the professors in Stringfellow Barr's novel (1958) who, when together socially, lecture past one another alternately and sometimes simultaneously. There is no real self-to-self or person-to-person meeting in such transactions.

Now what does it mean to know a person, or, more accurately, a person's self? I don't mean anything mysterious by "self." All I mean is the person's subjective side —what he thinks, feels, believes, wants, worries about, his past and so forth—the kind of thing one could never know unless one were told. We get to know the other person's self when he discloses it to us.

Self-disclosure, letting another person know what you think, feel or want, is the most direct means (though not the only means) by which an individual can make himself known to another person. Personality hygienists place great emphasis upon the importance for mental health of what they call "real self being," "self-realization," "discovering one-self" and so on. An operational analysis of what goes on in counseling and therapy shows that the patients and clients discover themselves through self-disclosure to the counselor. They talk, and to their shock and amazement the counselor listens.

I venture to say that there is probably no experience more horrifying and terrifying than that of self-disclosure to "significant others" whose probable reactions are assumed but not known. Hence the phenomenon of "resistance." This is what makes psychotherapy so difficult to take and so difficult to administer. If there is any skill to be learned in the art of counseling and psychotherapy, it is the art of coping with the terrors which attend self-disclosure, and the art of decoding the language—verbal and non-verbal—in which a person speaks about his inner experience.

Now, what is the connection between self-disclosure and healthy personality?

Self-disclosure, or should I say "real" self-disclosure, is both a symptom of personality health (Jourard 1958, 218–21) and at the same time a means of ultimately achieving healthy personality. The discloser of self is an animated "real self-be-er." This, of course, takes courage—the "courage to be" (Tillich 1954). I have known people who would rather die than become known, and in fact some did die when it appeared that the chances were great that they would become known. When I say that self-disclosure is a symptom of personality health, what I mean really is that a person who displays many of the other characteristics that betoken healthy personality (Jourard 1958, Maslow 1954) will also display the ability to make himself fully known to at least one other significant human being. When I say that self-disclosure is a means by which one achieves personality health, I mean something like the following: It is not until I *am* my real self and I *act* my real self that my real self is in a position to grow. One's self grows from the consequence of being. People's selves stop growing when they repress them. This growth-arrest in the self is what helps to account for the surprising paradox of finding an infant inside the skin of someone who is playing the role of an adult.

In a fascinating analysis of mental distress, Jurgen Ruesch (1957) describes assorted neurotics, psychotics and psychosomatic patients as persons with selective atrophy and overspecialization in the aspects of communication. I have come to believe that it is not communication *per se* which is fouled up in the mentally ill. Rather, it is a foul-up in the processes of knowing others and of becoming known to others. Neurotic and psychotic symptoms might be viewed as smokescreens interposed between the patient's real self and the gaze of the onlooker. We might call the symptoms devices to avoid becoming known. A new theory of schizophrenia has been proposed by an anonymous former patient (1958) who "was there" and he makes such a point.

Alienation from one's real self not only arrests one's growth as a person; it also tends to make a farce out of one's relationships with people. As the ex-patient mentioned above observed, the crucial break in schizophrenia is with sincerity, not reality (Anonymous, 1958). A self-alienated person—one who does not disclose himself truthfully and fully—can never love another person nor can he be loved by the other person. Effective loving calls for knowledge of the object (Fromm 1957, Jourard 1958). How can I love a person whom I do not know? How can the other person love me if he does not know me?

Hans Selye (1946) proposed and documented the hypothesis that illness as we know it arises in consequence of stress applied to the organism. Now I rather think that unhealthy personality has a similar root cause, and one which is related to Selye's concept of stress. It is this: Every maladjusted person is a person who has not made himself known to another human being, and in consequence does not know himself. Nor can he find himself. More than that, he struggles actively to avoid becoming known by another human being. He works at it ceaselessly, 24 hours daily, and it is work! The fact that resisting becoming known is work offers us a research opening, incidentally (Dittes 1958, Davis and Malmo 1951). I believe that in the effort to avoid becoming known a person provides for himself a cancerous kind of stress which is subtle and unrecognized but nonetheless effective in producing not only the assorted patterns of unhealthy personality that psychiatry talks about but also the wide array of physical ills that have come to be recognized as the stock in trade of psychosomatic medicine. Stated another way, I believe that other people come to be stressors to an individual in direct proportion to his degree of self-alienation.

If I am struggling to avoid becoming known by other persons then of course I must construct a false public self (Jourard 1958, 301–302). The greater the discrepancy between my unexpurgated real self and the version of myself that I present to others, the more dangerous will other people be for me. If becoming known by another person is a source of danger, then it follows that merely the presence of the other person can serve as a stimulus to evoke anxiety, heightened muscle tension and all the assorted visceral changes which occur when a person is under stress. A beginning already has been made in demonstrating the tension-evoking powers of the other person through the use of such instruments as are employed in the lie detector, the measurement of muscle tensions with electromyographic apparatus and so on (Davis and Malmo 1958, Dittes 1958).

Students of psychosomatic medicine have been intimating something of what I have just finished saying explicity. They say (Alexander 1950) that ulcer patients, asthmatic patients, patients suffering from colitis, migraine and the like, are chronic repressors of certain needs and emotions, especially hostility and dependency. Now when you repress something, you are not only withholding awareness of this something from—yourself; you are also withholding it from the scrutiny of the other person. In fact, the means by which repressions are overcome in the therapeutic situation is through relentless disclosure of self to the therapist. When a patient is finally able to follow the fundamental rule in psychoanalysis and disclose everything which passes through his mind, he is generally shocked and dismayed to observe the breadth, depth, range and diversity of thoughts, memories and emotions which pass out of his "unconscious" into overt disclosure. Incidentally, by the time a person is that free to disclose in the presence of another human being, he has doubtless completed much of his therapeutic sequence.

Self-disclosure, then, appears to be one of the means by which a person engages in that elegant activity that we call real-self-being. But is real-self-being synonymous with healthy personality? Not in and of itself. I would say that real-self-being is a necessary but not a sufficient condition for healthy personality. It is in fact possible for a person to be much "nicer" socially when he is not being his real self than when he is his real self. But an individual's obnoxious and immoral real self can never grow in the direction of greater maturity until the person has become acquainted with it and begins to be it. Real-self-being produces consequences, which in accordance with well-known principles of behavior (Skinner 1953) produce changes in the real self. Thus, there can be no real growth of the self without real-self-being. Full disclosure of the self to at least one other significant human being appears to be one means by which a person discovers not only the breadth and depth of his needs and feelings but also the nature of his own self-affirmed values. There is no conflict between real-self-being and being an ethical or nice person, because for the average member of our society self-owned ethics are generally acquired during the process of growing up. All too often, however, the self-owned ethics are buried under authoritarian morals (Fromm 1947).

If self-disclosure is one of the means by which healthy personality is both achieved and maintained, we can also note that such activities as loving, psychotherapy, counseling, teaching and nursing all are impossible of achievement without the disclosure of the client. It is through self-disclosure that an individual reveals to himself and to the other party just exactly who, what and where he is. Just as thermometers, sphygmomanometers, etc. disclose information about the real state of the body, self-disclosure reveals the real nature of the soul or self. Such information is vital in order to conduct intelligent evaluations. All I mean by evaluation is comparing how a person is with some concept of optimum. You never really discover how truly sick your psychotherapy patient is until he discloses himself utterly to you. You cannot help your client in vocational guidance until he has disclosed to you something of the impasse in which he finds himself. You cannot love your spouse or your child or your friend unless he has permitted you to know him and to know what he needs to move toward greater health and well-being. Nurses cannot nurse patients in any meaningful way unless they have permitted the patients to disclose their needs, wants, worries, anxieties and doubts. Teachers cannot be very helpful to their students until they have permitted the students to disclose how utterly ignorant and misinformed they are. Teachers cannot even provide helpful information to the students until they have permitted the students to disclose exactly what they are interested in.

I believe we should reserve the term interpersonal relationships to refer to transactions between "I and thou," (Buber 1937), between person and person, not role and role. A truly personal relationship between two people involves disclosure of self, one to the other, in full and spontaneous honesty. The data that we have collected up to the present time (using very primitive data-collecting methods) have showed us some rather interesting phenomena. We found (Jourard and Lasakow 1958), for example, that women consistently are higher self-disclosers than men; they seem to have a greater capacity for establishing person-to-person relationships—interpersonal relationships—than men. This characteristic of women seems to be a socially-patterned phenomenon, which sociologists (Parsons and Bales 1955) refer to as the expressive role of women, in contradistinction to the instrumental role which men universally are obliged to adopt.

Men seem to be much more skilled at impersonal, instrumental role-playing. But public health officials, very concerned about the sex differential in mortality rates, have been wondering what it is about being a man, which makes males die younger than females. Here in Florida, Dr. Sowder, chief of the state health department, has been carrying on a long-term, multifaceted research program which he has termed "Project Fragile Male." Do you suppose that there is any connection whatsoever between the disclosure patterns of men and women and their differential death rates? I have already intimated that withholding self-disclosure seems to impose a certain stress on people. Maybe "being manly," whatever that means, is slow suicide!

I think there is a very general way of stating the relationship between self-disclosure and assorted values such as healthy personality, physical health, group effectiveness, successful marriage, effective teaching, effective nursing, etc. It is this: A person's self is known to be the immediate determiner of his overt behavior. This is a paraphrase of the phenomenological point of view in psychology (Snygg and Combs 1949). Now if we want to understand anything, explain it, control it or predict it, it is helpful if we have available as much pertinent information as we possibly can. Self-disclosure provides a source of information which is relevant. This information has often been overlooked. Where it has not been overlooked it has often been misinterpreted by observers and practitioners through such devices as projection or attribution. It seems to be difficult for people to accept the fact that they do not know the very person whom they are confronting at any given moment. We all seem to assume that we are expert psychologists and that we know the other person, when in fact we have only constructed a more or less autistic concept of him in our mind.

If we are to learn more about man's self, then we must learn more about self-disclosure—its conditions, dimensions and consequences. Beginning evidence (Rogers 1958) shows that actively accepting, empathic, loving, non-punitive responses—in short, love—provides the optimum conditions under which man will disclose, or expose, his naked, quivering self to our gaze. It follows that if we would be helpful (or should I say human?) that we must grow to loving stature and learn, in Buber's terms, to confirm our fellow man in his very being. Probably this presumes that we must first confirm our own being.

REFERENCES

Alexander, Franz, *Psychosomatic Medicine*. New York, Norton, 1950.

Allport, Gordon, *Becoming: Basic Considerations for a Psychology of Personality*. New Haven, Yale University Press, 1955.

Anonymous, "A New Theory of Schizophrenia," *Journal of Abnormal Social Psychology,* **57** (1958), 226–36.

Barr, Stringfellow, *Purely Academic*. New York, Simon and Schuster, 1958.

Buber, Martin, *I and thou*. New York, Scribners, 1937.

Davis, F. H. and R. B. Malmo, "Electromyographic Recording during Interview," *American Journal of Psychiatry,* **107** (1951), 908–16.

Dittes, J. E., "Extinction during Psychotherapy of GSR Accompanying 'Embarrassing' Sexual Statements," *Journal of Abnormal and Social Psychology,* **54** (1957), 187–91.

Dunn, H. L., "Higher-level Wellness for Man and Society," *American Journal Public Health,* 1959 (in press).

Freud, Sigmund, *The Interpretation of Dreams,* New York, Basic Books, 1955.

Fromm, Eric, *Man for Himself*. New York, Rinehart, 1947.

Fromm, Eric, *The Sane Society*. New York, Rinehart, 1957.

Groddeck, G., *The Book of It*. New York and Washington, Nervous and Mental Diseases Publishing Co., 1928.

Horney, Karen, *Neurosis and Human Growth*. New York, Norton, 1950.

Horney, Karen, *The Neurotic Personality of Our Time*. New York, Norton, 1936.

Jahoda, Marie, *Current Concepts of Positive Mental Health*. New York, Basic Books, 1958.

Jourard, S. M., *Healthy Personality: An Approach through the Study of Healthy Personality*. New York, Harper and Brothers, 1958.

Jourard, S. M., and P. Lasakow, "Some Factors in Self-Disclosure," *Journal of Abnormal and Social Psychology,* **56** (1958), 91–98.

Maslow, A. H., *Motivation and Personality*. New York, Harper and Brothers, 1954.

Parsons, Talcott and R. F. Bales, *Family, Socialization and Interaction Process*. Glencoe, Ill., Free Press, 1955.

Riesman, David, *The Lonely Crowd*. New Haven, Yale University Press, 1950.

Rogers, Carl R., *The Concept of the Fully-Functioning Person.* (Mimeographed manuscript, privately circulated, 1954.)

Rogers, Carl R., "The Characteristics of a Helping Relationship," *Personnel and Guidance Journal,* September 1958).

Ruesch, Jurgen, *Disturbed Communication.* New York, Norton, 1957.

Selye, Hans, "General Adaptation Syndrome and Diseases of Adaptation," *Journal of Clinical Endocrinology,* **6** (1946), 117–28.

Skinner, B. F., *Science and Human Behavior.* New York, Macmillan, 1953.

Snygg, D., and A. W. Combs, *Individual Behavior.* New York, Harper and Brothers, 1949.

Self-actualizing and Beyond*

Abraham H. Maslow

In this chapter, I plan to discuss ideas that are in midstream rather than ready for formulation into a final version. I find that with my students and with other people with whom I share these ideas, the notion of self-actualization gets to be almost like a Rorschach ink blot. It frequently tells me more about the person using it that about reality. What I would like to do now is to explore some aspects of the nature of self-actualization, not as a grand abstraction, but in terms of the operational meaning of the self-actualizing process. What does self-actualization mean in moment-to-moment terms? What does it mean on Tuesday at four o'clock?

The Beginnings of Self-actualization Studies

My investigations on self-actualization were not planned to be research and did not start out as research. They started out as the effort of a young intellectual to try to understand two of his teachers whom he loved, adored, and admired and who were very, very wonderful people. It was a kind of high-IQ devotion. I could not be content simply to adore, but sought to understand why these two people were so different from the run-of-the-mill people in the world. These two people were Ruth Benedict and Max Wertheimer. They were my teachers after I came with a Ph.D. from the West to New York City, and they were most remarkable human beings. My training in psychology equipped me not at all for understanding them. It was as if they were not quite people but something more than people. My own investigation began as a prescientific or nonscientific activity. I made descriptions and notes on Max Wertheimer, and I made notes on Ruth Benedict. When I tried to understand them, think about them, and write about them in my journal and my notes, I realized in one wonderful moment that their two patterns could be generalized. I was talking about a kind of person, not about two noncomparable individuals. There was wonderful excitement in that. I tried to see whether this pattern could be found elsewhere, and I did find it elsewhere, in one person after another.

*From Abraham H. Maslow, "Self-actualization and Beyond" in *Challenges of Humanistic Psychology,* (James F. T. Bugental (Ed.). New York: McGraw-Hill Book Company, Inc., 1967. Pages 279–286 reprinted by permission of the publisher.

By ordinary standards of laboratory research, that is of rigorous and controlled research, this simply was not research at all. My generalizations grew out of *my* selection of certain kinds of people. Obviously, other judges are needed. So far, one man has elected perhaps two dozen people whom he liked or admired very much and thought were wonderful people and then tried to figure them out and found that he was able to describe a syndrome—the kind of pattern that seemed to fit all of them. These were people only from Western cultures, people selected with all kinds of built-in biases. Unreliable as it is, that was the only operational definition of self-actualizing people as I described them in my first publication on the subject.

After I published the results of my investigations, there appeared perhaps six, eight, or ten other lines of evidence that supported the findings, not by replication, but by approaches from different angles. Carl Rogers' findings (1961, etc.) and those of his students add up to corroboration for the whole syndrome. Bugental (1965, pp. 266–275) has offered confirmatory evidence from psychotherapy. Some of the new work with LSD, some of the studies on the effects of therapy (good therapy, that is) some test results—in fact everything I know adds up to corroborative support, though not replicated support, for that study. I personally feel very confident about its major conclusions. I cannot conceive of any research that would make major changes in the pattern, though I am sure there will be minor changes. I have made some of those myself. But my confidence in my rightness is not a scientific datum. If you question the kind of data I have from my researches with monkeys and dogs, you are bringing my competence into doubt or calling me a liar, and I have a right to object. If you question my findings on self-actualizing people (Maslow, 1954, pp. 203–205; Maslow, 1962), you may reasonably do so because you don't know very much about the man who selected the people on whom all the conclusions are based. The conclusions are in the realm of prescience, but the affirmations are set forth in a form that can be put to test. In that sense, they are scientific.

The people I selected for my investigation were older people, people who had lived much of their lives out and were visibly successful. We do not yet know about the applicability of the findings to young people. We do not know what self-actualization means in other cultures, although studies of self-actualization in China and in India are now in process. We do not know what the findings of these new studies will be, but of one thing I have no doubt: When you select out for careful study very fine and healthy people, strong people, creative people, saintly people, sagacious people—in fact, exactly the kind of people I picked out—then you get a different view of mankind. You are asking how tall can people grow, what can a human being become? These are the Olympic goldmedal winners—the best we have. The fact that somebody can run 100 yards in less than ten seconds means that potentially any baby that is born into the world is, in theory, capable of doing so too. In that sense, any baby that is born into the world can in principle reach the heights that actually exist and can be described.

Intrinsic and Extrinsic Learning When you look at mankind this way, your thinking about psychology and psychiatry changes radically. For example, 99 percent of what has been written on so-called learning theory is simply irrelevant to a grown human being. "Learning theory" does not apply to a human being growing as tall as he can. Most of the literature on learning theory deals with what I call "extrinsic learning," to distinguish it from "intrinsic learning." Extrinsic learning means collecting acquisitions to yourself like keys in your pocket or coins that you pick up. Extrinsic learning is adding another association or another craft. The process of learning to be the best human being you can be is another business altogether. The far goals for adult education, and any other education, are the processes, the ways in which we can help people to become all they are capable of becoming. This I call intrinsic learning, and I am confining my remarks here entirely to it. That is the way self-actualizing people learn. To help the client achieve such intrinsic learning is the far goal of counseling.

These things I *know* with certainty. There are other things that I feel very confident about—"my smell tells me," so to speak. Yet I have even fewer objective data on these points than I had on those discussed above. Self-actualization is hard enough to define. How much harder it is to answer the question: Beyond self-actualization, what? Or, if you will: Beyond authenticity, what? Just being honest is, after all, not sufficient in all this. What else can we say of self-actualizing people?

B-values Self-actualizing people are, without one single exception, involved in a cause outside their own skin, in something outside of themselves. They are devoted, working at something, something which is very precious to them—some calling or vocation in the old sense, the priestly sense. They are working at something which fate has called them to somehow and which they work at and which they love, so that the work-joy dichotomy in them disappears. One devotes his life to the law, another to justice, another to beauty or truth. All, in one way or another, devote their lives to the search for what I have called (1962) the "being" values ("B," for short), the ultimate values which are intrinsic, which cannot be reduced to anything more ultimate. There are about fourteen of these B-values, including the truth and beauty and goodness of the ancients and perfection, simplicity, comprehensiveness, and several more. These B-values are described in the appendix to my book *Religions, Values and Peak Experiences* (1964). They are the values of being.

Meta-needs and Meta-pathologies

The existence of these B-values adds a whole set of complications to the structure of self-actualization. These B-values behave like needs. I have called them *meta-needs*. Their deprivation breeds certain kinds of pathologies which have not yet been adequately described but which I call *meta-pathologies*—the sicknesses of the soul which come, for example, from living among liars all the time and not trusting anyone. Just as we need counselors to help people with the simpler problems of unmet needs, so we may need *meta-counselors* to help with the soul-sicknesses that grow from the unfulfilled meta-needs. In certain definable and empirical ways, it is necessary for man to live in beauty rather than ugliness, as it is necessary for him to have food for an aching belly or rest for a weary body. In fact, I would go so far as to claim that these B-values are the meaning of life for most people, but many people don't even recognize that they have these meta-needs. Part of our job as counselors may be to make them aware of these needs in themselves, just as the classical psychoanalyst made his patients aware of their instinctoid basic needs. Ultimately, perhaps, we shall come to think of ourselves as philosophical or religious counselors.

We try to help our counselees move and grow toward self-actualization. These people are often all wrapped up in value problems. Many are youngsters who are, in principle, very wonderful people, though in actuality they often seem to be little more than snotty kids. Nevertheless, I assume (in the face of all behavioral evidence sometimes) that they are, in the classical sense, idealistic. I assume that they are looking for values and they would love to have something to devote themselves to, to be patriotic about, to worship, adore, love. These youngsters are making choices from moment to moment of going forward or retrogressing, moving away from or moving toward self-actualization. As counselors, or as meta-counselors, what can we tell them about becoming more fully themselves?

BEHAVIORS LEADING TO SELF-ACTUALIZATION

What does one do when he self-actualizes? Does he grit his teeth and squeeze? What does self-actualization mean in terms of actual behavior, actual procedure? I shall describe eight ways in which one self-actualizes.

First, self-actualization means experiencing fully, vividly, selflessly, with full concentration and total absorption. It means experiencing without the self-consciousness of the adolescent. At this moment of experiencing, the person is wholly and fully human. This is a self-actualization moment. This is a moment when the self is actualizing itself. As individuals, we help clients to experience them more often. We can encourage them to become totally absorbed in something and to forget their poses and their defenses and their shyness—to go at it whole hog. From the outside, we can see that this can be a very sweet moment. In those youngsters who are trying to be very tough and cynical and sophisticated, we can see the recovery of some of the guilelessness of childhood; some of the innocence and sweetness of the face can come back as they devote themselves fully to a moment and throw themselves fully into the experiencing of it. The key word for this is "selflessly," and our youngsters suffer from too little selflessness and too selfconsciousness, self-awareness.

Second, let us think of life as a process of choices, one after another. At each point there is a progression choice and a regression choice. There may be a movement toward defense, toward safety, toward being afraid; but over on the other side, there is the growth choice. To make the growth choice instead of the fear choice a dozen times a day is to move a dozen times a day toward self-actualization. Self-actualization is an ongoing process; it means making each of the many single choices about whether to lie or be honest, whether to steal or not to steal at a particular point, and it means to make each of these choices as a growth choice. This is movement toward self-actualization.

Third, to talk of self-actualization implies that there is a self to be actualized. A human being is not a *tabula rasa,* not a lump of clay or plastocene. He is something which is already there, at least a "cartilaginous" structure of some kind. A human being is, at minimum, his temperament, his biochemical balances, and so on. There is a self, and what I have sometimes referred to as "listening to the impulse voices" means letting the self emerge. Most of us, most of the time (and especially does this apply to children, young people), listen not to ourselves but to Mommy's introjected voice or Daddy's voice or to the voice of the Establishment, of the Elders, of authority, or of tradition.

As a simple first step toward self-actualization, I sometimes suggest to my students that when they are given a glass of wine and asked how they like it, they try a different way of responding. First, I suggest that they *not* look at the label on the bottle. Thus they will not use it to get any cue about whether or not they *should* like it. Next, I recommend that they close their eyes if possible and that they "make a hush." Now they are ready to look within themselves and try to shut out the noise of the world so that they may savor the wine on their tongues and look to the "Supreme Court" inside themselves. Then, and only then, they may come out and say, "I like it" or "I don't like it." A statement so arrived at is different from the usual kind of phoniness that we all indulge in. At a party recently, I caught myself looking at the label on a bottle and assuring my hostess that she had indeed selected a very good Scotch. But then I stopped myself: What was I saying? I know little about Scotches. All I knew was what the advertisements said. I had no idea whether this one was good or not; yet this is the kind of thing we all do. Refusing to do it is part of the ongoing process of actualizing oneself. Does *your* belly hurt? Or does it feel good? Does this taste good on *your* tongue? Do *you* like lettuce?

Fourth, when in doubt, be honest rather than not. I am covered by that phrase "when in doubt," so that we need not argue too much about diplomacy. Frequently, when we are in doubt we are not honest. Our clients are not honest much of the time. They are playing games and posing. They do not take easily to the suggestion to be honest. Looking within oneself for many of the answers implies taking responsibility. That is in itself a great step toward actualization. This matter of responsibility has been little studied. It doesn't turn up in our textbooks, for who can investigate responsibility in white rats? Yet it is an almost tangible part of psychotherapy. In psyclotherapy, one can feel it, can know the moment of responsibility. Then there is a clear knowing of what it feels like. This is one of the great steps. Each time one takes responsibility, this is an actualizing of the self.

Fifth, we have talked so far of experiencing without self-awareness, of making the growth choice rather than the fear choice, of listening to the impulse voices, and of being honest and taking responsibility. All these are steps toward self-actualization, and all of them guarantee better life choices. A person who does each of these little things each time the choice point comes will find that they add up to better choices about what is constitutionally right for him. He comes to know what his destiny is, who his wife or husband will be, what his mission in life will be. One cannot choose wisely for a life unless he dares to listen to himself, *his own self,* at each moment in life, and to say calmly, "No, I don't like such and such."

The art world, in my opinion, has been captured by a small group of opinion and taste makers about whom I feel suspicious. That is an *ad hominum* judgment, but it seems fair enough for people who set themselves up as able to say, "You like what I like or else you are a fool." We must teach people to listen to their own tastes. Most people don't do it. When standing in a gallery before a puzzling painting, one rarely hears, "That is a puzzling painting." We had a dance program at Brandeis not too long ago—a weird thing altogether, with electronic music, tapes, and people doing surrealistic and Dada things. When the lights went up everybody looked stunned, and nobody knew what to say. In that kind of situation most people will make some smart chatter instead of saying, "I would like to think about this." Making an honest statement involves daring to be different, unpopular, nonconformist. If we cannot teach our clients, young or old, about being prepared to be unpopular, we might just as well give up right now. To be courageous rather than afraid is another version of the same thing.

Sixth, self-actualization is not only an end state but also the process of actualizing one's potentialities at any time, in any amount. It is, for example, a matter of becoming smarter by studying if one is an intelligent person. Self-actualization means using one's intelligence. It does not mean doing some far-out thing necessarily, but it may mean going through an arduous and demanding period of preparation in order to realize one's possibilities. Self-actualization can consist of finger exercises at a piano keyboard. Self-actualization means working to do well the thing that one wants to do. To become a second-rate physician is not a good path to self-actualization. One wants to be first-rate or as good as he can be.

Seventh, peak experiences (Maslow, 1962; Maslow, 1964) are transient moments of self-actualization. They are moments of ecstasy which cannot be bought, cannot be guaranteed, cannot even be sought. One must be, as C. S. Lewis wrote, "surprised by joy." But one can set up the conditions so that peak experiences are more likely, or he can perversely set up the conditions so that they are less likely. Breaking up an illusion, getting rid of a false notion, learning what one is not good at, learning what his potentialities are *not*—these are also part of discovering what one is in fact.

Practically everyone does have peak experiences, but not everyone knows it. Some people wave these small mystical experiences aside. Helping people to recognize these little moments of ecstasy when they happen is one of the jobs of the counselor or meta-counselor. Yet, how does one's psyche, with nothing external in the world to point at—there is no blackboard there—look into another person's secret psyche and then try to communicate? We have to work out a new way of communication. I have tried one. It is described in another appendix in that same book *(Religions, Values and Peak Experiences)* under the title "Rhapsodic Communications." I think that kind of communication may be more of a model for teaching, and counseling, for helping adults to become as fully developed as they can be, than the kind we are used to when we see teachers writing on the board. If I love Beethoven and I hear something in a quartet that you don't, how do I teach you to hear? The noises are there, obviously. But I hear something very, very beautiful, and you look blank. You hear the sounds. How do I get you to hear the beauty? That is more our problem in teaching than making you learn the ABC's or demonstrating arithmetic on the board or pointing to a dissection of a frog. These latter things are external to both people; one has a pointer, and both can look at the same time. This kind of teaching is easy; the other kind is much harder, but it is part of our job as counselors. It is meta-counseling.

Eighth, finding out who one is, what he is, what he likes, what he doesn't like, what is good for him and what bad, where he is going and what his mission is—opening oneself up to himself—means the exposure of psychopathology. It means identifying defenses, and after defenses have been identified, it means finding the courage to give them up. This is painful because defenses are erected against something which is unpleasant. But giving up the defenses is worthwhile. If the psychoanalytic literature has taught us nothing else, it has taught us that repression is not a good way of solving problems.

Desacralizing

Let me talk about one defense mechanism that is not mentioned in the psychology textbooks, though it is a very important defense mechanism to the snotty and yet idealistic youngster of today. It is the defense mechanism of *desacralizing*. These youngsters mistrust the possibility of values and virtues. They feel themselves swindled or thwarted in their lives. Most of them have, in fact, dopey parents whom they don't respect very much, parents who are quite confused themselves about values and who, frequently, are simply terrified of their children and never punish them or stop them from doing things that are wrong. So you have a situation where the youngsters simply despise their elders—often for good and sufficient reason. Such youngsters have learned to make a big generalization: They won't listen to anybody who is grown up, especially if the grown-up uses the same words which they've heard from the hypocritical mouth. They have heard their fathers talk about being honest or brave or bold, and they have seen their fathers being the opposite of all these things.

The youngsters have learned to reduce the person to the concrete object and to refuse to see what he might be or to refuse to see him in his symbolic values or to refuse to see him or her eternally. Our kids have desacralized sex, for example. Sex is nothing; it is a natural thing, and they have made it so natural that it has lost its poetic qualities in many instances, which means that it has lost practically everything. Self-actualization means giving up this defense mechanism and learning or being taught to resacralize.[1]

Resacralizing

Resacralizing means being willing, once again, to see a person "under the aspect of eternity," as Spinoza says, or to see him in the medieval Christian unitive perception, that is, being able to see the sacred, the eternal, the symbolic. It is to see Woman with a capital "W" and everything which that implies, even when one looks at a particular woman. Another example: One goes to medical school and dissects a brain. Certainly something is lost if the medical student isn't awed but, without the unitive perception, sees the brain only as one concrete thing. Open to resacralization, one sees a brain as a sacred object also, sees its symbolic value, sees it as a figure of speech, sees it in its poetic aspects.

Resacralization often means an awful lot of corny talk—"very square," the kids would say. Nevertheless, for the counselor of older people, where these philosophical questions about religion and the meaning of life come up, this is a most important way

[1]I have had to make up these words because the English language is rotten for good people. It has no decent vocabulary for the virtues. Even the nice words get all smeared up. "Love," for instance.

of helping the person to move toward self-actualization. The youngsters may say that it is square, and the logical positivists may say that it is meaningless, but for the person who seeks our help in this process, it is obviously very meaningful and very important, and we had better answer him, or we're not doing what it is our job to do.

Put all these points together, and we see that self-actualization is not a matter of one great moment. It is not true that on Thursday at four o'clock the trumpet blows and one steps into the pantheon forever and altogether. Self-actualization is a matter of degree, of little accessions accumulated one by one. Too often our clients are inclined to wait for some kind of inspiration to strike so that they can say, "At 3:23 on this Thursday I became self-actualized!" People selected as self-actualizing subjects, people who fit the criteria, go about it in these little ways: They listen to their own voices; they take responsibility; they are honest; and they work hard. They find out who they are and what they are, not only in terms of their mission in life, but also in terms of the way their feet hurt when they wear such and such a pair of shoes and whether they do or do not like eggplant or stay up all night if they drink too much beer. All this is what the real self means. They find their own biological natures, their congenital natures, which are irreversible or difficult to change.

THE THERAPEUTIC ATTITUDE

These are the things people do as othey move toward self-actualization. Who, then, is a counselor? How can he help the people who come to him to make this movement in the direction of growth?

Seeking a Model

I have used the words "therapy," "psychotherapy," and "patient." Actually, I hate all these words, and I hate the medical model that they imply because the medical model suggests that the person who comes to the counselor is a sick person, beset by disease and illness, seeking a cure. Actually, of course, we hope that the counselor will be the one who helps to foster the self-actualization of people, rather than the one who helps to cure a disease.

The helping model has to give way, too; it just doesn't fit. It makes us think of the counselor as the person or the professional who knows and reaches down from his privileged position above to the poor jerks below who don't know and have to be helped in some way. Nor is the counselor to be a teacher, in the usual sense, because what teachers have specialized in and gotten to be very good at is the "extrinsic learning" I described above. The process of growing into the best human being one can be is, instead, intrinsic learning, as we saw.

The existential therapists have wrestled with this question of models, and I can recommend Bugental's book, *The Search for Authenticity* (1965), for a discussion of the matter. Bugental suggests that we call counseling or therapy "ontogogy," which means trying to help people to grow to their fullest possible height. Perhaps that's a better word than the one I once suggested, a word derived from a German author, "psychogogy," which means the education of the psyche. Whatever the word we use,

I think that the concept we will eventually have to come to is one that Alfred Adler suggested a long, long time ago when he spoke of the "older brother." The older brother is the loving person who takes responsibility, just as one does for his young, kid brother. Of course, the older brother knows more; he's lived longer, but he is not qualitatively different, and he is not in another realm of discourse. The wise and loving older brother tries to improve the younger, and he tries to make him better than he is, in the younger's own style. See how different this is from the "teaching somebody who doesn't know nothin' " model!

Counseling is not concerned with training or with molding or with teaching in the ordinary sense of telling people what to do and how to do it. It is not concerned with propaganda. It is a Taoistic uncovering and *then* helping. Taoistic means the noninterfering, the "letting be." Taoism is not a laissez-faire philosophy or a philosophy of neglect or of refusal to help or care. As a kind of model of this process we might think of a therapist who, if he is a decent therapist and also a decent human being, would never dream of imposing himself upon his patients or propagandizing in any way or of trying to make a patient into an imitation of himself.

What the good clinical therapist does is to help his particular client to unfold, to break through the defenses against his own self-knowledge, to recover himself, and to get to know himself. Ideally, the therapist's rather abstract frame of reference, the textbooks he has read, the schools that he has gone to, his beliefs about the world—these should never be perceptible to the patient. Respectful of the inner nature, the being, the essence of this "younger brother," he would recognize that the best way for him to lead a good life is to be more fully himself. The people we call "sick" are the people who are not themselves, the people who have built up all sorts of neurotic defenses against being human. Just as it makes no difference to the rosebush whether the gardener is Italian or French or Swedish, so it should make no difference to the younger brother how his helper learned to be a helper. What the helper has to give is certain services that are independent of his being Swedish or Catholic or Mohammedan or Freudian or whatever he is.

These basic concepts include, imply, and are completely in accord with the basic concepts of Freudian and other systems of psychodynamics. It is a Freudian principle that unconscious aspects of the self are repressed and that the finding of the true self requires the uncovering of these unconscious aspects. Implicit is a belief that truth heals much. Learning to break through one's repressions, to know one's self, to hear the impulse voices, to uncover the triumphant nature, to reach knowledge, insight, and truth—these are the requirements.

Lawrence Kubie (1953–1954), in "The Forgotten Man in Education," some time ago made the point that one, ultimate goal of education is to help the person become a human being, as fully human as he can possibly be.

Especially with adults we are not in a position in which we have nothing to work with. We already have a start; we already have capacities, talent, directions, missions, callings. The job is, if we are to take this model seriously, to help them to be more perfectly what they already are, to be more full, more actualizing, more realizing in fact what they are in potentiality.

REFERENCES

Bugental, J. F. T. *The Search for Authenticity*. New York: Holt, Rinehart and Winston, 1965.
Kubie, L. The forgotten man in education, *Harvard Alumni Bulletin,* 1953–1954, **56,** 349–353.
Maslow, A. H. *Motivation and Personality*. New York: Harper & Row, 1954.
———. *Toward a Psychology of Being*. Princeton, N.J.: Van Nostrand, 1962.
———. *Religions, Values and Peak Experiences*. Columbus, Ohio: Ohio State University Press, 1964.
Rogers, C. R. *On Becoming a Person*. Houghton Mifflin, 1961.

The Meaning of Emotional Maturity*

Walter S. Smitson

Knowing the direction to emotional maturity provides the basis for an inner security, for an understanding of oneself and others, and for full and productive interpersonal relationships. Yet, finding this direction proves to be an elusive experience for many.

The elusiveness is, in part, due to the abstract nature of emotional maturity along with the fact that it is not a static condition. Instead, emotional maturity is a process in which the personality is continually striving for a greater sense of emotional health, both intrapsychically and interpersonally. It is an attitude, a direction, never a destination.

We all experience fluctuation in our emotional states and in our interpersonal relationships. Periodically, for minutes, hours, days, or weeks we are unable to live up to the standards we have established for ourselves. Such substandard behavior should be considered normal and, therefore, should not become reason for self-imposed, harsh criticism or a feeling that on that basis alone one is immature.

On the other hand, if substandard behavior becomes a pattern, or a way of life, it is reason for concern, and thought should be given to ways of eliminating such counterproductive action. Corrections of immature behavior can often be made through increased self-observations and self-understanding. Insight can also be obtained through reading, learning to observe others with objectivity, increasing one's awareness of non-verbal cues, and through counseling or psychotherapy.

Such insight sets the foundation for making course corrections of intrapsychic and interpersonal behavior. More serious patterns of maladaptative behavior such as neurosis, character problems, and psychosis signify the personalities' strong preference for regressive reactions and, therefore, indicates a need for professional treatment.

TOWARD INDEPENDENCE

Everyone comes into the world totally on the receiving end, and some never change that position throughout their stay. The experiences of the infant and small child create a strong desire for a pleasure-oriented, *I want what I want when I want it* type of life.

*From Walter S. Smitson, "The Meaning of Emotional Maturity," *MH,* 1974, **58,** 1, 9–11. Reprinted by permission of the author and the Editor, *MH.*

Much of the struggle of adolescence pertains to the conflict between the drive for emotional maturity involving an increased capacity to take charge of one's life and the counter force of wanting to look continually to others to make one's life good. If the child continues too long in a dependent position, or if he misses too much of it, his normal progression toward full emotional independence is impaired.

The complex drawn-out relationship between child and parents greatly contributes to the difficulties humans in our society have in achieving independence. The tendency of many parents to hold on to their children, to relive their lives through their children greatly complicates the natural progression toward independence. Some youngsters never overcome these handicaps and, consequently, physically grow up only to remain emotionally dependent children trying to imitate adults.

ABILITY TO ACCEPT REALITY

Reality can be simply defined as the world we live in, with all its strengths and weaknesses, its joys, its satisfactions, and its contentments. Likewise, it includes the emotional hurts, the hostilities, the lack of understanding, the dishonesty, the disappointments, and the losses. The crucial issue for each of us is whether we acknowledge all these aspects of reality or deny them and take flight.

Mental hospitals are full of persons who have long histories of trying to run away from reality. Such persons may begin the denial-of-reality pattern by momentary escapes, such as unnecessarily postponing decisions or by pretending to ignore problems in hopes that they will go away. For most people, these temporary escapes do not lead to great difficulty. For others, a tragic pattern is set in motion that becomes more crystalized as stresses mount. The end result may be flight into a world of total fantasy.

In some fashion we all have to keep dealing with reality with whatever assets we have. We all have different abilities, different opportunities, and differing levels of intelligence. We have little control over having or not having certain assets. However, we can control the way in which we use whatever tools we do have and, together with a full acknowledgement of reality, can develop a pattern of behaving and relating in the most effective way.

ADAPTABILITY

This is perhaps the most crucial ingredient in emotional maturity and, subsequently, especially essential in relating in a healthy, satisfying manner. The most striking difference between emotionally healthy and unhealthy persons is their degree of flexibility.

The healthy person has the ability to easily adapt and accept a wide range of people and situations. By contrast, the unhealthy person is rigid, judgmental, defensive, and rejecting.

Adaptation in this framework does not necessarily imply agreement with the person or situation nor a reluctance to express one's own ideas. However, it does imply the necessary flexibility to relate to a particular person or situation in the most productive way.

Adaptability is based on a number of personality assets, all of which must occur through personal growth. These include self-confidence, comfort with one's own value system, and the inner security that makes acceptance of differences easy. Perhaps the most important ingredient in the ability to adapt is the establishment of an *observing ego*. Simply stated, this means the ability to observe oneself in a constructive, somewhat objective way.

It is important to identify differences between the person who is able to make adaptive changes in behavior versus one who approaches all situations in essentially the same way. Adaptive persons have an internal processing center that continually takes in data from daily experiences.

These data include self-observations, reactions of others to oneself, verbal and non-verbal cues, what one reads and hears, and what one senses by way of smell, touch and taste. Subsequently, data are examined, considered, retained, or rejected by the processor. From this process comes the basis for continual adaptive behavior that, in turn, equips the person to behave in the most productive way at all times.

In contrast, the person who is maladaptive and behaves in counterproductive ways has a faulty processor that is unable to receive and evaluate data. Consequently, there is no opportunity to tailor one's behavior to best meet a particular situation.

Faulty processors may stem from insecurity and defensiveness so that no data are internalized. Failure at processing can also be due to an excessive preoccupation with oneself or due to any prolonged internal or external conflict that ties up psychic energy.

READINESS TO RESPOND

This involves an awareness of the unique individuality of each person, a concern that each person should grow and unfold in his or her own right, and a perception of the inner feelings of others. The emotional maturity necessary to respond to others involves giving up the childhood wish of wanting to exploit others for one's own satisfaction.

The development of a capacity to derive satisfaction from productivity and caring for others was described by Freud as *object interest*. Such interest can only be achieved once a person is able to get beyond his inner concerns and use energy for loving others. This level of mature love is closely associated with the development of a healthy sexuality in the early developmental years.

People can be classified into three groups insofar as their responses to the emotional needs of others.

The first group comprises highly insensitive persons who show little or no response to the expressed or unexpressed needs of others. Individuals who are both sensitive and insensitive to other's needs compose the second group. Their sensitivity is reflected in their readiness to respond to the expressed needs of others. Their insensitivity is reflected in the absence of any response to unexpressed emotional needs. In the third group are those persons who are highly sensitive in that they readily respond to both the expressed and unexpressed needs of those around them. Most people fall into the second category.

People in the third group are able to attain the highest level of interacting because of their willingness to put forth the time and effort to engage in non-verbal communication. Their ability to interact at this level is also due to an assumption that certain basic emotional needs are present in everyone. Some of them had childhood conditioning that sensitized them to non-verbal cues, while others became sensitized after reaching adulthood—usually through psychotherapy, sensitivity training, or other similar growth-promoting experiences.

CAPACITY TO BALANCE

The immature person is continually looking at situations from the standpoint of *what's in it for me*. The mature person, on the other hand, looks at situations in terms of what he can contribute. There are many forms of emotional giving; all take time and energy.

Non-judgmental listening, for example, is an important form of giving at this level. Taking the interest, time and effort to affirm another human being is another form of emotional giving at this level of maturity. Finally, giving oneself to others is the ultimate way of finding oneself and, consequently, enjoying life to the fullest.

Giving consistently to others at the emotional level mainly depends on a comfort with oneself and the absence of a fear of being exploited. It is impossible to give to others and not be taken advantage of at times. A person who cannot tolerate this is necessarily always on guard and, consequently, unable to fully give of himself. All close, healthy relationships involve some degree of hurt, rejection, and unconscious exploitation. Emotional maturity depends on developing a tolerance for the frustration inherent in such interaction.

EMPATHIC UNDERSTANDING

Empathy can be defined as the ability to put oneself in the shoes of another person and sense how they feel or think. For example, it is not enough to merely know that another person is angry. Instead, one must know that underneath that anger are feelings of hurt, fear, sadness, or loneliness. Empathy can only be developed once the individual has grown beyond a preoccupation with self and self-fulfillment.

Children and adults can often be helped to develop this capacity through role play. Switching roles forces one outside one's own skin and into the skin of another. Another way to help children develop this level of maturity is to occasionally ask them how they think the other person felt after a particular interactional experience.

CHALLENGING ANGER

The first thing to recognize in successfully managing anger is that it is a natural emotion. Secondly, it is important to realize that anger is a gross emotion and is always a cover up for more subtle feelings such as hurt, rejection, sadness, and loneliness. An acceptance of one's anger, plus getting in touch with the underlying feelings, can go a long way toward successfully handling anger by channeling it into constructive outlets.

The most important factor in handling anger in an emotionally mature manner is a determination of one's vulnerability to external stress. Everyone has a buffer zone between the inner self and the external world.

For some, the buffer is too thin and, consequently, it renders them overly sensitive to external stimuli. This high degree of sensitivity comes about because the buffer zone allows too much of the world to come through to the inner self without adequately filtering out material that is too painful to the self. Other people have a buffer that is too thick, which renders them insensitive to others, since too little stimulation comes through to the inner self.

A workable, mature buffer zone is based on the development of feelings of security, self-worth, and a relative absence of competitiveness. The effectiveness of this zone can be greatly increased by sensitizing or desensitizing persons to external stimuli through reconditioning experiences.

These foregoing characteristics of emotional maturity are by no means all-inclusive. But they do spell out the most important ingredients of developing a healthy capacity to relate to others. Behavior at this level allows the person to not only relate at an adult level by having command of himself, but permits him to enjoy it as well.

Only a small percentage of adults in our society ever achieve the level of relating I've just outlined. Many have the capacity to do so, but they never are given the necessary help—either through mental health education, counseling, or psychotherapy. Many others do not have the capacity because of damaged self images through physical handicaps or because of having experienced sufficient emotional trauma early in life so as to render them emotional cripples.

All caretaking forces in our society should continue to conceptualize their experiences in helping others. Only in that way can we advance the efforts to prevent and correct emotional disorders and, in so doing, further man's quest for inner peace.

Section Five

Psychopathology and Adjustment Problems of Specific Groups

The readings in this section deal with both psychopathology and the problems that have been associated with specific groups of people. The study of the abnormal or pathological is extremely important to an understanding of the adjustment process. By focusing our attention on the abnormal, we hope to develop methods by which maladjusted behavior can be decreased and adjusted behavior increased. In addition, those members of our society who behave in ways that seem atypical, ineffective, or disturbed enable us to learn about the conditions likely to lead to adjustment difficulties.

The initial steps in the study of psychopathology are those of distinguishing between the normal and abnormal and classifying the abnormal into distinctive groups. This procedure is referred to as "diagnosis." However, in order for diagnoses to be useful in helping us prevent and alleviate adjustment difficulties, the specific groupings or classifications should be based on more than the differential descriptions of the ways people behave. We wish our diagnostic terms to be more than mere labels that sort individuals into groups. An ideal diagnosis should do the following: (1) provide us with a description of the difficulty; (2) give us an understanding of the factors that led up to it; (3) predict the consequences or future course of the difficulty; and (4) inform us of methods by which we can remedy, control, or alter these consequences.

Our present diagnostic terms hardly approach this ideal. All of the problems associated with research methods, terminology, and personality theory make the task difficult. Of particular significance in the area of psychopathology is the designation of meaningful concepts. In no other area of psychological inquiry have the difficulties of developing clear and useful concepts been highlighted so extensively. Numerous investigations have found that the agreements between diagnoses made by different workers are extremely low. Too often the specific diagnosis made by a psychiatrist, psychologist, or social worker depends more on his or her own theoretical and personal predilections than on the patient's condition. Even when different workers agree, the diagnostic classification provides little or no information about treatment techniques likely to be effective. Methods of treatment that are beneficial for many pathological conditions are not necessarily related to a given diagnosis. Our present diagnostic terms also encourage overgeneralizing from the observations we make and oversimplifying of the individual's condition. The tendency to overgeneralize and to assume that one basic factor or entity determines pathological behavior promotes serious limitations in our efforts to deal with these conditions.

Many of the problems associated with our diagnostic efforts can be traced to historical influences. Since early times human beings have attempted to explain behavior by postulating that one basic, all-influencing force compels us to act in a given way. Whether this force was attributed to a mystical being or to some internal factor, it represented human beings' attempts to explain everything about themselves in one easy sweep, i.e., with one basic idea. As science progressed, the notion was introduced that all psychological characteristics, including feelings, thoughts, and actions, are centered in the brain. Consequently it was thought that psychological disturbances must be caused by disturbances in the brain. This formulation, originally proposed by Hippocrates and expanded in the last century by Kraepelin, undoubtedly represented advanced thinking over the mystical connections drawn between behavior pathology and witchcraft. It should be noted, however, that attributing pathology to brain disturbance continues to involve the belief that one factor—in this case, one part of the body—can explain the psychological characteristics of human beings. In addition, the brain hypothesis attempts to explain psychopathology solely on the basis of anatomy and physiology and, in so doing, models itself along the lines of medicine's approach to disease. This approach equates a psychological disturbance with a state of disease and assumes that the disturbance is the result of an anomaly in the structure of the organism which causes a specific pattern of symptoms. Kraepelin attempted to classify pathology by seeking and labeling a unique feature of each condition. His classifications and the disease-entity logic on which they are based constitute the major approach to formal diagnosis today and often lead us to ignore the significance of motives, conflicts, experience, and learning in psychopathology.

Our present diagnostic concepts for psychopathology involve no systematic scheme of classification. Sometimes diagnostic terms represent a summary description of the individual's behavior *(depression, obsessive-compulsive, anxiety neurosis);* sometimes they are differentiated on the basis of a hypothesized cause *(psychosomatic illness, involutional melancholia, alcoholism);* and sometimes a term is used chiefly because it has become linked traditionally with the intensity of disturbance or with one or two predominant characteristics *(schizophrenia, manic-depressive psychosis, epilepsy).* In almost every case our terms fall short of the ideal and can hardly deserve to be called diagnostic concepts. For the most part diagnosticians today use the formal classifications of disorders as rough, summary descriptions of the individual's most apparent difficulty. In actual practice they have found it more fruitful to evaluate the individual patient's condition by considering the particular adjustment problems he or she is having, his or her typical approach in coping with them, and the consequences of the patient's actions. In other words, in order to make a useful diagnosis of an individual's adjustment difficulties, one must consider a complex of variables rather than a single diagnosis as the disease-entity approach suggests.

The first two papers in this section represent notable efforts to bring some order to the literature of behavior pathology by focusing on a variety of characteristics of disturbed behavior. Upon reviewing data both from clinical observations of disturbed human beings and from experimental investigations of pathology in animals, Wilson concludes that several major and similar features appear: the presence of intense anxiety, the development of stereotyped and repetitive symptoms, and fixation at an immature level. Wilson feels, therefore, that similar principles govern pathology in several species and that animal research can yield results applicable at the human level.

Strauss describes three approaches to the diagnosis of psychopathology. The *typological* model places disorders into distinct types. The *dimensional* model, which represents a scientific advance, accounts for individual differences by describing individuals quantitatively on one or more dimensions. A *mixed* model can incorporate both the typological and the dimensional. Consistent with Wilson's position, Strauss argues that data on psychopathology support a dimensional model despite the fact that the practice of categorizing patients into discrete groups remains popular. He anticipates that the application of a dimensional model will be more fruitful in diagnosis, treatment, and research.

The six papers that comprise the largest part of this section deal with the adjustment problems of specific groups of individuals. The reason for representing the problems of adjustment within specific groups is based on current concern with the criticism that traditional mental health concepts and practices have been based on middle-class whites and have little relevance to the problems of minority groups, such as blacks, women, homosexuals, and the poor. This possibility has encouraged many investigators to attempt to signal out the kinds of pressures and adjustment difficulties encountered by various groups.

Children continue to attract considerable attention from researchers and practitioners of psychopathology. In part, this attention is based on the belief that important antecedents of psychopathology occur in childhood and that prevention programs should be directed toward the events that occur early in life. Also, childhood disturbances appear to involve certain unique configurations. Jenkins has published a number of research papers aimed at developing a classificatory scheme of children's disorders based on clusters of behaviors or symptoms. In his paper presented here, he describes six categories of pathological reaction patterns in children. He associates each with factors that appear to promote it—and these usually pertain to the home and family relationships—and he discusses treatment approaches that have been effective with each category of disturbance.

The next paper, by Weiner, is directed to an analysis of modern adolescence and constitutes an evaluation of the extent to which the literature about the youth culture is valid. Some observers see the youth culture as alienated from and in conflict with adults and attribute "sloth, sloppiness, sexual promiscuity, drug abuse, and insistence on immediate gratification" to them, while others describe the adolescent generation as dull, stereotyped, and unimaginative. Weiner reviews the available research literature on alienation, sexuality, and drug abuse among adolescents and, in so doing, discusses the problems that confront them and the variability with which they resolve their problems. He concludes that modern adolescence is neither rebellious nor overconforming and that alienation, promiscuity, and the abuse of drugs do not constitute normative behavior for this group.

Weiner's commentary on the variability found among adolescents is followed by a discussion by Poussaint and Atkinson of one adolescent group, viz., blacks, and specific "problem areas" that exist for them. Their analysis is based on three motives, the needs for achievement, self-assertion, and approval, and they describe numerous environmental factors unique to black youth raised in a predominantly white society which influence the likely direction of the expression of these needs. In addition, they note that racist experiences are likely to provoke negative self-concepts in blacks, which in turn diminish their achievement efforts and actual performance. Still another significant point made is that the rewards offered by society for satisfactory performance frequently are withheld from blacks, which encourages their deviant efforts to achieve socially valued goals. The analysis by Poussaint and Atkinson supports the thesis that psychopathology cannot be understood without identification of the specific needs stimulated by the environment and the opportunities provided to satisfy these needs.

The women's liberation movement has pointed to numerous instances of inequality and unique pressures that women experience, and the women's claims have encouraged research investigations into the possibility that social roles and expectations for women foster emotional disturbance in this group. Gove reports that women have been found to experience higher rates of mental illness than men have. He cites three possible explanations for this finding, one based on biological differences, another on the hypothesis that women are more open in describing their psychological difficulties, and a third on distinctive pressures inherent in the roles of women which promote disturbance. He reviews a series of studies on rates of disorders according to sex and marital status, and he concludes that the higher incidence of mental illness in women is true only when married men and women are compared, but not when single, divorced, and widowed men and women are compared. His interpretation of these findings is that they implicate the significance of role differences between married men and women. In his review, he discusses many of the specific pressures on women and differences in sex roles which could influence the relative incidence of mental illness in men and women.

Bell's paper provides the reader with a rather comprehensive report of the experience of individuals who are classified as homosexuals. His research strategy is responsive to two sources of difficulty in other investigations: the fact that most samples of homosexuals which form the basis for generalizations do not include the broad range of individuals in the homosexual population and the fact that the scope of inquiry is usually narrow and restricted. The former difficulty is addressed by constructing the sample from a wide variety of sources: bars, personal contacts, steam baths, public advertisments, private bars, homophile organizations, public places, and mailing lists. The latter difficulty is addressed by seeking information regarding a wide range of homosexual experience in respect to such sexual parameters as level of sexual interest, conditions of sexual arousal, extensiveness of sexual experience, type of sexual problems, number of sexual partners, and the nature of the involvement with them. In addition, Bell provides us with data on etiology and the personal and social adjustment of his sample. From his data, Bell properly concludes that homosexuality involves widely divergent experiences and that the label "homosexual" provides little that can be predicted about a person on the basis of that label.

Another group that warrants the attention of mental health professionals is the aged. In the past, psychotherapists have tended to write off the aged as too rigid and lacking in potential for change to warrant much concern with their mental health. Also, diagnosticians have tended to use the term "old age" as if it explained different forms of deviant and disabled behavior rather than as merely a reference to a specific age group. In describing the emergence of the field of geriatrics, Sherman notes that the numbers of the aged have increased dramatically with advances in medicine and lengthened life expectancies. Consequently, concern with their health and general welfare has increased. Sherman discusses a number of specific problems that confront people as they move from maturity toward death which require special adjustments. The decline of bodily functions and physical attributes, susceptibility to diseases and illnesses, retirement, and changes in way of life associated with old age place new stresses on the individual which make him or her susceptible to emotional difficulties. Sherman points out that reactions to stresses associated with age often exaggerate the idosyncracies and maladjusted tendencies of individuals. He presents a number of suggestions for assisting the aged in dealing with their problems of living.

On Behavior Pathology*

Ronald S. Wilson

Investigation of behavior pathology has a long heritage, but perhaps two significant trends can be nominated as having substantially increased our understanding of functional disorders since the turn of the century. On the one hand, the advent of psychoanalysis laid the foundation for a dynamic theory of human pathology, and in a broader sense it recast the traditional conceptions of personality into a more kinetic form. Emotion, conflict, and anxiety received increasing emphasis as basic operators

*From Ronald S. Wilson, "On Behavior Pathology," *Psychol. Bull.* 1963, **60,** 130–146. Reprinted by permission of the author and the Managing Editor, the American Psychological Association.

in human behavior, and disturbances in emotional relationships became the focal point for interpreting behavior disorders. The theory was fashioned from data secured in the therapeutic treatment room, but as child psychiatry and clinical psychology developed, the domain of data expanded markedly and broadened the empirical framework on which the theory rested.

The transition from an organic view of pathology to a dynamic functional view was of inestimable significance for treatment and diagnosis. Nevertheless, the concepts introduced to account for pathological phenomena were not always clearly defined or open to verification; and some pointed criticisms were raised about the subjective bias of both patient and analyst that might enter into the interpretation of data.

The second major trend is of somewhat more recent vintage, dating from Pavlov's investigation of conditioned reflexes, and it can be referred to as the experimental investigation of behavior pathology. It is represented by the work of Gantt and Liddell on experimental neurosis, by Masserman's work on conflict, Maier on frustration, and the work of Solomon and his colleagues on traumatic avoidance learning. Although the conceptual schemata differ, these experiments share common properties in terms of the behavior disturbances produced, and within the limits of design differences they generally corroborate one another. As will subsequently become evident, the major features of pathology revealed in these studies also correspond to several important features of human pathology as seen in the clinic. Yet this body of research, which clearly satisfies the criteria of being objective and controlled, has not been embraced by clinicians, mainly because its significance for human pathology is somewhat obscure; and the experimentalists themselves have made only nominal efforts to integrate their results with clinical data.

The purpose of the present essay is to focus upon points of common agreement between the clinical and experimental areas, and to suggest that the same principles apply to both areas. To this end a selected group of clinical studies will be reviewed in an effort to establish some basic parameters that cut across the traditional categories of behavior pathology. Subsequently the experimental literature will be examined for concepts and empirical laws that will anchor our clinical concepts more securely. The final section will touch briefly on the implications of this review for the analysis of behavior pathology.

CLINICAL STUDIES OF HUMAN PATHOLOGY

Kubie on Neurosis

In an early paper Kubie (1941) analyzed the characteristics of neurotic behavior in search of a general principle that would unify the commonly recognized symptoms. He proposed the principle of *repetitiveness,* or more particularly, that distortions in the normal process of repetitiveness constituted the core of neurotic behavior. Kubie argued that the organization of the central nervous system provides for sustained impulses through the operation of open and closed circuits; consequently, the psychological development of the organism is rooted in repetition of experience. Motivated by diffuse tension, the infant responds with random efforts which gradually evolve into more economical forms until they finally become specifically goal directed. The acquisition of skills depends upon endless but flexible and spontaneous repetition of motor activity.

While these skills are developed primarily to relieve states of tension, they soon acquire secondary meaning as rewarding activities in their own right. Functions such as walking, talking, manipulating objects, exploring and mastering new situations are practiced time and again because the child is highly gratified by the exercise of these new functions. Great emotional significance attaches to these skills, either of delight and satisfaction in the case of uninterrupted practice, or of tension and rage where such activities are interfered with.

Kubie believes that frustration intervenes most markedly at this point, for the repetitive behavior of the child may stimulate inhibitory controls from his parents. When punishment or threats are applied to curtail such behavior, the child responds with rage and temper tantrums. If the parents vigorously suppress this outlet also, the stage is set for severe conflict.

It is at this point that the shift from normal flexible repetitiveness to rigid neurotic repetitiveness takes place. Successive expressions of the need are no longer modified by reward or punishment, but are cast rigidly as the only possible compromise solution of all the child feels in the conflict situation. Consequently, the repetitive act becomes irresistible to the child, and it displays a rigid intensity that eliminates flexible problem solving behavior.

In a later paper, Kubie (1954) sums up the basic distinction between normal and neurotic behavior:

> [Normal] patterns of behavior, no matter how varied they may be, will have one basic characteristic in common, namely that any repetitiveness which that behavior may exhibit with respect to impulse, thought, action or feeling, or any combination of these, will be flexible, modifiable, satiable. . . . [Neurotic behavior] will have precisely opposite characteristics; it will be repetitive, obligatory, insatiable, and stereotyped (pp. 202–203).

Alexander and French (1946) are also persuaded that repetitive behavior is a prominent feature of neurosis. Drawing on extensive therapeutic contacts with neurotic patients, they summarize the basic problem as follows:

> In normal development, patterns from the past undergo progressive modification. One learns from experience by correcting earlier patterns in the light of later events. When a problem becomes too disturbing to face, however, this learning process is interrupted and subsequent attempts to solve the problem must, therefore, assume the character of stereotyped repetitions of previous unsuccessful attempts to solve it. A neurosis may be defined as a series of such stereotyped reactions to problems that the patient has never solved in the past and is still unable to solve in the present (p. 76).

Frustration and Schizophrenia

In behavior disturbances more severe than neurosis, similar tendencies toward rigid repetition of certain acts, regardless of their consequences, have been noted.

Jenkins (1950, 1952) has proposed that frustration carried beyond the tolerance level of the individual stimulates disorganization, withdrawal, and stereotypy. Drawing on Maier's (1949) experimental work, Jenkins attributes the schizophrenic process to profound frustration that arises chiefly in the area of interpersonal relationships. After repeated rebuffs, the schizophrenic gradually withdraws from emotional contact with other people and dwells more and more in the realm of fantasy. Efforts to establish rewarding relationships are gradually replaced by regressive, stereotyped responses that further aggravate the problem.

Jenkins (1950) finds considerable support for his position in the published clinical literature, much of which assigns a prominent role to early frustrating experiences as a causal factor in schizophrenia. Studies of the schizophrenic's family often disclose an overpowering mother who is described by such adjectives as perfectionistic, dominating, aggressive, overanxious and overprotective—the type of mother who markedly interferes with the child's growth toward independent selfhood. The point is illustrated by a sample of statements chosen more frequently by mothers of male schizophrenics (Mark, 1953).

1 A mother should make it her business to know everything her children are thinking.
2 Children should not annoy parents with their unimportant problems.
3 A watchful mother can keep her child out of all accidents.
4 A devoted mother has no time for social life.
5 Playing with a child too much will spoil him.
6 A mother has to suffer much and say little.
7 Children who take part in sex play become sex criminals when they grow up.
8 Too much affection will make a child a "softee."

Jenkins (1952) reasons that pervasive control measures invade the day-to-day experience of the child throughout a wide range of situations and "make it more than usually difficult for a child to maintain a sense of his individuality, except in the autistic withdrawal of fantasy" (p. 740). Frustration at this stage interferes with the development of effective coping mechanisms and forces the child into regressive, stereotyped patterns of behavior.

A more phenomenological analysis of schizophrenia is offered by Guntrip (1952), who states that the primary danger for psychological development lies in early object-relationships that are frustrating for the child. When the mother is cross, impatient, and punitive with her child, or is emotionally detached and unresponsive, the child experiences such behavior as frustrating his most important needs. Consequently the mother becomes a bad object, and "an inner psychic world is set up . . . in which one is tied to bad objects and feeling, therefore, always frustrated, hungry, angry and guilty, and profoundly anxious" (p. 348).

Guntrip argues that a bad object cannot simply be dismissed. The most primitive reaction to early deprivation is to become pathologically attached to the object, and to continually rehearse these frustrating experiences in fantasy in an effort to make them turn out positively. They never do, though, and the schizophrenic remains fixated at a primitive level of emotional development, intensely preoccupied with problems of nurturance and support. He senses his own needs as being overwhelming and all-consuming, capable of exhausting the resources of anyone offering a supportive relationship. By the same token, the schizophrenic is acutely fearful of being rejected or exploited by a potentially gratifying object. He is therefore repetitively drawn into relationships offering support, but once established, the schizophrenic finds them too threatening to be maintained. He is terrorized by the prospect of a relationship which he perceives as mutually destructive, and his emotions are so poorly controlled that he is in constant danger of being overwhelmed by tension.

Set aside the mentalistic overtones of Guntrip's argument and it is evident that he is pointing in the same direction as Kubie and Jenkins. Frustration and deprivation in severe degree interfere with the normal course of development, and pathology is reflected in repetitive patterns of behavior and thought, in extreme tension levels, and in a freezing of emotional development, where needs of historical significance continue to plague the individual long beyond the stage they are appropriate. There is a loose consensus here about the important features of human pathology, a grouping that is amenable to further investigation. Since the foregoing studies have cast childhood frustration in a principal role, we turn now to a series of reports on behavior pathology in children, to see if disturbances at an early age are expressed in the same way.

BEHAVIOR PROBLEMS IN CHILDREN

Erikson (1940, 1953) has observed that repetitive sequences in a child's play activities are often traceable to conflicts being expressed with the toys. He suggests that play serves for the anxious child the same function as talking over problems or vicariously rehearsing them does for adults: it provides a limited sphere somewhat removed from the conflict situation in which the central features of the problem can be replayed, examined, and alternatives evaluated. But even here anxiety may intercede if the play activities too closely parallel the real life conflict. When the problem is of central significance to the child yet he cannot resolve it, play activities assume a repetitive, intense nature, inevitably leading to some emotional dead end and consequent play disruption. The problem may be defensively adjusted through unconscious transformations to avoid outright recognition, but its repetitive expression in play testifies to the position of prominence it occupies in the life of the child.

More serious behavior disturbances in children have been investigated by Bettelheim (1950) and by Redl and Wineman (1951, 1952). Bettelheim's children are notable for their withdrawal, their autistic reconstruction of reality, for serious problems with such fundamental processes as eating, elimination, and sleep; and they exhibit a host of repetitive behaviors that are heavily colored with symbolic significance. The prelude to these difficulties is suggested by the social history of the children, where deprivation and rejection are recurrent themes.

Perhaps the most significant change during treatment is the gradual freeing of needs and impulses that heretofore had been drastically inhibited. In the supportive atmosphere of the treatment center, where no restrictions are placed on regressive behavior, the child may experiment with indulging his primitive needs. If the problem touches on nourishment and security, as it does for most of these children, regressive behavior with food occupies a prominent role. Socialized eating habits are dispensed with in favor of manually stuffing the mouth full of food. Demands to be spoon fed or nursed from a bottle are not uncommon.

Yet the reactivation of these needs brings about a serious anxiety reaction that the child cannot cope with. It is particularly disruptive because his history is notably deficient of experiences wherein some behavior on his part was successful in relieving tension. Having only a limited repertoire of coping mechanisms, the child is overwhelmed by the strength of his impulses and he fears losing control of himself. As insurance he may institute compulsive rituals to protect himself from anxiety.

Behavior gradually becomes more flexible and reality-oriented as the child avails himself of unrestricted gratification. His emotional reactions are updated to conform to present circumstances, rather than being dominated by past experiences of frustration. He can enlarge his sphere of interests and more importantly, he develops inner controls to initiate and modify behavior in adaptive fashion—a series of coping mechanisms to operate on the environment and regulate impulse expression. Instead of being passively overwhelmed, the child now participates actively in growth experiences that promote a sense of confidence in his ability to manage his life.

The emphasis here upon inner controls recalls the point made by Jenkins and Kubie about the development of mastery skills—how these play a fundamental role in adjustment. Where circumstances combine to interfere with their growth, the child is seriously handicapped in his transactions with the environment and in the management of his impulses. The Pioneers of Redl and Wineman, to whom we turn next, also illustrate the point but with the unique twist of having a few mastery skills, or ego functions, overworked in the service of defense.

The children chosen for treatment by Redl and Wineman (1951, 1952) were highly aggressive and destructive, characterized by serious deficiences in behavior control. These delinquents were unable to handle reasonable amounts of tension without becoming disorganized. Fear, excitement, guilt, recall of past memories—even in minor doses these events sufficed to overwhelm the control system and stimulate violent acting out. The ego functions of appraisal, control, and delay were quickly swamped by unmanageable tension and the child's behavior exhibited regressive, stereotyped characteristics.

But in sharp contrast to their helplessness in coping with internal tension, the Pioneers exhibited a set of shrewdly developed defenses that protected their gratification outlets and insulated them from the implications of their behavior. It is exemplified by the delinquent's attempt to provoke restrictive, punitive action from adults, thereby justifying his belief that he is persecuted and is entitled to express his hatred and aggression against the persecutors. Distrust of adults is strongly rooted in early experiences of frustration and rejection, and techniques to close off interference from that quarter, to minimize potential danger to impulse expression, have been sharpened through a long history of warfare with a hostile environment. Concurrently, self-protective mechanisms develop as an armor against recognizing personal responsibility for the behavior in question. Thus fortified, the delinquent shrewdly gears his behavior to maintain free license and justify his delusional belief that all adults are out to get him. But the defensive nature of these activities is disclosed by their rigid repetitiveness even in the benign atmosphere of the treatment home, and by the appearance of regressive demands for gratification once a positive relationship with an adult is established.

Natural Experiment in Adult Frustration

The discussion thus far has emphasized the effects of frustration during early development. However, the same mechanism is conceived to be operative under conditions of stress at all stages of maturity, although during adulthood the effects on well established behavior patterns may be less marked. In particular, stereotypy of behavior is expected as an outgrowth of extreme tension, as well as a progressive breakdown in the more highly refined behavior controls.

Hinkle and Wolff (1956) have impressively documented this process in their study of Communist indoctrination techniques. Analyzing the prisoner's experience in the hands of the Communist police, Hinkle and Wolff emphasize that he is confronted with a continuous series of frustrations. They compare the indoctrination procedure with experimental studies of frustration and observe that the reaction of the prisoner is basically similar to that of the experimental subject, with the exception that the prisoner's reaction is more all-embracing and devastating. The sequence of behavior following imprisonment runs as follows: purposeful exploratory activity; random exploration, with a general increase in motor activity; excitement, anxiety, hyperactivity; gradual subsidence of activity, with the exception of isolated repetitive acts. Such acts are endlessly repeated although they can never provide a solution. If pressure is continued long enough, the ultimate response is one of total inactivity, accompanied by strong feelings of dejection. The prisoner is unusually receptive to approval or human support (adapted from Hinkle & Wolff, 1956, p. 160).

The prison situation is unique in the degree to which it interferes with the biological and social routines of the prisoner's life. In addition, the prisoner is subjected to repeated interrogations that play upon his emotional weak points and constantly pressure him to compromise his position on an issue he may not clearly understand. Effective use is made of stress, although seldom in the form of outright torture, until the prisoner's resistance eventually decays. Behavior becomes more primitive and psychological withdrawal accompanies the development of stereotyped responses. The entire process may be understood as a reaction to acute and unremitting tension.

Common Parameters

This brief survery of clinical research discloses three significant features that seem to cut across all classes of behavior pathology. There is on the one hand a rigid, intense manner of expressing symptomatic behavior, no matter what the content may be. Symptomatic behavior may be understood as a compromise activity that has been crystallized by its success in relieving tension, although it is demonstrably ineffective in securing need satisfaction. As an activity it pursues a stereotyped course and is relatively indifferent to control through reward or punishment. In form and function the symptoms may mirror a behavior pattern of historical significance, now no longer appropriate; they may express a conflict symbolically, or they may include postural and motor adjustments that bear no discernible relationship to the problem at hand.

In the second place, needs and emotions operative at the time of frustration seem to be fixated, and they furnish the individual with residual tensions that are chronologically out of step with his development in other areas. It is obvious that much surplus and subjective meaning attaches to the terms "need" and "emotion"; nevertheless, they are roughly descriptive of an internal state of affairs that exercises pressing control on the individual's behavior. The adult who is described as an oral character still maintains certain interests appropriate to an earlier phase of development, and the gratifications he seeks are thinly disguised holdovers from this period. The steady progression to mature, differentiated forms of emotional expression and impulse control is interrupted, and old problems of historical significance continue to bias all contemporary relationships. The individual cannot escape the past, and his techniques for coping with the environment likewise remain at a primitive, immature level.

The third important feature of behavior pathology is the presence of an intense anxiety reaction, and the manifold changes in behavior produced by anxiety. Due to its compelling drive properties, anxiety forces the individual into response patterns that ward off or alleviate anxiety, regardless of their adaptive value for other purposes. Precision and control give way to disorganization and panic. Flexible, goal directed adjustments are disrupted and behavior is crystallized into a stereotyped pattern. Subjectively, an anxiety reaction is accompanied by feelings of overwhelming dread and terror that are unpleasant in the extreme for the individual. His behavior is then dominated by primitive attempts to terminate the anxiety reaction and to ward off future attacks at all costs. These attempts will generally include internal defensive operations that process threatening thoughts or memories out of awareness, as well as the formation of stereotyped symptoms that forestall anxiety. Where anxiety is severe enough or is chronically sustained, it forces drastic changes in behavior of a pathological nature. From this viewpoint, anxiety appears to be the common denominator that underwrites the major features of behavior pathology.

These clinical phenomena serve as a basic point of reference for interpreting behavior pathology. But we are hindered at this stage by a certain looseness of terminology and concept, a vagueness about the exact nature and operation of these phenomena. The experimental literature on behavior pathology has made substantial inroads in this direction, and a survey of some of these studies may help to clarify the points in question.

EXPERIMENTAL INVESTIGATIONS OF BEHAVIOR PATHOLOGY

The transition from the clinic to the laboratory reveals some abrupt changes in design and procedure, as well as a shift from human to animal subjects. We shall be principally concerned with three overlapping categories of research that offer powerful concepts for interpreting human pathology. They are: frustration, traumatic avoidance learning, and experimental neurosis. While the procedures differ markedly in each case, the results uniformly reveal serious disturbances in behavior. A brief review of these studies may serve to illustrate the basic conditions that give rise to behavior pathology.

Frustration and Response Fixation

The most extensive work on frustration has been carried out by Maier, whose theory and experiments were reported originally in his 1949 monograph, and the theory has been extended in a more recent publication (Maier, 1956). The basic apparatus Maier uses is the Lashley jumping stand and the problem on which the animal is trained is a discrimination between two visual patterns. Once a discrimination is established, frustration is introduced by locking the two doors randomly, so that neither a position response nor a discriminated pattern response leads to reward more than 50% of the time. Maier's definition of frustration flows directly from this procedure: forcing the animal by means of an air blast or electric shock to respond to a presently insoluble problem.

Under these conditions, the jump latency increases and the animal may interpolate several abortive jumps into his response pattern. The tension under which the animal operates is reflected by the number of seizures experienced on the jumping platform. One response, usually a position response, becomes increasingly stereotyped and is routinely performed on each trial. As the stereotyped response is established, less resistance to jumping is manifest and seizures decrease; apparently it provides an outlet for tension. Once established, the response continues indefinitely. Even when the problem is made soluble again the animal does not break the pattern, although he may give evidence of recognizing what the correct response is. Short of some specialized therapeutic measures, the animal's behavior is remarkably invariant.

Maier (1956) has introduced the concept of frustration threshold to handle these data, suggesting that extreme frustration precipitates a sharp transition to massive and uniquely patterned autonomic reactions that override voluntary control. Maier reasons that tension pitched at a very high level may remove cortical inhibition of primitive neural mechanisms and facilitate gross emotional discharge in the form of seizures, tantrums, and rage. Tension functionally reverses the processes of individuation and specificity in neural control and pushes behavior towards more primitive forms. While Maier has not yet clearly coordinated these superthreshold tensions with the behavioral characteristics of frustration—response stereotypy, abnormal fixations—the evidence is strongly in favor of some mechanism by which internal tension transforms normally variable, goal oriented behavior into an immutable response pattern.

Traumatic Avoidance Learning

We turn now to a series of studies that have focused explicitly upon the behavior changes effected under acute pain-fear conditions. Using electric shock of just subtetanizing intensity, Solomon and his colleagues (e.g., Solomon & Wynne, 1953, 1954) have traced the course of avoidance learning and explored the physiological correlates of massive pain-fear reactions mobilized by shock.

The apparatus is a shuttle box with a gridded floor, separated into two compartments by an adjustable barrier and a drop gate. The dog is placed in one compartment, the conditioned stimulus (CS) is presented, the drop gate removed, and 10 seconds later shock is administered. After a period of intense panic activity, the dog scrambles over the barrier and by so doing terminates both shock and the CS.

The basic datum is the latency of the animal's jump over the barrier, measured from the onset of the CS. The first few trials are escape trials, the animal failing to jump until shocked, but by the fifth trial the average dog has executed an avoidance response within the 10-second interval and therefore is not shocked. By definition the animal is now in the extinction phase, and the experiment is continued indefinitely to assess resistance to extinction.

These animals manifest an abrupt shift from escape to avoidance responses, and of greater significance, the jump latencies gradually *decrease* while the animal is executing successful avoidance responses. As trials cumulate, the animal jumps with increasing rapidity until a stable latency of about 1.6 seconds is reached. It should be emphasized that latencies stabilize long after the last shock is received, i.e., during the extinction phase. Solomon and Wynne (1954) conclude that fear has replaced shock as the drive, and escape from the fear producing CS serves to strengthen and move forward the jumping response.

The persistence of the jumping response is remarkable. Animals carried through 600 or more extinction trials showed no sign of extinction. But during this period when the avoidance response is being precisely executed each time, the overt signs of anxiety rapidly disappear as the dog becomes more and more stereotyped in his jumping activities. A rather casual attitude replaces the acute panic reaction manifested earlier. If, however, the dog is forcibly prevented from jumping by means of a barrier, an intense overt anxiety reaction develops immediately (Solomon, Kamin, & Wynne, 1953).

Solomon and Wynne (1954) advance a carefully reasoned argument to account for their results. Their argument is derived from two-process learning theory, but with two additional principles: anxiety conservation, and partial irreversibility of high intensity pain-fear reactions. These additions form a conceptual base from which protracted resistance to extinction and the apparent loss of overt anxiety can be derived. The theory offers a major inroad to problems of human pathology and will be briefly outlined here.

Anxiety Conservation This principle grows out of observations that animals appear more relaxed as the response latency decreases to some stable value around 1½ seconds. Moreover, if an animal delays appreciably on one trial before jumping, he appears quite upset following the jump and responds very rapidly for the next few trials. On the strength of these observations, Solomon and Wynne suggest that the animal gradually establishes a stable response latency which is short enough to prevent full arousal of the anxiety reaction. When the CS is presented, a finite time lag intercedes before all components of the anxiety reaction are mobilized, and by virtue of a speedy instrumental response the animal terminates the CS and thus prevents full arousal of the anxiety reaction. Solomon and Wynne (1954) carefully evaluate the literature on latency of autonomic functioning and conclude that at least 2 seconds, perhaps longer, must elapse before feedback from the peripheral autonomic nervous system can appreciably affect central motor processes. Moreover, variations in latency exist for the several autonomic responses that constitute the anxiety reaction. Consequently, the intensity and scope of the anxiety reaction activated by the CS is a direct function of the exposure period and many elements of the anxiety reaction are not aroused.

Based on these considerations, the substance of the anxiety conservation principle is:

> *if nonreinforced exercise of a CS-CR relationship is the necessary condition for extinction,* then the extinction of the associational linkage and at least this [the unaroused] portion of the anxiety reaction cannot take place. In one sense, the amplitude of the anxiety reaction is being *conserved* as a relatively intact potentiality, a latent functional entity (p. 359).

Put another way, the animal does not test reality by remaining with the CS long enough to find that it is no longer followed by shock. The instrumental response, established under extraordinary levels of pain-fear, now is sustained by its efficacy in preventing full scale arousal of anxiety. So long as the animal can perform the avoidance response rapidly, he can control anxiety; he has, at the behavioral level, the equivalent of a defense mechanism. But the very act that prevents anxiety also eliminates the conditions that must obtain for extinction to occur, namely, repeated arousal of anxiety within the CS situation but with the original reinforcement absent. So anxiety continues as a latent but nonetheless potent state, supporting all manner of avoidance activities in a situation that has long since ceased to have its former significance.

This treatment is roughly analogous to the clinical interpretation of defensive mechanisms. When some event has been associated with severe anxiety, defense mechanisms are instituted to prevent subsequent arousal of anxiety. Defense mechanisms usually process out internal stimuli (thoughts, impulses), but they may also impose selective distortions upon the perception of external events that are threatening to the individual. Anxiety is thus the motivator of defense mechanisms, and at the same time it is the emotionally distressed state the individual avoids by dint of his defenses. By eliminating or disguising the internal stimuli that have become a signal for anxiety, the defense mechanisms successfully prevent an anxiety attack, just as withdrawal from the CS eliminated signs of anxiety in Solomon's dogs.

Partial Irreversibility of Intense Pain-Fear Reactions While anxiety may be conserved against extinction by a rapidly performed avoidance response, there are instances where the instrumental response either is not or cannot be executed quickly. A barrier may prevent jumping altogether, or on one trial the jump latency may lag below its usual stable value. On such occasions more anxiety should be aroused, and in the absence of pain as the unconditioned stimulus (UCS) the anxiety reaction should be fractionally reduced. Theoretically, a slow and gradual loss in the anxiety reaction would be expected. While extinction may be extended by the principle of anxiety conservation, it should not be permanently postponed.

On the strength of their data and related literature on avoidance learning, Solomon and Wynne (1954) believe that it is empirically possible to produce avoidance responses that will last for thousands of trials. They believe that ordinary extinction procedures will be ineffective for cases of severe trauma; anxiety will never be completely eliminated. They conclude, "Therefore, there must be a point at which the anxiety conservation phase is buttressed in some way; there must be some reason for such resistance to extinction . . ." (p. 361).

The second principle, *partial irreversibility,* constitutes the reason, and it means simply that when an intense pain-fear reaction of wide autonomic scope is classically conditioned to a CS, the stimulus is permanently invested with power to evoke a residual anxiety reaction. Repeated extinction trials may depress the anxiety reaction, but there is a fixed threshold value beyond which normal extinction procedures have no effect. Solomon thinks of partial irreversibility as a neurophysiological phenomenon, reflecting a relatively permanent reorganization within the central nervous system. The change is assumed to represent a decreased threshold of sensitivity, analogous to the partial reorganization of hormonal functioning that Selye (1950) incorporates in his concept of the adaptation syndrome.

With these two principles, Solomon and Wynne are able to interpret behavior that is functionally impervious to extinction. Clinicians have long since suspected that maladaptive behavior must be controlled by some such principles because it persists paradoxically even though causing distress and punishment. Of prime significance here is Solomon's observation that punishment may actually strengthen rather than weaken the instrumental avoidance response. Once the jumping response is firmly established, shocking the animal for performing the response seems to increase anxiety more than it inhibits jumping. This gives rise to the peculiar spectacle of an animal squealing vigorously as the CS is presented, yet inexorably jumping into shock. If our earlier equation of avoidance responses with human defensive activities is valid, it becomes increasingly clear why punishment does not eradicate anxiety-motivated behavior in clinical patients.

EXPERIMENTAL NEUROSIS

Behavior disturbances in animals have occupied a prominent research niche ever since Pavlov produced a "neurosis" in dogs who could no longer discriminate between positive and negative conditioned stimuli. Gantt (1944, 1953) and Liddell (1944, 1953) are among the principal American investigators using the conditioned reflex technique to study behavior disturbances, and their results are of considerable theoretical significance of the problem of anxiety.

Liddell on the Vigilance Reaction

Liddell has experimented extensively with sheep, goats, and pigs, using a feeble electric current applied to the foreleg to condition leg flexion. A metronome beat is introduced as the CS, and after a number of pairings the CR is firmly established. Subsequently, a second metronome beat is introduced but this beat is never followed by the UCS. After repeated trials a clear discrimination is established and the animal does not flex the leg to the negative stimulus. The animal does exhibit a sharp alerting reaction, just as for the positive stimulus, but in the negative instance he remains tense and vigilant although no response is performed. Paradoxically, the mild current applied following the positive stimulus produces relaxation and an abrupt decrease in tension.

By steadily converging the two metronome beats, the animal is required to make finer and finer discriminations until the threshold is passed. At this point the animal responds erratically, former discriminations are lost, and behavior disturbances appear. The animal may attack the apparatus, he may exhibit continuous tantrum behavior, or he may become cataleptic. Liddell has used several other procedures which are covered in detail in his 1944 article, but in all instances his conclusions are basically the same.

As a prelude to Liddell's basic thesis, we might note that the feeble electric current used here is in distinct contrast to the shock applied in traumatic avoidance learning. Liddell emphasizes that it is a startle stimulus rather than a pain stimulus; the current is set to be barely perceptible on the moistened fingers of the experimenter. Consequently, disruptions in behavior must be referred to the preliminary training procedures and the internal tension level of the animal, not to the traumatizing nature of the external stimulus.

Liddell (1953) proposes that the vigilance reaction is the emotional foundation out of which experimental neurosis develops. He documents his thesis by observing that a primordial function of the nervous system is vigilance, watchfulness, and generalized suspiciousness. This primitive sentinel activity is a behavioral equivalent of Cannon's emergency reaction. It is graded in intensity and reveals itself in qualitatively diverse behaviors, ranging from a startle reaction to panic. The vigilance reaction constitutes an emotional substrate for behavior, and when raised to disabling intensity it will disrupt prior habits and the flexible adjustments needed to insure adaptive behavior.

Conditioned reflex techniques lay the first stone by introducing the animal to an unfamiliar situation in which he is restrained by straps and has portions of the apparatus attached to his body. A long period of training is required for the animal to submit docilely to the conditioning regimen, during which impulsive behavior is gradually subordinated to habits of remaining alert yet self-contained and quiet while employed in the apparatus. Such restraints inevitably create tension in the animal, revealed by periodic outbursts of tantrum behavior. Measures of respiration, heart rate, and gastrointestinal activity similarly testify to internal arousal at the time the animal appears to be quietly responding to the CS. If training is continued long enough, emotional arousal reaches a disabling intensity and disrupts organic processes as well as overt behavior.

Whatever the neurological basis, behavior disturbances produced by this method seem to be facilitated by an absence of patterned motor activity which would relieve the aroused state of the animal. One might argue that the animal's spontaneous behavior, consisting mainly of efforts to escape, is gradually inhibited because it is ineffective in securing release from the confines of the Pavlov frame. But overt habituation does not signify a decline in emotional arousal. Self-restraint is maintained at some expense, and even a thoroughly trained animal is easily disturbed by events that increase arousal or otherwise depart from the normal training schedule. It appears that the animal can inhibit only a limited amount of tension before more primitive mechanisms in the nervous system effect a gross discharge. As Judson Herrick observed, the mammal is constructed to be active and cannot tolerate restrictions in this sphere indefinitely without pathological consequences.

Gantt on Experimental Neurosis

For a period of some 12 years, Gantt (1944) intensively studied the behavior disturbances produced in one dog by conditioned reflex techniques. Basically, Gantt used a procedure identical to that of Liddell except salivation was conditioned rather than leg flexion. After the neurosis was established, Gantt made extensive autonomic recordings and systematically altered features of the conditioning situation, always observing whether the animal's symptoms improved or degenerated. His conclusions have been validated with numerous other subjects, but Nick serves as the best focal point for discussion.

Once a discrimination between positive and negative conditioned stimuli had been established, Gantt gradually converged the two stimuli and forced the limits of discrimination. Under these circumstances a widescale emotional reaction developed that might be termed anxiety. The animal was extremely upset during the conditioning session and actively resisted being placed in the apparatus. Autonomic changes appeared that surpassed in intensity the effects produced by such natural trauma as fighting, attack by another animal, or painful insult to the body. Respiratory difficulties, cardiac acceleration, increased blood sugar, and chronic pollakiuria are representative of the changes at this level. Coincidentally, these reactions became keyed to the CS; whenever the stimulus was presented a widescale and abrupt acceleration in autonomic processes immediately followed. And these dysfunctions were intractable; once elaborated in the form of a widespread anxiety reaction, they persisted erratically long after the more obvious signs of pathology had disappeared. At a more molar level, the behavior of the animal fell into a stereotyped format of overt symptoms. Gantt refers repeatedly to the "marked character, regular manifestation and stereotypy of pattern of the symptom complexes."

It is a matter of some consequence to understand how a situation that does not include pain can produce such an intense, chronic level of anxiety. Disturbed behavior is intuitively reasonable when considerable amounts of punishment have been absorbed; but what is responsible for breakdown in the artificial world of reflex conditioning, where the most innocuous of stimuli are used?

Gantt and Liddell agree that conditioning in the Pavlov apparatus is essentially emotional in nature, and the nominal CR is but an incidental feature that best serves as an index of the underlying emotional state. Stable responses testify to reasonable stability and integration in the animal's emotional reaction; unstable and fluctuating CRs are an indicator of widespread autonomic and behavioral disruptions that may develop precipitately. Even in the traditional salivary conditioning experiments where no instance of behavior disturbance is reported, the emotional undertone is clearly revealed during extinction. When meat powder is omitted, the animal exhibits increasing agitation following the CS, and at a later stage he may become extremely upset and attack the apparatus. While the salivary response drops out under these circumstances, a simple report of the number of unreinforced trials to extinction hardly does justice to the complex features of the animal's behavior.[1]

Experimental neurosis capitalizes upon this emotional substrate of behavior; in Liddell's terms, upon the innate vigilance reaction the animal brings to the conditioning situation. It plays upon processes endogenous to the organism; processes, in fact, that are at the heart of adaptation and survival. But in this instance the emotional processes are not keyed to the contingencies of the environment. They are aroused in situations of no biological significance to the animal, and they cumulate because spontaneous escape activity is inhibited. So they pervert their normal function, contributing to disintegration rather than adaptation.

An Overview

With all their diversity of emphasis and procedure, the experimental studies nevertheless are tied together by certain recurrent themes. Taking the studies as a group, two significant features stand out in all cases of behavior pathology. On the one hand, the foundation for pathology is laid by a progressive state of emotional arousal that finally reaches disastrous proportions. Acute anxiety is the common denominator of these studies, and at early stages it is expressed in autonomic fluctuations, in panic reactions, and in behavioral disorganization. Whether initiated by traumatically painful episodes or elaborated out of the vigilance reaction, anxiety is the basic operator in behavior pathology.

Secondly, the constant feature of the behavioral symptoms is their stereotypy and repetitiveness. Once established, the symptoms are remarkably intractable to control by external reward or punishment. They may qualify as instrumental avoidance responses or they may simply include primitive response patterns that were incidentally fixated, but in either case the behavior is continued long after the task requirements have changed.

These two characteristics of behavior pathology, anchored as they are in careful experimental work, furnish substantial corroboration for the two similar features noted earlier in the clinical literature. We seem to be dealing here with principles of sufficient generality and power to produce consistent results even when a wide variety of species and procedures are sampled. The experimental studies do not provide any evidence on the third feature of clinical pathology, namely, the fixation of emotions and needs during early stages of development, but they were not designed to obtain data of this sort. Perhaps a group of experiments designed for this purpose, such as those of Hunt and his colleagues (1941, 1947), would produce the type of data desired.

If this be true, if in fact a set of principles can be established that apply to pathology in various species, then it would seem that we are in a more powerful position to isolate the basic conditions that underwrite pathology. Through animal studies the conditions that aggravate the emotional state of the organism can be explored, and nonverbal methods of therapeutic treatment can be systematically

[1]In quite a different context, O. R. Lindsley (1956) has applied operant conditioning techniques to a psychotic population and he reports that chronic schizophrenics often urinate or defecate during the extinction phase, again suggesting a strong emotional involvement.

examined. There are enough striking parallels in symptoms between man and other mammals to suggest that valuable insights might be derived from such studies, insights that could be transposed and beneficially applied at the human level.

This is not to suggest that human pathology is devoid of any distinguishing characteristics. Human pathology has many unique features, to be sure, features that are interwoven with the advanced mental processes available to man. One cannot fail to be impressed with the florid ideation and rich detail of schizophrenic thinking. But if disturbances in behavior are keyed principally to emotional conditioning, perhaps the cognitive processes serve chiefly to express the problem more complexly, to extend through language and ideation the range of relevant experiences that are associated with the pathological state. In this sense the peculiarly symbolic quality that enters into human disturbances may be considered a secondary phenomenon, just as the ability to cast the problem in verbal terms and communicate it to a therapist is. They are adjuncts that testify to man's ability to symbolically represent his experience at several different levels. But the indispensable feature of pathology is the state of anxiety keyed to significant portions of the individual's experience, not the special verbal or mental images through which the experience is elaborated.

SUMMARY

Two separate realms of discourse have contributed heavily to current conceptions of behavior pathology. The clinical realm, influenced largely by the theories of Freud, has offered dynamic interpretations of human disorders that are couched in a framework of drive, conflict, and defense. Its opposite number, experimental psychopathology, has been mainly occupied with animal studies in which behavior disturbances are methodically produced under carefully controlled conditions. There has been a noticeable lack of interchange between the two areas, yet a selective review of the literature suggests that behavior pathology in humans and animals may share some common principles.

In the clinical area there appear to be three general characteristics that apply to the functional behavior disorders. The first of these is the presence of an intense anxiety reaction that disrupts goal directed behavior and mobilizes defensive processes aimed at warding off anxiety. Secondly, behavior relevant to the anxiety provoking situation becomes stereotyped and repetitive, furnishing the individual with a set of symptoms that are remarkably intractable to change. Finally, needs and emotions operative at the point of severe frustration seem to be fixated, and consequently the steady progression to mature forms of emotional expression and impulse control is disrupted. The individual is preoccupied with residual interests that are appropriate to an earlier phase of development, and current experiences are refracted to conform with these themes.

The experimental literature reveals that the presence of acute anxiety and the formation of stereotyped, repetitive symptoms are typical characteristics of this area as well, and these data provide a firm experimental foundation for the two similar characteristics observed in the clinical realm. The experimental studies yield no evidence about the fixation of emotions and needs because they were not designed to obtain data of this sort, but some suggestive results in this direction have been obtained by other experiments on infantile feeding frustration.

In combination, the clinical and experimental research raises the possibility that the same principles control behavior pathology in more than one species. The unique features of human pathology seem to be traceable to the complex cognitive processes through which the problem is expressed, rather than a fundamental difference in how the pathology originates. We would tentatively conclude that the indispensable feature of pathology is a strong anxiety reaction keyed to significant aspects of the individual's experience; and if this be valid, suggest further that animal research on nonverbal techniques of therapy might yield results that could be translated and beneficially applied to the human level.

REFERENCES

Alexander, F., & French, T. M. *Psychoanalytic therapy.* New York: Ronald, 1946.

Bettelheim, B. *Love is not enough.* Glencoe, Ill.: Free Press, 1950.

Erikson, E. H. Studies in the interpretation of play: I. Clinical observation of play disruption in young children. *Genet. Psychol. Monogr.,* 1950, **22**(4), 557–671.

Erikson, E. H. Growth and crises of the "healthy personality." In C. Kluckhohn, H. A. Murray, and D. M. Schneider (Eds.), *Personality in nature, society and culture.* (2nd ed.) New York: Knopf, 1953. Pp. 185–225.

Gantt, W. H. *Experimental basis for neurotic behavior.* New York: Hoeber, 1944.

Gantt, W H. Principles of nervous breakdown: Schizokinesis and autokinesis. *Ann. N.Y. Acad. Sci.,* 1953, **56,** 143–163.

Guntrip, H. A study of Fairbairn's theory of schizoid reactions. *Brit. J. med. Psychol.,* 1952, **25,** 86–103. (Reprinted in C. F. Reed, I. E. Alexander, and S. S. Tomkins [Eds.], *Psychopathology.* Cambridge: Harvard Univer. Press, 1953. Pp. 344–369.)

Hinkle, L. E., Jr., & Wolff, H. G. Communist interrogation and indoctrination of "enemies of the states." *Arch. Neurol. Psychiat.,* 1956, **76,** 115–174.

Hunt, J. McV. The effects of infant feeding-frustration upon adult hoarding behavior. *J. abnorm. soc. Psychol.,* 1941, **36,** 336–360.

Hunt, J. McV., Schlosberg, H., Solomon, R. L., & Stellar, E. Studies of the effects of infantile experience on adult behavior in rats: I. Effects of infantile feeding-frustration on adult hoarding. *J. comp. physiol. Psychol.,* 1947, **40,** 291–304.

Jenkins, R. L. Nature of the schizophrenic process. *Arch. Neurol. Psychiat.* 1950, **64,** 243–262.

Jenkins, R. L. The schizophrenic sequence: Withdrawal, disorganization, psychotic reorganization. *Amer. J. Orthopsychiat.,* 1952, **22,** 738–748.

Kubie, L. S. The repetitive core of neurosis. *Psychoanal. Quart.,* 1941, **10,** 23–43.

Kubie, L. S. The fundamental nature of the distinction between normality and neurosis. *Psychoanal. Quart.,* 1954, **23,** 167–204.

Liddell, H. S. Conditioned reflex method and experimental neurosis. In J. McV. Hunt (Ed.), *Personality and the behavior disorders.* New York: Ronald, 1944. Pp. 389–412.

Liddell, H. S. A comparative approach to the dynamics of experimental neuroses. *Ann. N.Y. Acad. Sci.,* 1953, **56,** 164–170.

Lindsley, O. R. Operant conditioning methods applied to research in child behavior. *J. abnorm. soc. Psychol.,* 1953, **48,** 185–189.

Maier, N. R. F. *Frustration: The study of behavior without a goal.* New York: McGraw-Hill, 1949.

Maier, N. R. F. Frustration theory: Restatement and extension. *Psychol. Rev.,* 1956, **63,** 370–388.

Mark, J. C. The attitudes of the mothers of male schizophrenics toward child behavior. *J. abnorm. soc. Psychol.,* 1953, **48,** 185–189.

Redl, F., & Wineman, D. *Children who hate.* Glencoe, Ill.: Free Press, 1951.

Redl, F., & Wineman, D. *Controls from within.* Glencoe, Ill.: Free Press, 1952.

Selye, H. *The physiology and pathology of exposure to stress.* Montreal: Acta, 1950.

Solomon, R. L., Kamin, L. J., & Wynne, L. C. Traumatic avoidance learning: The outcomes of several extinction procedures with dogs. *J. abnorm. soc. Psychol.,* 1953, **48,** 291–302.

Solomon, R. L. & Wynne, L. C. Traumatic avoidance learning: Acquisition in normal dogs. *Psychol. Monogr.,* 1953, **67**(4, Whole No. 354).

Solomon, R. L., & Wynne, L. C. Traumatic avoidance learning: The principles of anxiety conservation and partial irreversibility. *Psychol. Rev.,* 1954, **61,** 353–384.

Diagnostic Models and the Nature of Psychiatric Disorder*

John S. Strauss

The widespread use in psychiatry of the typological model of diagnosis fosters the assumption that psychiatric disorders actually are discrete illnesses. The typological model describes distinct disorders such as schizophrenia, manic-depressive psychosis, and obsessive neurosis suggesting that each of these is a clinical entity with specific causes and treatments. In this way, the designation of types of psychiatric disorders influences psychiatric concepts, research, and treatment.

The typological model does not have established validity, however, and often fails to describe or explain psychiatric data adequately. It is important to evaluate further the limitations of the typological model and to reconsider the less popular alternatives: the dimensional and the mixed dimensional-typological models of diagnosis.

TYPOLOGICAL DIAGNOSTIC MODEL

The outstanding characteristic of the typological model is that it describes discrete categories of disorder. Since each category includes a circumscribed area of psychopathology, a number of categories must be defined so that together they include all kinds of psychiatric problems.(1) When this requirement of comprehensiveness is overlooked by a specialist who focuses on only one type of psychopathology and ignores other types, differential diagnosis often becomes impossible. For example, the diagnos-

*From John S. Strauss, "Diagnostic Models and the Nature of Psychiatric Disorder, *Archives of General Psychiatry,* 1973, **29,** 445–449. Reprinted by permission of the author and the Editor. Archives of General Psychiatry.

tic type, schizophrenia spectrum disorder,(2) appears to be valid on the basis of genetic findings but may often be impossible to distinguish clearly from other disorders.

Typological categories can have several kinds of relationships to each other. They can be mutually exclusive, so that having one disorder precludes having another. This would be the case in a diagnostic system in which a patient with schizophrenia could not also be manic depressive. In other diagnostic systems, more than one disorder may be considered present in a given individual at one time, as in the multiple diagnoses permitted in the *Diagnostic and Statistical Manual of the American Psychiatric Association (DSM II)*. In such a system, a patient with schizophrenia could also be manic depressive. Finally, types can be structured hierarchically into general categories and subcategories. An example of this is the general category of psychosis in which schizophrenia and manic-depressive illness are subtypes. Each of these kinds of interrelationships implies different characteristics of the nature of psychiatric disorder. In the examples given above, the different systems imply important characteristics about the relationships of schizophrenia and manic-depressive psychosis.

Typologies can use diagnostic criteria in several different ways. Most often, psychiatric typologies employ a small number of criteria to make a diagnosis(3) as with Schneider's first-rank symptoms of schizophrenia.(4) Other typological systems use a large number of variables to classify a patient. In psychiatry, this is most common in classifications derived from mathematical techniques such as cluster analysis.(5) A third kind of typological system uses profiles to classify a patient. This is especially common in diagnoses based on rating scales.(6, 7)

For diagnostic typologies to be useful, they must include necessary and sufficient rules for the assignment of individuals to the proper categories and for their exclusion from incorrect categories. This principle is carried out most successfully in Schneider's concept of pathognomonic symptoms where, if a patient has one or more first-rank symptoms in the absence of an organic psychosyndrome, he automatically is diagnosed as schizophrenic regardless of what other symptoms he might have. In most systems, diagnostic criteria are less absolute and less comprehensive. This is the problem in the *DSM II* where, for example, psychodynamic concepts are used as criteria for one category but not mentioned in another. Can patients with those psychodynamic characteristics also be assigned to diagnoses in which the characteristics are not mentioned either as present or absent?

Most current typologies in psychiatry have a common general structure in that they separate psychosis from other disorders, and divide psychosis—following the teachings of Kraepelin and Bleuler—into schizophrenia and nonschizophrenic conditions such as manic depressive and involutional psychoses. The neuroses and other disorders are also subdivided, usually on the basis of symptoms and behavior criteria. This basic typological framework, although at times seeming to represent a universal psychiatric truth, arose quite recently from 19th century European psychiatry and has since spread in various modifications throughout the world in a process Menninger labeled "the epidemiology of taxonomy."(8)

Typological models of diagnosis are among the most simple methods of classification. Because of their simplicity, these models lend themselves especially to use by psychiatrists who deal with large numbers of patients. In many cases these psychiatrists work in large hospitals, have relatively brief contacts with individual patients and, by preference or necessity, focus more on supposed diseases than individuals. In their purest form, typological models have been especially highly developed in Europe by such psychiatrists as Schneider and Langfeldt.(9)

The typological diagnostic model in psychiatry has many implications that frequently are uncritically accepted. For example, in suggesting that psychiatric disorders are discrete illnesses with specific causes and cures, the typological model fosters such research activities as the search for a biochemical or genetic factor that causes schizophrenia.(10) Different research approaches would be suggested if a model were used that focused on degrees of dysfunction, such as the degree of thought disorder.

Another by-product of the typological model is that it fosters the definition of discrete diagnostic criteria such as the "characteristic hallucinations" of schizophrenia.(11) Such pathognomonic characteristics are earnestly sought to satisfy the human need for simplicity as well as for their potential heuristic value. Frequently, description of such criteria has suggested that these characteristics represent discrete phenomena. Symptoms thus described are rarely interpreted as exaggerations of normal human behavior or as serving major communication or defensive functions.

The popularity of typological diagnostic models is almost universal. They are used as the basis for all standard systems of psychiatric diagnosis. The psychiatric section of the International Classification of Diseases (ICD) is a typological, diagnostic system which is widely accepted throughout the world. The American Psychiatric Association similarly has codified a standard typological system in the *DSM II*.

Although such standard classification systems represent important attempts to provide psychiatry with a universal nomenclature, they appear to reflect a more definitive consensus regarding categories of psychiatric disorder than actually exists. The ICD lists only diagnostic titles and does not provide a glossary, so that what appears to be a commonly accepted typology is primarily a nonmenclature without standardized definitions. The existence of basic disagreements regarding typological systems is reflected by the large number of competing typologies that have been used. Menninger(8) published a 70-page list of some of the more popular typological diagnostic systems that have been described over the years. Stengel(12) has listed 39 different typological systems in use in 20th century psychiatry alone.

Typological systems may be less definitive than they often seem for other reasons as well. They may not meet any of the standards that would confirm their appropriateness or utility. For such a demonstration at least one of the following criteria should be achieved: (1) types should be shown to be valid in terms of major clinical criteria; (2) there should be evidence for discontinuity of important variables to suggest a basis in reality for discrete types; or (3) there should be evidence for clumping in the distribution of key variables to suggest a basis for real types. In psychiatry, typological diagnoses do not fully satisfy any of these criteria.

Lack of Definitive Validity

No diagnostic model in psychiatry, typological or otherwise, has been definitely validated. To achieve such validity, a diagnostic system would have to relate closely to the key criteria of etiology, course of illness, or response to treatment. Other types of validation(13) and other criteria such as relationship to physiological or biochemical variables, would be valuable but less definitive.

Although some validity has been demonstrated for many systems of psychiatric diagnosis, such as a genetic factor,(2, 14) partial response to treatment,(15) or outcome,(16) no system has been validated to the degree common in other fields of medicine. There is no specific etiological agent, laboratory test, or treatment, for example, to validate schizophrenia as a distinct disorder. This absence of validity is in stark contrast to diagnoses in such fields as pulmonary disease where a patient diagnosed as having pneumococcal pneumonia will usually demonstrate a characteristic culture, x-ray film, and response to a specific antibiotic. The limited validity of psychiatric diagnosis is partly attributable to the absence of laboratory tests that could serve to validate ''functional'' psychiatric disorders. Even more, it is the reflection of the continuing difficulty in psychiatry in determining the fundamental clinical relationships.

Apparent Continuity of Psychiatric Variables

The appropriateness of typological models has often been supported by evidence for the apparent discreteness of crucial psychiatric variables. Frequently, such variables have been defined in dichotomized form contributing to the impression that patients being evaluated fall into discrete types. If patients either have hallucinations or they do not, it is easier to contend that they are psychotic or they are not. Combinations of symptoms into syndromes, such as a psychotic depressive syndrome, have also been described as discontinous phenomena as have variables like poor outcome that are used to validate diagnostic systems.

But description of these phenomena as discontinuous may have reflected more the level of development of the field of psychiatry than the nature of the phenomena being described. Hempel(1) has stated that sciences early in their history tend to categorize variables dichotomously as either present or absent. As a science progresses, methods become available to evaluate variables more precisely, resulting in their being dimensionally, rather than typologically, defined. This transition is occurring in psychiatry. Increasing evidence suggests that concepts previously considered dichotomous actually represent points on continua. This appears to be true of hallucinations which are easily represented as points on a continuum from normal perceptions,(17) psychotic depressive syndromes, which are on a continuum for neurotic syndromes,(18) and poor outcome which is on a continuum with good outcome.(19, 22) In fact, there is little evidence that any fundamental concepts in psychiatry are most accurately represented as dichotomous in nature.

Do more complex combinations of variables like types of patients or factors also appear to be continuous rather than discontinuous? Clinically, Langfeldt(16) and Leonhard(23) have described patients as defining discontinuous types. On the other hand, such discontinuities are not supported by more recent data. Menninger,(8) Beck,(24) and others have demonstrated repeatedly the existence of borderline cases between supposedly discrete types. Kendell,(18) Kendell and Gourlay,(25) and others have provided even more systematically collected clinical evidence for the existence of continua across dimensions and diagnostic types.

Besides clinical judgment, statistical techniques such as factor analysis have been used to determine whether combinations of psychiatric variables are discrete or continuous. In a series of painstaking studies, Eysenck described discrete psychopathological factors. However, these findings have been questioned on the grounds that independence of clinical factors derived by factor analysis is an artifact of redundancy of variables,(27) patient sampling and other methodological features. Questions have also been raised whether orthogonal factors really represent independent, reliable, clinically meaningful characteristics in real patients.(28, 29)

Cluster analysis techniques have been used as another means to determine the existence of naturally occurring discrete groups.(5, 6, 30) There is, however, much evidence to suggest that cluster analysis derived groups often do not actually reflect discrete types, but are mainly the product of subjecting data to a technique that forces types to appear even when the actual data do not represent discrete groups.(31–33) In fact, patients are assigned with great variability to particular groups by cluster programs, suggesting that discrete patient groups do not exist.(5, 33)

Modal Distribution of Psychiatric Data

Since data with two or more distribution peaks do not rule out small numbers of borderline individuals, they cannot support a concept of discontinuous types. Such data have been important, however, in supporting modified typological approaches. If a variable or group of variables is distributed bimodally, for example, this suggests two types of conditions and corresponding underlying processes. This would be a valid basis for defining two overlapping types of disorder.

However, the existence of such bimodal distributions has not been established. The modal distribution of data is easily distorted at every step in the diagnostic process. Although findings of bimodality of data have been reported, many of these appear to represent artifacts. For example, case records have often been used as a data source as in one study(34) where premorbid characteristics rated from case records defined a bimodal distribution. Since standardized forms had not been used for collecting data from informants, however, it seems likely that information was not recorded by interviewing psychiatrists unless it was at an extreme, or that the common tendency to clump data inaccurately at modal points was operating.(35)

Sampling problems have also tended to bias psychiatric data towards the appearance of bimodal or polymodal distributions since psychiatric research has often taken place in hospitals, clinics, or wards where only a specific subsample of the population requiring care was seen.

Halo effects in data collection also promote the erroneous appearance of polymodal distribution. These halo effects are fostered by the limited levels of interrater reliability of many key psychiatric concepts.(36, 37) This makes it easier for raters to fulfill their preconception of clear-cut syndromes and, thus, mistakenly appear to confirm the existence of stereotyped typological models.(38, 39) Although recent attention to problems of unreliability in collecting psychiatric data has resulted in great improvement, even with the best techniques, interrater reliability in psychiatry rarely insures that patient characteristics will account for more than 65% of total measurement variance. This renders halo effects a continuing problem biasing toward misleading impressions of diagnostic types.

Although the polymodal distribution often reported for psychiatric data is questionable, the actual distribution of these data is still not known with certainty. As the problems of data collection and sampling are better controlled, increasingly sophisticated multivariate techniques will provide a crucial tool for evaluating distribution. Some progress towards this goal has already been made.(18, 40, 41)

CLINICAL SHORTCOMINGS OF TYPOLOGIES

Besides the problems described above, typologies also have important shortcomings in clinical application. The first of these is the difficulty of assigning real patients to types. An axiom that reflects this problem is: "The better a clinician knows a patient, the harder it is to make a diagnosis." In the experience of many clinicians, pure typologies cannot do justice to the range of individual differences actually found. There are a great many patients who fall between typological categories or suggest entirely new types. This problem provides one source for Stengel's criticism: "If an essential tool is used grudgingly by workers who have a poor opinion of it, it is unlikely to prove useful and may even do more harm than good. This can be said of psychiatric classification today."(12, p. 603)

The other clinical weakness of the typological model is its implication that psychiatric disorders are specific diseases. This conception is closely related to the infectious disease model of illness and, like it, implies specific etiology, treatments, and treatment responses. This model can have misleading clinical ramifications in psychiatry.(42) Chafetz(43) has noted in dealing with alcoholism, for example, that the infectious disease model inappropriately applied in psychiatry suggests specific, stereotyped treatments that should lead to specific responses. These expectations are often both unrealistic and misleading for clinician and patient alike and may contribute to misguided treatment effort and goals.

For these reasons, the typological model in psychiatry, in spite of its potential clarity and simplicity, is not as strongly supported by the nature of psychiatric data and experience as has often been supposed.

DIMENSIONAL MODEL

Dimensional systems of psychiatric disorder have been suggested by many investigators but have never been widely accepted. In contrast to typologies, dimensional systems do not categorize, but locate individuals along one or more dimensions. Some dimensions used in this way have been degree of thought disorder, degree of depression, and degree of social competence. Dimensional models can have only one dimension such as Menninger's concept of the dimension of psychological disorganization,(44) or they can use several parameters so that individuals can be described in terms of their location on a point of intersection in a multidimensional framework.(40) Dimensions themselves can be defined as discrete from each other or they can be described as merging into each other, such as the junction between hallucinations (dimension of perceptual aberration) and delusions (dimension of thought content disorder) where patients find it impossible to distinguish whether a bizarre idea is a thought or a voice.

Dimensions can be defined as straight line where one pole is quite different from the other or as curvilinear where the two extremes of the dimension have certain similarities. Klein,(45) Menninger,(44) and others have described important examples in psychiatry supporting curvilinear dimensions where both extremes of a dimension such as activity or anxiety have similar disabling effects or response to drugs.

As with the typological model, the dimensional model implies many things about the nature of psychiatric disorder. Most important, it stresses quantitative interrelations among variables. Research strategies derived from dimensional models investigate such relationships as how an increase in variable A affects variable B rather than asking, as strategies derived from the typological model would, whether variable A causes variable B. The stress on degree of relationship is especially important when several major variables are involved in the process being studied. If, for example, several factors are related to degrees of psychological disorganization, the dimensional model permits description of how much of each, or what total level of factors, is necessary to cause a person to have a certain level of psychopathology.

A major advantage of dimensional systems is their ability to fit the individual differences of psychiatric patients. This contrasts with typologies which frequently distort patient descriptions to fit predefined categories.

The dimensional model in stressing a continuum with normal behavior also has the advantage of providing a useful conceptual framework for considering such common phenomena as culturally normal hallucinations or delusions. It permits these to be seen as nonpathologic processes in which certain tendencies to perceive or think are exaggerated along their continua by factors such as social permissiveness. It does not suggest that phenomena of this kind should necessarily be set apart as abnormal types.

Dimensional models also have many weaknesses. If only one dimension is used to describe patients—as in Menninger's use of the dimension, psychological disorganization—much information is lost. For example, in that system, it would be difficult to know from the identification of a patient as belonging to the groups with greatest disorganization whether either tranquilizing or antidepressant medications were indicated. On the other hand, if many parameters are employed, locating an individual on them is often so complex that involved rating scales and scoring methods are required. Dimensional models by their failure to define discrete types also fail to meet what seems to be an important psychological need to categorize with the feeling of mastery and knowledge that accompanies the bestowing of a name.(46, 47)

One way in which the flexibility of dimensions can be maintained without sacrificing the ability to categorize is by describing segments of dimensions. Such segmented dimensions have been described by Kendell(18) who suggests that archetypes of a disorder can be described and usefully studied even though they actually represent only the extremes of a continuum. These represent not types, but rather stereotypes, that can be used to define and study variables to clarify the properties of the continuum that exists in reality. Zigler and Phillips(48) describe a somewhat similar model defining one dimension of developmental progression for which not only the extremes but the entire dimension is divided into segments for descriptive purposes.

MIXED MODEL

The third kind of diagnostic model is the mixed model. In an attempt to utilize the advantages of both the typological and dimensional models, mixed diagnostic models have been described that incorporate both typological and dimensional features. Mixed models have the important potential for meeting the scientific need and human desire to categorize, while still accounting for the great individual variation demonstrated by individuals. One of the most widely used mixed models in psychiatry is Bleuler's concept of schizophrenia. Although this concept appears to be purely typological, it actually combines the orientations of typological and dimensional schools of psychiatry in a way that has often led to confusion.(49)

Recently, other mixed models have been proposed which have been theoretically more consistent. Since there are many ways in which dimensional and typological characteristics can be combined, these models have taken several different forms. One is characterized by defining broad types within which dimensions are specified. Conrad,(50) for example, described psychosis as a type of psychiatric disorder within which there are many dimensions of variation. Katz(15) described a sophisticated mixed model of this kind. He defines broad types of disorders which are partially validated by treatment response. He demonstrates that still greater validity is possible if dimensions within each type are considered. A similar mixed model is described by Kety et al(2) who define a type of disorder "schizophrenia spectrum disorder." Within this category is a broad dimension of pathology, ranging from severe schizophrenia to borderline schizophrenic conditions and personality disorder. Evidence for the validity of this concept is suggested by the finding that schizophrenia spectrum disorder occurs more frequently than chance in family members of patients with schizophrenia.

A final mixed model, one giving both typology and dimensionality equal importance has been described by Klein.(45) He demonstrated, using diagnostic categories and a depression-manic excitement dimension, that treatment response sometimes can only be predicted by using both types and dimensions.

Despite the apparent advantages of combining typological and dimensional models, mixed models have the severe disadvantage of being more complex than both. It is probably for this reason that such systems have only been used effectively by a limited number of psychiatrists or only applied to one or another circumscribed area of psychiatric disorder.

CONCLUSIONS

It is difficult without more definitive validation of any given diagnostic system, or more precise knowledge of the underlying structure of psychiatric data, to know which of the diagnostic models will ultimately be most useful. However, typologies appear to have been accepted more fully than is warranted by the data now available, and dimensional models appear to have more potential than has been realized.

This may support Hempel's view that as a science develops, it proceeds from a categorizing to a dimensional orientation. In psychiatry, there is increasing evidence for the validity of dimensional concepts.

One area, however, in which dimensional models may never be superior to typological concepts is in the description of new variables. The definition of the type, schizophrenia spectrum disorder, for example, appears to be an important concept that probably could not have been conceived using purely dimensional notions. Once described, however, the typological category can be redefined in dimensional terms to reflect more accurately the variables involved.

Because of increasing evidence supporting a dimensional model in psychiatry, it will be important to attempt more vigorously to develop a dimensional system that is simple, yet comprehensive enough to be useful, possibly a system with defined segments. The increased accuracy and applicability of such a system could provide a basis for more fruitful psychiatric diagnosis, treatment, and research.

REFERENCES

1 Hempel C. G.: Introduction to problems in taxonomy, in Zubin J. (ed.): *Field Studies in the Mental Disorders.* New York, Grune & Stratton Inc., 1967, pp. 3–22.

2 Kety S. S., et al: The types and prevalency of mental illness in the biological and adoptive families of adopted schizophrenics, in Rosenthal D., Kety, S. S. (eds.): *The Transmission of Schizophrenia,* Oxford, England, Pergamon Press, 1968, pp. 345–362.

3 Sokal, R. R., Sneath, P. H. A.: *Principles of Numerical Taxonomy.* San Francisco, W. H. Freeman, 1963.

4 Schneider K.: *Clinical Psychopathology.* (M. W. Hamilton, translator) New York, Grune & Stratton Inc., 1959.

5 Strauss, J. S., Bartko, J. J., Carpenter, W. T.: The use of clustering techniques for the classification of psychiatric patients. *Br. J. Psychiatry.* **122**:531–540, 1973.

6 Lorr, M.: *Explorations in Typing Psychotics.* Oxford, England, Pergamon Press, 1966, p. 22.

7 Katz, M. M.: The dimensional and typological approaches to assessment and prediction in psychopharmacology, in Efron, D. (ed.): *Psychopharmacology Review of Progress: 1957–1967,* No. 1838. Government Printing Office, 1968, pp. 1023–1027.

8 Menninger, K.: *The Vital Balance.* New York, Viking Press, 1963.

9 Stierlin, H.: Contrasting attitudes towards psychoses in Europe and the United States. *Psychiatry* **21**:141–147, 1958.

10 Durell, J., Schildkraut, J. J.: Biochemical studies of schizophrenic and affective disorders, in Arieti S., (ed.): *American Handbook of Psychiatry.* New York, Basic Books Inc., 1959, vol. 3.

11 Mayer-Gross, W., Slater, E., Roth, M.: *Clinical Psychiatry.* London, Cassell Press, 1954.

12 Stengel, E.: Classification of mental disorders. *Bull WHO* **21**:601–663, 1960.

13 Cronbach, L. J., Meehl, P. E.: Construct validity in psychological tests. *Psychol. Bull.* **52**:281–302, 1955.

14 Heston, L. L.: The genetics of schizophrenic and schizoid disease. *Science* **167**:249–256, 1970.

15 Katz, M. M.: A typological approach to the problem of predicting response to treatment, in Wittenborn, W., Jr., May, P. R. A. (eds.): *Prediction of Response to Pharmacotherapy.* Springfield, Ill., Charles C Thomas Publisher, 1966, pp. 85–101.

16 Langfeldt, G.: Schizophrenia: Diagnosis and prognosis. *Behav. Sci.* **14**:173–182, 1969.

17 Strauss, J. S.: Hallucinations and delusions as points on continua function. *Arch. Gen. Psychiatry* **21**:581–586, 1969.

18 Kendell, R. E.: *The Classification of Depressive Illnesses,* Maudsley monographs 18. New York, Oxford University Press, 1968.

19 Lewis, A. J.: Melancholia: Prognostic study and case material. *J. Ment. Sci.* **82**:488–558, 1936.

20 Astrup, C., Noreik, K.: *Functional Psychoses: Diagnostic and Prognostic Models.* Springfield, Ill., Charles C Thomas Publisher, 1966.

21 Brown, G. W., et al: Schizophrenia and Social Care. London, Oxford University Press, 1966.

22 Strauss, J. S., Carpenter, W. T.: Evaluation of outcome in schizophrenia, in Roff, T. A., Ricks, D. F. (eds.): *Life History Research in Psychopathology.* vol. 3, to be published.

23 Leonhard, K.: The cycloid psychoses. *J. Ment. Sci.* **107**:633–648, 1961.

24 Beck, A. T.: *Depression: Clinical, Experimental, and Theoretical Aspects.* New York, Harper & Row Publishers Inc., 1967.

25 Kendell, R. E., Gourlay, J.: The clinical distinction between the affective psychoses and schizophrenia. *Br. J. Psychiatry* **117**:261–266, 1970.

26 Eysenck, H. J.: Criterion analysis: An application of the hypothetico-deductive method to factor analysis. *Psychol. Rev.* **57**:38–53, 1950.

27 Lorr, M.: Classification of the behavior disorders. *Ann. Rev. Psychol.* **12**:195–216, 1961.

28 Armstrong, J. S., Solberg, P.: On the interpretation of factor analysis. *Psychol. Bull.* **70**:361–364, 1968.

29 Maxwell, A. E.: Multivariate statistical methods and classification problems. *Br. J. Psychiatry* **119**:721–727, 1971.

30 Grinker, R. R., Werble, B., Bryce, R. F.: *The Borderline Syndrome.* New York, Basic Books Inc. Publisher, 1968.

31 Fleiss, J. L., Zubin, J.: On the methods and theory of clustering. *Multivar Behav. Res.* **4**:235–250, 1969.

32 Ball, G. H.: Data analysis in the social sciences: What about the details? in *Proceedings of Fall Joint Computer Conference: American Federation of Information Processing Societies.* Washington, D.C., Spartan Books, 1965, vol. 27 (1), pp. 533–560.

33 Bartko, J. J., Strauss, J. S., Carpenter, W. T.: An evaluation of taxometric techniques for psychiatric data. *Class. Soc. Bull.* **2**:1–28, 1971.

34 Gittelman-Klein, R., Klein, D.: Premorbid asocial adjustment and prognosis in schizophrenia. *J. Psychiat. Res.* 735–53, 1969.

35 Marks, E. S., Maudlin, W. B.: Response errors in census research. *J. Am. Stat. Assoc.* **45**:424–438, 1950.

36 World Health Organization: *The International Pilot Study of Schizophrenia.* Geneva, WHO Press, vol. 1, 1973.

37 Achte, K. A.: *On Prognosis and Rehabilitation in Schizophrenia and Paranoid Psychoses.* Copenhagen, Munksgaard Press, 1967.

38 Arnhoff, F. N.: Some factors influencing the unreliability of clinical judgments. *J. Clin. Psychol.* **10**:272–275, 1954.

39 Kendell, R. E.: An important source of bias affecting ratings made by psychiatrists. *J. Psychiat. Res.* **6**:135–141, 1968.

40 Eysenck, H. J.: The classification of depressive illnesses. *Br. J. Psychiat.* **117**:241–250, *1970.*

41 Hamilton, M., White, J. M.: Clinical syndromes in depressive states. *J. Ment. Sci.* **105** 985–988, 1959.

42 Szasz, T. S.: The problem of psychiatric nosology. *Am. J. Psychiatry* **114**:405–413, 1957.

43 Chafetz, M. E.: Misconceptions about alcoholism mar therapeutic effectiveness. *Frontiers Psychiatry,* vol. 2, No. 6, 1972.

44 Menninger, K., et al: The unitary concept of mental illness. *Bull. Menninger Clin.* **22**:4–12, 1958.

45 Klein, D. F.: Importance of psychiatric diagnosis in prediction of clinical drug effects. *Arch. Gen. Psychiatry* **16**:118–126, 1967.

46 Raven, P. H., Berlin, B., Breedlove, D. E.: The origins of taxonomy. *Science* **174**:1210–1213, 1971.

47 Johnson, L. A. S.: Rainbow's end: The quest for an optimal taxonomy. *Proc. Linn. Soc. NSW* **93**:8–45, 1968.

48 Zigler, E., Phillips, L.: Social competence and the process-reactive distinction in psychopathology. *J. Abnorm. Psychol.* **64**:215–222, 1962.

49 Stierlin, H.: Bleuler's concept of schizophrenia: A confusing heritage. *Am. J. Psychiatry* **123**:996–1001, 1967.

50 Conrad, K.: Das problem der ''nosologischen einheit.'' *Der Psychiatrie Nervenarzt* **30**:488–494, 1959.

Behavior Problems of Children*

Richard L. Jenkins

The second edition of the *Diagnostic and Statistical Manual of Mental Disorders (DSM-II)* of the American Psychiatric Association utilizes the category *behavior disorders of childhood* from the eighth revision of the International Classification of Diseases. Since childhood is commonly conceived to include adolescence and yet the symptoms prone to occur in these two phases of immaturity may be perceptibly different, *DSM-II* permits the separation of behavior disorders of childhood and behavior disorders of adolescence. Each of these categories is subdivided into seven groups, the *hyperkinetic reaction,* the *withdrawing reaction,* the *overanxious reaction,* the *runaway reaction,* the *unsocialized aggressive reaction,* the *group delinquent reaction,* and *other reaction.* The last, of course, is a miscellaneous group without further definition which is included to avoid forcing cases into groups which they do not fit.

The manual states that this major category of behavior disorders ''is reserved for disorders occurring in childhood and adolescence that are more stable, internalized, and resistant to treatment than *Transient situational disturbances* but less so than *Psychoses, Neuroses,* and *Personality disorders.* This intermediate stability is attributed to the greater fluidity of all behavior at this age.''

This subdivision of behavior disorders of children takes its origin from groupings which appear repeatedly in statistical clusterings of large numbers of children brought to child psychiatry services and child guidance clinics(1, 3–8, 10–12, 17). These same groupings are recognizable in the clinical study of individual children(2).

Although these groupings are arrived at by a purely descriptive clustering of cases with similar behavior, an examination of the family backgrounds in which these different disorders of behavior develop reveals contrasting types of family situations

*From Richard L. Jenkins, "Classification of Behavior Problems of Children," *American Journal of Psychiatry,* 1969, **125,** 1032–1039. Reprinted by permission of the author and the Editor, *American Journal of Psychiatry.*

more or less specifically associated with five of these types of behavior disorder. A consideration of the behavior disorder in relation to the background factors makes it evident that each of these five groupings embodies a faulty way of endeavoring to cope with the world. One behavioral grouping, the *hyperkinetic reaction,* resembles the results of an organic handicap(5, 11).

THE HYPERKINETIC REACTION

The hyperkinetic or hyperactive reaction is widely recognized in child psychiatry. It is disproportionately frequent before the age of eight years and tends gradually to become less frequent and less prominent thereafter. It usually disappears by the middle teens.

The traits distinguishing this group are overactivity, restlessness, distractibility, and short attention span. Poor concentration, excitability, impulsiveness, mischievousness, and changeable moods are often present. These children tend to be socially immature and uninhibited. They are likely to talk incessantly. There is usually some general overreactivity and lack of self-control. Usually they do not appear anxious except as their hyperactivity may at times be interpreted as evidence of anxiety.

When organic brain damage can definitely be diagnosed, the diagnosis should fall under *mental disorders not specified as psychotic associated with physical conditions*. However, this reaction is certainly intensified in circumstances in which the child is under tension. This implies a functional element, and there is no present justification for assuming that all cases are due to organic brain damage.

When hyperkinetic children develop in a strong, understanding, and stable home, they usually become adequately trained and socialized, although their training requires more than the usual amount of patience, repetition, firmness, and consistency. In an unstable, inconsistent home they tend to develop increasing conflict with their parents and to get out of control.

Paradoxically, cerebral stimulants such as the amphetamines or methylphenidate characteristically have a quieting effect on these children, reducing their hyperactivity and distractibility and increasing their attention span. This often makes them tolerable in regular school classes when they have not previously been tolerable and typically increases their rate of school progress. This result appears to be obtained by improving their attention span and application. It does not typically improve their intelligence test performance, at least in individual testing.

Some clinicians consider a favorable response to cerebral stimulants and an unfavorable response to phenobarbital as clinical evidence of organic brain dysfunction.

There is particular need for patience, steadiness, understanding, restraint, and kindly repetition in the training of the hyperkinetic child. One should not expect to check the hyperkinesis but should rather seek to channel the activity constructively and to avoid unnecessary distracting stimuli and situations.

THE WITHDRAWING REACTION

The withdrawing reaction is characterized by "seclusiveness, detachment, sensitivity, shyness, timidity, and general inability to form close interpersonal relations. This diagnosis should be reserved for those who cannot be classified as having schizophrenia and whose tendencies toward withdrawal have not yet stabilized enough to justify the diagnosis of schizoid personality.''

The reaction of withdrawal and detachment has long been recognized as a defensive device utilized by the individual who is convinced he cannot win and who finds involvement too painful. It is one of the patterns which repeatedly emerge from cluster analysis of children's behavior traits(5, 8) and it quite common in the age range of five to seven years.

There are enormous differences among individuals in their tendencies toward the reaction of autistic withdrawal. It is not easy to produce such withdrawal either in vigorous persons who seem wedded to life or in dependent persons who have developed confidence in others and actively seek the support of others as a way of coping with life. However, at a certain point of hurt and frustration even hitherto dependent persons may, in emotional desperation, turn away from others, detach themselves emotionally, and defensively tell themselves that it really does not matter or that there is no help whatever to be had from turning to others.

The traits shown by the withdrawing children include seclusiveness, daydreaming, listlessness and apparent apathy(8), and an absence of close friendships or, indeed, of close relationships of any kind(5). Having given up hope of satisfaction in the human world and the real world, these children turn to daydreaming, fantasies, unrealistic thinking, or autistic thinking as a compensation. Impulsive destructiveness is not infrequent, apparently as an expression of frustration.

In turning away from objective reality, these children turn away from the normal practice of constantly checking their expectations against experience. With such turning away, their capacity to distinguish fact from fancy tends to deteriorate. They function inefficiently and fail to develop effective patterns of behavior. As they fail to check their thinking against the thinking of others, their own thinking becomes more and more idiosyncratic, and they are increasingly regarded as queer.

It is natural enough that this reaction of withdrawal and detachment is prone to occur when the child's relationship to his parents is unsatisfactory and lacking in warmth. Maternal ill health in the form of psychosis, instability, withdrawal, chronic illness, serious crippling, or physical impairment are disproportionately frequent(5). The mother is likely to report alcoholism or chronic illness or disability in her parental home. In any event, she has often failed to give the child any clear, consistent, understandable relationship. She is likely to be overly permissive toward the child, infantilizing and overprotective, and yet is frequently punitive in her attitude. If the child does not feel rejected by the mother, neither does he feel adequately supported or directed. He has no consistent relationship to a parent. He does not know what to expect and he has no confidence in human relations. The father's reaction to the child's problem is likely to be indifferent, detached, or minimizing. The parents may be suspicious and jealous of each other, but overt sexual conflict between them is not characteristic.

The problem of treating the withdrawn child involves developing a relationship or encouraging others to develop a relationship with him through which he can gradually be drawn out of his autistic fantasies and into the real world, and gradually helping him to deal more and more successfully with the real world until autistic withdrawal no longer effectively competes with living in the real world(2). While such withdrawal still may occasionally occur, it is used only for an occasional vacation from the hard realities of the real world.

One aspect of treating the withdrawn child is illustrated by Aesop's fable of the contest between the north wind and the sun as to which could make the traveler remove his cloak. The protective covering of the withdrawn child cannot be commanded away or torn away. It must be melted away.

THE OVERANXIOUS REACTION

Children showing the overanxious reaction are "characterized by chronic anxiety, excessive and unrealistic fears, sleeplessness, nightmares, and exaggerated autonomic responses. The patient tends to be immature, self-conscious, grossly lacking in self-confidence, conforming, inhibited, dutiful, approval-seeking, and apprehensive in new situations and unfamiliar surroundings"(1, 4, 8, 10, 11). Parents often describe these children as worrisome, sensitive, shy, nervous, and discouraged. They cry easily, often feel inferior, and may show disturbed sleep, being particularly prone to nightmares(5, 6, 17). They are likely to be submissive.

This is the pattern of the anxious, fearful child who feels inadequate and consequently feels very dependent upon others. He feels keenly a need to meet the expectations of others, particularly his parents, and so to please them, for this is his source of security(1, 10). Sometimes the child's anxiety is stimulated by an overanxious mother(6, 17). Sometimes illness of the child has contributed to his insecurity(1, 10). In general, the overanxious reaction tends to occur particularly in middle-class families with parents who are educationally ambitious(11) and who expect much of their children and hold them to high standards of behavior and achievement(1, 10, 14). The child is not freely given security for his position as a member of the family, but from an early age is made to feel he must earn his acceptance in the family by his conformity and his performance. Love, affection, and emotional support are made to seem conditional to the child. He is held to an exacting standard and comes to feel that his place in the family is dependent upon very controlled behavior and very superior performance. He incorporates severe standards for himself and becomes overly exacting and overly critical of himself. This results in an overinhibited, overdutiful adjustment to life which becomes his way of coping with the world.

The overanxious individual is in general responsive to those methods of individual psychotherapy which have been derived from psychoanalytic theory and which increase self-understanding and self-tolerance (1, 2, 4, 10). He needs initially a feeling of support and human warmth in the treatment relationship. Then, as he is asked to trace back in his own history and experience the elements which have led to his overanxious, overdutiful, self-critical tendencies, he finds the focus of his attention shifted from his severe and critical judgments of himself to a consideration of how these tendencies have developed in him through the experiences to which he has been subjected.

Such a shift of frame of reference involves a shift from his looking at himself as villain toward looking at himself as a victim of circumstances. When we are dealing with a person whose judgment of himself is unduly harsh and guilt-ridden, this shift in emphasis may have a very constructive, salutary, and therapeutic effect. The uncovering or exploratory methods of psychotherapy, if skillfully handled, commonly have a constructive and therapeutic effect in such cases, particularly if some more reasonable integration of objectives and values is encouraged in the latter stages of this process. A general anxiety and self-critical judgment tends to be replaced with a measure of self-tolerance and more discriminating self-judgment, with positive benefits.

It may be stated that one of our major problems in child psychiatry is that psychoanalytic thinking has attained such a dominance in our field that the psychoneurotic model has been overextended and that the treatment appropriate for the overanxious child has tended automatically to be extended to all types of children regardless of whether or not it is appropriate for their needs. Unfortunately, it is inappropriate to five of our six groups and thus leads to many poorly conceived treatment efforts.

THE RUNAWAY REACTION

The children who fall into this group all repeatedly run away from home overnight. They are timid and furtive and are inclined to stealing, particularly stealing in the home(7). Often the child will steal money in the home and then run away. These children are unhappy in their homes and stay out late at night. They tend to be discouraged. Frequently they are seclusive and apathetic. Often they seek the protection of peers whom they regard as stronger and more adequate than themselves. They may become involved in passive homosexuality, sometimes as a means of seeking a protector. In any event, they tend to associate with companions whom the community regards as undesirable and may become hangers-on of the delinquent gang(12), but they lack the loyalty or adequacy necessary to make or be accepted as good members of a well-knit delinquent gang. They are more furtive and more deceptive than most delinquents.

The home background of the chronic runaway children is typically one of parental rejection from birth or before birth(7) and one of parental severity and inconsistency. As a group these children do not show the muscular development that is fairly characteristic of children who develop a truly aggressive adjustment to life. As a consequence, any aggressiveness is less likely to be successful and is less likely to meet any reward than is the case with the unsocialized aggressive child. Typically there is a gross lack of self-confidence and a very poor self-image. The unwanted illegitimate child is very common in this group, and only child status is extremely common(7). This child has lacked socializing experiences with siblings as well as with parents.

The treatment of these children is difficult. Treatment of the home is essential. If the parents cannot be successfully encouraged toward a more accepting attitude than is usually present, at least temporary removal from the home is necessary. These children usually have conspicuously poor self-images(18), and the development of some sense of personal value is necessary.

If management in the home cannot be effectively and constructively modified, they will need a relatively prolonged period of treatment and training in a foster home or treatment institution. Even then, these children cannot be returned home successfully without very substantial modification of the home atmosphere and home management.

THE UNSOCIALIZED AGGRESSIVE REACTION

Unsocialized aggressive children are characterized by "overt or covert hostile disobedience, quarrelsomeness, physical and verbal aggressiveness, vengefulness, and destructiveness. Temper tantrums, solitary stealing, lying, and hostile teasing of other children are common"(1, 2, 4–12, 17). They are sexually uninhibited and inclined to be sexually aggressive(7, 9). There appears to be a basic defect in socialization, and the aggressive behavior itself appears to be in the nature of a frustration response. The work of Norman Maier(15) has demonstrated that in rats, at a certain level of frustration, adaptive behavior is replaced by what he calls frustration behavior. Frustration behavior is maladaptive, stereotyped, repetitive, and is typically increased by punishment. All of these characteristics are evident in the behavior of the unsocialized aggressive child(4, 16).

It is clear that the home life of the unsocialized aggressive child has typically been very frustrating. The parents are themselves typically unstable in their marital relationship(4, 11) and have never given the child any consistent acceptance or affection. The mother in particular has been immature and not ready for motherhood. Thus, rejection is not a product of his behavior for it predates it—in fact it commonly predates the birth of the child(1, 10). The most typical contributing factor in the background of such a child is that he was never wanted and knows it(1, 10). He has never experienced consistent acceptance, and he has never had a basis for developing trust in an adult(14). Because of family instability he is very likely to have a stepparent(6, 17). These children may be only children and are not likely to have many siblings.

A good musculature and male sex both show a significant association with the unsocialized aggressive reaction. Although rejected, these children are also often somewhat overprotected by their parents(7). These types of maternal behavior, rejection and overprotection may, in fact, be complementary, as David Levy pointed out 25 years ago(13). The rejecting mother may seek to redeem herself in her own and the public's eye by going through the gestures of maternity, but she may do so resentfully and in a way which actually restricts and frustrates the child. These parents not infrequently shield their children from the natural consequences of their delinquent acts. Such actions, and an inconsistent and unpredictable severity of punishment which may relate more to how the parent feels at the moment than to what the child has done, are characteristic. These parents are likely to alternate severity with bribery in the effort to control the child. They are unlikely to agree with each other and unlikely to support each other in discipline.

Persistent enuresis is a common problem(11).

Successful treatment of the unsocialized aggressive child is not possible without altering his management. The younger the age at which this can be undertaken, the better, for the longer it goes on the more hostility and distortion are produced in the personality of the child. Many women are not able to be maternal when overburdened in an unhappy marriage. Yet the maternal instinct is deeply rooted, and a combination of emotional support and guidance will improve the maternal behavior of most of these women. Some cases call for removal from the home. This ordinarily requires the intervention of a court. Sometimes a combination of some treatment in a hospital or other treatment institution and return to the home after a period of work with the parents is indicated.

When the child is hospitalized, he needs an environment that is warm, kindly, and accepting, yet firm and patient in its refusal to be bullied or blackmailed into making concessions to his aggressiveness. The limitations and the reasons for these limitations must be explained again and again and must be maintained effectively. The child's immediate response to a limitation is typically: "You don't like me!" The adult must reassure the child of his accepting attitude and give evidence of it as the occasion arises, while still maintaining the limits. Care must be taken to begin with first things first and not to try to bring on too many points at once, but rather to follow a step-by-step procedure at a gradual pace. Meanwhile, the family must be worked with and helped to show their acceptance of the child while maintaining a reasonable and consistent program of control. The extreme of the unsocialized aggressive reaction develops into the antisocial or psychopathic personality(3).

THE GROUP DELINQUENT REACTION

The groups of behavior disorders we have described to this point represent individual types of maladaptations. By contrast, the socialized delinquent represents group rebellion against the structure and limitations of our society. This group behavior is largely learned behavior and represents social group conflict more than individual psychopathology. Viewed from the short range, it is functional, adaptive, motivated, understandable behavior which has a goal.

This group of delinquents averages a bit older than the groups of children we have heretofore discussed. These delinquents are distinguished by group rebellion, with cooperation (and often loyalty) among the members of the group. They have typically been involved in group or gang delinquency, stealing (particularly cooperative stealing), and truancy from school(1, 3–12, 17).

Most socialized delinquents are boys. Girls are less prone to group rebellion, are not prone to "gang up," and when they relate to more or less organized delinquent gangs it is typically as the girl friends of gang members, although not infrequently girls may cooperate in shoplifting.

The socialized delinquent is distinguished from the unsocialized aggressive child and the runaway by his greater basic socialization, particularly by his capacity for loyalty. Usually he has experienced more or less normal mothering in his infancy and early childhood, but there has been a lack of parental supervision and particularly of paternal supervision during his later development(5). Group delinquency is a phenomenon that is more common in the impoverished and disadvantaged areas of our cities. The large family in poor housing on the wrong side of the railroad tracks, the working mother, the absent or alcoholic father, the broken home, the stepfather who has conflict with his adolescent stepson—these are all elements that appear with disproportionate frequency in this group(5).

The socialized delinquent represents not a failure of socialization but a limitation of loyalty to a more or less predatory peer group. The basic capacity for social relations has been achieved. What is lacking is an effective integration with the larger society as a contributing member.

The socialized delinquent needs to become a functioning and productive part of this larger society. He needs first of all a tie, a loyalty, to one or more socialized adults who can help him integrate himself to school and to the job world of adults(2). Elements which interfere with this integration are very important. Reading disability is an extremely common contributing factor to school maladjustment. Opportunities for earning money and for gaining status thereby are very important, and limitations of these opportunities because of minority status or educational deficiencies make major contributions to delinquency. Although employment of the juvenile appears constructive, periods of high employment tend to be accompanied by more delinquency than periods of low employment. This is presumably because in periods of high employment the children are more likely to be unsupervised.

Prevention is generally more successful than treatment and involves effective leadership in neighborhood youth activities. Juvenile delinquency tends to develop in a hiatus between effective schooling and integration with the adult society and may be combated by furthering such integration. The development of a personal relationship with a strong, interested, socialized man is most important in bridging the gap. Increasing maturity, interest in marriage, the establishment of family life all create powerful pressures tending to make the socialized delinquent give up his delinquency and get a job, thereby becoming a productive member of society. For the individual with an aptitude for it who has really developed group loyalty, military service may offer an alternative route.

SUMMARY

The six reactions listed under behavior disorders of childhood and adolescence represent clinically recognizable symptomatic clusters supported by different studies using different clustering methods.

The hyperkinetic reaction resembles the behavior seen in children with minimal brain damage.

The withdrawing reaction is prone to occur when real life offers too little satisfaction to the child, as may be the case for the child with inadequate parents who are detached, overly permissive in behavior, and yet punitive in attitude.

The overanxious reaction tends to occur particularly in middle-class, educationally ambitious families in which children are held to high standards of behavior and achievement and may come to feel that their acceptance in the family is dependent upon maintaining these standards.

The unsocialized aggressive reaction tends to occur as a reaction to parental rejection coupled with some parental overprotection.

The runaway reaction tends to occur as a reaction to simple undiluted parental rejection.

The group delinquent reaction tends to occur as a result of group rebellion in the adolescent years and in the absence of parental, and particularly in the absence of paternal, supervision.

Consideration is given to the problems of treating children falling in each of these groups. While the treatment of all children must be individualized, it can with advantage be individualized from a general pattern appropriate to the child's general type of problem. The widespread present tendency to generalize the treatment of all cases from the psychoneurotic model is self-defeating and humanly wasteful.

REFERENCES

1 Hewitt, C. E., and Jenkins, R. L.: Fundamental Patterns of Maladjustment: The Dynamics of Their Origin. Springfield: State of Illinois, 1946.

2 Jenkins, R. L.: Breaking Patterns of Defeat. Philadelphia: J. B. Lippincott Co., 1954.

3 Jenkins, R. L.: The Psychopathic or Antisocial Personality, J. Nerv. Ment. Dis. **131**:318–334, 1960.

4 Jenkins, R. L.: Diagnoses, Dynamics and Treatment in Child Psychiatry, Psychiat. Res. Rep. Amer. Psychiat. Ass. **18**:91–120, 1964.

5 Jenkins, R. L.: Psychiatric Syndromes in Children and Their Relation to Family Background, Amer. J. Orthopsychiat. **36**:450–457, 1966.

6 Jenkins, R. L.: The Varieties of Children's Behavioral Problems and Family Dynamics, Amer. J. Psychiat. **124**:1440–1445, 1968.

7 Jenkins, R. L., and Boyer, A.: Types of Delinquent Behavior and Background Factors, Int. J. Soc. Psychiat. **14**:65–76, 1967.

8 Jenkins, R. L., and Glickman, S.: Common Syndromes in Child Psychiatry: I. Deviant Behavior Traits, II. The Schizoid Child, Amer. J. Orthopsychiat. **16**:244–261, 1946.

9 Jenkins, R. L., and Glickman, S.: Patterns of Personality Organization Among Delinquents, Nervous Child **6**:329–339, 1947. Reprinted in Gorlow, L., and Katkovsky, W., eds.: Readings in the Psychology of Adjustment. New York: McGraw-Hill, 1959.

10 Jenkins, R. L., and Hewitt, L.: Types of Personality Structure Encountered in Child Guidance Clinics, Amer. J. Orthopsychiat. **14**:84–94, 1944.

11 Jenkins, R. L., NurEddin, E., and Shapiro, I.: Children's Behavior Syndromes and Parental Responses, Genet. Psychol. Monogr. **74**:261–329, 1966.

12 Kobayaski, S., Mizushima, K., and Shinohara, M.: Clinical Groupings of Problem Children Based on Symptoms and Behavior, Int. J. Soc. Psychiat. **13**:206–215, 1967.

13 Levy, D.: Maternal Overprotection. New York: Columbia University Press, 1943.

14 Lewis, H.: Deprived Children. London: Oxford University Press, 1954.

15 Maier, N. R. F.: Frustration: The Study of Behavior Without a Goal. New York: McGraw-Hill, 1949.

16 Saksida, S.: Motivation Mechanisms and Frustration Stereotypes, Amer. J. Orthopsychiat. **29**:599–611, 1959.

17 Shamsie, S. J., ed.: Adolescent Psychiatry. Pointe Claire, Quebec: Schering Corp., 1968.

18 Shinohara, M., and Jenkins, R. L.: MMPI Study of Three Types of Delinquents, J. Clin. Psychol. **23**:156–163, 1967.

Perspectives on the Modern Adolescent*

Irving B. Weiner

According to some authorities, today's teen-agers constitute a youth culture that is cut off from and at odds with the adult world. Among the imputed hallmarks of this youth culture are sloth, sloppiness, sexual promiscuity, drug abuse, and insistence on immediate gratification, mixed with a liberal dose of bad manners, disrespect for authority, and renunciation of traditional values. Whereas some writers view these aspects of youthful alienation with alarm, proponents of the "counter culture" and "Consciousness III" regard them as signs of social progress. A third group of writers disagrees entirely with the notion of a youth culture, asserting instead that adolescents as an essentially unique age group are a vanishing species. From this point of view the adolescent generation, beneath its superficial trappings, is a dull, stereotyped, unimaginative segment of our population that shrinks from individuality and prematurely adopts identities prescribed or modeled by their parents. Each of these positions has led to overdrawn conclusions about the nature of the modern adolescent, particularly with respect to his sex behavior and drug use, and a more balanced perspective is necessary to separate myth from reality.

THE YOUTH CULTURE

The notion of the youth culture in modern America emerged from the studies of Coleman *(The Adolescent Society),* Keniston *(The Uncommitted: Alienated Youth in American Society)* and Pearson *(Adolescence and the Conflict of Generations)* and has led to a recent spate of books decrying its existence, of which Feuer's *The Conflict of Generations* and Mead's *Culture and Commitment: A Study of the Generation Gap* are two of the more prominent. These writers attribute teen-age alienation to such influences as a breakdown of family organization and parental authority, a rapidly changing world that exposes teen-agers to experiences their parents cannot understand, the long apprenticeship between childhood and adulthood in a complex technological society, and teen-age disaffection for a hypocritical, materialistic adult generation that has failed to eliminate war, injustice, and human misery.

The youth culture is generally seen as arising because teen-agers have nowhere to turn except to themselves to find a sense of group belongingness and a set of values with which they can feel comfortable. Unappreciated by their elders and denied adult prerogatives, they look to each other for status and support and pointedly refuse to think, act, talk, dress, and comport themselves as the adult generation would like them to. "Don't trust anyone over 30" and "Screw the establishment" have become mottoes of the youth culture, and many observers feel that it is urgent that adults find some way to communicate across the generation gap before young people take over and tear down the institutions on which our society is founded. As contemporary as

*From Irving B. Weiner, "Perspectives on the Modern Adolescent," *Psychiatry,* 1972, **35,** 20–31. Reprinted by permission of the author and the Editor, *Psychiatry.*

such concerns are, it is interesting to note how closely they were shared by Shakespeare's old shepherd in *The Winter's Tale,* who had this to say about adolescents:

> I would there were no age between ten and three-and-twenty, or that youth would sleep out the rest; for there is nothing in the between but getting wenches with child, wronging the ancientry, stealing, fighting. [Act III, Scene iii]

In assessing the accuracy of this perspective on youth, it is first necessary to emphasize the oversimplification inherent in any reference to "the youth culture." To the extent that adolescents differ from adults in any uniform fashion, the teen-age population comprises not one but multiple cultures. There is a world of difference between the values and behavior of a group of 17-year-old black boys in New York's Harlem, a group of 13-year-old white girls in suburban Detroit's Grosse Point Shores, a group of teen-age 4H Clubbers in rural Kansas, and a group of adolescent Chicanos in southern California. The fact is that youngsters of different age and sex, representing different ethnic and social class backgrounds, and coming from different sections of the country, are likely to think and act as differently from each other as they do from adults.

Lipset and Raab have recently pointed out in this regard that no more than 10 percent of youth are really bent on renouncing or revamping the structure of our society, and that these youngsters are primarily college or college-bound students whose parents also hold liberal political attitudes. Thus revisionary youth protesting against the establishment comprise only a small segment of our adolescent population and are more likely to share political activism with their parents than to be rebelling against their parents' values.[1]

A less visible but equally large group of dissident youth comes from conservative working-class and lower-middle-class families whose major concern is preventing any erosion of their hard-won security and prerogatives. These young people, far from deploring traditional society, are as intent as their parents on preserving and intensifying societal norms and resisting any concession to liberal activists.

Still a third segment of dissatisfied youth consists mainly of black and other culturally disadvantaged youngsters who want to preserve the system essentially as it is but improve their chances of getting into it and enjoying a piece of the action. Thus most militant black leaders and their youthful followers are pressing not for doing away with the American system, but for more black power in it—blacks in government, blacks in the upper echelons of business and finance, black control of programs for black people, and equal educational and occupational opportunities for blacks.

The political gaps among these three elements in the youthful generation are considerably bigger than any gap between them and their parents: "Politically . . . the basic direction of the younger generation is in most cases the same as that of their parents; they go with the parental grain rather than against it" (Lipset and Raab, p. 38).

There is little evidence to support the widespread impression that most teen-agers are in revolt against the values of their family and society. The notion of a normative

[1]See also Block, Haan, and Smith.

"identity crisis" that causes teen-agers to behave in a confused, unpredictable, and undisciplined manner bordering on psychopathology has been laid to rest by a mass of empirical data, even though it persists in the thinking of many clinicians. These data, as reviewed by Offer (1969, Chaps. 11–13) and Weiner (Chap. 2), indicate (1) that adolescent turmoil is an infrequent phenomenon and reflects psychopathology rather than normal development when it occurs, (2) that most adolescents consolidate their personal identity gradually and without any major disruptions in the continuity of their self-concept or behavioral style, (3) that most adolescents respect their parents, want to be like them, and maintain relatively harmonious relations with them and other adults, and (4) that the majority of high school boys and girls feel that they are an integral part of the community in which they live and report that their main sources of concern are achievement and study habits, not sports or recreation or popularity or instant gratification.

THE COUNTER CULTURE AND CONSCIOUSNESS III

Two currently influential writers, Roszak and Reich, have taken positions that place the "youth culture" in numerical perspective, but at the same time extol and glorify those very aspects of youthful alienation that Feuer, Mead, and many other adults are concerned about. Roszak, a historian *(The Making of a Counter Culture),* and Reich, a law professor *(The Greening of America),* concur that revisionist or revolutionary youth comprise only a small minority of young people at present. However, both authors argue at length that radical youth capture what is best in the human spirit, that they are the wave of the future, and that they represent our only hope for survival.

According to Roszak, the counter culture is a revolt against the totalitarian, dehumanizing atmosphere of our contemporary technocracy, a society in which bigness and complexity compel its citizens to defer on all matters to those who know better. The counter culture calls into question the validity of the conventional scientific world view, it denies the existence of an objective consciousness, and it seeks to replace technical and industrial values with a "profoundly personalist sense of community." Roszak's views of the importance of the counter culture and of youth's role in it are unequivocal:

> . . . most of what is presently happening that is new, provocative, and engaging in politics, education, the arts, social relations (love, courtship, family, community), is the creation either of youth who are profoundly, even fanatically, alienated from the parental generation, or of those who address themselves primarily to the young . . . [p. 1]
>
> I am at a loss to know where, besides among these dissenting young people and their heirs of the next few generations, the radical discontent and innovation can be found that might transform this disoriented civilization of ours into something a human being can identify as home. . . . If the resistance of the counter culture fails, I think there will be nothing in store for us but what anti-utopians like Huxley and Orwell have forecast. [pp. xii–xiii]

Reich similarly sees the younger generation as the vanguard of revolt against a "Corporate State" that "dominates, exploits, and ultimately destroys both nature and man.'' The Corporate State is the heir of Consciousness I, which Reich defines as the every-man-for-himself, survival-of-the-fittest mentality, and is rooted in Consciousness II, which surrenders individuality to a dehumanized corporate hierarchy and responsibility to a bureaucracy that is accountable to no one. Consciousness III, which is the key to refurbishing or ''greening'' America so as to bring back our freedom, vigor, humanity, and sense of community, is difficult to define succinctly; Reich says that to describe it systematically and analytically would be to engage in an intellectual process that Consciousness III rejects. Essentially, Consciousness III liberates the person from automatically accepting the imperatives of society and frees him to build his own philosophy and values; it declares that the individual self is the only true reality; it postulates the absolute worth of every human being; and it rejects the concept of excellence and comparative merit by refusing to classify people or evaluate them by general standards (pp. 225–227).

Reich argues vigorously for the transcendental importance of Consciousness III: ''And only Consciousness III can make possible the continued survival of man as a species in this age of technology'' (p. 353). As for the role of youth in this revolution, and the gloriousness of ''youth culture,'' Reich is equally explicit:

> This is the revolution of the new generation. Their protest and rebellion, their culture, clothes, music, drugs, ways of thought, and liberated life-style are not a passing fad or a form of dissent and refusal, nor are they in any sense irrational. The whole emerging pattern, from ideals to campus demonstrations to beads and bell bottoms to the Woodstock Festival, makes sense and is part of a consistent philosophy. It is both necessary and inevitable, and in time it will include not only youth, but all people in America. [p. 4]

It is beyond the scope of this paper to debate the social philosophy advocated by Roszak and Reich. However, both authors extol a certain type of youthful behavior and exhort all young people, and indeed all America, to behave similarly, and in this regard they demonstrate a psychological naiveté that is quite germane to the topic of accurate perspectives on adolescence.

First, Roszak and Reich have an exaggerated impression of the innovativeness and depth of commitment reflected in many aspects of youthful behavior. In the quotation above, Reich includes tastes in clothes and music among adolescent behaviors that express a consistent philosophy and are not a passing fad. Later in his book he elaborates the selection of clothes by young people to express their freedom, affinity with nature, and rejection of affluence, and he pays particular attention to bell-bottom trousers as a means of expressing feelings through the body and giving the ankles freedom ''as if to invite dancing right on the street'' (pp. 234–237). What is missing here is the recognition that most teen-age tastes in clothes, music, and the like are not created *de novo* out of adolescent ingenuity and expressiveness. Rather, they are more often the product of adult inventiveness and opportunism, mainly in the form of entertainers, manufacturers, and promoters who are successful in convincing young people that what the merchandisers have to offer is ''now'' and ''with it.'' That the young decide what kinds of clothes and music they enjoy is neither here nor there. The point is that they are the *consumers* and not the *creators* of taste, and what they choose to consume is likely to change often enough to keep a step ahead of their boredom and satiation and the promoter's slacking profits—just as the bell bottoms with which Reich is enthralled were the pipe-stem jeans of a few years ago, and short skirts were long skirts and were short skirts before that, and the jerk was once the jitterbug, and so forth. Reich appears to feel that current tastes, because they are wedded to a whole new consciousness, are going to be permanent. History and our knowledge of adolescent psychology suggest that he is mistaken.

Second, both Roszak and Reich include among the youthful behaviors they glorify some that clinicians recognize as reflecting psychopathology—psychopathology not merely in the sense of being deviant, but also in the sense of previous interpersonal difficulty and underachievement and a current history of anxiety and depression, identity diffusion, inability to experience intimacy, failure of self-realization, and pervasive unhappiness. Thus Roszak pays tribute to youth "who are profoundly, even fanatically, alienated," and Reich credits psychedelic drugs as being "one of the most important means for restoring dulled consciousness" (p. 258) and lists them as among the necessary and rational elements of the revolution that is to green America. Yet clinicians have identified profound alienation as a symptom of psychological disturbance that may presage personality breakdown (Halleck; Weiner, Chap. 2; Wise), and there is mounting evidence, to be presented shortly, that drug use, aside from its possible harmful effects, is the pastime of the teen-age fringe and not of the masses or the likely leaders of the new generation.

THE VANISHING SPECIES

In striking contrast to writers who deplore the youth culture and all it is presumed to stand for or glorify it as our hope for salvation, other observers define the problems of today's youth as their lack of verve and cultural individuality. This view of contemporary youth was introduced by Friedenberg *(The Vanishing Adolescent),* whose thesis is that adolescent identity formation proceeds mainly through conflict with society, whereas modern technological society idealizes the organization man (Reich's Consciousness II) and has little tolerance for boat rockers. Thus our society no longer fosters "real" adolescents struggling to define themselves, but rather is turning out conformist youngsters homogeneously identified with school and other institutional values, and adolescence as a unique developmental period is becoming obsolete.

The main support for this view of adolescence is provided by Douvan and Adelson, whose research team interviewed a broadly representative sample of over 3,000 teen-agers. Douvan and Adelson concluded from their data that contemporary youth are indeed tending toward homogeneity, with a preference for conformity over conflict, for playing it safe and resisting change rather than experimenting or taking chances, and for premature identity consolidation. They also reported that apparent adolescent rebellion in their subjects consisted primarily of superficial disagreements with their parents about relatively trivial matters—hair length, style of dress, curfews, choice of friends, use of the family car—and did not involve major confrontations, disaffection, or controversy about fundamental standards of conduct and decency.

These data have served as an important corrective to the notion of a normatively alienated youth culture: ''What generation gap?,'' asks Adelson: ''an overwhelming majority of the young—as many as 80%—tend to be traditionalist in values.''[2] However, the implication that adolescents routinely turn out to be stodgy, stilted, overconforming carbon copies of their parents also needs some correction. First, premature identity consolidation does not appear to be any more universal than an identity crisis. Follow-up studies of the teen-agers interviewed by Offer and his colleagues suggest that relatively few adolescents opt for identity foreclosure. Even as 19- and 20-year-olds, the majority of these youngsters still had only a moderate sense of their personal identity and were constructively engaged in role experimentation and self-assessment (Offer, Marcus, and Offer).

Second, identity foreclosure, like identify diffusion, appears to reflect maladjustment rather than normal development when it occurs. In studies of college students, Marcia (1966, 1967) and Marcia and Friedman found significant differences between those who exemplified early identity foreclosure and those who had achieved identity gradually following an extended period of uncertainty about future commitments. Compared to identity achievement youngsters, identity foreclosure subjects were more authoritarian, more likely to set unrealistically high goals for themselves and maintain these goals even in the face of failure, and more vulnerable to experimental manipulations of their self-esteem. Other work suggests that college students with identity foreclosure tend to be less task-oriented and to receive lower grades than students of similar ability who have achieved identity gradually (Cross and Allen).

Third, the incompatibility that Friedenberg postulates between modern society and adolescence as a unique developmental period, whatever its sociological ramifications, makes little psychological sense. No degree of adolescent conformity or homogeneity alters the fact that teen-agers face certain developmental tasks peculiar to their age and that their lives are consequently oriented around different needs, different priorities, and different types of activities than the lives of children and adults. Adjusting to physical sexual maturation, learning to handle dating and heterosexual relationships, gaining psychological independence from parents, and planning one's educational and vocational future are tasks of adolescence that define it as a unique developmental period, regardless of how many youngsters prematurely foreclose their identity.

The uniqueness of adolescence brings us back to the question of the youth culture, and here there are some additional things to be said. Despite empirical evidence to the contrary, the notions of ''adolescent rebellion'' and the ''generation gap'' not only persist in clinical parlance, but also captivate the news media and become fixed in the public mind. The delinquent, the runaway, the addict, the Yippie, the flower person, the unwed mother, the malcontent, and the lost soul make better copy than the youngster who is unobtrusively going about the business of growing up. Likewise, the downtown shopper who see dozens of scraggly, unwashed, and boorish youngsters loitering on the street corners easily loses sight of the thousands who are at that moment sitting in a classroom, practicing with the football team, working at a part-time job, taking a music lesson, or helping around the house.

It is the focus of newspapers, magazines, television, and the movies on what is

[2]Joseph Adelson, *Time,* August 17, 1970, p. 35.

most spectacular and sensational rather than on what is most typical about adolescent behavior, together with the individual memory for what is most shocking and repugnant rather than what is most common and ordinary, that nourish overgeneralized conceptions of adolescent rebellion and the generation gap. Two areas of teen-age behavior that have come in for a lion's share of journalistic overemphasis and adult preoccupation are sex and drug use. A look at recent data in these two areas will further illustrate the need to balance current perspectives on adolescence against the weight of fact.

SEX BEHAVIOR

In this day of increasingly liberal attitudes toward nudity, pornography, and extramarital sexuality, it has become commonplace to accuse our youth in particular of moral decadence. The press dramatizes sexual swingers as if they were representative of all young people, and professional journals compound this fiction by carrying assertions that teen-agers no longer have any regard for virginity (Hurlock), and that premarital intercourse has become a perfunctory aspect of the adolescent dating system (Glassberg).

Such imprecations have little relation to reality. The most thorough assessment of premarital sexual behavior in the United States is provided by Reiss (1967, 1969), who reports that, contrary to widespread belief, there has been no appreciable increase in the proportion of nonvirginity among unmarried young people since the 1920s. Furthermore, the changes toward permissiveness that have taken place in recent years have been closely tied to affection and have neither fostered nor sanctioned promiscuity. Reiss emphasizes that permissiveness without affection has very few followers; unfortunately, however, it makes attractive grist for the popular media mill, and hence the public gets misled as to the number of people who endorse it.

Although Reiss's data and observations pertain to middle-class youngsters, lower-class youngsters hold similar attitudes. Rainwater (1966, 1969) reviews evidence that both lower-class boys and lower-class girls are more likely to have premarital sexual relations than middle-class boys and girls, but that a double standard is the rule among lower-class as well as middle-class youth. Fewer lower-class girls than middle-class boys have had premarital intercourse, and the virginity of lower-class girls is highly valued and protected within their family and peer group.

More recent data from selected samples suggest that the incidence of premarital intercourse among college girls may have risen in the past decade somewhat more than Reiss's earlier impressions. Studies by Kaats and Davis and by Luckey and Nass report a 60% frequency of intercourse among unmarried male college students, which is essentially the same figure that has existed since World War I, but an incidence approaching 40% for a sample consisting primarily of junior and senior co-eds, which represents an increase from the 20–30% figure observed in most studies of college girls during the 1950s and early 1960s. Yet these studies lend no support to the notion that adolescents have rejected virginity and accepted intercourse as a perfunctory aspect of dating.

In the Luckey and Nass study, which involved 1398 students drawn from a representative sample of 21 colleges and universities, 70% of the boys and 40% of the girls said it would "trouble" them to marry a person who had previously had intercourse with someone else. In the Kaats and Davis survey, only 28% of the co-eds felt that their having intercourse, even with someone they loved, would be approved by their friends. And Bell and Chaskes, studying co-eds in a large urban university, found a 39% incidence of premartial intercourse among girls who were engaged, 28% for those who were going steady, and 23% for those who had a dating relationship with their sexual partner.

In general, then, the evidence demonstrates that notions of rampant free love among teen-agers simply do not hold water. Young people have more permissive attitudes toward sex than in the past, but they link this new permissiveness to love and affection. Thus today's youth are more likely than previously to consider sexual intercourse within the context of a close, trusting, exclusive, and relatively enduring relationship, but they continue firm in their rejection of casual, indiscriminate, or promiscuous sexuality.

Two other recent sources of information help to distinguish normative patterns of teen-age sexuality from myths about youthful licentiousness. In a national survey by the Merit Publishing Company of 22,000 high-achieving high school juniors and seniors, 42% indicated their approval of premartial sexual intercourse but only 18% of the boys and 15% of the girls reported having participated in it. Although this sample of able students cannot be taken as representative of all adolescents, it does confirm how far nonvirginity is from being the norm among academically successful teen-agers.

Second, the problem of the unwed teen-age mother has not increased nearly as disproportionately as is commonly supposed. National statistics (U.S. Dept. of HEW) reveal that the rate of illegitimate births in the United States between 1940 and 1967 increased *less* among 15- to 19-year-old girls than for any other age range between 20 and 39. Over this period the illegitimacy rate per 1,000 unmarried women rose from 7.1 to 18.7 among 15- to 19-year-olds, but from 9.5 to 38.6 for 20- to 24-year-olds, from 7.2 to 41.4 for those 25–29, from 5.1 to 29.8 for age 30–34, and from 3.4 to 15.3 for age 35–39.

DRUG USE

There is little question that an increasing number of young people have been attracted to marijuana, amphetamines, LSD, and related drugs in recent years. This upsurge in drug use has led to enormous public concern and widespread belief that taking some sort of drug is fast becoming a universal teen-age fashion. We read in the *New York Times* that on the college campus "marijuana is the common denominator among all groups,"[3] and the Movement to Restore Decency Committee tells us that 25% of young Americans are on drugs and that their numbers are increasing by 7% per month[4] —which would mean 84%, or almost double, each year.

[3]J. Darnton, "Many on Campus Shifting to Softer Drugs and Alcohol," *New York Times*, Jan. 17, 1971.

[4]N. Hober, Letter to the Editor, *Rochester Democrat and Chronicle*, Jan. 9, 1971.

Teen-age drug addiction, when it occurs, is a grave clinical and public concern. However, reliance on less than adequate sampling has inflated the results of many incidence surveys of teen-age drug use, and highly publicized adolescent deaths due to drug overdose have led to exaggerated conclusions about the prevalence of youthful drug abuse. Imperi, Kleber, and Davie demonstrated this kind of discrepancy between fact and impression by comparing the actual incidence of drug use among Yale and Wesleyan students they surveyed with estimates of incidence given by students. The observed incidence was considerably lower than student estimates, and Imperi and her co-authors suggest that students who are involved with drugs overestimate campus use to justify their own behavior—that is, "everybody else is doing it." To the extent that this is the case, journalists who investigate campus drug use by interviewing student drug users will get responses that appear to justify captions like "Smoking Pot a Student Way of Life."

A somewhat different picture of teen-age drug use emerges if one excludes studies with restricted samples and polls reported in newspapers and magazines and looks just at recent large-scale studies done by reliable social scientists. Surveys of 10,364 students attending Sacramento State College (Morrison), 3,010 at Carnegie-Mellon University in Pittsburgh (Goldstein), 2,145 at Ithaca College, New York (Rand), and 26,111 at nine schools in the Denver area (Mizner, Barter, and Werme) indicate that approximately 25% of college students have used marijuana at some time, 12% have used amphetamines, and 5% have tried LSD. Furthermore, of students who report ever having used marijuana, amphetamines, or LSD, 40–50% state that they have stopped using them. In other words, it appears that three-fourths of college students have never tried drugs at all and that only half of those who have tried them have become repetitive users.

At the high school level, observed teen-age drug use has varied with the locale being studied (see table). Among 47,000 high school students in Utah, the reported incidence of any marijuana use was 12.2%, for amphetamine use 10%, and for LSD use 4.9% (Governor's Citizen Advisory Committee on Drugs). For 1,300 high school

Table 5 Percent of High School Students Reporting Any Previous Use of Marijuana, Amphetamines, or LSD

Locale and year	N	Marijuana	Amphetamines	LSD
Utah, 1969[1]	47,182	12.2	10.0	4.9
Montgomery County, Md., 1970[2]	1,348	18.7	7.8	5.9
Madison, Wis., 1969[3]	781	22.6	5.4	5.8
Suburban New York City, 1971[4]	1,704	24.0	12.0	10.0
San Mateo County, Cal., 1970[5]	25,756	42.9	20.0	14.4

[1] See Governor's Citizen Advisory Committee on Drugs.
[2] See Joint Committee on Drug Abuse.
[3] See Udell and Smith.
[4] See Tec.
[5] See San Mateo County Dept. of Public Health and Welfare.

youngsters in Montgomery County, Maryland (Joint Committee on Drug Abuse) and 800 in Madison, Wisconsin (Udell and Smith), about one fifth had tried marijuana; less than 8%, amphetamines; and less than 6%, LSD. For 1,704 respondents in a suburban New York City community, representing over 90% of that community's 15- to 18-year-old population, the rates of previous use were 24% for marijuana, 12% for amphetamines, and 10% for LSD (Tec). And in San Mateo County, California, 25,756 high school students reported previous use rates of 42.9% for marijuana, 20% for amphetamines, and 14.4% for LSD (San Mateo County Dept. of Public Health and Welfare). For high school as well as for college students, however, these reports of ever having used a drug do not necessarily indicate current use. In the Montgomery County study, for example, almost 40% of the youngsters who had used marijuana or LSD had quit after trying them, and two thirds of those who had experimented with amphetamines had never used them again.

The San Mateo County merits further comment in two respects: (1) it is the only large-scale study that has surveyed youthful drug use in the same population in three successive years—1968, 1969, and 1970—and provided comparisons over these years; and (2) the three-year data from the study indicate a leveling-off or decline in drug use rates. From 1968 to 1969 the San Mateo youngsters' reported incidence of any drug use during the previous year increased by 7.6% for marijuana, 4.3% for amphetamines, and 4.2% for LSD. For 1969 to 1970, however, the percent of reported use increased only 2.5% for marijuana and *decreased* for both amphetamines (by 0.9%) and LSD (by 1.5%). These changes may not be reliable enough to indicate a permanent downward trend in drug use. However, as Richards and Carroll point out in discussing these San Mateo data, west coast schools were the first to experience the onslaught of drug use, and the 1970 findings may well presage a general stabilization or rates of declining student interest in drugs.

Finally, in addition to demonstrating a lower rate of teen-age drug use than is commonly supposed, available data also indicate that drugs have relatively little appeal for well-adjusted youngsters. In a study of almost 9,000 junior and senior high school students drawn from throughout Metropolitan Toronto, Smart, Fejer, and White consistently found that the youngsters who were most likely to be using drugs were those who were doing least well academically, were least involved in school activities, and were most inclined to spend their evenings and weekends hanging around with friends rather than in organized activities.

This indication that the small minority of teen-agers who use drugs consists primarily of fringe youngsters who are not doing well in the classroom or in extracurricular activities is supported by the rates of marijuana use among the 22,000 able high school juniors and seniors in the Merit survey. These academically successful youngsters showed regional differences similar to those reflected in the Utah, Maryland, New York, and California studies, but in each case their incidence figures were lower than those for the general high school population. They reported higher rates of marijuana use in northeastern (15%) and western (13%) states than in the midwest (8%), south (5%), and southwest (5%), and their marijuana use was more common in suburban (13%) and urban (10%) communities than in rural and small-town America (5%).

In concluding this brief overview of teen-age drug use, I must report on the usual reaction when I present these kinds of data to professional colleagues: "Very interesting; but of course we know that drug use is a pervasive and spreading phenomenon, and there are probably other studies that show this more fully." But there is no such cache of "other studies" that I have steadfastly chosen to ignore or carelessly managed to overlook. I have kept reasonably abreast of the literature and have made use of current compilations of studies graciously supplied by the Drug Abuse Center of the National Institute of Mental Health (Berg). It seems to me that behavioral scientists may share with the general public some difficulty in hearing facts about teen-agers that conflict with impressions they have formed on some other basis.

I do not wish to minimize the presence and potential seriousness of drug abuse problems in substantial numbers of young people. However, I do wish to make the point that a proper perspective on drug use must be maintained so that (1) the use of drugs is not considered a normative feature of growing up in modern times and (2) the drug-abusing adolescent is recognized as a confused, disturbed, and probably alienated young person in need of professional help.

For a generally balanced perspective on the modern adolescent, then, it is necessary to recognize that he belongs neither to a rebellious youth culture nor to an overconfirming vanishing species; that the manner in which groups of young people approach the developmental tasks of adolescence often makes them as different from each other as they are from adults; and that alienation, protest, sexual promiscuity, and drug abuse are neither normal nor normative patterns of adolescent behavior, and assertions to the contrary suffuse reality with myth.

REFERENCES

Bell, Robert R., and Chaskes, Jay B. "Premarital Sexual Experience Among Coeds, 1958 and 1968," *J. Marriage and Family* (1970) **32**:81–84.

Berg, Dorothy F. "Illicit Use of Dangerous Drugs in the United States: A Compilation of Studies, Surveys, and Polls," Bureau of Narcotics and Dangerous Drugs, U.S. Dept. of Justice, 1970.

Block, Jeanne H., Haan, Norma, and Smith, M. Brewster. "Activism and Apathy in Contemporary Adolescents," in J. F. Adams (Ed.), *Understanding Adolescence: Current Developments in Adolescent Psychology;* Allyn and Bacon, 1968.

Coleman, James S. *The Adolescent Society;* Free Press, 1961.

Cross, Herbert J., and Allen, Jon G. "Ego Identity Status, Adjustment, and Academic Achievement," *J. Consulting and Clin. Psychology* (1970) **34**:288.

Douvan, Elizabeth, and Adelson, Joseph. *The Adolescent Experience;* Wiley, 1966.

Feuer, Lewis S. *The Conflict of Generations;* Basic Books, 1969.

Friedenberg, Edgar Z. *The Vanishing Adolescent;* Beacon, 1959.

Glassberg, B. Y. "Sexual Behavior Patterns in Contemporary Youth Culture: Implications for Later Marriage," *J. Marriage and Family* (1965) **27**:190–192.

Goldstein, Joel W. "The Social Psychology of Student Drug Use: Report on Phase One," Carnegie-Mellon Univ. Drug Research Project, June, 1970.

Governor's Citizen Advisory Committee on Drugs, State of Utah. "Drug Use Among High School Students in the State of Utah," Sept., 1969.

Halleck, Seymour L. "Psychiatric Treatment of Alienated College Student," *Amer. J. Psychiatry* (1967) **124**:642–650.

Hurlock, Elizabeth, B. "American Adolescents Today—A New Species," *Adolescence* (1966) **1**:17–21.

Imperi, Lillian L., Kleber, Herbert D., and Davie, James S. "Use of Hallucinogenic Drugs on Campus," *J. Amer. Med. Assn.* (1968) **204**:1021–1024.

Joint Committee on Drug Abuse, Montgomery County, Md. "A Survey of Secondary School Students' Perceptions of and Attitudes Toward Use of Drugs by Teenagers," Final Report, March 10, 1970.

Kaats, Gilbert R., and Davis, Keith E. "The Dynamics of Sexual Behavior of College Students," *J. Marriage and Family* (1970) **32**:390–399.

Keniston, Kenneth. *The Uncommitted: Alienated Youth in American Society;* Harcourt, Brace, & World, 1961.

Lipset, Seymour M., and Raab, Ernst. "The Non-Generation Gap," *Commentary* (1970) **50**:35–39.

Luckey, Eleanore B., and Nass, Gilbert D. "A Comparison of Sexual Attitudes and Behavior in an International Sample," *J. Marriage and Family* (1969) **31**:364–379.

Marcia, James E. "Development and Validation of Ego-Identity Status," *J. Personality and Social Psychology* (1966) **3**:551–558.

Marcia, James E. "Ego Identity Status: Relationship to Change in Self-Esteem, 'General Adjustment,' and Authoritarianism," *J. Personality* (1967) **35**:119–133.

Marcia, James E., and Friedman, Meredith L. "Ego Identity Status in College Women," *J. Personality (1970)* **38**:249–263.

Mead, Margaret. *Culture and Commitment: A Study of the Generation Gap;* Doubleday, 1970.

Merit Publishing Co. *National Survey of High School High Achievers,* 1970.

Mizner, George L., Barter, James T., and Werme, Paul H. "Patterns of Drug Use Among College Students: A Preliminary Report," *Amer. J. Psychiatry* (1970) **127**:15–24.

Morrison, Richard L. "Preliminary Report on the Incidence of the Use of Drugs at Sacramento State College," Sacramento State College, May 15, 1969.

Offer, Daniel. *The Psychological World of the Teenager;* Basic Books, 1969.

Offer, Daniel, Marcus, David, and Offer, Judith L. "A Longitudinal Study of Normal Adolescent Boys," *Amer. J. Psychiatry* (1970) **126**:917–924.

Pearson, Gerald H. *Adolescence and the Conflict of Generations;* Norton, 1958.

Rainwater, Lee. "Some Aspects of Lower Class Sexual Behavior," *Social Issues* (1966) **22**:96–108.

Rainwater, Lee. "Sex in the Culture of Poverty," in C. B. Broderick and J. Bernard (Eds.), *The Individual, Sex, and Society;* Johns Hopkins Press, 1969.

Rand, Martin E. "A Survey of Drug Use at Ithaca College," presented at the Amer. College Health Assn. Annual Convention, May, 1968.

Reich, Charles A. *The Greening of America;* Random House, 1970.

Reiss, Ira L. *The Social Context of Premarital Sexual Permissiveness;* Holt, Rinehart & Winston, 1967.

Reiss, Ira L. "Premarital Sexual Standards," in C. B. Broderick and J. Bernard (Eds.), *The Individual, Sex, and Society;* Johns Hopkins Press, 1969.

Richards, Louise G., and Carroll, Eleanor E. "Illicit Drug Use and Addiction in the United States," *Public Health Reports* (1970) **85**:1035–1041.

Roszak, Theodore. *The Making of a Counter Culture;* Doubleday, 1969.

San Mateo County Dept. of Public Health and Welfare. "Five Mind-Altering Drugs," Research and Statistics Section, 1969.

San Mateo County Dept. of Public Health and Welfare. "Five Mind-Altering Drugs (Plus One)," Research and Statistics Section, 1970.

Smart, Reginald G., Fejer, Dianne, and White, Jim. "The Extent of Drug Use in Metropolitan

Toronto Schools: A Study of Changes from 1968 to 1970,'' Toronto, Addiction Research Foundation, 1970.

Tec, Nechama. ''Drugs Among Suburban Teenagers: Basic Findings,'' *Social Science and Medicine* (1970) **5**:77–84.

Udell, Jon G., and Smith, Robert S. ''Attitudes, Usage, and Availability of Drugs among Madison High School Students,'' Univ. of Wis. Bureau of Business Research and Service, 1969.

U.S. Dept. of Health, Education and Welfare. *Vital Statistics of the United States, 1967,* Vol. 1, *Natality;* Govt. Printing Office.

Weiner, Irving B. *Psychological Disturbance in Adolescence;* Wiley-Interscience, 1970.

Wise, Louis J. ''Alienation of Present-Day Adolescents,'' *J. Amer. Academy of Child Psychiatry* (1970) **9**:264–277.

Black Youth and Motivation*

Alvin Poussaint and Carolyn Atkinson

The civil rights movement of the 1960's in America spawned a new and vibrant generation of young black people. The degree of their commitment and determination came as a surprise for most white Americans, who, if they thought of blacks to any extent, considered them to be a rather docile, acquiescent people. As the events of the early 60's moved on with inexorable force, another, still younger generation of blacks stood on the periphery watching and waiting their turn. Their intense coming-of-age has brought still more surprise and puzzlement not only to white Americans, but to some Negroes. So busy have many been in ''handling'' or ''coping with'' the complex behavior of these young blacks, that relatively little has been done in terms of examining the basis for this behavior. This paper represents an attempt to pause in the on-going melee for an exploration of some of the factors of particular relevance to the motivation of Afro-American youth. Our analysis will focus on some of the ''problem areas'' so of necessity will not detail the many strengths and positive features of the black socio-cultural environment. Of primary interest in our discussion will be the areas of internal motivation: the individual's self-concept; certain of his patterned needs; and the external motivators: the rewards offered by society for satisfactory performance in any of its institutional areas.

Of obvious importance to the functioning of any individual is his concept or vision of himself. And like it or not, this concept is inevitably a part of how others see him, how others tell him he should be seen. According to Mead,[1] Cooley,[2] and others,[3] the self arises through the individual's interaction with and reaction to other members of society: his peers, parents, teachers and other institutional representatives. Through

*From Alvin Poussaint and Carolyn Atkinson, "Black Youth and Motivation," *The Black Scholar*, March, 1970, 43–51. Reprinted by permission of the authors and the Editor, *The Black Scholar.*

[1]George H. Mead, *Mind, Self, and Society,* Chicago: University of Chicago Press, 1934, Part III.
[2]Charles H. Cooley, *Human Nature and the Social Order,* Glencoe, Ill: Free Press, 1956, passim.
[3]*Sociological Quarterly* (entire issue), Vol. 7, No. 3, Summer, 1966.

identification and as a necessary means of effective communication, the child learns to assume the roles and attitudes of others with whom he interacts. These assumed attitudes condition not only how he responds to others, but how he behaves towards himself. The collective attitudes of the others, the community or "generalized other" as Mead calls them, gives the individual his unity of self. The individual's self is shaped, developed and controlled by his anticipating and assuming the attitudes and definitions of others (the community) toward him. To the extent that the individual is a member of this community, its attitudes are his, its values are his, and its norms are his. His image of himself is structured in these terms. Each self, then, though having its unique characteristics of personality, is also an individual reflection of the social process.[4] This idea can be seen more succinctly illustrated in Cooley's suggestion of the self as a looking-glass, a looking-glass mirroring the three principal components of one's self-concept: "the imagination of our appearance to the other person; the imagination of his judgment of that appearance; and some sort of self-feeling, such as pride or mortification."[5]

For the black youth in white American society, the generalized other whose attitudes he assumes and the looking-glass into which he gazes both reflect the same judgment: he is inferior because he is black. His self-image, developed in the lowest stratum of a color caste system, is shaped, defined, and evaluated by a generalized other which is racist or warped by racists. His self-concept naturally becomes a negatively esteemed one, nurtured through contact with such institutionalized symbols of caste inferiority as segregated schools, neighborhoods, and jobs and more indirect negative indicators such as the reactions of his own family who have been socialized to believe that they are sub-standard human beings. Gradually becoming aware of the meaning of his black skin, the Negro child comes to see himself as an object of scorn and disparagement, unworthy of love and affection. The looking-glass of white society reflects the supposed undesirability of the black youth's physical appearance: black skin and wooly hair, as opposed to the valued models of white skin and straight hair. In order to gain the esteem of the generalized other, it becomes clear to him that he must approximate this white appearance as closely as possible. He learns to despise himself and to reject those like himself. From the moment of this realization, his personality and style of interaction with his environment become molded and shaped in a warped, self-hating, and self-denigrating way. He learns that existence for him in this society demands a strict adherence to the limitations of his sub-standard state. He comes to understand that to challenge the definition the others have given of him will destroy him. It is impressed upon him that the incompetent, acquiescent and irresponsible Negro survives in American society, while the competent, aggressive black is systematically suppressed. The looking-glass of the black youth's self reflects a shattered and defeated image.

Several attempts have been made to determine how this shattered self-concept affects the black child's ability to function in society, his ability to achieve, to succeed or

[4]Mead, *op. cit.*
[5]Cooley, *op. cit.*, p. 184.

"make good," particularly in the area of education. Though the conclusions of these varied attempts have differed on occasion, there has been general agreement as to the reality of the black child's incomplete self-image.[6,7,8] One notable exception to this agreement, however, is the Coleman Report, a 1966 study by the United States Office of Education on the "Equality of Education Opportunity."[9] This report maintains that the black child's self-concept has not been exceptionally damaged, and is in fact virtually no different from that of a white child. The report did, however, note that the white child is consistently able to achieve on a higher level than that of his black counterpart. The Coleman Study, therefore, concluded that self-concept has little to do with an individual's ability to achieve.[10] Other studies tend to disagree with these findings.

Another variation on this theme of the black child's self-concept is seen in a 1968 report on "Academic Motivation and Equal Educational Opportunity" done by Irwin Katz. Katz found that black children tended to have exaggeratedly high aspirations, so high, in fact, that they were realistically impossible to live up to. As a result, these children were able to achieve very little:

> Conceivably, their (low achieving Negro boys') standards were so stringent and rigid as to be utterly dysfunctional. They seem to have internalized a most effective mechanism for self-discouragement. In a sense, they had been socialized to self-impose failure.[11]

Katz presents evidence which indicates that the anticipation of failure or harsh judgment by adults produces anxiety in the child, and that in black children, this level of anxiety is highest in low achievers who have a high standard of self-evaluation.[12] Accordingly, a black child with an unrealistically elevated self-concept often tends to become so anxious concerning his possible failure to meet that self-concept that he does in fact fail consistently.

On the other hand, Deutsch's work has shown that Negro children had significantly more negative self-images than did white children.[13] He maintains that, among the influences converging on the black urban child,

[6]Poussaint, A. F., "The Dynamics of Racial Conflict," *Lowell Lecture Series,* sponsored by Tufts–New England Medical Center, April 16, 1968.

[7]Joan Gordon, *The Poor of Harlem: Social Functioning in the Underclass,* Report to the Welfare Administration, Washington, D.C., July 31, 1965, pp. 115 and 161 and Irwin Katz, "Academic Motivation and Equal Educational Opportunity," *Harvard Educational Review,* Vol. 38, Winter, 1968, pp. 56-65.

[8]While we recognize the limitations of many measures of self-concept and that self-concept is often defined by how it is measured, an exploration of these considerations within the scope of this paper is clearly impossible. Therefore for the purpose of our presentation here, we are taking the measures of self-concept at face-value.

[9]James S. Coleman and others. *Equality of Educational Opportunity,* U.S. Office of Education, Government Printing Office: Washington, D.C., 1966, p. 281.

[10]*Ibid.,* p. 320.

[11]Katz, *op. cit.,* p. 60.

[12]*Ibid.,* pp. 61–62.

[13]Martin Deutsch, "Minority Groups and Class Status as Related to Social and Personality Factors in Scholastic Achievement," in Martin Deutsch and Associates, *The Disadvantaged Child,* New York: Basic Books, Inc., 1967, p. 106.

> . . . is his sensing that the larger society views him as inferior and *expects* inferior performance from him as evidenced by the general denial to him of realistic vertical mobility possibilities. Under these conditions, it is understandable that the Negro child would tend strongly to question his own competencies and in so questioning would be acting largely as others expect him to act, an example of what Merton has called the "self-fulfilling prophecy" — the very expectation itself is a cause of its fulfillment.[14]

Similarly, Coombs and Davies offer the important proposition that:

> In the context of the school world, a student who is defined as a "poor student" (by significant others and thereby by self) comes to conceive of himself as such and gears his behavior accordingly, that is, the social expectation is realized. However, if he is led to believe by means of the social "looking-glass" that he is capable and able to achieve well, he does. To maintain his status and self-esteem becomes the incentive for further effort which subsequently involves him more in the reward system of the school.[15]

These views have been confirmed in such studies as that of Davidson and Greenberg.[16] In their examination of children from Central Harlem, these authors found that the lower the level of self-esteem, the lower the level of achievement; while consequently, higher levels of self-appraisal and ego strength — feelings of self-competence — were associated with higher levels of achievement. For example, high achievers were more able to give their own ideas and to express basic needs, suggesting that a stronger self-concept is associated with a greater willingness to risk self-expression, an obvious prerequisite for achievement.

Certainly these various studies cannot be considered as ultimately nor unanimously conclusive. However, it is important to note that none of these reports has found any evidence of high achievement resulting from a low self-concept. Obviously the black child with such a low self-concept competes at a disadvantage with white youth in the struggle to achieve in this society.

The question then arises as to why black youth bother to involve themselves at all in this struggle. If their negative self image handicaps them so greatly in achieving, why not simply abdicate and in fact adhere to society's definition of them as sub-standard? An attempted response to this question moves us into another area, that of patterned needs.

In the course of the socialization process, the individual acquires needs which motivate behavior and generate emotions. Three such needs concern us here: the need for achievement, the need for self-assertion or aggression, and the need for approval.

Among the attitudes of the generalized other which the individual in this society internalizes are the norms and values of the wider community, including, of course, the major tenets of the Protestant Ethic-American creed, i.e., with hard work and effort the individual can achieve success, and the individual's worth is defined by his ability

[14] *Ibid.*, p. 107.

[15] R. H. Coombs and V. Davies, "Self-Conception and the Relationship between High School and College Scholastic Achievement," *Sociology and Social Research*, Vol. 50, July, 1966, pp. 468–469.

[16] Helen H. Davidson and Judith W. Greenberg, *Traits of School Achievers from a Deprived Background*, New York: City College of the City University of New York, May 1967, pp. 133, 134.

to achieve that success. The individual who internalizes these values is motivated to act consistently with them, as his self-esteem is heightened or maintained through behaving in a manner approved by the community. Thus, the need for achievement develops in both white and black Americans. Consequently, the black youth's participation in the struggle for success is at least in part an attempt to satisfy his own needs.

This need to achieve may be very high as illustrated in the findings of Coleman[17] and Katz[18] who note the exceptionally high aspirations of Negro youth with regard to schooling and occupational choice. In addition, Katz[19] and Gordon[20] indicate that the aspirations and demands for academic achievement of the parents of these youth are also often exceptionally high. All of these sources agree, however, that the achievement of these youth is far from commensurate with either their own aspirations or those of their parents.[21] Thus, the problem does not seem to be, as some have suggested, one of insufficiently high levels of aspiration, but rather one of realizing these aspirations through productive behavior.[22] Gordon[23] and Katz[24] suggest that this discrepancy persists because the educational and occupational values and goals of white society have been internalized by black youth, but for one reason or another, the behavior patterns necessary for their successful attainment have not been similarly learned. Katz puts it succinctly:

> Apparently the typical Negro mother tries to socialize her child for scholastic achievement by laying down verbal rules and regulations about classroom (behavior), coupled with punishment of detected transgressions. But she does not do enough to guide and encourage her child's efforts at verbal-symbolic mastery. Therefore, the child learns only to verbalize standards of academic interest and attainment. These standards then provide the cognitive basis for negative self-evaluations . . . The low achieving Negro student learns to use expressions of interest and ambition as a verbal substitute for behaviors he is unable to enact . . . By emphasizing the discrepancy between the real and ideal performance, anxiety is raised in actual achievement situations.[25]

Thus, the black child's negative self-concept is further complicated by his internalization of white society's high-level goals, and the need to achieve them, without a true comprehension of how effectively to do so.

Further examination of the values of the Protestant Ethic leads to the conclusion that they imply that assertion of self and aggression is an expected and admired form of behavior. Through the socialization process, the individual internalizes those attitudes which reinforce his basic need to assert himself or express himself aggressively. Thus, random and possibly destructive aggression is channeled into a legitimate and rewarded avenue of achievement.[26]

[17]Coleman, *op. cit.,* pp. 278–280.
[18]Katz, *op. cit.,* p. 64.
[19]*Ibid.,* pp. 63–65.
[20]Gordon, *op. cit.,* p. 115.
[21]Coleman, *op. cit.,* p. 281; Katz, *op. cit.,* p. 63; Gordon, *op. cit.,* pp. 155, 160–161.
[22]David P. Ausubel and Pearl Ausubel, "Ego Development Among Segregated Negro Children," in A. Harry Passow, ed., *Education in Depressed Areas,* New York: Teachers College Press, 1963, p. 135.
[23]Gordon, *op. cit.,* pp. 115, 161.
[24]Katz, *op. cit.,* p. 63.
[25]*Ibid.,* p. 64.
[26]Davidson and Greenberg, *op. cit.,* p. 58.

What happens to the black child's need for aggression and self-assertion? What has been the nature of his socialization with respect to expressing aggression? Since slavery days and, to some extent, through the present, the Negro most rewarded by whites has been the "Uncle Tom," the exemplar of the black man who was docile and non-assertive, who bowed and scraped for the white boss and denied his aggressive feelings for his oppressor. In order to retain the most menial of jobs and keep from starving, black people quickly learned that passivity was a necessary survival technique. To be an "uppity nigger" was considered by racists one of the gravest violations of racial etiquette. Vestiges of this attitude remain to the present day, certainly in the South, but also in the North: blacks who are too "outspoken" about racial injustices often lose their jobs or are not promoted to higher positions because they are considered "unreasonable" or "too sensitive." It is significant that the civil rights movement had to adopt passive-resistance and non-violence in order to win acceptance by white America. Thus, the black child is socialized to the lesson taught by his parents, other blacks, and white society: don't be aggressive, don't be assertive. Such lessons do not, however, destroy the need for aggression and self-assertion.

One asserts oneself for self-expression, for achievement of one's goals, and for control of one's environment. Thus, an individual's success in satisfying his need for self-assertion is to some degree determined by his sense of control of his environment. Coleman found that the three attitudes measured, sense of control over environment showed the strongest relationship to achievement.[27] He further discovered that blacks have a much lower sense of control over their environment than do whites,[28] but that this sense of control increased as the proportion of whites with whom they went to school increased.[29] These findings indicate that for blacks, a realistic inability for meaningful self-assertion is a greater inhibitor of ability to achieve than is any other variable. These findings also suggest, however, that when blacks are interacting in a school situation which approximates the world in which they must cope, i.e., one with whites, their sense of control and achievement increases. Our emphasis here is not that black students' being in the presence of white students increases their sense of control and level of achievement, but that their being in a proximate real world suggests to them that they can cope in any situation, not just one in which they are interacting with others who, like themselves, have been defined as inferior.

Coleman's findings are supported by those of Davidson and Greenberg: high achievers were more able to exercise control and to cope more effectively with feelings of hostility and anxiety generated by the environment than were low achievers.[30] Deutsch points out that black male children for whom aggressive behavior has always been more threatening (compared with black girls) have lower levels of achievement on a number of variables than do black girls.[31] It is not surprising then that black people, objectively less able to control their environment than can whites, may react in abdicating control by deciding not to assert themselves. The reasons for this are clear. First, the anxiety that accompanies growth and change through self-assertion is

[27]Coleman, *op. cit.*, p. 319.
[28]*Ibid.*, p. 289.
[29]*Ibid.*, pp. 323–324.
[30]Davidson and Greenberg, *op. cit.*, p. 54.
[31]Deutsch, *op. cit.*, p. 108.

avoided if a new failure is not risked and thus, a try is not made. Second, the steady state of failure through non-achievement rather than through unsuccessful trial is a pattern which many blacks have come to know and expect. They feel psychologically comfortable with the more familiar.

However, this effort by black people to deny their need for control and self-assertion inevitably takes its toll. Frustration of efforts to control the environment are likely to lead to anger, rage and other expressions of aggression.[32] This aggression can be dealt with in a variety of ways. It can be suppressed, leading one to act on the basis of a substitute and opposing emotional attitude, i.e., compliance or docility. It can be channeled through legitimate activities — dancing, sports, or through an identification with the oppressor and a consequent striving to be like him. Aggression can also be turned inward and expressed in psychosomatic illness, drug addiction, or the attacking of those like oneself (other blacks) whom one hates as much as oneself. Or aggression can be directed toward those who generate the anger and rage — the oppressors, those whom the individual defines as thwarting this inclination to self-assertion. This final form of aggression can be either destructive or constructive: dropping out of school or becoming delinquent are examples of the former case, while participation in black social action movements is an example of the latter instance. This latter form of aggressive behavior amongst black people is increasing in extent. The old passivity is fading and being replaced by a drive to undo powerlessness, helplessness and dependency under American racism. The process is a difficult one for those black people who manage to make the attempt. For their aggressive drive, so long suppressed by the ruling power structure, is exercised to the inevitable detriment of still another exigency: their need for approval.

With the development of the self and through the process of identification, the individual's need for approval develops and grows as does his need to avoid disapproval.[33] As we have stated earlier, the Protestant Ethic of American society approves behavior which follows the achievement motive and expresses the need for self-assertion. An individual's behavior in accordance with this ethic is often tied to a need for approval. On the other hand, for blacks in American society, the reverse is often the case, i.e., behavior which is neither achievement-oriented nor self-assertive is often approved by both blacks and whites (for different reasons), and thus, the need for approval may be met through behavior unrelated to either achievement or self-assertion.

Katz's study maintains that in lower-class black homes, children do not learn realistic (middle class) standards of self-appraisal and therefore do not develop (as do middle class children) the capacity for gaining "satisfaction through self-approval of successful performance."[34] Accordingly, Katz suggests that achievement should be motivated and rewarded by approval not from the home, but from fellow students and teachers.[35] The extent to which black children are responsive to approval for achieve-

[32]Alvin F. Poussaint, "A Negro Psychiatrist Explains the Negro Psyche," *New York Times Magazine*, August 20, 1967, pp. 58–80.

[33]Davidson and Greenberg, *op. cit.*, p. 61.

[34]Katz, *op. cit.*, p. 57.

[35]*Ibid.*

ment in middle class terms is, however, problematic. Some evidence suggests that lower class black children are motivated to gain approval through physical characteristics and prowess rather than through intellectual achievement as are middle class white and black children.[36] Further, needs for approval, not often met in black children through the established institutional channels, may be met by others outside of these legitimate institutional areas. For instance, delinquent sub-cultures support and encourage the behavior of their members. As a result, such members are not often sensitive to the informal sanctions imposed by non-members of this sub-society.[37] If an individual's needs are not met by others to whose sanctions he is expected to be responsive, he will be less likely to fear their sanctions for non-performance and will seek to have his needs met by others to whose rewards of approval he will then be responsive.[38] Thus, for black youth no less than others, how the need for approval motivates behavior depends in large part upon how it is satisfied or rewarded.

The rewards which the institutions of this society offer to those whose behavior meets their approval or is "successful" consist of money, prestige, power, respect, acclamation, and love, with increasing amounts of each of these being extended for increasingly "successful" behavior. The individual is socialized to know that these will be his if he performs according to expectations. Hence, these rewards act as external motivators of behavior. Blacks have learned of the existence of these rewards. They have also learned, however, that behavior for which whites reap these rewards does not result in the same consequences for them. In the various institutional areas of society, blacks are often rewarded differentially from whites for the same behavior — if they are rewarded at all. How then can such a highly capricious system motivate their behavior?

That blacks orient some aspects of their behavior to society's reward system is evidenced by the fact that many studies have shown that lower class blacks, as opposed to middle class whites and blacks, have a utilitarian attitude toward education, viewing it primarily in terms of its market value.[39] The system provides no assurance, however, that once they obtain the proper education for a job, that they will in fact be allowed to get that job. This inability to trust society to confer rewards consistently no doubt makes it difficult for blacks to be socialized to behave in terms of anticipating future reward for present activity. Thus, it is that Deutsch found that young black children are unwilling to persist in attempting to solve difficult problems. They respond to such situations with a "who cares" attitude.[40] Similarly, another study showed that when a tangible reward was offered for successful work on a test, the motivation of the deprived youngsters increased considerably.[41] In a New York program, young men who had been working primarily as clerks and porters were motivated to join a tutorial program for admission to a construction trade union apprenticeship program when they

[36]Edmund W. Gordon and Doxey A. Wilkerson, *Compensatory Education for the Disadvantaged*, New York: College Entrance Examination Board, 1966, p. 18.

[37]Claude Brown, *Manchild in the Promised Land*, New York: Macmillan Company, 1965, passim.

[38]Talcott Parsons, *The Social System*, Glencoe, Ill.: The Free Press, 1951, Ch. 7.

[39]Gordon and Wilkerson, *op. cit.*, p. 18.

[40]Deutsch, *op. cit.*, p. 102.

[41]Elizabeth Douvan, "Social Status and Success Striving," cited in Frank Riessman, *The Culturally Deprived Child*, New York: Harper and Row, 1962, p. 53.

were promised that successful completion of the program (passing the union's examination) would definitely result in their being hired immediately at a salary often double what they were able to command previously.[42]

However, motivation to achieve certain rewards may have different consequences for behavior. As Merton explained, when the goals of society are internalized without a corresponding internalization of normative means for achieving these goals, what often results is the resort to illegitimate (deviant) means to achieve the socially valued goals.[43]

Just as a child unable to satisfy his need for approval through legitimate channels may turn to delinquent sub-cultures for support and encouragement, so too might such a child, unable to gain society's rewards by legitimate means, turn to illegitimate methods in order to attain them. Such forms of behavior as numbers running, dope pushing, and prostitution effectively serve to net the rewards of society. while circumventing the institutional channels for achievement of societal rewards. That Negro children early learn that such behavior is rewarded is suggested by Gordon's study in which young (9–13) Central Harlem boys were asked if they knew people who had become rich, and if so, how they thought they had managed to do so. Of those who responded affirmatively, a majority felt that they had become rich through illegitimate means or luck.[44]

Consequently, for many black youth, external rewards are weak motivators of behavior, as they are discriminatorily and inconsistently given. The more immediate and direct the reward is, the stronger a motivator it is likely to be.

It would appear from this analysis that the standards and rewards of white American society simply do not work effectively to motivate productive behavior in young blacks. Clearly there is urgent need for a fundamental restructuring of the system. First, with respect to self-concept, all institutional segments of society must begin to function in a non-racist manner. To the extent that the self is shaped with reference to a generalized other, to that extent will the black child's image be impaired as long as America remains racist. The growth of black consciousness and pride have had salutary consequences for the black's self-image. But this alone is not sufficient. The operation of self-image as a motivator for behavior is like a self-fulfilling prophecy: blacks are continuously told and some believe that they are inferior and will fail. Therefore, they fail. For the black child to be motivated to achieve in school, the school must negate everything that the society affirms: it must tell the child that he can succeed — and he will.[45]

The relationship between self-concept and achievement is not clear-cut, but it appears to be a weaker motivator of behavior than the motive to self-assertion and aggression. More attention should be given to examining this dimension of personality as a motivator of the black youth's behavior than to continuing inquiries into his self-image. It has been noted that the black youth's sense of control of his environment increases as the proportion of whites in his school increases. It is imperative to keep

[42]Personal Communication (C.A.)

[43]Robert K. Merton, *Social Theory and Social Structure,* Glencoe, Ill.: The Free Press, 1957. Ch. 4.

[44]Gordon, *op. cit.,* p. 164.

[45]Kenneth B. Clark, *Dark Ghetto,* New York: Harper and Row, 1965, pp. 139–148.

in mind, however, that participation in all-or-predominantly-black structures need not be self-destructive if the black youth chooses rather than is forced to participate in them. For if he chooses, he is asserting control over his environment. Those structural changes being made in American society in the direction of blacks having the opportunity to be more aggressively in control of their environment must be continued and expanded. The plans to decentralize New York City schools, to develop black business, and to organize and channel black political power are significant steps in this direction.

Most of the data indicate that black youth and their parents have high educational and occupational aspirations, which are not carried through to achievement levels. The reward systems of American society are often irrelevant to the lives and aspirations of most black youth. Approval is rewarded primarily for forms of behavior in which the black youth has managed to achieve little proficiency, making him less likely to make the effort. Something is obviously wrong with any school system which permits so much young potential to be wasted simply because it cannot be developed within the confines of traditional methods. New frameworks must be developed which will enable the educational aspirations of black youth to correspond to their interests and proficiencies. With the establishment of a pattern of consistent reward, there is every possibility that intellectual endeavors would have immediate relevance to their lives.

Certainly these suggested changes are sweeping, but so too have been the dangerous effects of the maintenance of the old systems. The time for being surprised at the behavior of black youth has passed. The time for lengthy, nonproductive attempts at understanding them has too, in its turn, come to an end. The time remaining must be effectively used in action to bring about these and similar changes. America cannot afford to wait for the next generation.

Sex Roles, Marital Status, and Mental Illness*

Walter R. Gove

In a recent paper Gove and Tudor (1972) looked at the proportion of men and women who were mentally ill in modern industrial societies as indicated by community surveys, first admissions to mental hospitals, psychiatric treatment in general hospitals, psychiatric outpatient clinics, private outpatient psychiatric care, and psychiatric illness in the practices of general physicians. All of these sources indicated that women are more likely to be mentally ill than men

As most studies indicate that never married and formerly married persons have higher rates of mental illness than those who are married, one might expect that the difference between the rates of men and women could be attributed to unmarried women having extremely high rates of mental illness. This would conform to the stereotype of the carefree bachelor and the rejected spinster (or former wife). However,

*From Walter R. Gove, "The Relationship Between Sex Roles, Marital Status, and Mental Illness," *Social Forces*, 1972, **51**, 34–44. Reprinted by permission of the author and the Editor, *Social Forces*.

in this article I will indicate that this expectation is incorrect and that it is the relatively high rates of mental illness in married women that account for the higher rates of mental illness among women. Furthermore, I will attempt to show that it is the roles confronting married men and women that account for the high rates among women and not some other factor such as women being biologically more susceptible to mental illness.

The Marriage Role

Let us start by briefly exploring what it is about marriage in modern industrial societies that might produce unusually high rates of mental illness in women. First, the married woman's structural base is typically more fragile than is the man's. Women generally occupy only one major social role, that of housewife, whereas men generally occupy two major roles, household head and worker. Thus, a married man has two major sources of gratification, his family and his work, and a woman only one, her family. If a male finds one of these roles unsatisfactory, he can frequently focus his interest and concern on the other role. In contrast, if a woman finds her family role unsatisfactory, she typically has no major alternative source of gratification.

Second, it seems reasonable to assume that a large number of married women might find that their major instrumental role, keeping house, is frustrating. Being a housewife does not require a great deal of skill; for virtually all women, whether educated or not, seem to be capable of being at least moderately competent housewives. Furthermore, it is a position of low prestige.[1] The occupancy of such a low-status, technically undemanding position is not consonant with the educational and intellectual attainment of a large number of married women in our society.

Third, the role of housewife is relatively unstructured and invisible. It is possible for the housewife to put things off, to let things slide, in sum, to perform poorly. The lack of structure and visibility allows her to brood over her troubles, and her distress may thus feed upon itself. In contrast, the jobholder must consistently and satisfactorily meet demands that constantly force him to be involved with his environment. For the jobholder, being forced to meet these structured demands should help draw his attention from his troubles and help prevent him from becoming obsessed with his worries.[2]

Fourth, even when a married woman works, she is typically in a less satisfactory position than the married male. Women are discriminated against in the job market and they frequently hold positions that are not commensurate with their educational backgrounds. (Epstein, 1970; Harrison, 1964; Knudsen, 1969). Furthermore, working wives are typically viewed by themselves and by others as supplementing the family income, and this orientation makes their career involvement fairly tenuous (Harrison, 1964:79; also see Hartley, 1959–1960). Perhaps most important, working wives would appear to be under a greater strain than their husbands. In addition to their jobs they

[1]Most authors routinely assume that the role of housewife has low prestige (e.g., Friedan, 1963; Harrison, 1964; Lopata, 1966; Mrndal and Klein, 1956; Parsons, 1942; Rossi, 1964), however, I know of no systematic evaluation that bears on this assumption.

[2]Evidence consistent with this analysis is provided by Langner and Michael (1963: 301–357), Phillips and Segal (1969), and especially Bradburn and Caplovitz (1965:95–127). Also see Gove and Tudor (1972).

apparently typically perform most of the household chores, and this means that they are putting in considerably more hours of work per day than their husbands.[3]

Fifth, several observers have noted that the expectations confronting women are unclear and diffuse (e.g., Angrist, 1969; Goode, 1960: Gross *et al.*, 1958; Kirkpatrick, 1936; Parsons, 1942; Rose, 1951) and many have argued that this lack of specificity in their role creates problems for women[4] (see especially Cottrell, 1942; Kirkpatrick, 1936; Parsons, 1942; Rose, 1951). Rose (1951) and Angrist (1969) have indicated that the feminine role is particularly characterized by the adjusting to and preparing for contingencies. Rose (1951), for example, found that women tend to perceive their career in terms of what men will do, whereas men perceive their career in terms of their own needs. At the minimum it is likely that women find their uncertainty and lack of control over their future to be frustrating. Probably one of the most serious problems confronting married women is that of finding something meaningful to do after their children grow up.

The results of the Gurin *et al.* (1960) study of mental health and happiness provide empirical evidence that women find marriage to be more difficult than men. Women report more marital problems than men and women tend to be less happy with their marriage. In light of the fact that they found women to be more introspective than men, it is surprising to note that women are more likely to blame their husbands for their marital problems and unhappiness than vice versa (Gurin *et al.*, 1960:84–116). Women are also less likely than men to get satisfaction out of being a parent, and they indicate that they have more problems in dealing with their children and that they more frequently feel inadequate as a parent (Gurin *et al.*, 1960:117–142). In general their information suggests that married women find their role limited and frustrating and that their circumscribed range of activities and introspective tendencies (and/or opportunities for brooding) tend to magnify their problems.

The Role of Single Men and Women

The roles of single men and women would appear to be much more similar than the roles of married men and women. Single persons generally only have one major societal role, that of jobholder. On the job, the visibility and structure of the demands confronting men and women are relatively similar. Furthermore, both single men and women tend to lack close interpersonal ties and are relatively isolated. It should be noted that such ties appear to be a major source of a feeling of well-being and that married persons, regardless of sex, are much happier than single persons (Gurin *et al.*, 1960:231–232).

In spite of the relative similarity of their roles, it is possible to argue that single women are in a more tenuous position than single men. As noted earlier, women, when compared to men, are less likely to hold jobs commensurate with their educational backgrounds. Furthermore, it is possible to interpret the single male's status as being a matter of choice while the single female's status is a matter of fate and is thus more

[3]The evidence indicates that this is the case in Europe (Haavio-Mannila, 1967; Jacoby, 1970; Prudenski and Kolpakov, 1962), and it appears to be the case in the United States (Hartley, 1959–1960).

[4]Some investigators (Friedan, 1963; Komarovsky, 1946; McGee, 1962; Mead, 1949) have suggested that the expectations confronting women are not merely diffuse but are in fact contradictory and that women are placed in a serious double bind (also see Steinman and Fox, 1966; Wallin, 1950).

frustrating. However, the evidence does not appear to support these arguments. First, single women who hold jobs have been found to be as satisfied with their jobs as men who hold jobs (Langner and Michael, 1963:308) and, if anything, are less likely to worry about their work (Langner and Michael, 1963:304). Second, single women are considerably happier than single men, and their mental health appears to be less impaired by their single status (Bradburn and Caplovitz, 1965:13; Gurin *et al.*, 1960:233–234).

It is also possible to argue the alternative, namely that the single woman is better situated than the single man. This argument follows along two lines, the first centering on the male's dominant role in courtship. As single men have the opportunity to court women, their failure to get married can be interpreted as a personal failure. In contrast, as women play a more passive role in courtship, it is easier for them to interpret their failure to get married as a failure of men.[5] The second line of reasoning focuses around a tendency for single women to form and maintain close interpersonal ties, while single men are more apt to be independent and isolated (Knupfer *et al.*, 1966:848). Evidence that single men are more socially isolated is provided by the fact that in 1968 there were *990,000* men between 25 and 45 living by themselves and only *690,000* women in the same age group living by themselves (Bureau of the Census, 1969). As noted earlier, close social bonds are related to a feeling of well-being and both such bonds and such feelings appear to be more frequent in single women than single men. Unmarried women, incidentally, are more likely to turn to others during unhappy periods than are unmarried men (Gurin *et al.*, 1960;232), which may in part be a reflection that unmarried women have persons close to them to turn to.[6]

Before we turn to the data that bear on the relationship between marital roles and mental illness, let me summarize the points that have been made. First, there are a number of reasons for believing that the role of the married woman is less satisfactory than the role of the married male and that it is more likely to lead to mental illness. In contrast, the roles of single men and women are fairly similar. In general we would expect that single persons would have higher rates of mental illness than married persons and that probably there would be relatively little difference between the rates of single men and women. If there is a difference between the rates of single men and women, the evidence reviewed suggests that it is single men who would have the higher rates.

RECENT STUDIES OF SEX, MARITAL STATUS, AND MENTAL ILLNESS

Many authors have argued that the woman's role has fairly recently undergone major changes in the industrial societies (Friedan, 1963; Gavron, 1966; Komarovsky, 1950; McGee, 1962; McKee and Sherriffs, 1959; Rossi, 1964). As these are changes which

[5]The fact that women are discriminated against in the job market can also be used by women to explain their failure to get ahead. Women can thus interpret their disadvantaged position as being due to the system and not to their own characteristics. In contrast, men who are relatively unsuccessful at work cannot as readily blame the system and may therefore be more apt to blame themselves.

[6]Married persons are much more likely than single persons to turn to someone else for help during unhappy periods. It is interesting to note that among the married, it is the *men* who are the most likely to turn to someone else for help (Gurin *et al.*, 1960:232).

A. Generally mild cases

Tauss. Community survey of the prevalence of mental illness. Cases identified by responses to a structured interview (*n = 707*).

Srole et al. Community survey of the prevalence of all forms of mental disorder. Cases identified by "clinical" evaluation of structured interview (*n = 1,660*).

Hagnell. Community survey of the incidence of all forms of mental disorder over a ten-year period. Cases identified by clinical diagnosis (*n = 2,550*).

Cooper. Incidence of all forms of mental disorder in persons consulting general physicians (*7,454* patients consulting).

Shepherd et al. Episodes of all forms of mental disorder in persons consulting general physicians during one year (*14,697* patients at risk). Rates calculated by author from data provided on pp. 81 and 88.

B. Generally moderate cases

Miles et al. Episodes of all forms of treated mental disorder during a one-year period as indicated by a psychiatric registrar. Rates for marital groups age adjusted (586,000 persons at risk).

Susser. Episodes of all forms of mental disorder treated by a psychiatric agency during a five-year period (*55,282* persons at risk).

Hollingshead and Redlich. Prevalence of all forms of mental disorder treated by a psychiatrist (*336,940* persons at risk). Rates calculated by author from data presented on pp. 411–413 on persons 20–49 years of age.

Zolik and Marches. Prevalence of all forms of mental illness. Cases are persons in contact with one or more of *32* health and service agencies in a one-week period who are judged to be emotionally or mentally ill (*1,516* cases).

Innes and Sharp. Incidence of referral to a psychiatrist for all forms of mental disorder during a one-year period (*2,103* referrals).

Kramer. Termination rates from the outpatient psychiatric clinics of the United States 1961. Data from *493* of *633* clinics in *23* states.

C. Generally severe cases

Jaco. Incidence of all treated psychoses in Texas during a two-year period (*7,711,194* persons at risk).

Thomas and Locke (New York). Incidence, ages 25–54, for all disorders admitted to *all* mental hospitals in New York State over a three-year period (24,652 cases)

Thomas and Locke (Ohio). Incidence, ages 25–54, for all disorders admitted to state mental hospitals in Ohio over a five-year period (14,249 cases).

Gregory. Incidence, of all persons, ages 20–69, admitted to Canadian mental hospitals over a three-year period with the exception of organic psychosis of senility in persons 60 years and over.

Kramer (1967). Incidence of functional psychosis in a *13* state area (n = 22,205).

D. Generally very severe cases

Frumkin. Incidence of all schizophrenics admitted to Ohio State Mental Hospitals during one-year period.

Figure 1. Sketch of Studies

bear directly on our analysis of marital roles, particularly the woman's role in marriage, we will limit our analysis to those studies which present the relationship between sex, marital status, and mental illness in industrial societies after World War II. A brief sketch of these studies[7] is presented in Figure 1. Four of the studies deal with the prevalence of mental illness, twelve with the incidence of mental illness and

[7]A study by Malzberg (1964) has been excluded because it uses essentially the same idea as Thomas and Locke (1963) while it is not as detailed in its presentation and does not have any age controls. The results of two community surveys (Dupuy *et al.*, 1970; Knupfer *et al.*, 1966) are also not reported here. Neither of these surveys develops an index of mental illness but instead presents each item separately, which makes it almost impossible to incorporate their statistics into a paper such as this. However, the data of both these surveys support the conclusion reached in the present paper.

one with the termination of treatment. Among the incidence studies, some deal only with new cases (indicated by "incidence" in Figure 1) and some with new cases and readmissions (indicated by "episodes" in Figure 1). As is indicated in Figure 1, the studies differ very markedly in the severity of the disorders investigated. The studies also differ in how narrowly or broadly they define mental illness. Because of the wide variations in severity, the different time periods involved, and the variation in definition of mental illness, the rates vary widely from study to study. We, therefore, will only make comparisons between categories within a particular study.

THE RESULTS

Married Men and Women

The rates of mental illness among married men and women are presented in Table 1. *All* of the studies found that married women have higher rates of mental disorder than

Table 1 Rates of Mental Disorder among Married Men and Women (persons per 100,000)

		Men	Women	Ratio W/M
	A Studies showing higher rates among married women			
1	Tauss (1967:122)	18,000	35,100	1.95
2	Srole *et al.* (1962:177)	19,300	19,900	1.03
3	Hagnell (1966:115)	900	2,500	2.78
4	Cooper (1966:9)	17,400	29,000	1.67
5	Shepherd *et al.* (1966)	8,934	16,154	1.81
6	Miles *et al.* (1964:472)	788	926	1.18
7	Susser (1968:364)	465	706	1.52
8	Hollingshead and Redlich (1958:411–413)	504	566	1.12
9	Zolik and Marches (1968:105)	Many more married females (414) than males (225)		
10	Innes and Sharp (1962:451)	495	651	1.32
11	Kramer (n.d.:71)	83	96	1.16
12	Jaco (1960:113)	62	92	1.48
13	Thomas and Locke (1963:148) New York	68	92	1.35
14	Thomas and Locke (1963:148) Ohio	65	66	1.02
15	Gregory (1959:138)*	45	59	1.31
16	Kramer (1967:26)	16.0	29.0	1.81
17	Frumkin (1954:384)	4.2	10.7	2.55
	B Studies showing higher rates among married men			
	None			

*For this study the married category includes persons who are separated but not divorced.

married men, and in most cases the preponderance of women is substantial. Twelve of the seventeen studies provide sufficient information (age standardized rates, age specific rates and the like) so that it is clear that for these studies the higher rates for married women cannot possibly be attributed to age differences between the sexes. And, in any case, when comparing populations, such as married men and married women, which have similar age distributions, it is very unlikely that these findings could be due to differences in the ages of the two populations. Furthermore, these findings are not affected by the severity of the cases investigated, nor by the means used to identify cases. In sum, these results do not appear to be due to some methodological artifact, and it seems reasonable to conclude that married women have higher rates of mental illness than married men.

Never Married (Single) Men and Women

The rates of mental disorder among men and women who have never married are presented in Table 2. Four studies found single women to have higher rates and eleven found single men to have higher rates. At the minimum this suggests that single women do not in general have higher rates of mental illness than single men. In fact, if there is a difference it appears that it is single men who have a greater tendency to become mentally ill.[8]

Table 3 presents a comparison of the rates of mental disorder of the married and the never married. In a very rough fashion the ratios indicate the relative likelihood that single persons as compared to married persons will become mentally ill. As would be expected, in the substantial majority of the studies, the rates of single persons are higher than those of married persons.[9] Perhaps the most striking thing about this table is the fact that for every study the ratio of single—married is larger for men than it is for women. In fact, on the average the ratio is almost twice as large for men.

Taken at face value, the data presented so far suggest that married women find their roles more difficult than married men and are more likely to become mentally ill. In contrast, the roles of single men and women appear to be more comparable, although it appears that single men find their role somewhat more difficult than single women and are slightly more likely to become mentally ill. Unfortunately, it is not clear that we should take these data at face value. There is fairly substantial evidence that one reason single persons have higher rates of mental illness than married persons

[8]I would note that Cooper's (1966) study, which was one of the four which found single women to have higher rates than single men, presents rates by age. This presentation shows that between the ages of 25 and 44 single men had higher rates of mental illness than single women, and between the ages of 45 and 64 single men and women had virtually the same rates. It was only at the age extremes (15 to 24 and 65+) that women had higher rates. Thus, for this study, during the adult working years single men, if anything, had higher rates than single women.

[9]In the study by Innes and Sharp (1962:451), the finding that single men and women have low rates of mental disorder is due solely to the low rates of the young. Single males over 25 have higher rates than married males and single females over 35 have higher rates than married females. In the study by Cooper (1966:9), which found single and married males to have similar rates, the result is again due to an age factor. In this study single males between 25 and 64 have much higher rates than married males. However, Cooper's finding that single women have lower rates than married women is not due to an age factor, for he found that in every age category single women had lower rates than married women. Similarly, age also does not account for single women having lower rates than married women in the Srole *et al.* (1962:177) study. Also see Dupuy *et al.* (1970).

Table 2 Rates of Mental Disorder among Men and Women Who Have Never Married

		Men	Women	Ratio W/M
	A Studies showing higher rates among single women			
1	Cooper	17,600	22,000	1.26
2	Shepherd *et al.*	11,580	17,464	1.51
3	Susser	938	976	1.04
4	Innes and Sharp	478	564	1.18
	B Studies showing higher rates among single men			
1	Srole *et al.*	29,700	16,800	1.77
2	Miles *et al.*	1,979	1,319	1.50
3	Hollingshead and Redlich	3,154	1,154	1.82
4	Zolik and Marches	Many more single males (418) than females (272)		
5	Kramer (n.d.)	208.1	82.6	1.14
6	Jaco	222	180	1.23
7	Thomas and Locke (New York)	299	228	1.31
8	Thomas and Locke (Ohio)	266	159	1.67
9	Gregory	164	123	1.33
10	Kramer (1967)	73.4	66.7	1.10
11	Frumkin	22.9	19.3	1.19

Table 3 Rate of Mental Illness of the Never Married Divided by the Rate of Mental Illness of the Married

	Men	Women
Srole *et al.*	1.54	.84
Cooper	1.01	.77
Shepherd *et al.*	1.30	1.08
Miles *et al.*	2.51	1.42
Susser	2.02	1.38
Hollingshead and Redlich	6.26	3.06
Innes and Sharp	.97	.87
Kramer (n.d.)	2.50	1.97
Jaco	3.58	1.96
Thomas and Locke (New York)	4.40	2.48
Thomas and Locke (Ohio)	4.09	2.41
Gregory	3.64	2.08
Kramer (1967)	4.59	2.30
Frumkin	5.45	1.80
Average Ratio	3.13	1.74

Source: Tables 1 and 2.

is that individuals who are unstable and prone to mental illness are less likely to get married (Adler, 1953; Klein and Klein, 1968; Odegård, 1946, 1953). Some persons have suggested that the differences in rates of mental illness between men and women who are married, and between men and women who are single are also due to selection processes (Malzberg, 1964:20; Srole *et al.,* 1962:179–182).

One argument for selective differences by sex is that as the man plays the dominant role in courtship, his faults (emotional instability) are more visible than a woman's, and the unstable man is thus less likely to get married than an unstable woman. A second possibility, suggested by Srole *et al.* (1962:180), is that men want to dominate women and thus bypass women with "strong, independent personalities." In the extreme form this argument suggests that the most competent and mentally robust women would not get married while the more passive (easily dominated) and unstable women would get married. In contrast to the above arguments, there remains the possibility that there is little selective difference by sex in the emotional stability of persons who get married. This alternative suggests that persons get to know each other fairly intimately before they get married, that at this intimate level there is little difference between the sexes in the visibility of emotional instability, and that neither men nor women want a spouse who is emotionally unstable. Fortunately we are able to at least tentatively evaluate the role and the selectivity explanations of the sex differences reported above. If the selectivity explanation explains most of the variance, we would expect that among persons who were once but are no longer married, the sex differences in mental disorder would be similar to those of married persons. In contrast, if the role explanation explains most of the variance, we would expect the sex differences in such persons to be more like persons who are single.

In our evaluation we will look at two marital statuses, the divorced and the widowed. We might expect the divorced to have unusually high rates of mental illness for at least two reasons. First, persons who are divorced have undergone a very trying experience which might be expected to promote an emotional disorder. Second, persons who get divorced may have been particularly unstable to begin with. Assume for the moment that a long-standing personal instability frequently leads to a divorce and that a long-standing instability is a major factor in the high rates of mental illness among persons who are divorced. If this is the case, and *if* more unstable women than men enter marriage, we would not only expect more divorced women than men to be mentally ill, but also that the disparity between divorced men and women would be even greater than among persons who were married. At the very minimum, if the selectivity hypothesis is correct, divorced women should consistently have higher rates of mental illness than divorced men. In terms of selective processes persons who are widowed should be very similar to persons who are married. Therefore, according to the selectivity hypothesis, widowed women should also have higher rates of mental illness than widowed men.[10]

[10]To provide a definitive evaluation of the selectivity hypothesis one should look at the formerly married without regard to whether or not they have remarried. Unfortunately, the studies reviewed do not allow us to do this. However, persons who are widowed or divorced have passed one selection barrier (i.e., they married) and it seems improbable that the effects of a second barrier (i.e., remarriage) would totally obscure the effects of initial selection. Furthermore, I would note that in a subsequent paper (Gove, n.d.)

In contrast, the role explanation would indicate that as widowed men and women are involved in relatively similar role networks, they should have relatively similar rates of mental illness. As with single persons there might be a slight tendency for the widowed woman to be slightly better situated than the widowed man, as she may be more apt to maintain close social ties. In general the same analysis can be made for the divorced, again leading to the expectation that the rates of mental illness for divorced women should be the same or possibly slightly lower than those of divorced men.

The rates of mental disorder for persons who once were but are no longer married are presented in Table 4. Unfortunately not all studies present rates for such persons.[11] Three categories are looked at, divorced, widowed, and divorced—widowed combined. In each category the majority of studies found higher rates of mental illness among men. In fact, the proportion of studies that found unmarried males to have higher rates than unmarried females is very similar for each of the three unmarried statuses (studies showing (1) never married males to have higher rates, *73* percent, (2) divorced males to have higher rates, *73* percent, (3) widowed males to have higher rates, *78* percent). These results support the role explanation.

In Table 5 the rates of mental illness of widowed and divorced males and females are compared with the rates of married males and females. As would be expected almost all of the studies found that the divorced and widowed had higher rates of mental illness than the married. In all but one case the difference between being married and being formerly married is greater for men than for women and in most cases this difference is quite large. In general the rates of the widowed are slightly lower than the rates of the never married (which provides some support for the argument that persons who are unstable are less likely to get married), while the rates of the divorced are noticeably higher than the rates of either the widowed or the never married (which suggests that either divorce is a very trying experience or that persons who get a divorce are unstable, or both). It is interesting to note that both Table 5 and Table 3 show a tendency for the difference between the married and the unmarried statuses to be greater in the studies dealing with a serious disorder than those dealing with a mild disorder.

Residence in Mental Hospitals

As noted previously, most of the studies reviewed have investigated the incidence of mental illness. Of the four studies that dealt with prevalence, all except one (Hollings-

---

I have explored the possibility that the pattern of mental illness presented here would be reflected in mortality due to specific causes (e.g., suicide, accidents, cirrhosis of the liver). In that paper it has been possible to show that selection due to remarriage is not the major contributor to the pattern found among the widowed and divorced—and the mortality pattern is the same as the one found here (also see Kraus and Lilienfeld 1959).

[11]Two studies that report some relevant information have been left out. As noted earlier Zolik and Marches (1968) present cases but not rates. If one uses U.S. census data to calculate the rates of divorced men and women and widowed men and women, the data indicate that widowers have notably higher rates of mental illness than widows, while divorced women have slightly higher rates than divorced men. Tauss (1967) had simply too few unmarried men in his community sample (7 single, 6 widowed, 3 separated or divorced) to draw any conclusions.

Table 4 Rates of Mental Disorder among Men and Women Who Were Once Married but Are No Longer Married (persons per 100,000)

	A Studies showing women have higher rates	Men	Women	W/M		B Studies showing men have higher rates	Men	Women	M/W
	Part I: Divorced								
1	Srole *et al.* (1962:185)	40,000	42,100	1.05	1	Shepherd *et al.* *	23,076	21,969	1.05
2	Kramer (n.d.)	284.2	295.1	1.04	2	Miles *et al.*	3,615	2,076	1.74
3	Kramer (1967)*	109.9	124.1	1.13	3	Susser	2,764	1,692	1.63
					4	Innes & Sharp	2,663	1,636	1.63
					5	Jaco (1960:114)	308	232	1.33
					6	Thomas & Locke (New York)	437	302	1.45
					7	Thomas & Locke (Ohio)	468	232	2.02
					8	Gregory	394	236	1.67
	Part II: Widowed								
1	Innes & Sharp	447	606	1.36	1	Miles *et al.*	2,530	1,418	1.78
2	Kramer (1967)	58.9	66.2	1.12	2	Susser	1,212	902	1.34
					3	Kramer (n.d.)	54.3	54.0	1.01
					4	Jaco	119	105	1.13
					5	Thomas & Locke (New York)	293	174	1.68
					6	Thomas & Locke (Ohio)	278	142	1.96
					7	Gregory	106	79	1.34
	Part III: Rates for divorced and widowed combined								
	None				1	Hollingshead & Redlich (1958:411–414)†	1,409	1,187	1.19
					2	Frumkin	14.8	13.0	1.14

*Rates for "other" category which, by the process of elimination must be divorced and separated.
†Rates also include separated.

Table 5 Rate of Mental Illness of the Formerly Married Divided by the Rate of Mental Illness of the Married

	Men	Women
Part I: The divorced and the married		
Srole *et al.*	2.07	2.12
Shepherd *et al.*	2.58	1.36
Miles *et al.*	4.59	2.24
Susser	5.94	2.40
Innes and Sharp	5.38	2.51
Kramer (n.d.)	3.42	3.09
Jaco	2.71	1.88
Thomas and Locke (New York)	6.43	3.28
Thomas and Locke (Ohio)	7.20	3.52
Gregory	8.76	4.00
Kramer (1967)	6.87	4.28
Average Ratio	5.09	2.80
Part II: The widowed and the married		
Shepherd *et al.*	1.34	1.17
Miles *et al.*	3.21	1.53
Susser	2.61	1.28
Kramer (n.d.)	.65	.56
Jaco	1.92	1.14
Thomas and Locke (New York)	4.31	1.89
Thomas and Locke (Ohio)	4.28	2.15
Gregory	2.36	1.34
Kramer (1967)	3.68	2.28
Average Ratio	2.53	1.43
Part III: The widowed and divorced combined and the married		
Hollingshead and Redlich	2.80	2.10
Frumkin	3.52	1.21
Average Ratio	3.16	1.66

Source: Tables 1 and 4.

head and Redlich, 1958) focused exclusively on persons living in the open community. Residents of mental hospitals, many of whom are very chronic cases, comprise a very different population. As a group they are probably more severely disturbed than the populations investigated by any of the studies reviewed. Furthermore, there is considerable interaction between length of stay in a mental hospital and marital status, with persons who are married tending to have a shorter stay than those who are not married (e.g., Kramer, n.d.:60). This means that any particular point in

Table 6 Rates of Residency in Mental Hospitals (persons per 100,000)

	Men	Women	M/W
Married	178.3	227.3	.78
Never married	1,275.0	849.3	1.48
Divorced	2,013.2	1,201.6	1.68
Widowed	997.7	684.0	1.46

time, mental hospitals will contain, relative to their admission rates, a higher proportion of unmarried than married patients. It is also the case that some persons who were married when they entered the hospital will have been widowed or divorced while in the hospital. An additional problem for our purposes is the (uninvestigated) possibility that the length of hospitalization of men and women within a particular marital category will differ.

Rates of residence in mental hospitals (state, county, city, private, and federal) by sex and marital status are presented in Table 6. These data are taken from a 25 percent sample of all such residents in the United States at the time of the 1960 census. They have been separated from that of the other studies in part because they are considerably more comprehensive, and in part because of the problems just noted. As can be readily seen, married women are more likely to be residents in mental hospitals than married men. In contrast, when we compare single men with single women, divorced men with divorced women, and widowed men with widowed women, in each case it is men who are much more likely to be residents of mental hospitals. Thus, the pattern associated with residency in mental hospitals corresponds exactly with the pattern found previously.

Marriage and Old Age

Our analysis of the roles of married men and women focuses on their roles prior to retirement. During this time one of the major differences between married men and women is that men have two major roles, jobholder and household head, while the women tend to have only one, housewife. However, after the male retires, his role network shrinks so that it becomes fairly comparable to his wife's. This suggests that the mental health of married men and women past retirement age might be more similar than it is before retirement age. Of the studies reviewed that provide sufficient data to explore this possibility, one (Kramer, n.d.:71) presents ambiguous data and three (Cooper, 1966:9; Kramer, n.d.:26; Susser, 1968:364) clearly indicate that the difference between married men and women is greater before the age of retirement than after. A fifth study by Bellin and Hardt (1958)[12] found virtually identical rates of mental illness for married men and women 65 and over. In sum, there is at least tentative evidence that the rates of mental illness of married men and women are more similar after the age of retirement.

[12]This study was not discussed before because it deals only with the aged.

Changes over Time

Earlier we noted that most authors who have analyzed the married woman's role in industrial societies have indicated that this role changed rather drastically in recent years. In general, they have argued that married women are in a more tenuous position than formerly. Because of this analysis we have only looked at studies conducted after World War II. If the married woman's role has changed, we might expect this to be reflected in changes over time in the rates of mental illness among married women. To investigate this possibility, I have reviewed Rose and Stub's (1955) summary of the studies of incidence of mental disorder. Of the four studies they cited that deal with mental illness prior to World War II which present rates for all disorders, three indicate that married women had *lower* rates of mental disorder than married men, while only one indicates that married women had higher rates.[13] This pattern is almost the precise opposite of the pattern following World War II and conforms to the argument that the married woman's role has not only changed but become more tenuous.

SUMMARY AND CONCLUSIONS

As was noted at the beginning of this paper, Gove and Tudor (1972) have recently demonstrated that in our society women are more likely than men to be mentally ill.[14] There are at least three plausible explanations for the high rates of mental illness in women. One is that women are biologically more susceptible to mental illness. Another is that there is some characteristic of the woman's generalized sex role that makes women more susceptible to the appearance of mental illness. Phillips and Segal (1969), for example, have argued that in some community surveys women might be more likely than men to appear to be mentally ill, for women may feel it is more appropriate to talk about their psychological symptoms. The third possibility is that there is something about the roles women occupy which is difficult and which promotes mental illness.

If women are biologically more susceptible to mental illness than men, we would tend to expect women to have higher rates of mental illness in each marital category. This is also true if the high rates among women were due to a characteristic of the woman's generalized sex role, such as women being more willing to seek help. It is, however, possible to retain a biological explanation and to account for equal or lower rates of mental illness in single women as compared to single men, by arguing that men have a greater tendency than women to marry persons who are likely to become mentally ill. However, both the biological and generalized sex role explanations suggest that divorced and widowed women should have higher rates of mental illness

[13]For these studies, within many of the particular diagnostic categories married women frequently had higher rates than married men.

[14]I would like to point out a major difference between the Gove and Tudor paper and the present paper. In the Gove and Tudor paper, mental illness is defined as a functional disorder involving severe distress and/or mental disorganization. Because relatively little data on mental illness is reported by sex and marital status, the present paper has been unable to develop its own definition but has had to rely on different definitions used by various sources.

than their male counterparts. As we have seen this expectation appears to be incorrect. Married women do tend to have much higher rates of mental illness than married men. But when single men are compared with single women, divorced men with divorced women, and widowed men with widowed women it is found that these women do not tend to have higher rates than their male counterparts. In fact, if there is a difference, it appears to be that women in these categories tend to have lower rates. The data thus suggest that the role explanation accounts for the differences between the sexes.

In summary, the married of both sexes have lower rates of mental illness than the unmarried. This relationship would appear to be due to both the nature of the roles of the married and the unmarried and to selective processes which kept unstable persons from marrying. When we look at the differences between the sexes it appears that, at least in terms of mental illness, being married is considerably more advantageous to men than it is to women, while being single is, if anything, slightly more disadvantageous to men than to women.

REFERENCES

Adler, L. 1953. ''The Relationship of Marital Status to Incidence of and Recovery from Mental Illness.'' *Social Forces* **32**(December): 185–194.

Angrist, S. 1969. ''The Study of Sex Roles.'' *Journal of Social Issues* **25**(January): 215–232.

Bellin, S., and R. Hardt. 1958. ''Marital Status and Mental Disorders Among the Aged.'' *American Sociological Review* **23**(April): 155–162.

Bradburn, Norman, and David Caplovitz. 1965. *Reports on Happiness*. Chicago: Aldine.

Bureau of the Census 1969. ''Marital Status and Family Status: March 1968.'' *Current Population Reports*. Series P-20, No. 187. Washington: Government Printing Office.

Cooper, B. 1966. ''Psychiatric Disorder in Hospitals and General Practice.'' *Social Psychiatry* **1**(1): 7–10.

Cottrell, L. 1942. ''The Adjustment of the Individual to His Age and Sex Roles.'' *American Sociological Review* **7**(October): 617–620.

Dupuy, Harold, Arnold Engel, Brian Devine, James Scanlon, and Linda Querec. 1970. *Selected Symptoms of Psychological Distress*. National Center for Health Statistics. Series 11, No. 37. Washington: Government Printing Office.

Epstein, Cynthia. 1970. *Woman's Place*. Berkeley and Los Angeles: University of California Press.

Friedan, Betty. 1963. *The Feminine Mystique*. New York: Norton.

Frumkin, R. 1954. ''Social Factors in Schizophrenia.'' *Sociology and Social Research* **38**(July–August): 383–386.

Gavron, Hannah. 1966. *The Captive Wife: Conflicts of Housebound Mothers*. London: Routledge & Kegan Paul.

Goode, W. 1960. ''Norm Commitment and Conformity to Role Status Obligations.'' *American Journal of Sociology* **66**(November): 246–258.

Gove, W. n.d. ''Sex, Marital Status, and Mortality.'' Article submitted for publication.

Gove, W., and J. Tudor. 1972. ''Adult Sex Roles and Mental Illness.'' *American Journal of Sociology* **78**(November): in press.

Gregory, I. 1959. ''Factors Influencing First Admissions Rates to Canadian Mental Hospitals III: An Analysis by Education, Marital Status, Country of Birth, Religion and Rural-Urban Residence, 1950–1952.'' *Canadian Psychiatric Association Journal* **4**(April): 133–151.

Gross, Neal, Ward Mason, and Alexander McEachern. 1958. *Explorations in Role Analysis.* New York: Wiley.

Gurin, Gerald, Joseph Veroff, and Alexander McEachern. 1960. *Americans View Their Mental Health.* New York: Basic Books.

Haavio-Mannila, E. 1967. "Sex Difference in Role Expectations and Performance." *Journal of Marriage and the Family* **29**(August): 368–378.

Hagnell, Olle. 1966. *A Prospective Study of the Incidence of Mental Disorder.* Sweden: Berlingska Boktryckeriet.

Harrison, E. 1964. "The Working Women: Barriers in Employment." *Public Administration Review* **24**(June): 78–85.

Hartley, R. 1959–60. "Some Implications of Current Changes in Sex Role Patterns." *Merrill-Palmer Quarterly* **6**: 153–164.

Hollingshead, August, and Frederick Redlich. 1958. *Social Class and Mental Illness.* New York: Wiley.

Innes, G., and G. Sharp. 1962. "A Study of Psychiatric Patients in North-East Scotland." *Journal of Mental Science* **108**(July): 447–456.

Jaco, E. Gartley. 1960. *The Social Epidemiology of Mental Disorders.* New York: Russell Sage Foundation.

Jacoby, S. 1970. "Women in Russia." *New Republic* (April 4; April 11): 16; 18.

Kirkpatrick, S. 1936. "The Measurement of Ethical Inconsistency in Marriage." *International Journal of Ethics* **46**(July): 444–460.

Klein, R., and D. Klein. 1968. "Marital Status as a Prognostic Indicator in Schizophrenia." *Journal of Nervous and Mental Disease* **147**(3): 289–296.

Knudsen, D. 1969. "The Declining Status of Women: Popular Myths and the Failure of Functionalist Thought." *Social Forces* **48**(December): 183–193.

Knupfer, G., W. Clark, and R. Room. 1966. "The Mental Health of the Unmarried." *American Journal of Psychiatry* **122**(February): 841–851.

Komarovsky, M. 1946. "Cultural Contradictions and Sex Roles." *American Journal of Sociology* **52**(November): 184–189.

———. 1950. "Functional Analysis of Sex Roles." *American Sociological Review* **15**(August): 508–516.

Kramer, Morton. 1967. "Epidemiology, Biostatistics, and Mental Health Planning." In Russell R. Monroe, Gerald D. Klee, and Eugene B. Brody (eds.), *Psychiatric Epidemiology and Mental Health Planning.* Washington: American Psychiatric Association.

———. n.d. *Some Implications of Trends in the Usage of Psychiatric Facilities for Community Mental Health Programs and Related Research.* Public Health Service Publication No. 1434. Washington: Government Printing Office.

Kraus. A., and A. Lilienfeld, 1959. "Some Epidemiologic Aspects of the High Mortality Rate in the Young Widowed Group." *Journal of Chronic Diseases* **10**(September): 207–217.

Langner, Thomas, and Stanley Michael. 1963. *Life Stress and Mental Health.* New York: Free Press.

Lopata, H. 1966. "The Life Cycle of the Social Role of Housewife." *Sociology and Social Research* **51**(October): 5–22.

Malzberg, B. 1964. "Marital Status and the Incidence of Mental Disease." *International Journal of Social Psychiatry* **10**(Winter): 19–26.

McGee, Reece. 1962. *Social Disorganization in America.* San Francisco: Chandler.

McKee, J., and A. Sherriffs. 1959. "Men's and Women's Beliefs, Ideals, and Self-Concepts." *American Journal of Sociology* **64**(January): 356–363.

Mead, Margaret. 1949. *Male and Female.* New York: Morrow.

Miles, H., E. Gardner, C. Bodian, and J. Romano. 1964. "Accumulative Survey of All Psychiatric Experience in Monroe County, N.Y." *Psychiatric Quarterly* **38**(July): 458–487.

Myrdal, Alva, and Viola Klein. 1956. *Women's Two Roles: Home and Work.* London: Routledge & Kegan Paul.

Odegärd, O. 1946. "Marriage and Mental Disease." *Journal of Mental Science* **92**(January): 35–59.

———. 1953. "New Data on Marriage and Mental Disease: The Incidence of Psychosis in the Widowed and the Divorced." *Journal of Mental Science* **99**(October): 778–785.

Parsons, T. 1942. "Age and Sex in the Social Structure of the United States." *American Sociological Review* **7**(October): 604–616.

Phillips, D., and B. Segal. 1969. "Sexual Status and Psychiatric Symptoms." *American Sociological Review* **34**(February): 58–72.

Prudenski, G., and B. Kolpakov. 1962. "Questions Concerning the Calculation of Non-working Time in Budget Statistics." *Problems of Economics* **4**(April): 29–33.

Rose, A. 1951. "The Adequacy of Women's Expectations for Adult Roles." *Social Forces* **30**(October): 69–77.

Rose, A., and H. Stub. 1955. "Summary of Studies on the Incidence of Mental Disorders." In Arnold Rose (ed.), *Mental Health and Mental Disorder.* New York: Norton.

Rossi, A. 1964. "Equality Between the Sexes: An Immodest Proposal." *Daedalus* **93**(Spring): 607–652.

Shepherd, Michael, Brian Cooper, Alexander Brown, and Graham Kalton. 1966. *Psychiatric Illness in General Practice.* London: Oxford University Press.

Srole, Leo, Thomas Langner, Stanley Michael, Marvin Opler, and Thomas Rennie. 1962. *Mental Health in the Metropolis.* New York: McGraw-Hill.

Steinman, A., and D. Fox. 1966. "Male-Female Perceptions of the Female Role in the United States." *Journal of Psychology* **64**(November): 265–279.

Susser, Mervyn. 1968. *Community Psychiatry: Epidemiology and Social Themes.* New York: Random House.

Tauss, W. 1967. "A Note on the Prevalence of Mental Disturbance." *Australian Journal of Psychology* **19**(August): 121–123.

Thomas, D., and B. Locke. 1963. "Marital Status. Education and Occupational Differentials in Mental Hospitals." *Milbank Memorial Fund Quarterly* **41**(April): 145–160.

Wallin, P. 1950. "Cultural Contradictions and Sex Roles: A Repeat Study." *American Sociological Review* **15**(April): 288–293.

Zolik, E., and J. Marches. 1968. "Mental Health Morbidity in a Suburban Community." *Journal of Clinical Psychology* **24**(January): 103–108.

Homosexualities: Their Range and Character*

Alan P. Bell

INTRODUCTION

Probably the outstanding characteristic of most of the research pertaining to the development and management of homosexuality, at least as reported in the literature since 1940, is the tendency to view homosexuality as a unitary phenomenon. Generally defined as "a definite preferential erotic attraction to members of the same sex" (Marmor, 1965), whether or not sexual relations with members of the same sex even occur, homosexuality has been viewed as a condition with but a single parameter, one's standing on the so-called Kinsey Scale. In most studies, the homosexual group is composed of males or females who have been rated (by the subjects themselves or by the experimenters) 6, 5, or 4 on the 7-point scale, indicating that they are more or less exclusively homosexual in their sexual behaviors and interests. When the study includes a control group of heterosexual men or women, this group is presumably made up of those who have received ratings of 0, 1, or 2 on the scale, which denote more or less exclusive heterosexual sexual behaviors and interests. Almost without exception, the researcher will proceed to collapse the categories which indicate subjects' standings on the homosexual-heterosexual continuum and to make comparisons between the dichotomized groups. The contention of this paper is that the failure of researchers to delineate their homosexual and heterosexual samples more precisely, even with regard to the one parameter used as the basis for assigning subjects to a given group, has tended to hide the nature and consequences of psychosexual development. To put it another way, before between-group differences are ever to emerge in ways that are truly enlightening, much more attention must be given to within-group differences than has been true of the past. If homosexuality (or heterosexuality) is to be understood, a more complete assessment of its range and character must be made (Hooker, 1959).

In order to make the kind of assessment I have in mind, special attention must be given to the two types of sampling issues which are basic to research in this and other areas. The first involves *people samples* and the extent to which a study sample includes, even if it does not exactly represent, the broad range of experience which can be found in the larger population of interest. The second issue pertains to what could be termed *item samples,* or the degree to which the measurements we use are not only valid but sufficiently comprehensive. It is the contention of this paper that most investigations of homosexuality have involved serious truncations with respect to both types of samples, and with predictable results. Homosexuality has been too narrowly defined by person samples offering too narrow a range of experience and who, in turn, have been investigated within too narrow a scope of inquiry. The paper will address itself to these issues with reference to some of the methodology employed

*From Alan P. Bell, "Homosexualities: Their range and character," in James K. Cole and Richard Dienstbier, (Eds.), *Nebraska Symposium on Motivation, 1973,* University of Nebraska Press, Lincoln, Nebraska, 1974, pages 1–26, reprinted by permission of the author, the editors, and the publisher.

in a current study of the development and management of human sexuality by the Institute for Sex Research and will include certain findings from that study which indicate the range and variation of homosexual experience as well as the importance of construing that experience more broadly.

PEOPLE SAMPLES

While it is unrealistic to suppose that in a ''homoerotophobic'' society such as ours (Churchill, 1967) a representative sample of persons whose sexual behaviors and/or feelings are homosexual could be obtained, this particular sense of the matter should hardly make us content with the fact that most of the samples so far obtained have been composed of people seeking psychological treatment or who have been incarcerated or who are members of homophile organizations. Relatively easy access to such groups has led to sometimes competing and equally erroneous impressions of homosexuality. While it has been pointed out to psychoanalysts frequently enough that it is a mistake to make generalizations about homosexuality on the basis of what they see in the life of a single patient, perhaps social scientists have not been warned sufficiently enough that larger numbers of subjects do little more than compound misimpressions if their findings are based upon an idiosyncratic sample. The importance of the nature of the homosexual sample in determining our view of the developmental or psychological correlates of homosexuality is illustrated by Schofield's findings (Schofield, 1965). Comparisons made between homosexuals and heterosexuals in prison, under psychiatric treatment and not under psychiatric treatment, indicated few differences between homosexuals and heterosexuals within a given group but large differences between homosexuals and heterosexuals across groups. For example, it was found that homosexuals and heterosexuals in treatment were more like each other developmentally and psychologically than they were like their counterparts not in treatment. Even if a majority of homosexuals seek psychiatric treatment, much smaller numbers do so in order to change their sexual orientation, and those who do apparently experience themselves as well as their homosexuality quite differently from those who do not. The even smaller numbers of homosexuals incarcerated for sexual offenses or belonging to homophile organizations make these kinds of samples even less representative of homosexuals in general.

The representativeness of a given sample is, of course, extremely important when one is attempting to estimate the incidence of a particular characteristic in the population. For example, if the interest is in determining the extent to which homosexuals in general display a given psychological characteristic or prefer one sexual technique over another, one would have to demonstrate the degree to which the sample represents homosexuals in general. Since all researchers in this area have failed to obtain such samples, any research which has the estimation of ''incidence'' as its aim must present its findings with extreme caution. Usually this is not what is done, or when the reader is warned not to generalize findings to the entire population of homosexuals, the words of caution appear more like a ritualistic gesture, a bone tossed in the direction of potential critics who are often more wary of others' findings than they are of their own.

When the primary aim of research is that of viewing relationships between various measures, the representativeness of a given (analytic) sample may be less crucial (Riley, 1963). For example, estimating the degree to which homosexuals are psychologically adjusted (i.e., an "incidence" study) is quite a different matter from estimating the degree to which psychological adjustment is related to various sociosexual life styles. It could be said, of course, that with a different sample, different indices of psychological adjustment might emerge, or that different sociosexual life styles would be represented, and even that relationships between the two measures might change; and yet, if the relationships which appear within a given sample make sense theoretically, the researcher's confidence in such findings can perhaps be more certain than those of the epidemiologist, despite the absence of a representative sample.

Finally, there is another related kind of research which does not rely at all upon representative samples, in which subjects are chosen beforehand or later classified on the basis of a given characteristic and then compared with other subjects who have been similarly chosen. This type of research, for example, can address itself to certain theoretical assumptions regarding homosexuality and go on to explore additional areas that are theoretically relevant. Hooker's work (1957, 1958) is of this kind. She deliberately chose for her homosexual sample those homosexuals who were not in therapy and who gave every evidence of "normal" adjustment, comparing their responses to various projective measures with those of a heterosexual sample chosen on the basis of the same criteria. Her studies did not demonstrate the extent to which homosexuals in general are better or worse adjusted than heterosexuals in general. What they did demonstrate, at least to her satisfaction, was that not all homosexuals are psychologically maladjusted and that, therefore, the theoretical assumption that homosexuality is ipso facto pathological could not be upheld. Williams and Weinberg (1971) did a similar thing. In their exploration of the relationship between "stigmatization" and various social and psychological consequences, they compared homosexuals who had received an honorable discharge from the military with those who had received a less-than-honorable discharge. Despite the fact that they did not have a representative sample of homosexuals who had served in the military, at the very least they were able to demonstrate that (a) not all homosexuals serving in the military receive a less-than-honorable discharge and (b) not all homosexuals who receive such a discharge and are stigmatized on that account suffer severe social or psychological consequences. The first point has implications for those who assume that a homosexual cannot function satisfactorily in the military. The second finding has important implications for labeling theory. Neither relies upon the representativeness of their particular sample.

Keenly aware of the sampling issues which I have just enumerated, we considered several sampling strategies for the institute's study of the development and management of human sexuality. The first possibility, involving a random sample of 10,000 to 20,000 persons from which both the homosexual and heterosexual samples would be drawn, was rejected because the cost of such an operation was prohibitive. Another, less costly, procedure would have involved generating homosexual and heterosexual "pools" of prospective interviewees through extensive publicity, limiting them to telephone volunteers. This plan was also rejected, in the belief that samples generated in this way would not have included the variety of persons which our study required. Still another plan would have involved recruiting homosexuals and heterosexuals from "equivalent" locales. It was decided not to proceed in this way, inasmuch as homosexuals and heterosexuals drawn from comparable locales are hardly equivalent. For example, the type of homosexual found attending church is not like the typical heterosexual churchgoer. The gay bar has a different place and purpose in the gay community than the neighborhood, or even "singles," bar has in a straight setting.

It was finally decided that we would generate stratified random samples of heterosexuals from the general population of San Francisco and Alameda counties by means of block-sampling techniques. Homosexuals—male and female, black and white— were to be recruited from as many different sources as possible: through public advertising, in public and private bars, steam baths, and other public places, through personal contacts, and by means of various mailing lists which were made available to us. Approximately two dozen recruiters, many of them homosexuals who could function comfortably in the role, were assigned to various locales with which they were familiar and were allowed the amount of time which we believed would be necessary to produce an adequate number of potential subjects. Over one entire summer, 4,639 individuals were recruited as potential respondents.

SAMPLE SOURCES

Public advertising consisted of paid advertising and feature articles in major newspapers, appeals made on radio and television, and strategically placed posters and matchbooks describing our study and the need for volunteers. Approximately 1,000 hours were spent recruiting persons in a total of 82 gay bars and restaurants in the San Francisco Bay Area. Although no bar was visited the same time and day every week, recruiters generally geared their activities to the times when the largest number of people could be informed of the study and recruited as potential respondents. The same was true of the three private bars where recruiting took place. Probably the most covert individuals were obtained by means of personal contacts, at small gatherings in private homes or contacts made on a one-to-one basis by persons who had been interviewed themselves or who, for whatever reason, had a special interest in the study. Using the mailing lists of various homophile organizations, bars, and bookstores, information about the study together with mailback cards were sent to almost 6,000 individuals. Posters and recruitment cards were placed on the premises of eight different steam baths, and eventually recruiting was done face to face in the hallways, steam rooms, and individual cubicles. The 23 homophile organizations in the Bay Area invited our recruiters to their meetings and to other social activities. Although we were accused of being "exploitative" or "establishment" by some of the more radical groups, our field work was supported by the vast majority of the homophile leadership. Probably the most difficult recruiting took place in what we termed "public places": men's rooms, theater lobbies and balconies, parks and beaches, and streets and public squares. Despite the fact that our recruiters made contact with several thousand males in these places, only 137 white males and 24 black males were recruited from these sources.

After much of the recruiting had been done, we determined what percentage of each homosexual sample (the white males, white females, black males, and black females) should come from each of the nine sources. This determination was based upon our estimate of the percentages of homosexuals likely to be found in a given locale and upon the actual number of persons recruited from each source. We also wanted each source to be sufficiently represented so that we could determine the influence of source upon our subsequent data, anticipating the possibility that it might be necessary to hold "source" constant in our multivariate analyses.

After determining the approximate percentage of persons we wanted derived from a given source for a particular sample, we then determined how many persons in a particular sample had been recruited from a given source and how many fell into a particular age and education cell. Interviewees were then selected at random from each of these mini-pools. On this basis, for example, of the 575 white male homosexuals who were eventually interviewed, approximately 20% had been recruited from bars, 14% each from personal contacts, steam baths, and public advertising, and 9% each from private bars, homophile organizations, public places, and mailing lists. Much larger percentages of the white females and the black samples were obtained from personal contacts. No females were obtained from steam baths or public places. While the sample is not representative of homosexuals in general nor even of homosexuals living in the Bay Area, we did make every effort to include persons from even the most difficult sources in order to ensure a variety of life styles and adjustments, all too often lacking in others' research.

Although we have no particular epidemiological interest, we are in a position to compare many of our subjects' responses with those of other institute samples interviewed in Chicago, New York, Amsterdam, and Copenhagen, thus increasing our confidence in estimating various incidences of homosexual experience on the part of those homosexuals most accessible to research of this kind. More important than the degree to which our sample may represent such a population is that it enables us to look at the relationship between homosexuality and a wide range of psychological processes and social characteristics, the next issue to which I would direct your attention.

An important question involves how homosexuality is to be defined, how broadly it should be construed, and what sexual, social, or psychological parameters it should include. Gagnon and Simon (1967), in reviewing the research that has been done in this area, quite correctly observe that homosexuality cannot be summed up by specifically sexual variables, that the erotic aspects of homosexuals' lives are but one, and perhaps the least important, of the reinforcing agents in their lives, and that if more is to be learned about this phenomenon, attention must be given to the social context in which it occurs. Before commenting on the extent to which the homosexual is more than a sexual creature, I would first like to underline the importance of delineating the homosexual's experience of his homosexuality and of sexuality in general more precisely than has been done in the past. I shall list some of the ways in which the homosexual's (or heterosexual's) experience of his sexuality can be delineated and then point out, on the basis of our data, the extent to which homosexuals differ with regard to that experience.

SEXUAL VARIABLES

As I have indicated elsewhere (1972), where a person stands on the so-called Kinsey Scale is probably not the most important indicator of where one is sexually. And if more is to be learned about the development and management of human sexuality, within-group differences with respect to other parameters of the sexual experience must be taken into account before between-group differences (homosexuals versus heterosexuals) on any other dimension can be properly reported. These other sexual parameters include: level of sexual interest (how important is sex vis-à-vis other areas of a person's life?); the conditions under which we become aroused sexually and the secondary feelings associated with that arousal; the extensiveness of sexual experience (how often does sexual activity occur and what is the range of one's sexual repertoire?); the number and type of sexual problems (does guilt or inferiority predominate?); the number of sexual partners; and the nature of our temporal and emotional involvement with them. Further important differentiations which can be made among homosexuals (and in comparable ways among heterosexuals as well) include the amount and kind of cruising they do, their feelings about and attitudes toward homosexuality in themselves and others, and the extent to which they are covert. Regardless of a person's sexual orientation, certainly the conscious and unconscious motivations underlying sexual behavior are another parameter with regard to which people can be differentiated. And until comparisons made between homosexuals and heterosexuals include controlling for one or another of these parameters, the exact size or nature of the between-group differences will never be known. For example, it might be that whatever differences one finds between homosexuals and heterosexuals with regard to a certain psychological characteristic will be increased or else ''wash out'' completely when the comparisons include controlling for ''sexual inhibition'' or ''extensiveness of sexual experience.''

THE HOMOSEXUAL-HETEROSEXUAL CONTINUUM

In our own study, a person's homosexual-heterosexual classification was based on ratings with regard to sexual behavior as well as to sexual feelings on the so-called Kinsey Scale, on the degree to which a person considered himself more homosexually than heterosexually responsive, on the proportion of dreams and masturbatory fantasies involving sexual encounters with members of the opposite sex, and on the number and frequency of various homosexual and heterosexual experiences which occurred during the past year. My general impression is that the white males tended to be more exclusively homosexual than the white females or either of the black samples. Among the white samples, 21% of the females and 28% of the males had never experienced heterosexual arousal; larger percentages of the black samples had. It seems that a person's standing on the homosexual-heterosexual continuum, shifts which occur in that standing over the course of a person's life, the ages at which these shifts have occurred, as well as the degree to which behavior and certain sexual feeling states have been incongruent, are crucial variables in the consideration of psychosexual development. And up until now, most of the researchers in this area have failed to report the nature of their samples with respect to these important dimensions. Developmentally and psychologically, it is not unreasonable to suppose that a person who has been exclusively homosexual throughout his or her life is quite different from one whose behaviors and feelings have varied. And it goes without saying that the implications of this variable for therapeutic goals and outcomes are enormous (Hatterer, 1970).

LEVELS OF SEXUAL INTEREST

Despite persisting notions that homosexuality involves primarily a sexual preoccupation, my impression of the data is that heterosexuals have *higher* levels of sexual interest and that among the homosexual samples the white males have the highest and white females the lowest levels of sexual interest. This latter fact is but further evidence that most people's impressions of homosexuality are based on the white males, whose characteristics cannot be generalized to either females or to blacks. Even among our white males we found differences in the levels of sexual interest. While 40% reported that sex was a very important aspect of their lives, 13% considered sex relatively unimportant. Thirty-seven percent thought quite a bit about sexual things during the course of a day, while 18% hardly did at all.

SEXUAL STIMULI

When asked what aspects of another person they found attractive or which they desired in a sexual partner, our white male homosexual sample tended to stress the less explicitly sexual stimuli. For example, the largest number (67%) reported that they would be very much attracted by a good-looking male stranger in a social situation, a smaller number (42%) by the naked chest of a male in real life, and even smaller numbers by seeing the buttocks of a male (37%) or male genitals in photos (36%). While the largest number (42%) specified 3 or 4 physical characteristics which they liked in a sexual partner, the number of characteristics specified ranged from none to 19. And again, the nature of those characteristics varied. In descending order of frequency were references made to weight or body frame (42%), a masculine appearance (26%), an athletic-type build (22%), a lack of baldness or a certain color hair (21%), a muscular body (15%), a pleasant face (13%), a tall stature (13%), and a large penis (12%). Less frequently specified preferences were for a lot of body hair on the part of the partner (8%), a lack of body hair (7%), eyes of a certain color (7%), a large scrotum (7%), and youthfulness or a younger age (9%). When asked if there were some special person from the past who possessed the preferred physical characteristics they had mentioned, approximately one-half (51%) could recall such a person, most often a past lover (37%).

SEXUAL REPERTOIRE

Although some homosexuals are locked into sociosexual roles, most simply prefer one technique over another and, depending on the circumstances, will engage in a variety of sexual activities. The largest number of our white male homosexuals preferred performing fellatio on their partners, followed by a slightly smaller number who preferred performing anal intercourse. The vast majority had never engaged in sadomasochistic activity. In addition to differences in technical preferences are the degrees of their sexual activity. For example, 16% of our white males reported that they had engaged in sexual activity of some kind with a partner four or more times a week; the same percentage reported having had sex once a month or less during the past year. I would guess that the range of a person's sexual repertoire as well as the frequency of sexual activity is related to age, the length of the homosexual career, and the extent to which he has been exposed to various sexual techniques and is involved with persons who represent a wide range of sexual life styles. Much would depend upon the extent to which the person has broken through stereotypical roles and behaviors, so often found in the more naive homosexual, and has managed to fashion a more realistic and viable identity.

SEXUAL PROBLEMS

Between 20 and 50% of our white male homosexual sample reported that nine different aspects of their sexual lives were problematic for them. In descending order of frequency, we find that difficulties associated with finding a suitable sexual partner are the most problematic, followed by a lack of frequency, coming too fast, the partner's failure to respond to his sexual requests, maintaining affection for his partner, concerns about his sexual adequacy, maintaining an erection, responding to his partner's sexual requests, and feeling that his sexual needs are exorbitant. In comparison with the white male heterosexuals, not only do we find more homosexuals reporting sexual problems, but also a difference in the nature of those problems. More heterosexuals are concerned about their partner's failure to reach orgasm and about coming too fast, while fewer report difficulties in finding a suitable sexual partner or are concerned with their sexual adequacy. Differences within the homosexual sample or between them and the heterosexual respondents are probably related to differences in the management of their sexuality. In a homoerotophobic culture such as ours which discourages anything more than surreptitious sociosexual encounters between homosexual males, we would expect to find the kinds of differences I have just reported. On the other hand, I would suspect that homosexuals whose sexual lives are lived out in less stressful circumstances, who are enjoying a relatively permanent relationship with a sexual partner, and who are generally relaxed about their homosexuality would report far fewer difficulties than those not in such circumstances.

SEXUAL PARTNERSHIPS

Differences between the male homosexual and heterosexual sample, and related to the same issue which I have just commented on, are most apparent when one looks at the number and nature of their sexual partnerships. A modal view of the white male homosexual, based on our findings, would be that of a person reporting 1,000 or more sexual partners throughout his lifetime, most of whom were strangers prior to their sexual meeting and with whom sexual activity occurred only once. Only a few of these partners were persons for whom there was much care or affection, and few were ever seen socially again. During the past year, 28% reported having had more than 50 partners; however, 31% claimed to have had 10 partners or less. A modal view of the white male heterosexual, on the other hand, would be that of a person who reports having had between 5 and 9 partners during his lifetime, only a few of whom were strangers but most of whom were cared about—people with whom sexual activity occurred more than once. While there has been much speculation about those factors responsible for such differences—the dynamics of homosexuality per se which reflect or result in an inability to integrate one's affectional and sexual needs—one must be ever mindful of the different set of social circumstances under which male homosexuals and heterosexuals pursue their sexual interests. One must also be aware of the differences in sexual transactions which occur between males as opposed to those between males and females. Female homosexuals present quite a different picture. And I would expect that the degree to which a homosexual community provides more than a gay bar or a public rest room for meetings would have an important bearing on the sociosexual encounters which take place.

Among our white homosexual males 17% reported that having a permanent living arrangement with a sexual partner is the most important thing in life and 20% did not consider it important at all. Nine percent reported never having had a relatively steady relationship (the "affair") with another male, while 57% were currently involved in such a relationship at the time they were interviewed, most of whom were living together with the partner. Only 39% were currently living with a roommate, and of these, two-thirds were having sex with him.

CRUISING

An important variable in this regard, and one in which we find considerable differences between homosexuals, is how often and where they "cruise," a term used to denote going out to look for a sexual partner. The most significant differences are found between the males and the females. Over 80% of the latter reported that they had not cruised at all during the last year, and those who do are apt to seek a prospective sexual partner in more private settings than the males. However, even among the males we find more than one-third reporting that they had gone out looking for a sexual partner once a month or less. Forty-three percent reported cruising once a week or more. In addition to differences in the amount of cruising reported are the locales in which it is done. The greatest number reported having cruised at least once in a gay bar, followed in decreasing order of frequency by steam baths, streets, private parties, parks and beaches, public toilets, and movie theaters. Needless to say, where one cruises has a bearing on the extent to which a sexual encounter is casual and anonymous as well as the kinds of social consequences which may be experienced. There may be an inverse relationship between the extent to which partners make themselves known to each other and the potential for exposure to the public authorities. Other aspects of those settings and circumstances under which sexual partners are pursued include the ease (or lack of it) with which a person can interact socially with others, the extent to which one is involved in the gay community, and, of course, the degree to which a person's homosexuality is covert. For example, it has been found (Humphreys, 1970) that many of those who frequent public toilets for sex are predominantly heterosexual, married males whose homosexual proclivities are unknown to others. Yet another factor which can account for differences between homosexuals with regard to their cruising practices is the age of those involved. An older male may avoid the bar scene altogether, either because he has settled into a relationship with another male or because his age has made him a less desirable commodity than the younger, more attractive male who is apt to frequent the bars. And finally, even the cruising behaviors employed may tell us a great deal about differences between male homosexuals in their psychological and social characteristics. Forty-one percent of our white males reported that they usually waited for the partner to approach them first; 28% reported that they more often made the first approach. And the reasons they give for the way in which they operate are also varied. Some indicate simply that they use a particular cruising technique because it works. Others describe themselves as too shy or passive, concerned about their personal safety, unwilling to take responsibility for what happens, wanting the partner to be more aggressive than they, or wishing to be sure the feeling is mutual.

ACCEPTANCE OF HOMOSEXUALITY

Another important way in which homosexuals differ is in the feelings and attitudes they have toward their own and others' homosexuality. Males tend to view their own homosexuality more negatively than females, but even among males there is a large variation. Twenty-seven percent of our white males tended to view homosexuality as an emotional disorder. Similar percentages tended to regret being homosexual and wished they had been entirely heterosexual from birth. A smaller percentage reported that if there were a magic pill that could make them completely and permanently heterosexual, they would take it. Twenty-nine percent had seriously considered discontinuing their homosexuality at one time or other, and of these, 63% had made at least one serious attempt to stop. Differing views of their homosexuality may be related to the extent to which they have experienced severe social consequences as a result of their homosexual status or behaviors, the degree to which their own personal moral value system departs from parental and various institutional evaluations of sexual behavior, and the degree of their acculturation in the homosexual community. In some persons, negative feelings about their homosexuality may represent phobic reactions to sex in general and/or a more pervasive lack of self-esteem. Needless to say, the extent to which homosexuality is ego-alien to a homosexual will powerfully affect the core feeling state he brings to his sexual encounters.

OVERTNESS AND COVERTNESS

Finally, an important dimension to the management of homosexuality has to do with the extent to which it is overt (or covert). Of some interest in this regard are the differences we found between males and females. More females reported that one or both parents knew about their homosexuality, but *fewer* females reported that their homosexuality was known or suspected by their heterosexual friends, neighbors, employers, or fellow employees. In both groups, mothers were more likely to know than fathers. Probably a variety of psychological and social correlates are to be found with respect to "knownaboutness." There is probably an inverse relationship between the degree to which one's homosexuality is known about and the size of the community in which a homosexual lives (Weinberg & Williams, 1974, in press). A positive relationship would be expected between "knownaboutness" and self-employment or employment in occupations associated with homosexual employees, the extent to which one's homosexuality is not ego-alien, and the degree to which one associates socially with other homosexuals or is apt to have a relatively enduring homosexual partnership. It would certainly be related to the way in which one has managed his homosexuality and whether or not his behaviors have resulted in an arrest or conviction. One's social status would also be expected to have a bearing on whether or not a person remains "in the closet"; lower-status individuals have less to lose if their homosexuality is made known by choice or by accident (Leznoff & Westley, 1956, Weinberg & Williams, 1974, in press). This last dichotomy may be an even more significant variable in differentiating homosexuals than simply the number or kinds of persons who know about their homosexuality. By way of summary, our study has probably delineated the experience and management of homosexuality more precisely than the evidence we find in others' work. Our interest is in developing a typology which includes far more than such simple dichotomies as inserter versus insertee. We are in a position to move beyond the trichotomous motivations for homosexuality posited by Ovesey (1963): homosexuality, dependency, and power. Homosexuality, in our work, is not viewed as narrowly, and the range of motivations which are thought to originate and/or maintain the homosexual experience is considerably broader than what has been conceptualized by him and others. It is our intention to determine the ways in which homosexuality serves a variety of psychological and social needs, to sort out the psychological and social correlates of various experiences of homosexuality, and to trace the origins of these experiences with reference to a variety of developmental variables.

It cannot be stressed too often that there are many different ways of being homosexual and that the experience includes far more than a series of sexual events. At the very least, it includes a variety of life styles and interpersonal transactions as well as the potential for both favorable and unfavorable social consequences. A careful delineation of homosexuality must therefore include a variety of social and psychological dimensions.

PSYCHOLOGICAL ADJUSTMENT

The questionnaire which we designed for our study incorporated, sometimes with modifications, items from others' psychological instruments which tapped a number of psychological dimensions. These include such feeling states as loneliness, depression, boredom, worry, anxiety, well-being, and suspiciousness, as well as level of self-esteem and various psychosomatic complaints. In addition, subjects were given the Dynamic Personality Inventory (Grygier, 1956) to fill out on their own at the conclusion of the interview. Following the general framework of the psychoanalytic approach to the study of personality, the inventory includes 325 items and 33 scales such as orality, anal dependence, narcissism, masculinity, femininity, phallic interests, ego strength, and compulsivity. A good deal of attention was also given to their experience with psychotherapy and to the nature of subjects's past suicidal ideation.

Unlike what the medical model of homosexuality might have predicted, our data reveal much greater differences within the homosexual and heterosexual samples than between them. For example, while 58% of the white male homosexuals had gone to a professional because of what they or others had construed as an emotional problem, 42% had not. Twenty-six percent had never imagined committing suicide; 37% had thought about it but had never considered it seriously; 19% did consider it seriously but never attempted it, while 18% reported that they had actually attempted suicide one or more times. Similar differences are found with regard to their current feeling states. During the year preceding the interview, 37% reported that they often felt on top of the world; 24%, that they rarely or never felt this way; 15%, that they often felt depressed; and 13%, that they never felt depressed. Twenty-eight percent described themselves as very happy, while 17% considered themselves either not too happy or very unhappy.

Although such data may do little to change the views of those who argue that the only valid data are those generated on the psychoanalytic couch (Socarides, 1970), and although even I am impatient with a methodology which does not include a more extensive clinical interview, the very least that can be said is that homosexuals differ from each other in their self-reports quite as much as heterosexuals do and that it may be possible to account for this variation on the basis of their developmental experiences, the management of their sexuality, and/or the nature of their social adjustments.

SOCIAL ADJUSTMENTS

Our data indicate a broad range of social characteristics and adjustments on the part of our homosexual samples. Occupationally we find few differences between the white male homosexual and heterosexual groups. These include more white male homosexuals employed in the field of organization than technology, fewer at the professional and managerial occupational levels, and a smaller percentage employed by government. We do not find large numbers employed in what are thought to be gay occupations. In terms of their religious involvement, we find 50% of the white male homosexuals describing themselves as not at all religious, but 22% as moderately to very religious. More than two-thirds (69%) do not attend church at all, while 18% attend at least once a month. Differences also appear with regard to their political involvement. Most (72%) vote regularly in local elections, and 27% describe themselves as active in politics. The largest number (42%) consider themselves Independent, 36% Democratic, and 17% Republican.

Even greater differences between the white male homosexuals can be found with regard to their social involvement. While 15% say that they spend almost every night at home, 17% go out almost every night. Twenty-three percent claim that more than half their leisure time is spent alone, while 38% spend almost none of their leisure time by themselves.

Homosexuals differ with respect to the number of close friends or acquaintances they have and the proportion of those friends, male or female, who are predominantly homosexual. Some associate only with homosexuals, others with equal numbers of homosexuals and heterosexuals—and in this last group some associate with their homosexual and heterosexual friends on separate occasions, while others report a more integrated friendship structure. Differences in this regard are related to other ways in which homosexuals can be categorized, having to do chiefly with how one copes with one's homosexuality in a predominantly heterosexual culture. Some leave the field entirely, becoming ghettoized occupationally, residentially, and emotionally. Such persons may live in one of the "lavender" ghettoes which can be found in any large urban center, seek employment in various enterprises where most of their fellow workers are known to be homosexual, frequent gay-owned business establishments, and limit their social contacts to those provided by various gay settings. At the other end of the continuum are those who are relatively uninvolved in, if not rejecting of, the gay subculture. How the disparity between the two worlds is experienced and managed would appear to reflect a variety of motivations and to be reflected in a variety of social postures, such as the nature of one's political or religious involvement.

Another more general set of categories which are useful in differentiating homosexuals in the social sphere has to do with the social consequences of their homosexuality. For some, the consequences may be so severely negative that it is possible to view their homosexuality as but one of many masochistic features in their personality. They may be rolled or robbed or arrested repeatedly. They may be fired from their jobs on more than one occasion. This experience of homosexuality may reflect and promote a growing sense of social isolation. At the other end of the continuum will be found perhaps even larger numbers of homosexuals whose experience of homosexuality does not even remotely resemble a masochistic enterprise. They may report that their homosexual, minority status has developed in themselves very useful and important capacities for social criticism, enhanced their creative abilities, or made them more sensitive to the needs of others. Many experience personal growth through a variety of social and sexual contacts. Others report a kind of freedom which they feel is seldom found by heterosexuals. Still others may report that their educational and occupational pursuits have benefited from their experience of homosexuality. Many describe a way of life replete with positive reinforcements quite apart from whatever sexual satisfactions they enjoy.

ETIOLOGIES

Although sociologists tend to emphasize the importance of current social circumstances in the maintenance of homosexuality, and while certain kinds of psychologists, at least, tend to view the maintenance of homosexuality as a reflection of ongoing oedipal issues in a person's life, I suppose I prefer to view homosexuality (like heterosexuality) as all of one piece, and in which temporal distinctions are acknowledged as arbitrary, artificial, and not always useful. We must always remind ourselves of the fact that our data are usually obtained from subjects at a single point in time and that what we choose to call antecedent variables are a function of our subjects' current needs and perceptions. In other words, the difference between reporting that the parents of *N* number of subjects possessed this or that characteristic and reporting that the parents of *N* number of subjects were *described* as possessing this or that characteristic must be clearly understood. We may never know the degree to which subjects' perceptions of persons or events in the past are distorted, but this uncertainty is of little consequence as long as it is understood that our data amount to no more than our subjects' current perceptions. This understanding also renders meaningless the debate over whether research conducted in the area of homosexuality should be concerned chiefly with the present or past circumstances of the subjects involved. A detailed description of the past is, in fact, a present circumstance. And whatever perceptions of the past have been filtered by more current life experiences (or vice versa) are quite beside the point.

Since homosexuality is most often viewed in the literature as a relatively undifferentiated (usually pathological) condition, the tendency has been to seek a single set of etiological factors to account for its development. Most, though not all, are thought to involve the original experiences of parents which are interpreted with reference to the psychoanalytic conception of the oedipal conflict. An overintense relationship with the mother together with an indifferent or hostile relationship with the father is thought by many to be the predominant, if not exclusive, etiological factor in male homosexuality. Some suppose that an opposite set of circumstances accounts for homosexuality in the female. Subsequent homosexual behaviors are then interpreted, often in different ways, as the result of these parental fixations. For example, male homosexual behaviors may be understood as the desire to be loved by the father or sometimes as a reaction formation designed to disguise a fear of or hostility toward all male figures (Bieber, 1965), beginning with the father. Others emphasize an exaggerated fear of the paternal phallic figure which results in an abandonment of females as sexual objects. Still others tend to emphasize the prehomosexual's guilt over his successful competition with an inadequate father for the mother's affections (Bell, 1969).

The mother-son relationship has been interpreted in as many different ways. A mother's dependency upon her relationship with the son may lead the son to avoid whatever contacts with females would disrupt that relationship, out of guilt over abandoning the mother. Some view a male's disinclination to become sexually or emotionally involved with females as reflecting fears of the kind of engulfment which was first experienced with the mother.

Hatterer (1970) lists 15 different etiologies stemming from the maternal relationship, 12 from the paternal relationship, 10 from the nature of the interparental relationship, and 6 which are a function of sibling relationships. He indicates 7 different aspects of the American culture and 5 characteristics of early peer relationships which increase the likelihood of a homosexual commitment. In addition, he gives 10 different motivations for a homosexuality associated with the search for a viable male identity.

Another, more behavioral, emphasis has concerned itself with the nature of a person's sexual conditioning. Early punishments of heterosexual behaviors or an early trauma resulting from a premature introduction to heterosexuality, especially when it has been unwillingly imposed, are thought to provide the original habit of avoidance of the opposite sex. Others, like Kinsey (1948), tend to understand homosexuality primarily as the result of positive reinforcement. They seek evidence of early satisfactions associated with a homosexual outlet as a sufficient condition for the maintenance of homosexual behaviors.

Finally, one sociological perspective on the development of homosexuality stresses the impact of labeling on the formation of a homosexual identity. It traces the experience of being sexually different through the process of being defined by others as sexually different to an outcome which usually involves a more or less exclusive association with others who have been labeled similarly.

A preliminary view of our own data which were gathered with reference to more than one theoretical perspective leads me to suppose that just as there is such a diversity of adult homosexuality (sufficient to speak, instead, of "homosexualities"), so there are multiple routes into this orientation, routes which may well account for differences in the way a particular person experiences and expresses his homosexuality as well as the nature of his psychological makeup and of his social adjustment.

For example, there is a considerable range of experiences and perceptions of parents reported by our white male homosexual sample, sometimes tending in a direction which contradicts previously held assumptions about homosexuals' parental relationships. Twenty-nine percent perceived their mothers as having been extremely involved with them during the time they were growing up, 25% as having been relatively uninvolved. Twenty-four percent described them as extremely overprotective, 21% as more nonprotective. While fathers tended to be viewed as less involved than mothers, 23% viewed their fathers as more involved than detached. Twenty-five percent described their fathers as not at all hostile toward them, and 14% as not at all rejecting. Mothers tended to be viewed as more feminine than masculine and fathers as more masculine than feminine. Only 39% reported that their mothers tended to dominate their fathers. Slightly less than half of the sample (46%) said they were very little or not at all afraid of their fathers; 78% stated that their mothers did not tend to be seductive. Since so many believe that homosexuality inevitably involves an impaired gender identity, often understood as the result of an identification made with a parent of the opposite sex, it is interesting to note that I was able to identify 17 white male subjects who reported that during the time they were growing up they did not feel similar to their mothers, did feel similar to their fathers, did not want to be the kind of person their mother was, but did want to be the kind of person their father was, and who described themselves as more masculine then feminine during childhood and adolescence, enjoyed boys' activities and did not enjoy girls' activities, and never engaged in cross-sex dressing. While a larger number, 37 of our white male subjects, had an opposite experience which conforms to a widely held view of homosexuality, it is clear that for a large number of our white male subjects there are varying degrees to which their homosexuality may involve an uncertain gender identification. Further evidence of this can be found in our subjects' responses to additional questions related to gender development. Seventy-three percent report having had a close same-sex friend during elementary school; the majority (55%) palled around with a group of boys during that period. Thirty-two percent reported having enjoyed boys' activities; only a minority (37%) ever engaged in cross-sex dressing. Nineteen percent had only sisters, 23%, only brothers.

In terms of their social relations during grade school, 38% described themselves as being very much loners, 30% as having felt very much different from their peers. Even if larger numbers of homosexuals than heterosexuals report a greater degree of social isolation during childhood and adolescence, what must be remembered is that large numbers do not. Again, differences between homosexuals become evident in their reports of sexual arousal and activity before, at, and after puberty. The majority (56%) report having had a prepubertal heterosexual experience; 28% report that they have never experienced heterosexual arousal. Thirty-eight percent experienced homosexual arousal by the age of 11, another 38% between the ages of 12 and 14, and 24% at age 15 or later. We find some reporting extensive prepubertal homosexual activity, many describing themselves as exclusively homosexual for as long as they can remember. On the other hand, there are those who begin their homosexual activity at later ages, who have engaged in a great deal of heterosexual experimentation, particularly during adolescence, and whose ratings on the Kinsey Scale, beginning at age 12, show considerable variation into young adulthood.

When we asked our subjects to enumerate the factors *they* thought were responsible for their homosexuality, the majority of the white males did not mention parental influence at all. Of those who did, the largest numbers mentioned an absent or distant father and/or a dominating or suffocating and overprotective mother. Of those who mentioned nonparental factors, 16% thought that their early homosexual experiences were responsible for their becoming homosexual, 15% said that they had simply been born that way, and 10% spoke of factors which resulted in an opposite-sex gender identification. Differences in these perceptions, regardless of their relationship to reality, may prompt or reflect an abiding sense of what one thinks one's homosexuality amounts to and the degree to which a person's perceptions correspond to conventional notions of what homosexuality involves.

SUMMARY

By way of summary, our data appear to indicate that homosexuality involves a large number of widely divergent experiences, developmental, sexual, social, and psychological, and that even after a person has been labeled "homosexual" on the basis of his or her preferred sexual object there is little that can be predicted about the person on the basis of that label. One's experience of homosexuality differs according to one's age, social status, sex, race, and geographical residence. It differs according to the time and culture in which it is expressed. In addition, the homosexual experience must be delineated much more precisely than has been done in the past and on the basis of parameters shared in common with heterosexuals.

Perhaps it is not sufficient even to explore relationships between a much larger number of variables than are found in past investigations or to develop a typology of homosexual experience based upon a variety of commonly held experiences on the part of one type versus another. It may be that an additional differentiation must be made on the basis of what is figure and what is ground for a given homosexual. For example, it is possible that for some homosexuals the most prominent feature of their homosexuality is their attempt to deal with the guilt which they experience over their behaviors; for others it may be the management of the tension they experience between the gay and straight worlds; for still others it might become experienced primarily as a social protest, as the search for a long-lasting relationship, or as an attempt to overcome sexual inhibitions. What is figure for some is ground for others; and for all, what is figure at one point in their lives may become ground at another. Clearly, where one is, homosexually, reflects and is accounted for by a wide range of experiences and motivations, none of which justifies a differentiation between a so-called real versus a pseudo homosexuality (Bergler, 1954). No homosexuality can be considered simply a function of sexual motivations nor of interests or conflicts arising either from the present or the past. Each expresses exactly where a given homosexual is, has been, and wants to go in his life—experiential strands involving discontinuities as well as continuities. And it is this wider view of the matter which, hopefully, will come to characterize whatever research addresses itself to the incredible variety of human sexual experience.

REFERENCES

Bell, A. P. The Scylla and Charybdis of psychosexual development. *Journal of Sex Research,* 1969, **5,** 86–89.

Bell, A. P. Human sexuality—a response. *International Journal of Psychiatry,* 1972, **10,** 99–102.

Bergler, E. Spurious homosexuality. *Psychiatric Quarterly,* 1954, **128,** 68–77.

Bieber, I. Clinical aspects of male homosexuality. In J. Marmor (Ed.), *Sexual inversion: The multiple roots of homosexuality.* New York: Basic Books, 1965.

Churchill, W. *Homosexual behavior among males: A cross-cultural and cross-species investigation.* New York: Hawthorn Books, 1967.

Gagnon, J. H., & Simon, W. The sociological perspective on homosexuality. *Dublin Review,* 1967, **512,** 96–114.

Grygier, T. G. *Dynamic personality inventory.* London: National Foundation for Educational Research, 1956.

Hatterer, L. J. *Changing homosexuality in the male.* New York: McGraw-Hill, 1970.

Hooker, E. The adjustment of the male overt homosexual. *Journal of Projective Techniques,* 1957, **21,** 18–31.

Hooker, E. Male homosexuality in the Rorschach. *Journal of Projective Techniques,* 1958, **22,** 33–54.

Hooker, E. What is a criterion? *Journal of Projective Techniques,* 1959, **23,** 278–281.

Humphreys, R. A. L. *Tearoom trade.* Chicago: Aldine, 1970.

Kinsey, A. C.; Pomeroy, W. B.; & Martin, C. E. *Sexual behavior in the human male.* Philadelphia: W. B. Saunders, 1948.

Leznoff, M., & Westley, W. A. The homosexual community. *Social Problems,* 1956, **3** (4), 257–263.

Marmor, J. (Ed.) *Sexual inversion: The multiple roots of homosexuality.* New York: Basic Books, 1965.

Ovesey, L.; Gaylin, W. M.; & Hendin, H. Psychotherapy of male homosexuality: Psychodynamic formulation. *Archives of General Psychiatry,* 1963 **9** (1), 19–31.

Riley, M. W. *Sociological research.* New York: Harcourt, Brace & World, 1963.

Schofield, M. G. *Sociological aspects of homosexuality: A comparative study of three types of homosexuals.* Boston: Little, Brown & Co., 1965.

Socarides, C. W. Homosexuality and medicine. *Journal of the American Medical Association,* 1970, **212** (7), 1,199–1,202.

Weinberg, M. S., & Williams, C. J. *Male homosexuals: Their problems and adaptations in three societies.* New York: Oxford University Press, 1974, in press.

Williams, C. J., & Weinberg, M.S. *Homosexuals and the military.* New York: Harper & Row, 1971.

Problems of the Aged*

E. David Sherman

"Not yet can I speak with the authority of the 'retired' from labour, a shadowy company who spend their time in regretting their retirement and criticising their successors. I am still at work with my hand to the plough, and my face to the future. The shadows of evening, it is true, lengthen about me, but morning is in my heart!"

Sir William Mulock, 1930

Old age and man's perpetual quest for youth have captivated the attention of physicians, priests, poets and philosophers from earliest times. To focus attention on the subject, Nascher (1) in 1909 coined the word "Geriatrics," derived from the Greek, geron, old man, and iatrikos, medical treatment. It denotes a special branch of medicine devoted to the diagnosis and treatment of disease in the aged. Although this word is approaching respectable middle age, it has only come into general use within the past decade. Disorders in older people constitute an essential part of general medicine. This has led to the adoption of another new term, "gerontology." This refers to the science of ageing in the broadest sense and involves all the biological, physical and social sciences. Geriatrics is part of the broader field of gerontology.

Gerontology is primarily concerned with changes occurring between maturity and death of the individual and factors that influence such changes. These range from hereditary to climatic differences and include the effects of social customs and usage. Gerontology is concerned not only with alterations of individual structure and function, but also with the effect of one upon the other, and the reaction of the individual to his environment. In Canada, as elsewhere, the growing number and proportion of older persons is creating new and complex problems. Bernard Baruch characterizes the increase in older citizens as one of the most momentous developments of modern times. The health and general welfare of these people along with their integration into the stream of national life presents a major challenge.

In 1900 the average North American could expect to live about 50 years.By 1960 the life span increased to nearly 70 in the United States and Canada. In 1961 the number of Canadians 65 and over was estimated at 1,435,000—more than triple the number in 1921. They comprised 7.8 per cent of the nation's population, compared

*From E. David Sherman, "Geriatrics: An Emerging Challenge to the Health Professions," *Journal of the American Geriatrics Society,* 1971, *19,* 199–207. Reprinted by permission of the author, the Editor, American Geriatrics Society, and the Editor, *Journal of the Canadian Dental Association.*

to only 4.8 per cent in 1921. By 1971 there will likely be 1,845,000 Canadians 65 and over.

The dramatic increase in longevity in the western world is due to a combination of factors including new drugs, improved hygiene, and improved control of childhood infections, tuberculosis, respiratory diseases and numerous other illnesses. Continuing advances in medical, hygienic and dietary knowledge indicate that the life span will increase beyond the three-score-and-ten.

Life has depth and breadth as well as length. Consequently, geriatric medicine aims to improve the quality of life, not merely increase longevity, in the declining years. These goals are attainable through greater health during maturity, the prevention and retardation of progressive disabling disorders of senescence, and continued cultivation of the mind through better adult education.

The problems (2–5) that stem from an ageing population are by no means limited to the biological sciences and clinical medicine—social, economic and environmental aspects have equal importance. Indeed, the older citizen may have more social and economic difficulties than medical problems.

Anticipating old age with assurance calls for good health, financial security, social adjustment and a receptive environment. The all-important goal is the preservation of usefulness for as long as possible: an awareness of uselessness is the real tragedy of old age. All of us have a responsibility in achieving this end.

Though none of the current theories of ageing (6–15) fully explain all of the phenomena associated with ageing and death, we do have some important clues.

Although some functions do not change with age, there is generally a gradual decrement beginning at age 25 and 30 and extending to death. The rate of decrease varies widely with different functions, being usually greater for complex performances or responses to stresses and displacing stimuli. Thus the maximum excretory capacity of the kidney falls by 50 per cent between the ages of 30 and 90, whereas the speed of conduction of a nervous impulse diminishes by only 15 per cent over the same span.

Shock (16–18) has shown that ageing is associated with a reduction in reserve capacities. This increases the probability that environmental demand may strain the individual's capacity and result in death. Diminished performance of organs or organ systems is also associated with progressive loss of cells or function units. This phenomenon is well illustrated in the kidney where there is a loss of nephrons as well as muscle and nerve fibres with advancing age.

But why do the cells die? A cell population at any time represents a balance between the rate of formation of new cells and the rate of loss. All organ systems do not age at the same rate. Some cells such as those of the skin, the lining of the gastro-intestinal tract, and liver retain their capacity to divide even in late adult life and senescence, but the rate of division may diminish with age. Cellular ageing in these tissues may be considerably lower than that of the entire animal so that few age differences in cellular metabolism can be detected. On the other hand, brain, muscle and kidney cells do not undergo division with advancing age. In these cells we can therefore observe changes in cellular metabolism which precede death. Losses or changes in such fixed cells cannot be restored or replaced.

Some cells undoubtedly die from anoxia or starvation due to impairment of the blood supply and deprivation of oxygen and nutrients. Ageing and death may also be due to intracellular factors. At least three mechanisms (18) have been postulated: 1) exhaustion of some essential material: 2) eversion, that is the accumulation of alterations in macromolecules concerned with cellular structure or function: and 3) the error mechanism. The latter assumes that the DNA (desoxynucleic acid) molecule contains the information required to form the many complex materials that are essential for life. As cells age, the DNA molecule becomes altered, thereby interfering with the production of materials indispensable to the functioning of the cells.

CHRONIC ILLNESS

Though chronic illnesses are more frequent and severe in older people, there are few diseases which may not occur at any age. The acute communicable diseases of childhood are not unusual late in life. After maturity, however, infectious disorders become less frequent and degenerative disorders take precedence. These are chronic, slowly progressive disorders. They constitute the gravest menace to continued health and usefulness of those reaching maturity. Today, over 60 per cent of the deaths in Canada and the United States are attributable to chronic disease. The frequency of the degenerative disorders is increasing because more people survive through youth to fall into the vulnerable period after 40.

According to the Canadian Sickness Survey, there were 684,000 year-long illnesses in 1950–51. They represent a year-long illness for every 20 persons in the country. The age group 65 and over, representing only 7.8 per cent of the population had nearly 25 per cent of all these disorders.

Four major disorders are significant in geriatric medicine: 1) circulatory impairments, 2) metabolic dysfunctions like diabetes and gout, 3) arthritis, and 4) neoplasms.

The 10 principal causes of disability in persons 65 and over are heart disease, arthritis, hypertensive vascular disease, nephritis, tuberculosis, disease of bones and joints (except tuberculosis and arthritis), accidents, diabetes, cancer and eye disease. Five of these are also leading causes of death in people 65: heart disease, cerebral haemorrhage and other vascular lesions affecting the central nervous system, cancer, general arteriosclerosis and accidents.

PSYCHOLOGICAL AND PSYCHIATRIC ASPECTS OF AGEING

Intelligence, as measured by the Bellevue Scale, declines very slowly in later years. Certain qualitative changes compensate for the quantitative depreciation. Moreover, such factors as motivation, interest, practice or disease alter and distort the quantitative values on those in later maturity (19). The result is that general intelligence, having reached its peak, stays at this level, especially if people continue to be active and suffer no physical and neurological deterioration. Since education is an intellectual stimulus, continued learning throughout life presumably exerts a similar effect. Indeed, a high level of intelligence, a good education and continuous practice in exercising one's learning capacity delay the onset of any loss of ability to learn.

Memory for past events is often less impaired than retention and recall of recent experience. Failure in immediate recall, perhaps associated with inability to register what is new, characterizes memory failure in old age. Healthy older people, however, show much less deficit in short term memory than do those who are in poor health.

Ageing, moreover, is asymmetrical. As certain physical attributes decline, others become stronger. Memory may decline, but judgement in the appraisal of significance improves with age. Visual acuity obviously diminishes, but the ability to comprehend that which is seen improves with experience. Experience is dependent on time and therefore inevitably grows with age.

The older individual is under a load of accumulated past experiences. Some of these are no longer useful. He experiences some decrement of function. Changes in his appearance advertise his advancing age. He must face up to new circumstances such as retirement, reduced income, bereavement, loss of status and recognition and an overabundance of leisure. Successful ageing depends upon one's ability to cope with internal physiological changes as well as with external social changes and the capacity to achieve a harmony of the two (20).

Older people exhibit increasing concern with bodily symptoms and diminished interest in physical activities. They are more withdrawn and less emotionally responsive. As a person ages, his individual characteristics are intensified. Dependencies and inadequacies, camouflaged in earlier years by supporting social factors, emerge when later years take away job, spouse, friends and a tolerant milieu. Rigidity in thinking develops when the ageing person relies too heavily on old habits of response and rejects new ideas that seem to imply that long-held notions were wrong. Anxiety, too, accompanies psychological ageing. Some people are apprehensive about their jobs, their social position or diminished sexual attractiveness. Others who are excessively dependent fear pain, mutilation and death. Many tend to regress to earlier stages of emotional development. Geriatric patients, like those of any other age group, should be treated at the level of their personality function.

Care of elderly patients is more than just their medical supervision; it includes suggestions on how to improve the quality of living and of the environment. Activity enhances the quality of living. To be truly therapeutic, activity must be purposeful; the more it absorbs the energies and the more deeply it stirs the emotional life of the patient, the more beneficial it will be. All patients, regardless of the nature of their illnesses, respond favourably to participatory activities. A sheltered workshop, for example, provides through work the only contact they have with the real world because it involves working with a well-known product. Activity promotes interaction between patients; isolation is thereby significantly reduced and satisfying groups are formed. A further benefit is that drug and treatment needs decrease when psychological and social requirements are satisfied.

The preventive implications of such therapy are self-evident. The goals were aptly defined by Gitelson (21): "To die with one's boots on is the keynote of mental health in old age. Never to know that one is through, never to feel superfluous, never to lack significance, never to be without use, never to be without an outlet for creative urge, never to be without a word in the affairs of man." These goals, reflecting the wellsprings of human dignity, must be achieved in a more restricted life-space than that of younger persons.

Often, the physician is the only person to whom the lonely patient turns for aid in his struggle against illness and old age. An elderly person is apt to cast him in the parent role in his search for security and reassurance. Understanding the nature and depth of his patient's needs as well as his own capacity for satisfying them makes the physician more patient and compassionate in treating the whole person.

Emotional strain accentuates the difficulties of those who are more or less disabled. In contrast, older people who maintain their interests even in the presence of physical limitations are likely to live longer, more happily and more productively.

RETIREMENT

As the human life increases, it opens up new potentials heretofore undreamed of. When 65 was selected as an arbitrary retirement age, the average retirement expectation was approximately five years. Modern medicine has extended the life span by another five to 10 years. The further possibility of lowering the retirement age to 60 or 55 indicates that even more time may be spent in retirement.

Since work plays such an important part in life, retirement often has a devastating effect on those who are unprepared for it. The elderly should therefore participate in the creative, social, economic and political life of the community, in keeping with their capacities, for as long as possible.

Partial and gradual retirement from work and the cultivation of hobbies and other interests are sound psychiatric principles. Older people have much to contribute to our civilization; their ideas and cultural development deserve greater recognition. A more constructive attitude toward the ageing will emerge when we learn to appreciate what they can really do.

Factors that bear on retirement include compulsory retirement, pensions and income maintenance. Pre-retirement programs can aid workers to relinquish work relatively free from anxiety. They reduce the fear of retirement, enhance positive attitudes toward retirement, encourage constructive planning for this event and promote desirable behavior in retirement preparation (22). Pre-retirement guidance is most effective in relation to financial planning, health and nutrition, and retirement living. Retirement should offer an activity routine, opportunity for personal contacts, status derived from performance of a culturally defined role, perhaps opportunities to serve others, as well as intrinsic satisfaction in the activity itself (23).

Self-employed professionals usually do not retire; therefore retirement planning does not have the same urgency for dentists and physicians. As a rule, their interests are so varied and their work so interesting that they develop a maturity and judgment that makes their service to patients more valuable with time.

Retirement should furnish larger opportunities for the enjoyment of life. The fight against growing old is not so much a matter of duration as it is for preservation of the capacity for happiness and interesting living.

Retirement from a job need not bring about retirement from society. Skills and experience acquired over the years may be profitably directed to various perplexing problems of community life.

Adequate financial planning is the key element in preparation for retirement; without it, hardship is inevitable.

Retirement means different things to different people (24). Trouble must ensue when it is approached with apprehension as a final time of uselessness and dependency on others. A barren and unproductive period between regular employment and death must at all cost be avoided. Retirement should be a time for taking up new and useful duties which are adapted to the older person's capabilities and which do not demand his participation beyond voluntary limits. The man himself must develop his interests as resources over the years against the day when he is free to leave his regular job. At all ages, men seek for self-realization and have the desire to carry on. Although physical activity slows moderately, mental processes may carry on at a higher level of performance into the upper advanced years.

The factors that limit longevity are a man's inherent genetic make-up, disease (principally cardiovascular and respiratory disease and cancer), obesity and the gradual changes in organs and tissues which reduce their reserve capacity (25). These changes do not proceed uniformly in all organ systems. Many can be compensated by devices such as eye glasses, hearing aids and dentures. Some can be retarded by systematic exercise and physical activity. We can learn to live with others simply by avoiding the strain of excesses.

NUTRITION AND AGEING

Life-diminishing obesity is associated with an increase in cardiovascular disease. McCay (26) has shown that diet can retard ageing and that certain diets actually lengthen the life line of rats. He increased their life span by feeding them a diet containing all essential substances for normal growth but low in calories. This diet retarded the development of inflammatory, neoplastic and degenerative diseases common to this species in old age. When exercised, the rats were even healthier. This has obvious implications for man. By consuming only the amount of food required, maintaining an active muscular tone and carrying out a well balanced active program every day, the average person increases his chances of living longer. Most people who attain a ripe old age have a low, rather than a high body weight.

The foregoing is even more crucial in view of the significance ascribed to fat intake in the genesis of arteriosclerosis and coronary artery disease. A reduced fat intake or a shift from the consumption of animal (saturated) fat to vegetable oils (unsaturated fats) limits the deposition of cholesterol in the arterial walls. Among Eastern peoples often less than 10 per cent of the diet is in fat, and Snapper (27) has emphasized the rarity of arteriosclerosis in North China.

Decreased muscular activity in old age results in diminished basal oxygen consumption and energy expenditure. The total caloric requirement of old people is therefore less. Consequently, caloric intake may be reduced by as much as 30 per cent from age 25 to old age.

Though they need less calories, the aged require the same ingredients in the same proportions as the young. They must be furnished adequate calories from the proper percentages of protein, fat and carbohydrate as well as sufficient minerals and vitamins.

PHYSICAL EXERCISE AND MAINTENANCE OF GENERAL FITNESS

Physical activity contributes to the maintenance of health and the prevention of disease by enhancing the functional and reserve capacities of the cardiovascular and respiratory systems and strengthening adaptability to the stress of modern living. Recent physical activity is more important than activity earlier in life; even lighter or moderate physical activity can be significant for cardiovascular health (28).

LIFETIME APPLICATION OF HEALTH MEASURES

The basic measures of health maintenance and disease prevention carry with them the promise of generally improved health, a sense of well-being and the avoidance of certain disorders which could be fatal. However, these measures will not reverse any degenerative changes that have already occurred. The requisite steps must therefore be adopted in youth. To appraise basic health maintenance measures in relation to the diseases of old age, one should consider not just the effects of last minute applications, but the sum total of influences which a lifetime application of such measures may have on the human organism (29).

SUMMARY

In the past two decades ageing has been accepted as a human experience and geriatrics has become a major challenge for the health professions.

The problems of ageing are not confined to the biological sciences and clinical medicine; social, economic and environmental aspects are equally important. A total approach to this many-faceted topic is obligatory to attain the perspective of "the whole person."

Ageing is associated with reduced reserve capacity due to cellular loss in the organ tissues.

The frequency and severity of chronic illness are more pronounced in older people.

General intelligence, having reached its peak, is maintained in old age, especially if one continues to be active and exercises the capacity to learn throughout life. Education must become a life-long discipline.

Emotional strain accentuates the difficulties of those who are healthy as well as those who are disabled. Yet, older people who maintain their interests even in the presence of physical limitations can anticipate a longer, happier and more productive life.

Partial and gradual retirement from work with the cultivation of hobbies and other interests are sound psychiatric principles. For the employed, pre-retirement programs are beneficial. Retirement should furnish larger opportunities for the enjoyment of life and those interests which are significant for the individual. It should be a time for taking up new and useful duties adapted to one's capabilities.

Basic measures for health maintenance beginning in youth should include proper nutrition, prevention of obesity, systematic exercise and physical activity, and avoidance of the strain of excesses.

REFERENCES

1 Nascher, I. L.: Geriatrics, *New York Med. J.* **90:** 358, 1909.

2 Sherman, E. D.: Present day problems of aging, *Can. Jew. Rev.* **41:** 39, 1959.

3 Idem: Relationship of geriatrics to chronic illness, *L'Hopital d'Aujourd'hui* **7:** 1961.

4 Idem: Some clinical aspects of geriatrics, *Canad. Serv. Med. J.* **18:** 801, 1962.

5 Idem: A physician's view on the aging process. Canada, 26th Parliament, 2nd session. In: Proceedings of the Special Committee of the Senate on Aging, No. 6. Queen's Printer, Ottawa, 1963.

6 Bjorksten. J.: The crosslinkage theory of aging, *J. Amer. Geriat. Soc.* **16:** 408, 1968.

7 Harman, Denham: Role of free radicals in mutation, cancer, aging, and the maintenance of life, *Radiation Res.* **16:** 753, 1962.

8 Verzar, Frederic: The aging of collagen, *Scient. Amer.* **208:** 104, 1963.

9 Strehler. B., Mark, D. D., Mildvan, A. S., and Gee, M. V.: Rate of magnitude of age pigment accumulation in the human myocardium, *J. Geront.* **14:** 430, 1959.

10 Pearl, Raymond: The rate of living, New York, A. A. Knopf. 1928.

11 Selye, Hans: The stress of life, New York, McGraw-Hill, 1956.

12 Carpenter, D. G.: Diffusion theory of aging, *J. Geront.* **20:** 191, 1965.

13 Curtis, H. J., and Gebhard, K. L.: Comparison of life-shortening effects of toxic and radiation stresses, *Radiation Res.* **9:** 104, 1958. Abstract.

14 Walford, R. L.: Auto-immunity and aging, *J. Geront,* **17:** 281, 1962.

15 Still, J. W.: The physiology of aging—a research approach. *J. Washington Acad. Sci.* **48:** 224, 1958.

16 Shock, N. W.: Age changes in physiological functions in the total animal: the role of tissue loss. In: Strehler, B. L., ed. The biology of aging. Washington, American Institute of Biological Sciences, Publication No. 6, p. 258, 1960.

17 Idem: The physiology of aging. *Scient. Amer.* **206:** 100, 1962.

18 Idem: Intrinsic factors in aging. In: Age with a future. Proceedings of 6th International Congress of Gerontology, p. 13. 1963. Copenhagen, Munksgaard, 1964.

19 Kleemeier, R. W.: Psychological aspects of the health care needs of the elderly patient. In: Coppinger, W. W., ed. Proceedings of Institute on Health Care Needs of the Elderly Patient. Kecoughtan, Virginia. Veterans Administration Centre, 1968.

20 Donahue, Wilma: Psychologic aspects. In: Crowdry, E. V., ed. The care of the geriatric patient. Ed. 3. St. Louis, Mosby, 1968.

21 Gitelson, Maxwell: The emotional problems of elderly people. *Geriatrics* **3:** 135, 1948.

22 Mack, Margery J.: An evaluation of a retirement-planning program, *J. Geront,* **13:** 198, 1958.

23 Friedmannn, E. A., and Havighurst, R. J.: The meaning of work and retirement. Chicago, University of Chicago Press, 1954.

24 Bortz, E. L.: Retirement and the individual, *J. Amer. Geriat. Soc.* **16:** 1, 1968.

25 Shock, N. W.: Age with a future. *Gerontologist* **8:** 147, 1968.

26 McCay, C. M., Crowell, Mary F., and Maynard, L. A.: The effect of retarded growth upon the length of life span and upon the ultimate body size. *J. Nutrition* **10:** 63, 1935.

27 Snapper, I.: Chinese lessons to western medicine. New York, Interscience Publishers, 1941.

28 Fox, S. M., and Skinner, J. S.: Physical activity and cardiovascular health, *Amer. J. Cardiol.* **14:** 731, 1964.

29 Hrachovec, J. P.: Health maintenance in older adults, *J. Amer. Geriat. Soc.* **17:** 433, 1969.

Section Six

Therapeutic Interventions

The basic goal in the treatment of adjustment difficulties is the alteration of the patient's behavior. The behavior to be changed may involve both the overt actions of the individual, such as his or her manner of interacting with others, and internal characteristics, such as the individual's self-perception or conflicting attitudes and motives. Numerous methods of effecting changes in behavior are employed in the treatment of adjustment problems. Some of these are chemotherapy (tranquilizing drugs, sedatives, stimulants, etc.), physical therapy (sports, physical exercise, etc.), psychosurgery (lobotomies and various other surgical operations on the brain), and electroshock therapy. The interest here is in the use of psychological approaches to the treatment of adjustment problems, and these are called "psychotherapy." Because of the wide variety of techniques that are based on the application of psychological principles and which are referred to as psychotherapy, it is extremely difficult to define the term in more than a broad fashion. In general, psychotherapy refers to a controlled interaction between a person seeking psychological assistance and another person who is professionally trained to provide it. The goal is to bring about a more effective adjustment on the part of the individual seeking aid. Usually psychotherapy is associated with talking, since most of the interaction between the persons involved is of a verbal nature. Some psychotherapeutic techniques, however, stress a planned program of physical activity in the context of which the interaction between patient and therapist takes place.

Psychotherapies may be classified in numerous ways. Sometimes the types of therapy are identified on the basis of the theoretical ideas underlying them *(psychoanalytic therapy, client-centered therapy, Adlerian therapy);* sometimes by the particular groups of people or type of problem for which the approach was designed *(child-guidance therapy, marriage counseling);* sometimes by the methods employed *(play therapy, dance therapy);* and sometimes by the goal that the therapy establishes *(supportive therapy, reconstructive therapy).* The readings that follow present a sample of the various therapeutic approaches in common use. In addition they illustrate the thinking underlying the three major theoretical approaches that have most influenced psychotherapy: *psychoanalysis, phenomenological theory* or *client-centered therapy,* and *learning theory.*

The first paper, by Arnold Allen, presents a case study, using *psychoanalytic techniques,* of a young man experiencing a number of personality difficulties and poor adjustment, including stealing, marital problems, passivity, inefficiency, and inner rage over frustrations of his strong dependence and acceptance needs. The interaction between patient and psychoanalyst illustrates several of the procedures that distinguish psychoanalysis from other forms of psychotherapy. A brief statement of some of these procedures may help the reader identify significant features of the interaction. The most distinctive feature is the use of *free association;* i.e, the patient is requested to state everything that comes to mind and to avoid asserting conscious control over his or her thoughts. To the extent that the patient is able to do this without censoring thoughts or imposing logic on them, his or her feelings, desires, fears, and impulses that are usually suppressed are likely to be revealed to both the patient and the analyst. Often in the psychoanalytic session, the content of the patient's free association deals with important events in his or her life or with significant feelings while lying on the couch in the psychoanalyst's office. In addition, the patient's dreams frequently are used as a starting point for free association and, as seen in the case presented, serve as a rich source of material for examining the patient's repressed feelings and desires. Patients usually are unable to see the relevance of their free association and dreams to their problems on their own, since awareness of their repressions is extremely threatening; in fact, patients are apt to resist and defend against understanding. It is only through the psychoanalyst's interest, support, and objectivity that the patient gradually becomes less resistant and willing to accept things about himself or herself which he or she previously censored from awareness. The primary method that the psychoanalyst uses to help the patient gain insight is *interpretation.* In effect, interpretation refers to the analyst's giving words to the patient which express feelings that are not totally conscious, thereby facilitating the patient's awareness of them. In this way the psychoanalyst attempts to make unconscious material conscious. However, awareness per se is not likely to alter the patient's behavior or remove his or her problems. The feelings, desires, or conflicts that have been causing the emotional difficulties must be considered again and again in connection with many different experiences and areas of life before the patient is able to alter his or her way of behaving. This is a slow process, which is called the *working-through stage* and which accounts for a large part of the extensive period, usually years, which Freudian psychoanalysis requires.

As stated in the papers by Freud and Dollard and Miller in previous sections of this book, psychoanalysis postulates that emotional problems are associated primarily with childhood experiences, and consequently much of the psychoanalytic discussion (the patient's free association and the analyst's interpretations) pertains to the patient's childhood. The case presented by Allen clearly illustrates the psychoanalyst's emphasis on family experiences and relationships during childhood. The analyst endeavors to learn as much as possible about the patient's early experiences from his or her spontaneous verbalizations, but in addition, the analyst anticipates that gradually the patient will begin to perceive and respond to the analyst as he or she perceived and responded to significant people and events in his or her early life. This projection on the part of the patient to the analyst is referred to as *the transference* and constitutes another distinctive feature of the psychoanalytic treatment process. The analyst endeavors to remain an interested, but neutral, figure in the relationship with the patient and in so doing provides the patient with a stimulus on which to project many of his or her needs, fears, and desires experienced in early life. These projections enable the analyst to observe directly the patient's perceptions of and reactions to past experiences, and through the interpretations of them, the therapist helps the patient better understand the part they play in his or her emotional disturbance and gain greater control over them. In Allen's paper, the patient's reactions to the analyst—his fluctuating dependence and competitiveness, his unwarranted feelings of being rejected, and his presentation of a gift to the analyst—are interpreted as transference reactions that were used to help the patient become aware of painful desires and impulses that unconsciously were motivating his maladjusted behavior.

The article by Carl Rogers which follows describes the characteristics that constitute the essential features of the *client-centered* approach to psychotherapy. Rogers's purpose in counseling is to promote development and growth in his client, since he regards the troubles, emotional conflicts, and maladjustments of persons who seek professional assistance as the result of a block in personal development. His focus is on the personal relationship between the individual seeking help and the professional worker, and he believes that the attitudinal characteristics that the latter brings to the relationship are most important in determining whether or not the meetings will be effective in helping the client. In his paper he discusses the attitudes that he believes the counselor must experience and communicate to the client in order to promote the client's growth. The most important of these he calls *congruence,* by which he means the genuineness of the counselor in revealing his or her real feelings to the client. Unless the counselor enters the relationship with a willingness to examine his or her feelings about and reactions to the client and to communicate these honestly and sincerely to the client, Rogers believes the therapeutic interaction will not be a meaningful one. *Empathy* is the second necessary condition of the therapeutic relationship. It is important that the counselor experience "an accurate empathic understanding of his client's personal world" and communicate this to the client. The third characteristic cited by Rogers is that the counselor experience *positive regard* for his or her client in an unconditional way. The counselor's attitude of warmth, regard, and acceptance should be based on respect for the client as a separate individual with potential for growth.

Especially interesting in the client-centered approach to psychotherapy, and one of its distinctive features, is the lack of importance given to professional knowledge, training, and the theoretical orientation of the therapist. Whereas the psychoanalyst regards as crucial to successful treatment the therapist's ability to conceptualize the patient's conflicts and dynamics and to deal effectively with the transference situation, Rogers regards as more important the therapist's positive attitude toward the client and the candor and sincerity with which he or she communicates feelings and thoughts in the therapeutic relationship. Another group of psychotherapists, the existentialists, have taken an even stronger position than Rogers concerning the idea that the therapist's theories, techniques, and efforts to achieve specific goals are not important to therapeutic progress; in fact, most existential psychotherapists regard the therapist's concern with what he or she should do as likely to lead to unnatural and contrived behavior that will interfere with effective psychotherapy. Instead they regard the essence of the therapeutic interaction as the openness, spontaneity, and sincerity of the participants with each other. Only by renouncing preconceived ideas and methods in dealing with patients can the therapist bring to the meeting freedom and flexibility of thought and thereby promote similar qualities in the patient. The theoretical rationale for existential psychotherapy is described in Pervin's article in the personality-theory section of this book.

The paper by Ellis on rational-emotive therapy presents another approach to psychotherapy which, while employing both affective and behavioral methods, stresses "the cognitive element in self-defeating behavior." Ellis takes the position that a fair share of personal difficulty derives from a person's holding irrational beliefs about activities or people which result in fear of devastating and irrational consequences. The course of therapy here involves teaching the patient to dispute his or her irrational beliefs whereupon he or she concludes that they are "unverifiable, unempirically based, and superstitious. . . ." Rational-emotive therapy is viewed as having a great many therapeutic applications, and it is also seen as having potential for forestalling emotional disturbance.

The papers by Wolpe and Liberman which follow constitute behavior-therapy approaches to psychological treatment. These approaches are grounded in psychological learning theories and represent efforts to apply the principles of learning to the treatment of maladaptive behavior. The essential strategy here is to approach behavior by way of direct intervention. This procedure is in contrast to the practices of so-called dynamic therapies, which view maladaptive behavior as a group of symptoms of underlying anxiety and conflict that must be acknowledged and resolved to result in behavior change. Wolpe's paper provides us with an account of some of the direct methods that are based upon general principles of learning. He argues that therapy based upon conditioning and learning principles is a fundamental therapy and not simply a superficial procedure failing to deal with "basic dynamic conflict."

Liberman's paper describes behavioral approaches to family and couple therapy in which the procedure involves the specification of problems in concrete and observable terms for the purpose of direct behavioral intervention. In addressing couples and families seeking assistance, Liberman advances two questions: (1) What behavior is maladaptive or problematic? (2) What environmental and interpersonal contingencies currently support the problem behavior? He presents a number of cases involving family problems which illustrate the use of such techniques as discontinuing reward of undesirable behaviors, "shaping" or teaching desirable behaviors, modeling, and role playing.

In contrast with behavior therapies, which attempt to isolate specific problem behaviors and alter the conditions that encourage them, the next two papers present descriptions of therapies that attempt to remediate maladjustment through the patient's self-awareness and confrontation with unpleasant aspects of himself or herself which he or she has tried to avoid. Levitsky and Perls define "the rules and games" associated with gestalt therapy, the latter representing an effort to unify the individual by achieving a state of harmony between his or her feelings and actions. This approach to therapy places great significance on the individual's participation in and experiencing of interpersonal relationships in the here-and-now and involves techniques for identifying feelings and emotions elicited in the therapy. Eric Berne's paper presents a brief statement of transactional analysis, which was popularized in his best seller, *Games People Play*. Transactional analysis endeavors to identify for the patient his or her three modes of relating to others, viz., as parent, child, and adult, and the inappropriateness of each of these "ego states" under some conditions. In addition, Berne's therapy identifies and analyzes the "scripts" and "games" the patient plays that restrict self-awareness and personal freedom.

The practice of group therapy, in which one therapist interacts with a number of patients at the same time, initially became popular because of the limited number of therapists available and the costliness of individual therapy. Through evaluations of group procedures, however, their many special advantages over dyadic therapy were recognized. These advantages include the experiences the group situation provides the individual in social interaction, the opportunity to compare one's own problems with those of others, the development of supportive and constructive relationships, etc. Bugental notes that a variety of disparate procedures are included under the heading of "group therapy," and he proposes a schema for classifying groups based on their purposes and activities. He describes five different kinds of groups and indicates how the behavior of the group members and the therapist in each differs. He also evaluates the value of each type of group in bringing about particular therapeutic experiences for its members.

The selections presented on psychotherapy offer only a limited number of the large variety of ideas and practices that currently are being used to help emotionally disturbed persons. Innovations and experimentation are characteristic of the field of psychotherapy. Investigations of the effectiveness of treatment have suggested that many different kinds of practices have proved equally successful in helping people, but that all practices have an appreciable number of failures. Consequently, despite differences of opinion, psychotherapists of all schools are in the process of studying their ideas and procedures and are searching for new methods with the hope of expanding their success in helping persons overcome emotional and adjustment problems.

Psychoanalytic Treatment of a Patient Utilizing Stealing as a Defense*

Arnold Allen

CLINICAL MATERIAL

. . . My interest in the subject of stealing was first stimulated by a patient in psychoanalysis in whom stealing was not the primary problem. When first seen, the patient, a professional man, was twenty-seven years old. Even in his first interview he repeatedly made interpretations about himself and his wife that suggested that his intellectualization and his ambivalence about accepting the role of a patient would present difficulties in his analysis. His stated reasons for seeking analysis were that he was "functioning at only ten per cent of capacity" and "did not produce without pressure." For three years he had had all the data needed with which to finish his Ph.D. thesis but had done nothing with it. He realized that without his degree he could not obtain a good professional position. He felt his negligence about completing his thesis was due in part to his fear of producing an inadequate paper; also, he could remain in a passive, dependent role if he did not obtain a good position. This difficulty began during college and increased as the years went by. He managed by maneuvering people with "diplomacy, charming personality, and even temper," which, of course, was the way he related to me.

Other complaints were difficulties with his wife, with constant arguments and mutual provocation, and with his parents, particularly his mother; he could not decide whether to assume the masculine role of husband and father or to remain "mother's boy."

The patient was the older of two children; his sister was nine years younger. He denied any particular feeling about her birth but he had regularly showered her with gifts, many of which he had stolen. He felt that his mother, an aggressive, ambitious, controlling woman, had castrated his father, always nagging at him to be more of a man and depreciating him. She early turned to the patient to make up for disappointments in her husband, but at the same time she infantilized him and blocked his efforts at growth and masculinity. The weak, passive father was uncompetitive and content to work in a factory. The patient never felt close to him and joined his mother in deriding him. Nevertheless he was sorry for him because of all the mortification he suffered at the hands of his wife. The stage was set early for the patient's problems in identification: strength and feminity were embodied in the mother, weakness and masculinity in the father. Even more confusing his mother incited him to fierce competition in school; indeed he won many awards in the early grades with compositions written for him by his mother. Despite the constant push to achieve, his mother kept him a baby. She took milk to him at school until he was nine or ten years old and one summer, confined him to the house lest he be exposed to poliomyelitis.

*From Arnold Allen, "Stealing as a Defense," *Psychoanal. Quart.*, 1965, *34*, 572–583. Pages 576–583 reprinted by permission of the author and the Editor, *Psychonalytic Quarterly*.

His life was spent as an only child in this setting until the age of nine, when his sister was born. With his peers he felt he did not fit in; he thought of himself as a sissy and was never sure of his role. Faced with the threat of mother's disapproval, he always "did well" at school.

In his marriage he overtly assumed a passive and nonaggressive role while covertly he seethed with rage at the least slight or deprivation. His choice of a wife seemed to have been determined largely by her being weak, not especially feminine, and not threatening to him as a sexual partner. Prior to his marriage he had had no sexual contacts and his relations with women had been casual and shallow, he playing a passive role in the relationships. His parents objected strongly to his marriage. When he was twenty-four years old, they finally agreed but then became involved in constant discord with his wife. During these arguments the patient would stand by passively, wishing to act somehow but not daring, and secretly rather enjoying his central position.

A dream on the night before his first analytic hour gave some indication of things to come.

> I was in a laboratory conducting an experiment. A girl entered and we went out together. I was apprehensive because I was not supposed to be away, but later I returned and nobody was any the wiser.

This dream apparently represented his need to isolate himself from the analysis and indicated also the first entry into the analytic situation of the defense of reversal, of protecting himself against a dependent striving by an aggressive act.

Stealing, which to this patient had no connection with seeking analysis and was not a major problem, had begun following the birth of his sister. He would steal trifles and toys from five-and-ten-cent stores, giving some to his sister and keeping some himself. This stealing appeared to fulfill a variety of functions. First, in the face of intense dependent strivings stirred by his displacement by the younger sister, it served as a denial: "I don't want what she is getting; on the contrary I enjoy having this rival around so much that I even want to give her things myself." Thus he both identified with her and denied the identification at the same time. (Anna Freud describes this as an altruistic identification.) At another level he was defending against the anxiety stirred by his strong wish to be given things. By aggressively taking, he was saying in a sense: "It's not true that I am weak; as a matter of fact I am quite strong, like mother" (identification with the aggressor). Not to be overlooked of course was the dependent gratification in his providing for himself something of which he felt deprived.

The stealing served still another function: after it was discovered by mother, she would punish him. He would then be filled with remorse but relieved of his guilt and temporarily close again to mother of whom he felt deprived. The act thus entailed all of the motivations described in the earlier literature on stealing: dependent id gratification, gratification of superego demands, rivalry with the envied object, and revenge or spite. At the same time it revealed the defensive aspect of stealing; it protected him from the anxiety mobilized by his dependent strivings.

In later years he took more and more pride in his ability to "get away with things," considering this a real accomplishment and a demonstration of strength. His petty thievery continued throughout life, even in his current job where he pilfered from the laboratory. He rationalized "there is so much, it will never be missed," and he used the stolen items to avoid buying things for various home projects, feeling that only a "weak sucker" would fail to take advantage of the situation. Except for cookies he stole while baby-sitting with his sister, the objects stolen never had particular symbolic significance. It is noteworthy that the stealing was more apt to occur when he felt deprived or humiliated in some way. His great pleasure was to find "bargains" and "put one over" on the seller. Humiliation was a recurrent theme in this man's analysis.

The analytic relationship mirrored the situations just described. It was marked by a constant seesaw between overwhelming dependency and his reactive competitiveness, always flavored with dishonesty—getting something for nothing or shirking the work involved—, followed by mounting anxiety. He would then return to passive dependency, feeling small, weak, and humiliated. His greatest fear was of being humiliated by being considered weak and inadequate, which was gradually related to a fear of facing and exposing his intense passive-dependent feminine wishes. Any confrontation with his dependent needs called forth shame and humiliation. The role of patient was for him a humiliation, to keep an appointment on time was a sign of weakness. He had repeatedly to affirm his strength by keeping another person waiting, and this was acted out early in his analysis. A good grade in school was for him not the result of effort but evidence of his having "put something over," which then was a source of pride. To work on his thesis and acknowledge his wish and need for a Ph.D. was to admit to weakness. The strong thing to do, he felt, was to make it appear he had no need for the degree. Guilt connected with aggressive acts was manifest only when he was caught and faced with disapproval. The recognition of his strong need for approval again led to feelings of weakness and humiliation. His stealing abated as he came to recognize its aggressive defensive nature, and as he made me the forbidding superego to whom he would have to confess and from whom he would meet disapproval. In time he came to think of the stealing itself as a weakness rather than a strength; in other words, it became ego alien.

After the analysis had been in progress for nearly two years, he reported an interesting, hitherto unmentioned matter: when he went to his own refrigerator to take out food (as he often did when he felt frustrated or rejected), he had the feeling that he was stealing, and he would look around to see if he were being watched. This material confirmed the idea of the defensive nature of his stealing. In the face of a feeling of rejection or frustration, his wish to receive was directly expressed in a wish to eat. Yet the feeling of smallness and shame stirred by the awareness of a dependent need, and the resultant anxiety, were defended against by the fantasy that he was stealing; that is, aggressively grabbing rather than expressing a passive need. It was as if he had a fleeting unconscious fantasy of being fed at the moment before he decided to "steal" from his own refrigerator. His ego seemed to prefer facing superego anxiety rather than anxiety stirred by infantile id needs.

An illuminating incident occurred in the patient's third year of analysis which illustrated some of the behavior described earlier. One day he arrived a half hour early and asked that I be informed of his presence. He was told that I would see him when

I had completed the session with the patient now in my office, who he was aware was a young woman who had begun her analysis some time after he began treatment. As he sat in the waiting room he became increasingly angry. He explained his behavior by the following reasoning: I would like to know he was there so that I could start earlier with him and thus go home earlier. (He had repeatedly denied the fact that another patient followed him.) He saw the previous patient leave and I called him in ten minutes earlier than usual. As soon as he got into my office he expressed strong disapproval of my secretary for failing to inform me of his presence. Ignoring that he had seen my patient leave, he believed that he had waited fifteen or twenty minutes for me after her departure. When I confronted him with the fact that not over two or three minutes had elapsed between her leaving and his coming in, he was amazed. Analysis revealed his wishful fantasy that I be interrupted while with my previous patient, that I discharge her and immediately take him in so that he would not have to wait. Associations led to his feeling ''left out'' as though he did not exist, repeating his childhood feeling when mother was preoccupied with his little sister. He became aware of the intensity of his own dependent needs and that his early arrival was not for my benefit but for his. His response to this was a feeling of shame, weakness, and humiliation. In the next hour he offered me as a gift a pipe he had just acquired—''a terrific bargain.'' A friend had smuggled it into the country. This chain of events is clear-cut illustration of strong defensiveness mobilized by his awareness of dependent strivings in his relationship with me, followed by an aggressive pseudomasculine act.

Among other such sequences was a dream of stealing which followed an argument with his wife that ended in her refusal to speak to him and his feeling ''out in the cold.'' Another dream was of an act of sabotage which came after a humiliating recognition of dependency, stirred by my not giving him a ''special reception'' upon his return from a vacation.

Psychic operations similar to this have been observed in at least two other patients who were seen in brief psychotherapy. Basic intense, unresolved dependency strivings were seen in both. One, a potentially successful business man of great ability, repeatedly failed in what could have been very profitable business ventures when, in the face of possible realistically motivated dependency on other men, he felt compelled to steal, with consequent disastrous results. He identified himself with his father, who took more pride in wealth acquired by theft and subterfuge than in legitimately earned money. Another patient, a physician, damaged his practice by losing patients because he kept no records. The reason for this was to avoid paying income taxes—the evasion of which did more to bolster his faltering concept of himself as a man than could a more adequate income easily achievable by realistic and legitimate means. A colleague has told me of a patient who had great difficulty in accepting his dependency which he attempted to handle by stealing something immediately before coming to each therapeutic hour.

SUMMARY

As suggested by Alexander, Fenichel, and others, there is little doubt that my analytic patient's stealing represented an expression of infantile oral receptive attitudes, a spite reaction, a superego bribe, and a way of re-establishing a lost relationship. However, I should like to emphasize the concept, introduced by Alexander, elaborated by Menaker, and supported by Waelder, that many functions can be served by a single act. In certain cases, particularly where there is a strong need to reject underlying dependent strivings, stealing primarily represents an ego defense against anxiety. As in Menaker's boys, the psychopathological family setting, with weak father and phallically perceived mother, was clearly illustrated in my patient. The attempts to solve the bisexual gratification, the fluctuation between masculine and feminine roles, and confusion about them, were also clearly seen. Further he illustrated the type of superego defect which results from inability to identify successfully with the father and from fixation on the pregenital level. His passive homosexual attitude to the father, his failure to identify with him but his wish to be loved by him, and the attempt to identify with a phallic mother were also demonstrated. The most striking finding, however, was the reversal of a desire to be given into active taking, and the use of symptomatic stealing as a defense against passive pregenital wishes for immediate gratification. Rather than the ego's operating passively as a mere tool for instinctual and superego expression, all of this implies definite defensive ego action.

REFERENCES*

1 Abraham, Karl: *Selected Papers.* London: The Hogarth Press, Ltd., 1942.

2 Alexander, Franz and Healy, William: *Roots of Crime.* New York and London: Alfred A. Knopf, 1935.

3 Fenichel, Otto: *The Collected Papers, First Series.* New York: W. W. Norton & Co., Inc., 1953.

4 Freud, Anna: *The Ego and the Mechanisms of Defense.* New York: International Universities Press, Inc., 1946.

5 Glover, Edward: *Selected Papers on Psychoanalysis, Vol. II.* New York: International Universities Press, Inc., 1960.

6 Kirkpatrick, M. and Tiebout, H.: *Psychiatric Factors in Stealing.* Amer. J. Orthopsychiatry, II, 1932, p. 114.

7 Menaker, Esther: *Contribution to the Study of the Neurotic Stealing Symptom.* Amer. J. Orthopsychiatry, IX, 1939, pp. 368–376.

8 Rado, Sandor: *Fear of Castration in Women.* This quarterly, II, 1933, pp. 425–475.

9 Socarides, Charles W.: *Pathological Stealing as a Reparative Move of the Ego.* Psa. Review, XLI, 1954.

10 Waelder, Robert: *The Principle of Multiple Function: Observations on Over-Determination.* This quarterly, V, 1936, pp. 45–62.

11 Zulliger, Hans: *Eine Diebin aus fehlgeleiteter Gewissenreaktion.* Psyche (Heidelberg), VIII/IX, 1954, pp. 545–558.

**Editor's note:* Since the paper has been edited, not all references remain in the body of the paper. For reasons of general interest, however, we have chosen to leave the *list* of references intact.

The Interpersonal Relationship in Client-centered Therapy*

Carl R. Rogers

I would like to share with you in this paper a conclusion, a conviction, which has grown out of years of experience in dealing with individuals, a conclusion which finds some confirmation in a steadily growing body of empirical evidence. It is simply that in a wide variety of professional work involving relationships with people—whether as a psychotherapist, teacher, religious worker, guidance counselor, social worker, clinical psychologist—it is the *quality* of the interpersonal encounter with the client which is the most significant element in determining effectiveness.

Let me spell out a little more fully the basis of this statement in my personal experience. I have been primarily a counselor and psychotherapist. In the course of my professional life I have worked with troubled college students, with adults in difficulty, with "normal" individuals such as business executives, and more recently with hospitalized psychotic persons. I have endeavored to make use of the learnings from my therapeutic experience in my interactions with classes and seminars, in the training of teachers, in the administration of staff groups, in the clinical supervision of psychologists, psychiatrists, and guidance workers as they work with their clients or patients. Some of these relationships are long-continued and intensive, as in individual psychotherapy. Some are brief, as in experiences with workshop participants or in contacts with students who come for practical advice. They cover a wide range of depth. Gradually I have come to the conclusion that one learning which applies to all of these experiences is that it is the quality of the personal relationship which matters most. With some of these individuals I am in touch only briefly, with others I have the opportunity of knowing them intimately, but in either case the quality of the personal encounter is probably, in the long run, the element which determines the extent to which this is an experience which releases or promotes development and growth. I believe the quality of my encounter is more important in the long run than is my scholarly knowledge, my professional training, my counseling orientation, the techniques I use in the interview. In keeping with this line of thought, I suspect that for a guidance worker also the relationship he forms with each student— brief or continuing— is more important than his knowledge of tests and measurements, the adequacy of his record keeping, the theories he holds, the accuracy with which he is able to predict academic success, or the school in which he received his training.

In recent years I have thought a great deal about this issue. I have tried to observe counselors and therapists whose orientations are very different from mine, in order to understand the basis of their effectiveness as well as my own. I have listened to recorded interviews from many different sources. Gradually I have developed some theoretical formulations (4, 5), some hypotheses as to the basis of effectiveness in relationships. As I have asked myself how individuals sharply different in personality,

*From Carl R. Rogers, "The Interpersonal Relationship: The Core of Guidance," *Harvard Educ. Rev., 1962,* **32**, 416–429. Pages 416–424 reprinted by permission of the author and the Editor, *Harvard Educational Review.*

orientation and procedure can all be effective in a helping relationship, can each be successful in facilitating constructive change or development, I have concluded that it is because they bring to the helping relationship certain attitudinal ingredients. It is these that I hypothesize as making for effectiveness, whether we are speaking of a guidance counselor, a clinical psychologist, or a psychiatrist.

What are these attitudinal or experiential elements in the counselor which make a relationship a growth-promoting climate? I would like to describe them as carefully and accurately as I can, though I am well aware that words rarely capture or communicate the qualities of a personal encounter.

CONGRUENCE

In the first place, I hypothesize that personal growth is facilitated when the counselor is what he *is,* when in the relationship with his client he is genuine and without "front" or facade, openly being the feelings and attitudes which at that moment are flowing in him. We have used the term "congruence" to try to describe this condition. By this we mean that the feelings the counselor is experiencing are available to him, available to his awareness, that he is able to live these feelings, be them in the relationship, and able to communicate them if appropriate. It means that he comes into a direct personal encounter with his client, meeting him on a person-to-person basis. It means that he is *being* himself, not denying himself. No one fully achieves this condition, yet the more the therapist is able to listen acceptantly to what is going on within himself, and the more he is able to *be* the complexity of his feelings without fear, the higher the degree of his congruence.

I think that we readily sense this quality in our everyday life. We could each of us name persons whom we know who always seem to be operating from behind a front, who are playing a role, who tend to say things they do not feel. They are exhibiting incongruence. We do not reveal ourselves too deeply to such people. On the other hand each of us knows individuals whom we somehow trust, because we sense that they are being what they *are,* that we are dealing with the person himself, and not with a polite or professional facade. This is the quality of which we are speaking, and it is hypothesized that the more genuine and congruent the therapist in the relationship, the more probability there is that change in personality in the client will occur.

I have received much clinical confirmation for this hypothesis in recent years in our work with randomly selected hospitalized schizophrenic patients. The individual therapists in our research program who seem to be most successful in dealing with these unmotivated, poorly educated, resistant, chronically hospitalized individuals, are those who are first of all real, who react in a genuine, human way as persons, and who exhibit their genuineness in the relationship.

But is it always helpful to be genuine? What about negative feelings? What about the times when the counselor's real feeling toward his client is one of annoyance, or boredom, or dislike? My tentative answer is that even with such feelings as these, which we all have from time to time, it is preferable for the counselor to be real than to put up a facade of interest and concern and liking which he does not feel.

But it is not a simple thing to achieve such reality. I am not saying that it is helpful to blurt out impulsively every passing feeling and accusation under the comfortable impression that one is being genuine. Being real involves the difficult task of being acquainted with the flow of experiencing going on within oneself, a flow marked especially by complexity and continuous change. So if I sense that I am feeling bored by my contacts with this student, and this feeling persists, I think I owe it to him and to our relationship to share this feeling with him. But here again I will want to be constantly in touch with what is going on in me. If I am, I will recognize that it is *my* feeling of being bored which I am expressing, and not some supposed fact about him as a boring person. If I voice it as my *own* reaction, it has the potentiality of leading to a deeper relationship. But this feeling exists in the context of a complex and changing flow, and this needs to be communicated too. I would like to share with him my distress at feeling bored, and the discomfort I feel in expressing this aspect of me. As I share these attitudes I find that my feeling of boredom arises from my sense of remoteness from him, and that I would like to be more in touch with him. And even as I try to express these feelings, they change. I am certainly not bored as I try to communicate myself to him in this way, and I am far from bored as I wait with eagerness and perhaps a bit of apprehension for his response. I also feel a new sensitivity to him, now that I have shared this feeling which has been a barrier between us. So I am very much more able to hear the surprise or perhaps the hurt in his voice as he now finds *him*self speaking more genuinely because I have dared to be real with him. I have let myself be a person—real, imperfect— in my relationship with him.

I have tried to describe this first element at some length because I regard it as highly important, perhaps the most crucial of the conditions I will describe, and because it is neither easy to grasp nor to achieve. Gendlin (2) has done an excellent job of explaining the significance of the concept of experiencing and its relationship to counseling and therapy, and his presentation may supplement what I have tried to say.

I hope it is clear that I am talking about a realness in the counselor which is deep and true, not superficial. I have sometimes thought that the word transparency helps to describe this element of personal congruence. If everything going on in me which is relevant to the relationship can be seen by my client, if he can see "clear through me," and if I am *willing* for this realness to show through in the relationship, then I can be almost certain that this will be a meaningful encounter in which we both learn and develop.

I have sometimes wondered if this is the only quality which matters in a counseling relationship. The evidence seems to show that other qualities also make a profound difference and are perhaps easier to achieve. So I am going to describe these others. But I would stress that if, in a given moment of relationship, they are not genuinely a part of the experience of the counselor, then it is, I believe, better to be genuinely what one is, than to pretend to be feeling these other qualities.

EMPATHY

The second essential condition in the relationship, as I see it, is that the counselor is experiencing an accurate empathic understanding of his client's private world, and is able to communicate some of the significant fragments of that understanding. To sense the client's inner world of private personal meanings as if it were your own, but without ever losing the "as if" quality, this is empathy, and this seems essential to a growth-promoting relationship. To sense his confusion or his timidity or his anger or his feeling of being treated unfairly as if it were your own, yet without your own uncertainty or fear or anger or suspicion getting bound up in it, this is the condition I am endeavoring to describe. When the client's world is clear to the counselor and he can move about in it freely, then he can both communicate his understanding of what is vaguely known to the client, and he can also voice meanings in the client's experience of which the client is scarcely aware. It is this kind of highly sensitive empathy which seems important in making it possible for a person to get close to himself and to learn, to change and develop.

I suspect that each of us has discovered that this kind of understanding is extremely rare. We neither receive it nor offer it with any great frequency. Instead we offer another type of understanding which is very different, such as "I understand what is wrong with you" or "I understand what makes you act that way." These are the types of understanding which we usually offer and receive—an evaluative understanding from the outside. It is not surprising that we shy away from true understanding. If I am truly open to the way life is experienced by another person— if I can take his world into mine—then I run the risk of seeing life in his way, of being changed myself, and we all resist change. So we tend to view this other person's world only in our terms, not in his. We analyze and evaluate it. We do not understand it. But when someone understands how it feels and seems to be me, without wanting to analyze me or judge me, then I can blossom and grow in that climate. I am sure I am not alone in that feeling. I believe that when the counselor can grasp the moment-to-moment experiencing occurring in the inner world of the client, as the client sees it and feels it, without losing the separateness of his own identity in this empathic process, then change is likely to occur.

Though the accuracy of such understanding is highly important, the communication of intent to understand is also helpful. Even in dealing with the confused or inarticulate or bizarre individual, if he perceives that I am *trying* to understand his meanings, this is helpful. It communicates the value I place on him as an individual. It gets across the fact that I perceive his feelings and meanings as being *worth* understanding.

None of us steadily achieves such a complete empathy as I have been trying to describe, any more than we achieve complete congruence, but there is no doubt that individuals can develop along this line. Suitable training experiences have been utilized in the training of counselors, and also in the "sensitivity training" of industrial management personnel. Such experiences enable the person to listen more sensitively, to receive more of the subtle meanings the other person is expressing in words, gesture, and posture, to resonate more deeply and freely within himself to the significance of those expressions.[1]

[1]I hope the above account of an empathic attitude will make it abundantly clear that I am not advocating a wooden technique of pseudo-understanding in which the counselor "reflects back what the client has just said." I have been more than a little horrified at the interpretation of my approach which has sometimes crept into the teaching and training of counselors.

POSITIVE REGARD

Now the third condition. I hypothesize that growth and change are more likely to occur the more that the counselor is experiencing a warm, positive, acceptant attitude toward what *is* in the client. It means that he prizes his client, as a person, with somewhat the same quality of feeling that a parent feels for his child, prizing him as a person regardless of his particular behavior at the moment. It means that he cares for his client in a non-possessive way, as a person with potentialities. It involves an open willingness for the client to be whatever feelings are real in him at the moment—hostility or tenderness, rebellion or submissiveness, assurance or self-depreciation. It means a kind of love for the client as he is, providing we understand the word love as equivalent to the theologian's term "agape," and not in its usual romantic and possessive meanings. What I am describing is a feeling which is not paternalistic, nor sentimental, nor superficially social and agreeable. It respects the other person as a separate individual, and does not possess him. It is a kind of liking which has strength, and which is not demanding. We have termed it positive regard.

UNCONDITIONALITY OF REGARD

There is one aspect of this attitude of which I am somewhat less sure. I advance tentatively the hypothesis that the relationship will be more effective the more the positive regard is unconditional. By this I mean that the counselor prizes the client in a total, rather than a conditional way. He does not accept certain feelings in the client and disapprove others. He feels an *unconditional* positive regard for this person. This is an outgoing, positive feeling without reservations and without evaluations. It means *not* making judgments. I believe that when this nonevaluative prizing is present in the encounter between the counselor and his client, constructive change and development in the client is more likely to occur.

Certainly one does not need to be a professional to experience this attitude. The best of parents show this in abundance, while others do not. A friend of mine, a therapist in private practice on the east coast, illustrates this very well in a letter in which he tells me what he is learning about parents. He says:

> I am beginning to feel that the key to the human being is the attitudes with which the parents have regarded him. If the child was lucky enough to have parents who have felt proud of him, wanted him, wanted him just as he was, exactly as he was, this child grows into adulthood with self-confidence, self-esteem; he goes forth in life feeling sure of himself, strong, able to lick what confronts him. Franklin Delano Roosevelt is an example . . . "my friends. . . ." He couldn't imagine anyone thinking otherwise. He had two adoring parents. He was like the pampered dog who runs up at you, frisking his tail, eager to love you, for this dog has never known rejection or harshness. Even if you should kick him, he'll come right back to you, his tail friskier than ever, thinking you're playing a game with him and wanting more. This animal cannot imagine anyone disapproving or disliking him. Just as unconditional regard and love was poured into him, he has it now to give out. If a child is lucky enough to grow up in this unconditionally accepting atmosphere, he emerges as strong and sure and he can approach life and its vicissitudes with courage and confidence, with zest and joy of expectation.

> But the parents who like their children—if. They would like them if they were changed, altered, different; if they were smarter or if they were better, or if, if, if. The offspring of these parents have trouble because they never had the feeling of acceptance. These parents don't really like these children; they would like them if they were like someone else. When you come down to the basic fundamental, the parent feels: "I don't like *this* child, this child before me." They don't say that. I am beginning to believe that it would be better for all concerned if parents did. It wouldn't leave such horrible ravages on these unaccepted children. It's never done that crudely. "If you were a nice boy and did this, that and the other thing, then we would all love you."
>
> I am coming to believe that children brought up by parents who would like them "if" are never quite right. They grow up assuming that their parents are right and that they are wrong; that somehow or other they are at fault; and even worse, very frequently they feel they are stupid, inadequate, inferior.

This is an excellent contrast between an unconditional positive regard and a conditional regard. I believe it holds as true for counselors as for parents.

THE CLIENT'S PERCEPTION

Thus far all my hypotheses regarding the possibility of constructive growth have rested upon the experiencing of these elements by the counselor. There is, however, one condition which must exist in the client. Unless the attitudes I have been describing have been to some degree communicated to the client, and perceived by him, they do not exist in his perceptual world and thus cannot be effective. Consequently it is necessary to add one more condition to the equation which I have been building up regarding personal growth through counseling. It is that when the client perceives, to a minimal degree, the genuineness of the counselor and the acceptance and empathy which the counselor experiences for him, then development in personality and change in behavior are predicted.

This has implications for me as a counselor. I need to be sensitive, not only to what is going on in me, and sensitive to the flow of feelings in my client. I must also be sensitive to the way he is receiving my communications. I have learned, especially in working with more disturbed persons, that empathy can be perceived as lack of involvement; that an unconditional regard on my part can be perceived as indifference; that warmth can be perceived as a threatening closeness, that real feelings of mine can be perceived as false. I would like to behave in ways, and communicate in ways which have clarity for this specific person, so that what I am experiencing in relationship to him would be perceived unambiguously by him. Like the other conditions I have proposed the principle is easy to grasp; the achievement of it is difficult and complex.

THE ESSENTIAL HYPOTHESIS

Let me restate very briefly the essentially simple but somewhat radical hypothesis I have set forth. I have said that constructive personality growth and change comes about only when the client perceives and experiences a certain psychological climate in the relationship. The conditions which constitute this climate do not consist of knowledge, intellectual training, orientation in some school of thought, or techniques. They are feelings or attitudes which must be experienced by the counselor and perceived by the client if they are to be effective. Those I have singled out as being essential are: a realness, genuineness, or congruence in the therapist; a sensitive, empathic understanding of the client's feelings and personal meanings; a warm, accepting prizing of the client; and an unconditionality in this positive regard.

SOME LIMITATIONS

. . . I regard it as entirely possible that there are other conditions which I have not described, which are also essential. Recently I had occasion to listen to some recorded interviews by a young counselor of elementary school children. She was very warm and positive in her attitude toward her clients, yet she was definitely ineffective. She seemed to be responding warmly only to the superficial aspects of each child and so the contacts were chatty, social and friendly, but it was clear she was not reaching the real person of the child. Yet in a number of ways she rated reasonably high on each of the conditions I have described. So perhaps there are still elements missing which I have not captured in my formulation.

I am also aware of the possibility that different kinds of helping relationships may be effective with different kinds of people. Some of our therapists working with schizophrenics are effective when they appear to be highly conditional, when they do *not* accept some of the bizarre behavior of the psychotic. This can be interpreted in two ways. Perhaps a conditional set is more helpful with these individuals. Or perhaps—and this seems to me to fit the facts better—these psychotic individuals perceive a conditional attitude as meaning that the therapist *really* cares, where an unconditional attitude may be interpreted as apathetic noncaring. In any event, I do want to make it clear that what I have given are beginning formulations which surely will be modified and corrected from further learnings.

THE PHILOSOPHY WHICH IS IMPLICIT

It is evident that the kind of attitudes I have described are not likely to be experienced by a counselor unless he holds a philosophy regarding people in which such attitudes are congenial. The attitudes pictured make no sense except in a context of great respect for the person and his potentialities. Unless the primary element in the counselor's value system is the worth of the individual, he is not apt to find himself experiencing a real caring, or a desire to understand, and perhaps he will not respect himself enough to be real. Certainly the professional person who holds the view that individuals are essentially objects to be manipulated for the welfare of the state, or the good of the educational institution, or "for their own good," or to satisfy his own need for power and control, would not experience the attitudinal elements I have described as constituting growth-promoting relationships. So these conditions are congenial and natural in certain philosphical contexts but not in others. . . .

CONCLUSION

Let me conclude with a series of statements which for me follow logically one upon the other.

The purpose of most of the helping professions, including guidance counseling, is to enhance the personal development, the psychological growth toward a socialized maturity, of its clients.

The effectiveness of any member of the profession is most adequately measured in terms of the degree to which, in his work with his clients, he achieves this goal.

Our knowledge of the elements which bring about constructive change in personal growth is in its infant stages.

Such factual knowledge as we currently possess indicates that a primary change-producing influence is the degree to which the client experiences certain qualities in his relationship with his counselor.

In a variety of clients—normal, maladjusted, and psychotic—with many different counselors and therapists, and studying the relationship from the vantage point of the client, the therapist, or the uninvolved observer, certain qualities in the relationship are quite uniformly found to be associated with personal growth and change.

These elements are not constituted of technical knowledge or ideological sophistication. They are personal human qualities—something the counselor *experiences,* not something he *knows*. Constructive personal growth is associated with the counselor's realness, with his genuine and unconditional liking for his client, with his sensitive understanding of his client's private world, and with his ability to communicate these qualities in himself to his client.

These findings have some far-reaching implications for the theory and practice of guidance counseling and psychotherapy, and for the training of workers in these fields.

REFERENCES*

1 Barrett-Lennard, G. T. Dimensions of therapist response as causal factors in therapeutic change. *Psychol. Monogr.* (In press)

2 Gendlin, E. T. Experiencing: A variable in the process of therapeutic change. *Am. Jour. Psychother.* **15,** 1961, 233–245.

3 Halkides, G. An experimental study of four conditions necessary for therapeutic change. Unpublished doctoral dissertation, University of Chicago, 1958.

4 Rogers, C. R. The necessary and sufficient conditions of therapeutic personality change. *Jour. Cons. Psych.,* **21,** 1957, 95–103.

5 ———. A theory of therapy, personality, and interpersonal relationships as developed in the client-centered framework. In S. Koch (ed.) *Psychology: A Study of a Science, Vol. III*. New York: McGraw-Hill, 1959, 184–256.

6 Wisconsin Psychiatric Institute: Research Reports (unpublished)

a Spotts, J. E. The perception of positive regard by relatively successful and relatively unsuccessful clients.

**Editor's note:* Since the paper has been edited, not all references remain in the body of the paper. For reasons of general interest, however, we have chosen to leave the *list* of references intact.

b Truax, C. B. Comparison between high conditions therapy, low conditions therapy, and control conditions in the outcome measure of change in anxiety levels.

c ———. Constructive personality change in schizophrenic patients receiving high-conditions therapy, low-conditions therapy, and no-therapy.

d ———. Effects of therapists and effects of patients upon the amount of accurate empathy occurring in the psychotherapeutic interaction.

e ———. Effects of therapists and effects of patients upon the level of problem expression and experiencing occurring in the therapeutic interaction.

f ———. The relationship between the patient's perception of the level of therapeutic conditions offered in psychotherapy and constructive personality change.

g ———, Liccione, J., and Rosenberg, M. Psychological test evaluations of personality change in high conditions therapy, low conditions therapy, and control patients.

h van der Veen, F. The effects of the therapist and the patient on each other's therapeutic behavior early in therapy: A study of the beginning interviews of three patients with each of five therapists.

i ———. Perceived therapist conditions and degree of disturbance: A comparison of conditions perceived by hospitalized schizophrenic patients and counseling center clients.

j Wargo, D. G. The Barron Ego Strength and LH4 Scales as predictors and indicators of change in psychotherapy.

The A-B-C's of Rational-Emotive Therapy*

Albert Ellis

Rational-emotive psychotherapy is a comprehensive approach to psychological treatment and to education that not only employs emotive and behavioristic methods but also significantly stresses and undermines the cognitive element in self-defeating behavior. Humans are exceptionally complex, so that there is no simple way in which they become "emotionally disturbed," and no single manner in which they can be helped to overcome their disturbances. Their psychological problems arise from their misperceptions and mistaken cognitions about what they perceive; from their emotional underreactions or overreactions to normal and to unusual stimuli; and from their habitually dysfunctional behavior patterns, which encourage them to keep repeating nonadjustive responses even when they know they are behaving poorly. Consequently, a three-way, rational-emotive-behavioristic approach to their problems is desirable; and rational-emotive therapy provides this multifaceted attack.

Primarily, RET employs a highly active cognitive approach. It is based on the assumption that what we label our "emotional" reactions are mainly caused by our conscious and unconscious evaluations, interpretations, and philosophies. Thus, we feel anxious or depressed because we strongly convince ourselves that it is not only unfortunate and inconvenient but that *it is terrible and catastrophic* when we fail at

*From Albert Ellis, *Humanistic Psychotherapy: The Rational-Emotive Approach,* McGraw-Hill Book Company, Inc., New York, 1974. Pages 55–67 reprinted by permission of the author and the publisher.

a major task or are rejected by a significant person. And we feel hostile because we vigorously believe that people who behave unfairly not only *would better not* but *absolutely should not* act the way they indubitably do and that it is *utterly insufferable* when they frustrate us.

Like stoicism, a school of philosophy which originated some twenty-five hundred years ago, RET holds that there are virtually no legitimate reasons for people to make themselves terribly upset, hysterical, or emotionally disturbed, no matter what kind of psychological or verbal stimuli are impinging on them. It encourages them to feel strong *appropriate* emotions—such as sorrow, regret, displeasure, annoyance, rebellion, and determination to change unpleasant social conditions. But it holds that when they experience certain self-defeating and *inappropriate* emotions—such as guilt, depression, rage, or feelings of worthlessness—they are adding an unverifiable, magical hypothesis (that things *ought* or *must* be different) to their empirically based view (that certain things and acts are reprehensible or inefficient and that something *would better* be done about changing them).

Because the rational-emotive therapist has a highly structured and workable theory, he can almost always see the few central irrational philosophies which a client is vehemently propounding to himself and through which he is foolishly upsetting himself. He can show the client how these cause his problems and his symptoms; can demonstrate exactly how the client can forthrightly question and challenge these ideas; and can often induce him to work to uproot them and to replace them with scientifically testable hypotheses about himself and the world which are not likely to get him into future emotional difficulties.

The cognitive part of the theory and practice of RET may be briefly stated in A-B-C form as follows:

At point A there is an ACTIVITY, ACTION, or AGENT that the individual becomes disturbed about. Example: He goes for an important job interview; or he has a fight with his mate, who unfairly screams at him.

At point rB the individual has a RATIONAL BELIEF (or a REASONABLE BELIEF or a REALISTIC BELIEF) about the ACTIVITY, ACTION, or AGENT that occurs at point A. Example: He believes, ''It would be unfortunate if I were rejected at the job interview.'' Or, ''How annoying it is to have my mate unfairly scream at me!''

At point iB the individual has an IRRATIONAL BELIEF (or an INAPPROPRIATE BELIEF) about the ACTIVITY, ACTION, or AGENT that occurs at point A. Example: He believes, ''It would be catastrophic if I were rejected at the job interview. ''Or, ''My mate is a horrible person for screaming at me!''

Point rB, the RATIONAL BELIEF, can be supported by empirical data and is appropriate to the reality that is occurring, or that may occur, at point A. For it normally *is* unfortunate if the individual is rejected at an interview for an important job; and it *is* annoying if his mate unfairly screams at him. It would hardly be rational or realistic if he thought; ''How great it will be if I am rejected at the job interview!'' Or: ''It is wonderful to have my mate scream at me! Her screaming shows what a lovely person she is!''

Point iB, the IRRATIONAL BELIEF, cannot be supported by any empirical evidence and is inappropriate to the reality that is occurring, or that may occur, at Point A. For it hardly would be truly catastrophic, but only (at worst) highly inconvenient, if the individual were rejected for an important job. It is unlikely that he would never get another job, that he would literally starve to death, or that he would have to be utterly miserable at any other job he could get. And his mate is not a horrible person for screaming at him; she is merely a person who behaves (at some times) horribly and who (at other times) has various unhorrible traits.

His iB's, or IRRATIONAL BELIEFS, moreover, state or imply a *should, ought,* or *must*—an absolutistic *demand* or *dictate* that the individual obtain what he wants; for, by believing that it is catastrophic if he is rejected for an important job, he explicitly or implicitly believes that he *should* or *must* be accepted at that interview. And by believing that his mate is a horrible person for screaming at him, he overtly or tacitly believes that she *ought* or *must* be nonscreaming. There is, of course, no law of the universe (except in his muddled head!) which says that he *should* do well at an important job interview, or that his mate *must* not scream at him.

At point rC the individual experiences or feels RATIONAL CONSEQUENCES or REASONABLE CONSEQUENCES of his rB's (RATIONAL BELIEFS). Thus, if he rigorously and discriminately believes, "It would be unfortunate if I were rejected at the job interview," he feels concerned and thoughtful about the interview; he plans in a determined manner how to succeed at it; and if by chance he fails to get the job he wants, he feels disappointed, displeased, sorrowful, and frustrated. His actions and his feelings are *appropriate* to the situation that is occurring or may occur at point A; and they tend to help him succeed in his goals or feel suitably regretful if he does not achieve these goals.

At point iC the individual experiences IRRATIONAL CONSEQUENCES or INAPPROPRIATE CONSEQUENCES of his iB's (IRRATIONAL BELIEFS). Thus, if he childishly and dictatorially believes, "It would be catastrophic if I were rejected at the job interview. I couldn't stand it! What a worm I would then prove to be! I *should* do well at this important interview!" he tends to feel anxious, self-hating, self-pitying, depressed, and enraged. He gets dystunctional psychosomatic reactions, such as high blood pressure and ulcers. He becomes defensive, fails to see his own mistakes in this interview, and by rationalization blames his failure on external factors. He becomes preoccupied with how hopeless his situation is, and refuses to do much about changing it by going for other interviews. And he generally experiences what we call "disturbed," "neurotic," or "overreactive" symptoms. His actions and feelings at point iC are *inappropriate* to the situation that is occurring or may occur at point B, because they are based on magical demands regarding the way he and the universe presumably *ought to be*. And they tend to help him fail at his goals or feel horribly upset if he does not achieve them.

These are the A-B-C's of emotional disturbance or self-defeating attitudes, and behavior, according to the RET theory. Therapeutically, these A-B-C's can be extended to D-E's, which constitute the cognitive core of the RET methodology.

At point D, the individual can be taught (or can teach himself) to DISPUTE his iB's (IRRATIONAL BELIEFS). Thus, he can ask himself, "*Why* is it catastrophic if I am rejected in this forthcoming job interview? How would such a rejection *destroy* me? Why couldn't I *stand* losing this particular job? Where is the evidence that I would be a *worm* if I were rejected? Why *should* I have to do well at this important interview?'' If he persistently, vigorously DISPUTES (or *questions* and *challenges)* his own iB's (IRRATIONAL BELIEFS) which are creating his iC's (INAPPROPRIATE CONSEQUENCES), he will sooner or later come to see, in most instances, that they are unverifiable, unempirically based, and superstitious; and he will be able to change and reject them.

At point cE the individual is likely to obtain the COGNITIVE EFFECT OF HIS DISPUTING his iB's (IRRATIONAL BELIEFS). Thus, if he asks himself, ''Why is it catastrophic if I am rejected in this forthcoming job interview?'' he will tend to answer: ''It is not; it will merely be inconvenient.'' If he asks, ''How would such a rejection destroy me?'' he will reply, ''It won't; it will only frustrate me.'' If he asks: ''Why couldn't I stand losing this particular job?'' he will tell himself: ''I can! I won't like it; but I can gracefully lump it!'' If he asks: ''Where is the evidence that I would be a worm if I were rejected?'' he will respond: ''There isn't any! I will only feel like a worm if I *define myself as* and *think of myself as* a worm!'' If he asks, ''Why *should* I have to do well at this important interview?'' he will tell himself: ''There's no reason why I should *have* to do well. There are several reasons why *it would be nice*. *It would be very fortunate* if I succeeded at this job interview. But they never add up to: 'Therefore I must!' ''

At point bE the individual will most likely obtain the BEHAVIORAL EFFECT of his DISPUTING his iB's (IRRATIONAL BELIEFS). Thus, he will tend to be much less anxious about his forthcoming job interview. He will become less self-hating, self-pitying, and enraged. He will reduce his psychosomatic reactions. He will be able to become less defensive. He will become less unconstructively preoccupied with the possibility or the actuality of his failing at the job interview and will more constructively devote himself to succeeding at it or taking other measures to improve his vocational condition if he fails at it. He will become significantly less ''upset,'' ''disturbed,'' ''overreactive,'' or ''neurotic.''

On the cognitive level, then, rational-emotive therapy largely employs direct philosophic confrontation. The therapist actively demonstrates to the client how, every time he experiences a dysfunctional emotion or behavior or CONSEQUENCE, at point C, it only indirectly stems from some ACTIVITY or AGENT that may be occurring (or about to occur) in his life at point A, and it much more directly results from his interpretations, philosophies, attitudes, or BELIEFS, at point B. The therapist then teaches the client how to scientifically (empirically and logically) DISPUTE these beliefs, at point D, and to persist at this DISPUTING until he consistently comes up, at point E, with a set of sensible COGNITIVE EFFECTS, cE's, and appropriate BEHAVIORAL EFFECTS, bE's. When he has remained, for some period of time, at point E, the individual has a radically changed philosophic attitude toward himself, toward others, and toward the world, and he is thereafter much less likely to keep convincing himself of iB's (IRRATIONAL BELIEFS) and thereby creating iC's (INAPPROPRIATE CONSEQUENCES) or emotional disturbances.

In addition to its cognitive methods, RET has exceptionally important behavioristic techniques that it consistently uses. It especially uses activity homework assignments, which the therapist or the client's therapy group assign to him during various sessions, and later check to see whether he is doing them. Such assignments may consist of the client's being asked to initiate contacts with three new people during a week's period, to visit his nagging mother-in-law instead of trying to avoid her, or to make a list of his job-hunting assets and of several means of his looking for a better job. These assignments are given in order to help the client take risks, gain new experiences, interrupt his dysfunctional habituations, and change his philosophies regarding certain activities.

A third major emphasis in RET is on emotive release. Thus, the rational-emotive therapist usually takes a no-nonsense-about-it direct confrontation approach to the client and his problems. He forces or persuades the client to express himself openly and to bring out his real feelings, no matter how painful it may at first be for him to do so. Frequently, he ruthlessly reveals and attacks the client's defenses—while simultaneously showing him how he can live without these defenses and how he can unconditionally accept himself whether or not others highly approve of him. The therapist does not hesitate to reveal his own feelings, to answer direct questions about himself, and to participate as an individual in rational marathon encounters. He does his best to give the client unconditional rather than conditional positive regard and to teach him the essence of rational-emotive philosophy; namely, that no human is to be condemned for anything, no matter how execrable his acts may be. His *deeds* may be measurable and heinous, but he is never to be rated or given a report card *as a person*. Because of the therapist's full acceptance of him as a human being, the client is able to express his feelings much more openly than in his everyday life and to accept *himself* even when he is acknowledging the inefficiency or immorality of some of his *acts*.

In many important ways, then, RET uses expressive-experiential methods and behavioral techniques. It is not, however, primarily interested in helping the client *feel* better, but in showing him how he can *get* better. In its approach to marathon group therapy, for example, RET allows the participants plenty of opportunity to encounter each other on a gut level, to force themselves to stay in the here and now, to face their own emotional and sensory reactions to themselves and to other members of the group, and to be ruthlessly honest with themselves and others. Instead, however, of beginning and ending on a purely basic encounter or sensitivity training level—and thereby risk opening up many people without showing them how to put themselves together again—the rational-oriented marathon also shows the participants exactly what they are telling themselves to create their negative feelings toward themselves and others. They are further told how they can change their internalized and uncritically accepted iB's (IRRATIONAL BELIEFS) so that ultimately they can feel and behave spontaneously in a less self-defeating manner and can actualize their potential for happy, nondefeating lives.

Basically, RET is an extension of the scientific method to human affairs. People, for biological as well as environmental reasons, tend to think superstitiously, unrealistically, and unscientifically about themselves and the world around them. In science, we teach them to set up hypotheses about external reality and then to vigorously question and challenge these hypotheses—to look for empirical evidence for and against them, before they are cavalierly accepted as truths. In rational-emotive therapy, the therapist teaches his client to question scientifically and to dispute all self-defeating hypotheses about himself and others. Thus, if he believes—as, alas, millions of people tend to believe—that he is a worthless person because he performs certain acts badly, he is not taught merely to ask: "What is truly bad about my acts? Where is the evidence that they are wrong or unethical?" More important, he is shown how to ask himself: "Granted that some of my acts may be mistaken, why am I a totally bad *person* for performing them? Where is the evidence that I must always (or mainly) be right in order to consider myself worthy? Assuming that it is *preferable* for me to act well or efficiently rather than badly or inefficiently, why do I *have* to do what is preferable?"

Similarly, when an individual perceives—and let us suppose that he correctly perceives—the erroneous and unjust acts of others, and when he makes himself (as he all too frequently does) enraged at these others and tries to hurt or annihilate them, he is taught by the rational-emotive therapist to stop and ask himself: "Why is my hypothesis true that these error-prone people are absolutely no good? Granted that *it would be better* if they acted more competently or fairly, why *should* they have to do what would be better? Where is the evidence that people who commit a number of mistaken or unethical acts are doomed to be forever wrong? Why, even if they persistently behave poorly, should they be totally damned, excommunicated, and consigned to some kind of hell?"

Rational-emotive therapy teaches the individual to generalize adequately but to watch his *over*generalizing; to discriminate his desires, wants, and preferences from his assumed needs, necessities, or dictates; to be less suggestible and more thinking; to be a long-range hedonist, who enjoys himself in the here and now *and* the future, rather than merely a short-range hedonist, who thinks mainly of immediate gratification; to feel the appropriate emotions of sorrow, regret, annoyance, and determination to change unpleasant aspects of his life, while minimizing the inappropriate emotions of worthlessness, self-pity, severe anxiety, and rage. RET, like the science of psychology itself and like the discipline of general semantics, as set forth by Alfred Korzybski, particularly teaches the client how to *discriminate* more clearly between sense and nonsense, fiction and reality, superstition and science. While using many behavioristic and teaching methods, it is far from being dogmatic and authoritarian. Rather, it is one of the most humanistically oriented kinds of therapy, in that it emphasizes that man can fully accept himself just because he is alive, just because he exists; that he does not have to prove his worth in any way; that he can have real happiness whether or not he performs well and whether or not he impresses others; that he is able to create his own meaningful purposes; and that he needs neither magic nor gods on whom to rely. The humanistic-existentialist approach to life is therefore as much a part of rational-emotive psychotherapy as is its rational, logical, and scientific methodology.

RET, like many other modern forms of psychotherapy, is backed by a good many years of clinical experience by the present author and various other rational-emotive therapists. It is supported by several studies demonstrating its clinical effectiveness under controlled experimental conditions.

Rational-emotive psychotherapy has a great many therapeutic applications, some of which are unavailable to various other modes of psychotherapy. For one thing, it is relevant and useful to a far wider range of client disabilities than are many other therapies. Robert Harper, Cecil H. Patterson, and others have shown that many techniques, such as classical psychoanalysis, can only be effectively employed with a relatively small number of clients and are actually contraindicated with other individuals (such as with schizophrenics). Rational-emotive therapy, however, can be employed with almost any type of person the therapist is likely to see, including those who are conventionally labeled as psychotic, borderline psychotic, psychopathic, and mentally retarded. This is not to say that equally good results are obtained when it is employed with these most difficult individuals as are obtained with less difficult neurotics. But the main principles of RET can be so simply and efficiently stated that even individuals with very serious problems, some of whom have not been reached by years of previous intensive therapy, can often find significant improvement through RET.

Prophylactically, rational-emotive principles can be used with many kinds of individuals, to help prevent them from eventually becoming emotionally disturbed. At a school for normal children operated on the principles of rationality, the pupils from the first grade onward are taught a rational-emotive philosophy by their regular teachers, in the course of classroom activities, recreational affairs, therapy groups, and other games and exercises. They are taught for example, not to catastrophize when they do not achieve perfectly, not to enrage themselves against others when these others act badly, and not to demand that the world be nicer and easier than it usually is. As a result of this teaching, they seem to be becoming remarkably less anxious, depressed, self-hating, and hostile than other children of equivalent age.

Rational-emotive ideas also have application to politics, to problems of the generation gap, to the treatment and prevention of violence and murder, and to various other areas of life. Because it is deeply philosophic, because it realistically accepts individuals as they are and shows them how they can obtain their fuller potentials, and because it is not only oriented toward individuals with emotional disturbances but toward all types of people everywhere, RET is likely to be increasingly applied to the solution of many kinds of human problems.

Is RET really more effective than other forms of psychotherapy? The evidence is not in that will answer this question. Clinical findings would seem to indicate that it benefits more people than do most other methods; that it can obtain beneficial results in surprisingly short order in many instances; and that the level of improvement or cure that is effected through its use is more permanent and deep-seated than that obtained through other methods. But this clinical evidence has been haphazardly collected and is now being substantiated through controlled studies of therapeutic outcome. My hypothesis is that RET is a more effective procedure for clients and therapists because it is active-directive, it is comprehensive, it is unusually clear and precise, and it is hardheaded and down to earth.

More important, rational-emotive therapy is philosophically unambiguous, logical, and empirically oriented. This can be especially seen in its viewpoint on the most important of therapeutic problems: that of human worth. Nearly all systems of psychotherapy hold that the individual is worthwhile and can esteem himself because he discovers how to relate well to others and win the love he needs and/or learns how to perform adequately and to achieve his potentials for functioning. Thus, Sigmund Freud held that man solves his basic problems through work and love. Alfred Adler emphasized the necessity of his finding himself through social interest. Harry Stack Sullivan stressed his achieving adequate interpersonal relations. William Glasser insisted that he needs both love and achievement. Nathaniel Branden demanded competence and extreme rationality. Even Carl Rogers, who presumably emphasized unconditional positive regard, actually has held that the individual can truly accept himself only when someone else, such as a therapist, accepts him or loves him unconditionally; so that his self-concept is still dependent on some important element outside himself.

RET, on the contrary, seems to be almost the only major kind of psychotherapy (aside, perhaps, from Zen Buddhism, if this is conceptualized as psychotherapy and not exclusively as a philosophy) that holds that the individual does not need *any* trait, characteristic, achievement, purpose, or social approval in order to accept himself. In fact, he does not have to rate himself, esteem himself, or have any self-measurement or self-concept whatever.

It is not only undesirable but it is impossible for the individual to have a self-image, and it is enormously harmful if he attempts to construct one. Ego ratings depend on the summation of the ratings of the individual's separate traits (such as his competence, honesty, and talents, for example), and it is not legitimate to add and average these traits any more than it is legitimate to add apples and pears. Moreover, if one finally arrives, by some devious means, at a global rating of the individual (or of his "self"), one thereby invents a magical heaven (his "worth," his "value," his "goodness") or a mystical hell (his "worthlessness," his "valuelessness," his "badness"). This deification or devilification (note that this word is devil-ification, not de-vilification) of the individual is arrived at tautologically, by definition. It has no relation to objective reality; it is based on the false assumption that he *should* or *must* be a certain way and that the universe truly *cares* if he is not what he *ought* to be; it refuses to acknowledge the fact that all humans are, and probably always will be, incredibly *fallible;* and it almost always results in the self-rating individual's harshly condemning and punishing himself or defensively pretending that he is "worthy" and "good" in order to minimize his anxiety and self-deprecation. Finally, since self-ratings invariably involve ego games wherein the individual compares his self-esteem to that of others, they inevitably result in his deifying and damning other humans in addition to himself; and the feelings of intense anxiety and hostility that thereby occur constitute the very core of what we usually call "emotional disturbance."

Rational-emotive therapy, by solidly teaching the individual to avoid *any* kind of self-rating (and only, instead, to measure his characteristics and performances, so that he may help correct them and increase his enjoyment), gets to the deepest levels of personality change. It offers no panacea for the termination of human unhappiness, sorrow, frustration, and annoyance. But it importantly reveals, attacks, and radically uproots the major sources of needless self-defeating and socially destructive behavior.

Basic Principles and Practices of Behavior Therapy of Neuroses*

Joseph Wolpe

Behavior therapy or conditioning therapy was formally introduced to American psychiatry 14 years ago(21). The term *behavior therapy* was first used by Skinner and Lindsley(16) and subsequently popularized by Eysenck(3, 4, 5). It denotes the use of experimentally established principles of learning for the purpose of changing unadaptive behavior. Behavior therapy is thus an applied science, in every way parallel to other modern technologies and in particular to the technologies constituting medical therapeutics. Therapeutic possibilities emerge when we know the lawful relations of organismic processes. In the psychotherapeutic field the lawful relations that are most often relevant are those established by experimental psychology.

Persistent maladaptive (unadaptive) *anxiety* responses are the nucleus of most cases that are labeled "neurotic," and therefore much of the effort of behavior therapists has been directed toward overcoming them. "Anxiety" is defined as a particular organism's characteristic pattern of autonomic responses to noxious stimulation(22). Anxiety is conditionable; conditioned anxiety responses are in fact far more common than unconditioned ones. Anxiety responses are called maladaptive when they have been conditioned to stimulus situations that do not pose any objective threat. It is implicit in this formulation that neurotic responses are not ways of avoiding stress; they *are* stress responses.

Behavior therapy of human neuroses had its origin in observations of animal neuroses (20, 22). An animal placed in a confined environment and subjected to either strong ambivalent stimulation or noxious stimulation acquires a persistent habit of responding with marked anxiety to the environment concerned, and with weaker anxiety to other environments according to their similarity to the original one.

The most effective way of procuring unlearning is to feed the animal repeatedly while it is in an environment which evokes *weak* anxiety. The effect of this is to diminish progressively—ultimately to zero—the strength of the anxiety response to the particular stimulus. Increasingly "strong" stimulus situations are successively dealt with in the same way, so that finally the animal shows no anxiety to any of the situations to which anxiety has been conditioned.The basis of this gradual elimination of the anxiety response habit is considered to be an example(22), at a more complex level, of the phenomenon of *reciprocal inhibition* described by Sherrington(15). Each time the animal eats, the anxiety response is to some extent inhibited, and each occasion of inhibition diminishes the anxiety habit. Apparently the evocation of a response that inhibits anxiety weakens the bond between the anxiety-evoking stimulus and the anxiety response.

*From Joseph Wolpe, "Basic Principles and Practices of Behavior Therapy," *American Journal of Psychiatry*, 1969, **125**, 1241–1247. Reprinted by permission of the author and the Editor, *American Journal of Psychiatry*.

Human neuroses resemble those of the animal in all basic respects(26). Even though not all human neuroses present themselves as anxiety states, anxiety underlies most of them. For example, the patient with a stutter is not as a rule aware of the stimuli that produce the anxiety that is usually a necessary condition for stuttering. Indeed, he may not realize that he has any special anxiety in the situations in which he stutters, even though he can contrast them with other situations in which his speech is normal. Investigation generally shows that there is an emotional undercurrent, the intensity of which determines the degree of stutter.

The same is true of a host of other conditions in which the main presenting complaint is not anxiety—obsessions and compulsions, psychosomatic states, character neuroses, impotence, frigidity, homosexuality, and many others. The key to recovery is generally the deconditioning of anxiety. This is why a detailed behavioral analysis is an essential prerequisite to effective behavior therapy. The behavior therapist makes a practice of obtaining a detailed life history and a full account of the present life situation and administers various questionnaires designed to reveal stimulus situations conditioned to neurotic anxiety responses(27).

METHODS OF BEHAVIOR THERAPY

Many of the methods of behavior therapy derive from the therapeutic experiments with animals described above. They exemplify reciprocal inhibition (counterconditioning). Other methods derive from positive reinforcement, experimental extinction, and various other experimental paradigms(27).

Counterconditioning by the Emotions of Life Situations

Where neurotic responses are conditioned to situations involving direct interpersonal relations, the essence of reciprocal inhibition therapy has been to inhibit anxiety by the instigation of patterns of motor behavior that express anger (or whatever other feelings may be relevant). The repeated exercise of these patterns in the proper context weakens the anxiety response habit.

For example, a patient may need to be taught how to stand up for his rights when somebody gets in front of him in a line. The teaching will be either by direct instruction and exhortation or by actual rehearsal of the desired new behavior in the consulting room. A recent patient had become so intent on acceding to his wife's requirements that his own needs were completely subordinated. He repeatedly went into states of depression that he attempted to relieve by heavy drinking. He was shown how to assert himself appropriately—for example, by refusing to allow whatever he might be doing, such as reading the newspaper, to be interrupted by his wife's demands for conversation. By dint of a program along these lines he achieved reasonable control of this interpersonal situation and stopped having depressions.

Sexual responses are used to overcome anxiety responses to sexual situations that are the basis of impotence or premature ejaculation. The essence of treatment is to control sexual approaches so that anxiety is never permitted to be strong. Inhibition of anxiety can then be obtained by the parasympathetic dominated sexual arousal and the anxiety response habit can consequently be weakened.

Tactics vary from case to case but always involve the cooperation of the spouse. The therapist must determine at what point in the patient's sexual approach there are the first indications of anxiety. He then instructs the patient to take love-making no farther than this point, having obtained the acquiescence of the spouse. In the course of a few amorous sessions, anxiety usually ceases to be felt at the permitted point, and then the patient is permitted to go on the next stage. Usually several preliminary stages need to be passed before coitus is attempted; and it, too, requires a succession of graded steps.

Systematic Desensitization Based on Relaxation

Neurotic anxiety responses conditioned to stimuli other than those arising from direct interpersonal relations (e.g., phobic responses) do not lend themselves to behavioral treatment in the life situation of the patient. In such cases, reciprocal inhibition of anxiety must be obtained by methods that do not involve motor activity on the part of the patient toward the fearful object. In the earliest deliberate example of therapy on this basis, the anxiety of phobic children was inhibited by eating(8), very much as in the case of the experimental neuroses described above.

Deep muscle relaxation(7) has had the widest use in this way, mainly in a method known as *systematic desensitization*(21, 22, 27). In brief, desensitization consists of repeatedly presenting to the imagination of the deeply relaxed patient the feeblest item in a list of anxiety-evoking stimuli until no more anxiety is evoked either as reported by the patient or as psychophysiologically recorded. The next higher item in the list is then presented—again until the anxiety response to it is extinct. The procedure is continued until eventually even the strongest of the anxiety-evoking stimuli fails to evoke any stir of anxiety in the patient. It is almost always found in those subjects in whom imagined scenes have initially evoked anxiety that a situation that no longer evokes it in imagination also ceases to evoke it when encountered in reality.

Variants of Systematic Desensitization

Other inhibitors of anxiety may also be employed therapeutically in a systematic way. In some patients the therapeutic situation itself evokes anxiety-inhibiting emotions. These are very likely the usual basis of whatever therapeutic changes result from therapies other than behavior therapy. They must also account for part of the success of behavior therapy(22). But they can in addition be deliberately used in behavior therapy—usually in what is called desensitization in vivo, in which real stimuli take the place of imaginary ones, and the anxiety may be inhibited by these emotions.

For example, a patient who has a fear of humiliation at making mistakes is made to perform minor errors and then progressively more serious ones in the presence of the therapist—in each instance until all feelings of anxiety disappear. To the extent that this succeeds it is probably due to the anxiety being inhibited by competing interpersonal emotions. Tests of this assumption are now being planned.

Use has also been made of the observation that anxiety can be inhibited by cutaneous stimulation by nonaversive electric shocks. The therapist arranges for these to break in on the anxiety evoked by images from hierarchies by getting the patient to signal when the image is clear, and then delivering two or three shocks in quick succession. This apparently weakens anxiety on the basis of *external inhibition*(13).

Another method of procuring inhibition of anxiety depends on presenting a neutral stimulus just before the cessation of a strong continuous current to the forearm. The effect of this is to condition cessation (inhibition) of anxiety to the neutral stimulus(21, 22, 27). The conditioned stimulus can then be systematically used to inhibit neutrotic anxieties in the life situation.

Avoidance Conditioning

Avoidance (aversive) conditioning is an application of the reciprocal inhibition principle to overcoming responses other than anxiety. A noxious stimulus—usually a strongly unpleasant electric shock—is administered to the patient in an appropriate time relation to the stimulus to which avoidance conditioning is desired. It has been effectively used to overcome obsessional thinking, compulsive acts, fetishes, and homosexuality. It is, however, not always successful for reasons that are often quite clear.

Homosexuality, for example, is often based on neurotic interpersonal anxiety, which should be treated by deconditioning the anxiety(17). But when aversion is used for homosexuality, the most promising technique consists of administering a very unpleasant shock as long as a homosexual figure is projected onto a screen and terminating the shock at the appearance of an attractive female(6). Further details and other applications have been discussed in my book, *The Practice of Behavior Therapy*(27).

Experimental Extinction

Experimental extinction is the breaking of a habit through repeated performance of the relevant response without reinforcement (reward). The therapeutic use of extinction was formally introduced by Dunlap(2) under the name "negative practice."

The method did not then achieve much popularity, but recently there has been renewed interest in it, mainly in the context of the treatment of tics. The patient is instructed to perform deliberately the undesired movement very many times, and in the course of some weeks it may be found that spontaneous evocations of the tic have decreased, perhaps markedly(14, 18, 28). Kondas(10) has reported that many resistent tics can be cured if the negative practice is accompanied by a strong aversive stimulus that is terminated each time the practice stops (cf. anxiety-relief conditioning described above).

Positive Reinforcement

The deconditioning of unadaptive autonomic response habits is the central approach to behavior therapy of neuroses, but it is often also necessary to condition new motor habits. This often occurs as a result of the same measures that break down the anxiety habit. For example, in assertive training (see above), simultaneously with the counter-conditioning of anxiety, motor (operant) habits of assertion are conditioned. They are reinforced by the rewarding consequences of the assertive act, such as gaining control of a situation.

But operant conditioning can also be effected on its own. Anorexia nervosa has been successfully treated by arranging for eating to be followed by social rewards such as the use of a radio or company and withholding the rewards when the patient does not eat(1). The same principles have been effective in a variety of cases. For example, Williams(19) has described how tantrum behavior is completely under the control of the adult attention it elicits.

RESULTS OF BEHAVIOR THERAPY

The distinctive feature of behavior therapy is that the therapist selects his targets and plans his strategy in respect to each of them. He can sometimes—for example, in desensitization of classical phobias—even calculate the quantitative relations between number of therapeutic operations and amount of change(24).

Statistical Data

R. P. Knight's(9) five criteria—symptomatic improvement, increased productiveness, improved adjustment and pleasure in sex, improved interpersonal relationships, and ability to handle ordinary psychological conflicts and reasonable reality stresses—have been generally adopted by behavior therapists. By these criteria, the results of behavior therapy of neurosis have been quite notably good. For example, in several series of neurotic patients totaling 618 cases, about 87 percent either apparently recovered or were much improved(27). In the last published series of my own(22), the median number of sessions for 88 cases was 23. Follow-up studies in this as in other series have shown neither the spontaneous relapses nor the symptom substitutions that psychoanalytically oriented colleagues have prognosticated.

Compare these results with the 60 percent "cured" or "greatly improved" among the *completely analyzed* patients in the study of the Central Fact-Finding Committee of the American Psychoanalytic Association. While the psychoanalyzed patients were treated an average of four times a week for three to four years, i.e., about 700 sessions, and the average course of behavior therapy covered about 30 sessions(22), it is fair to point out that the comparison is not a controlled one.

A controlled comparative study is currently under way in the department of psychiatry at Temple University. Meanwhile, laboratory controlled studies have been distinctly favorable to behavior therapy. Paul(12) found that "dynamically" trained therapists did significantly better with systematic desensitization than with their own insight-giving techniques in treating fears of public speaking. Moore(11) reported a controlled study of cases of asthma in a London clinic. One schedule she employed was relaxation training; the second was support and suggestion under relaxation; and the third was systematic desensitization. In terms of both immediate and delayed effects, desensitization was clearly superior to the other two methods. In terms of maximum peak flow of respired air the difference was significant at .001.

One popular fallacy about behavior therapy is that it is useful in its place—for simple cases but not for complex ones. In 1964 I made a reexamination(25) of some previously published results dividing 86 cases into simple and complex. A neurosis was regarded as complex if it had one or more of the following features: a) a wide range of stimuli conditioned to neurotic responses (not just one), b) reactions to which the conditioned stimuli are obscure and determined with difficulty, c) reactions that include unadaptiveness in important areas of general behavior (character neuroses), d) obsessional neuroses, and e) reactions that include pervasive anxiety.

Of the 86 cases reviewed, 65 were complex in one or more of the senses defined. Fifty-eight of these (89 percent) were judged either apparently cured or much improved. This percentage was exactly the same as that obtained for the whole group. However, the median number of sessions for the complex group was 29 and the mean 54.8 in contrast to a median for the noncomplex remainder of 11.5 and a mean of 14.9. Thus, while complex cases responded to behavior therapy as often as simple ones did, therapy took longer.

HOW FUNDAMENTAL ARE THE EFFECTS OF BEHAVIOR THERAPY?

It is sometimes contended that behavior therapy is superficial and possibly even dangerous because it does not attempt to deal with the ''basic dynamic conflict'' that is alleged to underlie neuroses. In particular, it is prognosticated that recovery will be followed by relapse or symptom substitution sooner or later. A survey(23) of the results of follow-up studies on neuroses successfully treated by a variety of methods not concerned with the dynamic conflict revealed only a 1.6 percent incidence of relapse or symptom substitution. Skilled behavior therapists hardly ever encounter relapse or symptom substitution.

The weight of the evidence is thus that neuroses are indeed nothing but habits—the results of conditioning—often very complex conditioning. The implication is that a therapy based on principles of conditioning is fundamental therapy.

REFERENCES

1 Bachrach, A. J., Erwin, W. J., and Mohr, J. P.: ''The Control of Eating Behavior in an Anorexia by Operant Conditioning Techniques,'' in Ullman, L., and Krasner, L., eds.: Case Studies in Behavior Modification. New York: Holt, Rinehart and Winston, 1965.

2 Dunlap, K.: Habits, Their Making and Unmaking. New York: Liveright Publishing, 1932.

3 Eysenck, H. J.: Learning Theory and Behaviour Therapy, J. Ment. Sci. **105:** 61–75, 1959.

4 Eysenck, H. J.: Behavior Therapy and the Neuroses. New York: Pergamon Press, 1960.

5 Eysenck, H. J.: Experiments in Behavior Therapy. Oxford: Pergamon Press, 1965.

6 Feldman, M. P., and MacColloch, M. J.: The Application of Anticipatory Avoidance Learning to the Treatment of Homosexuality. I. Theory, Technique, and Preliminary Results, Behav. Res. Ther. **2:** 165–183, 1965.

7 Jacobson, E.: Progressive Relaxation. Chicago, Ill.: University of Chicago Press, 1938.

8 Jones, M. D.: A Laboratory Study of Fear. The Case of Peter, J. Genet. Psychol. **31:** 308–315, 1924.

9 Knight, R. P.: Evaluation of the Results of Psychoanalytic Therapy, Amer. J. Psychiat. **98:** 434–446, 1941.

10 Kondas, O.: The Possibilities of Applying Experimentally Created Procedures when Eliminating Tics, Studia Psychol. **7:** 221–229, 1965.

11 Moore, N.: Behaviour Therapy in Bronchial Asthma: A Controlled Study, J. Psychosom. Res. **9:** 257–276, 1965.

12 Paul, G. L.: Insight vs. Desensitization in Psychotherapy; An Experiment in Anxiety Reduction. Stanford, Calif.: Stanford University Press, 1966.

13 Pavlov, I. V.: Conditioned Reflexes, trans. by G. V. Anrep. New York: Liveright Publishing, 1927.

14 Rafi, A. A.: Learning Theory and the Treatment of Tics, J. Psychosom. Res. **6:** 71–76, 1962.

15 Sherrington, C. S.: Integration Action of the Nervous System. New Haven, Conn.: Yale University Prss, 1906.

16 Skinner, B. F., and Lindsley, O.: Studies in Behavior Therapy, Status Reports II and III. Naval Research Contract N5 ori-7662, 1954.

17 Stevenson, I., and Wolpe, J.: Recovery from Sexual Deviations Through Overcoming Nonsexual Neurotic Responses, Amer. J. Psychiat. **116:** 737–742, 1960.

18 Walton, D.: Experimental Psychology and the Treatment of a Tiquer, J. Child Psychol. Psychiat. **2:** 148–155, 1961.

19 Williams, C. D.: The Elimination of Tantrum Behavior by Extinction Procedures, J. Abnorm. Soc. Psychol. **59:** 269, 1959.

20 Wolpe, J.: Experimental Neuroses as Learned Behavior, Brit. J. Psychol. **43:** 243–268, 1952.

21 Wolpe, J.: Reciprocal Inhibition as the Main Basis of Psychotherapeutic Effects, Arch. Neurol. Psychiat. **72:** 205–226, 1954.

22 Wolpe, J.: Psychotherapy by Reciprocal Inhibition. Stanford, Calif.: Stanford University Press, 1958.

23 Wolpe, J.: The Prognosis in Unpsychoanalyzed Recovery from Neurosis, Amer. J. Psychiat. **118:** 35–39, 1961.

24 Wolpe, J.: Quantitative Relationships in the Systematic Desensitization of Phobias, Amer. J. Psychiat. **119:** 1062–1068, 1963.

25 Wolpe, J.: Behavior Therapy in Complex Neurotic States, Brit. J. Psychiat. **110:** 28–34, 1964.

26 Wolpe, J.: "Parallels Between Animal and Human Neuroses," in Hoch, P., and Zubin, J., eds.: Comparative Psychopathology. New York: Grune & Stratton, 1967.

27 Wolpe, J.: The Practice of Behavior Therapy. New York: Pergamon Press, 1968.

28 Yates, A. J.: The Application of Learning Theory to the Treatment of Tics, J. Abnorm. Soc. Psychol. **56:** 175–182, 1958.

Behavioral Approaches to Family and Couple Therapy*

Robert Liberman

The current splurge of couple and family therapies is not simply an accident or passing fad. These increasingly used modes of treatment for psychiatric problems are anchored in a sound foundation and are not likely to blow away. The foundation of these newer therapies lies in the opportunity they offer to induce significant behavioral change in the participants by a major restructuring of their interpersonal environments.

Couple and family therapy can be particularly potent means of behavior modification because the interpersonal milieu that undergoes change is that of the day-to-day, face-to-face encounter an individual experiences with the most important people in his life—his spouse or members of his immediate family. When these therapies are successful it is because the therapist is able to guide the members of the couple or family into changing their modes of dealing with each other. In behavioral or learning terms, we can translate "ways of dealing with each other" into consequences of behavior or *contingencies of reinforcement*. Instead of rewarding maladaptive behavior with attention and concern, the family members learn to give each other recognition and approval for desired behavior.

Since the family is a system of interlocking, reciprocal behaviors (including affective behavior), family therapy proceeds best when each of the members learns how to change his or her responsiveness to the others. Family therapy should be a learning experience for all the members involved. For simplification, however, this paper will analyze family pathology and therapy from the point of view of the family responding to a single member.

Typically, families that come for treatment have coped with the maladaptive or deviant behavior of one member by responding to it over the years with anger, nagging, babying, conciliation, irritation, or sympathy. These responses, however punishing they might seem on the surface, have the effect of reinforcing the deviance, that is, increasing the frequency or intensity of the deviant behavior in the future. Reinforcement occurs because the attention offered is viewed and felt by the deviant member as positive concern and interest. In many families with a deviant member, there is little social interaction and the individuals tend to lead lives relatively isolated from each other. Because of this overall lack of interaction, when interaction does occur in response to a member's "abnormal" behavior, such behavior is powerfully reinforced.(14)

Verbal and nonverbal means of giving attention and recognition can be termed *social reinforcement* (as contrasted with food or sex, which are termed *primary reinforcement*). Social reinforcement represents a most important source of motivation for human behavior. (6, 19) Often massive amounts of such "concern" or social reinforcement are communicated to the deviant member, focused and contingent upon

*From Robert Liberman, "Behavioral Approaches To Family and Couple Therapy," *American Journal of Orthopsychiatry,* 1970, **40,** 106–118. Reprinted by permission of the author and the Editor, *American Journal of Orthopsychiatry.*

the member's maladaptive behavior. The deviant member gets the message: "So long as you continue to produce this undesirable behavior (symptoms), we will be interested and concerned in you." Learning the lesson of such messages leads to the development and maintenance of symptomatic or deviant behavior and to characterological patterns of activity and identity. Sometimes, the message of concern and interest is within the awareness of the "sick" member. Individuals with a conscious awareness of these contingencies are frequently termed "manipulative" by mental health professionals since they are adept at generating social reinforcement for their maladaptive behavior. But learning can occur without an individual's awareness or insight, in which case we view the maladaptive behavior as being unconsciously motivated.

Massive amounts of contingent social reinforcement are not necessary to maintain deviant behavior. Especially after the behavior has developed, occasional or *intermittant reinforcement* will promote very durable continuation of the behavior. Laboratory studies have shown that intermittant reinforcement produces behavior that is most resistant to extinction.(6)

Many family therapists(7, 8, 21) have demonstrated that the interest and concern family members show in the deviance of one member can be in the service of their own psychological economy. Maintaining a "sick" person in the family can be gratifying (reinforcing) to others, albeit at some cost in comfort and equanimity. Patterson(15) describes how this reciprocal reinforcement can maintain deviant behavior by using the example of a child who demands an ice cream cone while shopping with his mother in a supermarket. The reinforcer for this "demand behavior" is compliance by the mother, but if she ignores the demand, the effect is to increase the rate or loudness of the demand. Loud demands or shrieks by a child in a supermarket are aversive to the mother; that is, her noncompliance is punished. When the mother finally buys the ice cream cone, the aversive tantrum ends. The reinforcer for the child's tantrum is the ice cream cone. The reinforcing contingency for the mother was the termination of the "scene" in the supermarket. In this reciprocal fashion, the tantrum behavior is maintained. I shall return to this important aspect of family psychopathology—the mutually reinforcing or symbiotic nature of deviance—in the case studies below. Indeed, the balance between the aversive and gratifying consequences of maladaptive behavior in a member on the other family members is the crucial determinant of motivation for and response to treatment.

Changing the contingencies by which the patient gets acknowledgment and concern from other members of his family is the basic principle of learning that underlies the potency of family or couple therapy. Social reinforcement is made contingent on desired, adaptive behavior instead of maladaptive and symptomatic behavior. It is the task of the therapist in collaboration with the family or couple to (1) specify the maladaptive behavior, (2) choose reasonable goals which are alternative, adaptive behaviors, (3) direct and guide the family to change the contingencies of their social reinforcement patterns from maladaptive to adaptive target behaviors.

Another principle of learning involved in the process of successful family therapy is modeling, also called imitation or identification. The model, sometimes the therapist but also other members of the family, exhibits desired, adaptive behavior which then is imitated by the patient. Imitation or identification occurs when the model is an esteemed person (therapist, admired family member) and when the model receives positive reinforcement (approval) for his behavior from others.(3) The amount of observational learning will be governed by the degree to which a family member pays attention to the modeling cues, has the capacity to process and rehearse the cues, and possesses the necessary components in his behavioral experience which can be combined to reproduce the more complex, currently modeled behavior.

Imitative learning enables an individual to short-circuit the tedious and lengthy process of trial-and-error (or reward) learning while incorporating complex chains of behavior into his repertoire. Much of the behaviors which reflect the enduring part of our culture are to a large extent transmitted by repeated observation of behavior displayed by social models, particularly familial models. If performed frequently enough and rewarded in turn with approval by others, the imitated behavior will become incorporated into the patient's behavioral repertoire. The principles of imitative learning have been exploited with clinical success by researchers working with autistic children,(12) phobic youngsters,(4) and male, chronic psychotics.(18) How modeling can be used in family therapy will be illustrated in the cases cited below.

I will limit the scope of the case examples to couples and families; however, the same principles of learning apply to group therapy(11, 17) and with some modification to individual psychotherapy.(9) Although learning theory has been associated in clinical psychiatry with its systematic and explicit application in the new behavior therapies, it should be emphasized that learning theory offers a generic and unitary explanation of the processes mediating change in all psychotherapies, including psychoanalytic ones.(1, 13)

TECHNIQUE

Before getting to the case material, I would like to outline the main features of an application of behavior theory to family therapy. The three major areas of technical concern for the therapist are: (1) *creating and maintaining a positive therapeutic alliance;* (2) *making a behavioral analysis of the problem(s);* and (3) *implementing the behavioral principles of reinforcement and modeling in the context of ongoing interpersonal interactions.*

Without the positive therapeutic alliance between the therapist and those he is helping, there can be little or no successful intervention. The working alliance is the lever which stimulates change. In learning terms, the positive relationship between therapist and patient(s) permits the therapist to serve as a social reinforcer and model; in other words, to build up adaptive behaviors and allow maladaptive behaviors to extinguish. The therapist is an effective reinforcer and model for the patients to the extent that the patients value him and hold him in high regard and warm esteem.

Clinicians have described the ingredients that go into this positive therapist-patient relationship in many different ways. Terminology varies with the "school" of psychotherapy to which the clinician adheres. Psychoanalysts have contributed notions such as "positive transference" and an alliance between the therapist and the patient's "observing ego." Reality therapists call for a trusting involvement with the patient. Some clinicians have termed it a "supportive relationship" implying sympathy, respect, and concern on the part of the therapist. Recent research has labeled the critical aspects of the therapist-client relationship: nonpossessive warmth, accurate empathy, and genuine concern.(20) Truax and his colleagues(20) have been able to successfully operationalize these concepts and to teach them to selected individuals. They have further shown that therapists high on these attributes are more successful in psychotherapy than those who are not. Whatever the labels, a necessary if not sufficient condition for therapeutic change in patients is a doctor-patient relationship that is infused with mutual respect, warmth, trust, and affection.

In my experience, these qualities of the therapeutic alliance can be developed through a period of initial evaluation of the patient or family. The early therapist-family contacts, proceeding during the first few interviews, offer an opportunity to the therapist to show unconditional warmth, acceptance, and concern for the clients and their problems.

Also during the first few sessions, while the therapeutic relationship is being established, the therapist must do his "diagnostic." In a learning approach to family therapy, the diagnostic consists of a *behavioral* or *functional analysis* of the problems. In making his behavioral analysis, the therapist, in collaboration with the family, asks two major questions:

1 What behavior is maladaptive or problematic—what behavior in the designated patient should be increased or decreased? Each person, in turn, is asked, (1) what changes would you like to see in others in the family, and (2) how would you like to be different from the way you are now? Answering these questions forces the therapist to choose carefully *specific behavioral goals*.

2 What environmental and interpersonal contingencies currently support the problematic behavior—that is, what is maintaining undesirable behavior or reducing the likelihood of more adaptive responses? This is called a "functional analysis of behavior," and also can include an analysis of the development of symptomatic or maladaptive behavior, the "conditioning history" of the patient. The mutual patterns of social reinforcement in the family deserve special scrutiny in this analysis since their deciphering and clarification become central to an understanding of the case and to the formulation of therapeutic strategy.

It should be noted that the behavioral analysis of the problem doesn't end after the initial sessions, but by necessity continues throughout the course of therapy. As the problem behaviors change during treatment, so must the analysis of what maintains these behaviors. New sources of reinforcement for the patient and family members must be assessed. In this sense, the behavioral approach to family therapy is dynamic.

The third aspect of behavioral technique is the actual choice and implementation of therapeutic strategy and tactics. Which interpersonal transactions between the therapist and family members and among the family members can serve to alter the problem behavior in a more adaptive direction? The therapist acts as an educator, using his value as a social reinforcer to instruct the family or couple in changing their ways of dealing with each other. Some of the possible tactics are described in the case studies below.

A helpful way to conceptualize these tactics is to view them as "behavioral change experiments" where the therapist and family together re-program the contingencies of reinforcement operating in the family system. The behavioral change experiments consist of family members responding to each other in various ways, with the responses contingent on more desired reciprocal ways of relating. Ballentine(2) views the behavioral change experiments, starting with small but well-defined successes, as leading to (1) a shift toward more optimistic and hopeful expectations; (2) an emphasis on doing things differently while giving the responsibility for change to each family member; (3) "encouragement of an observational outlook which forces family members to look closely at themselves and their relationships with one another, rather than looking 'inside' themselves with incessant why's and wherefores"; and (4) "the generation of empirical data which can be instrumental to further change, since they often expose sequences of family action and reaction in particularly graphic and unambiguous fashion."

The therapist also uses his importance as a model to illustrate desired modes of responding differentially to behavior that at times is maladaptive and at other times approaches more desirable form. The operant conditioning principle of "shaping" is used, whereby gradual approximations to the desired end behavior are reinforced with approval and spontaneous and genuine interest by the therapist. Through his instructions and example, the therapist teaches shaping to the members of the couple or family. Role playing or behavioral rehearsal are among the useful tactics employed in generating improved patterns of interaction among the family members.

The therapist using a behavioral model does not act like a teaching machine, devoid of emotional expression. Just as therapists using other theoretical schemas, he is most effective in his role as an educator when he expresses himself with affect in a comfortable, human style developed during his clinical training and in his life as a whole. Since intermittant reinforcement produces more durable behavior, the therapist may employ trial terminations, tapering off the frequency of sessions prior to termination and "booster" sessions.(1) The strategy and tactics of this behavioral approach to couples and families will be more clearly delineated in the case studies that follow. A more systematic and detailed outline of the behavior modification approach is presented in Table 1. The specification and implications of the items in this outline can be found in the manual by Reese.(16)

Case #1

Mrs. D is a 35-year-old housewife and mother of three children who had a 15-year history of severe, migranous headaches. She had had frequent medical hospitalizations for her headaches (without any organic problems being found), and also a 1½-year period of intensive, psychodynamically oriented, individual psychotherapy. She found relief from her headaches only after retreating to her bed for periods of days to a week with the use of narcotics.

After a brief period of evaluation by me, she again developed intractable headaches and was hospitalized. A full neurological workup revealed no neuropathology. At this time I recommended that I continue with the patient and her husband in couple therapy. It had previously become clear to me that the patient's headaches were serving an important purpose in the economy of her marital relationship: headaches and the resultant debilitation were the sure way the patient could elicit and

Table 1 A Behavioral Model for Learning
(Adapted from E.P. Reese[16])

1 Specify the final performance (therapeutic goals):
- Identify the behavior.
- Determine how it is to be measured.

2 Determine the current baseline rate of the desired behavior.

3 Structure a favorable situation for eliciting the desired behavior by providing cues for the appropriate behavior and removing cues for incompatible, inappropriate behavior.

4 Establish motivation by locating reinforcers, depriving the individual of reinforcers (if necessary), and withholding reinforcers for inappropriate behavior.

5 Enable the individual to become comfortable in the therapeutic setting and to become familiar with the reinforcers.

6 Shape the desired behavior:
- Reinforce successive approximations of the therapeutic goals.
- Raise the criterion for reinforcement gradually.
- Present reinforcement immediately, contingent upon the behavior.

7 Fade out the specific cues in the therapeutic setting to promote generalization of acquired behavior.

8 Reinforce intermittently to facilitate durability of the gains.

9 Keep continuous, objective records.

maintain her husband's concern and interest in her. On his part, her husband was an active, action-oriented man who found it difficult to sit down and engage in conversation. He came home from work, read the newspaper, tinkered with his car, made repairs on the house, or watched TV. Mrs. D got her husband's clear-cut attention only when she developed headaches, stopped functioning as mother and wife, and took to her bed. At these times Mr. D was very solicitous and caring. He gave her medication, stayed home to take care of the children, and called the doctor.

My analysis of the situation led me to the strategy of redirecting Mr. D's attention to the adaptive strivings and the maternal and wifely behavior of his wife. During ten 45-minute sessions, I shared my analysis of the problem with Mr. and Mrs. D and encouraged them to reciprocally restructure their marital relationship. Once involved in a trusting and confident relationship with me, Mr. D worked hard to give his wife attention and approval for her day-to-day efforts as a mother and housewife. When he came home from work, instead of burying himself in the newspaper he inquired about the day at home and discussed with his wife problems concerning the children. He occasionally rewarded his wife's homemaking efforts by taking her out to a movie or to dinner (something they had not done for years). While watching TV he had his wife sit close to him or on his lap. In return, Mrs. D was taught to reward her husband's new efforts at intimacy with affection and appreciation. She let him know how much she liked to talk with him about the day's events. She prepared special dishes for him and kissed him warmly when he took initiative in expressing affection toward her. On the other hand, Mr. D was instructed to pay minimal attention to his wife's headaches. He was reassured that in so doing, he would be helping her decrease their frequency and severity. He was no longer to give her medication, cater to her when she was ill, or call the doctor for her. If she got a headache, she was to help herself and he was to carry on with his regular routine insofar as possible. I emphasized that *he should not, overall, decrease his attentiveness to his wife, but rather change the timing and direction of his attentiveness.* Thus the behavioral contingencies of Mr. D's attention changed from headaches to housework, from invalidism to active coping and functioning as mother and wife.

Within ten sessions, both were seriously immersed in this new approach toward each other. Their marriage was different and more satisfying to both. Their sex life improved. Their children were better behaved, as they quickly learned to apply the same reinforcement principles in reacting to the children and to reach a consensus in responding to their children's limit-testing. Mrs. D got a job as a department store clerk (a job she enjoyed and which provided her with further reinforcement—money and attention from people for "healthy" behavior). She was given recognition by her husband for her efforts to collaborate in improving the family's financial condition. She still had headaches, but they were mild and short-lived and she took care of them herself. Everyone was happier including Mrs. D's internist who no longer was receiving emergency calls from her husband.

A followup call to Mr. and Mrs. D one year later found them maintaining their progress. She has occasional headaches but has not had to retreat to bed or enter a hospital.

Case #2

Mrs. S is a 34-year-old mother of five who herself came from a family of ten siblings. She wanted very badly to equal her mother's output of children and also wanted to prove to her husband that he was potent and fertile. He had a congenital hypospadius and had been told by a physician prior to their marriage that he probably could not have children. Unfortunately Mrs. S was Rh negative and her husband Rh positive. After their fifth child she had a series of spontaneous abortions because of the Rh incompatibility. Each was followed by a severe depression. Soon the depressions ran into each other and she was given a course of 150 EST's. The EST's had the effect of making her confused and unable to function at home while not significantly lifting the depressions. She had some successful short-term supportive psychotherapy but again plunged into a depression after a hysterectomy.

Her husband, like Mr. D in the previous case, found it hard to tolerate his wife's conversation, especially since it was taken up mostly by complaints and tearfulness. He escaped from the unhappy home situation by plunging himself into his work, holding two jobs simultaneously. When he was home, he was too tired for any conversation or meaningful interaction with his wife. Their sexual interaction was nil. Although Mrs. S tried hard to maintain her household and raise her children and even hold a part-time job, she received little acknowledgment for her efforts from her husband who became more distant and peripheral as the years went by.

My behavioral analysis pointed to a lack of reinforcement from Mrs. S's husband for her adaptive strivings. Consequently her depressions, with their large hypochondrical components, represented her desperate attempt to elicit her husband's attention and concern. Although her somatic complaints and self-depreciating accusations were aversive for her husband, the only way he knew how to "turn them off" was to offer sympathy, reassure her of his devotion to her, and occasionally stay home from work. Naturally, his nurturing her in this manner had the effect of reinforcing the very behavior he was trying to terminate.

During five half-hour couple sessions I focused primarily on Mr. S, who was the mediating agent of reinforcement for his wife and hence the person who could potentially modify her behavior. I actively redirected his attention from his wife "the unhappy, depressed woman" to his wife "the coping woman." I forthrightly recommended to him that he drop his extra job, at least for the time being, in order to be at home in the evening to converse with his wife about the day's events, especially her approximations at successful homemaking. I showed by my own example (modeling) how to support his wife in her efforts to assert herself reasonably with her intrusive mother-in-law and an obnoxious neighbor.

A turning point came after the second session, when I received a desperate phone call from Mr. S one evening. He told me that his wife had called from her job and tearfully complained that she could not go on and that he must come and bring her home. He asked me what he should do. I indicated that this was a crucial moment, that he should call her back and briefly acknowledge her distress but at the same time emphasize the importance of her finishing the evening's work. I further suggested that he meet her as usual after work and take her out for an ice cream soda. This would get across to her his abiding interest and recognition for her positive efforts in a genuine and spontaneous way. With this support from me, he followed my suggestions and within two weeks Mrs. S's depression had completely lifted.

She was shortly thereafter give a job promotion, which served as an extrinsic reinforcement for her improved work performance and was the occasion for additional reinforcement from me and her husband during the next therapy session. We terminated after the fifth session, a time limit we had initially agreed on.

Eight months later at followup they reported being "happier together than ever before."

Case #3

Edward is a 23-year-old young man who had received much psychotherapy, special schooling, and occupational counseling and training during the past 17 years. He was diagnosed at different times as a childhood schizophrenic and as mentally subnormal. At age 6 he was evaluated by a child psychiatry clinic and given three years of psychodynamic therapy by a psychoanalyst. He had started many remedial programs and finished almost none of them. He, in fact, was a chronic failure—in schools as well as in jobs. His parents viewed him as slightly retarded despite his low normal intelligence on IQ tests. He was infantilized by his mother and largely ignored or criticized by his father. He was used by his mother, who was domineering and aggressive, as an ally against the weak and passive father. When I began seeing them in a family evaluation, Edward was in the process of failing in the most recent rehabilitation effort—on evening, adult high school.

The initial goals of the family treatment, then, were (1) to disengage Edward from the clasp of his protective mother, (2) to get his father to offer himself as a model and as a source of encouragement (reinforcement) for Edward's desires and efforts towards independence, (3) to structure Edward's life with occupational and social opportunities that he could not initiate on his own. Fortunately the Jewish Vocational Service in Boston offers an excellent rehabilitation program based on the same basic principles of learning that have been elucidated in this article. I referred Edward to it and at the same time introduced him to a social club for ex-mental patients which has a constant whirl of activities daily and on weekends.

During our weekly family sessions, I used modeling and role-playing to help Edward's parents positively reinforce his beginning efforts at the J.V.S. and the social club. After three months at the J.V.S., Edward secured a job and now after another seven months has a job tenure and membership in the union. He has been an active member of the social club and has gone on weekend trips with groups there—something he had never done before. He is now "graduating" to another social club, a singles' group in a church, and has started action on getting his driver's license.

The family sessions were not easy or without occasional storms, usually generated by Edward's mother as she from time to time felt "left out." She needed my support and interest (reinforcement) in her problems as a hardworking and unappreciated mother at these times. Because of the positive therapeutic relationship cemented over a period of nine months, Edward's parents slowly began to be able to substitute positive reinforcement for his gradually improving efforts at work and play instead of the previous blanket criticism (also, paradoxically, a kind of social reinforcement) he had received from them for his failures. I encouraged the father to share openly with Edward his own experiences in a young man reaching for independence, thereby serving as a model for his son.

The parents needed constant reinforcement (approval) from me for trying out new ways of responding to Edward's behavior; for example, to eliminate the usual nagging of him to do his chores around the house (which only served to increase the lethargic slothful behavior which accrues from the attention) and to indicate instead pleasure when he mows the lawn even if he forgets to rake the grass and trim the hedge. They learned to give Edward approval when he takes the garbage out even if he doesn't do it "their" way. And they learned how to spend time listening to Edward pour out his enthusiasm for his job even if they feel he is a bit too exuberant.

Our family sessions were tapered to twice monthly and then to once a month. Termination went smoothly after one year of treatment.

Case #4

Mr. and Mrs. F have a long history of marital strife. There was a year-long separation early in their marriage and several attempts at marriage counseling lasting three years. Mr. F has paranoid trends which are reflected in his extreme sensitivity to any lack of affection or commitment toward him by his wife. He is very jealous of her close-knit relationship with her parents. Mrs. F is a disheveled and unorganized woman who has been unable to meet her husband's expectations for an orderly and accomplished homemaker or competent manager of their five children. Their marriage has been marked by frequent mutual accusations and depreciation, angry withdrawal and sullenness.

My strategy with this couple, whom I saw for 15 sessions, was to teach them to stop reinforcing each other with attention and emotionality for undesired behavior and to begin eliciting desired behavior in each other using the principle of *shaping*. Tactically, I structured the therapy sessions with an important "ground-rule": No criticism or harping were allowed and they were to spend the time telling each other what the other had done during the past week that approached the desired behaviors. As they gave positive feedback to each other for approximations to the behavior each valued in the other, I served as an auxiliary source of positive acknowledgement, reinforcing the reinforcer.

We began by clearly delineating what specific behaviors were desired by each of them in the other and by my giving them homework assignments in making gradual efforts to approximate the behavioral goals. For instance, Mr. F incessantly complained about his wife's lack of care in handling the evening meal—the disarray of the table setting, lack of tablecloth, disorderly clearing of the dishes. Mrs. F grudgingly agreed that there was room for improvement and I instructed her to make a start by using a tablecloth nightly. Mr. F in turn was told the importance of his giving her positive and consistent attention for her effort, since this was important to him. After one week they reported that they had been able to fulfill the assignment and that the evening meal was more enjoyable. Mrs. F had increased her performance to the complete satisfaction of her husband, who meanwhile had continued to give her positive support for her progress.

A similar process occurred in another problem area. Mr. F felt that his wife should do more sewing (mending clothes, putting on missing buttons) and should iron his shirts (which he had always done himself). Mrs. F was fed up with the home they lived in, which was much too small for their expanded family. Mr. F resolutely refused to consider moving to larger quarters because he felt it would not affect the quality of his wife's homemaking performance. I instructed Mrs. F to begin to do more sewing and ironing and Mr. F to reinforce this by starting to consider moving to a new home. He was to concretize this by spending part of each Sunday reviewing the real estate section of the newspaper with his wife and to make visits to homes that were advertised for sale. He was to make clear to her that his interest in a new home was *contingent* upon her improvements as a homemaker.

Between the third and sixth sessions, Mrs. F's father—who was ill with terminal lung cancer—was admitted to the hospital and died. During this period, we emphasized the importance of Mr. F giving his wife solace and support. I positively reinforced Mr. F's efforts in this direction. He was able to help his wife over her period of sadness and mourning despite his long-standing antagonism toward her father. Mrs. F in turn, with my encouragement, responded to her husband's sympathetic behavior with affection and appreciation. Although far from having an idyllic marriage, Mr. and Mrs. F have made tangible gains in moving closer toward each other.

DISCUSSION

There is too much confusion in the rationales and techniques underlying current practices in family therapy. Although attempts to convey the method of family therapy always suffer when done through the written word, I do not share the belief that "the vital communications in all forms of psychotherapy are intuitive, felt, unspoken, and unconscious."[7] Although this article is not meant as a "how to do it" treatise for family therapists, I do intend it as a preliminary attempt to apply a few of the basic principles of imitative learning and operant conditioning to couple and family therapy.

Although the rationalized conceptualization of family therapy practiced by psychoanalytically oriented therapists differs from the learning and behavioral approach described here, closer examination of the actual techniques used reveals marked similarity. For example Framo,[7] in explaining the theory behind his family therapy, writes: "The overriding goal of the intensive middle phases consists in understanding and working through, often through transference to each other and to the therapists, the introjects of the parents so that the parents can see and experience how those difficulties manifested in the present family system have emerged from their unconscious attempts to perpetrate or master old conflicts arising from their families of origin. . . . The essence of the true work of family therapy is in the tracing of the vicissitudes of early object-relationships, and . . . the exceedingly intricate transformations which occur as a function of the intrapsychic and transactional blending of the old and new family systems of the parents. . . ."

Despite the use of psychoanalytic constructs, Framo describes the actual process of family therapy in ways that are very compatible within a learning framework. He writes: "Those techniques which prompt family interaction are the most productive in the long run. . . . It is especially useful to concentrate on here-and-now feelings; this method usually penetrated much deeper than dealing with feelings described in retrospect. . . . As we gained experience in working with families we became less hesitant about taking more forceful, active positions in order to help the family become unshackled from their rigid patterns."

Framo goes on to give illustrations of his work with families in which differential reinforcement for behavior considered more desirable and appropriate is given by the therapists. In dealing with angry and aggressive mothers, "we learned to avoid noticing what they did (e.g. emotional in-fighting) and pay attention to what they missed in life." Trying to activate passive fathers, "the therapists make every conscious effort to build him up during the sessions. . . . A number of techniques have been tried: forcing more interaction between the husband and wife; assigning tasks; having a female therapist give encouragement in a flattering way; occasional individual sessions with the father." Zuk[23] describes his technique of family therapy in ways that fit into a reinforcement framework. He views the cornerstone of the technique the exploration and attempt to shift the balance of pathogenic relating among family members so that new forms of relating become possible." Zuk further delineates the therapist's tactics as a "go-between" in which he uses his leverage to "constantly structure and direct the treatment situation."

It should be emphasized that the behavioral approach does not simplistically reduce the family system and family interaction to individualistic or dyadic mechanisms of reinforcement. The richness and complexity of family interaction is appreciated by the family therapist working within a behavioral framework. For instance, Ballentine[2] states: ". . . behavior within a system cannot be so easily modified by focusing on the behavioral contingencies existing within any two-person subsystem, since one person's behavior in relation to a second's is often determined by behaviors of others within the system . . . the behavioral contingencies within a family system are manifold and constitute a matrix of multiple behavioral contingencies.''

The complexity of family contingencies is exemplified by a transient problem which arose in Case #3. As Edward developed more independence from his parents and spent less and less time at home, his parents began to argue more angrily. Edward had served as a buffer between them—taking sides, being used as a scapegoat for their hostility, and serving as a ''problem child'' who required joint parental action and solidarity. With their buffer gone, the husband-wife relationship intensified and friction developed. Since the therapeutic goals were limited to Edward's emancipation from his parents and since it seemed that the parents were sufficiently symbiotic to contain a temporary eruption of hostility, the therapist's major efforts at this point were aimed at protecting Edward from backsliding in response to guilt or family pressure. The strategy worked, and within a few weeks the parents had reached a new modus vivendi with each other while Edward continued to consolidate and extend his gains.

A behavioral and learning approach to family therapy differs from a more psychoanalytic one. The therapist defines his role as an educator in collaboration with the family; therefore, the assigning of ''sickness'' labels to members, with its potential for moral blame, does not occur as it does under the medical model embodied in the psychoanalytic concept of underlying conflict or disease. There is no need for family members to acknowledge publicly their ''weaknesses'' or irrationality since insight per se is not considered vital.

The behavioral approach, with its more systematic and specific guidelines, makes it less likely that a therapist will adventitiously reinforce or model contradictory behavior patterns. The behavioral approach, consistently applied, is potentially more effective and faster. When patients do not respond to behavioral techniques, the therapist can use his more empirical attitude to ask why and perhaps to try another technique. The orientation is more experimental and ''the patient is always right,'' with the burden on the therapist to devise effective interventions. In the psychoanalytic approach, the tendency has been for the therapist to decide that their failures are caused by patients who were inappropriate for the technique rather than viewing the technique as needing modification for the particular patient.

The work of behaviorally oriented family therapists is not restricted to the here-and-now of the therapy sessions. As the cases described reveal, much of the effort involves collaboration and involvement with adjunctive agencies such as schools, rehabilitation services, medication, and work settings. Family therapists are moving toward this total systems approach.

The advantages of behavioral approaches to family therapy sketched in this paper remain to be proven by systematic research. Such research is now proceeding.[5, 10, 15, 22] Much work will go into demonstrating that family processes are ''essentially behavioral sequences which can be sorted out, specified and measured with a fair degree of accuracy and precision.''[2] Hopefully, further clinical and research progress made by behaviorally oriented therapists will challenge all family therapists, regardless of theoretical leanings, to specify more clearly their interventions, their goals, and their empirical results. If these challenges are accepted seriously, the field of family therapy will likely improve and gain stature as a scientifically grounded modality.

REFERENCES

1 Alexander, F. 1965. The dynamics of psychotherapy in the light of learning theory. Internat. J. Psychiat. **1:** 189–207.

2 Ballentine, R. 1968. The family therapist as a behavioral systems engineer . . . and a responsible one. Paper read at Georgetown Univ. Symp. on Fam. Psychother. Washington.

3 Bandura, A., and Walters, R. 1963. Social Learning and Personality Development.

4 Bandura, A., Grusec, J., and Menlove, F. 1967. Vicarious extinction of avoidance behavior. Personality and Soc. Psychol. **5:** 16–23.

5 Dunham, R. 1966. Ex post facto reconstruction of conditioning schedules in family interaction. *In* Family Structure, Dynamics and Therapy, Irvin M. Cohen, ed.: 107–114. Psychiatric Research No. 20, Amer. Psychiat. Assn., Washington.

6 Ferster, C. 1963. Essentials of a science of behavior. *In* An Introduction to the Science of Human Behavior, J. I. Nurnberger, C. B. Ferster, and J. P. Brady, eds. Appleton-Century-Crofts, New York.

7 Framo, J. 1965. Rationale and techniques of intensive family therapy. *In* Intensive Family Therapy, I. Boszormenyi-Nagy, and J. L. Framo, eds. Hoeber Medical Division, New York.

8 Handel, G. (ed.). 1967. The Psychosocial Interior of the Family. Aldine, Chicago.

9 Krasner, L. 1962. The therapist as a social reinforcement machine. *In* Research in Psychotherapy, H. Strupp, and L. Luborsky, eds. Amer. Psychol. Assn., Washington.

10 Lewinsohn, P., Weinstein, M., and Shaw, D. 1969. Depression: a clinical research approach. *In* Proceedings, 1968 Conference, Assn. Advan. Behav. Ther., San Francisco. In press.

11 Liberman, R. 1970. A behavioral approach to group dynamics. Behav. Ther. In press.

12 Lovaas, O., et al. 1966. Acquisition of imitative speech by schizophrenic children. Science, **151:** 705–707.

13 Marmor, J. 1966. Theories of learning and psychotherapeutic process. Brit. J. Psychiat. **112:** 363–366.

14 Patterson, G., et al. 1967. Reprogramming the social environment. Child Psychol. and Psychiat. **8:** 181–195.

15 Patterson, G., and Reid, J. 1967. Reciprocity and coercion: two facets of social systems. Paper read at 9th Ann. Inst. for Res. in Clin. Psychol. Univ. of Kansas.

16 Reese, E. 1966. The Analysis of Human Operant Behavior. Wm. C. Brown, Dubuque, Iowa.

17 Shapiro, D., and Birk, L. 1967. Group therapy in experimental perspectives. Internat. J. Group Psychother. **17:** 211–224.

18 Sherman, J. 1965. Use of reinforcement and imitation to reinstate verbal behavior in mute psychotics. J. Abnorm. Psychol. **70:** 155–164.

19 Skinner, B. 1953. Science and Human Behavior. Macmillan, New York.

20 Truax, C., and Carkhuff, R. 1967. Toward Effective Counseling and Psychotherapy: Training and Practice. Aldine, Chicago.

21 Vogel, E., and Bell, N. 1960. The emotionally disturbed child as the family scapegoat. *In* A Modern Introduction to the Family, N. W. Bell, and E. F. Vogel, eds. Free Press, New York.

22 Zeilberger, J., Sampen, S., and Sloane, H. 1968. Modification of a child's problem behaviors in the home with the mother as therapist. J. Appl. Behav. Anal. **1:**47–53.
23 Zuk, G. 1967. Family therapy. Arch. Gen. Psychiat. **16:**71–79.

The Rules and Games of Gestalt Therapy*

Abraham Levitsky and Frederick S. Perls

The techniques of Gestalt therapy revolve largely around two sets of guidelines which we will call "rules" and "games." The rules are few in number and are usually introduced and described formally at the outset. The games, on the other hand, are numerous and no definitive list is possible since an ingenious therapist may well devise new ones from time to time.

If we are to do justice at all to the spirit and essence of Gestalt therapy, we must recognize clearly the distinction between rules and commandments. The philosophy of rules is to provide us with effective means of unifying thought with feeling. They are designed to help us dig out resistances, promote heightened awareness—to facilitate the maturation process. They are definitely *not* intended as a dogmatic list of *do's* and *don'ts;* rather, they are offered in the spirit of experiments that the patient may perform. They will often provide considerable shock value and thus demonstrate to the patient the many and subtle ways in which he prevents himself from fully experiencing himself and his environment.

When the intention of the rules is truly appreciated, they will be understood in their inner meaning and not in their literal sense. The "good boy" for instance, totally incapable of understanding the liberating intent of the rules, will frequently follow them exactly but to absurdity, thus endowing them with his own bloodlessness rather than with the vitality they seek to promote.

True to its heritage in Gestalt psychology, the essence of Gestalt therapy is in the perspective with which it views human life processes. Seen in this light, any particular set of techniques such as our presently used rules and games will be regarded merely as convenient means—useful tools for our purposes but without sacrosanct qualities.

THE RULES

The Principle of the Now

The idea of the now, of the immediate moment, of the content and structure of present experience is one of the most potent, most pregnant, and most elusive principles of Gestalt therapy. Speaking from my own experience [A.L.], I have been at various times intrigued, angered, baffled, and exhilarated by the implications of the seemingly simple idea "being in the now." And what a fascinating experience it is to help others

*From Abraham Levitsky and Frederick S. Perls, "The Rules and Games of Gestalt Therapy." In *Gestalt Therapy Now.* (Eds.) Joen Fagan and Irma Lee Shepherd. Palo Alto, California: Science and Behavior Books, 1970, 140–149. Reprinted by permission of the author, the editors, and the publisher.

become aware of the manifold ways in which they prevent themselves from having true immediate awareness.

In order to promote *now* awareness, we encourage communications in the present tense. "What is your present awareness?" "What is happening now?" "What do you feel at this moment?" The phrase "What is your *now*?" is an effective one from therapist to patient.

It would not be accurate to say that there is no interest in historical material and in the past. This material is dealt with actively when it is felt to be germane to important themes of the present personality structure. However, the most effective means of integrating past material into the personality is to bring it—as fully as possible—into the present. In this way we avoid the bland, intellectualized "aboutisms" and strive vigorously to give all material the impact of immediacy. When the patient refers to events of yesterday, last week, or last year, we quickly direct him to "be there" in fantasy and to enact the drama in present terms.

We are active in pointing out to the patient how easily he leaves the now. We identify his need to bring into the dialogue absent individuals, the nostalgic urge to reminisce, the tendency to get preoccupied with fears and fantasies of the future. For most of us, the exercise of remaining in present awareness is a taxing discipline that can be maintained only for short periods. It is a discipline to which we are not accustomed and which we are inclined to resist.

I and Thou

With this principle, we strive to drive home as concretely as possible the notion that true communication involves both sender and receiver. The receiver often behaves as if his words are aimed at the blank wall or at thin air. When he is asked, "To whom are you saying this?" he is made to face his reluctance to send his message directly and unequivocally to the receiver, to the *other*.

Thus the patient is often directed to invoke the other's name—if necessary, at the beginning of each sentence. He is asked to be aware of the distinction between "talking to" and "talking at" the listener. He is led to discover whether his voice and words are truly reaching the other. Is he really touching the other with his words? How far is he willing to touch the other with his words? Can he begin to see that this phobic avoidance of relating to others, of making genuine contact with others is also manifested in his voice mechanisms and his verbal behavior? If he has slight or insufficient contact, can he begin to realize his serious doubts as to whether others actually exist for him in this world; as to whether he is truly *with* people or feeling alone and abandoned?

"It" Language and "I" Language

This rule deals with the semantics of responsibility and involvement. It is common for us to refer to our bodies and to our acts and behaviors in distantiated, third person, *it* language:

> What do you feel in your eye?
>
> *It is blinking.*

What is your hand doing?
It is trembling.
What do you experience in your throat?
It is choked.
What do you hear in your voice?
It is sobbing.

Through the simple—and seemingly mechanical—expedient of changing *it* language into *I* language we learn to identify more closely with the particular behavior in question and to assume responsibility for it.

Instead of "It is trembling," "*I* am trembling." Rather than "It is choked," "*I* am choked." Going one step further, rather than "I am choked," "I am choking myself." Here we can immediately see the different degree of responsibility and involvement that is experienced.

Changing *it* to *I* is an example in microcosm of many of the Gestalt game techniques. As the patient participates, he is far more likely to see himself as an active agent who does things rather than a passive creature to whom things somehow "happen."

A number of other semantic games are available. If the patient says, "I can't do that," the therapist will ask, "Can you say, I *won't* do that?" As the patient accepts and uses this formulation, the therapist will follow with "And what do you experience now?"

T.: What do you hear in your voice?
P.: My voice sounds like it is crying.
T.: Can you take responsibility for that by saying, "I am crying"?

Other gambits in the semantics of responsibility are having the patient substitute verbs for nouns and frequently use the imperative mode of speech as the most direct means of communication.

Use of the Awareness Continuum

The use of the so-called awareness continuum—the *"how"* of experience— is absolutely basic to Gestalt therapy. With it we often achieve effects both striking and startling. The frequent return to and reliance on the awareness continuum is one of the major innovations in technique contributed by Gestalt therapy. The method is quite simple:

T.: What are you aware of now?

P.: Now I am aware of talking to you. I see the others in the room. I'm aware of John squirming. I can feel the tension in my shoulders. I'm aware that I get anxious as I say this.

T.: How do you experience the anxiety?
P.: I hear my voice quiver. My mouth feels dry. I talk in a very halting way.
T.: Are you aware of what your eyes are doing?
P.: Well, now I realize that my eyes keep looking away—
T.: Can you take responsibility for that?
P.: —that I keep looking away from you.

T.: Can you be your eyes now? Write the dialogue for them.

P.: I am Mary's eyes. I find it hard to gaze steadily. I keep jumping and darting about. . . .

The awareness continuum has inexhaustible applications. Primarily, however, it is an effective way of guiding the individual to the firm bedrock of his experiences and away from the endless verbalizations, explanations, interpretations. Awareness of body feelings and of sensations and perceptions constitutes our most certain—perhaps our only certain—knowledge. Relying on information provided in awareness is the best method of implementing Perls's dictum to "lose your mind and come to your senses."

The use of the awareness continuum is the Gestalt therapist's best means of leading the patient away from the emphasis on the *why* of behavior (psychoanalytic interpretation) and toward the *what* and the *how* of behavior (experiential psychotherapy):

P.: I feel afraid.

T.: How do you experience the fear?

P.: I can't see you clearly. My hands are perspiring. . . .

As we help the patient rely on his senses ("return to his senses"), we also help him distinguish between the reality *out there* and the frightening goblins he manufactures in his own fantasies:

P.: I'm sure people will despise me for what I just said.

T.: Go around the room and look at us carefully. Tell me what you *see,* what your eyes—not your imaginings—tell you.

P.: *(after some moments of exploration and discovery)* Well, actually people don't *look* so rejecting! Some of you even look warm and friendly!

T.: What do you experience now?

P.: I'm more relaxed now.

No Gossiping

As is the case with many Gestalt techniques, the no-gossiping rule is designed to promote feelings and to prevent avoidance of feelings. Gossiping is defined as talking about an individual when he is actually present and could just as well be addressed directly. For example, let us say the therapist is dealing with Bill and Ann:

P.: *(to therapist)* The trouble with Ann is she's always picking on me.

T.: You're gossiping; say this to Ann.

P.: *(turning to Ann)* You're always picking on me.

We often gossip about people when we have not been able to handle directly the feelings they arouse in us. The no-gossiping rule is another Gestalt technique that facilitates direct confrontation of feelings.

Asking Questions

Gestalt therapy gives a good deal of attention to the patient's need to ask questions. The questioner is obviously saying, "Give me, tell me . . ." Careful listening will often reveal that the questioner does not really need information, or that the question is not really necessary, or that it represents laziness and passivity on the part of the patient. The therapist may then say, "Change that question into a statement." The frequency with which the patient can actually do this validates the action of the therapist.

Genuine questions are to be distinguished from hypocritical questions. The latter are intended to manipulate or cajole the other into seeing or doing things a particular way. On the other hand, questions in the form of "How are you doing?" and "Are you aware that . . ." provide genuine support.

THE GAMES

Following is a brief description of a number of "games" used in Gestalt therapy. They are proposed by the therapist when the moment—in terms of either the individual's or the group's needs—seems appropriate. Some of the games, such as the "I have a secret" game or the "I take responsibility" game are particularly useful as group warm-ups at the beginning of a session.

It is, of course, no accident that some of the major techniques of Gestalt therapy are couched in game form. This is evidently a basic metacommunication on the part of Perls, highlighting one of the many facets of his philosophy of personality functioning. The game language (itself a game) can be seen as a commentary on the nature of all or most of social behavior. The message is *not* to stop playing games, since every form of social organization can be seen as one or another game form. Rather the message is to be aware of the games we play and to be free to substitute satisfying for nonsatisfying games. Applying this view to any two-person relationship (love, marriage, friendship), we would not be inclined to seek out a partner who "does not play games" but rather one whose games fit comfortably with our own.

Games of Dialogue

In trying to effect integrated functioning, the Gestalt therapist seeks out whatever divisons or splits are manifested in the personality. Naturally, whatever "split" is found is a function of the therapist's frame of reference and his observational powers. One of the main divisions postulated is that between the so-called top-dog and under-dog. Top-dog is roughly the equivalent of the psychoanalytic superego. Top-dog moralizes, specializes in *shoulds,* and is generally bossy and condemning. Under-dog tends to be passively resistant, makes excuses, and finds reasons to delay.

When this division is encountered, the patient is asked to have an actual dialogue between these two components of himself. The same game of dialogue can, of course, be pursued for any significant split within the personality (aggressive versus passive, "nice guy" versus scoundrel, masculine versus feminine, etc.). At times the dialogue game can even be applied with various body parts such as right hand versus left, or upper body versus lower. The dialogue can also be developed between the patient and some significant person. The patient simply addresses the person as if he were there, imagines the response, replies to the response, etc.

Making the Rounds

The therapist may feel that a particular theme or feeling expressed by the patient should be faced vis-à-vis every other person in the group. The patient may have said, "I can't stand anyone in this room." The therapist will then say, "OK, make the rounds. Say that to each one of us, and add some other remark pertaining to your feelings about each person."

The "rounds" game is of course infinitely flexible and need not be confined to verbal interaction. It may involve touching, caressing, observing, frightening, etc.

Unfinished Business

Unfinished business is the Gestalt therapy analogue of the perceptual or cognitive incomplete task of Gestalt psychology. Whenever unfinished business (unresolved feelings) is identified, the patient is asked to complete it. Obviously all of us have endless lists of unfinished business in the realm of interpersonal relations, with, for instance, parents, siblings, friends. Perls contends that resentments are the most common and important kinds of unfinished business.

"I Take Responsibility"

In this game we build on some of the elements of the awareness continuum but we consider all perceptions to be acts. With each statement, we ask patients to use the phrase, ". . . and I take responsibility for it." For example, "I am aware that I move my leg . . . and I take responsibility for it." "My voice is very quiet . . . and I take responsibility for it." "Now I don't know what to say . . . and I take responsibility for not knowing."

What seems at first blush a mechanical, even foolish procedure is soon seen as one heavily laden with meaning.

"I Have a Secret"

This game permits exploration of feelings of guilt and shame. Each person thinks of a well-guarded personal secret. He is instructed *not* to share the secret itself but to imagine (project) how he feels others would react to it. A further step can then be for each person to boast about what a terrible secret he nurses. The unconscious attachment to the secret as a precious achievement now begins to come to light.

Playing the Projection

Many seeming perceptions are projections. For instance, the patient who say, "I can't trust you," may be asked to play the role of an untrustworthy person in order to discover his own inner conflict in this area. Another patient may complain to therapist, "You're not really interested in me. You just do this for a living." He will be told to enact this attitude, after which he might be asked whether this is possibly a trait he himself possesses.

Reversals

One way in which the Gestalt therapist approaches certain symptoms or difficulties is to help the patient realize that overt behavior commonly represents the reversal of underlying or latent impulses. We therefore use the reversal technique. For example, the patient claims to suffer from inhibition or excessive timidity. He will be asked to play an exhibitionist. In taking this plunge into an area fraught with anxiety, he makes contact with a part of himself that has long been submerged. Or, the patient may wish to work on his problem of extreme touchiness to criticism. He will be asked to play the role of listening very carefully to everything that is said to him—especially criticism—without the need to defend or counterattack. Or, the patient may be unassertive and overly sweet; he will be asked to play the part of an uncooperative and spiteful person.

The Rhythm of Contact and Withdrawal

Following its interest in the totality of life processes, in the phenomena of figure and ground, Gestalt therapy emphasizes the polar nature of vital functioning. The capacity for love is impaired by the inability to sustain anger. Rest is needed to restore energy. A hand is neither open nor closed but capable of both functions.

The natural inclination toward withdrawal from contact, which the patient will experience from time to time, is not dealt with as a resistance to be overcome but as a rhythmic response to be respected. Consequently when the patient wishes to withdraw, he is asked to close his eyes and withdraw in fantasy to any place or situation in which he feels secure. He describes the scene and his feelings there. Soon he is asked to open his eyes and "come back to the group." The on-going work is then resumed, usually with new material provided by the patient who has now had some of his energies restored by his withdrawal.

The Gestalt approach suggests that we accept withdrawal needs in any situation where attention or interest has lagged but that we remain aware of where our attention goes.

"Rehearsal"

According to Perls, a great deal of our thinking consists of internal rehearsal and preparation for playing our accustomed social roles. The experience of stage fright simply represents our fear that we will not conduct our roles well. The group therefore plays the game of sharing rehearsals with each other, thus becoming more aware of the preparatory means employed in bolstering our social roles.

"Exaggeration"

This game is closely allied to the principle of the awareness continuum and provides us with another means of understanding body language. There are many times when the patient's unwitting movement or gesture appears to be a significant communication. However, the gestures may be abortive, undeveloped or incomplete—perhaps a wave of the arm or a tap of the leg. The patient will be asked to exaggerate the movement repeatedly, usually making the inner meaning more apparent. Sometimes the patient will be asked to develop the movement into a dance to get more of his self into integrative expression.

A similar technique is used for purely verbal behavior and can well be called the "repetition" game. A patient may make a statement of importance but has perhaps glossed over it or in some way indicated that he has not fully absorbed its impact. He will be asked to say it again—if necessary a great number of times—and, where necessary, louder and louder. Soon he is really hearing himself and not just forming words.

"May I Feed You a Sentence?"

In listening to or observing the patient, the therapist may conclude that a particular attitude or message is implied. He will then say, "May I feed you a sentence? Say it and try it on for size. Say it to several people here." He then proposes his sentence, and the patient tests out his reaction to the sentence. Typically, the therapist does not simply interpret for or to the patient. Although there is obviously a strong interpretative element here, the patient must make the experience his own through active participation. If the proposed sentence is truly a key sentence, spontaneous development of the idea will be supplied by the patient.

Marriage Counseling Games

We will mention only a few of the great number of possible variations on these games.

The partners face each other and take turns saying sentences beginning with, "I resent you for . . ." The resentment theme can then be followed by the appreciation theme, "What I appreciate in you is . . ." Then the spite theme, "I spite you by . . ." Or, the compliance theme, "I am compliant by . . ."

Lastly, there is the discovery theme. The partners alternate describing each other in sentences beginning with "I see . . ." Many times this process of discovery involves actually seeing each other for the first time. Since, as Perls points out, the most difficult problem in marriage is that of being in love with a concept rather than an individual, we must learn to distinguish between our fantasied image and the flesh-and-blood person.

Finally, we should mention a particular approach that does not fall under the heading of either rules or games but which can well be included at this point. It is an important gambit in Gestalt therapy and symbolizes much of Perls's underlying philosophy. We might call it the principle of "Can you stay with this feeling?" This technique is invoked at key moments when the patient refers to a feeling or mood or state of mind that is unpleasant and that he has a great urge to dispel. Let us say he has arrived at a point where he feels empty or confused or frustrated or discouraged. The therapist says, "Can you stay with this feeling?"

This is almost always a dramatic moment and a frustrating one for the patient. He has referred to his experience with some sourness and an obviously impatient desire to get on with it, to leave this feeling well behind him. The therapist however asks him deliberately to remain with whatever psychic pain he has at the moment. The patient will be asked to elaborate the *what* and *how* of his feelings. "What are your sensations?" "What are your perceptions, fantasies, expectancies?" At these moments, it is frequently most appropriate and necessary to help the patient distinguish between what he imagines and what he perceives.

The stay-with-it technique illustrates par excellence Perls's emphasis on the role of phobic avoidance in all of neurotic behavor. In his view, the neurotic has habitually

this life plan is not unconscious, it is pre-conscious and we call it the script—a drama of life, so the next thing we got into was script analysis, analysis of a person's whole life plan in which you could predict the great scheme of their lives. For example, whether they would kill themselves, kill somebody else, whether they would become successful or psychotic, this was all decided beforehand. So it is just like a big theatrical script or a play people have in their heads.

At this point you have a rough outline of this system. Let me talk about some of the people who have had similar ideas. Now the fact that someone has had a similar idea does not mean necessarily that it is the same thing. All good clinicians are good observers and there are people who are going to see the same things, but the advantage of Transactional Analysis, I think, is that it has named these things and enabled us to have a consistent theory of human behavior. For example, when someone comes on and talks like the child he once was and switches over and talks like a reality testing grown up and then switches again and talks like a typical mother or father would to a little boy or girl, what should we call them? Well I called them ego states because I happen to know Dr. Paul Feder (he knew me better than I knew him), but anyway I knew about his work on ego states. He says things like "ego states" and "to repress" and "to fixate" which is exactly what we are saying except we are not so interested in repression as the fixation. That child ego state diagram on the blackboard can be fixated at a certain point in childhood by a variety of things, perhaps by a trauma but not necessarily.

We never use the word "mature," which has no meaning. When we speak of Adult, we mean the ability to look out to reality or to an inner reality and process the data very much like a computer. The parental ego state is borrowed from other people by imitation, by introjection and by incorporation. Now ego states to us are not merely constructs, they are phenomenological realities. When people learn how to distinguish them, they can feel them. They say "now I really feel my child" or "now, I can really feel my adult" (data processor) or "now, I can really feel my parent coming on" is the expression we use which means they are working. They are social realities and it is very easy to diagnose which ego state a person is in by watching his behavior and the behavior of those who respond to him. For example if you have in a group what we could call a rebellious Child (or someone who is in a rebellious Child ego state) he functions as a kind of litmus paper for other people. The moment someone comes on with a Parent ego state, he will get angry at that person. Ego states are also behavioral realities—there are all sorts of muscular tensions and gestures and manners of speech which go into each ego state. Let me talk about these aspects very briefly. The phenomenological problem in Transactional Analysis, or in this particular aspect which is called structural analysis is "Who am I?" "Which is my real self?" Well, they are all real selves. In other words, everybody has three real selves, and so we postulate a kind of a cathexis we call pre-cathexis which can move from one ego state to the other and give the experience of real self. Since this can reside in any of the three ego states you can say then that the person has three real selves. Each of these selves has its own way of experiencing. At the time a person is coming on Parent he experiences his parent as his real self or his Parent ego state. His data processing adding up a column of figures, for example, he experiences that Adult ego state as his real self. Here we get into different ways of experiencing the self. Each ego state has its own way of experiencing. The social reality of these ego states falls in the realm of social psychology but we have a very different approach because social psychology very often tends to account for itself by Freudian mechanisms, such as defenses. We are interested in motivations and gratifications rather than defenses, and that is why we like the word transaction in which you talk to someone because you get something out of it. The most complete defense is to just not say anything, just to sit still. But there is more to life than defenses. There are motivations and gratifications and that is what we are interested in.

Ego states are not roles. A little boy or girl can take the role of the parent, the role of the little boy or the girl or the role of the data processor. For example, a classical form of children's play is "you be the mommy, you be the little girl and I will be the doctor." Now the mommy is the parent, the doctor is the computer, the data processor, who figures out what is wrong with you and the other person will be the little girl and she acts like the little girl. Now those are roles, but you see all the roles are played in a child's ego state. It is very important that we distinguish ego states from roles. Ego states are not roles. So I often get my feelings hurt by people referring to ego states as roles and my feelings get hurt easily, so I hope that during this discussion no one will refer to ego states as roles!

Now the behavioral reality which has to do with muscular activity and the manner in which you speak is because of the fact that postures and gestures are reinforced in early childhood and other postures and gestures are forbidden. For example, in family life, particularly for very small infants, the mother's or father's smile, and conversely, their frowns, are in a sense, Pavlovian reinforcers of behavior. There are also verbal reinforcements which we are very much interested in. These are the things parents say which determine what I referred to before as the script. The whole life plan is decided upon at a very early age in its most rudimentary archaic form, probably by the age of four. Then it is elaborated in a more practical kind of life plan between the ages of four and eleven and refined during early adolescence. Since behavior is in a sense a conditioned reaction, it can be changed by outside influences, and that is the job of the therapist. Now having postulated that there are three different selves we then run into the Freudian concepts. One of the problems is the difference between Parent, Child and Adult ego states and superego, ego and id. We say the super ego, ego and id are concepts, whereas ego states are phenomenological behavior and social realities. In other words, I can show you a Parent, I can show you a Child. I can show you someone in an Adult ego state. We feel that this terminology which we have devised is much more suitable for social psychology and for talking about groups than the Freudian terminology. I know this attitude has aroused some antagonism that I am anti-Freudian. All I am saying is that Freud did not design psychoanalysis as a social psychology, he designed it as individual psychology. In order to find out something about social behavior in Freudian language you have to read a whole paragraph of polysyllables, whereas in Transactional language you can say the same thing in one sentence of very short words, so it is just easier. Now I will talk briefly about the difference between the Freudian concepts and ego states.

The child ego state is different from the id. The child's ego state has all the feelings, experiences and behavioral patterns of the child. The id, as Freud said, has no organization and can't say "No." The ego, as reality testor, is very much like the Adult. The super ego is essentially a negative concept. In order to account for certain forms of behavior by using the concept of super ego, we have to go through a kind of a reversal. In other words, first we postulate that there is a superego and then we postulate that there are holes in it. We do it differently, we do it transactionally with phenomenological directness. Children are delinquent because their parents tell them to be delinquent.

Psychologically we have two kinds of energy, bound and unbound. We postulate a third kind which we call free energy which can move from one ego state to the other and is a carrier of all things that philosophers talk about, the feeling of self, the feeling of inspiration, etc. The repetition compulsion we see in people playing games, we also see in the script. Most scripts are designed for a whole lifetime and they are essentially repetitive. In other words, let's say a man may have three divorces in a row or go to the hospital three times for alcoholism—that's part of the script—and that's where the repetition compulsion comes in. The concept of transference we expand to mean all archaic reactions of the child. Again we have one advantage in that there is no word in psychoanalysis for the original situation from which the transferences are derived, like what did father and mother do. We call that the protocol of the script.

In TA therapy, we speak of winners and losers. Now, therapy is designed to make winners out of losers, or, to use fairy tale terminology, to make princes out of frogs, and that is our job. We take it very seriously. We do not want better frogs, we want princes to come out of the treatment. Obviously, the script has a lot to do with the life style barometer based to a large extent on the family. This has a lot to do with things that Adler and Jung and Horney have said on the role of the parent in forming the script. In therapy, we get into a lot of existential things. TA therapy is directed toward autonomy and the recovery of intimacy. Another existential element we like to establish the clarity of, is the self. To do that, we recognize that there are three different selves. The problem of people sitting around saying "Who am I? Who am I?" is based on the fact that they want to be one person and they are not one person. There is no way to be one person. Everybody is three different selves. The moment we realize that, we have very little trouble with the problem of the self.

Then we have the problem of free will as opposed to the script. The fact that everyone is programmed and programs himself is the opposite of freedom and of spontaneity, and for that matter, of authenticity. An analogy is when a person is sitting at a player piano. Now a player piano is a piano with a roll of paper in it and the paper turns and the piano plays. So most people spend their time sitting in front of a player piano going like this with their fingers and saying, "How do you like the music I am making?", under the delusion that they are making the music. Whereas, the music is being made for them by a roll of a bunch of computer tapes which were put into their head by their parents when they were very young. When they say "How do you like what I am playing?" we say to them "How would you like to get away from the player piano and learn to play your own piano?" You might be embarrassed at first, a little awkward, but really, it's much more worthwhile than sitting at a player piano saying "How do you like what I am playing?" So that's how we handle the problem of free will versus that fact that everybody is programmed by a script. Now, in order to demonstrate all this, of course, we have to have lots of confrontations and we're pretty tough.

A lot of transactional analysts are healthy, happy, rich and brave. Which they are. They take trips all over the world. They're all here. The brave part comes in because you take chances that other therapists won't take and you do. And they're not a gamble. Oftentimes, you can say the most amazing things to patients, things that would make outsiders shudder until they see it two or three times, then they start doing it, and the patients get well faster. You don't stand for any nonsense from the patient. If he says something that doesn't make sense to you let him know about it. That's why we have heterogeneous groups. We don't like homogeneous groups, because in a homogeneous group, there's no confrontation. If there's a group of eight alcoholics and one therapist who doesn't drink, his confrontations are very poor, because he is one against eight. Whereas if everybody in the group is different, they confront each other, because to each one, the other person's game seems strange. If you're going to cure people, you have to make them individual. Therefore, we are not entirely in accord with using group analytical therapy because to us, what the group does may be interesting, but it does not cure schizophrenia. The way to cure a schizophrenic is to talk to the schizophrenic as a person.

These encounters of talking straight are back on the idea that most people are really in a fog and if they get in a certain kind of group, things become real and that's what we believe and it also works.

In America, we have trading stamps at the grocery store. When you buy groceries you get trading stamps, you put them in a book, and when you get enough you turn them in for a prize. We call certain kinds of feelings "trading stamps." A person may go around and arrange that people kick him verbally or physically so that way he collects his trading stamps. When he gets one thousand kicks, he gets a "free" suicide. If a person throws away the trading stamps instead of going on with the project, he goes into a state of despair, which is an existential thing. It looks like depression, but it isn't.

Depression in our language is an inner dialogue between the Parent and the Child ego states, which is not too dissimilar from the way Freud said it. Despair is a dialogue between the Adult and the outside world. "What do I do now? I gave up my project: All the people that I know that so obligingly hurt my feelings and are my good friends because they hurt my feelings I have to give them up if I'm going to give up hurt feelings. What do I do now? How do I relate to people in some other way than getting them to hurt my feelings?" So what we call hurt feelings, we call that a racket. Because in our experience, not in our philosophy, 90% of all human feelings are spurious and we call them rackets. The "hurt feelings" racket is where you can get a free suicide; the "guilt" racket is where you get people to make you feel guilty, and then commit suicide, or the "anger" racket, where you collect anger. "That would make anybody angry, wouldn't it?" and I say, "No, it wouldn't," and that really upsets people. So if you collect a thousand "angries" you get a free homicide.

So despair means giving up these "rackets," and you have to find a new way of feeling. In other words your parents not only tell you how to stand, how to sit, how to talk, but they also tell you how to think, how to listen, and how to feel. You do exactly what they tell you. If your mother says, "In our family, when the going gets tough, we feel guilty," you'll feel guilty. If mother says, when the going gets tough, "We'll feel angry," then you feel angry.

Now the only thing we are interested in is the choice of the therapist as part of the script. They come to you if the script calls for someone like you. The sooner you realize that or the sooner we realize it, the sooner we can start curing the patient. Now I want to stop in about seven minutes, so I'll go a little quickly.

Now we have a strong relationship with Gestalt therapy which is most prominently promoted in America by Fritz Perls, who lives in California. Many of his ideas are very congenial with us and many of our ideas are very congenial with him. One difference is we don't allow closure. If the closure is to kill yourself we don't allow that. We say no closures, you have to start over, and that's how you get your despair, by not allowing the closures. We're very interested in semantics and non-verbal manifestations. In fact one of our models is sphincter. Which spincter is the patient holding tight. One criteria of getting well, rather than making progress is that he relaxes that particular sphincter.

We also very often interpret dreams functionally rather than symbolically which is also very similar to the Gestalt way of interpreting a dream. We also believe in positive affects which Adler gave. In America, by affects people usually mean anger or crying. They say we had a good group meeting if somebody got mad or cried. I don't know why that's a good group meeting. People don't get better. I know people who have cried in groups for twenty years or got angry in groups for twenty years; they make good group meetings, but they are not getting better. We believe in positive affects. Laughing is an affect and it's more fun to have a group where everybody is laughing than a group where everyone is getting angry, and they get better faster. We do not believe in solemnity. There is no scientific evidence that if the therapist looks solemn, that a patient will get better faster than if he laughs. There's absolutely no evidence to this effect. Nevertheless, 95% of the therapists take to looking very solemn. Our people don't. I think our people get better faster. It's much easier to give the patient permission to get better than it is to give therapists permission not to look solemn. Some therapists sit very nervous as they try to look solemn and grim. Well, okay then, the actual thing that Gestalt therapists do, we don't do in our groups.

Okay, now we have a lot of psychodrama. For instance, what we call regression therapy, in which you say to the patient, "Okay, I want to talk to your five year old child, I'm a five year old child. Now let's talk." So there is a certain amount of role playing. There are certain experiments you can do with patients. For instance, the patient says "You ought to see what my wife did" and etc., and tells you a long story and what you're supposed to say is "Gee whiz, yes you're right" so what I say is "You're right—how do you feel now?" and then I say "You're wrong—how do you feel now?" and it doesn't make any difference. Usually it works this way in that particular experiment. "You were wrong," so he feels guilty. . . . Let me start over. You say to the patient, "You're right," so if he looks happy, then you say "No, you're wrong;" he says, "Well, I knew that all the time."

So what happens there is one thing we've discovered. The Child part of the personality does not understand jokes, even if the Adult part knows you are doing something on purpose, even if you have done it before, the response will nevertheless be real and spontaneous. So you try that sometime, it may surprise you how well that principle works.

Again, I want to emphasize that ego states are not roles. Also we do not believe in weak egos. The ego is always there, it can be cathected strongly or weakly. If you tell the patient he has a weak ego, he will obligingly have a weak ego. My patients are very good sports. They'll believe anything I tell them, almost. If I say, "have a weak ego," they'll have a weak ego, or "have a strong ego," they'll have a strong ego. There's no such thing as a weak ego. There is such a thing as a weakly cathected ego. If you cathect the Adult, it is going to be just as strong as anybody else's, maybe stronger than the therapist. One reason why a lot of people have weak egos is that their patients have weak egos and they do not know what to do if their patient had a stronger ego than they did. It is a harrowing experience to have happen, believe me. The worst thing that can happen to a therapist is to have a patient who is more honest than he is. And I have had that experience. Really scares you. (Laughter).

We also believe in giving the patient permission. The patient does not need advice or exhortation, he needs permission. The classical example, of course, is the man who is a gambler. Now, what he needed was not an exhortation to stop gambling, but what he needed is permission to stop gambling, because he gambled because his Parent ego ordered him to gamble.

I'm going to spend the last four minutes summarizing Transactional Analysis. First of all, ego states are the key to Transactional Analysis. If you can't break it down to ego states, it is not Transactional Analysis, and this distinction is well worth making.

Secondly, our therapy is contractual. It is the only way to tell what you are doing. And you do not make contracts with words like "relationship," "interpersonal," "social anxiety." Those words are meaningless. The patient has to come with something that you can understand, operationally.

When he talks about "relationships" trouble, say "What do you mean?" and he says, "Okay, I go into a room with strangers, my stomach contracts." That leads to a contract. You say, "Okay, what you are here for is that when you go into a room and strangers are there your stomach will no longer contract," and he says "yeah." That's a contract. We know when he's better, he knows when he's better, everybody else in the group knows he's better, and his stomach stops contracting. He gets along much better socially, obviously, and all the other things go along with it.

Or . . . "I want to be cured of my headache." Now the contract. . . . You make a tentative contract with the patient. The patient says "I want to be cured of my headache." Okay, "let's try to cure you of your headache," and you're geared to cure the headache. That's what he's paying you for. Yes. Then you can modify the contract. Six months later you've cured him of his headache. Then you could say to him, "Would you also like to be cured of having auditory hallucinations?" (Laughter).

My staff consultations are all held in the presence of the patient, no matter what we are talking about. Even if we are talking about shock treatment, our patients are present. In other words, patients are people like us.

Then we analyze the transactions, not the content, what does the person get out of it. My position is that 90% of things people call unconscious are really preconscious. So we don't call it unconscious unless it really is unconscious. Probably the original oedipal rage is really unconscious. Everything else is pre-conscious unless it is proven otherwise.

We have a small colloquial vocabulary. I use archeo psyche, neo psyche and extero psyche here to show that I once took Greek in school and like big words. They are not necessary to the theory. But they are there.

We also believe that neuroses arrive from playing games and the cure is to stop being crooked. We believe that the therapist should be potent, we're not afraid to be potent. We're not afraid when people come around and say, "Are you omnipotent?" We say, "No, I'm not omnipotent, but man, I sure am potent." (Laughter). We gotta be more potent than the patient's Parent. Obviously, this potency enables us to give the patient permission to get better. When the patient is in a state of despair, we also have to be potent enough to protect him from himself.

I want to end up by saying, we are not interested in making progress. I'm sure many therapists or all therapists have patients who have been making progress for ten, fifteen, and twenty years, and it is really wonderful to see them making progress in ten, fifteen or twenty years. We're not interested. We want to cure the patient. That's what we are trying to do. That's why we have to be potent.

Five Paradigms for Group Psychotherapy*

J. F. T. Bugental

The literature of group psychotherapy is apt to prove frustrating to the informed and conscientious reader because of the evident range of phenomena which are lumped together under the single name "group therapy" (1, 2, 3, 4, 5, 6, 7, 8, 9). To be sure, such adjectives as "analytic," "intensive," or "activity" are sometimes used to try to denote more specifically what a particular author is discussing; nevertheless, no assurance is available that two different writers, both nominally dealing with, say, "intensive group therapy," have indeed the same sort of program in mind. It is manifest that this situation makes it difficult for the student, the teacher, and the professional journeyman.

It is the purpose of this paper to describe five paradigms for group therapy. In addition to the aid to clearer communication which it is hoped this may provide, it is likely that it will enable group therapists to exercise greater precision in conducting their work and greater flexibility in adapting it to the needs of their patients. An adequate taxonomy is an essential of a disciplined procedure.

Let us imagine five different groups among which we may draw contrasts. For our purposes we will focus only on what goes on in the groups. We will be trying

*From J. F. T. Bugental, "Five Paradigms for Group Psychotherapy," *Psychol. Rep.*, 1962, **10**, 607–610. Reprinted by permission of the author and the Editor, *Psychological Reports*.

to get five different answers to the question, "What does a therapy group do?" Let us recognize at the outset that we will overdraw each of these portraits of the groups in order to highlight contrasts. Here are thumbnail descriptions of the five. *Process-centered group:* First we may think of a group that is close to the so-called "group dynamics" or "training" groups though in one way or another such procedures are used also in therapy. *Activity-projects group:* Some groups center their activity around projects of various kinds which are used for instigating activities thought to be therapeutic. *Interpersonal discussion group:* This group concerns itself primarily with expressing and seeking to understand the actual relations among the members of the group itself. *Expressive-projective group:* In this form, emphasis is placed on catharis through projections upon ambiguous materials and activities. *Analytic group:* This approach seeks to examine the reinstatement of early emotional conditioning in the transferences among the patients and upon the therapist. Having these first, hasty pictures of the five models, let us next contrast them in terms of characteristics of their functioning, recognizing the while that we are overemphasizing differences in order to understand the phenomena more readily.

TYPICAL ACTIVITIES

What does each group do when it is functioning most nearly as the therapist thinks productive?

The *process* group reviews and looks for underlying implications in an immediately preceding discussion segment. Thus it may look at the sorts of member behaviors that facilitated and blocked understanding, at the patterns of relative frequency of participation, or at competition for group leadership.

The *projects* group may watch a film on different forms of parental discipline and then share memories of the punishments and rewards they received from their own parents or that they mete out to their children. They may each respond to a projective question (such as naming three impossibilities) and then compare the kinds of responses they have given. They may role play a problem in giving sex education to a teen-ager and then compare the ideas, memories, and concerns stimulated.

The *interpersonal discussion* group members share their emotional responses to an interchange which has just occurred among some of the group. They try to bring out candidly the impacts experienced in terms of anger, competition, affection, empathy, and so on, and then seek to understand these in terms of other aspects of their own personalities with which they are becoming familiar.

The *expressive* group uses a variety of media to stimulate and reveal feelings, impulses, fantasies, and unconscious material generally: thus they may all work on a composite drawing with crayons or finger paints, each following the dictates of his own impulses and then reacting to the contributions of the others. They may exchange roles and play out their perceptions of each other. Their participation is encouraged to be freer and will be more characterized by shouting, cursing, weeping, grimacing, etc.

The *analytic* group gives subjective associations to a dream of one of its members; notes and interprets slips of speech or metaphors, and seeks to make explicit the projection of familial identities upon each other and upon the therapists.

Next let us look at *typical therapist functions* in each of these types of groups. The lists are not exhaustive and there is much overlap, but we will try to pick out a few of the most important and most distinguishing.

The *process* group therapist must set an example as a sensitive listener and perceptive reporter. He teaches the importance of the implicit and helps the group get over its content-boundness. He frequently will provide observation schedules and will coach members in their uses.

The *projects* group therapist will supply the projects around which the group centers and guide the group in using them. He may give lecturettes to illuminate aspects with which the group needs help or to encourage greater involvement and to demonstrate the universality of certain experiences.

The *discussion* group therapist tends to be much less active, limiting his interventions more to those of helping the group maintain a here-and-now focus, of encouraging greater candor in interpersonal exchanges, and of pointing out commonalities and differences among reactions.

The *expressive* group therapist will be a resource to his group for media upon which to project. He will interpret resistances to free expression, enforce limits to the acting out, and support patients who verge on being overwhelmed, either from within themselves or from the group.

The *analytic* group therapist tends to be more passive than most of the others as he provides a screen upon which transferences may be projected. However, from time to time, he will interpret resistances or transferences, particularly pointing out the parataxic distortions which may be involved.

Next let us examine the *patient's* role in each of these models.

The *process* group tends to maintain a here-and-now, group-centered, rational orientation in which the patient seeks to increase his interpersonal sensitivities. He is rewarded by the group for subtlety of perception and for manifest changes in his skills in dealing with others.

The *projects* group is more apt to use an historical perspective with a consequently greater attention to the individual than to the group as a group. Availability of memories is encouraged, and there is an emphasis on manifest reasonableness and pertinence.

The *discussion* group maintains an orientation to what is going on now in the group but focuses particularly on relationships. Logic is valued but not to the exclusion of feelings, which the group usually insists must also be expressed. The patient who can sense emotional parallels and contrasts with others' experiences especially gains group approval.

The *expressive* group similarly maintains a here-and-now emphasis but with more attention to the individual as such. Depth and even exoticness of production is prized, and affective coherence far outweighs logical consistency. The patient who most plumbs his emotions and most clearly overthrows super-ego censorship is apt to be most rewarded.

The *analytic* group tends to have a much stronger individual focus and to seek historical materials. The patient is alerted to symbolic meanings in the contributions, and the ability to share dreams and readily associate to them is valued. Similarly a moderate degree of regression in explicitly relating to the therapist as a parent and the other patients as siblings frequently is encouraged.

Although each of these models of group therapy has its proponents, no present evidence exists to demonstrate that one is more universally effective than another. Rather it seems highly probable that each has its values. We will close our descriptions of these five paradigms with some preliminary and highly tentative speculations about the possible functional values of each. It is hoped that in the future, clinical reports and research investigations will provide sounder bases for selecting one form or another in a particular treatment situation.

The *process* group seems to be useful in providing not-too-threatening introductions to behavioral uniformities among superficially different people, to the significance of the implicit and preconscious, and to the values and satisfactions of sharing and interacting with others. As such it can provide a kind of training in socialization and human interaction.

The *projects* group moves more toward a focus on the inner life of the individual as it extends the "introductions" to the psychological world mentioned for the previous group. It may bring about a shallow dipping into the unconscious with the recovery of some less stringently repressed materials. It can aid in achieving insights into one's own processes through demonstrating the uses of introspection, the pertinence of historical material, and the inevitability of ambivalence toward emotionally important figures. In common with all group therapy forms, it offers the reassurance of demonstrations of the universality of certain emotional experiences.

The *discussion* group moves into the inner life more truly than either of the preceding two models. The unconscious is more frequently tapped although still not to the deepest levels. The patient may perceive how he "sets up" the interactions which have long been punishing to him, may become more aware of his distortions of perception, and may discover how much of his behavior has been compulsive rather than truly elective. Similarly—and especially when the patients have individual sessions also—discussion group patients can be introduced to awareness of the functions of symbols and to the reality of transference.

The *expressive* group is particularly suited to freeing overly repressed creative and emotional resources, and, through the catharsis which it encourages, to providing probes to the characterological roots of neurosis (although the method does not provide for a real "working through" of these in most instances). The patient also is apt to be made aware of the more infantile elements underlying his conscious life.

The *analytic* group, through its focus on transferences and symbolic material, is most likely to provide the climate necessary to genuine "working through" of unconscious material. In this group the deep, or truly familial, parataxes may be stimulated repeatedly, leading to the establishment of the transference neurosis and its eventual resolution.

SUMMARY

And so we have set forth five paradigms of therapy groups. For each we have tried to suggest the usual nature of group activity, the roles of therapists and patients, and finally we have advanced some notions about the possible functional values of a successful group experience in each. There is much more that might be said. We have not dealt with such crucially important questions as patient selection, therapist preparation, frequency of meetings, and so on. However, if we have made a first step toward developing a nomenclature which will improve our communications with each other about group therapy, we will have accomplished our purpose.

REFERENCES

1 Bach, G. R. *Intensive group therapy*. New York: Ronald, 1954.

2 Corsini, R. J. *Methods of group therapy*. New York: McGraw-Hill, 1957.

3 Hinkley, R. G., & Hermann, L. *Group treatment in psychotherapy*. Minneapolis: Univer. of Minnesota Press, 1951.

4 Klapman, J. W. *Group psychotherapy: theory and practice*, (2nd ed.) New York: Grune & Stratton, 1959.

5 Powdermaker, F. B., & Frank, J. D. *Group psychotherapy*. Cambridge: Harvard Univer. Press, 1953.

6 Slavson, S. R. *An introduction to group therapy*. New York: Commonwealth Fund, 1943.

7 Slavson, S. R. Group psychotherapies. In J. L. McCary, & D. E. Sheer (Eds.), *Six approaches to psychotherapy*. New York: Dryden, 1955. Pp. 127–178.

8 Spotnitz, H. Group therapy. In G. Bychowski, & J. L. Despert (Eds.), *Specialized techniques in psychotherapy*. New York: Basic Books, 1952. Pp. 85–102.

9 Ziferstein, I., & Grotjahn, M. Psychoanalysis and group psychotherapy. In F. Fromm-Reichmann, & J. L. Moreno (Eds.), *Progress in psychotherapy: 1956*. New York: Grune & Stratton, 1956. Pp. 248–255.

Section Seven

Preventive Interventions

Historically the development of intervention procedures involving mental health problems has been directed to remediation. Thus the mental health professions have concerned themselves chiefly with treating psychopathology and eliminating undesirable behaviors and conditions. Yet the ideal of the mental health movement is to promote adjustment, happiness, and well-being and to prevent the development of abnormal conditions. While few professionals would question the desirability of pursuing the goal of prevention, specific recommendations for its accomplishment have been too vague, conjectural, and controversial to constitute highly supported prophylactic programs. Many professionals argue that our knowledge of antecedents of levels of psychological adjustment lacks sufficient precision and detail to enable us to develop preventive programs. Consequently, for the most part the literature on prevention has consisted of theoretical statements rather than empirical investigations or applied efforts.

The first paper in this section, by Lawrence Kubie, deals with the prevention of emotional and adjustment disturbances and describes many of the problems and difficulties associated with preventive efforts. He notes that before large-scale preventive work can be undertaken, the following are needed: a better understanding of childhood development and the factors that provoke psychological disturbances, an increase in the number of professional workers devoted to helping persons who display early stages of maladjustment, the development of new educational techniques, and the reexamination of many cultural institutions that appear to play a part in promoting adjustment and emotional difficulties. Kubie points out that a variety of characteristics of our culture, including practices associated with education, religion, industry, and government, appear to exploit and intensify psychopathology. His enumeration of the myriad ways in which society encourages and supports emotional problems makes us aware of the complexity of prophylactic efforts. In effect Kubie reminds us that the prevention of emotional disturbances requires an ambitious and courageous attack on many social processes and institutions, and the scope of the task invites the question that he raises, Is prevention possible?

In recent years, increased attention has been given to techniques and programs of intervention involving persons who are not seriously troubled or disturbed, but who are motivated for or are thought likely to benefit from programs designed to aid general adjustment and effectiveness. In a sense, the kinds of programs to which we refer represent ones that have attempted to deal with commonplace difficulties in living and have aimed to introduce remediations at early stages in order to prevent the difficulties from developing into major maladjustments. These programs have taken a variety of forms and represent diverse theoretical orientations. One type of program that has received considerable attention during the past ten years, to the extent that today many professionals regard it as a distinct field, is community mental health. In his paper, Brickman describes a preventive program in Los Angeles County which attempts to increase the community's acceptance of deviation and to promote interaction between opposing parties where conflicts occur between individuals and social institutions. Brickman notes that psychiatrists, as well as other mental health workers, often are perpetuators of the social system and thereby contribute to the adjustment problems of many individuals whose problems stem directly from conflicts with the social system. He argues that mental health programs need to be flexible and to strike a balance between social control and social change. Community programs should promote social change and discourage clashes between individuals and the social order and, by so doing, prevent these clashes from mushrooming into major maladjustments and pathological conditions.

Another type of program which has as its aim preventing the development of adjustment problems consists of group meetings where individuals interact in semicontrolled ways in order to improve their life-styles. Some of these programs are called "sensitivity training," some are known as "T-groups," and some are called "encounter groups." The paper by Bach describes one such approach known as "marathon groups," in which participants engage in a live-in retreat for two to four days devoted to an intensive examination of their personality characteristics and interactions with others. He describes the program as "a practicum in authentic communication" where participants share "subjective truths," and intimate and competent behavioral patterns are substituted for irrational and ineffectual behavior. While the effectiveness of such programs is questioned by some professionals, who caution that their intensiveness may be harmful to some participants, marathon groups represent one of the many types of encounter programs designed to promote effectiveness and thereby prevent psychological disturbance.

The next two papers describe very different approaches, but ones with the same aim of promoting positive mental health by means of programs that incorporate preventive procedures with remedial ones. A growing trend in mental health fields is training paraprofessionals who work in a variety of settings and with different people to promote conditions likely to enhance mental health. Paraprofessionals may be trained assistants who work with psychiatrists and psychologists, or they may be important people in the real lives of patients who assist the professional in his efforts to help the patient. One example of the use of adjunct persons is described by Tavormina in programs in which parents are trained "to work on present problems as well as to prevent future behavioral problems in their children." He describes two models for such programs, one which he calls "reflective counseling," in which parents are trained to understand their children and to express and deal with their own feelings about them, and the other called "behavioral," in which parents are taught learning principles to assist them in teaching their children desirable behaviors and in eliminating undesirable ones.

The final paper in this section pertains to the development and management of social skills to increase effectiveness and satisfaction and to diminish personal inadequacies in persons who otherwise function adequately. Kazdin describes the success with which behavior-modification techniques have been used in helping individuals cope with diverse types of social problems. Here he focuses on the areas of assertive behavior and heterosexual interaction, describing techniques of behavioral rehearsal, modeling, and imagery which have been found to be effective in enhancing social skills. This kind of specific and directed training is likely to increase an individual's effectiveness and overall adjustment, thereby preventing everyday problems of living from growing.

Is Preventive Psychiatry Possible?*

Lawrence S. Kubie

There are no easy answers to any of the difficult questions with which preventive psychiatry confronts us; but questions to which we have no answers can nonetheless be useful. It is valuable to recognize the presence of an illness long before we can diagnose its precise nature, much less cure or prevent it. Physicians are reconciled to this fact. Even laymen accept this in medicine, yet tend to be resentful of it in social issues, or in such medico-social problems as the present topic.

Preventive psychiatry derives its vision, its data, and some of its techniques and strategy from the study of mental illness and from the therapists' attempts to interrupt and reverse the causal chains producing psychological illness. The larger goal of preventive psychiatry is a human nature released from the rigidity that limits our freedom to change, destroys our capacity for happiness even under favorable circum-

*From Lawrence S. Kubie, "Is Preventive Psychiatry Possible?" *Daedalus,* 1959, **88,** 646–668. Reprinted by permission of the author, the Editor, *Daedalus* and the American Academy of Arts and Sciences. Edited.

stances, and distorts our creative potential in science, in art, music, and literature, in scholarship in general, and in politics and economics. Indeed, this is the most difficult problem in human culture: to learn how to bring ourselves up freed from the tyranny of stereotyped, rigid, unlearning, unconscious psychological mechanisms.

The implementation of any such vision will demand several things:

a A more precise knowledge of the psychological development of the human infant, leading to the discovery of new techniques for guiding, modifying, and controlling that development. This implies the introduction of measures to prevent the neurotic process *before* its onset.

b The application of methods to correct and reverse the neurotic process in its early stages. This will require the training of many more individuals in the diagnosis of potential illness before frank illness has crystallized, and in its treatment in its larval stages. This is no "minor" psychiatry, comparable to "minor" surgery. It is "major" psychiatry, precisely because it concerns itself with subtle early deviations from the normal, rather than those more obvious, late disturbances which bring most patients to the psychiatrist's consulting room or to the psychiatric hospital (12, 15). Furthermore, these early manifestations occur largely in nonmedical situations; and their recognition and treatment must take place where they are found. To meet this challenge will require an increase in the number of behavioral scientists educated, certified, and licensed as qualified psychodiagnosticians and psychotherapists, without requiring that they be physicians. The medical profession alone cannot meet this need because there will never be enough medical specialists for this task. This is the bottleneck which must be broken.

c The development of new educational techniques to help reunite psychological processes which had become dissociated, instead of increasing repressive dissociations, as occurs in education as we have known it (10, 13, 14).

d Finally, preventive psychiatry will demand a critical re-examination of the influence all cultural institutions exercise on the evolution of the neurotic process. Among the factors to be studied are: the structure of the modern family; the impact of longevity and of over-all increases in the population and in population density; the changing age distribution and regional and occupation distribution of the population; the mixed constellation of therapeutic and noxious influences emanating from the several religions as presently organized and practiced; the effects on the neurotic process of various movements within the visual arts, music, and literature; the exploitation, reinforcement, and rewarding of the neurotic component in human nature by every type of economic system man has devised; and the many psycho-noxious influences that emanate from every political influence known. Even this incomplete list makes it obvious that merely to conduct an objective inquiry into these problems will arouse the opposition of every vested interest in our complacent society (17, 19).

When Henry Adams returned to Boston after a long absence, he remarked on his surprise at finding that the Unitarians who dominated the Boston culture of that day seemed to believe they had solved every great philosophical conundrum that had ever convulsed the human spirit (1). Were he to revisit America today, he would be moved to make a parallel comment about our illusions as to the perfection of our political, economic, educational, artistic, literary, and religious systems, each of which interacts in its own way with the ubiquitous but masked neurotic ingredients in so-called "normal" human nature.

NEUROSIS AND REPETITION

In another connection (5) I have pointed out that a neurotic potential exists in every child, not so defective as to be incapable of learning symbolic thinking, feeling, and action. This potential becomes entangled in the neurotic process when under stress any dissociative repression occurs, i.e., when the link is severed between memory traces of events and their appropriate affects, or when the link becomes distorted or repressed between the symbolic representatives of inner or outer experience and that which the symbol originally stood for. The neurotic process is manifested primarily in personality disturbances. Under special and critical conditions of decompensation, the neurotic state precipitates out of the neurotic process as a constellation of symptoms.

Clearly, prevention must concern itself with the neurotic potential and the neurotic process. It cannot hope to achieve any material reduction in the toll of neuroses if it waits for the imminent occurrence of the neurotic state—the final and most easily recognized, but in a sense the least important, step in the series.

Every moment of behavior is produced by a constellation of concurrent forces. Whenever this constellation is of such a nature that it predetermines the automatic repetition of any pattern of action, thought, or feeling, the result is neurosis. This is our most precise and concise definition of what we mean by "neurotic" as distinct from "normal"; it is an obligatory repetitiveness, predetermined by the pattern of the forces that produce the act (8, 9, 11).

Yet repetitiveness is necessary to life. From the first moment, we breathe and suck, not once but repeatedly. Every bodily need makes itself felt many times. Every gesture, thought, and feeling, and their communication, are repeated. Therefore, repetition is an essential attribute of behavior. Furthermore, data from modern neurophysiology indicate that the organization of the brain is such that its processes tend to continue and to recur unless some active process arises to divert them. It is "easier" for the brain to go on doing the same thing than to change.

This is normal as long as the inherent tendency to repeat alters in response to the changing demands of body chemistry as signaled from the body to the brain through its internal afferent signaling system, both conscious and preconscious. Normal repetitiveness must also be free to alter in response to signals reaching us from outside the body (signals we see and hear and apprehend through all modalities of sensation) and to the signals called symbols.

Organic injuries to the brain can render it nonresponsive to both external and internal signals, thus producing organically determined repetitiveness. Such injuries can be structural, through direct injury or infection, or they can be chemical, through fever, intoxication, and drugs. But the frozen repetitiveness resulting from organic damage is not the object of our concern.

In the neuroses, the capacity to change in response to changing external or internal stimuli is impaired without the interposition of any of these organic variables which can impose automatic repetition on behavior (8). Even with a normal nervous system and a normal biochemistry of the whole body, an obligatory repetitiveness can be imposed on human conduct by psychological variables alone. As already stated, this occurs whenever behavior is dominated by symbolic processes whose roots and relationships are unconscious. Again, neither conscious nor unconscious symbolic processes ever operate alone, but always act concurrently, though with a varied distribution of influence. Moreover, they always exert their influence on thought, feeling, and behavior largely through the continuous central stream of preconscious processing. Where conscious processes exercise the dominant influence on preconscious processing, the resulting behavior is continuously adaptive and responsive to experience, past, present, and future. Consequently, the resulting behavior can be altered by rewards and punishments, by argument, exhortation, and reason. It can respond to success and failure. It can achieve satiation. It can alter after testing the usefulness and the effectiveness of effort. In short, it can learn, since it is flexibly responsive to signals both from the outer world and from the body. Where conscious processes dominate, any repetitions which occur are normal expressions of voluntary choice or of the recurrent tidal needs of body chemistry, or else they are part of the learning process.

On the other hand, where the preconscious processes that mediate behavior are under the preponderant influence of unconscious purposes and conflicts, any pattern will become stereotyped, inflexible, and insatiable, uninfluenced by any appeal to feeling or to reason, incapable of learning from experience and of assembling data creatively into new combinations. Whenever unconscious influences dominate, it becomes impossible for preconscious functions to create anything new. They are restricted to restating the old in a variety of more or less interchangeable symbolic languages. This, of course, is precisely what occurs in much of the neurotogenically overdetermined "modern" modes of art and literature (18). Unconscious psychological processes impose this rigid stereotype on preconscious processing precisely because the symbols representing them are distorted and dislocated from their roots. Since we communicate by means of symbols, wherever such a distortion of the symbolic process occurs we become walled off from the corrective, guiding, feed-back influences of internal or external realities.

This is where psychogenic psychological illness starts. No isolated or transient episode—whether a moment of rage, terror, elation, or depresssion, or a quick explosion of odd or inappropriate behavior—constitutes an illness. Only if the response becomes an emotional position to which the individual returns like an automaton, only if the individual begins to show fear, rage, depression, or anxiety in an insistent or repetitive manner irrespective of the stimulus, only if any triggered pattern becomes automatic, stereotyped, and repetitive, can we say that certain mechanisms have taken over to predetermine the automatic and obligatory repetitiveness which is the core of that which is neurotic in human nature (5, 7, 9, 11).

From this point of view, the neurotic ingredient in human nature results from the enslavement of behavior by psychological processes inaccessible to our own conscious self-inspection and control. This is the unhappy consequence of the dichotomy of symbolic processes into two systems, in one of which the roots and ramifications are predominantly conscious, whereas in the other they are predominantly unconscious. It is this dichotomy which must be one of the primary targets of preventive psychiatry.

The early manifestations of neurotic repetitiveness are seen in the repetitive play of infancy, or in the familiar wailing, thumb-sucking, rocking, head-bumping, toy-dropping, and night terrors, or in the regurgitation, retention, breath-holding, etc., which characterize some of the transitory neurotic episodes of infancy. We are so accustomed to these events that until recently they were dismissed an unimportant. Yet such transient examples of obligatory repetitions of behavior and feeling are warning signals. Each represents an inner disturbance which will remain active unless it is fully resolved. Otherwise, a constellation of symptomatic acts may disappear, but it will be replaced by another.

These buried and unconscious processes become time bombs with slow fuses. Their masked effects are cumulative, coalescing in the end to form the neuroses and ultimately the psychoses of adult life. These residues may be explosive charges which can be touched off by appropriate trigger stimuli into frank neurotic and psychotic states, or they may exercise a continuously deforming influence on the quality of an entire personality, on the quality of his creations, and on the patterns of his living.

Since they are first laid down in fragmentary fashion during infancy and early childhood, it is at this early age that we must search for the key to prevention, learning how to limit the dissociations that can occur between the symbolic process and what it attempts to represent. After such a split has occurred, it must be detected at once and a resynthesis achieved before cumulative injury occurs to the developing personality of the infant and child. But there are important differences between limiting, checking, or preventing fission when it threatens, on the one hand, and a therapeutic re-fusion after the initial fission has occurred, on the other. If the effort is made early enough, both fall within the field of preventive psychiatry. But if fusion is undertaken only after many secondary consequences of the initial fission have already accumulated, then the process of therapeutic fusion requires those heroic investments of time and effort which constitute psychotherapy and psychoanalysis as we know them today.

PREVENTION AND THE HUMAN FAMILY

The family is a protective environment arising around one or more adults on whom the infant, the toddler, or the child depends, to whom he becomes attached, with whom he identifies, whose images he builds into himself, and who become the objects of intense rivalry, love, fear, hate, and envy. Only a small part of this struggle is experienced on a fully conscious level. Most of its goes on preconsciously; even a great deal of that part of the struggle which receives symbolic representation is subjected to dissociative (i.e., repressive) processes, so that it is represented in partial and distorted fashion by symbols of whose true nature we may be unaware.

Consequently, although the family is necessary for human life, it is at the same time the soil in which the neurotic process takes root. It is out of the tense interpersonal and growth struggles of the nursery years in the family that illness and feuds arise. It is an area for basic research to determine how the family as a necessary institution can be modified so as to yield a larger crop of health and a smaller crop of illness.

There has been a small beginning in this direction. In fact, there is a cultural revolution even in the implications of such a change of phrase as this: whereas former generations said, "What did I do to deserve a brat like that?" the present generation says, "What did I *do*?" This is a valid and moving expression of humility and search. Although at times it goes too far and involves us in fantasies of parental omniscience, omnipotence, and guilt, it represents a trend in a healthier direction, and the overswing will soon be corrected.

Yet to ask this question is one thing. To define what we could have done to prevent illness is another, involving considerations of education, of religion, of social structure, of population growth and density, of sex and age distribution within the population, of economic influences, of family size and units. The family is not an isolated or static entity. In every conceivable aspect the family as a breeding ground of health and of illness is changing rapidly in an intricate network of cultural processes which are also changing. All we can say now about the effects of these changes is that we do not yet know enough to guide them in a preventive direction (4, 19).

We know that love is essential, yet that alone is not enough: we see many children with severe neuroses coming even out of loving families. We know that faith is not enough—many neuroses arise among the devout. We know that doubt and skepticism are not enough, because they too afford no protection against the neurotic process. Similarly, we can say of simplicity or education, wealth and comfort, poverty and deprivation, ease or suffering, overwork or underwork, that none of these serves a preventive function. If any one factor plays a crucial determining role, it would seem to be the openness with which experience is shared among the generations, since it is the level of awareness on which experience is lived through and on which memory and feeling reverberate which determines whether or not it will give rise to obligatory and repetitive patterns of neurotic distortion. Here the child needs help from the adult world, in thinking and speaking out what is painful to recall and put into words, in place of silent acquiescence in unhealthy pseudo-forgetting.

THE CONSPIRACY OF SILENCE

Early analytic insights engendered naiv̈e hopes that merely to allow a child to act out his spontaneous impulses would protect him from the cumulative neurotogenic effects of repression. It soon became clear that this was not so, but that on the contrary in the child who acts out his primitive, destructive, lustful, insatiable,and unattainable needs, the very violence of the impulses of which his behavior is a partial expression engenders deep terror and guilt, with spontaneous repressive repercussions. On the other hand, where timid adults shroud the critical inner experiences of childhood in silence, the neurotogenic effects of these experiences are intensified. Indeed, this is precisely where the conspiracy of silence enters into the evolving neurotic processes of youth. The conspiracy of silence, therefore, may perhaps be looked upon as a central target for research into prevention. There is still no general appreciation of how subtle and complex is this conspiracy, how insidiously it irradiates every aspect of child life, how difficult it is to correct, and how much basic research must be done before anybody can hope to offer better alternatives. As usual, it is easier to recognize that something is wrong than to correct it. Nevertheless, its recognition is an essential prerequisite to future prevention.

The conspiracy of silence establishes the basic pattern of that type of fragmentation and dissociation called repression. It implies in the first place a silent acquiescence in a child's confusions. Moreover, these confusions actually tend to be greater for the bright child who acquires words early than for the verbal laggard, because the linguistically precocious child picks up many verbal symbols whose meanings to him are obscure and overlapping. Yet instead of being helpfully and quietly corrected, his verbal precocity is hailed and his confusion is thereby increased. Every bright child harbors countless confused thoughts and confused fantasies, many of which he himself does not even apprehend clearly enough to express in words, unless he is helped to do so by the adult world. If the world does not deliberately bring them out into the open by helping the child to become articulate about his confusions, spoken or unspoken, the child mistakes adult silence for agreement, and they remain uncorrected until at length they are repressed. Furthermore, what the adult world does not talk about becomes itself taboo, just as those parts of the body which the adult covers automatically become taboo.

There are many subtle irradiations from this taboo of silence. Consider the words "private," "privacy," "private parts"—the nameless parts which are special and peculiar to "me" and which "I" must never acknowledge, explore, think about, name, or compare. The mere impulse to inquire and to find out about them is in itself a sinful proof of an inner evil of heart and mind. This feeling spreads to include all body functions. Something happens to the baby's image of himself when the potty ceases to be a proud, happy, social function, but is moved from its dais in the center of the nursery floor and shut away behind closed doors in a room that resembles an operating room in its aspirations to cleanliness. Under the euphemism of modesty, shame is born—shame about the body, its apertures, its products, its smells. The toilet becomes a room to which we refer only by guarded, nice-nelly euphemisms—"the john," the *lavatory* (to stress cleansing instead of excreting), the *little* boy's room or *little* girl's room, as if it becomes slightly less filthy when dedicated to the child's excretory rites.

Moreover, the concept of the privacy of dirt comes to include the family. For each small child there are things he does, talks of, smells, and experiences, but only in "my family." This means to him that only *my* family is dirty, dirtier than the rest of the world. One wonders how much of social snobbery, how much of the cult of the untouchable, is at least in part a compensatory reaction to the child's feeling that "my family is dirty," a thought so painful that it usually is repressed (3).

Nor are these wordless taboos restricted to sex or to bodily things in general. They are operative also in regard to death, disappearance, desertion, and pain. In television, movies, and comics we expose our children to vicarious participation in primitive, gory, and sadistic brutalities, and with all the artful simulation of the sight and color and sound of blood and death and agonizing tortures. Everything but the smell of death is reproduced; and if this becomes sufficiently profitable, Madison Avenue and Hollywood will add that too. We immerse children in a facsimile blood bath—but we are much too nice to talk to children about such things. Consequently each child buries his mixed responses to all this deep in his angry, frightened, and suffering heart. He cannot share it: therefore he cannot clarify it with anyone. Instead, so as to leave our own comfort undisturbed, we pretend that what the child does not ask about has no effect on him. This is the measure of the immaturity and moral complicity of the adult world. If we talked about it, we then would have to do something about it. This would bring us face to face with the entrenched interests of Hollywood and the advertising sponsors of crime television.

In sum, by our silence we create a hierarchy of evil for the child. There are things he can touch and put in his mouth. These are clean. They are not dangerous. Next are the things he can touch but cannot put in his mouth. These are the first degree of danger and dirt. Next are the things he cannot touch but can look at—though perhaps a bit askance. These are the second degree of dirt. Then there are the things he must not even look at, followed in quick succession by the things that must not be talked about, the nameless things about which he must not think or feel.

What the child cannot feel, or talk about, or name, or even think about, automatically becomes repressed. The nameless loses its link to any conscious symbol, and it can be represented only by distorted, masking, dissociated symbols. This is the essential step in the process of repression because it isolates objects, acts, impulses, events, and inner conflicts from those verbal symbols by means of which we are enabled to think, to communicate, and to inquire. This makes correction impossible. Furthermore, although the conspiracy of silence severs or distorts the links between the symbol and its roots, the emotions *are there still*. Yet because they too focus around the unnamable, the wordless, the unthinkable, the untouchable, they also become detached from anything the child can think about and correct. They become free-floating emotions, balloons floating in the air of the child's psychic life. This is what the conspiracy of silence does to the evolving verbal, symbolic, and affective life of childhood.

It is not the trauma of experience or the stress of inner conflicts among irreconcilable impulses that determines sickness or health—this depends on the psychological level on which the reverberations of trauma and the stress of inner struggle are lived out, and this level in turn derives mainly from the adult conspiracy of silence. To all this, of course, the adult adds still further confusion by never bringing his own mistakes out in the open, thus making sure that neither he nor his children nor his children's children will ever learn from past errors, our only potential source of wisdom.

The moment one begins even to contemplate an attack on this multiform and subtly pervasive conspiracy of silence, he finds himself up against taboos that have been strongly entrenched, sometimes for centuries, not only in each individual's separate feelings, but also in laws, traditions, rituals, religious taboos and pronouncements, and above all in our family life, the universal breeding ground for neurotogenic unconscious conflicts. The details of this conspiracy, its form and impact, vary from culture to culture, but no culture is free of it. Nor have our cultural anthropologists or social psychologists made objective comparisons of cultures, specifically in terms of the variations to be found in the conspiracy of silence, the variations in the repressive mechanisms it imposes, and the consequent variations in the forms of the neurotic processes which evolve.

PREVENTION AND EDUCATION

If we wish to make education an ally of psychological health, we will have to weigh the effects of every ingredient in the conventional educational scene and in the customary educational techniques on the activity of neurotogenic forces (10, 14, 18). We must develop methods to counteract the tendency to fragment experience into unrelated parts, to dissociate thinking, feeling, and action from one another,to bury one fragment and then to represent it in distorted form by means of symbols which are dissociated from their origins. Since creative preconscious processes become imprisoned in the dichotomy between conscious and repressed symbolic processes, any control of dissociation and repression will profoundly influence emotional maturation, intellectual development, and above all the free play of creative imagination.

Such efforts would begin in the nursery school and kindergarten, since here the child first acquires his capacity for symbolic thinking, for feeling and communicating through gesture, mimicry, and sound, even before he learns to use the more highly developed symbolic functions of speech, reading, and elementary arithmetic. To free a child in this way will also free his acquisition of the basic tools. The three R's, as well as the plastic, rhythmical, and musical arts, will benefit. Thus the prevention of neurotogenic processes at their sources would enhance the efficacy of our entire educational system.

From the toddler years to the top levels of postgraduate education, we need school techniques by which dissociation and repression among the various ingredients of psychological function would be limited or reversed as quickly as they start, so that thinking, feeling, and acting would develop as well-synthesized and unitary expressions of an evolving personality, instead of as erratic outcroppings from fragmented and dissociated functions.

Let me repeat that to limit fission is not identical with psychotherapy, which aims at reuniting components which have already been split. In psychological matters, as in physics, the process of fission can release destructive energy, and again as in physics the process of fusion may be accompanied by dramatic explosive discharges. There is no reason to believe, however, that this would be true of procedures by which the primary fission itself was limited or prevented. Therefore, although we have learned our basic principles from the treatment of the neuroses and psychoses, the implications of early psychotherapy are not identical with, and should not be confused with, psychotherapy.

INTERACTIONS BETWEEN SOCIAL PROCESSES AND THE SECONDARY AND TERTIARY CONSEQUENCES OF THE NEUROTIC PROCESS

Resistance to change is deeply entrenched in all institutions, and the history of all preventive medicine is marked by opposition. An unsparing effort toward the preventive use of psychiatric knowledge and techniques would challenge every human institution. In the face of this challenge, education, religion, industry, and government will have to manifest a humility and honesty to which they are not accustomed.

In addition, it is in the essential nature of that which is neurotic to stay put. Self-examination that might lead to change is therefore opposed with fear, with the anger born of fear, with tenacity and desperation. Everything sick in human nature manifests this obstinate reluctance to change. Individually, this is evidenced by our patients. Socially, it is shown by our defense of cultural institutions that have repeatedly demonstrated their impotence or their actual pathogenicity. Therefore it is not surprising that the ubiquitous yet masked neurotic process struggles to go on being and doing, just as in the past.

We have no evidence that social forces per se are responsible for the ubiquitous neurotic potential, or that they generate the neurotic process that derives from it (5, 9, 11). We do know that they help to shape it, and that in every known culture man is surrounded by social forces that interact in complex ways with both the neurotic process and the fully developed neurotic state (17). The present inquiry will be clearer, therefore, if it distinguishes among these social forces: (a) those that conceivably generate neuroses (an uncertain and debatable claim); (b) those that exploit and prey upon neurotic trends extant in human nature; (c) those that intensify such trends by actively rewarding them; (d) special vested interests that oppose change; (e) deeper individual biases, both conscious and unconscious in origin, that oppose any change even for the better.

By implication this position challenges many frequent assumptions about the ease with which the neurotic process can be averted or limited. I want to underscore this. There can be no doubt that the cultural organization of any society influences both the neurotic process and the price its citizens pay for their neuroses. This, however, is far from claiming that cultural differences can either initiate or prevent the neurotic process. Yet it is always tempting to blame neuroses on aspects of life which for other reasons may be undesirable. Thus we find people who in the same breath say that neuroses are due to poverty and that they are due to wealth, that they are due to overwork and to leisure, to sleeping too much or too little, to ignorance or to excessive education, to superstition or to supersophistication. Others blame neuroses on a lack of love or on excessive loving, on neglect or on overprotection. Neuroses are blamed on the simplicity, barrenness, and isolation of country life; or on the complexity, congestion, and pace of urban existence. Primitivism is blamed, or the rarefied and precious atmosphere of a highly cultivated society. Some blame neuroses on doubt and cynical skepticism, others on credulity or an overcompliant and passive acceptance of religious faith. Thus we find neuroses blamed with splendid impartiality on religion and on skepticism, on puritanism or on license. There was a period not long past when neuroses were blamed on close family ties. This is implicit in certain novels of Louis Couperus, Henry James, G. B. Stern, Louis Golding, Wasserman, and Thomas Mann. In all this fiction we find the masked manifestations of secret accumulations of inexpressible patricidal, matricidal, fratricidal, and incestuous rivalries and tensions within close-knit family units. Conveniently forgetting all this, however, people today place the emphasis on domestic turbulence, family disruption, and the loosening of family ties. Superficial observers blame the breakdown or attenuation of family life, rather than viewing these as important manifestations of the ubiquitous neurotic process.

In this connection we should consider the statistics of the situation, if only as a warning against the kind of fallacy which is so easily substituted for thinking. I have in mind two basic facts: (a) that nearly 20 per cent more of the total population are married today than seventy years ago (18); and (b) that in 1890 families were disrupted and reshuffled by early deaths at a greater rate than occurred through divorce in 1940 (4). During the half-century between these dates the rising divorce rate did not keep up with the falling death rate. One would not hold that the impact of reshuffling because of divorce and the impact of reshuffling because of early deaths are necessarily the same. Certainly, when the reshuffling is because of early deaths it presumably follows a shorter period of family tension, since people may die before intrafamilial tensions have had time to reach explosive states. But which does the major damage to the progeny: the divorce, or the prolonged intrafamilial stress which precedes divorce and which is made possible by longevity? To such questions no one has any right to answer either *ex cathedra* or out of preconceptions, since no one yet has objectively, carefully, and without passion or prejudice explored the influence of these complex psychosocial phenomena.

Let me illustrate other ways in which our thinking has been hobbled. We have assumed that parents are necessarily the best people to bring up their own children. Yet in earlier days when large families with many children and many adults lived under the same wide roof, responsibility for child-rearing was spread thin among the adults. Every child then had an adult ally to whom he could turn when needed, whether against his age peers or against any oppression by the adult group. Few children were "brought up," as today, solely by their inexperienced parents. The child does not have such an ally any more, unless arranged for him outside the family group. Instead, today's family is built like a pyramid, with all the intrafamilial rivalries, tensions, jealousies, angers, hatreds, loves, and needs focused on the untrained, vulnerable, insecure, young, inexperienced, and incompetent parental apex of this pyramid, about whose incompetence our vaunted educational system does nothing. It is, to say the least, foolhardy to take it for granted that this is a healthy way to bring up children. The issue merits objective investigation.

Longevity (an amazing achievement of modern medicine) puts on human ties still other strains never before experienced. For the average man his earning span has not increased, but, if anything, has diminished, while the number of older and younger dependents he must carry has increased. Moreover, the family (like most individual communities) is no longer a producing unit but only a consuming unit. This increases the rivalries and decreases the loyalties, the cooperative spirit, within the family, just as it does in the community. In this and other ways the family has become a source of economic and emotional insecurity instead of a source of strength. The center of security has thus shifted from the individual's effort to earn his own way to a sharing of risk through group insurance, social security, group health, union pension plans, etc. Consequently some remote impersonal agency (i.e., the government, the management, the union, the voluntary mutual insurance group) has taken over what was once a function of the parents, the clan, or the family. What are the effects on human development of replacing individual risk by group risk? What do all such changes do to the human spirit, and to the secondary and tertiary consequences of what is neurotic in all human nature?

Many other profound changes are at work in the family today. The shrinking size of the family unit creates new problems. The increase in population causes more people to live in smaller space. It is harder to smile politely every morning across an apartment-house hall at the neighbor who opens his door as you do yours than to greet such a neighbor once a month when you visit him five miles down the road. When he is that far away you do not have to pretend so often that you always feel like smiling at him. Congestion can reach a saturation point, a threshold beyond which the human spirit cannot breathe. This consideration, however, is singularly unimportant to real estate operators. The more human beings who can be crowded onto the point of an urban pin, the more money can be made, no matter what the cost to the human spirit.

Or take the profound change in the leverage of direct human responsibility for one another. This change results directly from the fact that in his life at home, at work, at play, and in government man has become increasingly detached from his fellows, increasingly faceless. Even on the battlefield, you shoot an enemy you cannot see and are shot by an enemy who cannot see you. In the labor union as in the industrial plant, working life is depersonalized by magnitude. The home itself has become impersonalized, a place for sitting side by side, facing, not one another, but a ground-glass screen to watch imaginary catastrophes happening to someone else. All this creates a gap in what used to be the close-linked chain of human responsibility, a gap filled destructively by the impersonal monolithic structures of labor and industry, religion, states, "entertainment," and gangs—and monoliths are built on the destructive organization of rivalry, envy, acquisitiveness, hate, or fear.

Organized religion is deliberately included in this listing, since so much of the churches' strength rests on the organization, not of loving and individual responsibility, but of mass hating. We are rapidly moving into an era of choice between faith and the sword, forgetting that the right to believe as conscience dictates must include the right to question and doubt also as conscience dictates. Too often religion displays a strange fusion of hucksterism and evangelism, as in the substitution of the shopping list for the manger in our modern degradation of the Christmas festival.

In the meantime, as the entertainment industry and the advertisers take over, ours becomes a spectator culture. The increasing perfection with which the techniques of entertainment simulate reality increases our passivity. It requires a lesser effort of imagination to watch a television show that it once did to read a nickel novel. Nor is this transformation of our culture into a spectator culture attributable to the entertainment industries alone: the art dealers, the picture galleries, couturiers, and decorators are all likewise involved.

Finally, we must consider our economy, increasingly gambling its success or failure on consumption by the installment plan. Has anyone since Veblen asked what would happen to such an economy if what is neurotic in human nature were by sudden magic to be eliminated? What would happen to the fashion cults, the beauty cults, the food and drink and tobacco cults with their exploitation of orality, the excretory cult, the cleanliness cults, the size cults, the height cults, the strip-tease cults? Consider the exploitation of hypochondriasis through the drug houses and even our more elite publishing houses. Take also the endless whetting of consumer cravings, the exploitation of the "gimmies" of childhood by transmuting them into the "gimmies" of adult life. Consider the ministering to neurotic needs through size and power: the knight of old has been replaced by Casper Milquetoast in General Motors armor, complete with chromium, unneeded size, unused seating capacity, and a pointless, illegal, and unusable capacity for speed. Or consider the search for happiness anywhere else than where one is, and how the travel industry abets it by vacations on the installment plan.

To repeat, what would happen to our economy if we got well? And what does the exploitation of neurosis by so many forces in our culture do to the neurotic process itself? Is this a culture that breeds health? Is this a culture we can afford to be complacent about? Or have we allowed the enormous creative potential of private enterprise to be enslaved by greed to the neurotic process in industry, exactly as the creative process in art, literature, music, even science, has become the slave of neurosis?

Lest you think I am singling out our culture, our economy, for attack, I repeat that I do not believe that human ingenuity has yet devised any economic system that does not exploit, intensify, and reward much that is neurotic (potentially even psychotic) in human nature. If the profit-driven economies exploit subtle manifestations of neurotic self-indulgence and short-term needs, so do totalitarian systems, whether Fascist or Communist, exploit power needs and power fantasies in a still more primitive fashion, rewarding the sadistic lusts and the paranoid components of human nature. As Freud once pointed out, man is still frail enough to need competition for money and for conspicuous display as a buffering device with which to protect himself and his fellows from more brutal forms of the struggle for power.

The paradox here is that primitive cultural, political, and economic forms are inevitably transmuted into more sophisticated forms. But, because of the persistent influences of the masked neurotic forces in human nature, sophistication leads to its own weakening and self-destruction, so that the cycle returns to the primitive again. This is perhaps the most vicious cycle in the history of culture, and the one to which least attention is paid: namely, how the initial idealism of a totalitarian economy leads from the struggle for naked power, through perceptible transitions, back to the struggle for the glutting of personal yearnings. This in turn brings in the neurotic weakening of a profit-motive economy, and thence, through "The Degradation of the Democratic Dogma" (2), to self-destruction, and back once more to the primitive forms of power struggle. The world would be a safer place if on both sides of the Iron Curtain men would turn their attention to the ways in which each system sows the seeds of its own neurotic destruction. For these seeds of destruction can be eliminated only if we recognize and attack the subtle, pervasive influence of the concealed neurotic processes in so-called normal men and women, who, in their confused and immature and inept ways make up all human society, whether East or West.

SUMMARY

1 Preventive medicine has always encountered obstacles that are rooted in socially entrenched prejudices. Preventive psychiatry must overcome obstructive forces even more tenacious than those now vanquished in other fields of medicine. These forces are built into social institutions, but have their deeper roots in the tendency of the neurotic process itself to resist change.

2 This manifests the basic fact that the neurotic process is interwoven with our growth processes and our highest intellectual and cultural aspirations, giving rise to a tendency to defend this all-pervasive aspect of the neurotic process as something to be prized, rather than disowned as something alien. Consequently the attitudes of the individual and of society toward the neurotic process differ materially from their attitudes toward other forms of illness.

3 We must attempt to prevent psychiatric disorders on three levels.

   a The organization of society in part determines the price we pay for our neuroses. Therefore certain elements of our social organization should be altered so as to alter the cost of the neurotic process, both to the individual and to society. In this connection, every phase of group living influences the fate of the neurotic process—economic differences, population density, longevity, housing, the organization of work and play, educational and religious processes, political and economic processes, the changing structure of the family, etc. Consequently, to limit the disastrous secondary and tertiary consequences of the neurotic process demands an objective consideration of every aspect of human society.

b Preventive psychiatry also depends on the earliest possible application of psychodiagnostic and psychotherapeutic methods. The adult neurosis and indeed the adult psychosis are in large measure the cumulative secondary consequences of the unresolved neurotic process of infancy. Therefore the early introduction of therapy constitutes one of the primary techniques of prevention in an effort to resolve the neurotic process so early and so completely that no residues remain to produce cumulative distortions in the maturing personality.

Our ability to do this depends first upon the sharpening and refining of our techniques of early psychodiagnosis, and second upon the training of a large number of experts competent to make early and precise psychodiagnoses and to give psychotherapy in situations not ordinarily reached by the psychiatrist. The training of a new profession, that of a doctorate in medical psychology, must therefore be an integral part of any all-out effort toward preventive psychiatry.

c The ultimate objective of preventive psychiatry, however, goes even deeper: it aims to limit or reverse the first steps in the neurotic process as these arise in infancy and childhood. To attain this goal will require much basic research to enable us to recognize those first deviations from the path of normal development which occur in childhood and which subsequently and in varying degrees influence every human life.

In our present stage of knowledge we can recognize several ingredients that require preventive manipulations: (a) a control of those experiences which impose on the infant persisting central emotional positions; (b) a control of those conditioning experiences which link these central emotional positions to trigger mechanisms; (c) a control of the processes of identification by which the developing personality makes destructive and conflicting identifications with destructive and conflicting persons; (d) finally and most important, there must be a significant measure of control of the processes of repression which produce a dichotomy in the symbolic process itself, i.e., the fateful dichotomy into conscious and unconscious components.

None of these goals is easy to achieve; but the recognition of their importance is a step forward. In coming years the course of preventive psychiatry will depend in part on the development of techniques aimed at these objectives.

4 A further complication is introduced by the fact that in some ways the most important part of the story of the neurosis deals not with an illness from which the patient himself experiences pain, but rather with concealed illness, which has a destructive effect on the lives of those around the patient and on society as a whole while leaving the patient relatively comfortable, at least until the neurotic process catches up with him in later years. . . .

Yet precisely because these most universal of all manifestations of the neurotic process also cause the patient the least immediate suffering, they are the most difficult to bring into therapy or under control.

5 Psychotherapy (the attempt "to heal a man through the influence of his own mind," as Austen F. Riggs defined it) is part of the age-old struggle for freedom, especially the freedom to change. In contrast, psychonoxious processes enslave the human spirit. . . .

The most searching test of the creative value of any ingredient in our culture is whether it increases man's capacity to change or entrenches his resistance to change. This might well become our ultimate criterion of "greatness," in whatever cultural field (18). . . .

6 There are complex technical issues and tough practical obstacles impeding the elimination of the roots of the neurotic process. . . . The idea that we "outgrow" these difficulties without help, or that a happy home and an intact family are enough, or that better high schools, or more formal education, or love alone is enough; the muddled notion that believing is more creative than doubting, faith more powerful in advancing human culture than skepticism, the accepting spirit healthier than the challenging spirit—all these oversimplifications have been tried, and all have failed. As we face both the critical problems of the inner world and the devastating problems of the outer world, one asks whether we dare lull ourselves any longer with these ancient quarter-truths. . . .

Let us now return to the question we asked at the beginning: is preventive psychiatry possible?

Unquestionably it is possible to alter materially the secondary consequences of the neurotic process, that is, to interrupt those social forces whose consequences reactivate the original process so that it builds up to greater tragedy. It is possible to ameliorate the secondary and tertiary manifestations of the neurotic process by changes in the shape of our society. Note that this is "possible"—"probable" is another matter. The least maneuver toward this goal requires an unsparing, critical re-examination of every element in our culture. If this is to be more than an empty intellectual exercise, it implies a willingness to experiment with changes in those elements in our social structure that reward, exploit, and thus intensify the neurotic process. Yet men live by their affiliation with institutions, and in turn the institutions themselves live by these various cultural stereotypes. It would be naïve, therefore, to imagine that changes can come easily in the face of strongly entrenched vested interests.

To pinpoint these as specific challenges for basic research on the techniques of prevention is an advance. But to turn the theoretically "possible" into an ongoing process toward a well-defined goal requires instruments we do not yet possess. In school, we need instruments of education based on self-knowledge in depth (10). In the home, we require new techniques of child-rearing which will no longer reinforce the neurotic process as our homes do today. Our children need skilled adult allies outside the family circle, such as those who once graced every large household but who disappeared as the family unit shrank to its present sharply pyramidal structure. To this end the community needs prepayment plans for intensive education in the basic principles of child care and in the psychopathology of family living, plus periodic psychotherapy for parents and children (6).

To develop such new devices will require many pilot tests, along lines elsewhere described in detail but never yet subjected to adequate experimental investigation. Though we have no ready panaceas, we can diagnose much that is wrong. This is worth doing, but only if it initiates uncompromising efforts to find better ways and better substitutes for many of our self-adulating institutions.

REFERENCES

1 Henry Adams, *The Education of Henry Adams* (Washington, D.C., privately printed, 1907), p. 453.

2 ———, *The Degradation of the Democratic Dogma* (New York ,The Macmillan Company, 1919), p. 317.

3 Lawrence S. Kubie, "The Fantasy of Dirt," *Psychoanalytical Quarterly,* 1937, **6**:388–425.

4 ———, "Husband-Wife," in M. M. Hughes, ed., *The People in Your Life* (New York, Alfred A. Knopf, Inc., 1951), p. 278.

5 ———, "The Neurotic Potential, the Neurotic Process, and the Neurotic State," *U.S. Armed Forces Medical Journal,* January 1951, **2**:1–12.

6 ———, "A Research Project in Community Mental Hygiene: A Fantasy," *Mental Hygiene,* 1952, **36**:220–226.

7 ———, "Neurosis and Psychosis," *Journal of the American Psychoanalytic Association,* 1953, **1**:59–86.

8 ———, "Some Implications for Psychoanalysis of Modern Concepts of the Organization of the Brain," *Psychoanalytical Quarterly,* 1953, **22**:21–68.

9 ———, "The Concept of Normality and Neurosis," in M. Heiman, ed., *Psychoanalysis and Social Work* (New York, International Universities Press, Inc., 1953), p. 346.

10 ———, "The Forgotten Man of Education," *Harvard Alumni Bulletin,* 1954, **56**:349–353.

11 ———, "The Fundamental Nature of the Distinction Between Normality and Neurosis," *Psychoanalytical Quarterly,* 1954, **23**:167–204.

12 ———, "The Pros and Cons of a New Profession," *Texas Reports on Biology and Medicine,* 1954, **12**:692–737.

13 ———, "The Impact of Behavioral Medicine on Pre-Professional Education for the Future Student," Conference on Pre-Professional Education for Medicine, 18–19 October 1956 (New York, State University of New York, Downstate Medical Center, College of Medicine), p. 106.

14 ———, "Education and the Process of Maturation," in *Today's Children Are Tomorrow's World,* Fifth Annual Conference, February 1957 (New York, Associates of the Bank Street College of Education), p. 68.

15 ———, "The Need for a New Subdiscipline in the Medical Profession" (read before the Strecker Society, Philadelphia, 10 December 1956), *Archives of Neurology and Psychiatry,* 1957, **78**:283–293.

16 ———, "Freud's Legacy to Human Freedom" (read in part before the Rudolf Virchow Medical Society, 7 May 1956), *Proceedings of the Rudolf Virchow Medical Society,* 1956, **15**:34–48; reprinted in *Perspectives in Biology and Medicine,* 1957, **1**:105–118.

17 ———, "Social Forces and the Neurotic Process," in Alexander H. Leighton, ed., *Explorations in Social Psychiatry* (New York, Basic Books, Inc., 1957), p. 452.

18 ———, "Neurotic Distortion of the Creative Process" (Porter Lectures, series 22; Lawrence, University of Kansas Press, 1958), p. 151.

19 ———, *The Disintegrating Impact of "Modern" Life on the Family in America; and Its Explosive Repercussions* (in press).

Community Mental Health and Social Change*

Harry R. Brickman

Psychiatry's usefulness pivots on its function in the social system of which it is an integral part. If "adjustment" is our touchstone, what have we to say to those who cry in ever-increasing numbers: "Adjustment to what? To human and natural exploitation? To racism? To Viet Nam? To Czechoslovakia? To Chicago? To a dehumanizing, violence-ridden society in which the affluent prosper at the expense of the have-nots?" Is it normal *not* to be depressed, anxious, and alienated in these troubled days? As society is being confronted by pressures for change, so is psychiatry itself.

Psychiatry is never practiced in a social vacuum. Few psychiatrists realize that the charismatic mantle placed on their shoulders has been put there by society, which looks to psychiatrists to perform certain vital social functions related to the control of deviant behavior. Psychiatry's embeddedness in society makes it important to examine the ecology of mental health.

In order to develop an ecological perspective, it is necessary first to identify the ecosystem of which we as psychiatrists and mental health professionals are a part. Our ecosystem is perhaps most evident to us in its physical aspect. We are all aware of the growing crisis in our physical ecology. The air we breathe is being increasingly polluted by products of the internal combustion engine, the water we drink by industrial waste, the land we supposedly love by progressive defoliation and macadamization. We are generally aware also of many features of our social ecology. At the domestic level we witness grave current upheavals such as urban crises, school revolts, and many aspects of rapid social transition: changes in behavioral norms, in sexual standards, in political affiliations, and many other developments such as the decline of the extended and even the nuclear family.

At the international level we see struggles between the "haves" and the "have-nots," resurgent nationalism, and mini-nationalism. We are perhaps least aware of our ideological ecology, the great belief systems held in common by millions of people that are the infrastructure of our perceptions of the world, of awareness of self and others, of the meanings we attach to life and to death, and of man-made changes in physical and social ecology.

THE PSYCHIATRIST AS SOCIAL CONTROL AGENT

Viewed in social perspective, the psychiatrist wears his charisma only because he is an officially recognized agent of social control. He is vested by society with the role of identifying those who are peculiarly disruptive to smooth societal functioning. He is given the power to grant these deviants a social role known as mental illness, thereby allowing them to be exempted from many social obligations. He is then expected to resocialize these deviants in such a way as to return them to undisruptive social functioning.

*From Harry R. Brickman, "Mental Health and Social Change: An Ecological Perspective," *The American Journal of Psychiatry,* 1970, **127,** 413–419. Reprinted by permission of the author and the Editor, *The American Journal of Psychiatry.*

Some psychiatrists may have difficulty in perceiving this statement as the sociological analogue of diagnosing, treating, and rehabilitating the mentally ill. Many psychiatrists are convinced that behavioral disorder is a "real illness." Whether or not most of our psychiatric patients are "truly" suffering from an illness, the medical model as a pattern for social control is relatively humane and humanistic as it is presently practiced. It should not be discarded until a wholly more effective and at the same time humane model is developed and tested.

And so we diagnose and treat our patients according to the medical model within which we so comfortably function. Wearing our charisma, we practice our profession generally as advocates and agents of the social system. Respecting authority, the family, the community, and the nation, and appreciating the benefits of our technological society, we have implicitly reinforced these social values in our patients. In doing so, we have been assisting them to adjust to become better functioning members of our society.

In our middle- and upper-class psychotherapeutic private practices, our patients, well acculturated like ourselves, are content to come regularly to our offices for varying periods of time. Our ministrations, ideologically embedded in determinism, tend to seek out causes, to enlist rationality in our patients, and to help them attain the limited liberation that they seek. This limited liberation is generally perceived as relative freedom from self-defeating behavior known as neurotic symptoms so that social, sexual, and material success can be better attained.

Those of us who are psychoanalysts view our work as assisting the individual toward the twin Freudian criteria of mental health—*lieben und arbeiten,* to love and to work. We assist our patients in this direction through some variant of the classical model of resolution of the transference neurosis and attainment of genitality, through rational insight and working through of pregenital fixations. Others follow behavioral or biological models, but most psychiatrists measure therapeutic success in terms of social adaptation and generally by the patient's relinquishment of the emotionally sick role.

MENTAL HEALTH FOR THE POOR

Our preoccupation with the intrapsychic—and our accompanying lack of awareness of our social roles as duly anointed control agents and perpetuators of the social system—have extended themselves into the well-meaning efforts of psychiatrists and other middle-class professionals in what is now called the field of community mental health. Psychiatric clinics, many of them of high professional competence, have sprung up, supported by voluntary agencies, to dispense "psychiatry for the masses." Since long-term treatment is economically difficult to provide, shorter-term crisis, group, and family techniques have been developed to serve greater numbers of people. However, most clinics for the socioeconomically disadvantaged are ideological offspring of middle-class psychotherapeutic psychiatry. The chief justification for community mental health programs continues to be, in the minds of most professionals, the inability of the poor to pay for psychiatric treatment services. The goal of these programs, to the extent that a goal is ever made explicit, is to assist the socioeconomically disadvantaged neurotic or psychotic individual in attaining a state of mental health, as conceived chiefly by affluent Judeo-Christian professionals.

This desired state of mental health for the poor, if examined more closely, is conceptually identical to the middle-class model applied to private patients: a limited liberation from obstacles, conceived as intrapsychic, interfering with an implicitly desirable adjustment to the very society which, though trembling with shocks of multiple confrontations by the "have-nots," is a society that in turn looks to the psychiatrist to pursue his goals of *lieben und arbeiten,* so that deviants may return to the fold. Is it any wonder that not only community mental health but psychiatry in general is being currently challenged? Can we, as psychiatrists practicing in the black ghetto, comfortably dismiss the violently angry as having "affective disorders" or the destructively manipulative as "sociopathic personalities?" Can we as psychiatrists, in group discussions with drug-using disaffiliated youth, be satisfied with our labels of "inadequate personality" or "depersonalization neurosis?"

PRESSURES FOR SOCIAL CHANGE

We may very well apply these labels, and thus psychopathologize social discontent, but not for long. A mighty struggle is now taking place between the forces of the status quo and those demanding drastic change. At times the seesawing contemporary battles seem to favor the status quo in which we were raised and so comfortably function. It is impossible, however, to seriously expect that current revolutionary pressures will be completely nullified by reestablishment of an ultimately unchanged social milieu. Change is the very essence of the dimension of time. Change is inevitable, and those social institutions that do not change are destined to disappear.

Pressures for social change and their reactionary counterpressures include those concerned with authoritarianism, the human family, the significance of work, and the fate of dynamic pluralism.

The phenomenon of awareness is rarely dealt with in the classical psychiatric literature, especially if it is seen as consciousness colored by acculturated meaning. Awareness of the environment, of the world in general, has been communicated for tens of thousands of years by word of mouth—in myth, fable, story, and song. In this form, acculturative coloring of the events described was inevitable, and the spoken word undoubtedly served as the major vehicle of socialization.

The advent of printing expanded knowledge of the world materially, although removing it a step farther from immediate awareness. Intellectualization, rationalization, the scientific, industrial and technological revolutions—all these have been shown by MacLuhan(1) and others to have been crucially facilitated by the dissemination of the printed word. The printed word, moreover, has been a powerful acculturative force, as shown throughout the range of present-day printed material from the often distorted history of the average grade school textbook to viciously manipulative propaganda. The advent of radio brought the dissemination of knowledge back to the auditory level—a more immediate, more emotional plane of awareness. It has been the advent and widespread use of film, and particularly of television, that has provided the individual with opportunities for immediate awareness rather than indirect, rationalized, predigested awareness. Again we can thank MacLuhan(2) for some of these insights.

Television, combining auditory and visual impacts, arrests the attention of the viewer and stimulates his emotional participation in the events he is perceiving. He can witness the actual shooting of a prisoner or a soldier in Viet Nam minutes after it occurs. He can witness a campus disturbance when it happens. Certainly editorializing and selectivity limit his perceptions somewhat, but the acculturative screen is full of holes. Immediate, graphic, emotionally significant information about his world is now at hand. Furthermore, a whole generation has grown to early maturation experiencing this type of education—an education only briefly interrupted by the traditional authoritarian, acculturating, rationalizing, and intellectualizing pedagogy encountered in school. Tradition, authority, the wisdom of elders—all embedded in the printed page—seem less relevant to young people than the immediate awareness of the human drama.

Linear thinking, the serial links in the chains of psychological causality characteristic of psychoanalysis, is being seriously challenged by the "here-and-now" approaches of humanistic psychology. The greatly increased interest in Gestalt therapy(3) is entirely consistent with new social patterns of awareness. Gestaltists practice their form of liberation with the conviction that regardless of causes related to childhood neurosis, man tends to be fragmented and alienated from himself at the emotional level.

The emphasis embodied in the slogan "I and thou, here and now," typifies a new emphasis on confrontation, immediate awareness, and the values of openness, honesty, and direct emotional expression in intrapersonal relationships. The general trend toward immediate emotional experience that characterizes humanistic psychology is also being expressed in ever-widening applications of encounter techniques(4), body awareness exercises, and group marathon experiences. Psychiatry can ill afford to hide its head, or worse, to condemn out of hand, in its reaction to these developments.

CHALLENGE TO AUTHORITY

Authoritarianism is being seriously challenged almost everywhere. Loyalty to nation (or symbolically to the flag), to leaders, to elders in general, and to almost every established social institution is viewed by the revolutionary as supportive of the socially stratifying exploitative status quo. In California the authority of psychiatry itself has been socially challenged, but not from the expected quarter of wild-eyed, long-haired revolutionaries. Curiously enough, ultraconservative forces fearful of the social control aspects of psychiatry have combined with civil libertarians of the left to produce a drastic change in the commitment laws in this state. Thanks to the new Lanterman-Petris-Short Act(5), no longer will the respected authority of the psychiatrist be sufficient to hospitalize a patient against his will. Clear and present danger to self or others or total disablement must be demonstrated, and the psychiatrist is under repeated warning in the new law against the misuse of his drastically limited authority. Throughout all his dealings with his involuntary patient he is at repeated risk of becoming his patient's adversary in a court proceeding. The authority and to some extent the charismatic mantle of psychiatry have been further tattered by the total elimination from the California statute books of the term "mentally ill." The medical model is moribund in California state law.

Authority is yielding to destratification and egalitarianism in many quarters of psychiatry. To some extent it is responsible for the declining prestige of orthodox Freudian psychoanalysis, although traditional psychoanalysts' own ostrich-like ignoring of social realities is also responsible for its apparent decline. Yet psychoanalysis is still the most comprehensive and at the same time the most humanistic frame of reference for understanding man's individual psychology. Its theory and clinical practice, aimed at richer and freer individuation, are all too often paradoxically juxtaposed to its encrusted authoritarian social structure as a collectivity.

The vicissitudes of the family are of clear and pressing relevance to the practice of psychiatry and community mental health. Can we come to grips with the decline not only of the extended family but the nuclear family as well? Are we going to continue to apply status quo social judgments to the unmarried mother, the deliberately childless couple, the woman who is single by choice, or to the experiments with new familial arrangements involving less permanent sexual attachments? Are we to continue to assign highest sexual prestige to genitality when the population explosion and decline of the family call it into serious question? Are we to favor increased attention to recreation as jobs become increasingly automated, and yet balk at pregenital, pansexual implications of the idea of play? Can we accept the possibility that sexuality can be enjoyed at varying levels of interpersonal commitment without affixing to it our familiar label of "acting out?"

Our incorporation of societal standards is well illustrated in the value attached to "work" in psychiatric circles. Sublimation has become the most sublime of mental mechanisms only because the work ethic is implicit in the acculturation or socializing function of the psychiatrist. While the phenomenon of work is not likely to disappear in our lifetime, its primacy in our value system is being challenged. An ever-increasing encroachment by automation forces us to reconsider the place of work in our society. While sublimatory goals can indeed be met through play, it is clear that one of the twin Freudian criteria of mental health, *lieben und arbeiten,* requires serious reconsideration in the light of current developments.

The trend toward dynamic pluralism of the population is being resisted by those forces that wish to sustain our own brand of social apartheid. Nevertheless, broader educational experiences and increasing awareness of the diversity of mankind are continuing to impinge on us. It is consistent with a humanistic outcome of contemporary social struggle that our society will accept and even eventually love the diversity of appearance, dress, skin color, speech, and life patterns embodied in the current expression"everyone doing his thing." Psychiatry and mental health must contend openly with the expectation of status quo forces that it help turn out a homogenized human being who will adjust, conform, live his life unobtrusively, and tolerate his alienation in silence. Is there a prospect more dreary than that of a society of completely adjusted conforming individuals everywhere?

AN EXAMPLE OF ECOLOGICAL AWARENESS

The community mental health program that has been under way in Los Angeles County for the past ten years(6) has attempted to reflect an ecological awareness through its application of the concept of dynamic pluralism to the emotionally and behaviorally deviant. The philosophy of our program aims for increased tolerance for behavioral deviation by the community rather than the automatic identification, social isolation, and eventual homogenization of the individual whose ideas, perceptions, or emotional patterns are different. For this reason the provision of direct treatment services, although expanded markedly, has been given less emphasis than prevention.

Prevention, in turn, has been conceptualized as prevention of the assignment of the mentally ill role to those who are deviant. Our attempt has been to increase the community's acceptance of deviation while at the same time enhancing its ability to assist the deviant through life crises—short of assignment of the sick role. In some cases, of course, removal of the individual from a psychologically noxious environment is essential for his recovery from critical personal disorganization; inpatient psychiatric wards, day and night hospital services, and special living and working environments for the critically disorganized will continue to be necessary.

However, never in the history of mankind has an illness been eradicated by increased treatment of the ill alone(7). The prevention of mental illness, a phenomenon so thoroughly contingent upon social events, must reflect the most sophisticated ecological awareness of the social structure in which the deviant exists, as well as an awareness of how that social structure can accept his deviation while assisting him to overcome whatever personal or interpersonal disorganization he may be experiencing.

A clear choice becomes apparent when one views psychiatry and mental health in ecological perspective. Since the official sanction is for social control, must psychiatry go the way of inflexible social institutions, or can it become a force for social change? Certainly some sensitively balanced combination of the two societal functions must be developed.

The problem of developing a social change function is particularly critical for a public community mental health program where the social control expectation is more explicitly defined. Yet if the public mental health program is to survive, it must be attuned to the ecological dynamics of the community. It must avoid the image of "old wine in new bottles" justifiably assigned to conventionally conceived mental health centers, which are chiefly centers for recruitment and social processing of deviant persons. If conventional concepts dominating the planning of community mental health centers are followed and patient recruitment operations are developed, we will see yet another anachronistic state hospital system, albeit geographically closer to home. A network of clinical services, continuous within their own components but basically discontinuous with a changing social ecology, will guarantee nothing but its own fossilization(8).

The public trust in psychiatry hinges not upon what the private practitioner does with his middle-class client in his office, but rather on the fate of the community mental health movement throughout the nation. Public attention and public funds have at last been mobilized in considerable quantities so that psychiatry can have a chance to make an impact on the phenomenon of mental illness. If this opportunity leads to only another halting, unimaginative, and unresponsive social device labeled "community mental health center," it will be psychiatry that will suffer, and such a setback may be irreparable.

Acutely aware of the necessity to justify the public trust, our Los Angeles County community mental health program has been attempting to tread the fine line of balance between acknowledged social control functions and the urgent need to function as agent of social change without subverting duly constituted governmental functions in the community.

Realizing that personal disorganization is closely correlated with socioeconomic distress, we have given highest priority to the development of new mental health services in the black and brown ghetto areas. It is, of course, a great challenge for professional staff working in our ghetto area regional services to adapt their middle-class psychotherapeutic orientation to problems presented by people whose emotional difficulties exist in an ecosystem of racial discrimination, limited educational and vocational opportunity, familial disorganization, and other well-known alienating features of ghetto life. Although challenged in this manner, psychotherapists in these centers uniformly report professionally gratifying experiences with clients. Many different clinical techniques are employed, but the crucial factor seems to be the quality of the special mixture of human compassion and objectivity that is provided.

The goal of treatment with the socially victimized client cannot realistically be total reintegration into his alienating milieu. This is even more true of community consultation and educational efforts. In one instance a professional staff member of one of our ghetto services served as consultant to a group of parents who were angrily confronting local school administrators over the issue of inflexible school rules. A strictly status quo orientation would have led our staff member to attempt to quiet down the dissidents and assist them to accept the inevitability of bureaucratic rigidity. Instead, our staff member chose to serve as the catalyst for bringing frightened parents and defensive school administrators together and facilitating free and open dialogue.

As a result of this dialogue, both sides found to their relief that they shared a common view of the inapplicability of regulations imposed from a central office removed from the community and insensitive to its needs. It was resolved to work together to eliminate the offending restrictions. The parent group felt fulfilled in bringing about needed social changes, and the school administrators were happy to have community support in their desire to change burdensome rules that they themselves considered oppressive. The new entente of school administrators and parents was successful in accomplishing the desired changes. The mental health consultant in this instance functioned as an agent of social change while fulfilling his social control function by successfully helping to avoid a potentially destructive community confrontation.

THE PRINCIPLE OF "REHUMANIZATION"

Perhaps the principle of rehumanization can best underlie the community mental health service that wishes to survive in a changing ecology and to do so by striking the proper balance between social control and social change. Ruesch(9) has stated that the only worthwhile function of psychoanalysis is the continued redefinition and reaffirmation of those qualities of people that are ultimately and uniquely human. A humanistic psychiatry, a humanistic mental health orientation would harmonize with ecological changes by taking on the responsibility of helping preserve the human qualities of those who are buffeted by these disruptions of the status quo.

Sigmund Freud's philosophical contributions may be as great as those in individual psychology. In *Civilization and Its Discontents*(10) Freud the philosopher and ecologist stated:

> Men have brought their powers of subduing the forces of nature to such a pitch that by using them they could now very easily exterminate one another to the last man. They know this—hence arises a great part of their current unrest, their dejection, their mood of apprehension.

This insight into present-day alienation was expressed not in 1968 or 1969, but almost 40 years ago! Freud's genius was characterized by his ability to change his ideas. One finds all too little of this ability in those who have formed a quasi-religious movement around him.

A rehumanizing function for psychiatry, then, might guarantee it survival in the face of active social change. To the extent that the choice is ours to make, it must be made soon.

REFERENCES

1 MacLuhan, M.: The Gutenberg Galaxy. Toronto, University of Toronto Press, 1962.

2 MacLuhan, M.: The Medium is the Message. New York, Random House, 1967.

3 Perls, F.: Gestalt Therapy. New York, Dell Publishing Co., 1951.

4 Schutz, W.: Joy: Expanding Human Awareness. New York, Grove Press, 1967.

5 Brickman, H. R.: The new mental health system. Calif. Med. **109**:403–408, 1968.

6 Brickman, H. R.: Community mental health—the metropolitan view. Amer. J. Public Health **57**:641–650, 1967.

7 Ryan, W.: Community care in historical perspective. Canada's Mental Health **17** (suppl. 60), 1969.

8 Brickman, H. R.: Community mental health—means or end? Psychiat. Dig. **28**:43–50, 1967.

9 Ruesch, J.: The future of psychologically oriented psychiatry, in Sexuality of Women. Edited by Masserman, J. H. New York, Grune & Stratton, 1966.

10 Freud, S.: Civilization and its discontents, trans. by Riviere, J., in International Psycho-Analytical Library. Edited by Jones, E. London, Hogarth Press, 1930.

The Marathon Group*

George R. Bach

I

Like all effective group psychotherapeutic programs, the *Marathon* is a group practicum in intimate, authentic human interaction. One of the unique aspects of the Marathon technique is an intensification and acceleration of transparency and genuine encounter by a deliberate instigation of group pressure focused on behavioral change.

In the course of conducting over 12,000 therapeutic group hours with a great variety of patients, it is clinically observable that for many patients the 50-minute individual hour or the 1- or 2-hour group sessions are not long enough for either patient or therapist to take off their social masks, i.e., to stop playing games and start interacting truthfully, authentically, and transparently. It takes a longer session for people in our culture to switch from the marketing stance of role-playing and image-making, which they must practice in the work-a-day world, to feel free to "come out" straight and strong, not hidden behind oblique "sick" roles or other so-called "resistance."

Clinical experience has shown that *group-pressure,* rather than the therapist's individual interventions and interpretations given privately, is a major vehicle which can move people effectively and quickly from impression making and manipulative behavior toward honest, responsible, spontaneous *levelling* with one another. But it takes time for the therapeutic group to generate influence-pressure in intensity and work-oriented kind, sufficient to produce behavioral change. It takes time, also, for group members to display their individual ways of acting within the group which stimulates their ways of being and acting in the world. It takes time for therapists and peers to discern the potential for therapeutic change in each person and then to focus on this potential and to suggest change. Finally, it also takes time to experience the change, experiment with it and practice it here and now while participating in shaping the learning culture of the therapeutic group. All of this, becoming transparent, levelling, exposing to influence-pressure, attempting changes and practicing new behavior, we believe, is a *natural Gestalt,* i.e., *a unit* of learning experience which should not be broken up into bits and pieces but should occur as a whole, mediating a significant turning-point, a big step toward becoming what one can be!

Customary schedules of group therapy tend to break up this experiential learning unit. One-, two-, or even three-hour office meetings are not enough therapeutically, although staff time and fee economics make them universally accepted schedules. We have tried long hour groups and also week-end retreats and closely spaced groups (every other evening). With each of these schedules we noticed that there are always a few patients who "slip by" the experience, always waiting and ready to level truthfully with their peers, but never quite coming out openly transparent in time for the group to get hold of them fully for feedback, confrontation, and pressure to change.

*From George R. Bach, "The Marathon Group: Intensive Practice of Intimate Interaction," *Psychological Reports,* 1966, **18**:995–1002. Reprinted by permission of the author and the Editor, *Psychological Reports.*

These brief interrupted groups rarely generate the right amount and kind of *influence-pressure* to make a crucial impact on the resistant learner. The brief group is an ideal play-ground for time-wasting, psychiatric games, such as diagnosing (labelling) safaris into phantasias, psychological archeology, playing psychoanalysis with "transference" interpretation, collusive acceptance of people's irrational self-propaganda as to "who is the best therapist," "best patient," etc., etc.

Searching for a practical solution, we were delighted to discover last year (in 1963) that a group of younger colleagues (Roger Wickland and Frederick Stoller) had independently developed in a psychiatric hospital setting all-day-long types of group therapeutic sessions which were effective in producing therapeutic changes in "difficult" patients. Adopting this approach to our private practice patients, we re-activated our old week-end retreat program but with a new twist: no interruptions, continuous meetings for 2 days, no sub-grouping, no socializing, minimal breaks, clear-cut ground rules, and admission of people seriously interested in changing themselves rather than the universe. The revision is a success thanks to our consultant, Dr. Frederick Stoller, who working as my co-therapist in the very first Marathon ever done with private patients, has helped me significantly to improve our old week-end live-in program.

Currently, our *Marathon* group therapy retreats take place in a secluded private setting where a selected group of 10 to 14 participants can stay together for 2, 3, or 4 days.[1]

The actual schedule of a particular Marathon varies, depending on setting and the members' goals and values. In the standard procedures members meet non-stop throughout the first night, i.e., without sleeping for 24 hr. or longer. The Marathon terminates in non-verbal, silent communication exercises, conducted in pairs. This is followed by a "closure-party" in which sub-grouping is resumed. Thus, a gradual re-entry into the conventional social atmosphere is reluctantly made. The entire session may be recorded and a feedback follow-up is scheduled 4 to 8 weeks later, which is designed to reinforce those decisions for change which have been emerging during the Marathon itself. In our Institute practice the Marathon retreats for private patients are systematically integrated with the regular group therapy program. Most patients are first seen individually (briefly) and then assigned to a regular 2- to 4-hour weekly therapy group. Marathon retreat experiences are interspersed at intervals of 3 to 6 months. Some Marathons are "specialized" for marital couples, executives of business organizations, or an advanced training session for group psychotherapists or social science researchers.

We conceptualize the Marathon therapeutic process as a practicum in authentic communication, based on freedom from social fears conventionally associated with transparency.

The unique opportunity of participating in honest encounter on a day-and-night basis produces psychological intimacy among the participants. This gives them a taste for what can be achieved with significant others everywhere.

As subjective truths are shared, irrational and ineffectual behavior appears incon-

[1]The enrollment fee, which includes room and board, ranges from \$90.00 to \$300.00 per participant depending on duration, setting, and staff. The minimum fee per actual group therapy hour is \$3.00.

gruent, to be dropped in favor of new, more intimate, and competent behavioral patterns. The latter emerge and are practiced in the course of the Marathon. Orientation is ahistorical, emphasizing "what" and "how now" rather than "why" and "where from."

The genuine productivity of every group member is the therapist's mission which he procures by whatever means at his disposal. One of the other missions of the therapist is to maximize group feedback and enhance the opportunity for genuine encountering of and exposure to group pressure. For these reasons the Marathon is not unlike a *"pressure cooker"* in which phoney steam boils away and genuine emotions (including negative ones) emerge. The group atmosphere is kept focused every moment on the objectives at hand: to produce *change in orientation* and new ways of dealing with old crucial problems (creativity).

Every member is a co-therapist and co-responsible for the relative success or failure of any given Marathon meeting. Thus, the two or more professional co-therapists will, if and when they genuinely feel it, take their turns to participate "patient-wise," that is, as whole persons rather than just in a technical role-wise form. Decisions for change and serious commitment to follow though in life action are frankly elicited. Follow-up sessions will inquire into their validity.

Concerning *selection,* prospective Marathon participants are not sorted out in the traditional psychiatric-diagnostic sense, but rather on the basis of (1) attitudes toward self-change and (2) group constellation. Before admittance "Marathonians" must convince one and preferably both professional co-therapists that they are anxious to make significant *changes* in their customary ways of acting and being in this world. This presumes some degree of basic self-understanding of what one *now* is and what one can potentially become. The purpose of the Marathon is to awaken and strengthen further feelings for new directions and *movement* toward self-actualization in mutual *intimate concert* with others who are growing also. Marathons create a social climate for inter-peer growth stimulation, a sort of *psychological fertility*!

The Marathon group-therapeutic experience is most fully effective with those who wish to exchange their own ways of acting and being in this world and who are ready to quit blaming others and environment for their present unsatisfactory lot. New patients who initially tend to play the psychiatric game: "*I* am sick—*YOU* cure me" may be admitted to *initiation types* of *Marathons* whose specific mission is to knock out blamesmanship and other false, irrational, socially destructive operations (Bach, 1954) by which people preserve, cuddle, and justify their sick-roles. A patient who has given up his game of "I am sick—You, Doctor, and you-all (group) do something and take care of me" is a person ready to behave like a problem-solving adult. Such an individual can quickly learn to accept rational group-pressure as a useful means of strengthening his still weak and new "character." Therapeutic group pressure need not be misused irrationally (Bach, 1956) and immaturely as a substitute for individuality or as some social womb into which one may regressively crawl and hide there in fearful alienation from the big, bad competitive world of adult "fighters!" The regressive tendency to depend on the group is counteracted by the demand for *everyone to act as therapist to everyone*.

The work-burden of trying to be an effective co-therapist and agent of change to others *fatigues* all Marathonians over the long work hours. It takes devotion mixed with CONSTRUCTIVE AGGRESSION to get people to take off image-masks and put on honest faces. It takes patience and energy to break down resistances against change which all well-entrenched behavioral patterns—however irrational—will put up as part of a person's phoney "self-esteem." The exhaustion and *fatigue* produced by the Marathon procedure leads to refusal to spend any energy on "acting up" or "acting out." Tired people tend to be truthful! They do not have the energy to play games.

Therapeutic Effects of Marathon Therapy

It also takes disciplined, concerted group-cooperation to create properly *focused* selective group pressure. Behavioral change is not created by uni-lateral influence, or chaotic, disorganized "free-for-all," cathartic "group-emotions" *per se*. Marathons are *not* tension-relieving, cathartic acting-out groups. They generate rather high levels of emotional tensions which stimulate cognitive re-orientation for their relief! Generally two new modes of acting, feeling, and being emerge during a Marathon: (1) *transparency of the real self,* which (being accepted and reinforced by the peer-group) leads to (2) *psychological intimacy*[2] within the peer-group. This sequence from transparency to intimacy is a natural development because what alienates people from one another are the masks they put on, the roles they take, the images they try to create, and many of the games they play. Parenthetically, there are a few intimacy-producing games played by explicit mutual awareness and consent. These inter-personal stances alienate because they make it harder to know a person and to know where one stands with him. Inter-personal uncertainty is experienced as psychologically dangerous and anxiety-evoking until authenticity and transparency are reciprocally practiced. One or both parties may have hidden ulterior motives which usually turn out to be exploitive or destructive. Unless a person displays himself transparently, one never knows when to come on with him and when to get off or when to give, when to get or when to give up! One must remain alienated, on guard against the possibility of *psychological ambush,* i.e., to be seduced into spilling one's guts, to expose one's vulnerability, to get one's expectations up, only to be let down, even "destroyed." The con-artist's use of the double bind, i.e., you are damned if you do and damned if you don't, is psychologically lethal, for friends have no effective defenses against the double bind.

In the course of the long work hours of Marathon therapy, a transition from this self-defensive alienation and exploitive game-playing to psychological intimacy is revealed for everyone present to see.

II

Entering a Marathon group implies submitting to a set of *ground rules*. The importance of these rules is such that they have been termed *Ten Marathon Commandments*. How explicit these rules are made depends upon the sophistication of the particular group;

[2]Part II was drafted by Dr. Bach and edited by Dr. F. Stoller after both had worked together and also independently with Marathon groups for 2 years. The 10 Marathon Commandments, their purpose and evolution will be discussed in detail in a forthcoming book, *The 300 year weekend,* by G. R. Bach, J. Gibb, G. Hoover, and F. Stoller.

many participants grasp them without their having to be concretely outlined. However, there are groups which require that the rules be clearly laid out, and individual participants may behave in such a manner as to force the rules to be spelled out. In any case, these rules must be crystal clear in the minds of the group leaders and will act as a guide for their direction of the sessions. The following, then, are the basic group rules of the Marathon.

The Ten Marathon Commandments

1 To stay together in the same place and not leave until the group breaks or ends at its prearranged time. Everyone communicates with the *whole* group. Everyone attends to and reacts to how each individual acts in the group situation. This means that there must be *no sub-grouping*, such as is common at ordinary social gatherings and parties. Only during official group breaks and at the end of the session do people break up into sub-groups.

2 Creature comforts are to be taken care of on a self-regulatory basis. Eating will be done within the rules of the group, usually on a buffet basis *without disrupting the continuity of the group proceedings*! Participants can move about to different chairs, lie down on the floor, indulge in exercises within the sights and sounds of the group arena. Brief breaks for exercising, sleeping or changing clothes will be decided on by each group as a whole. There will be no alcohol or drugs taken during the Marathon proper. At the conclusion, most groups treat themselves to a ''closure-party'' and some groups schedule a follow-up meeting.

3 The group leader is bound by the same rules as everyone else, except that in order to keep his services alert he has the privilege, during every twenty-four hours of work, to rest up to four hours away from the group. During his absence, the group continues the meeting on a self-regulatory basis with every group member responsible for the uninterrupted continuation of the group proceedings and the enforcement of the ground rules. (A group leader in top physical condition may become so involved in the proceedings that he may choose not to exercise his resting privilege.)

4 All forms of physical assault or threats of physical violence are outlawed. Attacks must be confined to verbal critiques. However, there are no limits as to the straightforward use of Anglo-Saxon words or slang.

5 Legitimate, professionally correct group procedures such as Psycho-Drama, Awareness-expansion Exercises, ''Sensitivity Training,'' Transactional Games Analyses, etc., may be used temporarily during a Marathon, but only under *very* special circumstances. We have found that the use of a ''technique'' may retard rather than facilitate the slow, natural emergence of trust, transparency, and intimacy. Any routine use of any group-process ''technique,'' however valuable it may be in other settings, is definitely contra-indicated in the Marathon group situation.

6 The encountering experience is a four-phase process. Individual expressions are (a) reacted to, and (b) these reactions are shared in a ''feedback.'' (c) The ''feedback'' in turn generates counter-reactions (d) from the original expressors as well as from the rest of the group. Members are expected to facilitate each of these phases by active participation in the following manner.

i Members share true feelings as clearly and transparently as possible. The expressor is himself responsible for drawing and keeping the full attention of the group onto himself. No one should wait to be ''brought out.'' Every participant is expected to put himself voluntarily into the focus on the group's attention, to seek out the group and to turn attention to himself, preferably a number of times. This applies to *everybody* including the official group leaders. There are *no observers,* only active participants!

By being an attentive audience, the group rewards the expressor. The expressor will remain in focal-position (or ''hot-seat'') until his feeling-productivity wanes and/or until the expressor himself has had ''enough'' of the ''hot-seat,'' or until group-interest and group-pressure are dissipated.

ii In the ''feedback'' reactions to the expressor, no holds are barred! Candid *''levelling''* is expected from everyone, which means participants explicitly share and do *not* hide or mask their here-and-now, on the spot reactions to one another! Tact is ''out'' and brutal frankness is ''in.'' Any phony, defensive or evasive behavior (such as playing psychiatric games or reciting old ''lines'') is fair game for the group's critique and verbal attack. ''Ought's-manship'' (advising others how to solve their problems) can deteriorate into a time-consuming, dulling routine which suppresses spontaneous encounter. Excessive advice-giving is, therefore, undesirable.

iii Trying to make people ''feel better'' is *NOT the purpose of the Marathon.* Self-appointed, tactful diplomats, amateur ''protectors,'' and ''Red Cross nurses'' distract and dilute the levelling experience. Any kind of protective ''cushioning'' or cuddling spoils (for the central ''hot-seat'' person) the experience of standing up alone to the group, as he must to the world. Cushioning interventions should be held in abeyance until a participant has had the opportunity to express the full range of his Being in the group and to feel the group's reaction to him.

7 ''SHOW ME NOW . . . DO NOT TELL ME WHEN'' is *the* Marathon Leitmotif. Owning up to feelings *here and now* and sharing them is *the* mode of participation. Telling the group about how one behaves outside the group and how ''he'' then and there reacted in bygone times and other places, back home or back at the office —is only warm-up material. The thing to do is for each member to let himself feel his presence in the group and let the *currently active impact* of the others get to him!

The modes of participation recommended in the four paragraphs above (6i, 6ii, 6iii, and 7) provide each group member with the opportunity to become better aware of how he *IS* in the group and in what directions he may want to *change,* and to try out new ways of being in the group.

8 ''AS YOU ARE IN THE GROUP, SO YOU ARE IN THE WORLD.'' As the members learn to exchange feelings in the group, a pattern of participation automatically emerges which the group will mirror back to the individual member. In the long hours of a Marathon one cannot help being seen for what he really is and to see what he may become. The Marathon group simulates the world of emotionally significant others; and the ways in which the member relates to this world reflect the core pattern of his Being. The group members' reactions give cues as to the effect his behavior patterns have on the world. He has the option to try out new, improved ways of Being.

9 Group members' changes and improvements in participation will be attended to by the group. Giving affectionate recognition to growth and new learning is as much in order as cuddling, defensive behavior is out of order (cf. Rule 6iii).

Reinforcement of new learning is the loving side of critical levelling (cf. rule 7 for the "attack" part).

10 While nothing is sacred within the group, the information gained during a Marathon week-end is confidential in the nature of professionally privileged communication. Nothing is revealed to anyone outside. Objective research reporting in anonymous format is the only exception to this "rule of discretion."

The "Ten Commandments," the ground rules for Marathon participants given above, are not arbitrary "rules" or "conventions." Rather, they emerged gradually and painfully in years of clinical experience with interaction groups generally and with Marathon groups in particular. Respecting these basic ground rules does not necessarily guarantee success for a given Marathon. But, we do know that respecting the work-spirit of the situation facilitates the exciting metamorphosis of an assembly of role-playing strangers into a creatively intimate, authentically sharing communion. Since the Marathon leader likes to facilitate and partake of this metamorphosis, he has a vested, professional and personal interest in keeping anybody from distracting him and the group from this beautiful and valuable experience.

REFERENCES

Bach, G. R. *Intensive group psychotherapy.* New York: Ronald, 1954.

Bach, G. R. Pathological aspects of therapeutic groups. *Group Psychotherapy,* 1956, **9,** 133–148.

Bach, G. R., & Alexander, S. *Intimate enemies: principles of therapeutic aggression.* New York: Doubleday, in press.

Basic Models of Parent Counseling*

Joseph B. Tavormina

In recent years, there has been an increasing trend toward the use of parents as "therapists" for their own children. Either singly or in groups, parents have been taught to work on present problems as well as to prevent future behavioral problems in their children. This trend is part of the broader attempt to develop effective and more economical means for both intervention and prevention of mental health problems in light of shortages of therapeutic manpower. This strategy focuses on teaching parents more effective ways to deal with child rearing and child management issues and consequently stands in contrast to the more traditional child- or parent-therapy-oriented approaches.

Auerbach (1968) defined the goals of these parent counseling or parent education procedures as (a) helping parents to become more familiar with basic concepts of child growth and development; (b) helping them clarify their own role and that of their

*From Joseph B. Tavormina, "Basic Models of Parent Counseling: A Critical Review," *Psychological Bulletin,* 1974, **81,** 827–835. Reprinted by permission of the author and the Managing Editor, American Psychological Association.

children; and (c) increasing parental understanding of the complexities of everyday situations to enable them to make better management decisions.

Within this framework, there are two basic counseling models. One emphasizes feelings, while the other emphasizes behavior as the primary starting point. The first is termed reflective counseling in light of the emphasis placed on parental awareness, understanding, and acceptance of the child's feelings (Auerbach, 1968; Ginott, 1957). This model uses cognitively mediated variables (feelings) as a means of affecting the child's behavior and the parent-child interaction. The second method, behavioral counseling, attempts to eliminate cognitive variables in its emphasis on actual behavior. Counseling is geared toward teaching parents to manipulate their responses to the child in order to affect the child's subsequent behavior (Patterson, 1971).

Each model takes a different perspective for defining and assessing counseling outcome. Although both strategies have been used to deal with similar problems across similar populations, the focus of intervention, the issues addressed in counseling, and the criteria for measuring counseling success differ for each. Consistent with its assumptions, changes in parental cognitions have been the primary success criteria for reflective counseling. Similarly, behavioral counselors key on measuring change in target behaviors, again consistent with their major focus. This article presents a critical evaluation of the effectiveness of each model to determine whether each meets its own criteria for success and also makes suggestions for future research on their comparative utility.

RESEARCH ON REFLECTIVE COUNSELING

The reflective counseling model offers many different approaches in terms of group size, homogeneity of membership, length of groups, number of meetings, and the process of the group (Gabel, 1972). There are some basic similarities (Auerbach, 1968; Brim, 1959; Ginott, 1957): (a) an exchange of information between parents; (b) development of a group agenda based on interests and problems specific to group members; (c) encouragement of the expression of feelings; and (d) creation of a climate of trust and safety in which all can participate freely and honestly. The basic goals are also similar: (a) understanding the child's needs at various stages of growth; (b) examination of what group members expect of themselves as parents; (c) a focus on feelings within the parent-child interaction; and (d) recognition of the children as reacting and feeling individuals.

There have been three lines of research on this counseling model: parent testimonials and clinical impressions; evaluation of parental attitudes, knowledge, and feelings; and changes in parent and child behavior. Many nonsystematic, noncontrolled studies endorse the efficacy of reflective counseling. For example, Cary and Reveal (1967) cite clinical impressions of the benefits their program had in helping mothers gain an understanding of their children. Parental reactions to Bricklin's (1970) groups were highly favorable in terms of more reported understanding of their learning-disabled children. In all of these studies, the absence of controlled measures significantly detracts from the scope and applicability of the reported results.

Shapiro (1955, 1956) was among the first to test the hypothesis that counseling affects parental attitudes and feelings. Twenty-five parents received a series of 12 monthly group discussions and 25 served as the control. Parts of the University of Southern California Parent Attitude Survey (Shoben, 1949) were administered before and after the group discussions. Results showed a significant change for treated subjects and no change for controls. Shapiro concluded that the groups were effective in modifying child-rearing attitudes. He added that group participants also seemed to benefit in their social, marital, and religious group relationships.

Balser, Brown, Brown, Laski, and Phillips (1957) used the same instrument in a similar design. The nonparticipant controls improved more than the group members, who only demonstrated a slight tendency toward attitude change. Similarly, results from the St. Louis School Mental Health Project (Gildea, Glidewell, & Kantor, 1967; Glidewell, 1961) show no significant effect of parent groups on attitudes.

However, in the most definitive study in the area, Hereford (1963) reported highly favorable results. He included four experimental conditions: a group whose members attended six weekly parent education sessions (n = 370); a lecture control whose members (n = 102) attended six weekly lectures on parent-child relations; a nonattendant control (n = 160) made up of parents who initially volunteered but failed to attend; and a random control group of parents selected from school files (n = 271). Attitudes were assessed by the Hereford Parent Attitude Survey Form prior to and following the intervention. Counseled parents showed significant positive changes, which were significantly greater than those of the control groups. The number of meetings attended, the amount of participation in discussions, and the individual group leader did not affect the outcome. Hereford concluded that the treatment method per se was the critical change agent.

Gabel (1972) also used Hereford's scale in his assessment of counseling effects. Subjects were 98 mothers of normal kindergarten children who volunteered to participate. There were 12 hourly discussion sessions geared toward maternal expression of concerns around child rearing. Results showed that experimental subjects increased their emphasis on mutual parent-child understanding significantly more than controls. Counseled subjects also showed greater though nonsignificant improvements in the other four Hereford subscales: confidence in parental role, causation of the child's behavior, acceptance of the child's behavior, and mutual trust.

These studies showed mixed results for the efficacy of reflective counseling, perhaps because of the different instruments used to measure attitudes, the differences in group content, or the different types of group interactions. There is a need for systematic control and more rigorous definition of these variables in order to determine the effective components of the reflective procedure.

Friedman (1969) correlated parents' attitudes from the Hereford scale with their children's social behavior as assessed by raters who observed the children while they attended summer camp. Leadership in the child was significantly correlated with parental trust. However, the lack of any other significant relationships between any of the other six rated areas and the five Hereford subscales suggests that changing parental attitudes may not lead automatically to similar changes in parent or child behavior. Similarly, Hereford (1963) reported that sociometric ratings of the children of counseled parents improved more than those of control children, but teacher ratings showed no changes across groups. He claimed that the three-month treatment period was not long enough for changes to be seen by teachers. Swenson (1970) and Stearn (1971) reported similar results. Some parental attitude change also resulted in child improvement, but across all subjects this improvement did not reach statistical significance.

While the previously mentioned studies had mixed results, some investigations have shown that reflective counseling had a positive effect on child behavior, especially in a school setting. These studies have examined the effects of counseling parents on the actual school behavior of their children. Dee (1970) found that child-centered parent counseling enhanced the overall treatment effectiveness for 40 children with school adjustment problems, as measured by a personality questionnaire and a behavior rating scale taken at school and at home. McGowan (1968) divided 32 underachieving tenth-grade boys into four groups: a no-treatment control, parent counseling only, student counseling only, and both parent and child counseling, each done separately. The focus of the parent groups was to hlep the participants better understand their children's behavior. All treatmen groups improved on home improvement ratings and on the ability to express feelings, but *only* the boys whose parents received counseling significantly improved their academic achievement. This improvement was maintained on a five-month follow-up. Perkins (1970) and Perkins and Wicas (1971) reported similar results in their study of 120 ninth-grade male underachievers. The design included four groups similar to McGowan's. The group leaders received 40 hours of training in nondirective techniques, especially to offer minimal levels of empathy, warmth, and genuineness to their clients. All three treatment groups (mothers only, boys only, or both counseled) significantly improved over controls on academic achievement. However, most of these results were not maintained on the five-month follow-up, except for the mothers-only treatment group. In addition, the boys whose mothers were counseled made greater gains in their own self-acceptance as measured by a rating scale. Radin (1969) isolated home counseling geared toward making the mother see herself as a resource person for the child as the critical variable in improving the academic assessment of a group of disadvantaged students. Palmo (1971) found that parent and teacher consultations were the most effective tool in decreasing the adjustment problems of 56 primary school children, as measured by teacher and observer ratings in the school setting. These studies demonstrate the importance of counseling the parents to better understand the child's problems in order to achieve lasting changes in the child's school behavior. Consequently, reflective counseling for the parents can have a generalizable effect on the child's behavior, even as measured in a non-home setting.

Another reflective technique is represented by Guerney's filial therapy (Andronico, Fidler, Guerney, & Guerney, 1967; Guerney, 1964; Guerney, Stover, & Andronico, 1967; Shah, 1969), which attempts to bridge the gap between parent attitude change and resultant parent and child behavior. Parents are trained to conduct client-centered play therapy with their own children. The basic goal is to allow the child to work through his emotional problems via play in a therapeutic atmosphere of parental empathy and acceptance. Stover and Guerney (1967) attempted to evaluate the procedure by rating the tape recordings of sessions. Parents trained in filial therapy increased their reflective statements and decreased directive statements, while the untrained parents did not change. In addition, the children of trained parents increased their verbalization of negative feelings toward their parents, while control children did not. Even though these results were highly favorable, this is the only research to date on the method, and no conclusions can be drawn until more data is generated.

Carkhuff and Bierman (1970) drew some conclusions which are relevant in the present context. They stated that parents must be *directly* trained in ways of interacting with their children in order to effect actual behavioral changes. They added that one must work specifically on a particular problem in order to change it. Consequently, it is highly probable that some reflective counseling procedures are too vaguely defined or applied to have practical importance. The lack of precision in definition, the use of many different instruments to assess change, and the lack of a specific problem focus seem to interfere with the outcome of these counseling techniques. However, the existence of positive outcomes in the literature, especially in the child's social behavior, suggests the importance of further assessment of the reflective model.

RESEARCH ON BEHAVIORAL COUNSELING

Behavioral counseling stresses the importance of the principles of learning theory in understanding parent-child behavior. Patterson (1971) isolates two critical steps in the process: (a) training parents to carefully observe and record the child's behavior and (b) training them to reinforce the child's behavior appropriately. The common denominators in the process are teaching the principles of conditioning and their application in specific circumstances. Most of the research on behavioral counseling can be divided into single-subject or multiple-family designs.

Williams (1959) introduced the topic of parents' use of operant principles to alter their child's behavior. He trained the parents to ignore and thereby eliminate the child's temper tantrums at bedtime. In another classic article (Wahler, Winkel, Peterson, & Morrison, 1965) mothers were trained as "behavior therapists" for their own children. The mothers were taught to decrease the frequency of deviant behaviors by not attending to them and by reinforcing competing responses. Patterson and Brodsky (1966) stressed the importance of reprogramming the social environment in order to achieve lasting behavior change. For example, Patterson, McNeal, Hawkins, and Phelps (1967) taught the parents of a withdrawn, aggressive five-year-old how to apply behavioral principles. Using home observations as the dependent measure, they demonstrated that the mother increased the number of warm (positive reinforcement) responses to the child and the child spent less time engaging in deviant behavior.

Cone and Sloop (1971) reviewed 49 other single-subject studies, all of which reported successful treatment outcomes for a variety of problem behaviors. Each study stressed the need to involve the parents in the treatment process by teaching them new ways of responding to the child. Many of these investigations pointed to the durability of change, typically over a 4- to 7-month follow-up. In addition, some authors suggested that there were beneficial side effects in the improvement of the quality of family functioning. Subjective reports on this issue included more warmth, more affection in the family, and an increase in parental self-esteem.

In spite of the wide range of positive results, two critical questions merit exploration: the type of design used and the generality of the setting. The single-subject studies typically use treatment only, baseline to treatment (AB) or ABA reversal (baseline to treatment and back to baseline follow-up) designs. Such designs contrast with the no-treatment control and multisubject designs used to evaluate reflective counseling. Although these designs viably demonstrate the efficacy of work with single families, they do not provide a workable clinical model. Working with single families is both costly and time consuming for hard-pressed and understaffed clinics. In addition, there have been few systematic attempts to determine how the parents use their new knowledge in areas other than those targeted. The previously cited studies claim, but have not experimentally demonstrated, that the behavioral principles are put into generalized use. In fact, Wahler (1969) presents evidence that even when parents become effective managers of the child's behavior at home, this does not automatically guarantee control over those behaviors in other settings. In contrast with the effects of reflective parent counseling on resultant child school behavior, the generalization of change from home to school has not been reliably demonstrated by behavioral counseling. Until the issues of generality across behaviors and across settings are suitably addressed, one can only conclude that behavioral counseling may be limited in scope to dealing with specific target behaviors, rather than as a general educative tool for parents.

In order to package behavioral procedures in a less costly way, two major trends have developed. The first has been for professionals to treat only the parents and not the children. The second has been group or multiple-family counseling. This approach adds the use of group process as a helpful therapeutic agent.

The basis of the group is some presentation of didactic material or programmed texts that outline principles of reinforcement theory and child management. Two such texts are *Living With Children: New Methods for Parents and Teachers* (Patterson & Gullion, 1968) and *Parents Are Teachers: A Child Management Program* (Becker, 1971). However, Patterson (1971) emphasized that mere presentation or parental reading of these principles will not in itself change their behavior. The basic work of the group is the application of the didactic principles to the particular needs of each participating family.

One of the first investigations of the group approach to behavioral counseling of parents was done by Walder, Cohen, Breiter, Daston, Hirsch, and Liebowitz (1969). They used a combination of didactic group meetings plus individual consultations with parents to set up specific programs within the home. Hirsch and Walder (1969) evaluated this method in a controlled study with 30 white, self-referred upper-middle-class mothers. Mothers were divided into two groups of 15 such that one group received immediate counseling and the other formed a waiting list control. The treatment group was further divided into two, one of 10 and the other of 5 mothers. At the end of the nine-session program, the controls were then given counseling in the same fashion. Dependent measures included maternal responses to objective tests as well as maternal frequency counts of target behavior. Results indicated that treatment mothers gained a significant amount of knowledge about principles of behavior modification and decreased their frequency counts of inappropriate behavior. Neither group size nor maternal intelligence affected the outcome, a result which suggests that the process of behavioral counseling is both flexible and consistent enough to be applicable in a variety of situations. However, since improvement was also noticed for the control group, the authors felt that maternal reports might have been a biased account. Perhaps mothers who want to see improvement will do so in spite of the circumstances. Indeed, it is possible that involved parents might tend to report improvements, even when the target behaviors are not changing. This finding demonstrates the need for unbiased observations by impartial observers as true indices of change.

A number of writers have pointed out shortcomings in the early use of group counseling. Salzinger, Feldman, and Portnoy (1970) studied two groups, one with 8 and the other with 7 parents of brain-injured children. Four of the 15 parents reported complete success in altering target behaviors; 4 had limited success; while 7 were failures. The authors attributed these failures to the parents' inability or lack of motivation to carry out programs designed for them. They concluded, as did Patterson (1971), that parents must be reinforced for their attempts, just as they are expected to reinforce the child's attempts to change his behavior.

Mira (1970) reported on group versus individual behavioral interventions. Subjects were 82 families of children with self-care, social behavior, education, or self-mutilation problems. Thirty-nine percent of the families failed to successfully change their two target behaviors. In addition, it was more expensive in terms of expenditure of professional time per success to work with groups rather than single families. In this case, the group procedure seemed to lose some of the precision afforded by individual counseling. Finally, McPherson and Samuels (1971) concluded that group methods may be useful, but they are not a panacea for parental child-rearing problems. The authors used the *Living With Children* text in a 10-week group for four sets of parents of aggressive, acting out, and hyperkinetic children. Although the parents reported feeling less helpless at the conclusion of treatment, they added that the sessions were not enough to help them deal with the problems they were facing. The authors concluded that the group helped cue parents to some important dimensions, but that such groups must be supplemented with play therapy for the child and reflective counseling for the parents to increase their effectiveness.

These studies highlight the differential effectiveness of single-family versus group counseling. However, one must consider whether the features that led to group counseling success can be identified and enhanced. For example, Wiltz (1970) attempted to validate the group procedure (Patterson, 1971) versus a matched no-treatment control ($n = 6$ per group). Although the results were not statistically significant, they showed a strong trend toward decreases in deviant behavior for the experimental group versus no change for the controls. Wiltz called for a replication with a larger sample to allow for an evaluation of the most beneficial aspects of the program. Walter and Gilmore (1973) extended the Wiltz study by comparing the group counseling procedure with a placebo treatment condition that emphasized the status-attention and expectancy variables inherent in the procedures ($n = 6$ per group). The group counseling method led to significant reductions in targeted deviant behavior as measured by both parent and observer frequency counts, while the placebo group did not improve. Walter and Gilmore concluded that the systematic and contingent application of behavioral principles, rather than merely therapist contact or parent expectancy of improvement, is crucial for successful counseling outcome.

Our recent investigation into the essential features of group counseling evaluated the effects of behavioral counseling on parental attitudes. In addition to frequency counts, Howard[1] measured parents' confidence in handling their children and obtained parents' ratings on the discrepancy between their views of their present versus ideal child. Parent who attended the six 2-hour sessions (n = 10) became significantly more confident and reduced the discrepancy ratings, while the no-treatment controls (n = 10) did not change. These data provide objective evidence that group counseling can have an advantageous effect on parental attitudes and feelings.

Another recent approach to this work has involved a greater sophistication in both group procedure and measurement methodology. Patterson and his associates have developed a program which begins with home observations to gather baseline data on child behavior and parental modes of reinforcement. They then require the parents to study a programmed text on the principles of child management. After successfully passing a test on the didactic material, parents are taught to observe and record rates of target behaviors. Then training groups are formed to help parents set up and execute programs at home. Finally, repeated follow-ups are made to determine the stability of treatment effects.

Patterson and Reid (1973) used this method with 11 families of highly aggressive boys. They used multiple criteria to evaluate treatment outcome, including parent ratings, parent frequency counts, and frequency counts by objective observers. Significant improvement was demonstrated on all variables, but Patterson still called for further development of various criterion measures to demonstrate the range of effectiveness of his procedure. In any event, Patterson underscored the benefits of using both parent report and observer variables to more fully evaluate group counseling.

Still another improvement has been the direct measurement of mother-child interaction patterns. In a series of papers, Mash and his associates (Cone & Sloop, 1971; Mash, Terdal, & Anderson, 1973) have developed a methodology to evaluate the antecedent-consequent relationship between mother and child. Observations are taken in a three-term contingency model, including mother starting an interaction, child responding, and mother consequating. The authors directly trained mothers how to command appropriately, reinforce compliance, and ignore noncompliance. Across a number of studies, they demonstrated that their observational system measured increases in child compliance and appropriate maternal consequation, while the control groups did not change significantly. These results point to the importance of using interactional data to gauge counseling effects. It seems logical that, if the parents can reliably demonstrate *use* of appropriate child management procedures in observational settings, this behavior should generalize to other settings.

These developments have begun to demonstrate the potential utility of group counseling. New research should be geared toward incorporating these newly developed methodologies, especially the interactional systems, into more comprehensive designs.

[1]O. F. Howard. Teaching a class of parents as reinforcement therapists to treat their own children. Paper presented at the meeting of the Southeastern Psychological Association, Louisville, Kentucky, April 1970.

COMPARATIVE EFFECTIVENESS OF REFLECTIVE VERSUS BEHAVIORAL COUNSELING

There have been numerous attempts to compare the effectiveness of behavioral, reflective, and other models of therapy and counseling with adult patients. In a review of this literature, Mettzoff and Kornreich (1970) concluded that there was no clear-cut evidence that any one school of therapy yielded a better outcome than another. Analogously, Hartmann[2] argued for the necessity of comparative utility studies in work with children. He stated that it was essential for behavior therapists to begin demonstrating the relative effectiveness, efficiency, and durability of the behavior change produced by their techniques. Cost efficiency studies are needed to compare behavioral methods to alternative treatment approaches.

This argument holds for parent counseling procedures. Both reflective and behavioral counseling are somewhat similar in that they focus on specific child-rearing issues. However, the behavioral model places a direct focus on concrete, observable behavior, while reflective techniques involve the use of cognitively mediated variables, like warmth and understanding. Both key on behavioral issues, but one uses behavior, while the other uses the constructs of feelings in order to effect change in the child. Comparison of the two methods should help determine their relative effectiveness and may also shed some light on the issue whether one or the other is the treatment of choice for certain types of parents.

Nevertheless, differences in design and measurement techniques have been barriers to comparative research on behavioral and reflective counseling. One basic problem has been the lack of comparative measures of outcome derived from the two procedures. To eliminate this obstacle, it is feasible to incorporate the measures typically used by each counseling model as multiple criterion variables. A combination of parent report, attitudinal measures, and observer variables will provide a broad-based, representative comparison of effectiveness. This multimethod approach hopefully will minimize the effects of bias of distortion inherent in the use of single criterion measures (Lytton, 1971; Patterson & Reid, 1973; Tramantana, 1971).

Only one study (Johnson, 1970) has attempted to compare these two modes of treatment. Subjects were 45 essentially normal first and second graders, described by their parents as having trouble with obedience. Five conditions were studied: (a) reflective treatment of the mother; (b) reflective treatment of the child; (c) behavioral treatment of the mother; (d) behavioral treatment of the child; and (e) no-treatment control. Results on parent ratings of specific obedience behaviors showed that behavioral and reflective treatment of the mother and behavioral treatment of the child resulted in improvement by the child. Indices of general adjustment did not indicate significant change for any group. Therefore, both counseling modes when applied to the patient's mother had similar effects in this study, a finding which left the question of their comparative utility as yet unanswered.

[2]D. P. Hartman. Some neglected issues in behavior modification with children. Paper presented at the meeting of the American Association of Behavior Therapy, New York, December 1972.

CONCLUSION

In conclusion, both reflective and behavioral counseling have in the main enjoyed a successful reputation as intervention strategies, even though the literature contains a significant number of negative outcomes and problems in research methodology. Currently both, although they differ in focus, are used in a variety of settings to work with many types of behavioral problems as well as with divergent populations. Consequently there is a need for comparative utility and cost efficiency studies on these models to determine (a) which approach is more appropriate for which population of parents and for which types and ages of children; (b) which behavioral problem can each model best deal with; and (c) whether particular combinations of the two models might enhance overall counseling effectiveness. If parent counseling is indeed a useful intervention strategy, there is need to closely define the parameters relevant to the appropriate use of each counseling model.

REFERENCES

Andronico, M. P., Fidler, J., Guerney, B. G., & Guerney, L. The combination of didactic and dynamic elements in filial therapy. *International Journal of Group Psychotherapy,* 1967, **17,** 10–17.

Auerbach, A. B. *Parents learn through discussion.* New York: Wiley, 1968.

Balser, B. H., Brown, F., Brown, M. L., Laski, L., & Phillips, D. K. Further report on experimental evaluation of mental hygiene techniques in school and community. *American Journal of Psychiatry,* 1957, **113,** 733–739.

Becker, W. C. *Parents are teachers: A child management program.* Champaign, Ill.: Research Press, 1971.

Bricklin, P. M. Counseling parents of children with learning disabilities. *Reading Teacher,* 1970, **23,** 331–338.

Brim, O. G. *Education for child rearing.* New York: Russell Sage Foundation, 1959.

Carkhuff, R. R., & Bierman, R. Training as a preferred mode of treatment of parents of emotionally disturbed children. *Journal of Counseling Psychology,* 1970, **17,** 157–161.

Cary, A. C., & Reveal, M. T. Prevention and detection of emotional disturbances in preschool children. *American Journal of Orthopsychiatry,* 1967, **37,** 719–724.

Cone, J. D., & Sloop, E. W. Parents as agents of change. In A. Jacobs & W. W. Spradlin (Eds.), *Group as agent of change.* Chicago: Aldine-Atherton, 1971.

Dee, G. The effects of parent group counseling on children with school adjustment problems. *Dissertation Abstracts International,* 1970, **31,** 1008A.

Friedman, S. T. Relation of parental attitudes toward child rearing and patterns of social behavior in middle childhood. *Psychological Reports,* 1969, **24,** 575–579.

Gabel, H. D. Effects of parent group education and group play psychotherapy on maternal child rearing attitudes. Unpublished doctoral dissertation, University of Rochester, 1972.

Gildea, M. C., Glidewell, J. C., & Kantor, M. B. The St. Louis school mental health project: History and evaluation. In E. L. Cowen, E. A. Gardner, & M. Zax (Eds.), *Emergent approaches to mental health problems.* New York: Appleton-Century-Crofts, 1967.

Ginott, H. G. Parent education groups in a child guidance clinic. *Mental Hygiene,* 1957, **41,** 82–86.

Glidewell, J. C. (Ed.), *Parental attitudes and child behavior.* Springfield, Ill.: Charles C. Thomas, 1961.

Guerney, B. G. Filial therapy: Description and rationale. *Journal of Consulting Psychology,* 1964, **28,** 304–310.

Guerney, B. G., Stover, L., & Andronico, M. P. On educating disadvantaged parents to motivate children for learning: A filial approach. *Community Mental Health Journal,* 1967, **3,** 66–72.

Hereford, C. F. *Changing parental attitudes through group discussion.* Austin: University of Texas Press, 1963.

Hirsch, I., & Walder, L. Training mothers in groups as reinforcement therapists for their own children. *Proceedings of the 77th Annual Convention of the American Psychological Association,* 1969, **4,** 561–562. (Summary)

Johnson, S. A. A comparison of mother versus child groups and traditional versus behavior modification procedures in the treatment of "disobedient" children. *Dissertation Abstracts International,* 1970, **31,** 2989B.

Lytton, H. Observational studies of parent-child interaction: A methodological review. *Child Development,* 1971, **42,** 651–684.

Mash, E. J., Terdal, L., & Anderson, K. The response-class matrix: A procedure for recording parent-child interactions. *Journal of Consulting and Clinical Psychology,* 1973, **40,** 163–164.

McGowan, R. J. Group counseling with underachievers and their parents. *School Counselor,* 1968, **16,** 30–35.

McPherson, S. B., & Samuels, C. R. Teaching behavioral methods to parents. *Social Casework,* 1971, **52,** 148–153.

Mettzoff, J., & Kornreich, M. *Research in psychotherapy.* New York: Atherton Press, 1970.

Mira, M. Results of a behavior modification training program for parents and teachers. *Behaviour Research and Therapy,* 1970, **8,** 309–311.

Palmo, A. J. The effect of group counseling and parent-teacher consultations on the classroom behavior of elementary school children. *Dissertation Abstracts International,* 1971, **32,** 1863–1864A.

Patterson, G. R. Behavioral intervention procedures in the classroom and the home. In A. E. Bergin & S. L. Garfield (Eds.), *Handbook of psychotherapy and behavior change: An empirical analysis.* New York: Wiley, 1971.

Patterson, G. R., & Brodsky, G. A behavior modification programme for a child with multiple problem behaviours. *Journal of Child Psychology and Psychiatry,* 1966, **7,** 227–295.

Patterson, G. R., & Gullion, M. E. *Living with children: New methods for parents and teachers.* Champaign, Ill.: Research Press, 1968.

Patterson, G. R., McNeal, S., Hawkins, N., & Phelps, R. Reprogramming the social environment. *Journal of Child Psychology and Psychiatry,* 1967, **8,** 181–195.

Patterson, G. R., & Reid, J. B. Reciprocity and coercion: Two facets of social systems. In C. Neuringer & J. Michael (Eds.), *Behavior modification in clinical psychology.* New York: Appleton-Century-Crofts, 1970.

Patterson, G. R., & Reid, J. B. Intervention for families of aggressive boys: A replication study. *Behaviour Research and Therapy,* 1973, **11,** 383–394.

Perkins, J. A. Group counseling with bright underachievers and their mothers. *Dissertation Abstracts International,* 1970, **30,** 2809A.

Perkins, J. A., & Wicas, E. Group counseling with bright underachievers and their mothers. *Journal of Counseling Psychology,* 1971, **18,** 273–278.

Radin, N. The impact of kindergarten home counseling program. *Exceptional Children,* 1969, **36,** 251–258.

Salzinger, K., Feldman, R. S., & Portnoy, S. Training parents of brain-injured children in the use of operant conditioning procedures. *Behavior Therapy,* 1970, **1,** 4–32.

Shah, S. A. Training and utilizing a mother as the therapist for her child. In B. G. Guerney, Jr. (Ed.), *Psychotherapeutic agents: New roles for non-professionals, parents, and teachers.* New York: Holt, Rinehart & Winston, 1969.

Shapiro, I. S. Changing child-rearing attitudes through group discussion. *Dissertation Abstracts,* 1955, **15,** 538–539.

Shapiro, I. S. Is group parent education worthwhile? A research report. *Marriage and Family Living,* 1956, **18,** 154–161.

Shoben, E. I. The assessment of parental attitudes in relation to child adjustment. *Genetic Psychology Monographs,* 1949, **39,** 101–148.

Stearn, M. B. The relationship of parent effectiveness training to parent attitudes, parent behavior, and child self-esteem. *Dissertation Abstracts International,* 1971, **32**, 1885–1886B.

Stover, L. & Guerney, B. G. The efficacy of training procedures for mothers in filial therapy. *Psychotherapy: Theory, Research, and Practice,* 1967, **4**, 110–115.

Swenson, S. S. Changing expressed parent attitudes toward child-rearing practices and its effect on school adaptation and level of adjustment perceived by parents. *Dissertation Abstracts International,* 1970, **31,** 2118–2119A.

Tramantana, J. A review of research in behavior modification in the home and school. *Educational Technology,* 1971, **11,** 61–64.

Wahler, R. G. Setting generality: Some specific and general effects of child behavior therapy. *Journal of Applied Behavior Analysis,* 1969, **2,** 239–246.

Wahler, R. G., Winkel, G. H., Peterson, R. F., & Morrison, D. C. Mothers as behavior therapists for their own children. *Behaviour Research and Therapy,* 1965, **3,** 113–124.

Walder, L. O., Cohen, S. I., Breiter, D. E., Daston, P .G., Hirsch, I. S., & Liebowitz, J. M. Teaching behavioral principles to parents of disturbed children. In B. G. Guerney, Jr. (Ed.), *Psychotherapeutic agents: New roles for non-professionals, parents, and teachers.* New York: Holt, Rinehart & Winston, 1969.

Walter, H. I., & Gilmore, S. K. Placebo versus social learning effects in parent training procedures designed to alter the behavior of aggressive boys. *Behavior Therapy,* 1973, **4,** 361–377.

Williams, C. D. The elimination of tantrum behavior by extinction procedures. *Journal of Abnormal and Social Psychology,* 1959, **59,** 269.

Wiltz, N. A. Modification of behaviors of deviant boys through parent participation in a group technique. *Dissertation Abstracts International,* 1970, **30,** 4786–4787A.

Developing Social Skills with Behavior Modification*

Alan E. Kazdin

Many individuals experience difficulty or discomfort in aspects of their social interaction with others. Such individuals usually function adequately in everyday life and are not immobilized by their difficulties but are unsatisfied with their social behavior. Social behaviors which may lead to dissatisfaction include the apparent inability to converse comfortably with others, to handle situations where confrontations or conflicts exist, or to express positive feelings such as friendship, love, affection, and approval. The discomfort individuals experience in social encounters sometimes re-

*This paper was written for *The Psychology of Adjustment: Current Concepts and Applications,* 3rd edition.

sults from a lack of appropriate social skills. The deficits in behavior may not be pervasive but rather restricted to one or a few types of situations. For example, a business executive might be socially adept with peers but have difficulty in communicating with his or her spouse. Similarly, a college student may freely express feelings to his peers but feel completely inhibited in expressing feelings in the presence of his parents.

Recently, behavior modification techniques have focused upon developing social skills with diverse types of problems. Social skills refer generally to those behaviors which are likely to enhance an individual's receipt of positive consequences in the context of social interaction. The range of behaviors included in appropriate social interaction is great. Two areas which have received particular attention are assertive behavior and heterosexual interaction. The present paper discusses areas of social skills training, the behavior modification techniques employed to develop social skills, and the effects of treatment.

ASSERTIVE TRAINING

Assertive training has been used with individuals who experience difficulty in speaking up for their rights, refusing unreasonable demands, expressing their true feelings, and communicating positively to others (Hersen, Eisler, & Miller, 1973). Most assertive training programs have focused upon interactions which pertain to areas of conflict (e.g., expression of anger, refusal, or disappointment). There are several ways individuals can respond to express feelings such as anger. For example, one can subject someone to physical or verbal abuse. Yet, interactions such as these are not included in assertive training. To clarify the nature of assertive training, it is important to distinguish assertive from aggressive behavior.

Assertive training focuses on helping an individual express himself in a socially appropriate fashion. Assertive expressions can be made in a tactful manner rather than at the expense of another individual. Aggressive interactions which might be characterized by caustic and belligerent remarks, are likely to alienate and offend others. In contrast, assertive responses are designed to express one's own feelings in a reasonable fashion. Many individuals who behave inassertively are the victim of the wishes of others without ever expressing their own views. Assertive training merely helps them express their own preferences and needs so they can handle sources of conflict appropriately. The goal of assertive training is to make the individual more effective socially. Thus, the individual must know how to maximize the positive effects he has on others. Aggressive confrontations would be counterproductive in the long run. Thus, assertive behavior differs from aggressive behavior by the *manner* in which the responses are made.

There is another major difference between assertive and aggressive behavior. Assertive behavior, at least in social skills training programs, does not merely include negative statements. Rather, positive statements such as expressions of friendship, love, approval, and affection are included as well (Lazarus, 1971). Unfortunately, relatively little research and clinical applications of assertive training have focused upon developing the expression of positive feelings. Individuals who seek assertive training or participate in assertive training programs usually are interested in overcoming anxiety, frustration, or inhibitions in making socially appropriate confrontations and developing the relevant social skills.

The type of behavior for which assertive training would be recommended is illustrated in one description of a 45-year old housewife who lived with her husband, son, and mother (MacPherson, 1972). The woman was dominated by her mother who apparently controlled several aspects of her life. For example, the mother decided what the weekly shopping would include and interfered with disciplining the child. The control of the wife by her mother appeared to disrupt the family. The boy was becoming "spoiled" which seemed to result from the interference of the grandmother in the discipline. Also, the wife appeared to be extremely critical of her husband who was the brunt of her frustration with the mother. In any case, the woman expressed the desire to respond to her mother and to terminate her dominance but was unable to do so. Assertive training was used to alter her interaction with both her mother and husband.

While most of assertive training is used to develop expressions of feelings which would otherwise remain unexpressed, this is not always the case. Some individuals readily express their feelings and, indeed, are overexpressive and hostile. Assertive training for individuals who are overcritical or cannot control their temper (e.g., resulting in abusive language or breaking objects) focuses on the re-expression of such feelings in a more appropriate and productive fashion (e.g., Wallace, Teigen, Liberman, & Baker, 1973). For example, in the case described above, the woman was simultaneously trained to be more assertive toward her mother and to be less critical and negative with her husband. Both the interaction with the mother and husband required expression of feelings in a more appropriate fashion.

HETEROSEXUAL INTERACTION

Social skills training has encompassed aspects of heterosexual interaction. Two areas focused upon are developing dating skills and enhancing marital interaction. Developing dating skills generally has been restricted to male college students who experience anxiety in heterosexual encounters or do not have the requisite skills to procure dates (e.g., conversing with others, inviting others out for a date). A low frequency of attempts to procure and obtain dates attests to the need for social skills training. The goal of training is to increase dating behavior and feelings of competence. In most reports, males have been trained to engage in a variety of behaviors which approximate dating. For example, individuals initially may be trained to engage in behaviors such as taking a seat next to someone of the opposite sex. Eventually, training leads up to calling others, asking them for dates, and behaving appropriately on a date (e.g., Rehm & Marston, 1968).

Developing social skills in the context of marital interaction usually focuses upon a specific communication pattern which is problematic between spouses. Prior to training, the interaction between spouses may be observed to determine the specific behaviors which are unproductive. For example, in one case, the husband failed to respond to his wife (Eisler, Miller, Hersen, & Alford, 1974). Videotapes of the couple's interaction revealed that the husband failed to express either positive or negative feelings about any of his wife's behavior. Training focused upon his expression of feelings. The wife was not seen in treatment. Interestingly, not only did the husband improve in his communication skills, but both spouses increased in the frequency of positive verbal expressions (e.g., agreement, approval) and reciprocal smiling and decreased in their negative expressions (e.g., criticism, disagreement).

OTHER APPLICATIONS OF SOCIAL SKILLS TRAINING

Social skills training usually has been restricted to individuals who function adequately in everyday life except in relatively delimited types of social situations. However, the role of inappropriate or a lack of social skills has been emphasized as important in various psychiatric disorders. In diverse psychiatric disorders, problems in social interaction are acknowledged. For example, inadequate and problematic social interaction has been suggested to play a major role in depression. Some authors characterize certain forms of depression as a result of a low rate of positive interactions with the environment (Lewinsohn, 1975). Indeed, evidence suggests that depressed individuals tend to initiate fewer communications with others, make fewer positive statements, and communicate with fewer individuals than do nondepressed individuals (Libet & Lewinsohn, 1973). This is not to say that social inadequacies necessarily cause depression. Yet, at the very least, inadequate social skills appear to be concomitants of depression. In any case, investigators have developed social skills (e.g., positive social interaction) in depressed individuals with favorable results. Increasing social interaction has been associated with reductions in depression (Lewinsohn, 1975; McLean, Ogston, & Grauer, 1973).

Aside from depression, social skills training has been effectively employed with hospitalized schizophrenic patients who often are characterized as compliant, submissive, and generally socially inhibited. Although few individuals regard the lack of social skills as the basis of disorders such as schizophrenia, training appropriate social interaction as in assertive training is associated with a decrease in various psychotic symptoms (Lomont, Gilner, Spector, & Skinner, 1969). Many problems for which psychiatric and psychological treatment are sought relate directly to social interaction. Social withdrawal, aggressive outbursts, failure to communicate coherently, and other behaviors are problematic social behaviors. Thus, it is no surprise that social skills training has been applied to psychiatric patients. There is another reason which makes social skills training appropriate for hospitalized patients. Such training may facilitate posthospital adjustment which typically is problematic. The absence of deviant behaviors alone (e.g., hallucinations, delusions) does not ensure that expatients can effectively sustain posthospital adjustment. Severe response deficits in appropriate social skills, if not corrected, may lead to rehospitalization.

TECHNIQUES FOR DEVELOPING SOCIAL SKILLS

Several behavior modification techniques have been used to develop social skills. The techniques are characterized as behavioral techniques because they focus directly upon the behaviors which appear problematic rather than supposed psychological, motivational, or unconscious underpinnings of such behaviors. Training usually focuses upon verbal and nonverbal behaviors which form social skills. Verbal aspects of particular skills such as assertive behavior or dating are obvious. Yet, effective communication entails nonverbal behaviors which often dictate whether the appropriate verbalizations will have their intended effect. Nonverbal behaviors focused upon include loudness of voice, fluency of spoken words, eye contact, facial expressions, bodily expression and body distance (Serber, 1972).

Three techniques which have received attention in social skills training include behavioral rehearsal, modeling, and imagery. Sometimes the techniques are combined. Behavioral rehearsal, also known as role-playing, consists of having the client practice social behaviors in the therapy sessions. The client role-plays behaviors with the therapist which pertain to those situations in which the client experiences difficulty. For example, in assertive training, the therapist may enact the role of someone who encroaches upon the client's rights. The client is asked to respond as he normally would. In another situation, the therapist may play the role of a prospective employer while the client attempts to exhibit appropriate job-interview behaviors. By practicing in this fashion, the therapist can suggest improvements for effective interaction to the client. Over time the client can practice diverse simulated situations and receive feedback from the therapist. The therapist provides praise to the client for gradual improvements as the client approximates increasingly appropriate social interactions over time. Thus, feedback plays a crucial part in behavioral rehearsal.

In some situations, the client's role-playing responses are tape recorded or videotaped and played back to him. The client can evaluate his own responses and rectify obvious inadequacies. The feedback provided by the therapist and client self-evaluation of previously recorded performance probably contribute extensively to behavioral rehearsal.

Modeling is another technique used to train assertive behavior. Modeling requires that a client observe someone else engage in the behavior the client wishes to develop. The client need not respond directly but only observe someone perform appropriate responses across a number of situations. In modeling, the individual usually views a film of someone performing appropriate social behaviors. Thus, modeling typically involves both audio and visual presentations to the clients. Yet, audio modeling where the client listens to appropriate social interaction sequences has been effective in its own right. Clients merely hear responses of others to diverse situations rather than see and hear the model. Modeling effects probably are best achieved with audio and visual components because not all of the components of effective social interaction (e.g., gestures, facial expressions) can be conveyed by tape recordings.

While modeling has been used alone, it is sometimes combined with behavioral rehearsal. Frequently the client and therapist alternate roles in simulated situations. Sometimes the therapist takes the role of the individual to whom the assertive response is made; other times the therapist models the appropriate response. For example, in a dating situation, the therapist may act as if he or she is opposite sexed from the client in a situation in which approach responses might be appropriate. The client could role-play the responses he or she actually might make. After the client responds, the therapist would provide feedback to assess the adequacy of the client's response. Also, the therapist might take the role of the client and model an appropriate response. With the client role-playing and viewing the therapist as a model for the same situations, training can develop competence across a variety of situations.

A final technique to be discussed is based upon imagery. Rather than role-playing or observing a model, individuals can imagine a select sequence of social responses. For example, in assertive training individuals can imagine rather than observe a model engage in assertive responses across diverse situations. The client never actually performs assertive behavior in therapy. The therapist describes various situations to the client. The client imagines a number of situations repeatedly. A typical situation which might be described to the client in the context of assertive training might be:

> Imagine a person [the model] eating in a restaurant with friends. He orders a steak and tells the waiter he would like it rare. When the food arrives, the person begins to eat and apparently finds something wrong with the steak. He immediately signals the waiter. When the waiter arrives, the person says, "I ordered the steak rare and this one is medium. Please take it back and bring me one that is rare." In a few minutes, the waiter brings another steak and says he is very sorry this has happened.

After several opportunities to imagine situations in which someone engages in assertive behavior, the clients' own behavior actually improves (Kazdin, 1974). Because the procedure in which the client imagines the behavior of someone else resembles modeling (where the behavior of someone else actually is observed), the procedure has been referred to as a variation of modeling (Cautela, 1971). Specifically, the procedure is called covert modeling because the modeling takes place covertly, i.e., privately in imagination.

Currently, the appropriate investigations have not been conducted to determine the most effective technique for social skills training. However, evidence for the treatment of other problems suggests that training is most effective when the client actually is allowed to practice the situations in which behavior change is to be developed. Thus, it is likely that behavioral rehearsal would be superior to modeling or covert modeling alone (see Bandura, Blanchard, & Ritter, 1969; Friedman, 1971). In fact, many of the social skills training programs incorporate diverse techniques to ensure the maximum behavior change.

The majority of social skills training programs have been conducted on an individual basis. Recently group training has been shown to be effective (Lomont et al., 1969; Rimm, Hill, Brown, & Stuart, 1974). There are some obvious advantages of conducting treatment on a group basis. First, group treatment simply is more efficient. In a group situation, several individuals can be treated simultaneously with the use of one therapist. Second, the group serves as a useful forum for evaluating the extent to which one's behavior is socially effective and appropriate. For example, if behavioral rehearsal is used in treatment, clients can rehearse their response in the presence of the entire group. The therapist as well as members of the group can provide diverse feedback and suggest alternative responses. In individual treatment, only the therapist would provide feedback. At present, both individual and group social skills training have been effective. There is no clear evidence supporting their differential effectiveness.

EFFECTS OF SOCIAL SKILLS TRAINING

Two areas crucial for evaluating the effects of social skills training are the extent to which behavior change actually is achieved and the extent to which these changes are maintained after treatment is terminated. With respect to the first issue, relatively consistent changes have been effected with treatment. Interestingly, diverse behaviors change in the process of training. Not only do the clients change in the behaviors focused upon (e.g., assertiveness, dating skills) but they evaluate themselves differently as well. At the end of treatment clients see themselves as having much less of a problem interacting with others, and less anxiety in social situations in general (Kazdin, 1974; McFall & Lillesand, 1971). Also, clients change in behaviors not always focused upon in treatment. Disruptions of speech, duration of social responses, and eye contact, even when not focused upon often are altered as a function of training (Kazdin, 1974; Hersen, Eisler, & Miller, 1974).

Other changes which sometimes occur pertain to the effects that training one individual in social skills has on others. As noted earlier, the behavior of both spouses sometimes is altered by providing social skills training for one of the partners who has difficulty in expressing him or herself (Eisler et al., 1974).

Although social skills training has been shown to alter diverse behaviors, relatively few investigations have examined whether the gains made in treatment are maintained after treatment is terminated. Usually, it is assumed that once an individual responds appropriately in everyday social interaction, the favorable consequences which result from this interaction (e.g., increased comfort, attainment of goals, self-confidence) will maintain these behaviors. The few investigations which have been concerned with long term maintenance reveal that therapeutic gains are maintained at least up to several months after treatment is terminated (Kazdin, 1974; McLean et al., 1973). Thus, it would appear that there are no immediate losses after treatment is terminated. Insufficient research has been completed to make statements about protracted therapeutic effects of social skills training.

CONCLUSION

Several investigations and clinical cases have shown that diverse social behaviors, a few of which were sampled in the present paper, can be readily altered. The interesting feature of social skills training is that its utility extends from individuals with little impairment in everyday life to those whose impairment may be severe. Recent research suggests that behavior modification techniques are effective in altering social behaviors with diverse populations. Of course this is not to say that only behavioral techniques are effective. However, at the present time relatively few techniques have been carefully studied.

At the present time, social skills training has been used to alter specific areas of concern to individual clients who seek treatment. However, this is not necessarily the only application of social skills training. Problems of social interaction are sufficiently pervasive that training in diverse social skills might be used in a preventive fashion.

In a sense, most individuals might profit from preparatory training to cover situations involving interactions with parents, siblings, peers, colleagues, employers, spouses, lovers, friends, and enemies. By preparing individuals in diverse skills, some of the problems which precipitate seeking treatment might be forestalled or eliminated entirely.

REFERENCES

Bandura, A., Blanchard, E. G., & Ritter, B. Relative efficacy of desensitization and modeling approaches for inducing behavioral, affective, and attitudinal changes. *Journal of Personality and Social Psychology,* 1969, **13,** 173–199.

Cautela, J. R. Covert modeling. Paper presented at Fifth Annual Meeting of the Association for the Advancement of Behavior Therapy, Washington, D.C., September, 1971.

Eisler, R. M., Miller, P. M., Hersen, M., & Alford, H. Effects of assertive training on marital interaction. *Archives of General Psychiatry,* 1974, **30,** 643–649.

Friedman, P. H. The effects of modeling and role-playing on assertive behavior. In R. D. Rubin, H. Fensterheim, A. A. Lazarus, & C. M. Franks (Eds.), *Advances in behavior therapy.* New York: Academic Press, 1971. Pp. 149–169.

Hersen, M., Eisler, R. M., & Miller, P. M. Development of assertive responses: Clinical, measurement and research considerations. *Behaviour Research and Therapy,* 1973, **11,** 505–521.

Hersen, M., Eisler, R. M., & Miller, P. M. An experimental analysis of generalization in assertive training. *Behaviour Research and Therapy,* 1974, **12,** 295–310.

Kazdin, A. E. Effects of covert modeling and model reinforcement on assertive behavior. *Journal of Abnormal Psychology,* 1974, **83,** 240–252.

Lazarus, A. A. *Behavior therapy and beyond.* New York: McGraw-Hill, 1971.

Lewinsohn, P. M. The behavioral study and treatment of depression. In M. Hersen, R. M. Eisler, & P. M. Miller (Eds.), *Progress in behavior modification, Vol. 1.* New York: Academic Press, 1975.

Libet, J., & Lewinsohn, P. M. Concept of social skill with special reference to the behavior of depressed persons. *Journal of Consulting and Clinical Psychology,* 1973, **40,** 304–312.

Lomont, J. F., Gilner, F. H., Spector, N. J., & Skinner, B. F. Group assertion training and group insight therapies. *Psychological Reports,* 1969, **25,** 463–470.

MacPherson, E. L. R. Selective operant conditioning and deconditioning of assertive modes of behaviour. *Journal of Behavior Therapy and Experimental Psychiatry,* 1972, **3,** 99–102.

McFall, R. M., & Lillesand, D. Behavior rehearsal with modeling and coaching in assertion training. *Journal of Abnormal Psychology,* 1971, **77,** 313–323.

McLean, P. D., Ogston, K., & Grauer, L. A behavioral approach to the treatment of depression. *Journal of Behavior Therapy and Experimental Psychiatry,* 1973, **4,** 323–330.

Rehm, L. P., & Marston, A. R. Reduction of social anxiety through modification of self-reinforcement: An instigation therapy technique. *Journal of Consulting and Clinical Psychology,* 1968, **32,** 565–574.

Rimm, D. C., Hill, G. A., Brown, N. N., & Stuart, J. E. Group-assertive training in treatment of expression of inappropriate anger. *Psychological Reports,* 1974, **34,** 791–798.

Serber, M. Teaching the nonverbal components of assertive training. *Journal of Behavior Therapy and Experimental Psychiatry,* 1972, **3,** 179–183.

Wallace, C. J., Teigen, J., Liberman, R. P., & Baker, V. Destructive behavior treated by contingency contracts and assertive training: A case study. *Journal of Behavior Therapy and Experimental Psychiatry,* 1973, **4,** 273–274.